A HISTORY OF THE HIGHLAND CLEARANCES

Volume 2: Emigration, Protest, Reasons

Eric Richards

CROOM HELM
London • Sydney • Dover, New Hampshire

Croom Helm Ltd, Provident House, Burrell Row,
Beckenham, Kent BR3 1AT
Croom Helm Australia Pty Ltd, First Floor,
139 King Street, Sydney, NSW 2001, Australia

British Library Cataloguing in Publication Data
Richards, Eric
    A history of the Highland clearances.
    Vol. 2: Emigration, protest, reasons
    1. Crofters—Scotland—Highlands—History
    2. Eviction—Scotland—Highlands—History
    I. Title
    333.33'5   HD1511.G72

    ISBN 0-7099-2259-0

Croom Helm, 51 Washington Street,
Dover, New Hampshire 03820, USA

Library of Congress Cataloging in Publication Data
Richards, Eric.
    A history of the highland clearances.

    Vol. 2 Published: London = Dover, N.H.
    Includes bibliographies and indexes.
    Contents: (1) Agrarian transformation and the
    evictions, 1746–1886—V. 2. Emigration,
    protest, reasons.
    1. Crofters—History.   2. Farm tenancy—Scotland—
    Highlands—History.   3. Eviction—Scotland—Highlands—
    History.   4. Highlands (Scotland)—Economic conditions.
    I. Title
    HD1511.G7R53   1982   333.33'5   81-208122
ISBN 0-85664-496-X (V.1)
ISBN 0-7099-2259-0 (V.2)

The publishers acknowledge the financial
assistance of the Scottish Arts Council in
the publication of this book.

Typeset by Leaper & Gard Ltd, Bristol, England
Printed and bound in Great Britain

CONTENTS

To Ngaire May Naffin

PREFACE

The Highland clearances may begin to look like an excellent story ruined first by an excess of historical documentation,[1] and now by a flood of analysis. The justification is the importance of the subject itself, and the controversy that has always raged about it. It is important because the clearances determined the shape of the modern Highlands and the fate of generations of its people; it is important also because the Highlands represents the recurrent and universal problem of regional maladjustment during modernisation. The subject is controversial because anger and recrimination continue to burn in the memory of the community, and because the clearances are entangled in eternal moral questions of power, loyalty, justice and truth.

The first volume of this work was primarily descriptive in purpose; it sought to establish the chronology and geography of the events, and to evaluate the surviving evidence. It tried to establish a broadly agreed document of the clearance story. The present volume is a different kind of book: it contains far less descriptive detail, it employs a quite different density of evidence, and is altogether more analytical, speculative and argumentative. It is about various types of communal and intellectual responses, contemporary and retrospective, to the experience of the clearances. It is divided into five sections which deal with aspects of the response.

The first section considers the legacy of two hundred years' debate about the Highland problem and the place of the clearances therein. It tells a story that ran parallel to the actual experience of agrarian transformation, about the intellectual currents which have flowed into and out of the Highlands. It attempts to account for the indignation and intellectual confusion that have marked the effort to understand the unhappy history of the Highlands. Amongst other things it shows that the history of the Highlands was much more than the history of the clearances.

The middle sections of the book deal with varieties of collective response to the clearances. Emigration was a logical but contentious reaction to the transformation of the Highland economy: here some effort is made to gauge the scale, range and timing of the emigrations of the Highlanders, as well as some of the motivations. The third section contemplates the direct popular response to the clearances, the collective memory and the tradition of physical resistance. It examines the various symptoms of communal breakdown and withdrawal of co-operation, and the failure of resistance. The fourth section is about Patrick Sellar, his career, trial and reputation, which together embodied much of the social history, the ruling ideas and the necessary mythology of the clearances. Since this study is organised thematically rather than along a continuous narrative, some events recur in successive chapters, but the repetition of material has been kept to an unavoidable minimum.

The last part of this volume is about the fundamental economic problem of the Highlands in the age of the clearances, and about the moral and economic alternatives that faced the community, the landlords and the nation. To this task are brought the uncertain advantages of historical perspective and modern economic analysis. At that point the reader will have travelled through many pages to reach conclusions which are perhaps relatively undramatic. They yield an interpretation which gives prominence to the forces of demographic crisis and to the economic imperatives of the age of industrialisation. It is an interpretation which stresses the inability of the society to activate itself into an effective response to the demands of agrarian transformation and social dislocation. It identifies also signs of poor leadership by the landlords, of communal introversion by the people, of failure by the intellectuals to elucidate the basic problems, and a certain supineness in government which refused to acknowledge any positive role for state intervention. It remains for the reader to say whether modern explanations penetrate any deeper than those offered over the previous two hundred years.

Several caveats must be stated. This book, and its predecessors, were meant to open rather than close the account. The ground is prepared for better work. I am thinking of more precise analysis of the economic variables, and their quantification, without which much of the discussion remains educated guesswork. The time is now ripe for work on Scotland to match that on Ireland by, for instance, Joel Mokyr — work in which quantitative values are attached to key propositions in order to verify causal relationships.[2] We need also a more thorough evaluation of the literary record. For instance, it is possible to rewrite the history of Patrick

Sellar in a manner far beyond the limits of this volume. Just as important will be a more systematic history of the different elements of Highland society, a subject already opened by James Hunter. The agenda for future research is large: there remains much to be discovered about, for instance, the impact of famine, the demographic mechanisms, and trends in living standards. Needless to say there are dozens of Highland estates still unvisited by the tribes of modern historians. But the significance of the Highland experience can only be fully fathomed in a context much wider than the confines of northern Scotland. These two volumes will have served their function if they draw the Highlands into the wider debate about the process of agrarian transformation and the consequences of industrialisation.

Notes

1. Eric Richards, *A History of the Highland Clearances: Agrarian Transformation and the Evictions 1746-1886* (London, 1982).
2. Joel Mokyr, *Why Ireland Starved. A Quantitative and Analytical History of the Irish Economy, 1800-1850* (London, 1983).

ACKNOWLEDGEMENTS

My debts have grown. The first volume caused correspondents in Canada, the United States, England and Scotland to offer assistance, and I am grateful to many reviewers for identifying problems. Some of the ideas in this book received beneficial comment in seminars: the economic interpretation was aired at Stirling University (1970), Queen's University, Belfast (1975), the University of New South Wales (1976) and the University of Warwick (1981), and draws on arguments outlined in a paper published in the *Economic History Review* (1973). Variants of the chapters on social protest were considered at the Universities of Glasgow and Aberdeen (1979), Monash University (1976), the Working Group in Social History in Adelaide (1977) and the Social History Society Conference at Bristol (1979). Material on emigration was discussed at seminars at Stirling and Strathclyde Universities (1979), Flinders University (1982) and Otago University (1984). I am grateful to the editor of *Scottish Studies* for permission to employ material from papers published in that journal. I have received unfailing help from the Scottish Record Office and the National Library of Scotland and wish to thank also the donors of documents to these repositories. I am thinking particularly of the recent deposit of the great Sutherland Collection which will help reconstruct the evidential foundation of modern Highland history. I wish to record my gratitude to Dr Ian Grimble, Professor Rosalind Mitchison, Mrs Monica Clough, Dr J. L. Campbell, Dr Leah Leneman, Mrs Joan Stephenson, Mrs M. W. Grant of Golspie, Mrs P. E. Durham and Mr David Graham-Campbell. My greatest individual debt is to Mrs Joan Hancock for her assistance, stamina and good humour. Mrs Hancock constructed the appendix and the graphs. The Australian Research Grants Scheme, the Scottish Arts Council and the Flinders University Research Committee have all provided much appreciated financial support.

Eric Richards
Brighton, South Australia

ABBREVIATIONS

NLS   National Library of Scotland
PP   *Parliamentary Papers*
SCRO Stafford County Record Office
SRO   Scottish Record Office
TGSI *Transactions of the Gaelic Society of Inverness*
THAS *Transactions of the Highland and Agricultural Society of Scotland*

Map 1: Scotland — Counties, Islands and Districts Mentioned

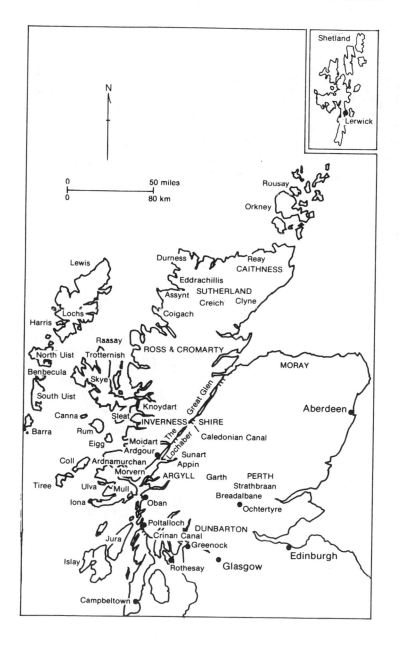

Map 2: Western Islands and Highlands

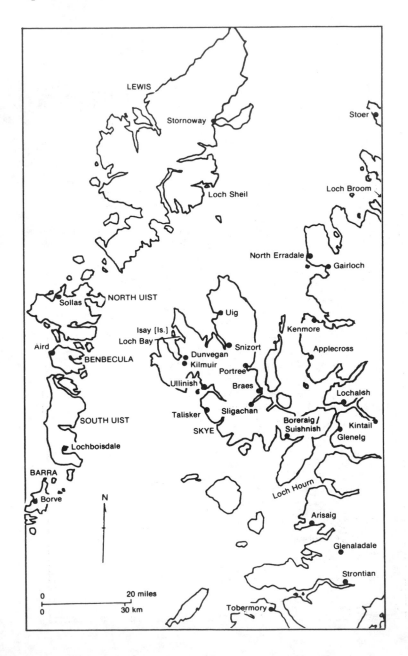

Map 3: Central and Eastern Highlands

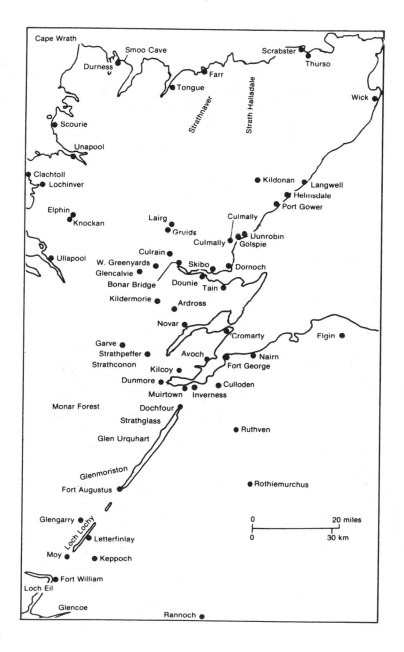

PART ONE

THE EFFORT TO UNDERSTAND

1

DR JOHNSON, DR SMITH AND THE IMPROVERS

I entered several of these huts [on Mull in 1797] which are even inferior to the generality of poor cottages in Wales. Their interior represents the most abject state to which human nature, by poverty and barbarism, can possible be reduced. The pig-sties of England are palaces to the huts of Mull; because the former admit at least fresh air, to which the latter are entirely strangers. But if anyone imagines happiness and contentment are strangers in these receptacles of abomination, they are much deceived, so relative is all human felicity. Surely, if anything can teach mankind the golden lesson of being contented with a small and peaceful competence, it is the spectacle of unfeigned satisfaction amidst poverty and want, such as this ... We do not visit the Hebrides to see stately palaces, and groves of citron, but to behold uncultivated nature, in the shed of the Highlander, or the solitude of mountains ... I found the untutored natives such as I expected them to be, and in their miserable mountains received a lesson of contentment, which future impressions will never be able to obliterate.

The Life and Remains of the Rev. Edward Daniel Clarke LL D, ed. William Otter

To the people of the Highlands the clearances that dominated the years between 1780 and 1855 were nothing less than a devastation of the old patterns of life. The foundations of their existence uprooted, the dispersed, disaffiliated peasantry met their fate without comprehension. For many landlords, the clearances were the means to improvement and profit, though for some the evictions were the last resort in an unavailing war against poverty and overpopulation. They, too, had little understanding of the reasons why. To the improvers of the eighteenth century, and their twentieth-century successors (planners and economists, historians and politicians), the question of Highland depopulation and undevelopment constituted a great intellectual challenge. Were the Highland clearances really necessary?

The clearances were part of a tragic problem entrapping the Highlands from at least 1800, and probably for much longer. By then it was already apparent to some that the people of the north were excluded from the benefits of industrialisation currently transforming the British Isles; it was becoming evident that population growth was outstripping the resources of that region. Realisation was dawning too that the landlords as a class would not, or could not, devise schemes capable of sustaining the swollen population. Thus the sheep came in by their thousands and pressed the human population out to the fringes of the land. Large numbers of people left the Highlands altogether, with or without direct compulsion from the proprietors; and those who remained lived in conditions of agricultural squalor which became a stain on the character of the Scottish (and indeed the British) nation. That this should happen during the age of improvement, when Britain cast off its pre-industrial shackles and eventually provided security of subsistence, and even affluence, to the masses was profoundly perplexing to the Victorian age. Whether the conundrum has yet been solved is a matter of some considerable controversy, and the subject of these chapters.

The effort to understand the 'Highland Problem' began in earnest when the intellectuals of the south ceased to dismiss the Highlands as barbarous, uncouth and literally unspeakable. The application of systematic analysis to the north of Scotland, not surprisingly, coincided with the rise of economic science, the doctrines of improvement, and the associated rational forces of the Enlightenment. And although few of the great Scottish intellects of the eighteenth century invested much direct attention in the Highlands, the general influence of their thinking saturated the ideas of virtually all observers of the time. The impact of the political economists may be juxtaposed with the direct observations of eye witnesses during the same period. The Highlands, soon after Culloden, began to exert a magnetic attraction for crusaders, the curious and the entrepreneurs. Between them, the political economists and the travellers shaped the definition and the diagnoses of the Highland problem during the age of the clearances.

I

For more than two hundred years there has been a procession of literary visitors to the Highlands and Islands of Scotland: tourists, journalists, missionaries, geologists, economists, sportsmen and, latterly, battalions of sociologists. The intrepid Samuel Johnson and his Lowland guide, James Boswell, aroused the nation's curiosity in the 1770s about this outlying culture, revealing the existence within a few hundred miles of the metropolis of a separate civilisation, as mysterious and exotic as any of the social systems recently discovered in the South Seas. The coexistence of breathtaking scenery, extraordinary social organisation and customs, and rank poverty was an attraction irresistible to southern visitors. The challenge was both aesthetic and intellectual. The effort to understand the nature of this society, to diagnose the 'Highland Problem', and to prescribe the proper direction of its development became the preoccupation of a succession of well-meaning outsiders who freely offered their thoughts to the Highland lairds and the government during the following two hundred years.

When Johnson and Boswell journeyed to the Hebrides in 1773 a structural transformation of the Highlands was already under way. In common with most of Western Europe, the Highlands was subjected to a series of pressures and opportunities which shifted the very foundations of life in the region. After the defeat of the Jacobite Rebellion in 1745-6, northern Scotland was comprehensively pacified by military and political power. A substantial part of the territory was expropriated from the rebellious landowners and administered on commercial principles for the government. Many private owners, already gripped by the propaganda of improvement, were conscious of the possibility of rapidly increasing rent-rolls. Rising prices for Highland products — notably cattle, kelp and wool, but also fish — encouraged the idea that the region could be made rich if directed rationally and supplied with enterprising capital investment. The extraordinary expansion of the industrial economy of Britain exerted profound effects on the Scottish Highlands: in essence the expansionary stimuli from the south ended northern isolation and created powerful economic incentives for new patterns of production, and for a radically changed society.

The 1770s witnessed the emergence of these trends in forms which were clear to the eyes of Johnson and Boswell: landowners and capitalists were experimenting with improved methods of agricultural organisation and new enterprise flowered in many parts of the region. The disruption of the old tenurial arrangements was already creating turmoil in the lives of the common people. Rents were rising and commercial sheepfarmers had begun to colonise the southern quarters of the Highlands. While the expansion of pastoralism intensified the pressure on landed resources, the phenomenal success of the potato (only very recently accepted into the common people's diet) worked to relieve land hunger, at least in the short run. The region had always been hostage to famine, and despite the new economic activity generated there in these decades, the iron grip of Malthusian forces was not broken. In part it was because population growth, already marked by 1770, outpaced the expansion of the Highland economy. In part it was a consequence also of the changing pattern of production and labour needs of the region which rendered redundant a large proportion of the swelling population. The poverty of the region was reflected in the recurrence of famine into the nineteenth century, and in the large seasonal and permanent emigrations remarked upon by most of the visitors who followed in the footsteps of Dr Johnson and his companion.

The story of the Highlands after Culloden was, therefore, one of failure. In contrast to most of the rest of Britain, where industrialisation eventually raised the average living standards of a vastly increased population, the Highlands seemed to regress. A region which had once supported practically half the population of Scotland, and had maintained a virtual autonomy of political structure and culture, was reduced by 1840 to a rural slum, frequently unable to feed itself and losing population at a time when growth was occurring elsewhere. In the context of British economic growth, the Highlands became 'the regional problem' *par excellence.*

The history of the 'Highland Clearances' is inseparable from the 'Highland Problem'. Two centuries of controversy have raged over their consequences, comprehending questions of morality, cultural decline, landlord obligation, racial autonomy, genocide, economic development and religion. At its core are propositions about landlord culpability for the tragedy of modern Highland history, the role of the church, the policy of the Westminster government, and the relations between the Highlands and the Lowlands, England and Scotland, Celt and Anglo-Saxon. It boils over in controversy

about the degree of violence employed by the Highland proprietors during the process of eviction. The literature is generally
emotive and polemical, intertwined in a series of criteria which are
extraordinarily difficult to disentangle.

Much of the obscurity and controversy in the debate is unnecessary. The character of the clearances, the attitudes of the landlords,
the methods of the evictions, the response of the people, even the
role of the factors and the ministers, and the posture of the government are — on the whole — not questions which can any longer
generate much disagreement.[1] The relevant questions for rational
debate are not what happened, or even how it happened, but why
the clearances happened and with what consequences? In effect
the important historical issues which remain are concerned with
explanation and interpretation and it is to these matters that this
volume is mainly addressed.

The Highland region has been a poor relation of England and
the Lowlands throughout the modern period: and, ever since the
clearances, it has been exceptionally difficult to generate balanced
economic development there. The great question for historians is
the degree of responsibility that may be attributed to the clearances
for Highland poverty and economic distress in the ninteenth and
twentieth centuries. The fact that there were other concurrent
causes renders the question at once more interesting and more
complicated.

It was natural that those controlling the resources of the Highlands, the landlords, should be held directly responsible for the
poverty of the people. This view was implicit, if not explicit, in
most contemporary accounts. In 1803, thirty years after Johnson
and Boswell, another tourist, the Rev. P. B. Homer, commented
on the current exodus of Highlanders from the north:

> I asked the landlady what was the cause of the emigrations; she
> answered 'oppression and poverty'... If the poor in England are
> discontented with their lot let them come to the Highlands of
> Scotland and compare their conditions with what they find here.
> The life of the poor is here the most destitute and the most
> deplorable that an imagination can conceive. In the supply of its
> necessary wants it is not raised one degree above that of the
> savages of Otaheite.[2]

Homer's view was unambiguous: the Highlanders were poor

because the landlords were oppressive. Underlying his diagnosis was the assumption that the region possessed genuine control over its own destiny, through the instrumentality of its landlords. It is a question which provides the primary focus for the present volume.

The debate about the Highland clearances and the causes of Highland poverty and undevelopment has been a living issue in Scottish politics almost since the first Blackface sheep crossed the Highland line. There exists, therefore, a substantial body of critical literature which, though it may not match the richness and depth of research that informs much discussion of the English and Irish land questions, is not inferior in passion and controversy. Much of it is based upon sketchy evidence and analysis innocent of alternate realities. It reflects both the changing currents of wider intellectual influences affecting governments' and landlords' policies, and the dogmatism which has consistently disfigured the debate. Above all, the long debate illustrates the power of myth in historical explanation.

II

No visitor or scholar served the Highlands better, nor repaid its hospitality more fully, than James Boswell and Dr Samuel Johnson. Accounts of their tour provide some of the earliest and most perspicacious thoughts on the transformation of the Highlands in the second half of the eighteenth century. Their itinerary took in Skye, Raasay, Coll, Mull and Ulva, as well as parts of the inland south of Inverness and Glenelg. Travellers' tales of the eighteenth century are an unreliable genre, often written mainly for literary effect and designed to leave the reader open-mouthed at the freakishness of distant places.[3] Johnson and Boswell were entirely exceptional. The journals of their tour[4] provide a marvellous introduction to the condition of the Highlands already in the throes of great change. They identified changes under way even before the impact of the clearances, and foreshadowed several of the key issues that recur in virtually all the subsequent literature on the Highland question.

Johnson described, in striking prose, a society in a state of degeneration and demoralisation, 'crushed by the heavy hand of a vindictive conqueror'.[5] Its humiliation after Culloden had left a hollow shell of the previous life: 'There was perhaps never any change of national manners so quick, so great, and so general, as that which operated in the Highlands, by the last conquest, and the subsequent laws.' Of the old Highland life, all the ferocity, the military ardour and the stern independence had gone:

> Of what they had before the late conquest of their country, there remain only their language and their poverty. Their language is attacked on all sides ... That their poverty is gradually abated, cannot be mentioned among the unpleasing consequences of subjection.

Johnson's optimism about the welfare of the common Highlander was based upon changes in the economic system which he regarded as both necessary and beneficial:

> They are now acquainted with money, and the possibility of gain will by degrees make them industrious. Such is the effect of the late regulations that a longer journey than to the Highlands must be taken by him whose curiosity pants for savage virtues and barbarous grandeur.[6]

Although Johnson was prepared to believe that the changes in Highland society were bringing material benefit to the people, and had reduced indolence among them, he found it difficult to gauge the actual poverty of the region. Indigence seemed to be universal — to this fact the shoeless beggary of the people bore witness — yet he suspected that they looked poorer than they were.[7] He was aware of some of the elementary facts of Highland life: he knew that seed produced only a threefold crop yield, and remarked that 'it is vain to hope for plenty, when a third part of the harvest must be reserved for seed'. The yield on barley was much higher but its labour requirements acted as a deterrent to extensive cultivation. Johnson knew also that famine was a reality that repeatedly stalked the Highlands, as in 'the black winter of seventy-one', the severity and length of which decimated the cattle. 'In countries like these', he observed, 'the descriptions of famine become intelligible.'[8] He judged the vulnerability of this peasant economy as well as any modern analyst:

> In Mull the disappointment of a harvest, or a murrain among the cattle cuts off the regular provision; and those who have no

manufactures can purchase no part of the superfluities of other countries. The consequence of a bad season is here not scarcity, but emptiness; and they whose plenty was barely a supply of natural and present need, when that slender stock fails, must perish with hunger.[9]

The two southern tourists were perfectly aware of the seductive charm of the older way of life and at one point Boswell exclaimed that 'my fellow traveller and I were now full of the old Highland spirit, and were dissatisfied at hearing of racked rents and emigration, and ... of a chief not surrounded by his clan'.[10] But generally Johnson's portrait of Highland society was little distorted by any romanticisation of the older forms, and he delivered sober judgements on the critical changes in the system, notably on the erosion of cultural identity in the Highlands, the roles of landlords and tacksmen, and the significance of emigration. He emphasised the destructive impact of the Jacobite Rebellion. The prevailing patriarchial life has been grounded on 'insular insubordination' in which

the inhabitants were for a long time perhaps not unhappy; but their content was a muddy mixtyure of pride and ignorance, an indifference for pleasures which they did not know, a blind veneration for their chiefs, and a strong conviction of their own importance.[11]

Humbled and broken after the rebellion, the chiefs

being now deprived of their jurisdiction, have already lost much of their influence; and as they generally degenerate from patriarchal rulers to rapacious landlords, they will divest themselves of the little that remains ... The Chief has lost his formidable retinue; and the Highlander works his heath unarmed and defenceless, with the peaceable submission of a French peasant or English cottager ... The Chiefs, divested of their prerogatives, necessarily turned their thoughts to the improvement of their revenues, and expect more rent, and they have less homage.[12]

Here indeed was the classic statement of social and psychological change in the post-1745 Highlands.

The transformation of the attitude of the chiefs was associated with three other changes at the time of Johnson's visit — one was rackrenting, which had raised rents by fourfold in twenty years in some places; another was the elimination of the 'middling class' of Highland life, known as the tacksmen; and the third was 'the fury of emigration'. Johnson believed that the general upward pressure on rents in the Highlands resulted from the combined effects of 'the philosophy of commerce' and the rapid expansion of kelp production. (Heavily taxed seaborne coal was used to produce calcined ashes from seaweed collected and burned on the seashore in iron pots, with vast labour effort.) Although he was highly critical of rackrenting landlords, Johnson warned against exaggeration:

> It seems to be the general opinion, that the rents have been raised with too much eagerness. Some regard must be paid to prejudice. Those who have hitherto paid but little, will not suddenly be persuaded to pay much, though they can afford it.[13]

He alluded also to the reluctance of the kelp-harvesters to pay the augmented rents because they believed their earnings to be 'the mere product of personal labour, to which the landlord contributes nothing'. But Johnson was fully familiar with the sacred rights of property for 'as any man may be said to give, what he gives the power of gaining, he has certainly as much right to profit from the price of kelp as of anything else found or raised upon his ground'.[14]

The exercise of these rights brought some chiefs into confrontation with their tenants, who refused to pay the higher rents and were ejected:

> The ground is then let to a stranger who perhaps brings a larger stock but who, taking the land at its full price, treats with the Laird upon equal terms, and considers him not as a Chief, but as a trafficker in land. Thus the estate perhaps is improved, but the clan is broken.

These developments were, of course, squarely in the pattern of the sheep clearances which followed during the next hundred years. Johnson's attitude to the new commercialism of the landlord was ambivalent. He expressed a repugnance at the calculating attitude that had become general, yet Boswell reported a conversation in which Johnson said:

A Highland Chief should now endeavour to do everything to raise his rents, by means of the industry of his people. Formerly, it was right for him to have his house full of idle fellows; they were his defenders, his servants, his dependants, his friends. Now they may be better employed.

He advocated that the great Highland lairds should improve their estates and emulate English aristocrats such as the Duke of Bedford, and become influential as great men in the king's dominion, by their wealth rather than their military strength.[15]

Dr Johnson was plainly impressed by what he identified as the remnants of the culture and social order of the older society, particularly the old tacksmen — the large leaseholders who acted as links between lairds and people and had sustained what he called 'the primitive stability' of the Highland life. The tacksmen were middlemen who came to be the *bête noire* of improvement thinkers — they allegedly impeded all change in agriculture and oppressed the people by the extraction of quasi-feudal services.[16] They were systematically eliminated by progressive landlords in the second part of the eighteenth century. Johnson reported that this destroyed the lines of authority in the hereditary system and left 'the tenants to the wisdom and mercy of a factor', i.e. the professional estate agent who acted on behalf of a landlord. He remarked, 'To banish the Tacksmen is easy, to make a country plentiful by diminishing the people is an expeditious mode of husbandry; but that abundance which there is nobody to enjoy, contributes little to human happiness.'[17] The great shift in attitudes had been bought at a high social cost: 'Since the islanders, no longer content to live, have learned the desire of growing rich, an ancient dependent is in danger of giving way to a higher bidder, at the expense of domestick dignity and hereditary power.'[18]

The effect of rackrenting and the assault on the tacksmen was the emergence of 'a general discontent' among the people of the Highlands which expressed itself in emigration. Johnson described it as 'this epidemick desire of wandering which spreads its contagion from valley to valley' and left a 'lasting vacuity' in the Highlands. Emigration was the antithesis of proper landlord policy. Johnson told Boswell that 'the Lairds instead of improving their country, diminished their people'. It was a great evil because the Highlands were, he thought, not thickly peopled: 'To hinder insurrection, by driving away the people, and to govern peaceably, by having no subjects, is an expedient that argues no great profundity of politicks.' Boswell quoted his mentor as saying that 'a rapacious Chief would make a wilderness of his estate.'[19] Throughout these remarks Johnson maintained an ironic tone, but he undoubtedly laboured under an assumption that the vacuum created by emigration would not be refilled by population growth and, therefore, it followed that emigration would ultimately defeat the landlord's own interest. Rents would eventually collapse. In this respect Johnson certainly miscalculated the more fundamental demographic changes beginning to alter the basic elements of Highland life.

The model landlord for Johnson and Boswell was the laird of Raasay, who was 'sensible, polite and a gentleman'. His lands, though they did not yield a great revenue, allowed him to live in some splendour — 'and so far is' he from distressing his people, that, in the present rage for emigration, not a man has left his estate'.[20]

The accounts of Johnson's tour to the Hebrides are full of luminous intelligence and judicious exposition. Much of the *Journals'* significance derives from Johnson's emphasis on the qualitative and psychological changes that had overcome the Highlands. He was prepared to allow that the material welfare of the people had improved as a consequence of the great transformation wrought since Culloden. He made no bones about the abject poverty of the region and the need for improvement. His main objection was to the extremism of some landlords' pursuit of gain. He identified, with crystal clarity, a spectrum of changes which, in fact, preceded the clearances, but he neglected the demographic elements at work in the Highland economy. Johnson's view of the Highlands rested, ultimately, on the belief that the lairds could shape the future, that all alternatives were open to them, and that they had no justification for behaving more avariciously than their English counterparts. In general, his was an optimistic perspective on Highland prospects for, though he regretted the passing of an elegant and picturesque culture, he foresaw improvement in material standards among the people, and an awakening from their traditional torpor. His basic assumption is plain enough: there was no special reason why the Highlands could not advance to the level of the better-developed parts of Britain. He believed that, in the old society, feudal values had placed a high priority on service, loyalty and valour and, correspondingly, a low premium on wealth, efficiency and application. In this he concurred with the prevailing prejudices of his time which contended that the feudal system had imprisoned, impoverished and enervated the people. The destruction of that system had not rendered the people happier, but it removed the impediments to material progress. It was a simple view of the sources of human development.

Towards the end of his journal Samuel Johnson wrote: 'after having seen the deaf taught arithmetick, who could be afraid to cultivate the Hebrides?'[21] His rhetorical flourish, re-echoed through the literature on the Highlands to the present day, was a remarkable expression of confidence in the possibility of Highland development from a man who had witnessed, at first hand, the after-effects of the famine of 1771.

Most of all, Johnson's *Journals* provided the classic account of the gains of economic progress juxtaposed with a sense of cultural decline. It was a model statement of the qualitative costs of material advance.

III

In the thirty years after Dr Johnson's tour of the Hebrides, the Highlands attracted public attention on a disproportionate scale, and came to be regarded as a region of promise, simply awaiting assistance and stimulation to bring it out of its 'feudal' past. 'Feudalism' became the epithet employed to derogate any arrangement appearing to stand in the way of commercial progress. The Highlands' case was advocated by several ideologues of improvement urging both government and private capitalists to consider the prospects for investment and enterprise in the north. The application of systematic analysis to northern Scotland, not surprisingly, coincided with the rise of scientific economics and the literature of agricultural improvement. Three men in particular — Adam Smith, George Dempster and Sir John Sinclair — were influential in moulding the intellectual and psychological context for the further transformation of the Highlands.

Adam Smith had only very slight personal knowledge of the Highlands,[22] and it remains a puzzle that he gave this part of his own country so little attention in *The Wealth of Nations*, although the Highlands provided Scots philosophers with what has been described as a 'sociological museum at Edinburgh's back door'. As

Jacob Viner has pointed out, Smith's focus on the plight of the Highlander was 'merely incidental to his search for illustrative material in connection with his general treatment of the problems of taxation, of bounties, of the economics of landlordism'.[23] The last is of special significance for a study of the Highland clearances and for Smith's evaluation of the causes of economic progess in the region.

For the most part Adam Smith employed the Highlands as the standard model of a backward society poverty-bound because the division of labour had been narrowly restricted. Specialisation of production in the Highlands had made virtually no progress, so that 'every farmer must be a butcher, baker and brewer to his own family'. He drew attention to the abysmal poverty and the primitive methods of cultivation of the cottars and small tenants. In a well-known passage he said that the advent of the potato was an important advance because it would improve the general nourishment and health of the population, and make the people less ugly in appearance. He attributed their appallingly high level of infant mortality to sheer poverty. Smith believed that, by its isolation, the region had been deprived of the main benefits of trade, and thus the people were kept poor and the archaic feudal regime had been preserved. In this respect the Highlands were to be compared with backward and insulated societies, such as the Arabs and the Tartars.[24]

Smith argued that the survival, until 1746, of the extraordinary powers of the local chiefs, for example Cameron of Lochiel, was evidence of the primitive character of the society and the economy. Of Cameron, he remarked: 'That gentleman, whose rent never exceeded five hundred pounds a year, carried, in 1745, eight hundred of his own people into the rebellion with him.' The economic effects of isolation were powerfully reinforced by the reigning patterns of consumption which further curtailed the possibilities of progress. Smith expressed the point in this way:

In a country [such as the Highlands] which has neither foreign commerce, nor any of the finer manufactures, a great proprietor, having nothing for which he can exchange the greater part of the produce of the lands which is over and above the maintenance of the cultivators, consumes the whole in rustick hospitality at home.[25]

This type of patriarchy, of which Samuel Johnson had been both witness and beneficiary, was an essential consequence of the economic isolation of the society. Smith argued that the old system had broken down only when the region was exposed to the trade of the outside world in the eighteenth century. He associated the widespread trend towards the consolidation of agricultural land with a 'general change in social habits on the part of the great barons, encouraged by the growing availability of fine manufactured goods'.[26] In this fashion Smith argued that a change in consumption habits caused the Highland proprietors to direct their energies towards the extraction of commercial rents for their lands. A decisive shift in consumption preferences was thus an initiating force for agricultural change and economic progress, and eventually it prompted Highland lairds to diminish the number of parasitic retainers and 'to dismiss the unnecessary part of the tenants'. Smith looked favourably on the whole process — 'Farms were enlarged, and the occupiers of land, notwithstanding the complaints of depopulation, reduced to the number necessary for cultivating';[27] landlords became more calculating; farming yielded greater produce; and trade was enlarged to the benefit of all. In essence he saw a society formerly hamstrung by compulsory services and deference and feudal waste transformed into a rational structure promoting increased output and reduced dependence and poverty.

Adam Smith contended that the great landowners had a moral responsibility to promote agricultural improvement, and was scathing about those who failed so to do. In 1759 he had written to Lord Shelburne:

We have in Scotland some noblemen whose estates extend from the east to the west sea, who call themselves improvers and are so called by their countrymen when they cultivate two or three hundred acres round the family seat, while they allow all the rest of their country to lie waste, almost uninhabited and actively unimproved, not worth a shilling a hundred acres, without thinking themselves answerable to God, their country and their posterity for so shameful as well as so foolish a neglect.[28]

But Smith, of course, had more faith in the operation of self-interest than of duty, and he had greater confidence in the newer breed of commercial landowners than in the traditional lairds who tended to squander their resources on unproductive pursuits. The advancement of agricultural improvement, though it might disrupt the old social order, was a high priority for general economic progress — 'Whatever measures discourage the improvement of this art are extremely prejudicial to the progress of opulence.'[29]

Smith stressed the beneficial effects derived by the Highlands from the Union of Scotland and England in 1707. This had opened a great market for Highland cattle and had altered the pattern of production in the north. Of cattle, he wrote, 'Their ordinary price is at present about three times that of the beginning of the century, and the rents of many Highland estates have been tripled and quadrupled in the same time.' Indeed Smith seemed to believe that the increased demand for meat and the resulting specialisation of production would promote regional differentiation of output — some regions would specialise in pastoral production, others in arable, in accordance with relative prices and factor costs and endowments.[30] In this he identified the mechanism which was to shape the future course of Highland development.

In his references to the contemporary Highland economy, it is clear that Smith was cognisant of the great windfall gains that had fallen to Highland landlords from the rapid rise in kelp prices, quite independent of any positive effort or investment on their part. Rent derived from kelp, he said, 'is not at all proportioned to what the landlord may have laid out upon the improvement of the land, or to what he can afford to take, but to what the farmer can afford to give'.[31] In making this point Adam Smith not only raised interesting problems in economic theory,[32] but also exposed important moral questions about the functions of the landlord class. By stressing the unearned character of kelp profits, Smith seemed to suggest an implicit moral denunciation which brought him closer than might be expected to the critics of the Highland lairds in the age of the clearances.

While Adam Smith spoke eloquently of the 'noble and important duty of attempting to introduce arts, industry and independency into a miserable country, which has hitherto been a stranger to them all',[33] it is nevertheless amply clear that he believed that the social good would be best promoted by the self-interested response of men of energy, capital and intelligence to the opportunities of trade and specialisation, as revealed in the market. The manifest opportunities which the Highlands had derived from the opening of the cattle trade with England was one of Smith's most telling illustrations of the benefits of an extended market. His references to the Scottish Highlands, taken together, amount to an indictment of feudal social relations, the associated narrowness of the market, and the restricted division of labour to which he attributed the proverbial poverty of the people. His prescription for Highland progress was, therefore, obvious. Smith, indeed, provided much of the inspiration, even a blueprint, for the rapid conversion of the Highlands to market economics in the following half century. *The Wealth of Nations* of 1776 yielded most of the economic propositions which justified the shift of the region towards sheep production, and away from the labour-intensive self-sufficiency which had characterised the old Highlands. His book was a bible to the Highland improvers.

In essence, Smith provided an implicit prescription for regional specialisation of production which became a standard, and virtually unchallenged, precept of classical economics. The classical economists, it has been suggested, were little concerned with the regional location of activity: it was taken for granted that capital and labour would simply migrate to those areas in which they would earn the highest attainable profit or wage: 'Capitalists therefore, would maximise profits by locating where their costs were lowest, and workers would maximise wages by moving to where jobs were to be found. In general, regional questions were relegated to the back of the classical stage.'[34] The classical economists simply assumed an automatic mechanism by which regions would adjust into balanced relations within the national economy, specialising in certain types of production, and attracting or throwing off the mobile factors of production in accordance with their factor endowments and market changes. It was a convenient set of assumptions which took small account of the immobility of factors, the social costs of adjustment, and the possibility of 'inherent imbalance' within the market system. As Stuart Holland has remarked, British development in the years after Adam Smith exposed major disparities of structure and employment between regions: 'The neo-classical theory of location became increasingly unreal as unbalanced capitalist development left behind a trail of wrecked regions and problem areas, which, according to the theory, should never have occured.'[35] The Scottish Highlands, in many respects, became the classic example of such a 'wrecked region', not fitting the theoretical framework created by either Adam Smith or his illustrious successors. The Highlands, it may be said, have not been well served by economic theory. The purpose of much of Smith's analysis of the Highlands was to accelerate the abolition of feudalism. In a recent study of the powerful intellectual forces which influenced the development of the Scottish economy in the eighteenth century, E.J. Hobsbawm has emphasised this aspect of contemporary thinking. He argues that agricultural transformation in Scotland was

> specifically formulated as one of the transition from a feudal to a capitalist system . . . The programme of the Scottish reformers aimed for the transformation of feudal lords into capitalist landowners by the offer of higher incomes, at the destruction of small scale peasant production and peasant communal practices, and at the transformation of a small section of the richer peasantry into an entrepreneurial rural bourgeoisie. It stressed not so much the creation of a market as structural changes which would make possible a more capital-intensive and technologically progresive agriculture.[36]

Smith provided a general model of agrarian transformation which entailed the elimination of the peasantry and the conversion of pre-capitalist landlords into the new approved variety. It was a radical programme repeated a hundred times by the improvement-thinkers of the late eighteenth century, all of whom, we may be certain, had been profoundly influenced by Adam Smith. Moreover, the prescription was so lucid and cogent that it seemed to allow virtually no alternative possibilities for the future of the Highland economy.

IV

The influence of Adam Smith on thinking about the Highlands was pervasive. Although his general recommendation against government intervention in economic life allowed for the exception of defence, his doctrine endorsed the improvement ideologues' insistence that the forces of the market should be liberated. In the decades both before and after the publication of *The Wealth of Nations*, landlords and writers grappled with the growing problem of what to do about the development of the Highlands.[37] The thinking of George Dempster (1732-1818) exemplifies the contemporary tension between the Smithian view and the continuing, but weakening, patriarchal tradition. Dempster, a prolific writer and a practical improver himself, was at one with the Smithian notion that the poverty and backwardness of the Highlands could be eliminated only by the mobilisation and liberation of the resources of the region, but believed that this could not be left to the mere exercise of market forces; rather, the progress of the Highlands required the leadership and promotional energy of 'men of patriotic zeal'.

Dempster was a propagandist and enthusiast for Highland development, fired by an almost Messianic belief in the future prospects of the region. A well-known opponent of sheep clearances, which he regarded as contrary to the long-term interests of both landlords and people, he advocated positive enterprise which would create wealth and employment and staunch the outflow of emigrants. Dempster's own record as an entrepreneur and politician is worth consideration. He had inherited a farmland estate of 6,000 acres in Forfarshire and he made a fortune in the east coast grain trade. He entered Parliament in 1761 after a severe contest for the Perth Burghs which cost him £10,000. In the Commons he was a vocal and highly independent member. When criticised for his unpredictable attitudes by Samuel Whitbread in 1774, he retorted with the memorable words: 'I sit here to change my mind just as often as my reason is convinced.'[38] In London he became a prominent spokesman for the cause of the Highlands.

Dempster was one of the founders of the 'British Society for Extending the Fisheries, and Improving the Sea Coasts of this Kingdom' (known as the British Fisheries Society), an ambitious enterprise designed to stimulate development, in the West Highlands in particular. In 1786 Parliament granted the Society a charter to operate as a joint-stock, limited liability company.[39] A curious blend of Utopianism, philanthropy and commercial optimism, it raised capital widely, including substantial contributions from the Highland lairds, and *émigré* Scots in India. It existed to create small towns and villages to act as depots for the fishing industry, the promotion of which would generate specialised employment and income, and then would initiate the process of the division of labour. Dempster particularly looked for the complementary promotion of improved cultivation by the people, and the introduction of diverse forms of industry into the Highlands. It was envisaged that these enterprises would end the flow of emigration from the Highlands, and break down the constricting feudalism of the old Highland ways. Dempster wrote of the prospects in December 1784:

> The seas abound with fish, the Highland with industrious and good people. It will be the business of the legislature to bring these two to meet. But I fear it would in that country be an easier task for mountains to melt, at least they are at present much nearer to one another. Should however the proper encouragement be given to the fisheries, it would produce still more important consequences to the nation, by the improvement the Highland is susceptible of in point in agriculture. If you can suppose potato substitutable in the place of corn, there is scarce a necessary of life that might not be produced in thousands of acres now covered with heath, or an island in the Hebrides that might not be as well cultivated and inhabited as Jersey and Guernsey.[40]

Dempster imagined that the advance of the Highlands would take several forms — there would be fishing villages certainly, but in addition new roads were required for 'piercing the north and west Highlands'. This activity, together with the introduction of cotton manufacturing, the encouragement of potato consumption and the creation of intensive arable production by the reclamation of moorland, would create the basic conditions of a populous and prosperous future for the Highlands. The role of the British Fisheries Society was to provide the initial thrust towards development. In a discussion of the rise of the new villages of Ullapool and Loch Bay, Dempster distilled the essence of his thinking in a striking metaphor:

> Tho' I am not for forcing our towns in hot beds, yet I think a gentle heat might be applied with great success to the walls, especially when the plant is only beginning to sprout in a cold climate and bleak country.[41]

His enthusiasm and optimism were unbounded: at one stage he declared that there was no reason why Sutherland should not be transformed into a second Lancashire.[42] He believed that, with the removal of institutional obstacles and the provision of appropriate assistance, virtually everything was possible. He reflected, in extreme form, the confidence of the age.

The Utopian mercantilism upon which George Dempster's views was based inevitably aroused great scepticism among the more hard-boiled political economists of his day. The British Fisheries Society seemed to some little better than a Highland version of the South Sea Bubble. Adam Smith was reported to have said with some cynicism that:

he looked for no other consequence from the scheme than the entire loss of every shilling that should be expended in it, granting, however, with uncommon candour, that the public would be no great sufferer, because he believed the individuals meant to put their hands only in their own pockets.[43]

Jeremy Bentham was scornful of the idea of giving special favour to an enterprise in the north of Scotland:

Supposing a greater profit might be made by a greater capital employed in this way, than by the same capital employed in any other (a point necessary to be made out, with at least some general share of probability), why am I, who am carrying on a flourishing manufacture at Manchester, to be taxed, to have money taken out of my pocket, to be given to you to catch fish in the isles of Scotland?[44]

These remarks on the question of the British Fisheries Society in the 1780s highlighted two great themes that recur in the debate about the clearances and the Highland problem. Dempster represented the view that the region deserved not only the attention of private enterprise but also the active promotion of the government; by contrast, Smith and Bentham could see no sense in any interference with the normal direction of capital and business — the only rational course was to leave the Highlands to the everyday operation of the market. By the turn of the century, except by indirect interference with Highland emigration, the advocates of minimal governmental activity had triumphed in official thinking about the Highland economy.

Dempster himself made a second and more immediate contribution to the question of Highland development. In 1786, the year of the parliamentary negotiations on the British Fisheries Society, Dempster bought the sizeable estate of Skibo in south-east Sutherland. Having by this purchase set himself up as a Highland laird, he proceeded to put into practice some of his ideas about economic progress in the north. He became a model landlord, an innovator and an experimenter. One of his principal acts was to lop away all the surviving feudal encrustations (such as labour services) which affected his tenants; in addition, he gave them individual security of tenure for life. He tried to encourage close settlement by intensive arable production in the form of an elaborate 'lotting' system. This involved the allocation of sections of waste heathland to small tenants at very low rents; they were given free materials to erect buildings and were expected to convert the land into good arable soil; in return Dempster gave the people leases and promised independently arbitrated compensation for any improvements they achieved during the span of the lease. 'Part of my object', he explained,

is to contribute my mite towards rendering the Highlands of Scotland, the Norway and Sweden of Great Britain, by inclosing and planting only such parts of it as have been *tirned* [i.e. pared of peat] to the bones by the industry of the people and at present is certainly not worth one farthing the 100 acres.[45]

Dempster, full of speculative enterprise, is said to have invented the idea of packing salmon in ice for export. He connected his elaborate lotting system with an ambitious project to introduce cotton spinning and weaving at Skibo, where a substantial mill was constructed in association with David Dale. All Dempster's initiatives were directed towards the task of lifting the common people out of their wretched poverty. He remarked that 'By these means, constant employment will be found for people of all ages and sexes, and a considerable market opened for the productions of the country.'

Dempster's manifesto of Highland development was propounded in his contribution to the *Old Statistical Account* published in the 1790s. His constant emphasis was that his schemes represented an *alternative* to the sheepfarming which, at that time, was believed to have devastating effects on the Highlands. His basic assumption was that any development which activated the energies of the common people would generate a cumulative growth of the local economy; sheepfarming, by contrast, would yield only a short-term gain and would have no lasting benefit for the Highlands.

Some have thought that it would be a fitter use for the Highlands, to convert them into sheep walks. That it might be better for the people to cultivate sheep instead of black cattle, is probably true ... But that the estates would ultimately become more valuable, is by no means so clear a proposition.

It was axiomatic with Dempster that a human population was preferable to one of sheep, and that the two were incompatible: 'The lower grounds, now occupied by people, must be reserved for the food and shelter of the flock in winter.' Where sheep did displace the people it was possible, he said, to think of locating them in new villages of the sort which he himself advocated, but he warned against the forced resettlement of people ejected from sheepwalks:

It is one thing to build a village, to which people may resort if they choose it, and another to drive them from the country into villages, where they must starve, unless they change at once their manners, their habits, and their occupations. How much better it would be, gradually to introduce spinning wheels and looms into their houses, than to drive them from their houses, their gardens and their little fields.[46]

Dempster insisted that landlords could achieve the same ends without recourse to sheepfarming: they could increase their returns by the promotion of manufacturing and agriculture which employed the labours of the existing people of the Highlands.

George Dempster's views represented a step beyond those of Samuel Johnson: while Dempster rejected the inevitability of sheepfarming and its consequent depopulating effects, he believed that positive, radical change was necessary. His opinions also diverged from those of Adam Smith in their reliance on the promotional intervention of government and benevolent capitalists. There were two fundamental premisses in Dempster's thinking. One was that the Highlands was in serious danger of a permanent population decline because of heavy emigration, from which it might take a century to recover. His second major premiss was that the conditions for the continuous growth of manufacturing which was being demonstrated in Lancashire could be replicated in the Highlands. This confidence about the possibility of a diversified economic structure was, indeed, a recurrent theme in the history of economic thought in the Highlands for the two centuries after the Forty-five. In fact Dempster's supreme optimism — despite his warnings about the danger of compulsion in the creation of villages — persuaded some landlords that the severe social effects of sheep clearances could be mitigated by the creation of fishing and manufacturing villages in parallel with the economy of the sheep-walks.

The history of Dempster's own improvements on his Highland estate at Skibo was not a happy one. The cotton mill at Spinningdale burned down in 1808, and the enterprise never recovered. Dempster gained a reputation for benevolence among his people and the intensive labour applied to the heathlands created an extension of cultivation on the estate.[47] But after Dempster's death in 1818 his heir found the estate congested with crofters and generally overpopulated. Although the younger Dempster never evicted crofters, he found it necessary to prohibit squatters and, on the death of each crofter, consolidated holdings and prevented the automatic succession of a relative. The population necessarily declined and the dreams of George Dempster dissolved; in 1865 the estate was sold off.[48] The story of the Dempster estate demonstrated the distance between theory and practice.

V

The most influential propagandist for the development of the Highlands at the time of the clearances was Sir John Sinclair. The improvement enthusiast *par excellence*, surpassing even the frenetically active Dempster, he probably did more than any other single person to introduce the latest methods — including new breeds of sheep — to the north of Scotland. He deluged the country with a flood of technical and moralising tracts. In particular he was responsible for the collection of a large body of basic and detailed information about the country on a parochial basis at the end of the century. This was the first *Statistical Account of Scotland*, a latter-day Domesday Book which constitutes the most important single source for the history of the clearances. Of Sinclair's own writing, three points may be made. First, his thinking stretches across the period of demographic transition in the Highlands and it is possible to trace the shift in his views from a fear of depopulation (through excessive emigration) towards fear of the Malthusian spectre of overpopulation. Second, Sinclair was himself a large landowner in the relatively favoured country of Caithness. Third, like Dempster, Sinclair wrestled with the inescapable moral problem of reconciling the imperatives of improvement with the severe social consequences of radical agrarian change. Towards the end of his career in improvement Sinclair's views seem to have hardened into a generally justificatory attitude towards landlord policy in the Highlands.

In terms of applied improvement, Sir John Sinclair appears to have done very well on his own estates in Caithness. In 1770 he inherited 60,000 acres which at that time yielded a rent of £2,300 per annum. According to his son's later recollection, the estate was then three-quarters bog and heath, saddled with debts of £18,000 and an annuity burden of £500. By 1795 Sinclair had managed to raise the rental value to £3,240.[49] In 1788 he bought, with the help of his wife's dowry, the estate of Langwell for £9,000 which, after much improvement expenditure and the introduction of sheep, he sold for £40,000 in 1811. A generation later the same estate was sold to the Duke of Portland for £90,000, to be converted into a deer forest.[50]

Sinclair maintained throughout that the poverty of the Highlands, and emigration from the region, were the avoidable consequences of gross inefficiency in the old system of agriculture, combined with the ignorance and indolence of the native population. His improvements were designed to remedy both problems. He set about the abolition of runrig agriculture and the residual labour services of the old system, and embarked on a great scheme of improvement encompassing enclosures, roads, new crops, coal imports, land reclamation and new breeds of sheep, notably the Cheviot. He conducted a virtual war against the wastelands; indeed his favourite toast was said to have been: 'May a common become an uncommon spectacle in Caithness.' He also brought to his Caithness estates advisers from Moray, one of the more progressive districts of the north. According to his modern biographer, Sir John Sinclair sought to demonstrate that 'there need be no long-term conflict between the interests of peasantry and landowner'. He was highly critical of the clearing landlord who converted the old cattle farms into sheep ranges. The depopulating form of sheepfarming he regarded 'a very dangerous and noxious' development in the northern economy. He wrote:

The first thing that is done is to drive away all the present inhabitants. The next is to introduce a shepherd and a few dogs; and then to cover the mountains with flocks of wild, coarse wooled, and savage animals, which seldom see their shepherd, or are benefited by his care.

However, he had no wish to prevent the introduction of sheep — he was in fact the greatest proselytiser of rational sheepfarming in the Highlands; but he believed that they could be assimilated into the old system of pastoralism. In 1791 he remarked:

A flock of 300 sheep ought be maintained on the generality of Highland farms as they are at present constituted, and the profit of such a flock, with a few cattle, is sufficient to maintain a family in the manner in which the natives of the Highlands are accustomed to live.[51]

Sinclair felt that the old Highland farms could accommodate to the great opportunities offered by sheepfarming in such a way that 'the value of the country might be at least doubled, without diminishing the numbers of the people'. He calculated that the Highlands under sheep production would produce an annual export of £4,200,000 as against the current export of cattle valued at £300,000.[52]

In practice Sinclair found his own counsel difficult to follow. When he introduced sheep on his own estates in Caithness, he could not avoid substantial displacement of the population. He discovered that about five hundred people would require alternative sources of subsistence: 'it was necessary to proceed with caution, in extending the system of sheepfarming, and to form some plan of provision for the people'.[53] Coming thus in his own experience face to face with the essential incompatibility of the new sheep and the indigenous human population, he turned to methods which would provide alternative accommodation for the people, in effect to a crofting system. The dislodged people were given 'minute divisions' of unimproved land which amounted to 2 Scotch acres of arable, a house, a garden and a 21-year lease at low rents. These 'crofts' would occupy the people for a substantial part of, but not the entire, year, and it would give the men time to engage as day labourers, while their women could spin wool for extra income. This type of improvement, as Professor Mitchison has noted, 'had to mean compulsory reorganisation'. Sinclair associated his changes with ambitious plans for the development of fishing and manufacturing in villages. He sank a great deal of capital in his estates, and though his rents eventually quintupled there 'is no evidence that the rise in rent had been purchased by any decline in the standard of living of the tenantry'.[54] Nevertheless it is abundantly clear that Sinclair — certainly one of the best motivated of landlords — was unable to reconcile the introduction of sheepfarming with the preservation of the best parts of the older system. He too removed the old peasantry and converted them into crofters and day labourers. Despite his eclectic improvements, the people became neither more vigorous nor more contented than before. Moreover, as Mitchison points out, Caithness was substantially better favoured in natural resources than most of the Highlands.

Sinclair made a virtue of the change in his views and believed that the transfer of the common people from the pastoral economy into fishing had been beneficial. In 1819, during the controversy about the great Sutherland clearances, Sinclair told one of the landlord's critics that resettlement schemes were perfectly practicable:

> I tried the experiment in the estate of Langwell and the result has been extremely satisfactory for the same people who on the old system often had not an ounce of meal in their coffers, under the new one where they have been industrious and careful they have rarely wanted meal and money. I understand from the most respectable authority that the fishermen of Avoch in Ross-shire last year put into the Bank no less a sum than £4000 arising from the profits of the herring fishing ... and the fisheries at Helmsdale and in Assint are likewise extremely prosperous. Why should not the people you allude to follow the same plan?[55]

It was typical of Sinclair that he offered to mediate in the Sutherland controversy, and even suggested the establishment of a colony at the Cape of Good Hope for the displaced people. The Sutherland managers regarded him as a meddling busybody.

In 1825 Sinclair attempted a grand synoptic review of the mountains of information which he had accumulated by the collective efforts of the ministers of Scotland in the first *Statistical*

Account.[56] This exercise required, *inter alia*, that he form a judgement on the impact of the introduction of commercial sheep-farming, which his own propaganda had done so much to promote. He could not ignore the fact that many of the ministers who contributed to the *Statistical Account* had expressed great regret and criticism about the changes:

> What can be more painful, it is said, than to see one person living on, and renting a property which formerly one hundred inhabitants were reared on to the state, and found a comfortable subsistence? and to see a few shepherds strolling over the face of a country, which formerly was the nurse of heroes, the bulwarks of their active soil, ever ready to brave danger and death in its defence?[57]

It was a measure of the alteration in his views over the previous thirty years that, in 1826, Sinclair was prepared to assert that the change had been both necessary and beneficial to all parties, even to the people who had been removed to make way for sheep. He remained critical of absentee landlords, and he was still prepared to exhort them 'to do everything in their power to foster village industry and population'.[58] Now, however, he was more conscious of the dangers of overpopulation and the crucial importance of persuading the people to emigrate to the towns where 'the great means by which employment is found for the increasing population.'[59] This was a critical and symptomatic change in his (and most of his contemporaries') thinking about the problems of agriculture in the Highlands, and in some other regions.

In 1826 Sinclair was prepared to stress the national gain from the greatly increased value and productivity of the north of Scotland, even though the sheep economy required far fewer hands. Moreover he contended, somewhat controversially, that the introduction of sheep had visibly improved the quality of Highland pastures so that they possessed 'a richer sward and a greener hue' than before. He was now absolutely convinced that the scientific production of sheep and the older methods of settlement could not coexist. The idea of joint farms, on the pattern of the traditional cattle farms, simply would not work in practice: Sinclair pointed out that proprietors in the Highlands had made repeated trials to introduce share-owning sheep systems among the common people. It was a record of total failure: 'It is indeed almost impossible that a multitude of people could agree in managing a joint stock of sheep, and selling the produce at market.'[60] Sinclair was convinced that sheepfarming necessitated a reduction of the population. He recognised that 'this alteration of system had certainly the appearance of great rigour, and was frequently attended with much private distress'; and acknowledged that 'it is to be lamented, that, in some cases, it was accompanied with a rapidity, which occasioned unnecessary distress to the former occupants, and depopulated some districts'.[61]

In compensation for the negative consequences of sheepfarming there were, said Sinclair, a number of manifest benefits for the people of the Highlands. He argued that by

> retiring to towns, and applying themselves to various branches of industry, [they] not only improved their mode of living, but were enabled to give education to their children, and to breed them to trades and professions, by which they earned so much, and to have it in their power, to send their parents gratefull remittances, sometimes from distant climes.

It was all to the good. Previously the people of the Highlands had contributed very little to the wealth or support of the nation, they had been prey to recurrent famine, and 'indolence was almost the only comfort they were accustomed to enjoy'. In consequence of the economic changes which Sinclair had first opposed, the Highlands had become a region which contributed strongly to the national interest by the production of the raw materials of industry; the people who had migrated had become 'better fed and clothed, than where they had formerly resided', and were very useful employees in the industrial towns. 'How different is their situation now! They enjoy the necessaries, comforts, and even some of the luxuries of life in abundance.' Sinclair also pointed out that, despite emigration, the population of the Highlands had actually increased between the censuses of 1811 and 1821; and he exulted in the fact that his native Caithness had recorded the greatest percentage increase in all Great Britain. He failed to connect the latter increase with the massive clearances that had taken place during that decade in the contiguous county of Sutherland.[62]

Sinclair eventually became the classic apologist of Highland landlordism in the age of the clearances. His career spanned the period of greatest dislocation in the Highlands and the transformation in his views over the period 1790 to 1825 accurately reflected the movement of moderate opinion on the Highland question and the triumph of the Smithian prescription for regional adjustment. But the shift of his opinions reflected also the altered perception of economic and demographic circumstances of the Highlands which swung from remarkable optimism in the 1780s to a pervasive pessimism by 1820. His ultimate defence of sheep-farming incorporated arguments which related to the great issues of the time — he stressed the problem of population pressure, the dismally low productivity of the old system, the dreadful poverty of the common people, and the national benefits which attended the introduction of commercial sheepfarming. The logical culmination of Sinclair's analysis was that the people of the Highlands would be best separated from the land which then would be better organised into great sheep farms. The people could become an urban proletariat either in the fishing villages of the north, or in the industrial cities of the south. Although this prescription was resisted by a diminishing number of contemporary economic thinkers it was, at all times, entirely unacceptable to the common people of the Highlands.

Notes

1. See Richards, *Highland Clearances*.
2. [P. B. Homer.] *Observations on a Short Tour Made in the Summer of 1803 to the Western Highlands of Scotland* (London, 1804).
3. See Frances Hutcheson, quoted in Richards, *Highland Clearances*, pp. 43-4.
4. All references are to *Johnson's Journey to the Western Islands of Scotland and Boswell's Journal of a Tour to the Hebrides with Samuel Johnson LL.D.*, ed. R. W. Chapman (Oxford, 1924).
5. Ibid., p. 81.
6. Ibid., p. 51.
7. Ibid., p. 37.
8. Ibid., p. 125.
9. Ibid., p. 125.
10. Ibid., p. 255.
11. Ibid., p. 81.
12. Ibid., p. 85.
13. Ibid., p. 255.
14. Ibid., p. 73.
15. Ibid., pp. 314-15.
16. See Richards, *Highland Clearances*, pp. 60ff.
17. *Johnson's Journey*, p. 78.
18. Ibid.

19. Ibid., pp. 85-9, 295-6.
20. Ibid., p. 361.
21. Ibid., p. 147.
22. He probably gained much of his knowledge from the published accounts of Thomas Pennant's tours of 1769 and 1772. See Tadao Yanaihara, *A Full and Detailed Catalogue of Books which Belonged to Adam Smith's Library* (Tokyo, 1951), pp. 47-8.
23. Jacob Viner, 'Guide to John Rae's *Life of Adam Smith*' in John Rae, *Life of Adam Smith* (reprinted, New York, 1965), pp. 88, 101. See also Andrew S. Skinner, *A System of Social Science* (Oxford, 1979), p. 2.
24. Adam Smith, *The Wealth of Nations* (Glasgow edition, 1976), I, pp. 31-2, 97, 133, 177, 209, 421.
25. Ibid., pp. 412-13, 416-17.
26. Samuel Hollander, *The Economics of Adam Smith* (London, 1973), p. 231.
27. Quoted in Hollander, *Adam Smith*, p. 388.
28. Quoted by Margaret M. McArthur in Introduction to *Survey of Lochtayside 1769* (Scottish History Society Publications, 3rd series, XXVII, Edinburgh, 1936), p. xvii.
29. Quoted in Hollander, *Adam Smith*, pp. 96, 232-4.
30. Smith, *Wealth of Nations*, I, p. 165.
31. Ibid., pp. 165ff.
32. See Hollander, *Adam Smith*, p. 164.
33. Ibid., pp. 232-3.
34. Stuart Holland, *Capital versus the Regions* (London, 1976), p. 1.
35. Ibid.
36. Eric J. Hobsbawm, 'Capitalism and Agriculture: the Scottish Reformers in the Eighteenth Century', *Annales*, vol. 33 (1978), p. 678.
37. See, for instances, A. J. Youngson's discussion of the contemporary debate in *After the Forty Five* (Edinburgh, 1973).
38. P. D. G. Thomas, *The House of Commons in the Eighteenth Century* (Oxford, 1971), p. 200.
39. See Viner, 'Guide', pp. 88-101; see also Jean Dunlop, 'The British Fisheries Society: 1787 Questionnaire', *Northern Scotland*, vol. 2, no. 1 (1974-5).
40. James Fergusson (ed.), *Letters of George Dempster to Sir Adam Fergusson, 1756-1813* (London, 1934), pp. 138-9.
41. Ibid., p. 192.
42. Ibid., p. 252.
43. Wilberforce quoted by Viner, 'Guide', p. 92.
44. W. Stark (ed.), *Jeremy Bentham's Economic Writings* (London, 1952), I, pp. 16-17.
45. Fergusson, *Letters*, p. 166.
46. *Statistical Account of Scotland* (21 vols., Edinburgh, 1791-9; reprinted, 1975-) (herein referred to as *Old Statistical Account*, VII, pp. 374-83.
47. Fergusson, *Letters*, p. 178.
48. George Dempster, *In Memoriam* (privately printed, 1889).
49. Rosalind Mitchison, *Agricultural Sir John. The Life of Sir John Sinclair of Ulbster 1754-1835* (London, 1962), p. 24.
50. Ibid., p. 190. See also *Memoirs of the Life and Works of the Late Right Honourable Sir John Sinclair, Bart*, by his son, the Rev. John Sinclair ((2 vols., Edinburgh, 1837), I, pp. 341, 350. The purchase price of Langwell is given as £8,000 in Sinclair, p. 350, and £9,000 in Mitchison, p. 109.
51. Sir John Sinclair, *Address to the Society for the Improvement of British Wool* (Edinburgh, 1791), p. 12.
52. Mitchison, *Agricultural Sir John*, p. 110; Sinclair, *Memoirs*, p. 349.

53. Mitchison, *Agricultural Sir John*, p. 111.
54. Ibid., pp. 111-12.
55. SCRO, Sutherland Collection, D593/K, Sinclair to Dudgeon, 29 July 1819.
56. Sir John Sinclair, *Analysis of the Statistical Account of Scotland* (2 vols., London, 1825).
57. Ibid., p. 168.
58. Ibid., pp. 177-9.
59. Ibid., p. 173. The most thoroughgoing exponent of these ideas was Sir George Steuart Mackenzie of Coul, who wrote:

Our only means of making the natives industrious, is to make them depend on each other for many of the necessaries of life, and this can only be done by collecting them in towns. This will, at first, be found extremely difficult, but a beginning is all that is required. If a few can be prevailed upon to study different trades, and commence business, many will follow their example. At the same time, when we collect tradesmen into a village we ought to endeavour to provide employment for the increasing numbers of useful people, and this is to be obtained by the establishment of some species of manufacture. (*Letter to the Proprietors of Land in Ross-shire* (Edinburgh, 1803), p. 17)

60. Sinclair, *Analysis*, p. 298.
61. Ibid., pp. 297-9.
62. Ibid., pp. 84, 297-301. See Richards, *Highland Clearances*, Ch. 10.

2
CONSERVATIVES AND RADICALS IN THE AGE OF THE CLEARANCES

Wherever cultivation may be heightened by the investment of new capital, the ... subdivision of land will be swept away for farmers of a different race, and wherever the extended territory of a thriving nation is diversified by a range of mountains, these will at length be appropriated to pasture walks.

The Writings of Francis Horner, ed. F. W. Fetter

We read with horror of the tyranny of William Rufus, who depopulated a country for selfish purposes, in days of darkness and cruelty; but, what is this to the crime of depopulating ten counties, in an age of high civilization, under every aggravating circumstance, and depriving the kingdom of those stamina which constitute to greatness.

David Lawrie to Sir John Sinclair, *Farmer's Magazine* (1808)

The relationship between the Highlands and the rest of the country was a matter of public controversy throughout the eighteenth century. Up till mid-century the question was dominated by the need to establish political control over the distant and unruly north. Thereafter most of the contemporary debate was concerned with the economic condition of the Highlands. It became primarily a question of how the region could be connected with the rest of the British economy and how best it could be brought to modern development. There was a conscious effort to direct enterprise and capital to the north, by both private and governmental initiative. As the previous chapter argued, these prescriptions were derived from a diagnosis influenced as much by paternalist and mercantilist notions as by the increasingly pervasive doctrines of Adam Smith.

By the end of the eighteenth century the circumstances of the Highlands had altered significantly. Public and private enterprise had introduced a diversified range of economic development, including fishing villages and new industries. In general the resultant industrial promotion was meagre and little permanent benefit accrued. On the other hand, however, the Highlands had attracted spontaneous expansion in two key areas. Kelp gathering and treatment in conjunction with potato production had permitted dense population settlement on many sites in the west, and created a rapid growth of income. In addition it had been demonstrated conclusively that sheep production was the most lucrative use for the main land mass of the region. For some time it seemed possible that the two developments were complementary — the kelp industry would employ the people in labour-intensive activity while releasing the straths and hills for the sheep. But the fragility of the kelp industry and the rapid growth of the population by the end of the century began to expose the underlying economic problems of the region. The controversy began to focus upon the conflict between sheepfarming and the retention of the expanded numbers of people in the region. Accordingly, the intellectual response to the problem shifted at the beginning of the nineteenth century. Opinion began to polarise as the full reality of the conflict emerged.

In their different ways Samuel Johnson, Adam Smith, George Dempster and Sir John Sinclair had adopted a sanguine attitude towards economic change in the Highlands; they believed that the north of Scotland could sustain improved living standards for the people, although Johnson was hesitant about the difficulties associated with a radical shift in the bases of the economy. These four writers represent the four main categories of evidence about the clearances at the end of the eighteenth century: these were, first, the reports of travellers to the north; second, the armchair speculations of the political and economic philosphers; third, the improvement manuals and memoirs of the landlords and their spokesmen; and, finally, the great body of information generated by the parish ministers which had been gathered together in the first *Statistical Account* by Sir John Sinclair and his successors.[1] It is plain that these sources convey the perceptions and diagnoses of the proprietorial orders. The other strata of Highland society — from the tacksmen downwards, but also the sheepfarmers, teachers and merchants — were seldom represented in the written record: these evidential lacunae persisted until the Napier Report appeared in 1884. Occasionally, it is true, the ordinary people of the Highlands emerge in the public record, usually in moments of crisis — as for instance during anti-clearance riots in Ross-shire in 1792 and 1820-1,[2] and during the famines of the 1830s and 1840s, when their highly expressive acts of resistance were given newspaper coverage: but even then their voice was rarely heard directly. It was only towards the middle of the nineteenth century that there emerged a small number of writers who claimed to speak on behalf of the people cleared from the glens. One of the more impenetrable aspects of the history of the Highland clearances is how the people most affected by that process perceived their world.

I

Emigration was a theme inextricably involved with the clearances. It emerged as an issue of public debate as early as the 1770s, some time before the invasion of the Highlands by the commercial sheep. Dr Johnson had remarked on the exodus of tacksmen and their followers at the time of his tour; in common with many later commentators, he regarded emigration as a symptom of landlord oppression and cultural breakdown. The debate continued throughout the nineteenth century and produced several private as well as parliamentary inquiries. But the question was most hotly contested in the first decade of the new century at a time when public knowledge of population trends remained scant, when national policy on emigration was itself unclear, and when Highland landlords remained ambivalent not only about their own economic and social roles, but also about the utility of a large population. It was in this context that Thomas Douglas, fifth Earl of Selkirk (1771-1820), published a set of opinions on Highland emigration which constitute a substantial analysis of the Highland problem. He advocated policies intended to benefit the anonymous people of the Highlands at a time when sheepfarming was spreading across the region at an accelerating rate. His tract became a major influence on the development of a 'philosophy of emigration'.

A substantial landowner in southern Scotland, Selkirk possessed only meagre knowledge of the north but he became an enthusiast (for philanthropic and commercial reasons) for the idea of sponsored and organised emigration of Highlanders to British possessions in North America. He believed that emigration was inevitable, that it did little harm to the Highlands or to the nation, and that the stream of migrants ought to be deflected away from the United States and towards British Canada, which would greatly benefit from the inflow. He contended that the exodus needed the direction and sponsorship of government without which the advantages would be lost to the nation. He had toured the Highlands in 1792 (about the time of the Ross-shire riots), had studied the literature and had learned the language of the north.[3] He warmly sympathised with the plight of the ordinary people, and organised schemes of emigration to Cape Breton Island in 1802-3, and more famously and tragically to the Red River settlement a decade later. His enthusiasm repeatedly collided with the opposition of the Colonial Office and the Highland Society (a pressure group of northern proprietors), a hostility which was given indirect legislative expression in the Emigration Regulation Bill of 1803.[3] His practical plans facilitating the exodus of several hundred Highlanders ran foul of rival interests in Canada, most notably the opposition of the North-West Fur Company. Political wrangles and appalling weather eventually turned his plans into tragedy and he died a broken man in 1820, some time before his efforts in Canada reached fruition.

Selkirk's belief that emigration was unavoidable rested upon a number of key propositions about the recent history of the Highlands. His basic assumption was that the Highlands had been fully populated even before the introduction of sheepfarming; the old clan system, in encouraging the growth of a great body of semi-military retainers, had produced a society 'teeming with the super-abundant population accumulated by the genius of feudal times'. This gloomy assessment contained no suggestion that the standard of life had ever been other than very low: 'the antient state of the Highlands differed remarkably from the rest of the kingdom — every spot was occupied by nearly as many families as the produce of the land could subsist'.[5]

The collapse of the old system and the emergence of a commercial attitude to land management had, according to Selkirk, rendered a large proportion of the Highland population redundant; in the crudest economic sense, they had lost their *raison d'être*. The problem was compounded by high population growth rates which he deduced from the evidence of Dr Webster's population count of 1755, and the *Statistical Account* forty years later. When landlords as a class sought to extract the full commercial rent for their property, they hastened the inexorable switch of land use towards sheepfarming. Rents were bid up beyond the means of the previous occupants who, inevitably, turned towards emigration. At first the rental increases had been gradual and, in the early phases, the rent levels had remained

> far below the real value of the lands, yet the circumstance was so unprecedented that great dissatisfaction ensued; and the removal of some of the tenants, who refused to comply, excited still more indignation. Accustomed to transmit their possessions from father to son, as if they had been their property, the people seem to have thought, that as they paid the old and accustomed rent, and performed the usual services their possessions were their own by legal right.[6]

Selkirk's account of the common people's perceptions accords with other meagre evidence of popular attitudes. He saw the process of change as not merely unpopular, but as having a revolutionary impact upon the region in its eventual substitution of the cash nexus for feudal ties. The values and priorities of the landlords continued to shift until 'all scruple seems to have been removed, and the proprietors in the Highlands have no more hesitation than in any other part of the Kingdom, in turning their estates to the best advantage'.[7] In this analysis sheepfarming and the consolidation of holdings led inescapably to a decline in the demand for labour which had formerly subsisted in a system of extraordinarily low rents and associated feudal services which had outlived their usefulness.

> When the Highland chieftain exacts the full value for his land his people, even if he could accommodate them all, will no longer be dependents; the relation between them must be the same as between a landlord and his tenants in other parts of the Kingdom.[8]

Selkirk qualified this view only to say that the effect of the French Wars had been to mask and delay the ongoing and relentless changes in the economic circumstances of the Highlands, an opinion which corresponds with modern research on the Highland economy.

While Selkirk recognised, and indeed stressed, the disruptive character of the recent events in the Highlands, he was not wholly opposed to all change. He regarded the clearances as part of the nation's progress, and a contribution to general improvement. The increased production of the Highlands was a net benefit to the world, and 'the produce of the country, instead of being consumed by a set of intrepid but indolent ancillary retainers, is applied to the support of peaceable and industrious manufacturers'.[9] By implication he accepted that regional division of labour within the British economy was, on balance, beneficial: advantages to the nation as a whole overwhelmingly compensated for the desolation that came upon the cleared parts of the Highlands. Indeed, it was his purpose to demonstrate 'the congruence of the Highlanders' needs and British interests'.

In Selkirk's analysis the emigration was a necessary consequence of sociological factors. The Highlanders were different: they were peasants whose ways of thinking and working were so dominated by possession of land that it was pointless to attempt retraining them into habits of industry in order to serve the manufacturers in the southern towns (or even to introduce them to industry in the north):

> The manners of a town, the practice of sedentary labour under the roof of a manufactory, present to the Highlander a most irksome contrast to his former life. The independence and irregularity to which he is accustomed, approach to that of a savage ... He is accustomed to occasional exertions of agricultural labour but without any habits of regular and steady industry; and he has not the least experience of sedentary employments, for which, most frequently, the prejudice of his infancy have brought him to entertain a contempt.[10]

This attitude produced the famous reputation that the Highlander 'never sits at ease at a loom; it is like putting a deer in a plough'. By concurring in the view that the peculiar psychology of the Highlanders justified special arrangements for their welfare, Selkirk reinforced a common stereotype of the Highland personality, which runs through the literature to the present day. Only by emigration to America could the Highlander (above the status of cottar) retain the independence that land conferred upon him, and to which he was accustomed, being a farmer not a labourer:

The small tenant who is deprived of his land has ... the question to ask himself ... whether he will remove into a different part of the country to earn his subsistence as a labourer, or go to America to obtain land.

Selkirk not only saw the choice as unavoidable; he believed that it would be an infringement of ideas of equity and liberty to prevent the natural exodus from the Highlands.[11]

At that moment, however, national policy was being manipulated specifically to block emigration from the Highlands. Much of Selkirk's ire was directed against Highland landlords who lobbied the government for the prevention of emigration. Among proprietors there was a fear of depopulation and labour scarcity even as late as 1815; they argued that the government should interfere on their behalf in the same spirit in which it protected manufacturers against the emigration of skilled labour. Selkirk derided the landlords as hypocritical and illogical:

They have no right to complain of a change which is their own work, the necessary result of the mode which they choose to employ their property. Claiming the right to use their lands as they see fit and most for their own advantage, can they deny their tenantry an equal right to carry their capital and their labour to the best market they can find?[12]

Selkirk asserted that the only way that landlords should dissuade the people from emigrating was by reducing their rents to the levels which prevailed in the pre-sheep economy. He maintained that the Highland lord had

no more title to expect public assistance for keeping his dependents on his estate, than any other proprietor would have, for establishing a village, and compelling people to inhabit it, on the summits of the Cheviot Mountains or of the Peak of Derby.[13]

Selkirk was unimpressed by the various remedies currently put forward to retain population in the Highlands. The reclamation and settlement of wasteland, advocated by George Dempster and many others, he regarded as a miserable business acceptable only to the lowliest cottar, and far too degrading to the rest of the Highland tenantry. He thought that while the development of fishing could provide some aid it had been generally over-rated, and, furthermore, grossly mismanaged by the British Fisheries Society. Moreover, he contended, even if the fishing was successful it could never cater for more than a small fraction of the displaced population. Similarly he scorned the introduction of manufacturing as impractical, Utopian and inapplicable to the Highland mentality.

Emigration, therefore, remained as the only sensible course. His examination of the population statistics indicated that an efflux was perfectly compatible with maintenance of current levels of population.[14] With strong emphasis, Selkirk warned that if emigration were obstructed the social consequences were likely to be grave.

> It is not to be overlooked that among the peasantry of the Highlands, and particularly among the tenants, a spirit of discontent and irritation is widely diffused ... The progress of the rise of rents, and the frequent removal of the ancient possessors of the land, have nearly annihilated in the people all the enthusiastic attachment to their chiefs which was formerly prevalent, and have substituted feelings of disgust and irritation proportionally violent.[15]

In the condition of contemporary Ireland, Selkirk saw an awful warning and parallel to the likely fate of the Highlands, already in an inflammatory state on the evidence of the Ross-shire riots of July and August 1792. Emigration would at least act as a safety valve by removing some of the discontented dispossessed. Otherwise, he predicted, the Highlands could so easily explode:

> There is scarcely any part of the Highlands that has not in its turn been in a state of irritation as great as that of Ross-shire in 1792; can any comment be necessary to show what have been the dreadful state of things, if this had come to a height of the same moment over all the country?[16]

This was the nightmare which periodically invaded the minds of the Highland lairds — the danger that popular opposition to the clearances would cohere into a general uprising against landlordism.

Selkirk believed that, having accepted a changed economic

system, the Highland landlords should follow the logic of their new status — they should actively promote emigration. He believed that the proprietors had simply failed to understand their own interest on this question, partly because they persisted in anachronistic notions about their functions in the Highlands: some landowners, sentimental about their old role in society, still shied away from the adverse publicity associated with the transformation. He observed:

> It would be difficult to find a proprietor in other parts of the Kingdom, who to please his tenants would accept a rent not half the value of his land. This has been done by many in the Highlands, yet these gentlemen have been generally reputed severe landlords.[17]

In this passage, Selkirk exposed the double standard that applied to Highland landlords moral criteria not used to judge the performance of other British proprietors; the duality indeed is apparent in much subsequent writing on the clearances. In the decades after the publication of Selkirk's book, despite heated controversy in the early stages, his views on emigration came to prevail.[18] The twin pressures of sheepfarming and demographic growth eventually persuaded virtually all landlords that the case for emigration was irresistible — even though it was never a popular strategy with those who condemned the clearances *in toto*. Selkirk's writing represented a transitional phase in the making of opinion, somewhat in advance of the full emergence of the 'Highland Problem' in the dimensions it assumed after 1815. In some degree he had not perceived the full sweep of the dynamic changes, especially in southern Scotland's ability to absorb the northern exodus. His own emigration schemes to Red River in Upper Canada were plagued by ill luck and suffered the costs of excessive optimism. His case was, in essence, an extension of the Smithian argument — that the factors of production should be allowed to adjust to their own level across the entire economy. Selkirk's contribution was to advocate some positive channelling of redundant Highland labour to Canada.

Selkirk's work, which stirred considerable debate in Scotland, gained unqualified support from Francis Horner (perhaps the finest mind of the intellectual movement that eventually hatched the *Edinburgh Review*). Horner's reaction was that of an unsentimental Smithian Scot who believed in the generally benign operation of the market. More penetratingly, he argued that the current changes in the Highlands, as described by Selkirk, were symptomatic of general changes of the sort that recurred throughout the history of progress. It was part of the creation of new opportunities in a system of economic advance. This, he argued, was a phenomenon which should surprise no government, and legislators should not be tempted to intervene. In the Highlands, adventurous individuals from the south of Scotland had demonstrated that, by the use of capital and enterprise, large profits would attend the new and successful modes of agriculture. Disruption of the old ways was inevitable:

Such a revolution ... in the system of landed property must be accompanied by an entire change in the distribution of the inhabitants ... During the operation of this change, and the temporary derangement it occasions, much individual distress will unavoidably be suffered. A great part of the inhabitants must, in one way or another, seek for means of livelihood totally different from those on which they have hitherto depended ... Thus it appears that in the subversion of the feudal economy, and the gradual extension of the commercial system over that quarter of the island, emigration forms a necessary part of the general change.

Horner's doctrine was the classical blueprint for economic transformation in which individual or regional adjustment, painful though it might be, was fully justified by the benefit which accrued to the nation at large. As he put it:

Emigration it must always be recollected, is one of the results or necessary conditions of this change, and which cannot be abstracted from its other concomitant effects ... We ought to judge of the whole effect, by taking the whole Kingdom into view.[19]

II

After 1815 the debate about the clearances and the future of the Highlands became more strident. Economic horizons in the Highlands had altered, as had the character of landlord policy, and there was a growing public awareness of events in the far north of Scotland. The critics of the clearances now became as vocal and angry as any formerly provoked by the enclosures in England. The change in the tone of debate had much to do with events in Sutherland in the second decade of the century: the scale and suddenness of the Sutherland clearances — where several thousand people were cleared a few weeks at a time — altered the dimension of the social transformation. Reports of arson, and allegations of brutality resulting in death, further changed the tenor of southern opinion. Patrick Sellar, a sheepfarmer and factor implementing the Sutherland clearances, was brought to trial for culpable homicide in 1816 and, though acquitted,[20] thereafter his name invariably evoked the notion of atrocity which was added to the indictment of the clearing landlords.

The events in Sutherland brought the clearances to national attention and proprietors lived in fear of parliamentary inquiry into their activities. At much the same time the long-run degeneration of vital sectors of the Highland economy was exposed and consequently altered entirely the context of landlord policy. The collapse of the kelp industry, the decline of cattle prices, the volatile condition of the fishing industry and the decline of wool prices combined to constrict the possibilities of progress in the Highlands. Added to these trends was the continuing rise of population, demonstrated unequivocally by the Census of 1811, which allowed defenders of clearance policies to invoke Malthusian arguments in support of their case. Increasingly it was contended that the clearances were essential to prevent a further deterioration in the condition of the people, and to prevent famine. The subsistence crisis of 1816-17 gave added credence to this line of argument. Clearances, it was argued by some, were necessary not only for the proper exploitation of the Highlands, but for the welfare of the people themselves. Landlord attitudes towards emigration were reversed and Selkirk's prescription became the conventional wisdom of the day.

In effect, the deterioration of economic conditions in the Highlands sharpened the conflict, and polarised interpretations of the Highland problem. Even Sir Walter Scott, who had many friends among the northern lairds, was critical of the execution of the changes in the Highlands. In one passage he tried to balance both ends of the contemporary controversy:

In many instances, Highland proprietors have laboured with laudable and humane precaution to render the change introduced by a new mode of cultivation gentle and gradual, and to provide, as far as possible, employment and protection for those families who are thereby dispossessed of their ancient habitations. But in others, and in but too many instances, the glens of the Highlands have been drained, not of their superfluity of population, but of the whole mass of the inhabitants, dispossessed by the unrelenting avarice which will be one day found to have been as shortsighted as it is unjust and selfish. Meanwhile the Highlands may become the fairy ground for romance and poetry, or subject of experiment for the professors of speculation, political and economic.[21]

III

The most eloquent contemporary critic of the great transformation in the Highlands was a landlord and soldier who identified himself with the traditional conception of the chivalrous, romantic, feudal Highland society of myth and fading memory. David Stewart of Garth (1768-1829) inherited landed estates in Perthshire and slave estates in the West Indies. His mother was descended from Jacobite stock, while his father's people had supported the Hanoverian side. It was said that 'Gaelic was his mother's tongue, and he had from his infancy an insatiable appetite for the Gaelic songs and stories.' He was a distinguished soldier, whose military career spanned most of the years of the French Wars. Captured at sea in 1798, he was imprisoned for five months, and then exchanged. In action once more, he was severely wounded in Egypt in 1801. In 1815 he retired on half pay and began to collect material for the lost history of the Highland regiments. The work, which extended into studies of the character of the Highland soldiery, the history of the clans and the evolution of the regiments, was published early in 1822 as *Sketches of the Character, Manners, and Present State of the Highlanders of Scotland.* Later that year he was asked by Sir Walter Scott to assist in the elaborate plans for George IV's visit to Edinburgh. Stewart organised the vast Highland Pageant, and designed new Highland outfits for those who could afford them; he was undoubtedly one of the makers of the rising cult of Celtic romanticism.[22] Despite his successes Stewart was ever in severe financial distress and, eventually, in 1825, he accepted the governorship of St Lucia, expressly to solve his problems. In the same year he was promoted to Major-General and the second edition of his *Sketches* was published. The book became an influential text, widely quoted by modern historians of the clearances. It contains some of the clearest statements directed against the new class of landlords. Nevertheless, as a later memorialist put it, Stewart 'was not a political economist but a Highland warrior'.[23]

Stewart of Garth believed that the Highland clearances were not merely inhuman and unnecessary but were the fundamental cause of poverty and unhappiness in the Highlands. He was perhaps the first writer to blame the clearances directly for the ills of the economy. By implication, he contended that, but for the clearances, the Highlands would have remained a prosperous and independent society; the difficulties into which it had fallen stemmed from the introduction of alien ways. Specifically he castigated 'the new system of statistical economy with its cold unrelenting spirit', and the new consumption habits of many lairds whose heads had been turned, and purses emptied, in Edinburgh and London. Stewart remarked:

> The minds of landlords were directed to the means of increasing their incomes, and of acquiring the funds necessary to support their new and more expensive mode of life in a distant country, while their own was impoverished by this constant drain of its produce.[24]

He regarded the change as entirely destructive of the qualities of the older society, a cultural invasion more deadly than any 'warlike intruder'. The spirit of commercialism undermined the old ways —

> [now] that none felt dignity and those social habits which formerly gave a nameless charm to the paternal seat of a Highland laird while he maintained an easy intercourse with the neighbouring proprietors, with the old retainers of the family, and with gentlemen farmers, or, was they are styled in the expressive language of patriarchal brotherhood, 'friendly tenants'.[25]

Stewart stated the standard propositions about the social consequences of the clearances. The elimination of the tacksmen had, he claimed, fractured the framework of Highland life and destroyed the connecting links between the top and bottom layers of society. Of the people cleared, many ended up in the hands of the emigration agents, whom he unselfconsciously likened to white slave-traders. Those who remained were thoroughly alienated — a despondent, agitated and broken people. He referred to this change as 'the revolutionised Highland character'. Worse still, the transformation constituted 'a check to exertion, or any attempt to improve'. This was a crucial point in Stewart's thinking: he argued that landlord policy itself generated the reputed indolence and shiftlessness of the common people, and explained their notorious resistance to all efforts to bring them to improvement. Stewart also rejected another basic premiss of improvement doctrine — that it was at all necessary to save labour. Of the protagonists of that mentality, he said:

> they endeavour to prove, that if one family can manage a tract of country, it is all useless waste of labour to allow it, as formerly, and is still the case in many parts of the Highlands, to be occupied by many families possessing much economy and industry, though with little capital.[26]

This, perhaps Stewart's most fundamental point, stood in diametric opposition to the rules of political economy. It caused him to wax satirical — he invited his readers to imagine the introduction of machinery 'to carry on manufactures of every description without the intervention of human labour', and then to ponder the question of whether 'the welfare of the state be promoted by the diminution of the population, which must be the necessary consequence of a want of employment'.[27]

Stewart was not opposed to sheepfarming as such, nor to improvement in general, but insisted that such change should be integrated with the old system. If done gradually, with wisdom and ordinary humanity, the transformation could benefit the entire population. Rents, he said, could be increased without resort to clearance; the people, given a reasonable chance, could improve their lands and pay higher rents:

> Rents might have been gradually increased with the increasing value of produce, and improved modes of cultivation introduced, without subverting the characteristic dispositions of a

race of men who inherited from their ancestors an attachment seldom equalled, and still more seldom exceeded, either in fidelity or disinterestedness.[28]

Sheep could be grazed by the small tenantry — the 'ancient race' as he called them. Depopulation was unnecessary: 'The quantity of grass required for sheep and cattle does not depend on the land being occupied by one, or by a number of tenants.' He pointed out that great increases of rent had been obtained in uncleared parts over the previous forty years, 'effected by far other means than the burning decrees'; he instanced increases of 1,000 per cent. In essence he argued that the trauma of the clearances was a tragic and stupid mistake:

> Although the wealth expected from the improvement might be delayed, it would be no less certain, had such a course been pursued. Instead of depopulated glens, and starving peasantry, alienated from their superiors ... we should still have seen a high-spirited and loyal people.[29]

This central propostion (usually in less explicit forms) has reverberated through the subsequent literature on the Highland problem. The people of the Highlands had been systematically denied access to the new-found wealth of their homelands: 'The original inhabitants were never thought of, nor included in the system which was to be productive of such wealth to the landlord, the man of capital, and the country at large.'[30] In these passages Stewart propounded an economic philosophy totally opposed to that of the Smithian world in which labour and capital flowed freely between regions to maximise output and equalise returns. For Stewart, Highland labour was almost as immobile a factor as land; efficiency of production, at least in the Highlands, was a secondary consideration in comparison with the distribution of wealth and the retention of the population. The implications of this viewpoint were more revolutionary than Stewart probably realised, and totally at odds with the credo of classical political economy.

Above all else, Stewart recoiled from the 'fatal rapidity' of the clearances and from the wantonly cruel means of ejecting the common people

from their possessions by force, or, as in some instances, by burning their houses about their ears, and driving them out, homeless and unsheltered, to the naked heath. It was a cold-hearted spirit of calculation, from before which humanity, and every better feeling shrunk, that induced men to set up for sale their loyalty, fidelity, and affection which, as they cannot be purchased, are above all price.[31]

He likened these violent proceedings to the treatment of slaves in the West Indies. Foreseeing poverty, immorality and crime among the evicted, he regretted that there had been no public outcry, only apathy, about the events in the north. The absence of public reprobation had worked to encourage landlords, and among them the evictions came to be 'hailed as an advantage, like ridding pasture ground of foxes and other vermin'. The agents of this transformation were strangers from the south

> who, detesting the people, and ignorant of their character, capability, and language, quickly surmounted every obstacle, and hurried on the change, without reflecting on the distress of which it might be productive, or allowing the kindlie feelings of landlords to operate in favour of their ancient tenantry.[32]

Stewart was aware that some landlords had made provision for their cleared people by way of small lots (or crofts), usually on the coast; but these, he claimed, had become 'thickly studded with wretched cottages, crowded with starving inhabitants' whose circumstances bore 'too near a resemblance to the potato gardens of Ireland'.[33]

To reinforce his denunciation of the landlords Stewart drew a sharp contrast between the new order and the Arcadian bliss which he claimed had prevailed in the pre-clearance period. In a striking passage, he described how, before the removals, the people 'passed the greater part of life in the enjoyment of abundance, and in the exercise of hospitality and charity, possessing stocks of ten, twenty, and thirty breeding cows, with usual proportion of other stock'. In the resettlement lots, he said, some people 'are now pining in one or two acres of bad land, with one or two starving cows'.[34] Once-happy communities had been desolated; those who had not been cleared remained 'contented and independent', but for the rest, 'a hardy and athletic race of men, easily induced by kindness to make a full exertion of their powers' had been entirely degraded. Those who had been cleared had sunk into the state of hapless cottars, and their peasant independence — crucial in Stewart's mind — had been destroyed, 'their being reduced from the state of independent tenants to that of cottagers and day labourers'.[35] Embedded in these propositions was a romantic vision of a peasantry, possessed of 'the spirit of independence, which is generated in countries where the free cultivators of the soil constitute the major part of the population'; and this independence was eventually 'founded on permanent property'.

David Stewart of Garth wrote the most important contemporary indictment of the clearances and exerted a substantial influence on later thinking about the Highland question. Unquestionably, his work was imbued with a historical romanticism about the old Highlands, and an unconventional (and untutored) interpretation of the economic problem of the region. Taken to a logical conclusion, his views would have led to the dispossession of the landlords and the creation of an independent peasantry; it is unlikely that he ever realised this corollary, even though his personal record as a landowner in the Highlands exposed the difficulties of practical humanitarianism. His Perthshire estates were unable to provide him with a sufficient rental income and he was desperate to raise a large flow of capital from his slave estates in the West Indies. Eventually the problems of overpopulation reached his own doorstep and by the mid-1820s Stewart found that he was encouraging his own small tenants to emigrate. Nevertheless his perspective on the Highlands opened an avenue of thinking which suggested (even if it did not actually demonstrate) an alternative to the clearances.

IV

When Stewart published his volumes, the great clearances in Sutherland and those on its border with Ross-shire were still recent events. In the first edition of his book Stewart alluded to them and made several statements about the trial of Patrick Sellar. Stewart made it perfectly clear that he believed Sellar guilty despite the exonerating verdict of the court. In his second edition, after Sellar had threatened to take legal action, Stewart eliminated these passages, but retained the full denunciation of the Sutherland clearances with which Sellar had been associated.[36] Stewart had returned to Sutherland in 1823 and examined the claims of the estate management that £210,000 had been expended by the landlord to ease the resettlement of the common people cleared from the sheep farms. He declared little had been spent for the benefit of the people — 'the ancient tenantry were to have no share in this expenditure'. Moreover he believed that in consequence of the recent sharp decline of most prices, the sheepfarmers were demanding large reductions of their rents, to a point 'so low as to be almost *on a level with what they were when the great changes occurred*'. Though this was a much exaggerated claim, it reflected the diminished confidence that had overtaken the pastoral economy, and helped Stewart to maintain the idea that the clearances were uneconomic, that they were based on a fallacious expectation of rent increase, and that 'no return is to be looked for from this vast expenditure'.[37]

Having rejected the economic rationale for the clearances, Stewart also dismissed the demographic justifications. The claim that the Highlands had been overpopulated before the clearances he dismissed on the grounds that public expenditure on poor relief had been slight. The people had been neither excessive in number nor indolent in character; Sutherland, for example, despite its unkind climate, had supported 15,000 people, who 'maintained the independence of their superiors, and enable them to preserve their title and property in a manner which no other family can boast of'. Stewart believed that this had been the normal condition of the Highlands for centuries and gave the lie to the idea of overpopulation. He contended that Highland population growth was effectively controlled by strict regulations on marriage. According to his reckoning (which took no account of population growth)60,000 Highlanders — 'faithful, blameless and industrious beings' — had already been cleared.[38] Unfortunately he offered no explanation of his calculation and, like his economic analysis, his demographic propositions raised more questions than they answered.

Stewart's book, the first and most influential attack on the clearing system, defined many of the perennial issues in the debate on the Highland question. By contrast, the literature in defence of the clearances has been smaller in volume and has generally suffered from its close and obvious association with the interests of the landlords. Certain general propositions, it is true, were derived from the political economists. But mostly it was assumed that, given the rights of property, little defence was necessary. Some occasional justification, however, issued from the factors and landlords themselves. The best-known example of this genre was the work of James Loch (1780-1855), an Edinburgh intellectual and lawyer who became commissioner to the Marquis of Stafford (whose wife was Countess of Sutherland) in 1812, when the Sutherland experiment was in full flood, and supervised the Sutherland estates for the following forty years. His defence of these policies, published anonymously in 1815 and republished in expanded form in 1820,[39] attempted to counteract the odium that was poured upon his employers, especially from the newspapers of the day. His *Account*, while espousing a number of general principles upon which the policy was based, relied primarily on a catalogue of the massive improvement expenditures undertaken by Lord Stafford in parallel with the clearances. This line of argument was rejected out of hand by critics such as David Stewart of Garth.

Loch's book encapsulated much of the basic philosophy of the improvement mentality, with its foundation of belief in progress and in the necessity for private property to remain free. Clearly believing that the clearances were part of an inexorable process of national progress, he took for granted — 'as matters upon which the publick mind seems to be in great measure made up' — that emigration, the consolidation of small farms into large, and the concentration of population into villages and towns, were all in the national interest, and no longer controversial.[40] Such processes had been delayed in their northward extension by the slow advance of law and order in the northern Highlands, but in the production of large amounts of wool the Highlands had at last found its true utility. In characteristic tones, Loch remarked that 'Luckily in this, as in every other instance of political economy, the interest of the individual [by which he meant the interest of the landlord] and the prosperity of the state went hand in hand.'[41] Moreover, despite their prejudice against it, the common people were equally the beneficiaries of the change.

Loch's assessment hinged largely upon his estimation of the condition of the Highlands before the clearances. In a standard denunciation of 'feudalism' he argued that the great burden of overpopulation had been exacerbated by the introduction of the potato, which had compounded the general wretchedness of the people. It had caused this result by allowing an increase in their numbers which it could not sustain year in, year out, being a less reliable but more easily raised staple than the traditional grains. Gripped in such a system the people had been credulous, ignorant, indolent and drunken. Smuggling was especially ruinous:

> It nursed them up in every species of deceit and idleness, by which they contracted habits and ideas, quite incompatible with the customs of regular society, and civilised life, adding greatly to those defects which characterise persons living in a loose and unformed state of society.[42]

These people, he believed, had been oppressed by labour services and the payment of rent in kind, both of which were extorted by the tacksmen, Loch's special enemy. The common huts were grotesquely dirty and as the men were 'impatient of regular and constant work, all the heavy labour was abandoned to the women, who were employed, occasionally, even in dragging the harrow to cover the seed'.[43] Yet worse was the fact that the very bases of life were precarious — 'crops failed on average ... every third or fourth year', throwing the people on the charity of their landlords. This, of course, was a cardinal point in the improver's case: Loch believed that the ordinary Highlanders were trapped in a social and economic system which was inappropriate to the natural resources of the Highlands; it was a way of life 'of irregular exertion, with intervals of sloth' which also rendered them vulnerable to famine. Loch was able to instance the famine years of 1807, 1812-13 and 1816-17, when

> they suffered the extremes of want and of human misery ... Their wretchedness was so great that after pawning everything they were possessed of, to the fishermen on the coast, such as had no cattle were reduced to come down from the hills in hundreds, for the purpose of gathering cockles on the shore.[44]

From such primitive degradation it was the mission of the improvers to rescue people.

The improvement policies in Sutherland, explained Loch, had two main objectives. One was to convert the mountainous districts into a great source of wool for 'the staple manufactory of England', so that the region could contribute to 'the general wealth and industry of the country'. The other was to convert the people 'to the habits of regular and continued industry' which would allow them not only to avoid recurrent famine but also to produce a surplus of economic output for the supply of southern towns. They would achieve this by resettlement on coastal lots where their employment would be promoted in activities such as fishing, agricultural improvement and manufacturing industry. With the assistance of great capital investments by the landlord, provision of sorts was made for all people cleared from the interior. It was the proud boast of the Sutherland planners that, throughout the upheaval of the clearances, nobody was required to leave the estate.[45] The inland grazing lands were unfit for dense settlement and therefore

> there could be no doubt as to the propriety of converting them into sheep walks, provided the people could be at the same time, settled in situations, where, by the exercise of their honest industry, they could obtain a decent livelihood, and add to the general mass of national wealth, and where they should not be exposed to the recurrence of those privations, which so frequently and terribly affected them, when so situated among the mountains.[46]

It was an important proviso because it represented a step back from the full logic of contemporary political economy which, it may be presumed, would have advised against any such benevolent intervention on behalf of the people cleared from the sheep-walks.

It was ironic that the Sutherland clearance scheme, incorporating the most elaborate arrangements for resettlement, should have provoked the greatest degree of resistance and negative publicity. Loch attributed this response to ignorance and prejudice, notably from the tacksman class which lost privileges in the transition. He conceded that the common people were not reconciled to the changes and that extraordinary inducements were necessary to shift them to the coast. However, he denied that they had been treated cruelly and throughout his life claimed repeatedly that the resettled people came to recognise the improvement in their condition.[47] He spoke of their increased wealth and prosperity, as demonstrated by the rise of a regular retail trade in the new village communities. Moreover, he reported that although the uncleared sections of the population in Sutherland had suffered extreme privations in the subsistence crisis of 1816-17, *it was hardly felt by those who had been settled upon the coast.* Their new occupation, as fishermen, rendered them not only independent of those which produced the misery of their neighbours, but enabled them at the same time, in some degree, to become contributors towards their support, both by the fish they were able to sell to them, and also by the regular payment of their rents.[48]

He insisted that the coastal lots of the new crofting system were perfectly adequate 'for the maintenance of the family, though not sufficient to admit of the young men remaining idle to the degree they were accustomed'.[49] He believed that the benefits were palpable, a perfect vindication of the policy: the people were better off, they were more useful to the nation, they were less prone to smuggling and famine, and they were placed within the reach of the 'benefits of education and moral instruction'. Loch obviously regarded the change as a civilising process of cumulative economic improvement; even more controversially (both then and since) he celebrated the concurrent decline of the Gaelic language among the people as a signal of the spread of civilisation.

There is no question that Loch's *Account* was written as an apologia for a clearing landlord. The time of his writing is also significant, for he wrote at the end of the great round of the Sutherland clearances, while the noise of controversy still rang in his ears. Moreover, at that time, the effects of the decline in the Highland economy had not yet been fully exposed. Ten more years of depression eroded much of Loch's confidence as they diminished the early benefits of the landlord's investment in resettlement facilities. Loch believed that clearances were inevitable and progessive agricultural improvements, that in Sutherland the change was to the benefit of landlord, people and the nation, and that it had been executed with the greatest humanity. In Loch's mind the landlord undoubtedly had absolute legal and moral rights to clear his land, but he was nevertheless critical of other Highland landowners who made no provision for the people removed in such changes.

Almost all Loch's propositions were in total opposition to those of Stewart of Garth and other critics of the clearances. To some degree the claims and counterclaims may be set against the contemporary record. In retrospect, for instance, it is obvious that the efforts of landlords to create a secure and decent existence on coastal crofts for the people removed by clearance never matched the confident, indeed facile, expectations. Loch believed that history would vindicate the radical transformation undertaken by the Sutherland landlord, but the record showed almost universal failure. These basic issues — such as the net economic effects of the change, and the demographic imperatives — remain as contentious today as they were when Loch defended his masters in 1820.

V

Public debate on the Highland clearances remained slight and superficial throughout the 1820s and 1830s. There were occasional newspaper reports but little editorial comment about the continuing transformation of the Highlands; parliamentary interest in national questions of poor relief and emigration sometimes extended briefly to the north of Scotland, and tourists continued to offer passing opinion on economic and social questions. But generally the political content of discussion remained undeveloped until the 1840s — only rarely was there reference to the question of land reform in the Highlands. Notwithstanding the surge of Celtic romanticism associated with the visit of George IV to Edinburgh in 1822 and with the popular works of Sir Walter Scott, it is evident that landlord policy in the Highlands attracted little attention and no restraining hand of government.

John MacCulloch was one of three prominent geologists who left useful accounts of social and economic conditions in the Highlands. In two multi-volume accounts of the Western Highlands and Islands (published in 1819 and 1824) he ruminated on the economy and social condition of northern Scotland. A friend of both Selkirk and Walter Scott, he adopted a severely utilitarian attitude to the needs of the region, and argued that sheepfarming was a logical extension of the improvement of agriculture as pioneered in England. Clearances were inevitable because sheepfarming required large-scale, capital-intensive methods beyond the capabilities of small producers. And the people of the interior were incompatible with progress: they were 'a race of starving and miserable tenants who ... impeded the application of what they could not use', producing nothing themselves and obstructing production.[50] MacCulloch was scornful of opponents of the rational development of the Highlands. He dismissed them as 'Celtic economists', assisted by 'the cant of a few idle poets and romancers', who caused 'the improvement of a whole country ... to be obstructed, and an indolent and half savage race preserved in misery and barbarism. It is easy to string words together, and write pathetic nonsense.'[51] In this same vein he denounced the excessive emotion and the lack of hard reasoning on the subject of the Highlands:

> Had Adam Smith by good fortune ... given one brief chapter to the Highlands, a world of ink and ill-humour would have been saved. Instead of this, the philosophy has been sought in the economics of Oliver Goldsmith ... It was by means of cabalistic words Emigration, Ejectment, Engrossing and Oppressive Rents, that all this perversion of judgement was produced: for it is by words that the world is swayed.

Yet, almost in the same breath, MacCulloch remarked of the unwisdom of applying political economy — 'a hypothetical science' — to the real world.[52]

MacCulloch simply could not understand why the clearances aroused such emotional agitation. He argued that, by comparison with the normal course of agricultural change in England and Scotland, many Highland landlords had been exceptionally solicitous and hospitable towards the people they removed to make way for sheep-walks. According to MacCulloch:

> It became imperative on the proprietors, to eject them, for the general benefit, as well as for their own. Yet those proprietors, so far from acting as had been formerly the case in England and Scotland, provided their displaced people with new farms in other places.

This was a reference to the lotting system which had been a prominent feature of the recent Sutherland clearances. He added:

> Instead of receiving their well merited praise for humanity, they have met nothing but obloquy [and] injurious writing from those who knew nothing of writing but how to hold a pen, with outcry and rebellion from their ungrateful tenantry, and, in some instances, even from those who were paying no rents, and who had become to consider the land as their own.[53]

The lotting scheme was estimable because it gave crofters an individual stake in the land and freed them from the constraints of communal 'servitude'. Where once they were a starving and redundant people whose best prospect was in emigration, they were now by way of fishing 'introduced to fresh wealth, to a new creation of wealth, on the sea shores'. MacCulloch dismissed the suggestion that the removal of the people to the sea shore had been painful; he asserted that the destruction of their houses was of small consequence because they were of trifling value. The resistance of the people to the plans was merely a symptom of their backwardness: 'The attachment of the wretched creatures in question was a habit; the habit of indolence and inexperience, the attachment of an animal little differing in feelings from his own horned animals.'[54]

MacCulloch gave short shrift to the belief that sheepfarming was causing depopulation. He pointed out that population had increased apace with sheepfarming and indeed appeared to be reaching dangerous proportions. He reasoned that 'The former frequency of famine is a sufficient proof of a redundant population in former days,' and attributed the decline in the incidence of famine largely to the beneficial effects of emigration. He contended that the rearrangement of the Highlands by clearance, resettlement and emigration was essential to prevent the deterioration of the population to a degree which would make their condition irredeemable. The urgency of the matter justified rigorous methods:

> It should be carried into effect, by any means, even by force, should that be necessary, while the people are yet rich enough to re-establish themselves, and before the period of real excess and want arrives. That which is called oppression is here, in fact, humanity. The longer a change is protracted, the more severe in every way it will be, because great numbers will be added to great poverty.[55]

MacCulloch's views represented a hardening of the diagnosis of the Highland problem: it specified an imperative for the transformation of the Highlands. Taken literally, MacCulloch's opinion left landlords no option: they were, on economic and moral grounds, obliged to clear their lands. It reflected the results of the first three censuses and also the influence of the Rev. Robert

Malthus. In almost every premiss MacCulloch's views contradicted diametrically those of the school associated with David Stewart of Garth. MacCulloch's harsh judgement on 'the procrastination, slovenly habits, and other defects of sea coast Celts excited vehement indignation', according to his biographer and the reception of his views was 'impaired by a want of condensation and clearness in style'. Nevertheless MacCulloch's voluminous writings gave formidable support to the pursuit of profit and improvement in the Highlands in the 1820s and 1830s.

VI

The pungency of John MacCulloch's prose, remarkable though it was, could not match that of William Cobbett's denunciation of the Highland clearances. His *Rural Rides*, regrettably, did not take him north of the Highland line, but he had resolved to investigate the various stories about the clearances that had come his way. He wrote in October 1832 that if he had the energy and time he would

> go and see how the Highlanders live, and how they raise those pretty sheep and oxen that they send to be devoured by others. I will go and inquire on the spot whether the natives of the country of Sutherland were driven from the land of their birth by the countess of that name, and by her husband the Marquis of Stafford; and if I be in Parliament, I will then endeavour to induce the nation, and through it the Parliament to come to some settled determination relative to the right of land-owners to drive away the natives of the land, or to refuse them a share of its produce. It is high time that we had some settled notions relative to this matter.[56]

Cobbett here raised the crucial question of whether landlord's exercise of their rights of property should be curbed by legislative action in Parliament. This question, surpringly, remained dormant in the debate on the Highlands until the 1870s.

William Cobbett was almost uniquely hostile to the classical political economists' doctrines, which appeared to sanction the very worst abuses perpetrated by landlords throughout the kingdom. He poured scorn on the 'Scotch *feelosofers* ... who preached up a doctrine tending to cause the people of England to be treated like cattle; even I could not make out how it was, that Scotland should spew forth so many of these monsters'.[57] His torrents of invective flowed without restraint: these *'feelosofers'* were rogues who sold their own country, and instructed the landed oligarchy 'how they should check the population and drive the people from the land'. They were 'renegade scoundrels ... base instruments of injustice, tyranny, and cruelty' who 'applauded the driving of the natives out of the country of Sutherland'; their advice incited 'insolent and stupid beasts of landowners to desolate the villages and drive out the people' in the south of England.[58]

Cobbett's desire to visit the far north of Scotland was frustrated and so, like many commentators on the Highlands, he had no direct knowledge of the circumstances. In one section of his journal he asked his readers a question which might well be echoed by modern historians of the clearances:

> My readers will recollect what was said at the time about the 'CLEARING' of the country [of Sutherland] ... I wish to possess authentic information relative to that CLEARING-affair; for, though it took place twenty years ago, it may be just as necessary minutely to inquire into it now. It may be quite proper to inquire into *the means that were used to effect* the CLEARING; and if any one will have the goodness to point out to me the authentic sources of information on the subject, I shall be extremely obliged to him.[59]

Lack of personal knowledge of the Highlands did not restrain Cobbett from a swingeing attack on the clearing landlords in the House of Commons in March 1833. The occasion was a debate directed to the condemnation of the Russian government for mal-treating 5,000 Poles, and transporting them to Siberia. Drawing a parallel, Cobbett told Parliament that there were equally pitiful objects for compassion closer to home. He referred to

> the driving out and almost extermination of nearly an entire county of Scotland ... And he wished that the cause of the poor and ill-used people in that case, had fallen into the same able hands, as the cause of the Poles.

He reminded members that 'the inhabitants of almost an entire county had had their houses burnt down, and themselves driven at the point of bayonet from the land in which they were born'. He told the House that monstrous crimes had been committed in the Highlands.⁶⁰ Yet Cobbett's outburst did not stimulate others to action in Parliament and it was seldom raised again for fifty years. His published writing on the question contained the recurring allegations of atrocity and wholesale eviction. As for the economic arguments justifying the clearances, Cobbett rejected them all in the same spirit as his famous attitude to the censuses — they were as credible as the belief that the moon was made of cheese.

Although mocked by Cobbett, the Highland proprietors continued to receive solace from the intellectual descendants of Adam Smith. From the towering authority of Malthus they were told that the Highlanders were 'probably more redundant in population' than anywhere else in Great Britain or, indeed, Europe;⁶¹ and J. R. McCulloch told them that they were not responsible for any depopulation (because the numbers had actually increased) and that the introduction of sheepfarming had been extraordinarily beneficial to all parties. The Highlands had been dragged out of the primitive economic plight of the previous century, vast territories had been rendered productive and the people had been presented with the fruits of the division of labour.

> The benefit has been truly national; and has redounded, despite the violence with which the change was, in a few instances, forced upon the poor occupiers, as much to their advantage as to that of the landlords ... The inhabitants, instead of being scattered over the country, have been collected into villages and towns, and from being lazy half-employed petty farmers and cottars, numbers have been converted into comparatively industrious artisans, fishermen etc.⁶²

The blessing of classical political economy was the reward of the improving landlord who had been prepared to break the grip of custom.

VII

The relative neglect of the Scottish Highlands in both newspapers and Parliament continued until the 1840s. The descent of famine conditions in 1836-7, it is true, had generated substantial interest in southern newspapers, but the concern did not outlive the crisis. The publication of the second *Statistical Account* towards the end of the 1830s yielded a vital body of information which prompted comparison with the account of the 1790s. In the 1840s there developed an increased national consciousness of the events and recent history of the Highlands, and with better communications it was possible to despatch reporters to the actual scenes of eviction. The emergence of public discussion of subsidised emigration in 1841-2 necesssarily drew some attention to the Highlands, and the debate on the Scottish poor-relief system had a similar effect.

The people most affected by the transformation of the Highlands, those shifted from their original lands, had found virtually no voice until Donald Macleod published a series of letters in 1841. Macleod had been an eye witness and victim of the Sutherland clearances two decades earlier, and his recollections, full of anger, are an important documentary source. Yet, on the whole, the common people remained, in a collective sense, extraordinarily quiet; their case was usually put to the world by outsiders. Most of the discussion, even in the 1840s, remained apolitical, but there began to emerge a literature which contained political implications of a distinctly radical and dangerous nature. The works of Cobbett provided some inspiration, and more came from the French-Swiss economist and historian Sismondi (1773-1842), of whom Sir Alexander Gray later said: 'Rightous indignation, such as inspired Sismondi, is a noble passion, and the indignant prophet fulfils a useful purpose, even if indignation not infrequently leads to bad logic.'[63] By drawing upon the example of the Highlands in his work on Celtic tenures Sismondi lent his authority to the idea that collective tenurial arrangements in the Highlands were of great antiquity, and were the historical foundation of the relationship between the land and the clan. They operated through the instrument of the 'tack', a type of lease, with subletting provisions, widespread in Scotland. Sismondi pointed out that while the ordinary Swiss peasant held his land with a 'guarantee of perpetuity', the Scottish Highlander had no security whatsoever because his ancient rights had been usurped by the landlords.

Hugh Miller, the geologist, took up the political implications of both Cobbett and Sismondi with enthusiasm. A self-made intellectual, he made his mark in radical religion and in science, and was a prolific writer of memoirs and travelogues. He was one of the first to realise the explosive implications of such doctrines. He knew that the recovery of the peasants' rights in the Highlands would be possible only 'in a time of revolution, when the very foundations of society would be unfixed, and opinions set loose, to pull down or re-construct at pleasure'. Miller's writing was calculated to give encouragement to a revolution in the north.

Miller's writings and memoirs provide valuable descriptions of conditions in the Highlands for the period 1820-45. A good part of his youth was spent in the Highlands where he acquired, as well as the basis of his geological education, an attachment to the Highlands and its culture. His work is full of nostalgia for the world of his youth and anger at its destruction. As one of his biographers points out, Robert Burns and Hugh Miller gave 'their joint authority in favour of the old system and against the new'.[64] Indeed Miller's main mode of argument was the juxtaposition of the circumstances of the Highlanders before the clearances with those of the 1840s, most notably for the case of Sutherland, for which he reserved most of his fire. He rejected the idea advanced by Smith, MacCulloch and Loch that the people had been locked in poverty and squalor before the clearances. Writing in 1843, he asserted:

> The country hears often of dearth in Sutherland now — every year in which the crop falls a little below average in other districts, it is a year of famine there; but the country never heard of dearth in Sutherland then [before the clearances]. There were very few among the holders of its small inland farms who had not saved a little money. Their circumstances were such, that their moral nature found full room to develope [*sic*] itself, and in a way the world has rarely seen. Never were there a happier or more contented people, or a people more strongly attached to the soil; and not one of them now lives in the altered circumstances on which they were so rudely precipitated by the landlord, who does not look back on this period of comfort and enjoyment with sad and hopeless regret.[65]

In this passage Miller reaffirmed the notion that the people had formerly existed in conditions which provided a cushion against periodic famine, in a society morally elevated above the new commercial and industrial world. He conceded that it was not a world of affluence, yet the Highlander possessed, on the average, his six, or eight, or ten head of cattle, and his small flock of sheep; and when, as sometimes happened in the high-lying districts, the corn crop turned out a failure, the sale of a few cattle or sheep more than served to clear scores with the landlord, and enabled him to purchase his winter and spring supply of meal in the Lowlands.[66]

The people, tenants from time immemorial, had always constructed their own houses, and had fought for their chiefs, until the most recent times. He pictured idyllic scenes of the old life: of the family gatherings round a cheerful turf fire on the long autumn evenings, listening to traditional tales and the poems of Rob Donn, or else happy contests of stone-throwing on the banks of trout-filled streams.[67] It had been a golden age before the fall.

For Miller, this picturesque world had been shattered by the clearing landlords. It was his repeated assertion, echoing Stewart of Garth, that the clearances were the cause rather than the consequence of the poverty and unhappiness of the Highland population in the mid-nineteenth century. He even spoke of 'annual famines' in the new age:

> The population, formerly spread pretty equally over the country, now exists as a miserable selvedge, stretched along its shores, dependent in most cases on precarious fisheries, that prove remunerative for a year or two, and disastrous for maybe half-a-dozen; and, able barely to subsist when most successful, a failure in the potato crop, or in the expected return of the herring shoals, at once reduces them to starvation.[68]

In the process the people had lost their gaiety and their enjoyment. Of the crofters, he claimed: 'When the fishing and their crops are comparatively abundant, they live on the bleak edge of want; while failure in either plunges them into a state of intense suffering.' He asserted that there had been a permanent deterioration in their condition: they had become a famished people eking out a living from the barren allotments along the coasts. In typically vivid terms he claimed that 'a singularly well-conditioned and wholesome district of a country had been converted into one wide ulcer of wretchedness'. Miller was sufficiently confident in his thesis, on the basis of his knowledge of the famine of 1836-7, to predict a catastrophe — he declared that 'the recurrence of this state of things no amount of providence or exertion on their own part, when placed in such circumstances, can obviate or prevent'.[69] Observations of the resettlement villages in Sutherland only confirmed this view.[70] He pointed out also that, in aggravation of the agony of the Highlanders, the landlords had chosen to attack their only means of solace, the Free Church (which was refused sites by many landlords after the Disruption in 1843).

Miller drew out the larger issues in the general conflict of interests. He believed that the large farm system must worsen the condition of the common people. They were transformed into wage labour, but 'Farm servants, must be lower in the scale than the old tenant-farmers, who wrought their little farms with their own hands.' He declared that unless the 'brute-making' process were arrested the Scottish people would 'sink, to a certainty, ... from being one of the most provident, intelligent, and moral in Europe, to be one of the most licentious, reckless and ignorant'.[71] Writing in the 1840s, when sheep-rents had been stagnant for many years, Miller claimed that the clearances had not been profitable despite the appalling upheaval that had occurred: 'there is but poor comfort ... to know, when one sees a country ruined, that the perpetrators of the mischief have not ruined it to their own advantage.' He singled out what he called the Sutherland experiment which he likened to vivisection — it was as though a dog had been carved up alive for the benefit of economic science.[72]

Hugh Miller meditated on the political circumstances that permitted such an outrage on humanity. It was, he insisted, a result of the power of the landlord reinforced by the passivity of the people. 'A combination of circumstances have conspired to vest in a Scottish proprietor ... a more despotic power than even the most absolute monarchs of the Continent possess.' Equally, he emphasised the 'natural obedience' of the Highland people to all authority: a theme much stressed by subsequent writers. Miller, however, was prepared to flirt with the idea of bolder advice to the people of the Highlands. In 1843 he contemplated more radical thoughts:

Were it suggested by some Chartist convention in a time of revolution, that Sutherland might be still further improved, — that it was really a piece of great waste to suffer the revenues of so extensive a district to be squandered by one individual — that it would be better to appropriate them to the use of the community in general, — that the community in general might be still further benefited by the removal of the one said individual [i.e. the Duke of Sutherland] from Dunrobin to a roadside, where he might be profitably employed in breaking stones ...[73]

— in such circumstances, Miller commented, it would not be much different from the fate that had actually overtaken the common people.

In fact, within a few years, Hugh Miller had travelled further along the road which led towards the doctrines of Karl Marx and the actively rebellious crofters of the 1880s. In a letter written in 1846, which contains an interesting link with the work of William Cobbett, Miller remarked:

> They [the Irish] are buying guns, and will be by-the-bye shooting magistrates and clergymen by the score; and Parliament will in consequence do a great deal for them. But the poor Highlanders will shoot no one, not even a site-refusing laird or a brutal factor, and so they will be left to perish unregarded in their hovels. I see more and more every day of the philosophy of Cobbett's advice to the chopsticks of Kent, 'If you wish to have your wrongs redressed, go out and burn ricks'; Government will yield nothing to justice, but a great deal to fear.[74]

Hugh Miller was one of the most eloquent and radical of the mid-century critics of the great Highland proprietors, and his work nurtured some of the main themes of the debate. His recourse to literary nostalgia and his dependence on key historical assumptions matched his dogmatism about the economic foundations of Highland life. He was no economist and most of his propositions rested upon assertion rather than analysis; nevertheless he contributed to the debate a powerfully articulated moral indignation combined with an exploration of some political possibilities within the crofter community. With his radicalism much in advance of opinion among the crofters of his day, his writings kept simmering a vast sense of grievance in the Highlands. It was to be three more decades before the political consciousness of the crofters reached an operational scale. In the 1840s, even the Potato Famine — which produced a small flood of pamphlets on the Highland question — did not arouse the type of response that Miller had favoured.

VIII

Neither Frederick Engels nor Karl Marx had any direct impact on the Highland question during their own lifetimes, but later historians and economists of the region have been much influenced by their work. Both writers were able to employ the events in the Highlands as vivid illustrations of their general propositions about the nature of long-run economic change and social conflict. Engels cited the case of the Highlands as a demonstration of the inexorable progress of industrialisation. He pointed out that the extension of roads into the far north in the beginning of the nineteenth century suddenly exposed the region to cultural and economic transformation:

The Highlanders had hitherto been chiefly poachers and smugglers; they now became farmers and hand-workers. And, though Gaelic schools were organised for the purpose of maintaining the Gaelic language, yet Gaelic-Celtic customs and speech are rapidly vanishing before the approach of English civilisation.[75]

Engels seems to have regarded the Highlanders in the same light as the Irish — a people who, by oppression, had been 'converted into an utterly impoverished nation' whose main function was to supply England, America and Australia with 'prostitutes, common labourers, pimps, pickpockets, swindlers, beggars and other rabble'.[76]

While Engels made no reference to the clearances as such, Marx himself regarded them as a particularly stark (and late-in-the-day) example of the process of the forcible expropriation of the land from the people of Britain. When, in 1853, Harriet Beecher Stowe had published a sympathetic account of the clearances undertaken by the father-in-law of the then Duchess of Sutherland (her hostess in Britain), Marx was one of several writers who ridiculed the author of *Uncle Tom's Cabin*. His articles on the question appeared in the *New York Tribune* and in some English newspapers,[77] and later provided the basis for a well-known passage in the first volume of *Capital*. Marx, not unlike Adam Smith and James Loch, regarded the Highlands as an anachronistic survival from the feudal world. The land had been divided amongst the greatest possible number of sub-feudatories who served, essentially, to maximise the power of the laird. In the nineteenth century the shift from feudalism to the capitalist mode of production was associated with the usurpation of ancient communal property rights, the embezzlement of land, and the eviction of the people from their homes. As a consequence, wrote Marx, 'a mass of free proletarians was hurled on the labour market by the breaking up of the bonds of feudal retainers'. Typically, 'thefts, outrages, and popular misery ... accompanied the forcible expropriation of the people'. The Highlands exemplified the most naked form of this general agrarian transformation:

> what 'clearing of estates' really and properly signifies, we learn only in the promised land of modern romance, the Highlands of Scotland. There the process is distinguished by its systematic character, by the magnitude of the scale on which it is carried out at one blow.

Areas as large as German principalities were swept suddenly clear of people, who were driven south as 'machine-fodder' for the Glasgow factories.

Marx gave specific attention to the events in Sutherland:

> This person [the Duchess of Sutherland], well instructed in economy, resolved, on entering upon her government, to effect a radical cure, and to turn the whole country, whose population had already been, by earlier processes of the like kind, reduced to 15,000, into a sheep-walk. From 1814 to 1820 these 15,000 inhabitants, about 3,000 families, were systematically hunted and rooted out. All their villages were destroyed and burnt, all their fields turned into pasturage. British soldiers enforced this eviction, and came to blows with the inhabitants. One old woman burnt to death in the flames of the hut, which she refused to leave. Thus this fine lady appropriated 794,000 acres of land that had from time immemorial belonged to the clan.[78]

Marx described the Countess of Sutherland as 'a female Mehemet Ali, who had well digested her Malthus'. He was scornful of the provision made by the Sutherland estate for the resettlement of the people on the coast: he believed the crofting system was merely a further device for squeezing from them the last drop of surplus value. 'The whole of the stolen clanland she divided into 29 great sheep farms, each inhabited by a single family, for the most part imported farm-servants. In the year 1835 the 15,000 Gaels were already replaced by 131,000 sheep.' Later on, he pointed out, the sheep-walks were converted into deer forests inhabited by animals as 'fat as London aldermen'. He quoted Robert Somers' pamphlet of 1848 which argued that the deer forests had created further pressure on the living space of the small tenants in the Highlands.[79]

It may be argued that the importance of Marx for the Scottish Highlands lies not so much in his denunciations of the landlords, as in his general analysis of the spatial consequences of capitalist industrialisation. Stuart Holland has contended that, unlike the classical economists, Karl Marx gave full recognition to the problems of regional retardation which, he says, were a systemic feature of economic growth in the *laissez-faire* world of the nineteenth century. Regions such as Ireland and the Scottish Highlands were fundamentally disadvantaged by the process that brought enormous development to the rest of Britain. Marx, writes Holland, provided an analytical framework for an understanding of this perennial problem in capitalist growth.[80]

In a section of his *Poverty of Philosophy* Marx briefly described the mechanism which transformed the Highlands. He linked the Highland clearances to the growth of English industry which, through the market, enhanced the profitability of wool production, and thereby altered the allocation of resources in northern Scotland. Land in the Highlands was switched to pastoral production which, in its turn, required the concentration of estates. Small holdings had to be abolished and 'thousands of tenants had to be driven from the native soil and a few shepherds in charge of millions of sheep installed in their place'.[81]

While Marx viewed the problem of regional imbalance as a structural deficiency of capitalist development, and as an aspect of the inevitable breakdown of the larger system of which it was part, he, like the classical economists, identified such phenomena as temporary problems of economic adjustment. It is worth stressing this point of concurrence in the two schools of thought. Malthus and Ricardo, for instance, both believed that the low living standards of the Irish (and, by extension, the Highlanders) were the result of 'the continuing tendency for population growth to outstrip capital increase'. Employment opportunities were few and wages low — but the subdivision of land and the extraordinary productivity of the potato permitted the people to subsist and multiply at a very low level of income. However, the system 'gave no incentive to produce more than this, and thus the great majority of the people were idle and indolent'. To raise a community out of this condition it was necessary to check population growth and promote an increase of capital.[82] In practice, in the Highlands, the increase of capital took the form mainly of sheepfarming, and the check to population growth occurred mainly by way of emigration. Consequently the region adjusted to the rest of the country by reducing its population until, in the long run, the level of income was almost equalised with other regions. The classical economists, no less than Marx himself, regarded the current upheaval in the Highlands as a transitional phase in general economic development.

IX

Marx, Sismondi, Miller and Cobbett were, in many ways, somewhat exotic commentators on the Highland experience. They were highly literary and articulate outsiders, men of obvious political awareness whose indignation speaks eloquently down the years into the modern debate on the Highland clearances. Yet the fact remains that there was little connection between these writers and the common people of the Highlands, who generally remain apolitical and unheard in the literary record in the entire period before 1870.

The perceptions of the common people are sometimes best identified by indirect means and there is, in the literature, an important strand of argument which maintains that it was through religion that the people of the Highlands gave expression to their view of the world that was being dislocated around them. The history of the Disruption of the Scottish church in the north is sometimes depicted as a dimension o the class-conflict between the people and the lairds. The tendency, even before the Disruption, towards millenarian or bizarre religious movements may have had some causal connections with the trauma of radical agrarian transformation. There can be no doubt that some of the most vehement castigations of the landlords voiced within the region came from the leaders of radical religion. One example among many was the Rev. John Kennedy of Dingwall, who published a stinging account of recent Highland history in the

1850s, full of the powerful Free Presbyterian antipathy to the clearances. He pointed out that 'the cruel work of eviction', which had laid waste the hillsides and plains of the north, had started at the time of the great revivalist movement of the 1780s, an era of 'spiritual prosperity' when the Highlanders were 'the most peaceable and virtuous peasantry in Britain'. The ungodly oppressors cleared the people in favour of 'strangers, red deer, and sheep. With few exceptions the owners of the soil began to act as if they were also the owners of the people, and disposed to regard them as the vilest part of their estate'. Hundreds of families were driven across the sea, 'or were gathered, as the sweepings of the hill-sides, into wretched hamlets on the shore. By wholesale evictions, wastes were formed for the red deer, that the gentry might indulge in the sports of three centuries before.'[83] For Kennedy the clearances had been a diabolical corruption of the community. This social disaster, however, yielded a triumphant spiritual response exemplified by the extraordinary austerity and vigour of Kennedy's own sect.

It is easy to match the moral outrage of the Rev. Kennedy against standard contemporary defences of Highland landlords. For instance, Alexander Russel (1814-76), editor of the *Scotsman*, published diametrically opposed propositions about the policies of the Highland clearances:

The sum of what the facts, so far as we can find them, establish, is that the population never was otherwise than usually wretched; that the removal of a portion of it, by one means or another, was absolutely necessary; that, after all, the population of the Highlands is at this moment greater than ever; that it is in many places greater than it ought to be, or than population is in districts much better fitted for employing and sustaining human beings; that the changes of position or employment undergone by portions of the population in some Highland counties are only similar in character and extent to what has taken place in non-Highland districts, not subjected to any compulsion; that the so-called 'cleared' districts are manifestly fitted by nature rather for Sheep than for Man; and that the Deer is no more of an intruder, and is less of a depopulator, than the sheep.[84]

Claims and counterclaims such as these create a number of difficulties. It is obvious, for instance, that the provenance of the contemporary evidence is unusually important for historical evaluation, mainly because Highland interests were profoundly divided. Furthermore the early debate on the Highland question was complicated by the confusion of levels on which the discourse was conducted. Many of the issues that emerged were of a philosophic nature, often related to implicit or explicit comparisons of the values and qualities of different styles of life. At the same time the debate encompassed factual questions — relating, for example, to allegations of atrocity, claims about the scale of population growth and loss, the extent of arable cultivation and long-run trends in living standards. Another cluster of questions dealt with the interpretation of old tenures and communal property, the vulnerability of the Highlanders to famine before and after the clearances, and to the profitability of sheepfarming. While historians in following generations were able to make inroads into the problems of historical verification, it was at all times unlikely that economic analysis would settle timeless questions of moral philosophy.

Notes

1. The second (or *New*) *Statistical Account* of Scotland was organised in the 1830s.
2. See Richards, *Highland Clearances*, chs. 9 and 11. Malthus himself complained that 'the histories of mankind that we possess are histories only of the higher classes', and consequently it was difficult to know the living conditions of the lower classes who did most of the breeding. Quoted in G. Himmelfarb, *Victorian Minds* (London, 1968), p. 94.
3. J. M. Gray, *Lord Selkirk of Red River* (London, 1963), p. 17.
4. See below, Ch. 8.
5. Thomas Douglas, Earl of Selkirk, *Observations on the Present State of the Highlands of Scotland* (Edinburgh, 1805), pp. 25, 37.
6. Ibid., p. 22.
7. Ibid., p. 23.
8. Ibid., p. 66.
9. Ibid., p. 77.
10. Ibid., pp. 38, 49, 83 and Appendix K.
11. Sidney Pollard, *The Genesis of Modern Management* (London, 1965), p. 191; Selkirk, *Observations*, p. 59.
12. Selkirk, *Observations*, p. 88.
13. Ibid., p. 90.
14. Ibid., pp. 96-113. In this opinion Selkirk was also influenced by the ideas of Malthus.
15. Ibid., pp. 118-19.
16. Ibid., pp. 122-4.
17. Ibid., p. 128.
18. Selkirk's book was generally well received, and praised by, amongst others, Walter Scott. It provoked an expected degree of controversy, the opposing ideas being represented in 'Amicus', *Eight Letters on the Subject of the Earl of Selkirk's*

Pamphlet on Highland Emigration as they Lately Appeared under the Signature of Amicus, in One of the Edinburgh Newspapers (Edinburgh, 1806).

19. *The Economic Writings of Francis Horner in the Edinburgh Review 1802-6*, ed. F. W. Fetter (London, 1957), pp. 119-23.
20. See below, ch. 15.
21. Quoted in G. M. Young, 'Scott and the Historians', *Sir Walter Scott Lectures, 1940-1948* (University of Edinburgh, 1946), p. 107.
22. See H. J. Hanham, 'Mid-Century Scottish Nationalism' in R. Robson (ed.), *Ideas and Institutions in Victorian Britain* (London, 1967), pp. 144-5. The most recent demolition of Highland mythology, and its cultural and historical pretensions, is at the hands of Hugh Trevor-Roper, 'The Invention of Tradition: the Highland Tradition of Scotland' in Eric Hobsbawm and Terence Ranger (eds.), *The Invention of Tradition* (Cambridge, 1983).
23. 'Proposed Memorial to General Stewart of Garth', *c.* 1898, Irvine Robertson Collection.
24. Colonel David Stewart, *Sketches of the Character, Manners, and Present State of the Highlanders of Scotland: with Details of the Military Service of the Highland Regiments* (2 vols., Edinburgh, 1822; 2nd edition, 1825), 2nd edition, p. 145.
25. Ibid., p. 144.
26. Ibid., p. 149.
27. Ibid., pp. 150-1.
28. Ibid.
29. Ibid., pp. 167-70.
30. Ibid., pp. 157ff, 165.
31. Ibid., pp. 152-3.
32. Ibid., p. 160.
33. Ibid., p. 169.
34. Ibid., p. 161.
35. Ibid., pp. 162-3, 168, 174.
36. Ibid., 1st edition (1822), pp. 156-8.
37. Ibid., 2nd edition (1825), pp. 175ff.
38. Ibid., pp. 19, 90-1, 167, 173-4, 194-5.
39. James Loch, *An Account of the Improvements on the Estates of the Marquess of Stafford* (London, 1815; enlarged edition, signed, London, 1820).
40. Ibid., pp. xi-xii.
41. Ibid., p. xvii.
42. Ibid., pp. 53, 114.
43. Ibid., p. 51.
44. Ibid., p. 63.
45. Ibid., pp. 33-4, 65, 99, 169.
46. Ibid., p. 70.
47. Ibid., pp. 74, 89-90, 93, 169.
48. Ibid., p. 78, Appendix, pp. 55-6.
49. Ibid., p. 106.
50. John MacCulloch, *The Highlands and Western Isles of Scotland* (4 vols., London, 1824), p. 111.
51. Ibid., p. 112.
52. Ibid., pp. 112, 124-5.
53. Ibid., pp. 111-12.
54. Ibid., p. 121.
55. Ibid., p. 134.
56. William Cobbett, *Rural Rides*, ed. G. D. H. and Margaret Cole (3 vols., London, 1930 edition), III, p. 301.

57. Ibid., p. 804.
58. Ibid.
59. Ibid.
60. *Hansard*, vol. 16, 1 March 1833.
61. T. R. Malthus, *An Essay on the Principle of Population* (London, 1972 edition), pp. 52, 261.
62. J. R. McCulloch, *A Descriptive and Statistical Account of the British Empire* (2 vols., London, 1854), I, pp. 287,302-4; *A Dictionary of Commerce* (London, 1834), pp. 590-2. Nassau Senior described the events in Sutherland as 'one of the largest and most beneficial clearings on record': N. S. Senior, *Journals, Conversations and Essays Relating to Ireland* (2 vols., London, 1868), II, p. 282.
63. Sir Alexander Gray, *The Development of Economic Doctrine* (London, 1931), p. 201.
64. Peter Bayne, *The Life and Letters of Hugh Miller* (2 vols., London, 1871), I, p. 88; see also Hugh Miller, *Essays* (Edinburgh, 1875), p. 201.
65. Hugh Miller, *My Schools and Schoolmasters* (Edinburgh, 1874 edition), pp. 292-5.
66. [Hugh Miller,] *Sutherland as it was, and is; or, How a Country may be Ruined* (Edinburgh, 1843), p. 15.
67. Miller, *Sutherland*, p. 16.
68. Miller, *My Schools*, pp. 292-3.
69. Miller, *Sutherland*, pp. 16, 26.
70. Bayne, *Life and Letters*, p. 359.
71. Ibid., p. 88.
72. Miller, *Sutherland*, p. 27.
73. Ibid., p. 19.
74. W. M. Mackenzie, *Hugh Miller. A Critical Study* (London, 1905), pp. 190-1.
75. Frederick Engels, *The Condition of the Working Class in England in 1844* (London, 1952 edition) pp. 13-14.
76. Engels to Marx, 23 May 1856, in *Ireland and the Irish Question. A Collection of Writings by Karl Marx and Frederick Engels* (New York, 1972), p. 84.
77. *The American Journalism of Marx and Engels* (New York, n.d.), pp. 57-65, 74-9.
78. Karl Marx, *Capital* (3 vols., Moscow edition, n.d.), I, pp. 718-31. See also Dr Charles Marx, 'Sutherland and Slavery, or The Duchess at Home', *The People's Paper*, 12 March 1853.
79. Karl Marx, *Collected works* (Moscow, 1976), VI, p. 173.
80. Holland, *Capital versus the Regions*, Ch. 2.
81. Karl Marx, *The Poverty of Philosophy* (New York, 1963 edition), pp. 119-20.
82. See R. D. Collison Black, 'The Classical View of Ireland's Economy' in A. W. Coats (ed.), *The Classical Economists and Economic Policy* (London, 1971), pp. 85-7.
83. J. Kennedy, *The Days of the Fathers in Ross-shire* 3rd edition (Edinburgh, 1861), pp. 15-16.
84. [A. Russel,] 'The Highlands — Men, Sheep and Deer', *Edinburgh Review*, vol. 106 (1857), p. 470.

3
THE NAPIER COMMISSION AND ITS AFTERMATH

... with everyone of those features is connected a crowd of associations of my early years ... and ... they are now almost wholly obliterated. The townships in every strath and glen, and on every hill, which once teemed with life are now desolate and silent; and the only traces visible of the vanished, happy population are, here and there, a half buried hearthstone or a moss grown graveyard.

Donald Sage, *Memorabilia Domestica*

The landlord invests his thousands mainly underground, and the passing idiot thinks that his rental is some kind of spontaneous return for which the owner has done nothing.

If such an act as the Irish Act of 1880 had been passed 150 years ago, Scotland would have been a rabbit warren of paupers worse than any part of Ireland ... The worst fallacies of PROTECTION are embalmed — alas! not mummified in the Act of 1880. The stupid, the idle, and the lazy are all protected, not against foreigners, but against the more intelligent and capable and industrious of their own neighbours.

George Douglas, eighth Duke of Argyll, KC, KT
(1823-1900), *Autobiography and Memoirs*

The second hundred years of debate on the Highland clearances began in the 1870s and 1880s with a remarkable flowering of writing. It coincided with, and became part of, the crofter agitation which led eventually to the establishment of the Napier Commission to inquire into tenurial conflict in the Highlands and, subsequently, to the passing of the Crofter Act of 1886. After several decades of relative quiet — not much disturbed even by writers — there was a rapid development of effective political pressure among the crofting community in the second half of the 1870s. The clearances were almost a thing of the past: true, there was renewed provocation in the widespread conversion of sheep runs into deer forests, but the clearances, as such, were virtually over. In a much heightened political atmosphere the crofters expanded their methods of resistance to landlords in a way which attracted national attention; their efforts were paralleled by a literary response of far greater depth and range than before. The efforts of rioters, land leaguers, land invaders and literary campaigners yielded surprising gains to the crofters. The resultant legislation placed unprecedented limitations on landlord autonomy and fundamental rights of property. While the crofter legislation did not initiate a golden age in the Highlands, it nevertheless undermined the authority of the landlords, and prevented them from pursuing the types of policies associated with the great clearances. It was inevitable that the political conflict should generate a debate about some fundamental elements of the Highland question. This debate was largely about the historical consequences of the clearances and the means by which the land could be regained from the landlords. The political temperature was maintained by repeated recollection of the alleged inhumanity of the clearances. But two further issues helped to quicken the debate in the 1870s and 1880s. One was the state of Ireland and the political campaigns which connected the land question and Irish nationalism: Ireland provided a powerful demonstration of the techniques and objectives of popular protest for the Highlanders. The second change in the context of the debate was the onset of depression in the sheepfarming sector of the Highland economy from the early 1870s. This undoubtedly helped to dislodge some long-standing notions about the inevitability of this type of land use in the north of Scotland.

No less important in the debate of the 1870s and 1880s was the manner in which the Highland question was levered open to make possible fresh discussion of the general problems of the Highland economy, and of new directions for the region's future. Once the authority of the landlords was curtailed, it became possible to consider alternative patterns of use for the region's resources. In a sense the past was exorcised and the debate turned towards the means of regional advance.

In the early nineteenth century most of the controversy about the Highlands had been couched in moral terms: Stewart of Garth was outraged at the chief's abnegation of their patriarchal obligations; James Loch had defended the landowners by demonstrating their continuing moral commitment to responsibilities attaching to the ownership of property. By the 1870s the very foundations of landlord authority were questioned not only in the Highlands, but in the rest of the country. The northern proprietors presented themselves for special attack — their record as evictors impinged directly on the national consciousness, and their vast acreages, as revealed by Bateman's *Great Landowners of Great Britain and Ireland* (1883), made them natural targets in the attack on 'land monopolies'. At the turn of the century Lloyd George conducted his self-appointed crusade against the lairds whom he excoriated without mercy, and sometimes without a full possession of the facts.

In the twentieth century the Highland question became entangled with wider arguments about the redistribution of income and wealth, problems of regional underdevelopment and the proper limits of socialist action. Frequently the Highland question surfaces in controversies about Celtic and Scottish nationalism which necessarily address such central issues as depopulation and regional retardation. Amid all such political debate, as also in the literature of Scotland, the events of the clearances have been drawn upon repeatedly as a potent source of inspiration. There are few better examples of the use of the historical experience for polemical purposes.

In the past several decades historians have introduced new elements into the analysis, in an attempt to provide a firmer theoretical and empirical basis for a discussion of the historical experience. Equally important has been the injection of new methods of interpretation, especially a greater recourse to economic theory, to regional economic analysis, and to Marxian class analysis. Historical sociology and demography have also been added to the tools of the historian. The overall effect has been to reveal the complexity of the issues, and the means of their elucidation. In general there has been no reduction in the passion invested in the study of the clearances.

I

In a paper on the Irish and Scottish Land Acts,[1] Clive Dewey has argued that the legislative victory of the cottars and crofters was underpinned by a crucial change in political philosophy. In both Ireland and the Highlands landlords had ridden rough-shod over traditional arrangements, and the clearances offered the best example of their wholesale elimination. Dewey argues that *laissez-faire* axioms which prevailed until the 1860s, together with the rise of 'utilitarian sociology', provided a compelling intellectual case for 'the abolition of such customary tenancy rights as survived'. But by 1881 the case had been almost entirely displaced by the rise of 'historicist axioms' which, as Dewey puts it, 'were sufficiently credible to justify the concession of tenant rights more comprehensive than those formerly conferred by custom'. Political economy of the classical sort was overturned by 'a historicist reaction'— that is, by the triumph of notions of historical determinism and evolution, and of the sanctity of historical institutions. Its employment of historical precedent brought it into strong association with Celtic Revivalism and the late-nineteenth-century cult of the peasant. In Scotland the 'historicist' programme was led by W. F. Skene, John Stuart Blackie and Cosmo Innes, intellectuals who created the basis for a philosophy which challenged the dominant assumptions of *laissez-faire*.[2]

In the Highlands the 'historicist' case was given local leadership by a self-educated ex-crofter who became the most effective, prolific and influential advocate of the crofters during their battle against the landlords during the seventies and eighties. Alexander Mackenzie (1838-98) provided most of the literary support for the crofters' movement: in his passionate advancement of their cause Mackenzie created an impressive corpus of historical writing on the Highlands. It has served two main purposes. In the first place it provided an influential retrospective on the crofter experience — in effect, the history of the two previous centuries was employed directly to give moral justification for the crofter agitation. In the second place, Mackenzie's work came to constitute the most important secondary source upon which much later writing on the clearances was based. He wrote the first comprehensive history of the clearances, and brought together a great deal of antiquarian material in a large series of clan histories. All this was additional to his important political and journalistic activity before, during and after the Crofter (Napier) Commission.

Mackenzie was by origin much closer to the people of the Highlands than many of their other spokesmen.[3] Although he claimed ancestry from the baronets of Gairloch and Kintail, he was born on a small croft at Tournaid on the estate of Sir George Mackenzie of Coul, a well-known propagandist of the most robust forms of Highland improvement. While he was an infant Alexander Mackenzie's entire township was evicted, and his family shifted to the Strath of Gairloch, and later to North Erradale. It was said that he spent his first twenty years on a four-acre croft, in a family of seven children. He learned both Gaelic and English, and used the *caschrom*, a clumsy-looking but effective Highland footplough which was the basis of crofter cultivation. According to another account, he left home in 1855, with 28 pence in his pocket, and eventually gained work on the Inverness and Nairn railway. He worked through a succession of jobs as crofter, ploughman, three seasons in the herring fishing, and as a grieve. He experienced the classic elements in the crofter's life — a large, poor family, a constricted and insecure life on a croft, eviction, the hard grind of crofting agriculture, and the almost inevitable seasonal employment in fishing and railway construction.

In the 1860s Mackenzie migrated to England and gained employment in the retail drapery trade in Ipswich. There he attended the Working Men's College, developed an admiration for the writing of Samuel Smiles, and turned his hand to journalism. Described as 'an able and astute businessman', Mackenzie prospered in Ipswich drapery and in 1869 sold his business to realise a capital of £900 with which he returned to Inverness where he established another drapery partnership. He was then in a position to develop his championship of Highland causes. In 1872 he stood as candidate for Town Councillor, was elected in the following year, and subsequently became a County Councillor, at a time when the crofting community was beginning to be aroused to a new degree of political awareness. In 1873 John Murdoch founded the newspaper *The Highlander* in Inverness; it transmitted many land league ideas from Ireland whence Murdoch had recently returned. Alexander Mackenzie himself started the *Celtic Magazine* in November 1875, a journal which strongly reinforced the case for land reform by placing the arguments in a cultural, and, most of all, a historical context. He was also a founding member of the Inverness Gaelic Society and subsequently established the *Scottish Highlander*, the most influential organ of the crofter movement in the 1880s. He carried on the work of propaganda and persuasion and gave 'expression to the legitimate aspirations of the people of the Highlands'. In the manifesto of the *Scottish*

Highlander Mackenzie declared that it was to be

> a temperate, but bold and independent spirit to advocate the
> rights and promote the interests of the Highland people. It will
> be impossible to do this effectively without at the same time
> advocating very great changes in the existing state of the law,
> but no changes will be urged except those based on the equit-
> able principle that every man, whatever his position, be he land-
> lord or tenant, employer or labourer, should be secured in the
> full enjoyment of the fruits of his labour, whether physical or
> mental.[4]

It was said that Alexander Mackenzie was the first to suggest a
parliamentary Commission of Inquiry into the Crofter Question. In
1881 he established the first Highland Land Law Reform Association. He came to be regarded as the standard-bearer of the
crofters and at the time of the Napier Commission he produced a
series of articles and pamphlets — often scholarly, well-written and
penetrating — which did much to promote the crofter's case. As
his own paper said in 1898:

> It is not too much to say that even so late as 1883 the most san-
> guine advocate of the reformation of the Land Laws as affecting
> the smaller tenants in the Highlands did not expect so far reach-
> ing a measure passed in a generation.[5]

Mackenzie's influence was widespread. His pamphlets sold very
quickly and his *History of the Highland Clearances*, published first
in 1883, passed through several editions and was, until recently,
the only comprehensive history that had been written. His radicalism was probably a shade in advance of the crofters for whom he
spoke. When, in 1888, he was asked, 'What do you think the
crofters really want?' he answered, 'The crofters want — and, in
my opinion, they never will be satisfied until they get it — all the
productive land, arable and pasture, of the Highlands.'[6] In this he
probably miscalculated the more modest aspirations and political
conservatism of the common man in the Highlands.

Mackenzie's fiery prose provoked indignation in his readers; his
turn of phrase was reminiscent of Cobbett. He accurately guessed
the power of history and myth to fuel the debate about Highland
land reform, and made no apology for resurrecting the old stories
of the clearances because, he claimed

the same laws which permitted the cruelties, [and] the inhuman atrocities ... are still the laws of the country, and any tyrant who may be indifferent to the healthier public opinion which now prevails, may legally repeat the same proceedings whenever he may take it into his head to do so.

It was the 'Iscariot-like sale' of the Highlanders by their landlords which inflamed his mind:

There is nothing in History so absolutely *mean* as the Eviction of the Highlanders by chiefs solely indebted for every inch of land they ever held to the strong arms and trusty blades of the progenitors of those whom the effeminate and ungrateful chiefs of the nineteenth century have so ruthlessly oppressed, evicted and despoiled.[7]

Mackenzie had begun his journalistic career in the *Celtic Magazine* in 1875 with relatively mild and gradualist proposals for reform in the Highlands, arguing that there was room enough for all in the region, including sheep and deer, so long as the land was managed under sensible regulations.[8] His historical work was, by contrast, polemical and vehement. His account of the Sutherland clearances, reconstructed mainly from the work of Donald Macleod, Donald Sage and Stewart of Garth, represented the whole process as a saga of atrocity verging on genocide. It had been 'a policy of extermination with a recklessness and remorselessness unparalleled anywhere the Gospel of peace and charity was preached — except, perhaps, unhappy Ireland'.[9] Sutherland was merely the extreme variant of the general Highland experience; in a heightened form it exemplified the main elements in his indictment of the clearing landlords. These included a recital of many atrocities allegedly committed during the clearances, and claims that a once-happy and prosperous people had been degraded in the process, that they had been forced to emigrate, and that they had been wickedly misled by their churchmen. Of the church in the Highlands during the clearances, he remarked: 'The professed ministers of religion sanctioned the iniquity.'[10] He also emphasised the impact of alien influences, specifically the English landlords, Lowland factors, southern sheepfarmers and foreign troops. He brought the name of Patrick Sellar into the gallery of Highland demonology by recounting the atrocity stories of 1813-16. In all, his *History of the Highland Clearances* was an effective fighting document in the political and populist campaign that preceded the establishment of the Napier Commission. Mackenzie sought not only to cure present ills, but to redress past wrongs.

Alexander Mackenzie gave cogent testimony before the Napier Commission in 1883. One of the landlords' complaints about the Napier Commission was that the crofters had colluded beforehand and had prepared their statements with the help of radicals, schoolmasters and Free Church ministers. Mackenzie had been rehearsing the case for a decade. The people of the Highlands, he said, had been robbed of the best arable land as well as their traditional grazing lands: while their territory was being reduced, their rents had been increased. There were stretches of land which, he claimed showed 'unmistakeable evidence of having been once under cultivation and occupied by a large number of people at no remote period'. Echoing the earlier propositions of Stewart and Miller, he contended that the loss of the land had demoralised the ordinary people of the Highlands: it had left them victims of periodic famine, destroyed their initiative, and cast them into a stupor of despair. Mackenzie drew on his own memory of the great famine of 1847-8, and of the factors' arbitrary oppression, as well as the cupidity of the landlords. He declared that the law itself was as fault for permitting the tragedy of the clearances.[11] Scottish landlords could do what they wished with their land. They could 'give it over, not only to deer forests, but to wolves and tigers. Is it not unjust', he asked, 'that a legal power like this should be virtually possessed by about thirty landlords born into such unnatural privileges?'[12] His remedy, of course, was to institute land laws which would thoroughly clip the wings of those thirty men. Yet he specifically rejected any romantic notion of a return to the past, and he conceded that the old runrig communal agriculture could provide no model for the future. But he believed that collective grazing was a perfectly feasible direction for land use.[13] He advocated five fundamental changes: the division of the deer forests into small holdings; the independent valuation of rented land on a basis of permanent tenure so that no eviction could ever occur so long as rent was paid; compensation for tenant improvement; government purchase of Highland estates which would then be granted to the people who, with the help of loans, would become peasant proprietors; and payment by the government of full compensation to the previous proprietors.[14] In some ways it was an 'emancipation of the serfs' in a British context.

Within Mackenzie's evidence, and in much of the contemporary discussion, there emerged a set of contested propositions about the possible capability of both the region and its people. Mackenzie believed, like many others, that the Highlands could sustain a collectivist or semi-collectivist form of economic life that could replace the sporting-cum-grazing economy of the latifundia of the great landlowners. Since Napier's time much public discussion of the Highland question has run along similar rails; the answer ultimately depends upon technical claims about, for instance, the viability of crofter agriculture, and the economics of competing and alternative forms of land use. These issues were deeply embedded in Mackenzie's evidence before the Napier Commission, which he regarded as the most important event in the Highlands since Culloden. Throughout his testimony Mackenzie made no effort to contest the *de facto* position of the landlords, or the present legality of their evictions. But he contended passionately that the people had a profound moral claim to better conditions, and that no scheme for Highland development would ever succeed until they were given full rights to the land.[15] He also voiced another warning about the crofters' anger: there was a danger, he said, that 'if no steps are taken almost immediately, you will have a social revolution in the Highlands'. He spoke darkly of Irish influene in the north of Scotland, and of the strength of support that the Highlanders could command in the towns of England, and in the colonies.[16] Mackenzie brought to the Napier Commission the moral fervour, the anger and the danger to public order that marked the crofter assault on the clearing landlords, past and present.

The utilisation of the Celtic past for intellectual and political purposes by Mackenzie and others did not pass unchallenged. It came under the penetrating gaze of the reviewer W. R. Lawson who, in 1884, claimed that 'As Radicals the crofters have learned, unfortunately, to regard their lairds as a burden on the land, and all connected with lairds — factors, gamekeepers and police included — as their natural enemies'; he believed the crofters were being openly incited by the Free Church ministers. Their inspiration was historical: 'The crofters are going back on the idea of a mythical age, and demanding their revival in an impossible present' generated by 'Patriotic bards and historians' who had 'started a theory that in the brilliant youth of the Celtic race the crofters formed village communities on the model of Sir Henry Maine's, and had a perpetual tenure of their lands'. Nevertheless, despite the vigour with which Lawson and others dismissed such theories as amusing speculations, the sympathy of the age for the Celtic peasantries continued undiminished.[17]

II

The volumes eventually published as the Evidence and Report of the Napier Commission in 1884 were landmarks in the political history of the Highlands. The Chairman was Lord Napier and Ettrick (1836-99), a relatively small landowner in the south of Scotland who had been Governor of Madras from 1866 to 1872. He was known to have made a number of 'socialistic' remarks at a social science congress in the year of his return from India and was visibly well-disposed to the common people of the Highlands. The other Commissioners were Sir Kenneth Smith Mackenzie and Donald Cameron of Lochiel, both large landowners in the north; Alexander Nicolson, Doctor of Laws, Advocate, Sheriff Substitute of the Stewartry of Kirkcudbright and a Celtic scholar who had been co-founder of the Chair of Celtic at Edinburgh University; Donald Mackinnon, another supporter of the Celtic view of the Highland identity and the first occupant of the Chair which Nicolson had created; and Charles Fraser-Mackintosh, Liberal MP, an active voice in the Highlands on behalf of the people, and a prolific antiquarian. Altogether the Commission, while spanning a wide range of opinion, was surprisingly balanced towards what Dewey calls the 'historicist' view of the world.[18] The composition of the Commission made it unlikely that the crofters would be rejected out of hand.

The Commissioners toured the Highlands and Islands, assisted by HMS *Lively*, which took them to their first port of call at Oban Bay in early May 1883. Their arrival was preceded by that of Alexander Mackenzie. They held a total of 71 meetings in 61 different locations, and received the testimonies of 775 people. They asked 46,750 questions, and the accumulated evidence and report amounted to 3,375 pages with a further 560 pages of appendices. The subsequent fate of the Napier recommendations and the passage of the Crofters Act in 1886 had much to do with the political problems of government in London, with the model created already by the Irish land reform legislation, and with the conflict between the *laissez-faire* and interventionist philosophies of the day.[19] The Napier Report effectively exposed the grievances and grinding poverty of the crofting community and attributed their problems mainly to the smallness of their holdings, the insecurity of their tenures, the absence of compensation for improvements, high rents and a defective economic infrastructure, especially of transport, which isolated the region from effective trading links for the crofters. The Commission advocated the resurrection of the 'highland township' as the central collectivist institution for the organisation of crofter land and resources, with powers of management, allocation of labour, payment of rents and taxes, and of compulsory purchase over adjacent land in private hands. The government jibbed at this recommendation which smacked too much of creeping socialism and passed instead a body of legislation in 1886 which accepted the less radical elements in the Napier proposals. Nevertheless the Crofters Act gave the people unprecedented security of tenure, and enabled them to apply to a statutory body for the arbitration of fair rents and compensation for improvements. Though it fell short of establishing a system of communal townships, the Act gave recognition to customary tenant rights relating to grazing. Perhaps most important of all, it prohibited the alienation of crofting land, which reduced critically the possibilities of economic adaptation to future circumstances. The crofter system was ossified from the start. The Crofters Act, always a controversial piece of legislation, has been largely blamed for the failure of crofting to provide adequate scope for material advance. But it nevertheless constituted a substantial set of concessions to the crofters and inaugurated a policy of government intervention in shaping the pattern of development in the Highlands. The Napier Report and the Act of 1886 were, therefore, substantial, though qualified, victories for the 'historicist' conception of Highland affairs.

The proceedings of the Napier Commission gave a unique opportunity for the ordinary people to speak directly into the historical record, sometimes with the aid of interpreters, sometimes by way of elected representatives. Their testimonies almost always recounted events several decades in the past and provided a sustained collective view of Highland history. Indeed, as Dewey has observed, 'much of the Napier Report was devoted to a critical examination of the interpretation of Highland history on which the crofters based their case'.[20] The evidence provides the authentic voice of the Highlands, silent for most of the decades of the clearances. It represents an unrivalled repository of popular declaration, the finest source for 'history from below' in the entire history of the Highlands (and better than available for most of the British Isles for this time). There are many problems in the interpretation of such data — problems common to oral history and all retrospective testimony. Much of the evidence is acrimonious and unbalanced.

The Report of the Commission contained a subtle exposition of the Highland problem. The historical case offered by so many of the crofters and their spokesmen was not swallowed whole, despite the sympathetic attitude of the majority of the Commissioners. The report began with some judicious remarks about the nature of the testimonies before it:

> In judging the validity of much of this evidence, we shall do well to remember that these depositions, regarding acts and incidents often obscure and remote, are in many cases delivered by illiterate persons seeking from early memory, or from hearsay, or from popular tradition, fleeting and fallacious sources even when not tinged by ancient regrets and resentments, or by the passions of the hour.

It is ironic that, one hundred years later, these popular traditions have come to be specially valued by scholars of the Highlands. Yet, despite their scepticism, the Commissioners delivered one of their most resounding judgements when they remarked that:

> The history of the economical transformation which a great portion of the Highlands and Islands has during the past century undergone does not repose in the loose and legendary tales that pass from mouth to mouth; it rests on the solid basis of contemporary records, and if these are wanting, it is written in indelible characters on the surface of the soil.[21]

The report proceeded to a consideration of the historical changes that had overtaken the Highlands, and noted the propensity towards 'retrospective fancy' among Highlanders, and the tendency to paint the past in attractive colours [which] will not easily be abandoned; nor is it likely to be obliterated by contemporary education or political training. A comparison of the present with the past is a favourite and effective instrument in stirring popular aspiration for enlarged right.

In this judgement, the Commission contended that most of the popular legend of the pre-clearance Highlands was idyllic and unrealistic, and excluded 'the dark realities' of existence — most notably the oppressive feudality of social and economic relations. The appeal to the past was invalid even in the sense that the 'old usage of the country' provided no foundation for claims of lost security of tenure. The crofters had not been able to furnish any documentary evidence of their alleged traditional rights of occupancy or communal ownership of land. It judged that no claim

> founded on the old usage of the country can now be seriously entertained. The clan system no longer exists. The chief has in many cases disappeared, and his property has been transferred by sale to another name and another race. The people have in many cases disappeared as a distinct sect or common extraction, under the influences of emigration, inter-marriage, and substitution. The relations of ancient inter-dependence have vanished.

This cold realism was considerably counterbalanced by the Report's heavy emphasis upon the moral claims of the crofters.

> It is difficult to deny that a Macdonald, a Macleod, a Mackenzie, or a Mackay, or a Cameron, who gave a son to his landlord eighty years ago to fill up the ranks of a Highland regiment, did morally acquire a tenure in his holding more sacred than the stipulations of written covenant.

This, of course, had been the forlorn belief of the common Highlanders over a century of clearances. The Napier Commission, despite its salutory scepticism, accepted a large part of the crofters' moral case, and the Crofters Act of 1886, as Fraser Darling later observed, 'wisely and justly gave legal status to the "indigenous impression" which pertains nowhere else in Britain than in the Highlands and Islands of Scotland'.[22] Hence the crofters won their suit even through their historical claims were rejected.

The clearances, in the verdict of the Napier Commission, had left the remaining crofters helpless at the hands of the landlords. Often restricted to inferior and exhausted soil, subject also to arbitrary rent increases, and without any security of tenure or compensation for improvements, the crofter lived in conditions 'of a character which would almost imply physical and moral degradation in the eyes of those who do not know how much decency, courtesy, virtue, and even mental refinement, survive amidst the sordid surroundings of a Highland hovel'. The Napier Report recognised that there had been a number of important countervailing benefits for the people, notably in higher wages, better communications, facilities for trade and emigration, and improved sanitary regulations. Nevertheless there remained the stark facts of great poverty among the Highlanders: they had lost land and the terms on which they occupied their crofts inhibited improvement of their conditions. The report observed that the current decline in the profitability of sheepfarming, having altered economic relativities in the Highlands, might provide an occasion for some rearrangement of land holding.[23]

On the question of land tenure the Commission recommended extraordinary regulations for the control of landlords' power. They acknowledged that the concept of government intervention in the rights of property was anathema to 'that school of economists, who, in dealing with social distresses, prefer to contemplate the operation of natural causes and tendencies, rather than the action of artificial remedies'. They knew also that government action of this sort would constitute

> a complex system of interference on behalf of a class in the community which is not numerous, which does not contribute a preponderant share to the aggregate sum of national wealth, and which does, after all that has been said, possess in ordinary times, conditions of welfare and happiness unknown to some others of the people, for instance to the poorer sort of rural day labourers in England, or those who depend on casual employment in great cities.[24]

In justification of such exceptional powers of intervention the Commissioners adduced several arguments, both economic and political. In terms of assisting development, they asserted that the fishing industry of the Highlands should not be allowed to run down any further because it was of national importance. They invoked the classic Smithian exception to the general rule of *laissez-faire* — that national defence was more vital than opulence, and that the northern fishermen were, in effect, part of a naval reserve for times of emergency. The Commissioners appealed also to the contemporary notion that the nation as a whole benefited when the common people achieved a material stake in the land: in part this reflected the increased esteem acccorded to peasant proprietors in the sentimentalised thinking of the mid-Victorians.[25] Thus, the encouragement and promotion of a secure tenantry in the Highlands would be 'a social experiment connected with the land of no common interest' — the more attractive, perhaps, because it would reverse the earlier experiment of the clearances.[26]

For this special treatment there were three further grounds. One was the continuing vulnerability of the crofting population to periodic climatic catastrophe which, in a subsistence agriculture, left the people close to famine. Another was the prevailing agitation and threat to order caused by the undiminished sense of grievance among the crofters. The government, it was true, had the power and means to crush the resistance, but such a policy was repugnant to the general public and would provide no solution to the basic problems. 'The land agitation of the Highlands is not likely to pass away without some adjustment of the claims of occupiers acceptable to the greater number who are not yet possessed with extravagant expectations.' The Commissioners told the government clearly enough that it should not underestimate the bitter feelings of the Highlanders, nor the likely support that their cause could draw upon from other parts of the world — in effect, they raised the spectre of another Ireland. Finally, the Commissioners pointed out that there was good precedent for special legislation on behalf of particular groups in the British polity. They contended that protection and regulation had been long introduced which safeguarded workers in mines, plantations and factories and on ships, and that the case for the Highlands was in no sense generically different from these well-accepted areas.[27]

British landed interests had been, for long, virtually immune from regulation of their conduct. The fact that many, though not all, of the Napier recommendations were incorporated into the Crofters Act of 1886 was a mark of their success in breaching that immunity. It was also a signal of the remarkable volte-face of the Liberals with regard to the sanctity of property rights in land, and a considerable reversal of the *laissez-faire* ideology.[28] It owed a great deal, of course, to the passage of the Irish Land Act in 1881 which Oliver MacDonagh has described as 'an undisguised acceptance of co-ownership, with the state permanently involved in the conflict between the wrangling partners through the institution of Land Courts empowered to fix rents'.[29] It is not surprising that Scottish landowners exhibited heightened anxiety over the debate on the Irish land question — but by the time of the crofter legislation many of them realised that total resistance was no longer politically feasible.[30] Although the eventual form of the Act was in important respects less comprehensive than the Napier recommendations, it represented a radical shift in tenurial relations in the Highlands. It provided a framework for the resolution of much conflict — by 1913 the Crofter Commission had reduced rents by an aggregate of 25 per cent, and cancelled 57 per cent of arrears. A set of rules now governed rents, tenure and size of holdings, but the legislation did little to tackle the greater problem of generating economic development for the crofters. This was the residual question which was to haunt all parties during the following century. The Napier Commission diagnosed the Highland problem primarily in terms of tenurial difficulties. Over the following six decades or so, the nature of the problem was revealed to have broader and more intractable causes.

III

The historical and economic axioms of the Napier Commissioners, the various crofters' propagandists, the Henry Georgites (whose leader had visited the north in 1884[31]) and the land leaguers did not, of course, pass uncontested. The Highland proprietors formed defence organisations and mounted a substantial campaign to limit the impending legislative changes. The most vigorous and prolific defender of the Highland lairds was the eighth Duke of Argyll, one of the great northern landowners. Even before the beginning of the crofter agitation, in June 1866, he had presented a paper before the Statistical Society in London, claiming that the record of improvement and economic development fostered by Highland landlords was as good as anywhere in Scotland. He stated

that the displacement of population by the introduction of great capitalists holding farms of very great value, has not taken place in the Highland counties to an extent nearly equal to that in which it has taken place in some of the richest counties of Scotland.[32]

Argyll subsequently wrote many more pamphlets and papers, and a book, *Scotland as it was and as it is* (1887), which was predominantly an explanation of the Highland experience, and a hymn of praise to the creative record of the landowners. In some ways his work was not so much a defence of the landlords as a positive statement of their collective agrarian achievements — he took the contest to the opposite camp.

Argyll, a vigorous exponent of classical political economy who had resigned from Gladstone's Cabinet over the Irish land legislation, was probably the best-known opponent of the philosophy of land reform. In 1870 he had warned Gladstone against ill-informed historical precedents:

I hope you will be *very careful* before you quote ancient Celtic usages, in a barbaric condition of society, as having any practical bearing upon legislation in the present day. If the known and admitted principles on which Property and Occupation have been based for the last two centuries are not to be admitted as having obliterated 'Tribal Rights' there can be no repose in Political Society.[33]

But eventually he chose not to resist the Crofter Bill mainly because, given the political condition of Westminster and the Highlands, opposition would be futile.[34] This did not prevent his public abuse of what he regarded as the retrogressive philosophy of the land reformers. John Mason, in a fine article on Argyll, has remarked that the Duke was

unusually frank in his defence of private property and inequality as the necessary preconditions for economic progress ... Argyll mounted an economic defence of the great landowner as the agricultural improver and the central archetypal figure in the history of material progress.[35]

He was scornful of the intellectual foundations of the opposing case for reform, and believed the proposed legislation would turn the Highlands back towards feudalism. His book, a sustained historical analysis of the Highlands since the Middle Ages, was designed as a systematic rebuttal of the work of Alexander Mackenzie and his supporters, who, Argyll believed, perpetuated myths and 'false sentiments' about the Highlands, past and present. His book was an important contribution, regardless of its propagandist function, to the emergent historiography of the Highlands, drawing upon considerably more primary historical documentation than had informed previous works. Argyll was much favoured in this respect because he had personal access to the great archives of the Campbells; he was also familiar with the antiquarian work of, for example, Fraser-Mackintosh and Cosmo Innes, and he drew upon earlier sources including Burt and the two *Statistical Accounts*. He was one of the few people at that time who attempted to meet the 'historicist' camp on its own empirical ground.

Argyll believed passionately in progress, more even than Macaulay. History to him was the epic struggle of the forces of civilisation against barbarity and backwardness; the price of progress was constant resistance to the dangers of sliding backwards into the feudal past. He entirely rejected the notion that the Highlands had ever been an Arcady; its past was one of oppression, cruelty and famine in which the 'domestic economy of the people ... had remained worse than stationary for more than a thousand years'. Much of his book was a detailed critique of the use of evidence by the historical 'sentimentalists'.[36] He believed indeed that the really extraordinary aspect of Highland history was that civilisation had been so slow to reach the north of Scotland, and regarded the elimination of the old social system — notably the abolition of the tacksmen, runrig and feudal services — as a profoundly beneficial and liberating process which had been in train long before the Forty-five. He dismissed altogether the view that, before the clearances, the townships had been in some sense communistic, or had subsumed individual interest into that of the community.[37]. Argyll maintained that progress came to the Highlanders via the instrumentality and positive efforts of certain landowners. He expressed the point plainly:

> Every single step towards improvement which has been taken during the last 150 years has been taken by the Proprietor, and not by the people. Not only so, but every one of these steps

without exception has been taken against the prevailing opinion and feelings of the people at the time.[38]

The great work of rural reform, he insisted, was always associated with enclosure and with an increasingly refined division of labour — 'a principle which runs through the whole of Nature' and which was the characteristic mark of progress in British history.[39] In conjunction with the great advances in trade and industry, the new agriculture, led by the creative spirit of the landowners, had conquered the ancient curses of poverty and famine. The only exceptions to the march of progress were

> the few remaining fastnesses of the ancient ignorance. These fastnesses have chiefly been in the Hebrides, and in a few Districts of the the Northern Highlands — always where, only where, and in proportion as, the old stupidities have resisted and survived.[40]

He repeatedly contrasted the resistance to change in the Highlands with the more advanced progress of the rest of the kingdom.

In this gospel of progress Argyll was emphatic that the greatest threat to economic and social advance in the Highlands had always been the danger of overpopulation. He observed that an established pattern of emigration already existed before 1745; and he drew attention to the 'natural' efflux of population experienced in many agricultural districts in Scotland. He asserted that the population of the Highlands, as elsewhere, had a tendency to outrun its resources. This had been evident in the eighteenth century when, under the influence of kelp production and short-sighted landowners who had encouraged the process, there had developed 'the terrible and then increasing disproportion between the old Celtic population and the legitimate means of subsistence', much exacerbated by the 'extreme unproductiveness' of the old Highland methods of agriculture. Argyll believed that population was the most fundamental issue in northern development since it created a crippling burden on the land — 'Every other cause was a mere consequence of this one cause.' The problem was not exclusive to the Highlands, for the growth of population pressure had been the same in Lowland parishes; but it was only in the Highlands that 'the stream was pent up longer, and was overflowing with a rush'. By virtue of the great rural reforms, Argyll maintained, the Highlands had been rendered far more productive and much less oppressive to the individual, and its population growth had adjusted, by means of emigration, to the economic opportunities which had been created within and beyond the Highlands. Any check to these sensible processes, he warned, would simply encourage a return to barbarism.[41]

Argyll put forward his case with outstanding clarity and vigour — even vehemence. Plainly he was much influenced by Malthusian and Darwinian thinking. He believed that the Highland population had been stranded by the collapse of the kelp trade and the deterioration of the potato crops. Many of them were effectively redundant: 'Sooner or later Nature finds out the sins and blindness of all her children.'[42] The Highlanders, instead of emigrating in sufficient numbers, had become objects of sentimentality and charity. It was axiomatic that

> wherever, in any area of country, the increase of population involves a lower and a lower standard of living — chronic poverty, and the necessity of periodic drafts upon the industry and property of other men — then the increase is an evil and not a good.[43]

At the core of Argyll's analysis was a belief that all human society was subject to irresistible forces which it was foolish to resist. It was absurd and damaging to attempt to thwart the operation of these universal rules of political economy in the Highlands. That region must pass through a transformation precisely the same as that of the rest of Scotland. He believed that there was nothing

> more curious about the agitation set up concerning these changes than the fact that men gape and stare over them when they see in the Highlands the very same agricultural conditions which have equally come to prevail around their own doors.[44]

He drew a parallel between the effects of rural change in the Highlands and adjustments that were the common experience of the industrial world:

> In all other countries when Mines are exhausted, or when Mills are closed, or when any other local industry is extinguished, the people who had been so employed invariably moved off to

other fields where their labour can be made remunerative to themselves, and useful to the world. But the Hebrideans never thought of this. There is, nevertheless, no suspension of the laws of Nature for the special and exclusive protection of any particular set of men, merely because they belong to a particular race, or because they live in an Island, or because they speak a particular language.[45]

To Argyll emigration was the obvious and beneficial consequence of progressive rural change at a time of population growth. He instanced the case of the people who left for Clydeside:

There at this moment, in the shipbuilding trade, a man, with no other skill than such as can be easily acquired, can earn as wages in a fortnight far more than the whole year's rent of the croft on which his father vegetated ... Those who have gone, and those who have remained, are all better off.[46]

The Duke devoted surprisingly little space to the actual record of the clearances, but his exposition contained several basic propositions, always stated pungently. He contended that, prior to the introduction of commercial sheepfarming, the old system of agriculture had seriously underutilised the landed resources of the Highlands. Hence sheep production represented 'an enormous addition ... to the natural produce of the country', and so 'added to the comfort and resources of Mankind'. The clearances, which facilitated this change, had been of small account: 'No doubt the new sheep farming involved some local displacement of population, because sheep could not be supported without access to low ground which was sometimes occupied by "clachans", liable to periodical distress and famine.' But, he maintained, the actual displacement required in the Highlands had been far less radical than had been the experience in either the Scottish Lowlands or the border counties. In fact in many parts of the Highlands the population had shown a net increase since 1801. Nor was it true (as was often claimed) that Lowland farmers had displaced the Highlanders — the new sheepfarmers were a cross-section of people, including many of northern stock.[47] Sheepfarming had represented a progressive shift in resource usage which was being threatened by the misplaced romanticism and ill-directed land-leaguism of the day.

To Argyll these changes had all be inevitable and, on balance, distinctly beneficial. The lairds, the energetic instrument of the change, had been maligned in the public imagination because the public was ignorant of the truth. He urged a comparative analysis of the modernised and unchanged sectors of the region, and claimed that the 'Highland Problem' was confined to those districts which had failed to modernise:

> Distress has existed, and has existed only, in the districts of the Highlands where the old conditions of society have not yet given way before the advance of sheep farming or of dairy farming, and those changes in the occupation of land which are a necessary step towards an improved husbandry.

He pointed out that on the evidence of the famines of the nineteenth century

> the distressed districts are precisely those in which the old crofting system is still lingering. Wherever the crofts have been consolidated into farms of moderate size, no distress has ever arisen from the failure of the potatoes. But this is a process which cannot be carried into effect without a reduction in the number of people who now derive from the land a scant and precarious subsistence.[48]

It was a generally unpalatable opinion in the climate of the 1880s; it suggested a comparative, almost counterfactual, approach to the Highland question which, a hundred years later, has hardly yet been put to an empirical test.

Argyll's other comparison was of a different sort: he considered the policies of Sir James Matheson on the island of Lewis. Matheson, who had made a vast fortune in the eastern (especially the opium) trade before the age of forty, returned to his native Highlands, bought the entire island of Lewis, and lavished his resources on schemes to retain the population and create a progressive economic structure for the crofters. Among Highland landlords he was a model of excellence whose good intentions and capital outlay had unfortunately not been matched by results. Argyll, sceptical of Matheson's benevolent plans, derided the manner in which he had 'poured out his immense capital like water upon the reclamation of peat-mosses'. By such foolish expenditure, he argued, Matheson had deliberately checked the natural emigration of the people from Lewis, and thereby increased their critical vulnerability to famine. Lewis was the most congested and desperate district of the West Highlands, and Matheson's philanthropy was an extremely dangerous model for Highland development.

This is the condition to which the whole of the Highlands would have been reduced if both the people and the proprietors had not taken warning in time. And this is the condition to which they would be reduced again, if they were to listen to the advice of those who would arrest the progress of civilisation and of improvement by establishing in the Highlands another population like that which is that which is now living half starved we are told, in the hovels of Donegal and Kerry.[49]

Argyll effectively reinforced his case with some interesting satire directed at the memory of Sir Walter Scott and at Lord Napier himself. Scott had been critical of 'the unrelenting avarice' of many Highland lairds during the clearances, and did more than anyone to romanticise the Highland past. Argyll, however, recollected that Scott himself became a substantial laird in the south of Scotland and had set himself up in a new baronial hall:

But he did not restore the Cottier Tenantry. He enclosed and planted. But he planted Larches. He did not invite the Workmen making high wages in Hawick or Galashiels to come back to starve on patches of corn and of potatoes along the once populous 'Houghs' of Tweed.

Yet this, according to Argyll, was the logical direction of current government policy — the reinstatement of small holders on Highland estates, as a revived peasantry, the effect of which would be to lock up the people in the region, create a population problem, and exacerbate the economic difficulties of the region. Even more ironic, he thought, was the fact that the creator of this policy was Lord Napier, a Scottish peer 'whose own Estate is situated among the long "cleared" sheep pastures of the Southern Highlands'. Argyll mocked Napier thus:

This distinguished Scotchman has given elaborate advice to

Highland Proprietors for the extension — not merely of small Holdings — but of the special form of these which is least advantageous — that of Joint or Township Farms. There is nevertheless not the slightest reason to believe that he himself or any of his brethren, would consent to cut up any of their comfortable and single arable Farms, for the purpose of restoring the population of the Middle Ages.[50]

He could imagine nothing more foolish or unrealistic. The entire burden of Argyll's literary outpourings was, indeed, that the Highland landlords were being singled out for discriminatory legislation which was entirely inequitable and, moreover, irrefutably retrogressive.

IV

While the Duke of Argyll fulminated, somewhat ineffectually, against the growing belief that the Highlands should be treated as a special case for government legislation, the opposing school maintained an unbroken stream of radical criticism of the landlords. Literary and political figures, too many to deal with individually, added their support to the case of the Highland crofter against his masters. There was a continuity of writing which, in the twentieth century, embraced Neil M. Gunn, Iain Crichton Smith, Eric Linklater, Sorley Maclean, John MacGrath and many others. The use of the history of the clearances in modern Scottish political debate has been widespread and potent; undoubtedly the invocation of the clearances has been effective in maintaining the temperature of debate on the Highland question, past and present. Literary dramatisation and political polemics have tended at all times to unbalance the historical perspective on the clearances. Two examples illustrate elements in the tradition.

Stimulus was given to the crofters' case in the 1880s by the powerful writings of John Stuart Blackie, Professor of Latin at Aberdeen University and of Greek at Edinburgh before his appointment as first occupant of a Chair of Celtic Literature in Scotland (in itself a symbolic moment in the consciousness of the Highlands' political cause). A major figure in the Gaelic revival movement — in Argyll's words, the leader of 'Gaelic sentimentalism' — he brought elevated literary style to the propaganda attacking the prevailing land laws. Blackie, in a heated combination of moral indignation, heavy satire, antiquarianism, literary criticism and Celtic revivalism, contributed a series of denunciations of Highland landlords. As Clive Dewey has said, 'Blackie's criterion of progress was moral: every society was "progressive or retrogressive" — in the highest sense of the word progress — only in proportion as the moral sand which holds the different classes together is becoming stronger or weaker.' On this criterion the old Highland social system possessed the highest virtues, in total contrast with the 'systematic selfishness' of the demoralised Lowland society which threatened the last remnants of Highland culture.[51] Blackie wrote about the cultural change that had debased eighteenth-century Highland lairds so that they became no better than land merchants — men who came to 'look upon their people as mere chattels to be sold or removed, with due form of law, at the pleasure of the proprietor'. He claimed that the moral fibre of the leaders of the Highlands had been weakened, notably by influences emanating from England. England was responsible for the new commercialism, and for the imported morality of London, Eton and Harrow, and for the absenteeism of the sportsman-landowner. It was a story of social decadence, exacerbated by 'the fashion of doctrinaire economy' and the 'haste to make rich'.[52] Blackie's work was an assault on the 'rampant individualism'[53] represented by the southern sporting landlord, and a spirited defence of the communal culture of the Highland village.

The literary and historical critique of the Highland lairds continued to exert considerable political influence even beyond the turn of the century. Ramsay MacDonald, for instance, ridiculed the Scottish aristocracy; he regarded the story of the clearances as a classic commentary on the misuse of power and wealth by a hereditary elite. At the time of the 1909 budget he derided the aristocratic slogan that the redistributive effects of the budget would be tantamount to 'exploitation, theft and robbery'. He suggested that if the origins of the wealth and broad acres of the landowners were closely examined they would have little claim on the title of honest men. He declared that many of the greatest men of the day had

> grown rich by laying their hands upon property that belonged to other people and ... increased their estates by a ruthless exploitation of smallholders and peasant owners — for such men to

speak of land taxation, compulsory land purchase, and other laws of a socialist land programme as injustice, is nothing but impertinence and hypocrisy.

MacDonald boasted that the Labour Party (and to a lesser extent, Lloyd George himself) were on the offensive, 'taking back from men who stole, withdrawing from men who stole, withdrawing from classes that expropriated, the wealth that originally belonged to the community, that had been made valuable by the community'.

MacDonald's radicalism was based upon an appeal to the past and to the record of the aristocracy's behaviour to the common people. He advocated that a twentieth-century 'domesday book' be prepared to provide the factual basis for a policy of restoring the land to the people, and also to provide the foundation for a scientific programme of socialism on land. He complained that there was no extant history of Scottish land and that

> the history of the people of Scotland yet remains to be written. The more impartially this is done, the more invaluable will it be as a propagandist manual. The story of the people in history is the best handbook for the guidance of the people in politics.[54]

V

From the time of the Napier Commission, when the crofter question became wholly politicised, the character of the treatment of the clearances had changed. A much clearer set of propositions emerged — for instance, about the alleged Malthusian necessity for systematic emigration, about the course of living standards of crofters in the nineteenth century, and about the impact of landlord policy on general levels of welfare. Already strongly implicit in the emerging debate were questions which, for their verification, required systematic comparative analysis of historical conditions before and after the clearances. Similarly the work of several influential writers in the late Victorian period depended unconsciously on a series of informal counterfactual propostions. For instance, both Hugh Miller and the eight Duke of Argyll employed reasoning which depended upon an imagined state of the Highlands in circumstances in which the clearances had not been executed. Both used implied 'hypothetical alternatives', and reached diametrically opposed conclusions about the net effects of the clearance policies.

By the end of the century the importance of the 'historicist' case in the Highlands had already been demonstrated; the powerful influence of a particular historical interpretation of Highland history was seen in the creation of an apparatus of government machinery which intervened in the relations between crofter and landlord. The Highlands had come to be regarded as a special case for administration, even as a place to attempt experiments in government and private initiatives in economic and social enterprise. It was inevitable that the Highlands would emerge as a *locus classicus* for the definition and analysis of regional problems in the United Kingdom.

Modern historical work on the clearances is best evaluated with regard to the degree to which the empirical basis has been extended and systematised beyond the state of knowledge at the time of the clearances. Where new theoretical insights or techniques of analysis are introduced, they need to be judged against their success in reinterpreting and clarifying the experience of the Highlands. For there is no question that much modern writing has tended simply to repeat the work of some of the nineteenth-century compilations, and has echoed the passions of the time without necessarily assisting in the understanding of the events. Some recent writers have come closer to a consideration of the counterfactual propositions which underlie much of the controversy about the clearances.

One writer who provides an interesting bridge between the debate about the Crofters Act and the modern discussion of the regional problem in the Highlands is J.P. Day, whose major treatise on Highland public administration appeared in 1918. He possessed considerable detailed knowledge of estate experience, but was mainly concerned in his book with the form and manner of public administration, of which he provided a sensitive account. He was primarily interested in the practical and philosophical limits of government responsibilities in such a region. He pointed out that the Highlands created special problems and that it already possessed, by virtue of the crofter legislation, a basic apparatus of administrative control.

The Highlands and Islands ... have become something of a laboratory for administrative and legislative experiments, and this makes them a peculiarly interesting field of study, inasmuch as experiments, thought to be successful, tend to be followed by the extension of the operation to wider areas. Moreover, some of the experiments, where proprietary rights and the interests of the community are opposed, are likely to bring up in an acute and practical form the question of the proper limits of State action. Already the Socialists regard the work of such bodies as the Congested Districts Board as 'pointing the way'.[55]

Day remarked that the nation had to decide whether or not it wished to maintain and subsidise the crofter population in the Highlands, and what price it was prepared to pay. In effect he gave expression to precisely the questions which eventually produced answers in the form of the Highlands and Islands Development Board some half a century later. The identification of the problem of regional economic development was crucial in this evolution of political priorities in the Highlands and the history of the clearances cast its shadow across the unending debate.

Notes

1. See Clive Dewey, 'Celtic Agrarian Legislation and the Celtic Revival: Historicist Implications of Gladstone's Irish and Scottish Land Acts 1870-1886', *Past and Present* no. 64 (1974).
2. Ibid., pp. 31, 50-5, 63-8.
3. This section is based on the *Scottish Highlander*, 27 January 1898, and the testimony of Mackenzie before the Napier Commission; see Report of Commissioners of Inquiry into the Condition of the Crofters and Cottars of the Highlands and Islands of Scotland, *PP* (1884), XXXII-XXXVI, Evidence, Qq. 41060ff.
4. Quoted in John Noble, *Miscellanea Invernessiana* (Sterling, 1902).
5. *Scottish Highlander*, 27 January 1898.
6. *Dundee Advertiser*, quoted in the *Scottish Highlander*, 24 May 1888.
7. Alexander Mackenzie, *The History of the Highland Clearances* (Inverness, 1883), pp. viii-ix.
8. See, for instance, the *Celtic Magazine* (November 1875).
9. Mackenzie, *History of the Clearances* (1966 edition), p. 20.
10. Ibid., p. 21.
11. Napier Commission, Q. 41060.
12. Ibid., Q. 41062.
13. Ibid., Qq. 41082-6.
14. Ibid., Q. 41063.
15. Ibid., Qq. 41097, 41124.
16. Ibid., Qq. 41147-50.
17. W. R. Lawson, 'The Poetry and the Prose of the Crofter Question', *National Review*, vol. 4 (1884-5).
18. Dewey, 'Celtic Agrarian Legislation', pp. 63-5.

19. Ibid., *passim.*
20. Ibid., p. 64.
21. Napier Report, p. 2.
22. Ibid., pp. 2-9; F. Fraser Darling, *West Highland Survey* (Oxford, 1955), p. 6; see Dewey, 'Celtic Agrarian Legislation', pp. 63-5.
23. Napier Report, p. 7.
24, Ibid., p. 108.
25. See, for example, Dewey, 'Celtic Agrarian Legislation', p. 42.
26. See Hugh Miller, quoted in Mackenzie, *Highland Clearances,* p. 182.
27. Napier Report, pp. 108-11.
28. Dewey, 'Celtic Agrarian Legislation', *passim.*
29. Oliver MacDonagh, *Ireland* (Englewood Cliffs, 1968), p. 39.
30. See Edward Bristow, 'The Liberty and Property Defence League and Individualism', *Historical Journal,* vol. 18 (1975), pp. 765-6.
31. See Henry George, *Scotland and Scotsmen* (Glasgow, 1884).
32. Duke of Argyll, 'On the Economic Condition of the Highlands of Scotland', *Journal of the Statistical Society of London,* vol. 26 (1883), p. 535.
33. Quoted from E. D. Steele in Clive Dewey, 'Celtic Agrarian Legislation', p. 59. See also *Autobiography and Memoirs,* ed. the Dowager Duchess of Argyll (2 vols., London, 1906), II, pp. 347ff.
34. See James Hunter, *The Making of the Crofting Community* (Edinburgh, 1976), p. 161.
35. John W. Mason, 'The Duke of Argyll and the Land Question in Late Nineteenth Century Britain', *Victorian Studies,* vol. 21 (1978), p. 157.
36. Duke of Argyll, *Scotland as it was and as it is* (2 vols., Edinburgh, 1887), II, p. 17. His detailed analysis of the use of evidence in the Napier Commission is contained in 'A Corrected Picture of the Highlands', *Nineteenth Century,* vol. 16 (November 1884).
37. Argyll, *Scotland as it was,* II, pp 25, 194-5.
38. Ibid., p. 48.
39. Ibid., p. 201.
40. Ibid., p. 251.
41. Argyll, 'On the Economic Condition', pp. 173-82.
42. Argyll, *Scotland as it was,* II, p. 261.
43. Argyll, 'On the Economic Condition', pp. 182-3.
44. Argyll, 'Corrected Picture', p. 686.
45. Argyll, *Scotland as it was,* II, p. 261.
46. Argyll, 'On the Economic Condition', p. 193.
47. Argyll, *Scotland as it was,* II, pp. 264-5.
48. Argyll, 'On the Economic Condition', p. 532.
49. Ibid., p. 198.
50. Argyll, *Scotland as it was,* II, p. 272.
51. Dewey, 'Celtic Agrarian Legislation', pp. 54-5.
52. J. S. Blackie, *The Scottish Highlanders and the Land Laws* (London, 1885), pp. 40, 44, 46, 54-5, 70.
53. J. S. Blackie, 'The Highland Crofters', *Nineteenth Century,* vol. 13 (1883), p. 616.
54. Ramsay MacDonald, Preface to Thomas Johnston, *Our Scots Noble Families* (Glasgow, 1926).
55. J. P. Day, *Public Administration in the Highlands and Islands of Scotland* (London, 1918), pp. 6-7.

4
ACADEMIC BEGINNINGS

New interpretations of the Highland experience began to emerge after the First World War, mainly, but not exclusively, from systematic empirically based historical research in the universities. Though the literature has remained impassioned, the automatic compulsion to attack or defend the landlord class has, occasionally, yielded place to analysis of the causes and consequences of the wider process. Though this altered the pattern of the historiography, perhaps more influential in moulding public opinion has been the substantial parallel popular literature of a fictional character. Novels, poems, films and plays about the history of the Highlands have continued to depend on a relatively small corpus of fully researched history.

Amongst historians two rival themes have tended to dominate the literature. One sees the clearances as an unavoidable conflict of class interests by which the common people of the Highlands were oppressed with uncommon ruthlessness. The other approach stresses the imperative of market forces which left the landlords and people of the region little choice beyond the actual course of events, and which maximised social welfare in the admittedly circumscribed geographical conditions of the Highlands. Apart from these stereotyped themes there have emerged in recent decades more adventurous lines of thought and analysis. A more critical attitude to the general corpus of documentary sources has been the growing mark of much new work; and systematic efforts have been made to employ statistical, archaeological and other non-literary evidence to complement and to test the written record. Similarly anthropology, geography, economics, sociology and demography have been drawn more fully into the question, and the Highland experience has been compared with similar regions within and beyond the British Isles. The analysis of popular disturbances in the Highlands and of the intra-regional demographic experience has brought greater depth to historical understanding, as have more precise studies of the role of the tacksmen and the church, the patterns of land use, the political awakening of the crofters, and the organisational framework of landlordism. None of this in any way dampens the passion that suffuses the question of the clearances; the main function of the new research has been to expose parts of the broader mechanisms which contributed to the transformation of the region. The evolution of some of these studies is traced in the following three chapters.

I

The work of Margaret Adam must count as one of the earliest efforts to pursue the historical evidence with relatively modern methods and with some explicit attempt to balance the weight of the contemporary documentation. In four articles published in the *Scottish Historical Review* between 1919 and 1922 Adam provided a clear and vigorous exposition of the problems confronting Highland landlords of the late eighteenth century. Based on a thorough and systematic reading of published sources, notably the accounts of tours, and the *Old Statistical Account,* her analysis was a methodical and persuasive attack on the 'unrealism' and 'sentimentality' of many previous writers who had attributed the poverty of the people and the economy simply to the avarice and inhumanity of the landlord class. Adam's work has undoubtedly influenced most of the works published in the inter-war years nothwithstanding the somewhat polemical and combative tone which pervades her writing. Her papers were challenging and unambiguous and it is surprising that they have never been squarely confronted by the opposing school. Indeed her views have been revived in the 1980s by the Canadian scholar J. M. Bumsted.[1]

Adam's work concentrated on emigration from the Highlands, its relationship to conditions in the region and the impact of landlord policies. Her quartet of articles began with an analysis of the Highland emigration of 1770 in which she argued against the suggestion that poverty and distress were the propellant forces behind the exodus. She examined the composition and social standing of the emigrants, and stressed the comparative affluence of the leaders of the migrant movement, often tacksmen and others of substantial capital. As she put it, there was 'no suggestion that the

Highland emigrants were being driven out by acute poverty'. It was a 'prosperous emigration', pre-dating the advent of large-scale sheepfarming. Adam believed that the main cause of the movement was the elimination of the tacksmen by progressive and often humane Highland proprietors who were modernising their estates. Many subtenants followed their tacksmen purely from 'habits of obedience [which,] engendered for generations, were not easily overcome'. It was Adam's central contention that the eradication of the tacksman class was altogether a beneficial development in the Highlands because 'despite their many virtues and accomplishments, [the tacksmen] had been largely instrumental in holding back the agricultural progress of the Highlands'. In her view, based on a broad array of eighteenth-century opinion, the tacksmen were 'little better than West Indian slave drivers'. They extorted rents and services, and were dictatorial, oppressive, extravagant and capricious. 'The lower classes in the Highlands did not stand to lose by any change which transferred them from the power of the tacksmen to that of the owner,' wrote Miss Adam.

To the unsentimental owner the whole system of which the tacksman was a part appeared a hopeless anachronism. The tacksmen were superfluous middlemen who farmed badly, paid inadequate rents, and by oppressive services prevented the under tenants from attending properly to their farms.

She was prepared to acknowledge the social prestige of the tacksman elite in Highland society, their association with the 'glamour of tradition', and 'their pleasing appearance in bridging the social gulf between owner and crofter'. But, in fact, it was all sham: 'the tacksman's capital was a means of oppression, not of development'. The tacksman, she insisted, had a vested interest in the maintenance of a tyrannical hierarchy and any regret 'expended on the emigration of the seventies is a tribute to romance rather than to economics'. The emigration of 1770, apart from the dismissal of the tacksmen, had nothing to do with landlord pressure.[2]

Having struck a blow for historical realism in her treatment of the 1770s, Miss Adam proceeded in her second instalment to an analysis of the resurgence of Highland migration in the period 1783-1803. It was, as she pointed out, marked by an independent movement of ordinary Highlanders to North America, possibly 12,000 people in all. Treating each possible cause in detail she gave special prominence to the effects of the periodic famines, pointing out that most landlords dealt out relief with signal generosity. She discounted the effects of sheepfarming: to a large extent, she claimed, the introduction of sheep simply filled in the blanks of the Highland economy and the previously underutilised lands — 'the extent of the displacement has been exaggerated, and where emigration occurred it was not inevitable'. She pointed out that, despite the rise of sheepfarming, the number of cattle sold at trysts continued to rise, and that where people were displaced by changes in grazing patterns, many simply resettled in the same parish. With the promise of higher rents landlords switched some of their land to sheep production.

The landlords got higher rents and more security for their payment. The new type of tenant could pay the increased rent and yet enjoy a prosperity unknown to his predecesors. The community gained by the development of natural resources hitherto untouched and by the increase of its food supply at a time when the latter was urgently necessary. It seems unfair to charge the proprietors with abnormal greed when they yielded to these arguments.

Adam contended that the Highland landlord was no more brutal (or self-denying) than other landowners, but he saw 'that the existing system brought neither profit nor prosperity to his tenants'.

Adam emphasised the growing demographic crisis, and condemned what she regarded as the quixotic gestures made by some landlords who refused to introduce sheep-walks and thereby 'deliberately sacrificed their own interests and the economic development of their estates to the immediate needs of their tenants'. She insisted that the causes of the emigration were not connected with sheepfarming, and lay outside the control of the landlords: 'the Highland population was overrunning its resources and, unless positive preventative measures were taken, emigration or migration on a fairly large scale was inevitable'. This, of course, was the classical popualation thesis *vis-à-vis* the clearances. The population, even before 1800, had increased to such a degree that a large proportion was 'but a dead weight on the scanty resources [of the Highlands] ... and a means of lowering the general standard of living of all the inhabitants'. In her explanation of the

108   Academic Beginnings

late-eighteenth-century exodus from the Highlands, the demographic 'facts' completely overshadowed the introduction of sheep
(though this indeed helped to bring the matter to a focus), and left
the landlord in a considerable quandary — for, as Miss Adam put it,
'he possessed neither the capital nor the brains to solve a problem
which, in a rather different form, is still perplexing the statesmen in
the twentieth century'. In a sense she believed that the 'Highland
Problem' of 1920 was not so much a consequence of the events of
1770-1800, as a continuation thereof. The great emigrations of the
late eighteenth century were the fault not of the landlords but of
the fecundity of a peasant population which outbred its means of
subsistence.[3]

Miss Adam's writing was distinctive in that she confronted the
most basic questions about the Highland experience. She extended
and reinforced her thesis in two further papers[4] which asked,
unambiguously, who or what was responsible for the poverty of the
Highlands in the age of the clearances? These were further exercises in demythologising the notion that it could all be set down to
the wickedness of the landlords. The Highlands, she began, had
always been poor and, given the explosive rate of population
growth in the eighteenth century, it was perfectly clear that the old
economy was incapable (both technologically and organisationally)
of accommodating the people: 'Highland unemployment and
Highland distress could not be wiped out merely by re-kindling the
ashes of a dying feudalism. A positive policy was wanted.' But a
persistent obstacle to positive action was the psychology of the
Highlander, particularly a propensity to inaction and voluntary
unemployment. Adam reviewed some of the contemporary proposals directed to the poverty problem which sought to raise the
standards of living without removing the majority of the people.
The ability of the people to pay economic rent was central to most
of the debates. Miss Adam herself was sceptical of the view that
rent increases had depressed living condiions, partly on the
grounds that there was no apparent correlation between high rents
and poverty. But she did concede two major points about the
getting and spending of Highland income:

> The saner critics of Highland estate management, while viewing
> some rents as excessive, did not greatly stress the point, though
> it was observed by them that in the Highlands, the general rise
> in rents was more in the nature of unearned increment than the

corresponding increase in the Lowlands, where the increases were much more spent on solid improvements beneficial to the tenants.

Here indeed were two crucial propositions: that the Highland proprietors appropriated a higher proportion of unearned income than elsewhere, and that they spent relatively less of their rent increases on their tenants and on productive investment. Neither proposition was subjected to quantitative verification by Adam nor indeed her successors. Moreover, throughout her exposition Adam highlighted examples of self-sacrifice, humanitarianism and considerate landlordism in the Highlands. (In fact she alluded to no example of any other sort.) Although she regarded better management and the elimination of services and certain types of leases as helpful, they did not penetrate to the real problem, 'the crux of which lay in a present excess of population'.

She examined also the more radical possibilities for the economy of the Highlands. The idea, for instance, that the old cattle farms might be converted to arable she regarded as impracticable: it was 'doubtful if it would have done much to solve the poverty and unemployment problems of the Highlands'. The economy did benefit from progressive changes in stock breeding and in methods of cultivation, both of which were enchanced by enclosure — but the range of improvement was widely impeded by the deficiency of capital in the Highlands. Few landlords, and fewer of the native tenantry, reserved enough income to finance this type of improvement. Moreover, she pointed out, any improvement in Highland agriculture was likely to require less, rather than more, labour. Still further, Adam argued, the profound psychological need of the people was not work (e.g. day labouring) but land. There existed a traditional peasant mentality: 'The only conceivable solution, then, of the Highland problem which was at the same time open to the landowners and desired by the people, was to plant the unoccupied persons upon the waste lands.' This, of course, was the widespread and much criticised method of letting crofts to individual small tenants, a plan adopted by many landowners, especially in the west. Adam noted the heavy investments in the development and reclamation of waste lands by Lord Kames, George Dempster and Lord Reay, and, on balance, she observed, 'Undoubtedly the crofting system of reclamation helped to solve some of the immediate Highland difficulties but whether, from a broad point of view, it was a success was a matter of much controversy at the time and later.' Adam agreed that there were cases of injustice and oppression in the resettlement of the crofters at the time of the clearances, and also that the crofts were often too small. But, she explained, most of the opposition to crofting was ill-judged. In part the resistance stemmed from 'an impossibly sentimental view of the previous situation of the crofter. At worst he was exchanging one life of poverty and hardship for another.' The smallness of the crofts mainly reflected a general shortage of land; subdivision of holdings was another symptom of land hunger: both were dangerous in an overpopulated society. Poverty was a fact of Highland life — the age-old condition of the people had been greatly compounded by the demographic explosion of the late eighteenth century, and was certainly beyond the power of the Highland landlord to cure. 'No manipulation of their estates by the owners could have provided employment for any length of time for all the people who wished to remain there.' The decline of Highland economic activity in the early nineteenth century — in kelp, fishing, canal construction and manufacturing — further exacerbated the demographic and employment problem. Moreover the location of many Highlanders on small and remote crofts virtually guaranteed a continuation of their abject poverty.

Margaret Adam's work on the Highland problem was a vigorous challenge to most prevailing thinking about the clearances. Her insistence upon the narrow limits constraining landlord action necessarily diminished the indictment of the lairds — they could hardly be blamed for circumstances which were beyond their control. Her criticism of the tacksmen and of the common people also set her work apart from the usual demonology of the clearances. But, most of all, her logical and robust specification of the arguments, and her unrolling of the evidence, helped to clarify some of the basic issues. On the whole, subsequent writers have not matched the clarity of her exposition and there has been little direct rebuttal of her points. Nevertheless Miss Adam's account of emigration undoubtedly understated the impact of famine in 1771-2. She neglected also the evidence of the general poverty of the people in the 1770s, on board the ships and in the Highlands. Her analysis did not fully articulate the mechanism which translated rising land hunger (from population growth, famine and the expansion of distilling and large-scale grazing) into windfall gains for the landlords. Miss Adam's claim that sheepfarming had very slight direct effect on emigration has not been fully explored, although Professor Rosalind Mitchison has more recently confirmed that, after 1790, population did indeed move out of areas which had *not* been turned over to sheep just as much as those that were. Moreover 'many landowners, wishing to restrain their peasantry from emigration, were unsuccessful in keeping them back'. Such evidence is cogent, but Mitchison adds: 'To dismiss the influence of sheep entirely is to ignore contemporary opinion of all the most informed observers ... [and] ... there is no reason to believe their appreciation of the part played by sheep to be in error.'[5] It is still possible, of course, to believe that most contemporary opinion was wrong — James Loch, Sir George Mackenzie and others thought it was — and the main significance of Mitchison's remarks is the direction to which they point in terms of comparative study of cleared and uncleared parts of the Highlands. Such research would address the counterfactual propositions embedded in the writings not only of Margaret Adam but also of her successors and opponents.

II

In 1913 any lecturer in Scottish economic history possessed an extremely narrow basis of scholarship upon which to ground teaching. J. F. Rees of Edinburgh University recollected that when he taught rural economy he simply avoided 'the complicated and forbidding subject of Scottish land tenure' because there was virtually nothing to read on the subject.[6] In the following two decades the wheels of scholarship began to turn, notably because of the efforts of I. F. Grant and Henry Hamilton, both of whom devoted a half a century to the study of Scottish economic history. Dr Grant brought to her work not only a great sympathy for the common culture of the Highlands, but also a command of a wide range of documentary sources. She was one of the first historians to examine the estate economy in detail by means of factors' records. To all this she added an intimate knowledge of the rich tradition of the north and an impressive familiarity with the forms of material life in the Highlands.

Miss Grant's treatment of the clearances emphasised the general circumstances which propelled economic change in the eighteenth century, while it also acknowledged the magnitude of the social consequences for the Highlanders. She pointed to various indisputable facts: that population growth continued despite the clearances, that emigration predated the Forty-five, and that the doubling of wool prices in the decade 1785-95 presented extraordinary opportunities to landowners keen to embark on economic enterprise.

Unfortunately, in order to utilise the hill pastures it was necessary to provide winter shelter in the glens, which were the only places fit for cultivation, and the lairds were tempted to clear out the tenants and turn their land into large sheep walks.

She judged that those who were resettled in fisher-crofter villages founded by their landlords 'lived in great misery'.[7] In her later studies Dr Grant demonstrated the absolute loss that the withdrawal of hill grazings implied for the old economy of the Highlands, and the aggravated land hunger that seemed to be a consequence of the clearances. The strength of her exposition was that it gave almost tangible substance to the notion that the old Highland economic structure was a balanced organism set in a particular ecology, the equilibrium of which was totally upset by the introduction of sheep. Nevertheless she did not argue that the old peasant economy had been immune from demographic or subsistence problems.

In essence, therefore, I. F. Grant brought to the study of change in the Highlands a convincing measure of realism, identifying salient weaknesses in both old and new economic structures, while offering an unusually sensitive account of the social transformations. She remarked in her best-known work that

> More than anything else the clearing for sheep broke the old ties of affection between the people who owned and those who lived on the land, and it has left an enduring feeling of bitterness that is part of the mental heritage of present day people.

Nevertheless, insists Dr Grant, the circumstances of the Highlands were never simple:

> It must be remembered that the clearing was not the sole cause of misery and congestion in the Highlands. Conditions were very serious in the Long Island before the large scale sheep-

farming reached there about the middle of the nineteenth century.[8]

In her close study of the documents of the pre-clearance economy in Aberdeenshire, in her differentiation of conditions within the Highlands, and in her tentative analysis of comparative consequences, Miss Grant achieved a considerable advance in the literature on the clearances. In so doing she began to develop a method which, perhaps, offers the greatest penetration of the chains of cause and effect in the economic history of the Highlands. These types of analysis, perhaps the most promising methods of unpacking the historical character of the Highland problem, have still to be fully exercised.

III

While general interest in the Highland clearances continued undiminished, no comprehensive history was written until the 1960s. The public desire for knowledge about the Highlands was satisfied by imaginative works of fiction which themselves suffered from a dearth of historical scholarship to draw on. Historians dealt with the clearances only by way of short sections of chapters on rural change during the Industrial Revolution. For example, Henry Hamilton, Professor of Political Economy at Aberdeen for many years, wrote two basic works on Scottish economic history during industrialisation. In both works (separated by 31 years) he delineated the broad determinants of change in Scotland, and sought the sources of, and obstacles to, industrialisation and development. His scholarship was based upon a thorough study of secondary sources. He was unsentimental about the condition of the Highlands before the clearances, and about its vulnerability to famine, the abiding problems of adequate winter feeding, and the general precariousness of life in the north. The inhospitable climate and terrain, and remoteness from the mainsprings of improvement, delayed agricultural progress. But, echoing the work of Margaret Adam, Hamilton specified the greatest impediment to progress as the figure of the tacksman: 'Tacksmen drew to themselves a considerable part of the meagre surplus income of their subtenants and, in so far as they spent it on extravagant living, they stultified progress and made no contribution to the advancement of farming.' He argued that it was usually only by the elimination of the tacksmen 'that improvements could be prosecuted'.

Hamilton believed that improvement in Scotland was a progressive process which reached the Highlands only when political conditions were stabilised after 1745, and was particularly consequent upon technical improvements in sheep breeding and winter feeding, and the gradual creation of an infrastructure for development. Once begun, its expansion was almost inevitable: 'The tendency of the improvements in agriculture was to push sheep-farming into the hilly districts and into the Highlands where they almost replaced cattle about 1800.' Hamilton provided a well-focused analysis of the technical imperatives which were involved in sheepfarming — notably in terms of economies of scale, and capital and labour requirements — and of the immense pressure of market incentives facing northern landlords in the last decades of the eighteenth century. Hamilton was also emphatic that the population of the Highlands had increased rapidly without any concomitant or prior improvement in the long-run condition of agriculture. The decline of the clan system, the curbing of smallpox and the introduction of potato cultivation had removed checks on demographic increase, and so generated conditions of congestion and overpopulation, in advance of sheepfarming. Hamilton suggested that the crisis harvests of 1763-4 and 1782-3, especially evident in the unusually large mortality of cattle, together with the large pre-clearance emigrations, were clear signals of demographic pressure on land resources. According to Hamilton, the sheep clearances simply exacerbated the already tragic circumstances of the Highland economy.[9]

Hamilton propounded the view that all economic change, by its nature, is disruptive. The case of the Highlands was an extreme example, and 'it was the impact on the small peasantry that was most serious and aroused bitter resentment in the hearts of the people'. He pointed out that the impact was not uniform and the intensity of the disruption depended on local circumstances, the ratio of arable to pastoral production, and the availability of alternative employment.

That townships in some parishes were absorbed in sheep walks, with consequent eviction of the tenants, is indisputable, but a great deal of the land which came under the control of graziers never contributed anything to the sustenance of the people.

He regarded the reception lots sometimes given to the people removed from the interior lands as mere footholds, providing no more than the minimum basis for a life which was 'indescribably hard'. He contended that the general process of migration from the land was no different from that of, for instance, the south of Scotland. Yet the Highland version was special, for 'this cruel process' came with thundering rapidity, and 'it is an incontrovertible fact that great hardship resulted from the clearing of the straths, and in some cases sheer cruelty when native resistance was crushed by rough handling and subsequent legal processes'.

Hamilton offered a judgement of a general character when he concluded that

> Eviction was a personal and human tragedy for the individuals concerned, but the problems of overcrowding and depopulation were not new. They were not the consequence of sheepfarming, but were simply intensified by it. Depopulation was a natural consequence of an expanding population within a rigid agrarian economy which offered no hope of a rise in the standard of living.[10]

This perspective was probably the most broadly held view in academic work on the Highlands until the mid-twentieth century, although it contained a number of controversial asumptions about the role of population growth, and the level of welfare before the clearances. Nevertheless Hamilton's view of the inexorability of economic forces pressing on the region was a dominant theme in the literature. It was echoed most strongly in Margaret Leigh's examination of crofting, written in 1928. She protested against the sentimentalisation of the problems of agrarian change in a capitalist system, declaring that

> well meaning reformers often fail to realise that the impersonal working of economic laws rather than human cupidity is responsible for the change, and that a mere redistribution of land will bring no remedy if the small holding system is in itself unprofitable.[11]

IV

Most people who visited the Highlands quickly developed an

opinion on the past and future of the region. No exception was George Orwell who, in a vain effort to recover his health, lived on the island of Jura from 1946 to 1948, during which time he wrote *Nineteen Eighty-four.* In a letter from this period he declared that

> The crofters ... would be quite comfortable if they could get a bit of help ... and could get the landlords off their backs and get rid of the deer ... everything is sacrificed to the brutes ... I suppose sooner or later these islands will be taken in hand.[12]

Orwell's supposition has not yet been fulfilled and the debate on the crofting problem continues to produce vigorous prose about the clearances, much of it appearing in the recurrent governmental reports on the state of the Highland economy. Some of the most important recent contributions to the historiography of the Highlands have come from geographers, sociologists and economists. Two outstanding examples are Adam Collier and Frank Fraser Darling, who wrote in the 1940s, neither a historian, but both passionately committed to the employment of systematic scholarship for the improvement of standards of life in the Highlands. Each saw the Highland problem as a historical as well as an economic problem.

Although Collier wrote his book, *The Crofting Problem*, in 1945, it was not published until 1953, several years after his premature death. An economist whose aim had been to unravel some of the basic issues connected with the optimisation of regional policy for the Highlands, he brought to his task a much more analytical approach than had hitherto been applied to the Highlands. As one reviewer noted of Collier's work: 'here, perhaps for the first time, an economist with wise sympathies and with the full measuring and analytical apparatus of his profession enters a field that has been too much in the hands of the propagandist and sentimental historian'.[13] Against a tradition of dogma, assertion and polemic, Collier offered a restrained and reasoned approach. 'As far as possible', he wrote in his Introduction, 'its approach is quantitative and relies on statistical measurement rather than on *a priori* generalisation.' He was critical of previous writing on the Highland question because it was essentially emotional and disputatious; he regretted that it had been neither quantitative nor comprehensive in scope, and had failed to pose the right questions. Collier therefore set a high priority on establishing the basic dimensions of economic life in the Highlands, though he acknowledged that precision was not always possible on even such elements as the number of crofters, their sources of income and standards of living, the resources of the region, and the economic history of the Highlands. His difficulties in this respect were far greater for the history of the economy than for contemporary data.

Although Collier applied systematic economic analysis to the Highland problem, he placed great emphasis upon the psychological component in the determination of economic behaviour, and made much of the unusual social values of Highland life.[14] He contended that the condition of the Highlands in 1945 remained exceedingly depressed — despite very substantial change since the Napier Commission. It was true that conditions of life had improved enormously, that education was widespread, that communications were far better, and that housing conditions were much improved. Yet the population had diminished by 40 per cent, congestion on the crofting land was a persistent problem, the fishing industry had contracted, and the local industrial structure had further declined. 'Probably worst of all', he claimed, 'the cultural integrity of the people has been invaded and their faith in the soundness of their way of life impaired.' In his examination of the evidence Collier was able to demonstrate that standards of life — for instance in diet and material well-being — were not significantly lower than national averages. But the society was not holding together: the forces of economic change (and especially external competition) had destroyed the traditional bases of the crofter's economic activity and this had caused what Collier identified as the common apathy of the Highlander:

> Living and working in new conditions uncongenial to his temperament, with the foundations of his economy undermined, competing with producers able to work on a larger scale, financially stronger, more efficient, and nearer the centres of consumption, it is little wonder that he exhibits signs of distress and his economy evidence of disintegration. Neither personal effort nor government intervention seems likely to raise him from his slough of despond.[15]

There were hints in Collier's work of a line of analysis which connected the difficulties of the Highlands with the peculiar regional consequences which flowed from the general industrialisation of the British economy. That is, Collier, notably in his historical sections, ventured a number of propositions which placed the Highland problem in a national context — as 'a dependent, underdeveloped economy', and a regional component of the wider process of British economic development.[16] One effect of the relationship was cultural disintegration, wrought by the impact upon the Highlands of a different way of life, and of thinking which he associated with the Industrial Revolution, and which was irresistible because of 'the disparity in power and pervasiveness of the two cultures'. The other effect was economic and signified the failure of the Industrial Revolution to take root in the north and north-west of Britain. Collier suggested that 'The form taken by the Industrial Revolution in its impact on the Highlands was the notorious Clearances,'[17] an altogether negative consequence which reduced economic activity in the region. Unfortunately Collier did not develop this line of reasoning any further, but it re-emerged in greater elaboration in the 1970s in the work of Michael Hechter and the present author.

Collier's treatment of the clearances as such was not extensive, but it contained several unusual points. One strength of his analysis was its emphasis on the considerable differences between the various parts of the Highlands. He observed that in some districts — such as Caithness, Orkney and Zetland — there had been only slight incidence of clearance; they, nevertheless, were in a similar economic plight to those zones which had experienced the full impact of clearance in the nineteenth century. Collier believed that in the pre-clearance period the Highlands had been essentially a tribal society in which the resources had been employed collectively. He accepted the common notion that the Jacobite Rebellion marked the great discontinuity in Highland development, after which individual land ownership and commercial relationships were established. He agreed that the clearance for sheep was the means towards the most economic use of the land, but he argued that the process was partly propelled by 'a powerful speculative influence which exaggerated and accelerated the dislocating effects of the new pastoralism'. The social disaster caused by the clearances was that the sheepfarmers took the land and yet had no use for the displaced labour of the Highlanders. Collier's analysis of the population statistics showed the differential growth of population in the congested coastal parishes in the west.[18] Indeed he conceded that the most basic cause of poverty was the general growth of population, a factor which he separated analytically from the clearances. His consideration of the historical consequence was summarised in these words:

> In passing judgement on the events of this time, the coarser temper of the age must be borne in mind; but certainly the correct note is struck in this quotation from the *Report* of the Departmental Committee on Deer Forests (1919): 'When their (i.e. the landlords') action is viewed now in the cold light of history, it is clear that the power of wholesale eviction by private persons was one which ought never to have been permitted and which was rendered doubly odious ... by contrast with the patriarchal relations which existed between chief and clansmen down to the rising of the '45.' Though their effect must not be underestimated, the Clearances are perhaps more remarkable for their injustice and the individual hardships they inflicted, and as an example of the remarkable licence enjoyed in a remote part of the Kingdom in the nineteenth century, than for their effect on the economy of the Highlands, though the bitterness of feeling which they provoked is still a factor of importance today.[19]

Collier's work was important because its rigorous analysis offered the promise of a more scientific and detached exploration of the problems of the region.

V

In some respects Adam Collier's work was quickly overtaken by a massive compilation of data and interpretative analysis, edited by the naturalist/ecologist Frank Fraser Darling: Darling's *West Highland Survey*, published only a year after Collier's book became available, had begun in 1944 as an ambitious multi-disciplinary study of 1,040 crofting parishes, a problem-oriented investigation of considerable sophistication. It was guided by a particular conception of the ecology of the Highlands which the editor developed particularly during a Crusoe-like sojourn in remote Hebridean islands for three years before the Second World War.[20] The *Survey* was, in terms of method, a demonstration of the analytical penetration that might be achieved by a combination of both social and physical sciences, based on a mass of statistical data. This attempt to diagnose the crofting problem and prescribe solutions was undertaken under the auspices of the Development Commission. The Commission established the project specifically 'to examine the Highland problem in the spirit of scientific enquiry'.

Fraser Darling insisted on seeing the Highland problem in its 'ecological totality' of the long-run interaction of human cultures and the environment, specifically in terms of the 'biological economics' of the Highlands.[21] From a welter of statistics, mainly those of population ratios and 'terrain values', Fraser Darling concluded that 'the Highlands and Islands are largely a devastated terrain, and that any policy which ignores this fact cannot hope to achieve rehabilitation'. The devastation, he believed, resulted from the destruction over time of an equilibrium in man's relation to the fundamental resources of the region. The entire exposition was drawn in the form of a metaphor about the balance of population — both human and animal — with the environment. After about 1700 this balance in nature had been lost, and the long process of decline produced the disastrous consequences which faced the crofters in the twentieth century. Fraser Darling's long-run perspective identified the clearances as one of the expressions of that process of historical devastation. In effect the clearances had been a major part of the physical deterioration of the Highlands, entirely disruptive of the ecological equilibrium. He therefore added a powerful scientific argument to the indictment of the clearances.

Fraser Darling invested his interpretation of the Highland problem with a strong regional dimension, accentuating the separateness of its circumstances. He believed that the contrast between the cultures of the Highlands and the rest of Britain had been extreme. Moreover, between the two there had been no protective buffer: the two unequal parts could not fairly coexist. 'Had Britain been physically three parts Highland', ventured the author, 'the problem would not have arisen, because the nation would have developed with this particular environment as a major part of its being instead of as a sore little finger.'[22] It was a view implicitly drawing an unfavourable comparison with Scandinavian parallels. In effect it located the origins of the Highland problem in ecological and historical causes.

The argument of the *West Highland Survey* hinged upon the relationship of population to the land, and the centrality of the productive capacity of the land and the sea to the welfare of the region. Fraser Darling simply dismissed the idea of secondary industry as totally irrrelevant to the Highlands. In the long historical perspective, he contended that medical improvements and the introduction of the potato in the eighteenth century had allowed the human population to expand to its Malthusian ceiling and, eventually, this radical alteration was connected with declining living standards and the imminence of famine.[23] This argument plainly implied a better, more prosperous time, presumably before about 1750, before the equilibrium had been broken. As important as the demographic factor was the fate of the land itself — its basic productiveness (and indeed that of the sea) had been undermined over many centuries by the elimination of the forests of the Highlands — a process which 'destroyed the continuum, the circulatory system, and the conserving value of the vegetation'. This debilitating process was vastly accelerated, first by the development of cattle production and then, more rapidly still, by the invasion of the sheep. 'The sheep-cattle ratio which had formerly been around unity now became very wide and set in train profound changes in the herbage complex.' The ecological devastation worked by way of overgrazing, burning, erosion, rabbits and other enemies of the balanced environment.[24] Fraser Darling observed the resurgence of sheep numbers in the twentieth century, spurred on by government subsidies which, he contended, had exacerbated the problem. He thought that cattle production, in the pre-clearance economy, had been a much better use of the Highlands: sheep were the greatest enemy of environmental regeneration and agricultural progress. He was not uncritical of crofting agriculture, though he spoke warmly of the classlessness and communalism of its society. He observed that the continuance of collective grazing was a durable cause of inefficiency, and thus the system favoured the least progressive members of the community. In this respect Fraser Darling echoed the improvement writers of 150 years earlier, and he indeed entertained little hope for the future of peasant proprietorship in the Highlands. His main concern, it seems, was not so much the economics of the Highlands as its ecology, more fundamental and more important for the future productivity of the region.

It is clear that Fraser Darling's diagnosis of the Highland problem was grounded on a perception of its historical roots. As he saw it, prior to the great and disastrous changes of the eighteenth century, the clan system had held its own. Resting on real or imaginary consanguinity, it was not to be confused with raw feudalism:

> The land upon which the clan lived was not the *property* of the chief; it belonged to the tribe and the chief was maintained by its members and given implicit obedience as the defender of the territory of the people and head of the race. Chieftainship of a clan was an hereditary personal dignity resting on a freely given allegiance of a family which considered itself one with the chief.

In this interpretation the old system had been essentially egalitarian, and in a fundamental balance with its environment — in 'a balanced reciprocal situation' which was, in essence, a socio-economic equivalent of a natural ecology: 'A Highlander could not help but feel independent and proud because he was so completely integrated with his society and place, sheltered yet defending, giving loyalty and receiving it, without question.'[25] It was all in splendid equilibrium: here was the Highland romanticism in modern dress.

This equilibrium was disturbed by the dismantling of the old clan system and the intrusion of external capital and new attitudes. The cattle economy, which had been much stimulated by the economic effects of the Union, had not been a definitive change because the cattle were 'reasonably compatible' with the forests. More corrosive, in the early stages of the new era, were the effects of large-scale sales of timber which typified the transformation of the patriarchal *mores* of the social leaders — towards ordinary landlordism, and the unashamed and unrestricted exploitation of Highland resources. The region entered 'this extractive period', much assisted by the southern flockmasters, who grasped the stored fertility of the hillsides from the centuries of pine and birch forests. The consequence was the clearances. As Fraser Darling put it:

> The breaks in the earlier ecological integration of laird and small tenant, chief and clansman, had been many and grievous, and what would have been unthinkable a hundred years earlier now seemed expedient and even right, namely, the eviction of the folk from the glens to inhospitable places on the coast, where, often enough, land had to be made anew.

He pointed out that there were cases of 'humane clearances', pursued in the interest of humanity. But more characteristic were others which 'were of the order of brutality expected of a Norse raid a thousand years earlier'. He instanced the cases of Sutherland and Knoydart as particularly atrocious examples, documented by 'well-attested eye-witness accounts'. They were made worse by the fact (which called to his mind Glencoe) that 'some of the surveyors for the flockmasters and proprietors had received food and shelter from the people of the glens'.

The clearances had scarred the collective mind, and exacerbated the congestion of the crofting community. But the overcrowding, Fraser Darling pointed out, was even more the product of 'the remarkable fertility and fecundity' of the people who became hostage to the potato, and who increased in numbers 'beyond the power of the land to feed' them. He observed that some of the lairds, throughout the changes, had remained entirely solicitous of the welfare of their people, but had been helpless in the face of the demographic burden on the Highland economy. He noted how Macleod of Macleod and Macdonald of Skye had virtually bankrupted themselves in their efforts to meliorate destitution during the great famine of the 1840s.[26]

The Highland problem was, at bottom, an ecological problem, a vicious circle of congestion and underemployment: there was simply insufficient arable land in the Highlands on which crofting could ever succeed at prevailing levels of population and agricultural expertise. The crofters were

the nearest approach to a peasantry which Britain can show: it is composed of a strictly indigenous bilingual people who were cut off from the industrial and social advances of the rest of the country until some time after the failure of the Rebellion of 1745.[27]

After the clearances the crofters formed 'a relatively primitive population on the fringe of a highly industrialised country. In the course of time the crofters had lost their simple self-sufficiency and had become dependent on manufactured goods — processed food, cheap dressing clothes, bijou furniture, cattle feed' — for which they exported 'the rawest of raw materials'.[28] He believed that the way forward for the crofters lay in the development of gardening and a more intensive husbandry of their limited arable grounds, the improvement of their common grazing and better techniques for the ensilage of winter fodder, together with the provision of part-time work in afforestation and road and harbour works. But he had little optimism for a vigorous development of the crofting economy.

In general terms, Fraser Darling identified a new dimension in the study of the Highlands, past and present. His evaluation of the physical and social ecologies introduced a greater degree of precision and indeed realism to the discussion of the limits of productive activity in the region. His strictures on sheepfarming provided further ammunition for the critics of landlordism. His concentration on the demographic and environmental circumstances also indicated the narrow constraints on social and economic activity in the Highlands. Few disagreed with his analysis of the devastation of the Highland environment, but there was dispute both about his economics and his social analysis. One dissentient reviewer commented:

> It is perpetuating a popular misconception to say that 'the land on which the clan lived was not the property of the chief: it belonged to the tribe'. The clan system as we know it seems to date from the breakdown of the Lordship of the Isles at the end of the fifteenth century; yet from that time at least precepts of sasine [Scots Law, the act of giving possession of feudal property] exist issued in favour of the heirs of chiefs, who were borrowing money on the security of their estates from early in the seventeenth century.[29]

The work of both Fraser Darling and Collier demonstrated the problems of striking a plausible balance between historical scholarship and theoretical analysis. They introduced methods of measurement and explicit theorising, and attempted to specify relationships between social and economic variables, partly in response to the needs of government planning in the north of Scotland, partly reflecting the growing confidence of the social sciences. Yet the historical scholarship which informed many of the key assumptions of this type of work remained shallow and unsatisfactory. The assumptions were mainly fed by the continuing literary tradition of romantic historical novels and popular writing for which the British and expatriate public appetite appeared insatiable.

Notes

1. J. M. Bumsted, *The People's Clearance: Highland Emigration to British North America 1770-1815* (Edinburgh, 1982)
2. Margaret I. Adam, 'The Highland Emigration of 1770', *Scottish Historical Review*, vol. 16 (1919), pp. 280-93.
3. Margaret I. Adam, 'The Causes of the Highland Emigrations of 1783-1803', *Scottish Historical Review*, vol. 17 (1920), pp. 73-89.
4. Margaret I. Adam, 'The Eighteenth Century Highland Landlords and the Poverty Problem', *Scottish Historical Review*, vol. 19 (1922), pp. 1-20, 161-79.
5. Mitchison, *Agricultural Sir John*, p. 108.
6. Introduction to I. F. Grant, *The Economic History of Scotland* (London, 1934).
7. Ibid., pp. 212-13. Miss Grant's most detailed analysis of eighteenth-century conditions was *Everyday Life on an Old Highland Farm, 1769-1782* (London, 1924).
8. I. F. Grant, *Highland Folk Ways* (London, 1961), pp. 50-60.
9. Henry Hamilton, *The Industrial Revolution in Scotland* (London, 1932), p. 27.
10. Ibid., pp. 27, 32, 66-75.
11. Margaret M. Leigh, 'The Crofting Problem 1790-1883', *Scottish Journal of Agriculture*, vol. 11-12 (1928-9).
12. George Orwell, quoted in John Mercer, *Hebridean Islands, Colonsay, Gigha, Jura* (London, 1974), p. 5.
13. Malcolm Gray, review in *Economic History Review*, vol. 7 (1954-5), p. 119.
14. See the mildly sceptical comments of Collier's editor, A. K. Cairncross in his Foreword to Adam Collier, *The Crofting Problem* (Cambridge, 1953).
15. Ibid., p. 9.
16. See a review of Collier by P. Deane, *Economic Journal*, vol. 64 (1954), p. 595.
17. Collier, *Crofting Problem*, pp. 8-9.
18. Ibid., pp. 38-45.
19. Ibid., pp. 45-6.
20. See Frank Fraser Darling, *Island Years* (London, 1940).
21. Fraser Darling, *West Highland Survey*, p. vii.
22. Ibid., p. viii.
23. Ibid., p. 408.
24. Ibid. This line of argument does not appear to command universal acceptance; cf. Grant, *Everyday Life on an Old Highland Farm*, p. 33: 'Before the introduction of sheepfarming in modern lines, the moorland in many parts of Scotland was probably far more barren, and with far less grass upon it, than at present.'
25. *West Highland Survey*, p. 408.
26. Ibid., pp. 1-13.
27. F. Fraser Darling, *The Story of Scotland* (London, 1945), pp. 35-6.
28. Ibid., pp. 37-8.
29. Anonymous review of *West Highland Survey* in *Times Literary Supplement*, 6 May 1955.

5
ECONOMIC HISTORIANS AND DRAMATISTS

Some of the circumstances which faced the Highland people and plagued their landlords during the age of the clearances had altered significantly by the twentieth century, most notably by the reduction of population levels; but much of the Highland problem remains essentially unchanged — the shortage of arable land, the deficiency of internally generated capital, the lack of self-sustaining secondary industry, underemployment, resource deficiencies and cultural decline. It is not fanciful to say that modern governmental instrumentalities, from the Crofter Commissions to the present Highlands and Islands Development Board, have been forced to grapple with economic problems substantially similar (apart from the reversal in population trends) to those of the nineteenth-century controllers of Highland property. Moreover there has been an almost uniform tendency to attribute many present problems to the malpractices of past landlords. The legacy of the Highland clearances continues to influence the approach of contemporary policy-makers: they have been influenced by historical assumptions as much as historians have been affected by the impact of economic theory which shapes the current policies for the Highlands.

The Highlands has been, on occasion, a laboratory for the development of regional planning in Britain. The Napier Commission Report in 1884 paved the way for the identification by government of 'the regional problem' in a general form. The intractability of the difficulties faced by the Highlands in the twentieth century led to a series of inquiries and eventually to government assumption of authority for the destiny of the region. Since the Second World War regional planning in Britain has emerged as a vital policy issue in the great debate on economic growth as a national objective — especially in the 1950s and 1960s. National attention has focused on the stubborness of the

Highland economy; the entry of Britain into the European Economic Community has widened the perspective by demonstrating the similarity to other European undeveloped regions on the periphery of a dynamic and affluent continent. Moreover the discovery of North Sea oil has created a further, though not unprecedented, problem: can the Highlands adapt to such powerful external pressure without further deterioration of its social and ecological structure? The establishment of the Highlands and Islands Development Board in 1965 was a recognition that the problems of the region have not solved themselves. The difficulties that have attended its operations indicate that the problem remains, notwithstanding the progressive intentions and capital backing of the government body.

The modern historiography of the clearances has begun to reflect the theoretical debates on growth and regionality engendered by present-day policy needs. The involvement of sociologists in the development programmes has influenced the content of the historical debate; but the historians' own focus has also shifted. There has been a great amount of popular writing which seeks to dramatise the Highland experience. Furthermore there has been a growing scholarly effort to search the primary archival foundations of Highland history and to map the quantitative boundaries of the Highland problem. Basic historical questions are being addressed, often enlightened by the use of theoretical concepts from other social sciences, and assisted by the increasing availablity of archives from the muniments of descendants of the clearing landlords. A less possessive and secretive attitude has developed towards private documents; additionally, many Highland proprietors, particularly if in financial decline, have come to realise that they have inadequate facilities for the efficient preservation of the documents of Highland history, and have deposited vital estate papers in public repositories.

I

The most penetrating contribution to the understanding of the transformation of the Highland economy in modern times has come from the economic historian, Malcolm Gray. In his book *The Highland Economy, 1750-1850*,[1] and in a series of associated papers, he raised the level of the entire debate; his work remains the most solid basis for discussion. Yet in many respects Gray's research has not been fully assimilated into the received wisdom about the Highlands. This arises partly because his dispassionate approach was strongly against the emotional grain of much writing on the subject, and partly because his work is more technical than most. He wrote as an economic historian when the influence of Sir John Clapham and T. S. Ashton was still strong; a high premium was set on rigorous economic analysis and measurement as applied to historical phenomena. Economic historians were paying increasing attention to the question of economic growth, and exploring the mystery of the Industrial Revolution with much more sophistication than before. Gray's *Highland Economy*, part of the new literature on the Industrial Revolution, placed the Highlands squarely within that wider experience. to this task he brought a broader knowledge of the archival sources than had been employed previously, and he developed also a series of basic statistical indices.

It was characteristic of Gray's work that it contained no description of any acts of clearance, little account of alleged atrocities, little attention to personal experience and motivation, no reference to riots, and no explicit defence or denunciation of landlords. His writing was in stark contrast to most other work on the clearances; some critics regarded his approach as clinical and bloodless. It was misjudged criticism, for Gray's purpose was fundamental to all the great questions about the Highlands: he sought, by careful analysis, to evaluate the strength of the economic forces at work in the Highlands in the century after Culloden. He brought into consideration the land-labour ratios, sheep numbers, population growth rates, production functions, inter-regional trade balances, the effect of weather, the mentalities of landlords and tacksmen, the force of tradition and, most of all, the pressures created by market circumstances. His book also contains some excellent pioneer work on the analysis of social class in the Highlands. By disaggregating the data on the regional economy, Gray was able to expose the markedly different impact of economic and demographic change on the various strata within the Highlands. This approach, which extended the methods of Fraser Darling, enabled Gray to expose some of the fundamental causes of the Highland problem, constituted a substantial advance in methodology, and promised further progress when applied in detail. It was an austere and precise analysis, and indispensable for any understanding of the Highlands in the age of the clearances;

not surprisingly it proved less than palatable to a public used to a tradition of overheated prose.

Gray examined in sequence the several phases by which the structure of the Highlands was transformed. He documented the limitations and inequalities of the pre-clearance system, pointing to the precarious equilibrium of life, and the stark dependence of the population on the variable caprice of their landlords, some of them prone to dissipating the meagre surplus which they extracted from the peasantry. The old system of agriculture was inefficient and 'there was constant conflict between the demands of productive efficiency and the old obligations of class to class'. Classic peasant land hunger endured in a social system in which 'little economic gain emerged ... from [the] strange mixture of neglect and sentimentality'. Even before the clearances, the Highlands were overburdened with a population living on minute holdings. The demographic expansion from 1750 to 1850 — which Gray seems to interpret as a quasi-autonomous force unresponsive to conditions within the region — 'thrust the whole economy on the Malthusian margins ... Every additional family in such a region necessarily added to the pressure on the land, and land pressure was the basic problem.' After 1815, he says, landlords succumbed to theories of overpopulation, and pursued policies of clearance. In its initial stage the demographic upsurge coincided with the expansion of the economy through kelp, fishing and sheep — the last of which created further pressure on arable and pasture resources. Gray also considered the role of the clearances among the causes of depopulation and destitution in the mid-nineteenth century. He argued that the proximity of the Lowlands was a more potent cause of migration than were the disruptive consequences of internal agrarian change. This conclusion derived from a study of the differential patterns of migration *within* the Highlands during the period of the clearances. In addition, he observed that the quantity of arable land declined very little during the clearances; the great empty tracts of the Highlands 'had always lain empty — the Highland population had always lived on the periphery of the main land mass, where the sheep farms were now spreading'. He further argued that some of the increment to rural income between 1790 to 1810 came from new men with new economic activity, and that the region benefited from the elimination of 'the parasitic middle ranks within the old system of subserviency'.

Gray followed the transformation into the period of 'growing strain, 1815-50' when the previous elements of growth, especially the labour-intensive industries of kelp and fishing, fell into catastrophic decline while population continued its upward trend. Great pressure was now placed on the shrunken economic base of the region, resulting in bankruptcy for many landlords, especially in the west. There was a decisive narrowing of the occupational base of the economy and a withering away of the traditional domestic handicrafts of the Highlands. As Gray said, 'The decline of industry had destroyed the possibility of employing any substantial body of landless labour just as it created the will to clear the land.'[2] The possibility of 'a populous and economically variegated' structure (which had been the landlord ideal of the last decades of the eighteenth century) gave way to the notion that emigration was the only available response to the new situation — 'cruel facts had killed the idea' of economic development. Landlords, where they survived, were saddled with difficulties vastly beyond their means. The peasant community, locked into crofting and excluded from the main commercial opportunities of the early Victorian economy, was trapped at a low level of income, and vulnerable to famine.

But all this masked important differences within the Highlands. Gray demonstrated a strong contrast between, on the one side, the south and east, and, on the other, the north and west. The arable production of the former was more efficient, rationalised and technically superior, and its ratios of population to arable land rendered it less prone to Malthusian crises of famine, Moreover, after 1815, the adverse forces at work there were less oppressive than in the north and west. As Gray put it:

> While the new economic power was removing the dangers of famine, both in towns and on the land, from the greater part of Britain and from the nearer Highlands, the more remote regions — along with Ireland — were approaching the great disasters of the potato famine.

In the north and west, tradition was more tenacious — but the economic cost of this tenacity was neglect of agricultural technique which left the periphery of the region in its 'age-old insecurity before the hazards of the seasons'. Population rose rapidly; former communal grazing land was engrossed by sheepfarmers, holdings were minute and the dependence on the potato almost total. The regional distinctions were epitomised by the differential incidence of famine in the 1840s: 'the varying extent of the catastrophe in each district', claimed Gray, 'gives us an index both of agrarian background and of underlying economic strength'.[3] The further north and west, the worse the disaster.

In his emphasis on the intra-regional differences, strongly documented with quantitative and literary evidence, Gray exposed the crucial circumstances which necessarily over-rode landlord action, either individually or collectively. Indeed this careful analysis reinforced his view that the problems of overpopulation and underemployment were not the consequences of landlord policy as such. The failure of the Highland economy in the north and west was structural; the peasantry had expanded its numbers almost entirely within the shell of the old system, and its continued vulnerability to harvest shortfall reflected the persistence of the pre-industrial structures of life. The nineteenth-century agrarian problem was in essence a legacy of previous conditions upon which had been superimposed the demographic burden. There had been no compensating industrial diversification which might have accommodated a growing population. As Gray pointed out, little had changed in the economy since the previous century:

> By the middle of the following century a much larger population was deployed over a somewhat wider arable acreage, was equipped with holdings no smaller than had been the common standard of former days, but still contained only a tiny minority of holdings any larger than the subsistence minimum.[4]

Malcolm Gray's treatment of the general problem of the Highlands recalls the closing words of T. S. Ashton's classic work on *The Industrial Revolution*:

> There are today on the plains of India and China men and women, plague-ridden and hungry, living lives little better, to outward appearance, than those of the cattle that toil with them by day and share their places of sleep at night. Such Asiatic standards, and such mechanised horrors, are the lot of those who increase their number without passing through an industrial revolution.[5]

Like most of Ireland, part of the Highlands had participated hardly at all in the benefits of industrialisation.

Gray tried to bring to light the realities of the Highland economy without recourse to sentimentality, apologetics or denunciation. Yet his book does not lack intellectual passion and all his analysis is imbued with a sombre sense of the Highland tragedy as well as an urgency to discover its roots. There is little retrospective comfort offered to Highland landlords in Gray's work, but his exposition of the objective conditions of the Highland economy makes any evaluation of landlord policies more problematic. His conclusion is carefully measured. He notes the tendency of writers to stress 'the special malignity of the landlords' and the idyllic and stable character of the pre-clearance Highlands. He agrees that there is some truth in the criticisms of landlords — their shortsightedness, their avarice, their precipitate policies. But, he contends,

> the impersonal forces — of prices and available technique — were more potent than the conscious will to destroy or preserve: and ... policies, opinion, and desires among the priviledged were themselves caused by an all-pervading climate of opinion, which saw nothing but good in change and rational unpicking of custom. The circumstances of change may have been over-violent; but the fact of change itself represented not the wayward greed of a small group of anti-social expatriates, but the total impact of the powerful individualism and economic rationalism of industrial civilisation on the weaker, semi-communal traditionalism of the recalcitrant fringe.[6]

Expressed in this way Gray's analysis does not depreciate the human tragedy of the Highland experience. Instead he had extended the meaning of its history.

Gray's work was pioneering because it led the way into many of the key propositions about the causes and consequences of the clearances. He asked about levels of regional income and their determinants, about the differential response to altered conditions, about the importance of distance from the centres of the new industrial economy, about the relative strengths of endogenous and exogenous forces for change, and about the experience of cleared and uncleared areas within the Highlands. Generally, it has to be said that, despite some work on income-generating effects of investment, on the rate of return on landlord outlays, and on some regional patterns, most later writers have not sustained Gray's analytical approach. His quantitative emphasis has been lost. Indeed his is perhaps the least read of the major modern works on the Highlands. His method has been regarded as too arid, too analytic, and too narrowly economic in style. The sociologist Donald Macrae claimed that Gray 'is not passionate' and that he had missed the essentially 'social' characteristics of Highland existence. Macrae contended that the most significant phenomenon of Highland history was the passivity of the people — they had not shot their oppressive landlords, they had submitted to 'expropriation, rent-racking and forced emigration'; and they had continued to believe in the traditional integrity of their society long after it had been sold out by the landlords. Macrae wrote of Gray's book:

> If moral factors explain the acquiescence of the highland peasantry in what was often a terrible and always an unpleasant fate, then the moral factors also — a moral failure — must be involved in the explanation of the behaviour of the landlord. It is very difficult not to be passionate when moral issues cannot be avoided. I am sure that it is a virtue in Mr. Gray not to be even a little moved.[7]

Macrae's response was tangential to the primary function of Gray's book, which was to establish the economic limits of Highland life. It was ill-judged to criticise Gray for not writing a sociology of the clearances, which had hardly been started even twenty years later. On the other hand, when Macrae likened the effect of change on the Highlands to the problems encountered in the 'so-called underdeveloped countries of the world', he offered a positive line of comparison which has been better pursued in recent years. His insistence on social analysis, while valuable, cannot diminish the priority of economic structure in understanding the Highland problem.

Reviewing the state of scholarship almost two decades after the publication of *The Highland Economy*, which was undoubtedly the most rigorous analysis available, Gray made a plea for greater intellectual modesty in the discussion of the Highland clearances. He remarked that his own work had beeen 'a holding operation ... in which somewhat crude generalisation hid the lack of detailed information underneath'. Secondly, he pointed out that despite the accretion of new scholarship in the intervening years, the central question of the age had remained unanswered. That is to say, historians had been unable, accurately and definitively, to evaluate the essential causes of Highland poverty. They had been able to identify influences such as 'the imbalance of economic proportions', planning failures, social dislocation, economic depression and resource deficiencies; but they had not been able to rank order such influences, still less settle the issue. Gray's was a salutary warning against the prevailing winds of dogmatism.[8]

II

The mainstream of Scottish historical writing after 1950 reflected an increasing awareness of the complexity of the Highland problem, though the dependence on a narrow base of research was changed slowly. For instance, George Pryde's textbook *Scotland from 1603* reflected Gray's influence and also Pryde's own emphases. He stressed the element of choice exercised by the Highlanders — in many ways they consciously clung to traditional ways and rejected southern values: 'the natives of the northern regions resisted or ignored the alien improvements that were generally welcomed in the south'. This resistance to integration with the rest of the country was the ultimate cause of the painful divergence in levels of welfare in the nineteenth century. He noted that the clearances produced contrasting consequences in different parts of the Highlands; in some parts overpopulation and congestion were exacerbated by clearance. While he emphasised the cupidity and savagery of some landlords, Pryde also acknowledged the widespread bankruptcy in their ranks: 'most of the Highland proprietors, between 1820 and 1846, had to sell their ancestral estates in whole or in part'. These financial difficulties caused positive policies for estate development to be reversed in favour of encouraging emigration which gave immediate relief from the population problem. Even the most humanitarian landlords eventually had to face the inevitability of emigration:

> The drastic case of eviction, to make way for sheepwalks, was still being applied here and there after 1850, but the more humane landlords tried to salvage the local economy by works of drainage and land reclamation, and by education in improved

methods of farming. The most prominent reformers also along such lines at mid-century were the Duke of Argyll in Tiree and James Matheson in Lewis, but it is significant that each of them was impelled in the end to persuade his tenants to emigrate, and so to relieve the intolerable congestion of these islands.[9]

Pryde argued plausibly that the unhappy record of humanitarian enterprise in the Highlands provided a measure of the fundamental problems facing the economy; it established a perspective also in which to place the consequences of the clearances.

Much controversy about the history of the Highland clearances arises from the repeated confusion of questions and criteria, and from a conflict of opposing values. There have been few attempts to unpack the prevailing propositions into logical order.[10] For instance, a discourse on the clearances may begin with premisses about the imperatives determining the growth of the national economy during the age of Industrial Revolution. Industrialisation, so the argument goes, in the long run undoubtedly improved the material life of the great majority of the British people. To this process the conversion of the Highlands to wool and sheep production made a significant contribution. Yet this line of argument, by its nature, necessarily tends to understate the social costs incurred locally in the pursuit of such a national goal. Moreover, it contains implicit assumptions about economic imperatives and the necessity of short-term sacrifices required for the greater long-run good, and imposes a hierarchy of values on the debate which raises philosophical questions about the nature of development itself. Undoubtedly the debate about the clearances is easily confused when such issues are run together, and where the criteria are unspecified.

The modern textbook *Scotland since 1707* by R. H. Campbell examines the recent Scottish past in terms of the development of its industrial structure. In this account of economic change there is no ambiguity about the author's priorities. Indeed Campbell believed that historians have expended too much time on the Highlands, to the neglect of the more developed and more populated part of the nation. The Highland problem, he argued, had pre-dated both the clearances and Culloden. Emigration was inevitable, despite the reluctance of many to accept change. The temporary opportunities (such as in fishing and kelp) merely deferred the necessary transformation. In the eighteenth century there had already emerged an ideological rift between the values of the traditional society of the Highlands and those of the new industrial world. Those landlords who pressed their people to emigrate were, he judged, 'frequently only forcing a tenant to act as he would have to do eventually'. The pressure of population on resources was more fundamental than the grasping after higher rents. Campbell wrote, 'It is not easy to substantiate the accusation that the landlords were forwarding their own ends selfishly at the expense of their tenants.' He contended that both landlords and tenants were at the mercy of economic forces beyond their control. The inevitable adjustment which was required of the Highland economy was impeded (and, by implication, exacerbated) by the people's tenacious attachment to the land, by the growth of population, and by the development of fishing, kelp, whisky distilling, the potato and the cattle trade — which, together, prolonged the life of 'an anachronistic economy', and built up further demographic pressure before the disintegration of the economy in the 1840s.

Campbell conceded that the landlords' demands for higher rents had forced a series of changes in land use, and had caused a desperate search among the people for non-agricultural sources of cash income. In the period before the collapse of the economy, the landlords had not employed the profits of the good times (especially the kelp revenues) to create a new structure for the region. This, rather than the clearances, was the true failure of the landlords. 'The clearances could be justified as a method, though an unhappy one, of attempting to improve the estates, and perhaps they could never have been avoided.' But, for Campbell, the landlords' greatest blunder had been their thoughtless encouragement of population growth: 'The greatest tragedy of the period was the ignorance of the landlords, and indeed of most of the people, that their prosperity represented only a temporary respite from the problems which had faced them throughout the eighteenth century.' Bankruptcy and the final disintegration of the old economy followed — and the clearances, in Campbell's view, were essentially only secondary to these developments. For though the old economy failed, sheepfarming was bound to make headway. The clearances, he remarked, were controversial because the publicity was concentrated on the worst cases, and because of 'a complete misapprehension of the grinding poverty which existed before the sheep came and which impelled emigration, sooner or later, unless the Highlands were to be left in squalor with the lowest standard of living in Scotland.' Campbell claimed that the reduction of arable land caused by sheepfarming was only 20 per cent and that most of the process was gradual. While the change worsened the population problem in some places, 'sheepfarming was not the cause of the clearances and of emigration'; it was merely the occasion for a change which was inevitable once the assumption that 'the land should support the largest number of people irrespective of their standard of living' was rejected. Emigration was common even without sheep. Campbell therefore argued that the depopulation of the Highlands was, in essence, a local version of the general rural experience of the age, and that it was entirely inescapable.[11]

According to William Ferguson, writing in 1968, 'the glamour of spurious romance' had obscured the real issues, namely the unquestionable fact of overpopulation, the concentration of landed wealth in a few hands, and the implacable resentment of the common people. Ferguson claimed that the populace offered virtually no resistance to the clearances: they were leaderless and stunned, and the clergy, for the most part, sided with the lairds. He also drew attention to the poor condition of some districts, for example Lewis under the Seaforths, which were not cleared, and pointed out that most landlords 'were relatively poor and faced difficulties, perhaps insuperable difficulties'. He concludes his few remarks on the subject with the opinion that

> However regarded, however palliated, it is not a pretty story; and when the question of the Clearances again came before the public in the 1840s it added to the ill reputation of landlordism and thus further strengthened the base of Scottish radicalism.[12]

Some of the most perceptive remarks on the clearances by a modern historian are contained in Rosalind Mitchison's *History of Scotland.* She suggests that the general absence of protest against enclosure and eviction in Scotland resulted from the extreme weakness of tenant right, and that the exodus to the beckoning towns should not be assumed to have been voluntary. The pressure of economic conditions (and of landlords) was stronger wherever the growth of population outstripped available resources. Mitchison emphasises the cultural transformation in the eighteenth-century Highlands and the consumption behaviour of landlords — both seriously affected the manner in which the region managed the economic problems that emerged at the end of the eighteenth century. She identifies the contradiction in the behaviour of those who attempted to retain their feudal pretensions as great chiefs while raising their standards of consumption to English levels. Their traditional prestige had depended on military and territorial power, not on net rental income. While a Lowland laird could realistically develop his estate to sustain consumption aspirations, his Highland counterpart was more likely to get himself into debt forcing him into desperate measures, incompatible with the traditional chief's relationship with his people. The miracle of kelp undoubtedly helped, and there were serious efforts in the development of fishing and cattle. But meanwhile rent burdens and population piled up and when regional income collapsed after 1815 emigration became inevitable. The clearances were, in effect, a means of accelerating the elimination of a starving peasantry. Mitchison observes that in some places the clearances were implemented with 'consideration and skill', and that 'in much of south Argyll and in Caithness, the population found other activities than farming and little real hardship was caused'. But a degree of brutality was also common, especially where the process was executed in haste by men wanting rapid returns on capital. She accepts the view that the landowners as a class 'did not measure up to the needs of a difficult situation', but points out that the word 'clearance' has been applied loosely and that often the departure of people was voluntary and rational: 'In all, probably some three times as many people left the Highlands voluntarily as from direct eviction.' The sheer pressure of circumstances had eased many out, but not enough. Indeed she goes further and implicitly condemns the 'beneficent' landlords who chose to retain their tenants — 'in a sort of privileged destitution' — to leave them victims to the Potato Famine of 1846-8.[13]

Most historians who have been critical of landlord and governmental policy in the Highlands have shied away from specifying an alternative policy that might have coped with the real problems of the nineteenth-century Highland economy. In general the implication has been that the landlords should have been more humanitarian, more patient, less prodigal with their resources, more attuned to the development needs of the region, and more responsive to the plight of the people. The repeated failure to specify realistic alternatives to the policy of clearance has always been a cardinal weakness in the indictment of the landlord class. The historical irony of the point has been well demonstrated by Professor Mitchison, who observes that the landlords have been widely criticised because they pushed the people off their lands and then, in the next breath, are condemned because they retained people vulnerable to famine.

One of the few historians who has made any effort to delineate alternatives to the policy of clearance is T. C. Smout, who devotes a respectable part of his influential *History of the Scottish People* to an exploration and definition of the Highland experience. For Smout the failure of the Highlands in the nineteenth century was the reciprocal of the success of the Lowlands; it reflected a contrast of culture, of society and especially of ideology. 'Half the drama of Highland history ... is caused by the clash and tangle of these two cultures, and by resolving the differences between them.'[11] Smout stresses the primitive, tribal, inefficient and poverty-stricken character of old Highland society, whose social structure was based on naked force. It could not easily adapt to the processes of modernisation, mainly because a cultural divide separated it from the values of the new era. Smout believes that the ethos of Highland society was a world removed from the 'new moral order' of the Lowlands. The strength of the old *mores* inhibited changes necessary for the improvement of Highland welfare. The clash of cultures was extreme and more traumatic for this region than elsewhere.

Smout's explanation of the Highland tragedy incorporates a theme akin to geographical determinism. He appears to define the economic failure of the North and West Highlands in terms of their inability to reproduce Lowland structural adjustments, in particular 'the emergence of a class of indigenous and wealthy capitalist farmers side by side with a class of landless labourers who lived by working for them'. This development can be discerned in some easterly and southerly parts of the Highlands, but in the remainder the adjustment was in the opposite direction, towards further congestion of peasant landholders on small plots, 'with few among them who could be regarded either as capitalists or as proletarians'. No one gained by this arrangement, and the Highlands became one of the fringe economies of Europe, at all times exposed to Malthusian dangers of overpopulation. These economies — which included West Ireland, the Balkans and much of the north of Europe — were overshadowed by 'the same demographic factors', and experienced the same types of 'geographical disadvantage', presumably in the sense of agricultural and general resource deficiencies.[15]

When the props of peasant agriculture collapsed in the early nineteenth century, Smout writes, the region faced a very restricted choice.

> Either the region reverted to subsistence husbandry and increasing numbers of people lived in a vast rural slum, existing off potatoes grown on tiny holdings, like their fellows in Ireland or Finland, or the region switched over in a big way to sheep, with the best ground engrossed by a handful of outsiders and the natives existing by digging plots on the edges.

In Smout's analysis the introduction of sheep was a response to and not a prime generator of the problem. This argument is especially persuasive with respect to the Lewis where clearances and sheep were hardly at all instrumental in social and economic change:

> the area suffered from the middle of the eighteenth century until the middle of the nineteenth century from the poverty of all its inhabitants who pressed against the edge of subsistence whether the economy was able to support only relatively few inhabitants or a great many.

Conditions comparable with those of peasant Ireland prevailed throughout the period — 'the misery of the Hebrides is primarily the misery of the congested, not of the dispossessed'. Smout notes varied and contrasting cases — of clearance both with and without resettlement provision, and cases where landowners rejected the policy of clearance. Yet everywhere the result was deprivation and despair — and by 1830 'the Highlanders had become a society of smallholders living in great poverty on congested holdings either on crowded islands or next to extensive sheepfarmers'. Famine and emigration became inescapable.

Notwithstanding this, Smout does not accept the notion that the Highland experience was predetermined. In a short but engaging end-piece to his exposition of the Highland tragedy, he offers positive alternatives which he believes could have been attempted fruitfully in the Highlands. He suggests, in the first place, that the abolition of the tacksman class robbed the region of its natural entrepreneurial talent and capital, the lack of which crippled the regional economy, even in the twentieth century. Secondly, the landlords failed to adjust their rental policies to meet current conditions and 'by squandering the resources of those who still had a little capital, all were reduced to the flat level of the crofter'. Most important of all, Smout ventures the idea that the co-operative modes of the old economy could have been adapted to the needs of the new era. The sheep farms could have been run by groups of co-operating Highland tenants, a mode of production which would have harnessed the capital and labour native to the region. This untried system, argues Smout, might have done the trick — but he concedes that the realities of economic geography, which defeated so much idealism and capitalism, might also have defeated crofter co-operation, if it ever emerged.

Smout's specification of the Highland problem employs two methods of positive benefit to the historical debate. One is to compare the consequences of different policies pursued in various parts of the Highlands, in a manner already suggested by the work of Malcolm Gray. The second is his explicit, albeit embryonic, consideration of alternative policies for the Highlands in the age of the clearances: he states a hypothetical alternative. The future debate on the Highlands will advance further only when the counterfactual is fully specified and subjected to basic tests of logical consistency. Then will follow the question of a quantitative verification. It is extraordinary that the few pages in Smout's book remain the only effort that has been made in this direction.

III

Scottish history had once held little interest for English readers: a general 'anti-Scotican rage' created great difficulties for any historian in 'winning the ear of an English audience to Scottish history'.[16] William Robertson, Sir Walter Scott, Robert Louis Stevenson and John Buchan reversed all that, and today there is a substantial literary industry producing historical fiction and popular history devoted to Scottish themes. The Highland clearances have attracted a disproportionate attention in this way — through the novels of Neil Gunn and Iain Critchton-Smith, for example. Two historians in particular — Ian Grimble and John

Prebble — have won the ear of a large audience. They highlight the dramatic and tragic aspect of the clearances; it is a signal of their success as writers that their view of the subject commands the widest acceptance with the modern public.

Ian Grimble's writing is shaped by socialist principles, by a close personal knowledge of the north of Scotland, and by a training at the feet of the influential Oxford historian, Christopher Hill. His work has been devoted to a study of the historical vicissitudes of a Celtic society to which he is fervently committed — but his knowledge of Scandinavian history often informs his writing on the Highlands in a constructive if not fully systematic manner. He views the Highland clearances as the climactic moment in the unparalleled destruction of a peasant civilisation. A vigorous, autonomous culture was destroyed for the sake of Anglo-Saxon gain. It was akin to genocide, a word from which Dr Grimble does not shrink. The clearances were a tragedy. He detects a racialist theme — 'a hidden strand through the whole of British history, [in] this antipathy of the English-speaking peoples for the surviving speakers of the Celtic language in our islands'.[17] The anti-Celticism of mid-nineteenth-century Britain sanctioned the atrocities of the Irish Famine and the Highland clearances. Much of Grimble's writing is an elaboration of this thesis of 'conflict of races'.[18]

A further theme in his work has been the identification of lines of continuity which connect the conflict of the nineteenth century to earlier periods. Part of his work traces the roots of modern antagonisms to events in the seventeenth century. Indeed much of his passion as a spokesman for Celtic society and culture derives ultimately from his conception of the pre-clearance world of the Highlands, and he has mapped out the virtues of eighteenth-century Highland culture — its 'joy and richness' in an 'elegant and untroubled poetic world'. His vision is in stark opposition to much modern writing on the period. On the actual clearances Grimble has concentrated on the case of Patrick Sellar and the momentous evictions in Sutherland in the decade 1811-21. This work is almost entirely innocent of archival research, but it has the unquestionable merits of causing questions to be asked of the political power of the landlords, and of demanding a proper consideration of Celtic cultural values. It is possible to see his influence even in the work of Smout, who is himself critical of Grimble's dramatic prose. But Grimble did not use the opportunity to deepen the foundations of historical research on the question.

The racialist theme was taken up by a more recent writer, Francis Thompson, who describes the clearances as 'the rape of the Highlands':

> Many thousands of Highland folk were driven away from their homes to seek solace in death; families were split up, many never to have the opportunity to unite again, murder and rapine were common, all carried out on instruction from the agents of the Duke of Sutherland.

It was all achieved by 'murderous bands of thugs whom Sellar used to empty the lands or Strathnaver'. Thompson drew wide historical parallels when he wrote that the clearances

> destroyed much of the foundation of a unique culture and ethnic grouping which was identified as being both Celtic and Gaelic — racial factors which made the victims of the Clearances objects of intense hatred such as the gypsies and the Jews were to experience under the Nazis and other groups in the Western World. All ethnic groups which differ in outlook, life styles, culture and language have had to bear the 'colonising' pressures of master races; and the Gaels were, and indeed are today, in no way different from the Red Indians, the Jews, the Eskimoes and the vanishing tribes of the Amazon River, all of whom face the prospect of extinction by process of assimilation before another century is out.[19]

The element of hyperbole in some of these statements derives from the vacuum of historical research which continued to mark the retelling of the clearances.

Indignation is also the prime mover in the work of John Prebble, a writer of considerable literary skills whose imaginative reconstructions of dramatic episodes in Highland history have been influential in sustaining a generalised scorn of the enemies of the old Highland culture — the Lowlanders, the English, the Anglo-Saxons, industrialism, avarice, landlords and capitalism. Written in a strikingly cinematic style, cumulatively impressionistic in method, Prebble's histories are literary and allusive. Their main focus is always individual personality and dramatic episodes. While Prebble eschews systematic analysis and the impedimenta of scholarship, his writing is nevertheless often informed by a sound knowledge of important and frequently neglected sources. His work, taken as a whole, has the force and sweep of a saga. It unfolds in four volumes devoted to an indictment of the people whom he considers responsible for the Highland tragedy.[20] Although Prebble's books are written in a form which proceeds by the accumulation of detailed cameos and impressions, they are nevertheless overarched by a general thesis about the nature of the Highland experience, of which the clearances were the last act. The interpretation, broadly, is that the integrity of the old Highland society and culture was cynically destroyed by external forces which were economically and technologically superior but, in every other way, crass and inferior. At one point, he summarised the theme as 'the spine-breaking blow of Culloden, the despoiling of the glens, the bloody scenes of the French Wars, the coming of the great Cheviot sheep ... eviction and dispersal'. In equally impassioned tones he wrote of the Highlands: 'Their society was torn away from the past by the use of rope, musket and bayonet, by prison and transportation, by the burning of the glens, the driving of cattle, the harrying of homeless men, women and children.'[21] Prebble makes a large point of telling his stories using as his focus 'the many ordinary men and women' of the Highlands. He achieves this mainly by leaps of the imagination — he invests elusive and obscure people with emotions, thoughts and feelings for which he possesses little or no direct evidence.

Prebble regards Culloden as the start of 'a sickness from which Scotland, and the Highlands in particular, never recovered' — and he adds, somewhat curiously, 'It is a sickness of emotions and its symptoms can be seen on the labels of whisky bottles.'[22] For Prebble, the clearances were a story of betrayal, neglect, exploit-ation and racial destruction. Memory of them must never be allowed to fade:

> The British government first defeated a tribal uprising and then destroyed the society that had made it possible. The exploitation of a country during the next hundred years was within the same pattern of colonial development — new economies introduced for the greater wealth of the few, and the unproductive obstacle of a native population removed or reduced. In the beginning the men who imposed the change were of the same blood, tongue and family as the people. They used the advantages given them by the old society to profit from the new, but in the end they were gone with their clans.[23]

Prebble's work has had a consciousness-raising effect which far outweighs his contribution to historical scholarship. There is no pretence at detailed analysis, or of a full exploitation of the sources; nor is there any clear model of causation. He is not interested in providing a dispassionate assemblage of data, or of comprehending the wider social and economic processes. For him the issues are self-evidently and inescapably moral issues; any other analysis would simply obfuscate the clear significance of the Highland experience from Glencoe to the clearances. It is all a story of man's inhumanity to man and there is no need to look for other sources of, for instance, the poverty of the Highlands in the nineteenth century. It is not surprising that Prebble's approach to Scottish history disconcerts other practitioners, unhappy with his dramatic mode of exposition or his idiosyncratic use of evidence. For all that, his influence on the interpretation of the clearances remains dominant.

IV

Many of the themes of Prebble's work have been taken up by other Scottish writers, particularly in works of drama and fiction. The most prominent recent example is John McGrath's successful satirical play, *The Cheviot, the Stag and the Black Black Oil.* It constitutes a direct extension of Prebble's thesis into the present day, employing similarly ironic imaginative devices to provoke political responses to the theme of the current exploitation of the Highlands. It is a work of protest against the dominance of the criterion of profitability over the 'well-being of the community'. Its philosophy is that capitalist enterprise can only benefit the owners of the means of production, and that therefore the operation of a free market economy is necessarily exploitative. This call to arms teaches 'the people' that they must organise themselves to resist the forces of capitalism. For McGrath, as for the other dramatists of the Highland past, the lessons of history are clear and simple.[24]

The work of James Hunter, the most recent professional historian to enter the fray, is written from a similar standpoint to that of Prebble and McGrath.[25] It differs in that the interpretation is erected on elaborate and scholarly analytical foundations and informed by a detailed study of archival sources which invests his propositions with considerable authority. He is also better acquainted with cognate and comparable findings from anthropology, Irish history and Scandinavian work. His book on *The Making of the Crofting Community*, written with great flair, has clearly advanced the study of the Highlands during the clearance period. He opens up entirely original lines of research on religion in the Highlands, on the impact of famine and deer farming, and on the origins and forms of crofter protest. It is impressive and path-breaking writing in the best tradition of Scottish social history. Hunter is himself critical of historians such as Grimble and Prebble who, despite their relevant sympathies with the crofters' tradition,

> have, by the very strength of their commitment to it, done it a disservice. Their published histories ... are largely made up of refurbished versions of their precursors' books and pamphlets. Thus abstracted from their historical context, the older works are deprived of purpose and effect, their message is distorted and their undoubted weaknesses highlighted.[26]

A new broom thus clears away the misunderstandings of the predecessors even where they erred on the right side.

But Hunter reserves a harsher indictment for another group of historians who, he claims, have wilfully neglected the common people of the Highlands: they have failed to do historical justice to the experience of the crofters. Malcolm Gray, Eric Cregeen, Phillip Gaskell and the present author have been criticised by Hunter for their excessive emphasis upon economic trends in modern history — 'the people upon whom estate management imposed their policies have been almost completely neglected'.[27] In part this damaging criticism is a technical question to do with historical method. In effect Hunter argues that these writers employ primary estate records and hence that they must necessarily construct pro-landlord history or interpretations which are ideologically tainted by their source. The historian becomes a prisoner of the archives. This is, naturally, a challenging proposition: it is surely a fundamental tenet of historical method that it is possible (and indeed necessary) to write the history of any group in society (elite or not) without identifying with the ideology of that body. As for estate records, they are the finest single source of evidence relating to the agricultural world of the nineteenth century and contain the richest material not only about the structure and finances of landed power, but also about the conditions of the people and the relations of the clan.[28] Alone they are an inadequate source of social realities, but so long as their provenance is kept centrally in mind, they are a vital treasury of the Highland past. It would be absurd to say that history from estate papers is landlords' history: this would be a negation of historical method.

The fundamental question of method raised by Hunter's criticisms is more problematical than he suggests. Any writer attempting a 'history-from-below', for the people of the Highlands or elsewhere, is invariably impeded by the dearth of direct primary sources. The inescapable fact is that the poor, the powerless and the illiterate leave very little residue of their lives amongst which a historian may seek material for their reconstruction. This presents a great challenge and there is a danger that, in the full flood of sympathy for the underdog, the historian will interpolate thoughts and emotions for people of whom there is no direct knowledge. Dr Hunter has by no means solved this problem, nor is he on safe ground assuming that other writers are any less well disposed to the Highland poor than himself. The assumption of moral superiority in historical debate is not easily conceded.

Hunter began his work with the premiss that there should be written a sustained history of the Highlands which deliberately and explicitly assumed the standpoint of the crofters:

A serious attempt is made to understand it and explain why the crofters' conception of his own part — as preserved in the nineteenth century books and pamphlets ... in Gaelic poetry, in press and policy reports of Highlands land league meetings and not least in the collective memory of the crofter community itself — is so radically different from the typical historian's portrayal of it. Such an explanation can be arrived at only by putting the crofter at the centre of his own history; and in essence, therefore, this book is an attempt to write the modern history of the Gaelic Highlands from the crofting community's point of view.

It is, as he claims, 'the first full length history of the crofting community', and its greatest strength is its empathy for the crofters, derived from the author's own upbringing, aided by his familiarity with the Gaelic language. Hunter's account examines the Highland experience essentially in terms of the impact of social and economic changes upon the victims of those changes. He is able to give powerful academic reinforcement to the older radical exposition of the roots of the Highland problem. In practice his analysis employs a conventional quasi-Marxist framework of class conflict. His major contribution is to express the continuity of political, social and economic tensions from the age of the clearances to the adjustments of the twentieth century.

Hunter's interpretation hinges upon the juxtaposition of the unequal elements of Highland life — he repeatedly identifies the diametrical opposition of the class interests of the powerful elite against the welfare of the common people in the nineteenth century. The making of the crofting community was constrained within a context of mounting class antagonism characterised by 'the excessive and ostentatious comfort of the privileged few; their oppressive and unjust conduct [and] the exploitation of man by man'.

The 'Highland problem', according to Hunter, was the creation of landlords who, under the impact of kelp profits, first encouraged the growth of population, and then cleared the people into inhuman concentrations on crofts, and finally exposed them to famine. The whole structure of small holding was, in this account, the specific and deliberate consequence of landlord policy, and had little connection with the old Highland society. Indeed the basic problem was a *new* phenomenon, the creation of the new age. The famine in its turn was the consequence of landlord policies; government policy was a mirror of the landlord's interests. Of the wider forces, 'it was only under the impact of capitalism and the associated imposition of a commercialised agricultural structure that a peasantry in the usual sense of the word was created from the lower strata of traditional society.' When economic conditions deteriorated they became far less tolerable to the community because there had been a collapse of 'the old Highland social and cultural unity, qualities which had to some extent compensated for the economically harsh conditions of the past and this gave it a retrospectively attractive aura'. Hunter is interested in economic processes in the Highlands only in the limited sense that they represented class interest and class conflict. While the latter is undoubtedly important to an understanding of the social milieu of the Highlands, it is nevertheless a partial view which fails to address the objective conditions of economic change in the region.

In essence, Hunter's eloquent and persuasive account is

grounded on three critical assumptions. The first is that the clearances were the catastrophic climax of the 'brutal betrayal of traditional custom and belief, a reckless assertion of the interests of the few at the expense of the many'. This thesis itself suggests a somewhat romanticised view of the pre-clearance circumstances in the Highlands. The second assumption is that the policy of clearance was worse than any feasible alternative. Hunter specifically eschews discussion of alternative directions which the region might have taken in the nineteenth century.[29] Finally he contends, usually by implication, that the nation at large should have made an economic sacrifice in order to nurse and regenerate crofting so that such communities could be sustained in their intractable territory. Beyond these premises Hunter entertains the wider (and older) dream of Highland reform by which the land and its allied resources would be returned to the common people. They would then be in a position to reap the benefits which eluded them in the past (for example, the profits of kelp, whisky and wool), and which promise well for the future (for example, aluminium and oil). Some of this credo derives from a particular reading of Highland history; some of it is contingent on judgements about political equity, economic justice and the rights of property.

Notes

1. Malcolm Gray, *The Highland Economy 1750-1850* (Edinburgh, 1957).
2. Ibid., p. 71.
3. Ibid., p. 240.
4. Ibid., p. 75.
5. T. S. Ashton, *The Industrial Revolution* (London, 1968 edition), p. 129.
6. Gray, *Highland Economy*, p. 246.
7. Donald G. Macrae, review of Gray, *Economica*, vol. 25 (1958), pp. 265-6.
8. Malcolm Gray, review article in *Scottish Historical Review*, vol. 53 (1974), pp. 94-9.
9. George S. Pryde, *Scotland from 1603 to the Present Day* (London, 1962), pp. 150-61.
10. See the discussion in Stewart R. Sutherland, 'Ethics and Economics in the Sutherland Clearances', *Northern Scotland*, vol. 2, no. 1 (1974-5).
11. R. H. Campbell, *Scotland since 1707* (Oxford, 1965), pp. 168-76.
12. William Ferguson, *Scotland 1689 to the Present* (Edinburgh, 1968), pp. 276-7.
13. Rosalind Mitchison, *A History of Scotland* (London, 1970), pp. 359, 375-8.
14. T. C. Smout, *A History of the Scottish People, 1560-1830* (London, 1969).
15. Ibid., p. 347.
16. Cosmo Innes, *Sketches of Early Scotch History and Social Progress* (Edinburgh, 1861), pp. vi-vii. Fashions change. Half a century before Walter Scott

had reported, no doubt accurately, that 'Everything belonging to the Highlands of Scotland has of late become peculiarly interesting. It is not above half a century since it was otherwise.' *Quarterly Review* (January 1816), p. 288, reviewing the *Culloden Papers.*

17. Ian Grimble, *The Trial of Patrick Sellar* (London, 1962), pp. 151-2.
18. See Ian Grimble, *Chief of Mackay* (London, 1965), Ch. 1; 'Gael and Saxon in Scotland', *Yale Review*, vol. 52 (1962).
19. Francis Thompson, *The Highlands and Islands* (London, 1974), pp. 61-2.
20. John Prebble, *Glencoe* (London, 1966); *Culloden* (London, 1961); *The Highland Clearances* (London, 1963); *Mutiny* (London, 1975).
21. *Mutiny*, pp. 27, 95.
22. *Culloden*, p. 1.
23. Prebble, *The Highland Clearances*, p. 304.
24. John McGrath, *The Cheviot, the Stag and the Black Black Oil* (Kyleakin, 1974).
25. Hunter, *Crofting Community.*
26. Ibid., pp. 4-5.
27. Ibid., p. 5. A similar categorisation is used by Ian Carter, 'The Changing Image of the Scottish Peasantry 1745-1980' in Raphael Samuel (ed.), *People's History and Socialist Theory* (London, 1981).
28. See the case for the preservation of English estate records made by Edward Hughes in 'The Eighteenth Century Estate Agent in H. A. Cronne, T.W. Moody and D.B. Quinn (eds.), *Essays in British and Irish History* (London, 1949), pp. 198-9.
29. Hunter, *Crofting Community*, p. 214.

6

NEW WAYS OF CONTROVERSY

I

Humane concern for the plight of the crofters — frequently seen as victims of an unequal history — has been a compelling motive in the work of many historians of the Highlands. Another, allied, concern has been for an explanation of the generic problem of peripheral regions such as the Highlands, which, though lying on the edge of a great industrial world, experienced deteriorating circumstances after the onset of modern economic growth. For anyone interested in the welfare of the mass of Highland people, the two approaches are complementary — the crofters and the ordinary folk of the towns and the land constitute 95 per cent of the population.

'The history of the people' is always frustrated by the poor availability of documentation. But the position is far from hopeless. There are several avenues of access to the various strata of society which have been little explored — for example, police and court records, petitions, letters, emigration registers, census returns and much material in estate papers. Recent exercises designed to penetrate the mental life of the people, their values and assumptions and the nature of their response to the clearances, to famine and to religion, have drawn their evidence from four main categories of documentation. One has been by way of the study of civil disorder at those moments of resistance and riot which, in some degree, expose the prevailing social structure, and give expression to otherwise inchoate popular feeling.[1] A second source has been the study of the physical remains of common life in the Highlands — the everyday materials of life which, for instance, are presented with great effect in Isobel Grant's book, *Highland Folk Ways*, and which may be seen in the local museums of the Highland region. Included in this category should be the archaeological findings, particularly of Dr Horace Fairhurst, who has sought to establish

151

the actual spatial patterns of pre- and post-clearance settlements in the Highlands. Fairhurst has also examined systematically the evidence of the use of fire in the evictions.[2] The third direction of research has been in the detailed local study, usually by geographers, for example J.B. Caird, of the fine detail of crofting life, much of which has been concerned with recreating the old patterns of the domestic economy.[3] Each of these modes of investigation adds a dimension to the study of the Highland problem, and the impact of the clearances.

The fourth type of research into the cultural heritage of the Highlands derives from the long-standing programme of literary, linguistic and folkloristic studies undertaken at the School of Scottish Studies at the University of Edinburgh. Of special significance have been the researches of the late Eric Cregeen, whose work initially concentrated upon the conventional records of the great Argyll estate. Subsequently Cregeen became a prominent advocate of the methods of oral history as promising high dividends for a history-from-below of the Highlands. Having contributed distinguished studies of Highland history from estate records, and explored the use of anthropology in historical writing, he contended that 'the oral tradition has a character of its own markedly distinct from written sources and ... [leads] to a conception of history in some respects fundamentally different from that produced by the records'.

Written records, Cregeen suggested, reflect the Highlands as seen through the eyes of outsiders, detached from the community by their status, education and outlook. (He had in mind estate factors, travellers, agricultural experts, solicitors, journalists and parliamentary inquirers.) By contrast, 'Oral tradition, handed on in successive generations in the native tongue, reflects the same scene as viewed from within the community by people who share its attitudes and values.' Cregeen argued further that there is inherent bias in the written sources for a society such as the Highlands — for instance, the perception of social and economic life derived from government reports and contemporary social investigations will yield only the 'problems of that society, the negative aspect of a community and not a rounded view of its life'. It is a point analogous to the interpretation of the Industrial Revolution drawn exclusively from the Blue Books of the day. Such sources for the Highlands, wrote Cregeen, would suggest that prevailing conditions would not sustain civilised life. Moreover, because of the deficiencies of the [written] sources, one begins to think of the Highlands after the eighteenth century as an anonymous mass of featureless peasants, passively suffering the blows of fortune and the injustices of the powerful, without sufficient initiative to comment on or react against them.

Oral history may therefore operate as a necessary corrective, to demonstrate that despite penury, eviction and emigration

> these same communities are seen to possess style and dignity in the midst of poverty, a rich and widely shared culture, and a complex and well-organised society which preserved the fundamental decencies of life and as far as possible protected the sick and aged.

Cregeen in effect argued that the realities of Highland history are absent from the written sources, or so obscured by them that it becomes extraordinarily difficult to perceive the truth of the matter. Nevertheless, as Cregeen himself pointed out, the oral tradition is itself highly selective in the opposite direction. He warned:

> One has to handle oral traditions as critically as written records and be assured of their bias and omissions and distortions. So far I have found oral tradition in this island [Tiree] very reticent about physical suffering and poor material conditions.

He found little in the surviving collective memory of one of the most traumatic episodes in modern Highland history — the great famine of 1847-9, about which the written record is, of course, replete with documentation of the people's suffering. Many years ago Isobel Grant testified to 'heart-rending tales ... told of the famines that followed the worst of the bad harvests'. Yet the oral record is now almost entirely silent on this great theme in the modern Highland experience.[4] Indeed the record is sparse in recording the cultural impact of the clearances, not simply on the patriarchal role of the landowners (which is relatively well documented) but also on the inner adjustments of the crofter communities. The consequences for social cohesion and moral values are usually perceptible only through the filter of religious behaviour, rarely through the words of the people directly.

An example of a more orthodox selection of sources, and a close analysis of a relatively circumscribed part of the Highland experience, was provided by Phillip Gaskell in 1968 in his study of a Highland parish, Morvern, in Argyll. Gaskell's announced purpose has been to counteract the main body of literature on the Highland clearances which, he observes, has been dominated by popular historians 'who have been interested chiefly in the propagandist or sensationalist aspects of the subject'. He argues that the published history of the clearances has been unbalanced and that

> few of us, in our guilt-obsessed century, can look back on the evictions without some feeling of responsibility for them, however mistaken, and a consequent urge to atone for it by coming out on the side of those who suffered.

Gaskell therefore deliberately eschews 'overemphasis on the misfortunes of the Highland peasantry'. He sees the clearances as a symptom of the inability of the old Highland economy to adapt to a changed world and not as a cause of the breakdown. The landlords, he believes, acted under extreme economic pressure and not necessarily without humanity — indeed, echoing a phrase of Malcolm Gray, he says that the clearances were the result of 'impersonal forces beyond the control of either landlords or tenants'.

Gaskell, of all historians, draws the starkest picture of the pre-clearance Highlands. The people 'lived not in picturesque rural felicity but in conditions of penury and squalor that can fairly be compared with those of a famine area in contemporary India, and that were tolerable only because they were traditional and familiar'. He depicts the life of the Highlands in the eighteenth century:

> a half-naked people living in mud-floored hovels, peat smoke blackening their faces before it drifted through a hole in the dripping roof, the sole room shared all the winter through with starving cattle, a tale of intermittent famine and endless poverty.[5]

Eventually, in the following century, it became clear that the resources of the parish could not support the people at an acceptable standard of living, regardless of the action of the landlords. By then the landowners were losing money, and sheep-farming became the only hope against further financial loss; and by then most responsible opinion urged the common people to emigrate. Gaskell judges that, though there were examples of culpable disregard of the people's feelings, the record of landlord behaviour is one of restraint, and indeed compares well with elsewhere.

Gaskell emphatically rejects the implicit counterfactual view which pervades the orthodox literature on the Highlands: he asserts 'that the inhabitants of the parish would have been prosperous and contented in 1881 if there had been no evictions ... was of course, absurd'. He contends that famine and emigration were the inevitable consequences of overcrowding and poverty. Gaskell indeed presents his own hypothetical alternative to the policy of clearances:

the actual alternative to the reorganisation imposed by sheep-farmers was chronic depression; and it is arguable that the drastic surgery of the clearance was preferable to the wasting of the population for a further fifty years, that the belief of the evicting landlords that they were acting for the greatest good of the greatest number was in fact justified.[6]

In essence, therefore, Gaskell is prepared to argue that the policy of clearance was probably correct in the circumstances of the nineteenth century; only the methods to which some landlords resorted in its implementation deserved condemnation.

Gaskell's most valuable contribution to the debate on the clearances is in his close attention to the facts of landlord-tenant relations, and in the careful elucidation of the local sequence of events in the unfolding crises of the Highlands. His documentation is stronger than any other study in the field, and his detailed consideration of estate records and memoirs gives his analysis of long-term tenurial changes unrivalled precision. His emphasis upon the 'Asiatic standards of life' in the pre-clearance Highlands highlights the critical importance of the *status quo ante* the changes for any interpretation of the subsequent events. His sympathy for the dilemmas of the landlords is by no means uncritical but the least persuasive element in his book is its lenient attitude to the squandering of the financial resources of Morvern by its successive landlords. Though some of them imported capital to the parish, and some ordained improvements and instituted charities, the story was generally one of extraction. The income generated in the area was disposed in ways which were far from optimal on any utilitarian criteria. The landlords and the great sheepfarmers lived handsomely simply because they controlled the resources of the land and lived off its surplus. In this respect they were no better (and perhaps no worse) than private landlords anywhere.

II

Embedded in most of the controversy about the clearances are propositions, usually implicit, about the economics of underdevelopment in the Highlands. It is natural therefore that this controversy should overlap into the contemporary discussion of the regional problem in the Highlands. The history of the Highlands is deeply involved in present-day prescriptions for the region. In his book on *Internal Colonialism* the North American sociologist, Michael Hechter, has drawn upon the literature of the clearances to provide evidence for a broad generalising thesis about the relationship of lesser racial minorities to the mainstream of development during industrialisation. In this work Hechter offered a general explanation of the fate of regions such as the Highlands.

Seeking inspiration and direction from Marx, from a notion of 'internal colonialism', and from the idea of a structural conflict of interest between regions during the evolution of industrial capitalism, Hechter addresses the question of the persistence of 'ethnicity' in modern Britain, specifically the retention of strong regional identities on the so-called 'Celtic fringe'. His overarching theory attempts to comprehend the divergence of experience in the regions of modern Britain. He speaks in terms of the exploitation of regions such as the Highlands by the centres of the southern industrial economy. 'The peripheral collectivity is seen to be already suffused with the exploitative connections to the core, such that it can be deemed to be an internal colony.' The economic structure of such an 'internal colony' depends mainly on a single primary 'export'; most of the economic characteristics of the region have been determined exogenously: for example, the movement of labour, standards of living and general social welfare are all beyond the region's control. Regional specialisation, Hechter argues, was forced upon the region in a manner which undermined economic welfare. In particular the narrowing of the foundations of economic life made it much more difficult to sustain and develop industry on the periphery of the national economy. Economic dependency is strongly reinforced by the political subjugation of the colony. Thus internal colonies became examples of underdevelopment within a wider economic structure: 'Political incorporation indirectly led to the development of economic dependence in the peripheral regions by facilitating the expansion of production for exchange.' Hence economic development became very selective, and disadvantageous to the Celtic regions and Hechter claims that 'While political incorporation undoubtedly stimulated investment in the Celtic regions, English capital was available only for those investments which would complement existing English industries.' The Highlands became, therefore, a mere primary-producing colony of English industrial capitalism — and the consequent underdevelopment of the region caused a 'forced emigration' to the south. Moreover the *laissez-faire* creed of the central government aided and abetted the imperialistic process: 'By denying these territories political independence, England made their increasing economic dependence inevitable.' In terms of economic development Britain became partitioned in structure between the core and its periphery. Hechter thereby posits fundamental propositions about the roots of regional retrogression and the arguments about 'economic inevitability'. The Highland clearances figure as the most obvious example of operation of these economic mechanisms in the relationship between 'core' and 'periphery'. Hechter goes on to argue at great length about the social and political consequences. In particular he contends that the economic conflict inherent in the regional relationship was essential in the preservation of what he terms 'the strength of ethnic solidarity' which has stunted the development of national cohesion and created fertile conditions for regional conflict. (Witness the conflict in Ulster and the growth of the Scottish National Party and Plaid Cymru.)[7]

Hechter's thesis is highly speculative in character and full of difficulties. Though the theory is an all encompassing analysis of long-term historical change, it offers little precise explanation of the mechanisms at work in regional relationships. It pays scant heed to the compensating benefits of trade to all participating regions, and his exposition allows too little volition to the owners of capital and resources in the region. Nor does he specify the policies (and their consequences) which autonomous instrumentalities within the region could have adopted to counteract the influence of external economic forces. Nevertheless, Hechter does offer a broad explanation of regional interdependence which lifts the discussion of the Highland experience from its usually insular approach. In some respects Hechter's thesis connects with nineteenth-century beliefs that the plight of the Highlands was a result of an invasion of southern sheepfarmers and sportsmen, and with Grimble's idea of racial exploitation at work. It also links into a wider literature on the 'economics of dependency' referred to below. For all its heroic and arguable assumptions, Hechter's work usefully draws attention to the importance of inter-regional analysis in any discussion of the clearances, and the associated 'Highland problem'.

The most clear-thinking and penetrating contribution to the literature since Gray's book has been A.J. Youngson's *After the Forty Five*. Youngson's account does not break new ground in its use of sources since it is based almost entirely on a close reading of secondary materials, the *Old Statistical Account* and contemporary descriptions. Nor is the interpretation particularly novel. Like most other writers, he locates the origins of the modern Highland problem squarely in the developments of the eighteenth century; he regards much of the story as the clash of ill-matched cultures in which a civilisation fought for its life and lost;[8] he sees the impact of external economic and social forces progressively tightening the range of choices open to the region; and his view of the central role of demographic upsurge is basically Malthusian. Youngson, however, introduces to the debate great clarity of thinking, and a consistent determination to analyse and evaluate, at each phase in the story, the economic and social options which faced the Highland region. He asks, 'Did it have to be so? Must it always be so?' Such questions require a view of the possible alternative policies, and a framework of comparison with other similar societies.

Youngson searches for the roots of economic development in the period 1750 to 1830, during which time the Highlands experienced radical structural changes associated with the rapid expansion of demand for certain local commodities and with growth of political concern in Edinburgh and Westminster for the future prospects of the northern economy. He provides a valuable commentary on the evolution of government policy in the Highlands since the eighteenth century, and evaluates some of the results of efforts made to stimulate and subsidise, for instance, the fishing industry, textiles and the development of the infrastructure (e.g. the Caledonian Canal). He considers the economic philosophy which persuaded the private sector, the improvers, as well as the government, to take initiatives in the Highlands at the end of the eighteenth century. Youngson is able to change our picture of the late-eighteenth-century Highlands by cataloguing an impressive range of positive attempts to bring economic development to the north of Scotland. There was, effectively, a concerted drive to foster an infrastructure for the regional economy amid the structural changes already under way. Most significant of the already established changes was the demographic upsurge — 'The old stability of highland population gave way to rapid growth for a complex of reasons.'[9] This is an interesting view because it assumes a prior demographic equilibrium in the old Highland economy, even though this is not easily demonstrated from any known evidence. The eighteenth-century population growth worsened the ratio of people to the land, which was also influenced by changing uses to which the land was put. And this, says Youngson, was 'the heart of the matter'. While the potato and kelp production enabled the common people to live off smaller plots of land, the advance by the sheep required a redistribution of the land.

In this account the clearances were essentially part of a long-run process of agrarian change, and the most visible and dramatic part of that change. Youngson contends that it is a gross distortion of history to talk of a sudden abnegation of paternalism by the Highland lairds, replaced simply by the cash nexus. 'There was a struggle — for many landowners a long and saddening struggle — between feelings of social obligation on the one hand and mounting economic pressure on the other.' In trying to delay the change as long as possible, many compounded the problems (such as congestion, overpopulation and technological backwardness) which had made the change inevitable. But, 'gradually the pressure to remove the occupiers of minute portions of land, those who could scarcely even in a good year produce enough for their own survival, increased; but for several decades landlords resisted, and did what they could to provide for their multiplying tenantry'.

As in Ireland, overpopulation (in the sense of negative marginal returns to labour) was expressed in the classic symptoms: subdivision, chronic rural unemployment and worsening levels of economic welfare. Youngson sees this as an indication of land and capital deficiencies (aggravated by the introduction of sheep-farming) and again asks the question: was there any realistic alternative? An injection of capital from outside was technically feasible, but the record of its effectiveness was very poor: the contemporary experience in both public and private ventures, gave little reason for optimism about the net benefits of capital import. The retention of the population was hardly practicable: 'Those who simply kept their tenants, and continued to parcel out their properties in tiny lots to people who, they know very well, had neither the capital nor the skill to improve them, were merely perpetuating stagnation and starvation.' Youngson repeated this point even more emphatically in another passage:

> On the face of it ... it seems unlikely that different policies of estate management could have produced a very much better result ... the removal of tenants was sometimes the only way to avoid the ruin of an estate, for if a famine occurred the landowners had to help, and thousands of pounds had to be spent on food supplies which, if not an outright gift, contributed a loan with very poor prospects of repayment.

Youngson therefore seems to imply that the role of the clearances was essentially secondary in this process, and not a first cause of the economic problem. It was, he remarks, 'no more than the visible breaking crest on a long travelled irresistible wave'.

In a national sense, sheepfarming was probably a beneficial advance in the utilisation of agricultural resources, but the human costs of the change were borne by those least able to shoulder them.

> It was irresponsible to suppose that poor tenants, accustomed to stagnant agricultural routine, could be dumped on the sea-shore or the shores of a sea loch, without skill, experience or equipment, and successfully wrest a living from the sea as fishermen, with or without the help of an acre or two of potatoes.

But Youngson also argues that small producers in the Highland economy (the old peasantry) could not have operated large-scale sheep production. This contention (supported by the earlier work of Margaret Leigh and Henry Hamilton) is at the heart of the historical controversy, and is strongly resisted in the unstated assumptions of many opposing historians of the Highlands. Moreover, says Youngson, the circumstances of resource and capital availability, and market possibilities made it exceedingly difficult for any landlord to try to establish new economic structures which might have accommodated the actual population of the Highlands at a reasonable standard of life. In effect, argues Youngson, population growth outstripped production despite the gains achieved by the forces of improvements. Emigration and deterioration of living standards were the natural consequences. Apart from the special cases of the improved villages of the east, the economy declined; debts increased and recurrent subsistence crises marked the end of the high hopes that had coloured the 1780s: 'the idea of building up the Highland economy was over, and it was not to be revived for more than a hundred years'.[10]

At the end of his book Youngson sets the Highland case in a wider perspective: he insists that the failure of public and private policy must be judged in the light of the extraordinary difficulties of the day. The contemporary context was profoundly unfavourable and acted to negate the beneficial effects of development promoted by landlords and government. The failure had little to do with the fabled indolence of the Highlander, or to any lack of education. The modernisation of agriculture and tenure, the promotion of fishing and transport, and especially of manufacturing, were unsuccessful for reasons beyond the control of the people of the Highlands. Positive deveopments could be achieved only with fewer, not more, people: at the centre of the discussion was the conflict 'between having the Highlands prosperous and having them populous'. All the solutions to this puzzle have failed.

Youngson is at his best where he draws out the inner conflicts of the Highland economy, and where he specifies the logical alternatives that might have been attempted within the Highland framework. He hypothesises about the effect of a completely new departure in the economy — the result of, say, the happy discovery of a lucrative mineral resource that might be exploited to sustain the people of the region. He makes relevant historical comparison with the experience of the Norrland region of Sweden where, in the middle of the nineteenth century, there was a rapid expansion of the timber industry (under the impact of a shifting demand schedule) which lead to a sizeable growth of the economy. It was a development not unlike a chance discovery of a mineral. Yet the subsequent history of Norrland revealed many undesirable features common also to Highland history, more especially the drift from the land, urban growth which siphoned off the people, and a loss of regional momentum.

Youngson's contribution to Highland history is, indeed, a dialogue between past and present problems of economic development. His historical and comparative analysis offers little comfort for those who would search for a single solution to the problem of economic and social revival. He shows that the planners in the decades after Culloden employed policies which were not radically dissimilar to those being followed two centuries later. Today, with the help of the discovery of off-shore oil, and a much reduced population, the Highlands and Islands Development Board operates in rather more propitious circumstances. Yet Youngson's account demonstrates that, in such a region, the achievement of most kinds of economic development, whether via oil, timber, wool, kelp or manufacturing industry, almost always alters the character of the region, and is likely to drain the agricultural population into a few growth points, or stimulate them to emigrate altogether.

III

The controversy over the economics of the clearances is paralleled by the present-day debate on optimal policies for Highland economic development. Indeed the difficulty of identifying the appropriate engines for growth in contemporary northern Scotland has persuaded some historians to give greater emphasis to the problems of landlords during the age of the clearances. And of course current problems are less severe than those of the overpopulated, constricted economy, of, say, the 1840s. Today the Highlands face difficulties of depopulation and rising unemployment, superimposed upon which has been the rapid growth of an oil industry.

This is not the place to rehearse the debate on recent Highland development, but several of the current lines of argument may be outlined. The government has acknowledged a positive role in the region for some years, and by the 1960s contributed one-half of total regional income; but until the creation of the Highlands and Islands Development Board in 1965 much of its programme was *ad hoc* and uncoordinated. In an article published in 1963, David

Simpson[11] claimed that the first priority of the region was to staunch the continuing depopulation. This could be achieved only by a co-ordinated system of policies designed to create employment and to neutralise the disadvantages of distance and small-scale production. He believed that 'Any programme of regional economic development must eventually rely upon the proliferation of new industries, which can frequently be classified as manufacturing,' and he advocated a much greater use of economic analysis in the design of the planning programme. He pointed out that the provision of social infrastructure had not been sufficient to promote economic development in a backward region; greater off-setting advantages were required to encourage enterprise into the region. Employment in the Highlands had declined despite large investments in, for example, hydro-electricity plant; expenditures in traditional industries had not been successful and there had been inadequate calculation of the relative productivity of alternative investments of government capital. Simpson stated 'that only the introduction of new industries can provide the savings and employment necessary to maintain a Highland population'. These arguments had been put at various times for two centuries.

One of the starting points of Simpson's exposition was that 'the political objectives in the Highlands are generally agreed', which implies that the rest of the country would, for a lengthy period, be prepared to subsidise the development of the region at considerable expense to the southern taxpayer. The evolution of government policy has, of course, indicated varying measures of acceptance of this doctrine, but it did not pass uncontested. Just as there were people in the early nineteenth century who said that there was no sensible alternative to clearance and emigration, so there have been economists who argue that government expenditure in the Highlands is a waste of money. The case was put by D. I. Mackay and N. K. Buxton in the mid-1960s. After considering the costs of generating and sustaining employment in the Highlands they reached the stark verdict that 'there is no economic case for the development of the Highland area; ... the economic solution to the "Highland problem" is to induce the movement of labour out of, and not the movement of capital into, the area'. In their estimation the economic cost of redevelopment in the Highlands was too high and further depopulation was inevitable; hence they decried the notion of 'bringing work to the workers' as an economic nonsense. They argued that the Highlands had been treated more favourably than other more deserving regions and that socio-political considerations had prevailed over economic criteria.[12]

In many respects the context of Highland development has been altered by the discovery of oil off the northern coasts. The finding of a prized raw material has tended to revive the debate about the politico-economic status of the region, and about the origins of its relative retardation within the national economy. Some of the recent debate, drawing upon notions of 'dependency', connects the Highlands to broader theoretical issues in economic development. The most sustained public discussion arose from the publications of a pamphlet on Highland policy-making by a visiting Canadian social anthropologist, J. I. Prattis, who sought to reassess the causes of 'marginality' and 'peasantness' in the Highland economy, and to challenge the alleged assumptions of regional policy. Prattis attacked what he regarded as the neo-classical errors of government policy, and cast his explanation in terms which recalled the internal colonialism thesis developed by Hechter. Prattis claimed that the Highlands had been, for several centuries, a dependent exploited region, 'an adjunct economy' of the dominant English economy. The modernisation of the national economy had created and compounded regional disparities in a fashion which was typical of, and inevitable in, a capitalist/industrialist system. Regional disparities were exacerbated as the market economy penetrated the outer zones such as the Highlands, and so 'the marginal sector is used instrumentally by the modern sector and indeed becomes functional to the maintenance of the continual growth of the modern sector'. In this system the dependent region provides resources (such as wool, cattle, kelp, fish, oil) which have little value added by any processing in that region; they are then converted into high-value commodities in the dominant region. Consequently the structure of the primary supplier remains narrow, undiversified and exceedingly vulnerable to market fluctuations — a feature of the Highland experience for two centuries — and inequalities between the regions are reinforced. National government policy has been geared, invariably, to the dominant sectors of the economy. For Prattis the history of the Highlands has been an example of excessive integration within the national economy since it rendered 'the Highlands particularly prone to boom and bust economic cycles with accompanying social and cultural consequences of a disastrous nature'. The relationship has been disadvantageous to the Highlands in leaving its people with few 'adaptive options'. The region, highly susceptible to external shock, has had no possibility of diversification when cycles of economic activity turned downwards. The successive exploitation of kelp, cattle, sheep, fishing and oil has yielded only short-term benefits to the region, but no lasting and self-generating economic structure. 'Once the boom has passed the local population will once more have to cope with and adapt for economic decline', because 'control' over capital power, and decision-making were not made available to producers of the area'.

Prattis extends his thesis further and contends that the social attitudes — i.e. 'peasantness' — have been an expression of 'a retreat response' of a people faced with repeated economic collapse. The policy of government towards the Highlands, in this analysis, is wrong, because it seeks to expose the region still more nakedly to the forces of the market. The only progressive policy for the region is one which seeks to alter the relationship of dependency between the Highlands and the rest of the nation. All in all, this interpretation is similar to that of Hunter and Hechter, which sees the Highlands as the victim of internal exploitation, as 'an undifferentiated colony of the United Kingdom'.[13] Prattis regards the Highland experience as a demonstration of the diametrical opposition of interests within (i.e. between classes) and beyond (i.e. between the region and the nation). Speculative and somewhat mechanical in operation, these ideas lack sufficient empirical testing to carry great persuasive power, but they are useful in bringing attention to the determinants of long-term economic and political change. They are part of a continuing debate about the relations between core and periphery in the process of economic development. Almost invariably the 'dependency' theorists neglect important elements of their case — notably the reciprocal character of economic interdependence, and the balance of costs and benefits between regions. Their thesis has its precursors in the long debate in the Highland question; it still cries out for historical testing. Nor can there be much doubt that an examination of inter-regional relationships is one of the most neglected areas in British economic development.

While the inspiration of Marx has moved many commentators on the Highlands, amongst economic historians there has been an interesting return to the doctrines of Thomas Malthus. The importance of a paper by Michael Flinn is twofold: one, because it follows the most comprehensive examination of Scottish population history yet mounted, and, two, because it provides a measure of the gulf that separates the opposing views on the origins of the Highland problem. The question of population scarcely enters the work of Prattis and Hechter, but to Flinn it was the principal determinant of the shape of social and economic development in the north and west Highlands. He believes that symptoms of overpopulation were clear enough already by 1770, marked by famine, emigration and increasing rents. The full impact was delayed by the increase in food productivity, or by the increased ability to import foodstuffs. Eventually the Malthusian pressures accumulated — worsened by bad harvests, the effect of smallpox vaccination, rising rents, subdivision and demobilisation. Emigration did not draw off enough people from the region. Landlords 'interfered with the natural playing out of the Malthusian drama in a variety of ways': at one stage they encouraged the growth of population, at others they evicted and/or resettled people, and they redistributed income towards themselves by kelp and sheep production. Generally their impact on the Malthusian juggernaut was marginal — the people became increasingly dependent on the potato until the famine of 1846-8 which demonstrated conclusively the reality of the population problem. Total famine was averted by the combined actions of the landlords and the government, and charitable organisations. But the only solution was emigration — 'the only escape from the Malthusian pincers'.

In many respects Flinn's revival of Malthus is a return to the line of argument which runs from Selkirk through Loch and Argyll to Malcolm Gray. It does not exonerate the landlords, but gives priority in any explanation of the Highland problem to an ostensibly autonomous variable. It is difficult, though perhaps not impossible, to reconcile this perspective with the view that the Highlands was continuously debauched by an imperial power to the south. Flinn concludes his case with a challenge:

Highland history of the eighteenth and nineteenth centuries has most commonly been written in terms of tenurial relationships and cultural clashes, but to leave the demographic development out of the pictures is like presenting Hamlet without the Prince of Denmark.[14]

IV

The academic debate about the Highland clearances has been keen enough but reflects only slightly the continuing inflammability of the question in the public mind. Popular excitability on the subject was amply demonstrated in controversy conducted mainly in the columns of the *Scotsman* newspaper in the early months of 1977. The occasion of the dispute was the current Countess of Sutherland's election as Honorary President of the National Mod, the prime celebration of Gaelic culture each year, programmed to be held at Golspie, in East Sutherland, the territorial centre of the aristocratic Sutherland family. In response to the election there was reported 'a storm of protest from Gaels who felt that the descendant of a family who cleared large numbers of Gaels from their land to make way for more profitable sheep should have nothing to do with a Gaelic festival'.[15] It was suggested by the editor of the *West Highland Free Press*, a relatively lively and radical newspaper in Skye, that 'holding the Mod in Dunrobin is a bit like the Jews holding the Festival of Pentecost in a stadium that gave Nuremburg a bad name'.[16] The campaign was successful in that the Countess chose to resign the presidency of the Mod: she agreed that the clearances had been high-handed and ill-advised but held that they were probably well-intentioned. She did not accept that her forebears were guilty, but resigned the honour of the Mod only to avoid demonstrations at Dunrobin during the festival. The debate generated around this question was long-winded and wide-ranging. It exposed not only the condition of the public mind on the question, but also the continuing power of the clearances to excite public feeling in Scotland.

The embattled Countess did not lack defenders. Sir Iain Moncrieff poured scorn on the idea that the sins of the fathers (or mothers perhaps) should descend upon an innocent woman 'who had been miserable about the clearances since she heard of them in childhood'. He abused the writer John Prebble (whose work helped to fire the controversy) for his highly selective history of the activities of nineteenth-century landlords, and for failing to give proper credit to the great financial sacrifices made during the famine of 1847-8 by many landlords, and for failing also to lay due blame on the consortia of creditors who often demanded clearances. Moncrieff pointed out a deficiency in knowledge in that nobody has yet bothered to publish a study of the numerous Highland estates where no clearances took place, nor why their glens are voluntarily just as empty today. Lord Lovat to take but one example not only did not clear, but sheltered many refugees who had been evicted elsewhere.[17]

The Countess herself suggested that the propaganda attack upon her had been the work of 'political journalists' — 'travelling minstrels' who used historical controversy as 'an item of present-day politics'. The clearances had occurred during an era of harshness which had witnessed the French Revolution: the new attack, she observed drily, was an attempt now 'to clear the landlords'. She believed that the controversy was political rather than historical.[18]

The Countess's husband, Charles Janson, complained that the public abuse of the Sutherland family had become a new light industry in Scotland. The clearances, he urged, had been prompted by Lowland and English advisers, in 'a high handed and unwise attempt to rush through agricultural and social reform'. The events needed to be seen in proper perspective; there had been too much sketchy history and worse economics applied to the whole subject.[19] The *Scotsman*'s editorial department also weighed in to support this 'innocent and vulnerable woman'. In its view the controversy had been 'one of the meanest and pettiest episodes to have disfigured Highland politics in recent years'. The attack on the Countess had been activated by 'class hatred', by 'advocates of class warfare' who wished to sweep away the landlord system but had been unable to force their opinions forward with any effect within a democratic society. An editorial offered the *Scotsman*'s own interpretation of the clearances:

for the record let it be stated that the main motive of the Sutherlands, one of the many other landlords who followed the same course, was to improve the wretched conditions of the people on their estates. A way of life was thereby destroyed, but it could probably not have survived in any case. All enlightened opinion agreed at the time that the numbers living on the congested lands in the North had to fall if any economic progress was to be achieved. The correctness of their opinion is proved by the fact that the districts not cleared have since largely cleared themselves through the natural processes of depopulation. The Clearances in fact probably saved the Highlands from the dreadful famines which in the nineteenth century affected rural Ireland, a region of much the same character. What was disgraceful was the manner in which the landlord's policy was carried out on an unresisting people.[20]

These words were greeted with approval by the Professor of Scottish History at the University of Edinburgh, Gordon Donaldson, who declared that the editorial was wholly admirable and refreshing at a time when 'so much that passes for history is the plaything of propagandists'.

These defences, if anything, served mainly to inflame feeling further. The Director of Club Leabhar commented that 'If the Countess and her family are so keen to do something for the Highlands why have they not taken up a land improvement scheme to improve the land they own for agricultural use and put people on it.'[21] Another correspondent asked the Countess to 'hand back to the Scottish people the reported 125,000 acres she inherited'.[22] Yet another angry writer said that the clearances had been hideously callous even if the Highlands were at the time overpopulated. He made the point also that the voluntary exodus from the Highlands, which had paralleled the clearances, had often been caused by 'the exorbitant rents demanded by landlords who had developed expensive tastes in the south'. He believed that the clearances would always rankle in the minds of all Scots.[23]

The newspaper debate was enlivened by a sideshow in which correspondents cited historians against each other. James Hunter also entered the controversy with several provocative contributions. He believed that the history of the clearances was important because it exemplified the general phenomenon of the destruction of traditional societies; moreover landlordism had survived into the twentieth century and continued to dominate the affairs of the region. He claimed that most historians offered intellectual mitigation of the actions of nineteenth-century landlords, and thereby gave succour to a system which had been responsible for atrocities which could be mentioned in the same breath as Dachau and My Lai. He rejected the view that the clearances had saved the Highlands from famine and asserted, without qualification, that the famine and the poverty of the region had been caused by the landlords' policy of clearance and coastal resettlement. He believed that most historians had supported the landlord case and has biased their history by their reliance on estate records — it was too much like constructing a history of the Third Reich from the archives of the Nazi Party. At bottom the issue was one of the ownership of the land, the control of resources and the power to perpetrate policies such as the clearances; it was not a question of individual humanity or cruelty, but rather a matter of the economic system and the structure of ownership.[24] John Prebble, accused of excessive emotion and a lack of balance in his historical judgement, was also moved to enter the debate. He contended that events during the clearances ought to stir the blood, and that as the descendants of the clearing landlords had inherited 'the residual comfort, station and influence', partly as a consequence of the clearances, they really should not 'object to the less tangible legacy of resentment left by those whose bitter misfortune made them possible'.[25]

Amid the polemics there were some correspondents who searched for 'a balanced view' of the clearances wherein there would be a juxtaposition of the positive and negative sides of the story. Another requested more historical research to clarify 'just how much wealth was used to sustain the starving population during the long series of crises'.[26] Another writer thought that much of the debate was merely 'a great deal of misplaced anger and sentimental nonsense'. The clearances were of an age which sent children down the mines for 15 hours a day and, she asked, were there not 'clearances in our city today, when thousands of people have been forcibly ejected (without proper recompense) from their homes and packed into high rise prisons in foreign neighbourhoods, equally reprehensible?' She thought that there was too much hypocrisy in the debate.[27] Another contributor thought that the Sutherland clearances 'were almost virginal in comparison with the diabolical and unpublished activities of other clan chiefs'.[28]

Virtually nothing was clarified by this noisy debate in the Scots newspapers. It certainly exposed a raw nerve in Scottish culture, and it exposed equally a confusion of issues that surround the question. It illustrated 'the deep and continuing feeling of the people involved and of their descendants'. As Rosalind Mitchison has remarked, there is 'a special heat that attaches to the clearances, to the neglect of the other wrongs of the propertyless', itself an interesting and mystifying phenomenon in modern Scotland. As she points out, there are many other examples in Scottish history of changes 'which broke up existing societies and forced difficult adjustments, yet relatively little sentiment is now expended over them. Recall with passion is solely for the highland changes.' And there is no obvious explanation. But the debate demonstrated best of all the difficulty involved in making sense of the history of the clearances — because of the moral, economic, legal, cultural and political issues which are so easily entangled in the issue. The confusion of issues is compounded when the history of the clearances is forced to yield lessons for present-day policies in the Highlands. The debate revealed the narrow base of historical knowledge upon which is built so much confident opinion. But one unequivocally positive benefit flowed from the debate: the Countess of Sutherland agreed to open to scholarship one of the greatest extant sources on Highland history, the Dunrobin Muniments.[29]

V

The public debate of 1977 displayed the inadequacy of historical research on the Highland clearances, as well as a set of philosophical difficulties in conceptualising the nature of the propositions. Among sceptics there had always been a suspicion that further academic research would yield merely quibbling qualification and a mass of detail which would serve only to obfuscate otherwise plain truths. Indeed there are points about the clearances which are patent and inescapable: no one can deny, for instance, that many people were evicted in the years 1780-1855, or that there was considerable suffering, or that the structure of authority in the Highlands permitted landlords to act without restraint, or that emigration and famine accompanied the great tenurial changes and that depopulation has been virtually continuous to the present day, or that the old Highland culture has diminished with the decline of the Gaelic-speaking population.

Unfortunately, awkward and unanswered questions remain, and press beyond the limits of the evidence. It is possible to identify several clusters of such questions. One category of questions relates to the *status quo ante* the clearances. Did the Highland problem pre-date the clearances? What were the levels of social and economic welfare in the old Highland economy? What was the incidence of famine? Was Highland population in an equilibrium which was disrupted only in the second half of the eighteenth century? Did the paternalism of the old system provide security and a humane form of life for the common people? What was the significance of emigration in the old economy? Was the old society moribund or was it capable of accommodating a much larger population and adjusting to radical changes in resource use? Was the demographic upsurge caused by landlord policy at the time of the kelp boom, or was it part of a wider phenomenon beyond the influence of the landowners? How dependent was this economy on externally generated supplies of income and food? Was the value system of the Highlands substantially different from that of the new era? How firm were the communal rights to land in the old system? Without answers to these questions no measure of the impact of the clearances can be achieved. It is the least explored area of Highland history.

The second cluster of questions concerns the actual process of clearance. The extent of violence, even atrocity, has yet to be fully accounted, and so has the degree of racialism that is often said to have accompanied the introduction of sheepfarming. Did the land-lords possess any real choice and were the limits of their actions severely constrained? Was the change in any sense inevitable? What considerations affected the timing and extent of clearance? Did Highland landlords behave with less humanity than landlords elsewhere? Was emigration entirely the result of landlord pressure? In what sense did landlords reap windfall gains and how did they employ such gains in relation to the long-run needs of the economy? What was the impact of differential price trends on the direction of change in the Highlands? Were rents raised more rapidly than in the rest of Britain? Did humanitarian considera-tions deter any landlords from a policy of clearance?

These questions lead into further puzzles about the conse-quences of the agrarian transformation. What was the comparative experience of cleared and uncleared zones within the Highlands? How great was the decline in arable acreage? What was the effect of sheep production on the level of regional income and the distribution thereof? Were the technical requirements of large-scale commercial sheepfarming (especially in the form of capital) so rigid that the economic benefits were almost bound to be restricted to a small proportion of the population? Did the social and economic impact of clearances depend upon conditions such as population density or the availability of alternative employ-ment? Where special provision was made for the people cleared, did such provision create any permanent benefits for sustaining life in the region? What leakages of income from the region were contingent upon the new economic structure? Were the crofts purely the result of clearances and did the levels of welfare diminish in consequence? How did the clearances affect the different layers of population in Highland society? Was there a widespread loss of status? Was there a larger than usual element of speculation in the pressure for clearance? What was the significance of the great flood of land sales in the region in the nineteenth century?

Some of the most fundamental questions are specifically economic: for instance, did the clearances yield a return on capital fully equal to alternative investments? Some questions are essentially demographic, most notably the scale and pace of rural depopulation an its results, compared with the rest of rural Britain. But there is also a series of questions which concerns the historical sociology of the Highlands, a field which James Hunter has begun to explore. The manner in which the people of the Highlands responded to the agrarian transformation is now a living issue in the debate, along with questions about social cohesion and leadership in the community. The roles of the tacksmen, the clergy and the landlords are now receiving systematic study. How capricious was the use of landlord power and how did it compare with its employment in the rest of Britain? Can the landlords as a class be regarded as a failure, and condemned both when they cleared their lands, and when they did not clear? To what degree were the Highlanders 'a depressed ethnic minority'? But perhaps the single most important question is the ever-present but counterfactural question: what would have happened had the clearances not occurred?

From the specific economic and social questions there emerge wider interpretative problems which seek to define the limits of political and economic manoeuvre in the nineteenth century. Central in the emerging literature is the problem of the regional place within national and international contexts — most notably, the question of whether the Highlands, as a peripheral region, was especially disadvantaged in the wider process of British and European industrialisation. Were the interests of this region (perhaps in company with other outlying areas) subordinated to the more powerful demands of the metropolitan pole of the industrial economy? There is an influential school of politico-economic thought which provides a tailor-made rationale of this proposition. In this view the Highland lairds were merely part of, the local agency for, a far larger system of capitalistic exploitation which denuded the

Highlands of the most vital elements for balanced economic development. Highland history is seen as the product of unrestrained market forces on a small region, though the mechanisms of its transmission and its specific forms are not well elucidated.

Few of these accumulating questions have been given clear answers (and the present volume is no exception to this view), and an account of the literature on the clearances over the past two centuries demonstrates the coexistence of contradictory opinions throughout the debate. Many of the questions overlap into areas of economics, ethics, agricultural technique, political theory and so on — in most of which the historian possesses no special competence to pronounce authoritatively on the issues. History has no exclusive wisdom by which, for instance, to judge the morality of past or present behaviour. Modern historians of the clearances may best be judged by their efforts to extend the empirical basis of Highland history, and the methods that have been developed to deepen the interpretation of the clearances.

At the end of two centuries of energetic controversy about the history of the Highlands, perhaps the most encouraging aspect of recent research has been the emergence of studies which are no longer comprehensively overshadowed by the problem of the clearances. The evictions have dominated the perception of the modern Highlands almost to the point of obsession, and have obscured many other vital elements in the explanation of the Highland experience. New studies of neglected aspects are beginning to shake northern studies out of their long-standing insularity. Hence the importance of work such as that of Dr Tom Devine into seasonal migration patterns of Highlanders, which goes far towards explaining the continuing tenacity of crofting in the second half of the nineteenth century.[30] Similarly there are new studies of emigrant Highlanders abroad which are able to explore the integrity (or otherwise) of Highland values in entirely new settings. It may come as a shocking revelation that the immigrant Highlanders sometimes treated racial minorities (for instance, American Indians and Australian Aborigines) with a savagery that is difficult to reconcile with the romantic pastoral image of the Gael. Still more, it is now possible to consult studies in demography which provides indispensable information about the structure of life in the Highlands. No less important have been a number of sorties into the pre-clearance world, notably in the work of David

Stevenson,[31] as well as ·in the sensitive resurrection of the folklore of the eighteenth century by J. L. Campbell, supported by further contributions from Ian Grimble.[32] Penetrating studies of the administration of the annexed estates and the British Fisheries Society have reinforced the work of A. J. Youngson.[33] The great bodies of estate archives for the nineteenth century have yet to be adequately assimilated into scholarship, but there has been good new writing on the history of the deer forests and the local experience of Rousay crofters in Orkney.[34]

Although the quantity of research remains relatively meagre, and although the Highlands has not attracted as sophisticated a body of historical research as, for example, the west of Ireland, nevertheless there has been a clear advance towards a better understanding of the transformation of the region in modern times. When the British universities recover from their present purgation they may be able to devote some resources to advance scholarship on the Highlands. Perhaps the most important priority on the agenda should be to draw the case of the Highlands into a wider and more systematic debate about the process of agrarian transformation and regional adjustment during industrialisation.[35] It is extraordinary that the Highlands figures so little in the history of European modernisation, and greater connection with this debate would benefit both the local and the wider discourse.

Notes

1. See for instance, Eric Richards, 'How Tame were the Highlanders during the Clearances?' *Scottish Studies*, vol. 17 (1973).

2. H. Fairhurst, 'The Surveys for the Sutherland Clearances 1813-1820', *Scottish Studies*, vol. 8 (1964); H. Fairhurst and G. I. Petrie, 'Scottish Clachans II: Lix and Rossal', *Scottish Geographical Magazine*, vol. 80 (1964).

3. J. B. Caird (ed.), *Park: a Geographical Study of a Lewis District* (Nottingham, 1958).

4. E. R. Cregeen, 'Oral Tradition and Agrarian History in the West Highlands' and 'Oral Sources for the Social History of the Scottish Highlands and Islands', *Oral History*, vol. 2 (1974).

5. Phillip Gaskell, *Morvern Transformed* (Cambridge, 1968), p. 9.

6. Ibid., pp. 9, 93, 117.

7. Michael Hechter, *Internal Colonialism: the Celtic Fringe in British National Development, 1536-1966* (London, 1975), p. 32 and Ch. 4.

8. Youngson, *After the Forty Five*, Preface.

9. Ibid., p. 162.

10. Ibid., p. 190.

11. David Simpson, 'Investment, Employment and Government Expenditure in

the Highlands, 1951-60', *Scottish Journal of Political Economy*, vol. 10 (1963).

12. D. I. Mackay and N. K. Buxton, 'The North of Scotland — a Case for Redevelopment?' *Scottish Journal of Political Economy*, vol. 12 (1965).

13. J. I. Prattis, *Economic Structures in the Highlands of Scotland* (The Fraser of Allander Institute Speculative Papers, no. 7, Glasgow, 1977). Mention should also be made of the contributions of a related type made by Ian Carter, e.g. 'The Highlands of Scotland as an Under-developed Region' in E. de Kadt and G. Williams (eds.), *Sociology and Development* (London, 1974), and John Bryden, 'Core-Periphery Problems — the Scottish Case' in Dudley Seers, Bernard Schatter and Marja-Lilsa Kiljunen (eds.), *Underdeveloped Europe* (London, 1979).

14. M. W. Flinn, 'Malthus, Emigration and Potatoes in the Scottish North-West, 1770-1870', in L. M. Cullen and T. C. Smout (eds.), *Comparative Aspects of Scottish and Irish Economic and Social History 1600-1900* (Edinburgh, 1977).

15. Quoted in the *Spectator*, 12 April 1977; see also *Scotsman*, 4 May 1977.

16. *West Highland Free Press* (January 1977).

17. *Scotsman*, 31 January 1977. On Lovat see the contrary evidence in Richards, *Highland Clearances*, p. 202.

18. *Scotsman*, 8 January 1977.

19. Ibid., 6 January 1977.

20. Ibid., 8 January, 1977.

21. Ibid.

22. Ibid., 11 January 1977.

23. Ibid.

24. Ibid., 20 January 1977, 22 January 1977, 2 February 1977.

25. Ibid., 20 January 1977, 5 February 1977.

26. Ibid., 22 January 1977.

27. Ibid., 14 January 1977.

28. Ibid., 17 January 1977.

29. Ibid., 21 January 1977, 5 February 1977, 15 February 1977, 1 May 1982; Rosalind Mitchison, 'The Highland Clearances', *Scottish Economic and Social History*, vol. I (1981), p. 11.

30. T. M. Devine, 'Temporary Migration and the Scottish Highlands in the Nineteenth Century', *Economic History Review*, vol. 32 (1979).

31. David Stevenson, *Alasdair Maccolla and the Highland Problem in the Seventeenth Century* (Edinburgh, 1980).

32. J. L. Campbell (ed.), *A Collection of Highland Rites and Customes, Copied by Edward Lloyd from the Manuscript of the Rev. James Kirkwood (1650-1709) and Annotated by him with the Aid of the Rev. John Beaton* (The Folklore Society, Cambridge, 1975); Ian Grimble, *The World of Rob Donn* (Edinburgh, 1979).

33. Jean Dunlop, *The British Fisheries Society 1786-1893* (Edinburgh, 1978); Annette M. Smith, *Jacobite Estates of the Forty Five* (Edinburgh, 1982); *The Rev. Dr John Walker's Report on the Hebrides in 1764 and 1771*, Margaret M. McKay (ed.), (Edinburgh 1980); Virginia Wills (ed.), *Reports on the Annexed Estates, 1755-1769* (Edinburgh, 1973), *Statistics of the Annexed Estates, 1755-1756* (Edinburgh, 1974).

34. W. P. L. Thomson, *The Little General and the Rousay Crofters* (Edinburgh, 1981); W. Orr, *Deer Forests, Landlords and Crofters* (Edinburgh, 1982).

35. It should become possible to relate the Highland experience to the recent revival of the primarily intra-Marxist debate about the transition from feudal modes of production to capitalism. Among the interesting contentions have been that there exist realistic alternatives to the simple elimination of the peasant as a requirement of economic progress, and that a peasantry can make positive adjustments to the imperatives of demographic and economic change. Related points are mentioned briefly in Ch. 19 below.

PART TWO

EMIGRATION AND THE HIGHLAND CLEARANCES

The Highland diaspora is a huge one, scattered all the way from Surbiton to San Francisco, and it clings tenaciously to the myth of the good life from which one's ancestors were rudely expelled.

Derek Cooper, *Hebridean Connection*

7
THE HIGHLAND EMIGRATIONS OF THE EIGHTEENTH CENTURY

The Country of Sutherland is the most remote in Great Britain, and also the most rugged and least improvable ... the misery of the inhabitants arising from the severity of the soil prompts them to frequent emigration.

Camden's *Britannia* (1586)[1]

A large, but unknown, proportion of the population of the Highlands departed the region in the age of the clearances. As always, the popular recollection of the story is dominated by dramatic images: the ragged remnants of a once-proud peasantry hounded from the hills by the factors and police were driven aboard disease-ridden ships bound for outlandish colonies, their families broken, their ministers compliant, and the collective agony sounded by the pibroch and the wailing of pathetic humanity. It is a tale of 'inconsolable anguish' which parallels the Irish orthodoxy identified and criticised by Patrick O'Farrell; it depicts emigration as draining the life blood of the country, inflicting untold heartbreak and misery on those who left and those who stayed, a monstrous continuing eviction contrived by the English.[2] The Highland version is no less histrionic than the Irish. A recent textbook of Scottish economic history claims that 'emigration from the Highlands became a major festering sore in Scottish social and economic life'.[3]

Emigration is a central and difficult issue in the history of the clearances not merely because it resides at the core of the emotional response, but because it suggests a possible measure of the abuse of power by the landlords. Were the Highlanders primarily expelled from the region or were other causes at work? Was landlord pressure exerted directly or indirectly? Was emigration greater from the Highlands than from other regions; more especially, was it greater than from other non-industrialised and

179

primarily pastoral regions of Western Europe? Was it part of the general evacuation of the increment of population growth from Europe's western periphery in the nineteenth century? Was emigration, by its nature, necessarily a tragedy for the people and the region? What became of the Highlanders? These questions are integral to the history of the clearances.

It is perfectly clear that emigration pre-dated the sheep clearances, and that the exodus from the Highlands continued after the period of the clearances, and has remained an important political issue to the present day. Indeed the modern perception of the 'Highland Problem' is dominated by the facts of depopulation. If the clearances were a cause of emigration, they were likely to have been part of a larger set of causes. There is good evidence of both seasonal and permanent emigration from the Highlands by the beginning of the eighteenth century. The long-established seasonal migration of Highlanders to the southern harvests was complemented by the emergence of an annual attendance at the northeastern fisheries, and the cattle trade also opened windows on another world. Each increased awareness of the possibilities existing outside the region, and indicated a surprising geographical mobility for a population which was fundamentally a traditional peasantry. Permanent emigration abroad emerged in the transatlantic exodus of the early eighteenth century, and even more strongly in the 1770s. In subsequent decades, the settlement of America helped to drain much of the demographic increase of the region, eventually aided by outflows to Australia, New Zealand and South Africa. Similarly, there can be no doubt that Highlanders were increasingly attracted to the Scottish Lowlands by the higher wages of the south and by the common processes of chain migration throughout these decades. But it is conventional to regard most of the emigration as a response to expulsive Malthusian pressures. The most visible force was, of course, the landlord policy of eviction. This was arguably only the most obvious expression of a broader range of pressures which extruded people from the region. In general terms it can be argued that the ongoing structural changes in the economy created an environment relatively inhospitable for a large part of a population which nevertheless continued to grow until the mid-nineteenth century.

Flinn, as we have seen in the previous chapter, indeed argues that the population of the Highlands continued to grow in the Highlands only because a number of essentially temporary factors permitted their retention — most notably the introduction of potatoes and the labour-intensive production of kelp; but, in the long run, a massive exodus was inevitable. Kelp and potatoes fostered an illusion of permanent improvement, but left the region repeatedly vulnerable to famine. Flinn claims that 'the demographic role of the potato in Scotland ... was almost certainly to retain populations that would have otherwise have emigrated'. In this interpretation the potato acted to raise production marginally above the minimum requirements of an expanding population, but failed utterly to create a long-run security of peasant subsistence.[4] Flinn's view, while not entirely discounting the exacerbating influence of sheepfarming and land availability, accords fundamental priority to the population variable: in essence, it was the growth of population beyond the real productive capacity of agriculture that made emigration inevitable.

The Malthusian interpretation of population and emigration trends in the Highlands faces some genuine difficulties when it confronts the significant (and not entirely consistent) variations in the pattern of dispersal from the region. Emigration was not solely a response to population pressure: the areas most threatened by demographic disaster were least assisted by emigration. The exodus of people from the north and north-west of the Highlands — where population pressure was severest — lagged far behind the migration from the better-off districts to the south and east. Distance from the cities and industries of the south appears to have been the most important single determinant of the rate of migration.

The dramatic emigrations of clansmen across the Atlantic were almost certainly of considerably smaller quantitative significance than the loss of Highland population to the Lowlands. From R. D. Lobban's close analysis of Greenock, and the Clyde, it is clear that the invasion of Highland migrants had begun as early as the seventeenth century and that by the 1790s between 20 and 30 per cent of the population of Greenock was Highland-born. This internal migration in Scotland occurred in a context of growing commercial contact between the north and south in the eighteenth century, doubtless assisted by radically reduced coastal transport costs between the regions. Lobban's work has undermined the notion that the main force causing migration was the behaviour of evicting landlords who expelled the people into the southern cities. Instead, he emphasises the magnetic attractive power of the south and increasing awareness of the benefits of town life as prime factors inducing the migrations. Equally, Lobban argues that demographic trends in the north were irresistible and that the old Highland society inhibited and restricted the people, and effectively crushed their upward mobility. To emphasise these elements necessarily diminishes the significance of the landlords' expulsive policies. Lobban argues that 'a substantial number of Highlanders ... were quite glad to shake the dust and mud of the glens from all their feet to seek a new life in more congenial climes'.[5] This view rejects the suggestion that emigration was in any sense a tragedy for either the people or the region. Its strength derives from its effort to see the full range of motivation and to avoid unicausal explanation.

The main questions which arise in the relationship between emigration and the clearances concern the dimensions and the avoidability of the exodus, and the balance of voluntary and involuntary departures from the Highlands.[6] The literature of the clearances has always been much concerned with the ethics and methods of induced emigration before and during the period of the famine of the 1840s. No less fundamental is the problem of whether the Highlands could have been organised to accommodate the much augmented population at a tolerable level of welfare without recourse to emigration. The destination of the emigrants and their subsequent history also merit attention. Much of the story has never been written. But the main themes concern the motives and timing of the departure of the Highland peasantry.[7] Their evacuation of the Highlands was a discontinuous movement and only with the greatest reluctance did the people obey Malthusian commands. The peasantry maintained a tenacious grip on what little land it retained, and for long it resisted the forces pressing it out of the region, and the attractions of a less tenuous life in the south. Between these two choices was the compromise which sustained the old life for many decades — as Dr Devine has argued recently, seasonal migration, even into the late nineteenth century, was 'a consequence of the desire to retain a foothold on the land and, as such, provided a vivid demonstration of the strength and resilience of an old established peasant society'.[8]

I

The incidence of migration, temporary or permanent, is not necessarily a definitive indication of a region's inability to support its people: much of the exodus from Britain in the nineteenth century occurred during periods of substantial improvement in the standards of living. Emigration was propelled by complex forces but almost invariably expressed a prospect of material betterment. In the history of Highland emigration it is likely that various expulsive pressures strengthened after the 1770s, and operated concurrently, and in shifting degrees, with 'pull forces' elsewhere, but at no point is the picture entirely clear.

Even before Culloden, North America was regarded both as a dumping ground for superfluous tenants, and as a great opportunity for investment and self-advancement. The prospect of profit from land grants persuaded proprietors in Scotland to promote emigration from their own estates; these ventures were sometimes given greater impetus by a desire to rid the land of the unwanted. Thus Maclean of Coll had endeavoured to ship away many of his clansmen when the colony of Georgia was being developed in 1733.[9] In 1735 the Governor of New York invited 'loyal Protestant Highlanders to settle in the lands between the Hudson River and the Northern lakes', and Captain Lachlan Campbell of Islay persuaded some 80 families to settle on a grant of 30,000 acres. In 1739 Neil McNeil led 350 Highlanders from Argyll to North Carolina.[10] There were other sporadic promotions before the more concerted migrations of the 1770s. How many Highlanders were shipped off as indentured labourers, it is impossible to say; in 1739 there were allegations that Macleod and other Skye landowners were still forcing unwanted tenants on to servant ships supplying American plantations. But some landlords were more reluctant; efforts to raise recruits for Georgia in Sutherland in 1735 faced resistance from gentry who were 'not so very favourable for fear of losing those poor creatures, who they took on to be their property as much as their Cattle'. Several early emigrations were led by tacksmen who organised large groups of kinsmen across the Atlantic, especially to North Carolina. One colonial developer appealed directly to proprietorial aspirations when he promised John Duncan Campbell 'a plan that will not only put money in your pocket with little trouble, but also secure you a property not unworthy of a Highland chieftain'.[11] Many Highlanders engaged in the Seven Years War in North America elected to remain and to attach themselves to larger settlement schemes. As Dr Johnson himself reported, 'Many men of considerable wealth have taken with them their train of labourers and dependants; and if they continue the feudal scheme of polity, may establish new clans in another hemisphere.' The poorest emigrants could always resort to the device of indenture which provided them with passage money in exchange for future labour.[12] The pre-1780 movements, either seasonal or permanent, cannot be attributed to the displacement effect of sheep but they may have been expressions of changing circumstances in the Highlands: there is evidence of varying degrees of land hunger, of the shadow of famine, or radical alterations in land use, and of the pressure of landlords on the backs of the people and the tacksmen. The context in which Highland emigration evolved was unusual, for here was a traditional peasantry committed to a perennial search for secure land tenure, yet increasingly involved in regular seasonal migration to the southern harvests and in the rapid expansion of military service at the end of the eighteenth century.[13]

Large groups of Highlanders from particular localities continued to cross the Atlantic to form new communities thoughout the century, especially in North Carolina. In 1739, for instance, 350 people from Argyll settled in the Cross Creek district of that colony, and between 1768 and 1772 it appears that a further 2,000 Highlanders went to the same colony. Georgia received 100 of the Mackintosh family in 1735 and there were other similar large migrations. It is generally thought that these people were led across the Atlantic by dissatisfied tacksmen, who refused to accept their loss of status in the changing world of 'improvement' in the post-Culloden years. The tacksmen were being pressed out of the social and economic system by landlords who were determined to reorganise their lands and to take advantage of increased cattle prices; the willingness of the people to follow their natural leaders reflected their poverty, the recurrence of famine, the goad of rising rents and the solidarity of social relations. The availability of land in America, the enticing propaganda of agents and letters of kinsmen completed the task of persuasion. It is significant that small tenants on the Forfeited Estates — men who held long secure leases — were not tempted to emigrate.[14] As Professor Donaldson has said, 'There were developments, which stimulated emigration long before clearance for sheep was so much as thought of,' and after 1775 'it was not difficult for a body of tenants, independent of the tacksmen's leadership, to initiate the technique which the tacksmen had pioneered'.[15] Yet, though these emigrations undoubtedly pre-dated the clearances, the manner in which they were generated was not necessarily different in kind from the later exodus. Both before and during the clearances, emigration was usually an expression of the pressure exerted both by landlord and by population growth on the meagre subsistence resources of the region. We do not know enough of the pre-1770 period to say whether or not the pressure of landlords operated in tandem with quasi-Malthusian forces. But it is clear that the people in general were in a highly suggestible state of mind for emigration.

By the time of the visit of Samuel Johnson and James Boswell to the West Highlands and Islands in 1773, the emigration to America had become large and disturbing. The whole question obsessed the mind of the proprietors, many of whom were caught in a dilemma of their own making. There was, according to Johnson, 'an epidemical fury of emigration', fed by a 'general discontent' in the Highlands, caused by a rapid increase in rents.[16] It was a clear indication of landlord pressure on the tenantry, a trend not exclusive to the Highlands but less tolerable at the prevailing levels of subsistence. The numbers of people involved were comparable to those associated with the clearances half a century later. In 1771, for instance, 500 people left Islay and 370 from Skye; in the next year 200 went from Sutherland, and, in 1773, 250 migrants embarked from Fort George, 308 from Fort William and a further 775 from northerly Stromness. Many of these groups were, apparently, guided abroad by well-to-do tacksmen, 'who thought in terms of reproducing in America the social conditions familiar in Scotland'.[17] They were in a position to buy property in America and to finance the entire migration, much attracted by publicity which extolled the freedom and prosperity of the colonies. The tacksmen were frequently men of substance who carried with them considerable capital, and were able to think positively of the advantages offered by America. With them were smaller tenantry, more likely to be pressed to the limits of their resources, who carried with them quite small savings. Others in these emigrant groups were more desperate, facing extreme privation if they remained in the Highlands under the new regime of rapidly inflating rents. These contrasts reflected the unequal distribution of income in the Highlands. The more affluent of the emigrants indeed carried with them substantial capital realised from the final sale of the cattle, the main asset of the community in the mid-eighteenth-century Highland economy.

The susceptibility of the common people to the idea of emigration was greatly intensified by recurrent shortfalls in the harvest, and the vicissitudes of the cattle trade. From Sutherland in 1763 and in the near-famine season of 1771-2, there was large-scale emigration to North America. It was described as 'a sort of madness among the Common People', who were provoked by 'the want of victuals' and 'the oppression they meet from their Masters the Tacksmen'.[18] This was one of several reports in these years suggesting that both tacksmen and landlords were oppressive, and that the source of the pressure made little difference to the smaller tenantry. The severity of the crisis of spring 1782 was attested by many reports from the Highlands. In Ullinish cattle had died and the people were without seed corn and were close to starving.[19] Cattle also died in Sutherland where Pennant describes crowds of poor people 'dispirited and driven to despair by bad management ... emaciated with hunger', trekking to the east coast in search of a meal ship. It was also reported that

> Numbers of the miserable of this country are now migrating: they wandered in a state of depression; too poor to pay, they mostly sell themselves for their passage, preferring a temporary bondage in a strange land, to starving for life on their native soil.[20]

There is, however, some discrepancy in the reports about the conditions of the migrants from Sutherland. The *Edinburgh Evening Courant* in November 1773 claimed that 1,500 people had left Sutherland for North America in the previous two years and that though the passage cost £3 10s each, every emigrant took an average of £4 in his pocket, an amount equal to the entire rental of the estate.[21] Yet it would be wrong to deduce that the departing peasants were wealthy: the money was almost certainly raised by the sale of the only source of income that the people possessed, that is their black cattle. Unable to compete with the large stock-farmers, they therefore sold off their only asset. As another newspaper reported of the Sutherland migrants in August 1772: 'The cause of this emigration they assign to be the want of the means of livelihood at home, through the opulent graziers engrossing the farms, and turning them into pasture.'[22]

Any analysis of the evidence about the emigrations of the 1770s must confront the mixture of adverse circumstances, desperation, opportunism and folly which generated the exodus. America indeed was a dream and a panacea to many. The settlement of Pictou, Nova Scotia, in July 1773 by the passengers of the ship *Hector* exemplified much of the story. Embarked from Loch Broom, Wester Ross, predominantly in family groups of five, they had been recruited by the agent of a land grantee in the new colony. They were given a farm lot and promise of provisions for a year. The historian of Pictou described how these people were 'allured by the prospect of owning a farm', and eagerly embraced the proposal. Smallpox and dysentry aboard the *Hector* took their toll of the human cargo, and the survivors of the voyage arrived to face uncleared forests, unknown Indians, extreme weather and inadequate provisions. Their early years were marked by privation: at the start they were forced to subsist on lobster and shellfish; in their frustration they mounted a brief rebellion against the store-masters, and it was not long before they became heavily dependent on potatoes. Nevertheless they were the vanguard of Scottish settlement in the region and their arduous pioneering story was repeated in many parts of the colonial world in the following 75 years. A chain of migration was established between Nova Scotia and the West Highlands.[23]

II

The poverty of the common Highland people was notorious throughout Scotland. In 1785 it was said that:

> The Highland poor have of late become so numerous in the Lowlands that some towns positively refuse them admittance — 'We are eat up, say they, with beggars.' Thus the poor creatures, especially women, children and old people are driven from place to place, as nuisances in society, and unworthy of existence, though they require nothing more than the coarsest gifts of nature, which Britons in general would spurn at.[24]

The emigrations of the 1770s were propelled by the revolt of tacksmen against rent increases and a loss of status, and by the general poverty of the small tenantry. To this was added some localised religious disaffection among the last vestiges of the Catholic population in the western isles. A departing tacksman leading Glenalladale people to Prince Edward Island in March 1772 expressed a general alienation. 'Emigrations', he said, 'are like to demolish the Highland Lairds and very deservedly.' He described the economic context of their departure: 'We have a very severe winter, last harvest failed entirely: Meal is scarce and our Cattle will be lost, and of Small Price, [and] under these Circumstances they have no reason to regret it who leave the Highlands.'[25]

The scale of the exodus created alarm among some of the leaders of Highland society. In Ross-shire in 1772 there was anger that certain landowners actively encouraged emigration, and one churchman exclaimed, 'What is a country without inhabitants, what are lands without people, what is … a minister's charge without parishioners?'[26] This pervasive fear of depopulation prompted the Earl of Seaforth to condemn the government's failure to appreciate the seriousness of the emigrations; he feared also that the disgruntled tacksmen were flitting the country without squaring their debts.[27] The unpublished journal of Mathew Culley's 'Tour in Scotland of 1775' provided some relatively unprejudiced observations of a well-informed and perspicacious Northumberland grazier. He had very little doubt about the causes of the recent expatriation of Highlanders:

> We found too good evidence that the chief reason why the poor people migrated to America, who had lately left this country, was entirely owing to the tyranny under which they groaned from Donald Macdonald of the Isles, and other chieftains who oppressed these poor vassals so much by raising their rents as to force them, by a voluntary Banishment to seek their bread which their native country denied them, in the inhospitable provinces of Canada.

Culley said that the lairds had increased rents without showing the people the means by which they could improve their lands. In one case, according to Culley, a landlord had refused to lower his rents or pay compensation for the houses left behind by the emigrants. In response, the people, 300 in all, had simply set fire to their own property to deny the landlord any gain from their departure. It was an unpublicised and unprecedented act of social protest, hardly equalled in the entire history of the Highland clearances.[28] Culley's references to emigration raise questions not only about the alleged passivity of the common Highlanders in face of adversity, but also about the inadequate distinction often made between voluntary and involuntary emigration. A radical elevation of rents was as effective as clearance in causing the people to leave; the effect of famine was not much different.

Unquestionably in the 1770s landlord pressure took the form of inflated rents rather than eviction. Fortunately there is specific and direct testimony about one group of 280 migrants who departed the Highlands in 1774 by a ship from Thurso, headed for Wilmington in North Carolina. The vessel ran into severe storms and was lucky to find shelter in Shetland where the distressed passengers were thrown on local charity. The passengers were closely interviewed in Lerwick before their re-embarkation for America, and a detailed report was forwarded to the Treasury.[29] Even allowing for the natural propensity of emigrants to focus upon their complaints, the evidence of the Lerwick interviews is graphic and convincing. They came from estates in Caithness and Sutherland and complained bitterly of the effects of famine, high rents and excessive labour services; their testimonies also demonstrated that a chain of emigration already operated between the Northern Highlands and Carolina. Elizabeth McDonald was an unmarried servant of Farr parish, aged 21, who was emigrating because her friends had already gone to America, and 'had assured her that she would get much better Service and greater Encouragement in Carolina than in her own Country'. Hector Macdonald was a 75-year-old farmer from Langwell, emigrating with three grown sons and two grandchildren, because his rent had been tripled at a time when cattle prices had halved and the cost of corn was rising steeply. 'He suffered much by the death of cattle, and still more by oppressive services exacted by the factor, being obliged to work with his people and cattle for 40 days and more each year, without a bit of bread'. William Macdonald of Lairg spoke of the failure of his crops, the inflation of rents and the excessive price of meal which he attributed to the demands of distilling in the locality: 'his Circumstances were much straitened, so that he could no longer support his Family at Home'. Hugh Matheson, a 32-year-old farmer of Kildonan with three small children, also faced ruin from the pressure of prices and rent.

Some of the respondents blamed the factors, some the tacksmen, some the landlords. George Grant, a young married farmer of Kildonan, said he emigrated 'because crops failed, so that he was obliged to buy four months provisions in a year, and at the same time the price of Cattle was reduced more than One half'. Alex Sinclair of Reay gave as his reason that 'the Tacksman of Sir John Sinclair's Estate demanded an advanced Rent and arbitrary Services, which in the present Distresses of the Country could not be complied with without ruin'. Shopkeepers and tradesmen emigrated because the people were too poor to buy their services. Aenas McLeod of Tongue 'Goes to Wilmington in North Carolina where he proposes to live by day labour, being informed that one day's wages will support him a week': he left behind high rents, lo cattle prices and a regime in which 'he was harrassed and oppressed with Arbitrary Services daily called for without wages or maintenance'. William Sutherland of Caithness was also prepared to exchange his status as farmer for that of day labourer: he had lost all his cattle in 1772 and since then was

> for a farm of 40/- Rent, obliged to perform with his Family and his Horses so many and so arbitrary Services to his Landlord at all times of the Year, but especially in Seedtime and Harvest, that he could not ... raise as much Corn as serve his Family for six months.

He had learned that Carolina was so fertile that it would raise three crops a year,

> so that one man's labour will maintain a Family of Twenty Persons. He has no Money, therefore proposes to employ himself as a Day labourer, his Wife can spin and sew, and he has heard of many going out in the same way who are now substantial Farmers.

The testimonies of the Lerwick emigrants demonstrated the depth of the subsistence crisis in the Highland cattle economy in 1772-3. The more stringent exaction of long-standing labour services clearly exacerbated their difficulties, while the price of grain, utterly crucial to cattle producers who depended upon imports from lowland Caithness, had reduced many to poverty.

The Lerwick evidence provides a penetrating focus upon the pressures of ordinary life in the Northern Highlands in the 1770s. Yet, though these people complained eloquently of their poverty, of the blighting effects of frost, and the aggression of their superiors, they were relatively middling people in the ranks of this peasant society, being farmers possessing cattle and employing servants, and able to pay their passages across the Atlantic. They were not the common people who were, presumably, several degrees worse off.

In the following year, 1775, Sir James Grant of Grant (one of the founders of the Highland Society) wrote to the Lord Advocate of Scotland to point out that the Highland emigrations were continuing despite the current political troubles that were convulsing the American colonies. The British government, he observed, had failed to prevent emigrant vessels departing for America, and indeed there were no regulations.

> for the preservation of his majesty's subjects, and more immediately of the poor deluded people, who in great numbers I am informed [intend] sailing with their wives and families this spring, without knowing to what hardships they may be exposed. My heart bleeds for them.

Humanitarian concern was much intensified by the rising fear of depopulation. Grant felt that the question was urgent because many more Highlanders were committed to depart in the coming May, and he said that the government should act to prevent it: 'it will show the Highlanders that his Majesty attends to their safety'. He advocated a policy by government that would create home employment because these people 'were a valuable set of people, who were always ready to fit [sic] for King and Country when required' — a sanguine remark only thirty years after Culloden. Grant predicted that the

> frenzy will extend universally if proper means are not taken to prevent it. It is in the power at present of any [pidling?] merch^t to carry off Hundreds and as the Highlanders are so connected by intermarrying, you will easily see how far that may extend. These sort of people hire a ship, and by enticing people to emigrate not only secure a free passage for themselves, but I am told make considerable profit besides — so that it is really now a species of low traffick.[30]

Grant's fears were matched by those of Lord Justice Clerk Miller, who was filled with concern about the emigration which affected not merely this lower class of people, 'but some of the better sort of farmers and mechanics, who are in good circumstances, and can live very comfortably at home'. He feared that, eventually, the transatlantic emigration would 'effectively depopulate this country as the mines of Peru have depopulated Spain'.[31] The ease with which the people were enticed may reflect their relations with the landlords, and the pressure of rising rents.

Hector St John Crevecoeur's description of the circumstances of an emigrant party from Barra to North America in 1770 is one of the most frequently cited accounts of a Highland emigration. The Barra folk had been 'driven by poverty, and other adverse causes, to a foreign land, in which they knew nobody'. They had travelled in a state wracked by distress and fear, pale and emaciated, and loaded with children. Elemental poverty rather than oppression was the cause of their departure. Of Barra, one man said: 'It is cold, the land is thin, and there are too many of us, which are the reasons that some are come to seek their fortunes here'; he added that 'could they have obtained but necessary food, they would not have left it; for it was not in consequence of oppression, either from their patriarch or the government, that they had emigrated'. He remarked, 'we have no such trees as I see here, no wheat, no kine, no apples ... [Here] We have no poor ... we are all alike, except our laird; but he cannot help anybody.'[32] In its sense of social harmony the story of the Barra emigrants seems to have contrasted with that of other people from the Hebrides.

The migrant passage was sometimes unalloyed horror. There exists a retrospective account of a passage from the Highlands to North Carolina in 1773. A ship had carried 451 people, of whom 25 had no berth or bed provided; their water supply had been totally inadequate, and the water barrels so contaminated with the residue of tobacco and indigo that the people could not drink it. Twenty-three people died, and the rest arrived 'in the most exhausted and debilitated state'.[33] Nevertheless the most recent historian of these emigrations has argued that opponents of the exodus exaggerated the squalor and dangers of the passage, and that the oral tradition has 'heightened for dramatic and polemic effect' the entire story of the early Highland settlers in North America.[34] Certainly, in the longer run, conditions in America proved sufficiently propitious to encourage a continuous chain of migration. Alexander Shaw described the settlement of a body of migrants in a letter to Lord Dartmouth in October 1775:

There is now a numerous body of the sons and grandsons of the first Scotch highland settlers, besides the later emigrants who retain that enthusiastic love for the country from which they are descended, which indeed scarce a highlander ever loses, that they will support its dignity at every risk. The Governor has attached them very strongly to him, as well as the later emigrants by many services he had had opportunities of doing them. Many highland gentlemen are now in that country, several of whom had been officers, and still retain their influence among the people.[35]

Subsequent historical research has confirmed the special identity which was retained by these early communities of North American Highlanders, even though the transatlantic feudalism predicted by some contemporary observers did not develop.[36]

The significance of the pre-clearance emigration, especially of the 1770s, has remaned contentious in the literature. Margaret Adam[37] argued that it was a gross error to regard these early migrations as the product of poverty and distress. She drew attention to the relative opulence and high social standing of many of the leaders of the movements, notably in 'the prosperous emigration of the seventies', and argued that the exodus was more the expression of the frustrated aspirations of the tacksmen whom she regarded as the true oppressors of the people. However, it is now more common to regard the emigration as symptomatic of a rising Malthusian pressure on a poor region which was failing to industrialise. There was, in the words of Michael Flinn, a recognition by the people that they were 'in danger of outgrowing their own capacity to feed themselves'.[38] Though there were periods of remission during the coming decades, there was a general continuity of pressure in the repeated release of population from the region, sometimes given local urgency by clearing landlords. Recurrent emigration was almost certainly the normal experience of this society even before the clearances, and it is likely that that upward surge in the rate of demographic increase at the end of the eighteenth century increased the propensity to leave the homeland. This was a common experience in the less favoured areas of Western Europe, but was subject to landlord policy which could either restrict or accelerate the movement.

Unfortunately the accounting of movements of people into and out of the region is incomplete. Much migration was temporary, much was associated with military service, some of it was illegal, and some of it passed without public notice. Contemporary estimates varied wildly and may have been inflated at the behest of politically motivated landlords wishing to hold back the tide. On the other hand a much used source, the *Scots Magazine*, recorded only about a quarter of all sailings when tested against Port Records. As Michael Flinn remarked, there is 'no means of knowing how many ships passed registration', and it is impossible to be either precise or comprehensive about Scottish emigration before 1825. Despite these manifold hazards, I. C. C. Graham has estimated that 9,511 people left the Highlands for America in the years 1768 to 1795. There were much greater contemporary guesses. Thomas Garnett thought that 30,000 emigrated in the years 1773 to 1775; John Knox said that more than 20,000 left between 1763 and 1773, and the modern American historian Meyer believes that Garnett's estimate was closest to the truth.[39] Even less is known about the exodus to the Lowlands during those years, though it may well have exceeded the external emigrations. A local report estimated that 4,000 people departed Skye in the years 1769 to 1773, probably accounting for more than 10 per cent of the total population of the island.[40] Taking even the lowest estimates of emigration it is clear that a significant proportion of the total population of the Highlands left in the dozen years before 1775. On more adventurous assumptions, and including the likely drain to the south, it is possible that a tenth of the population, or more, was lost by emigration. In either case it must have been a substantial alleviation of population pressure; it also increased opportunities for landlords to introduce the great sheepfarmers from the south. Throughout the period, however, it was rarely a steady flow, but one of rushes interspersed with times of relative stability.

III

The American War of Independence, in combination with relatively good harvests in the north of Scotland, slowed the flow of emigrants until the famine disasters of 1782-3. In those ill-famed years there was much talk of starvation in the western islands, and Michael Flinn and his colleagues describe it as 'an old-fashioned demographic crisis'.[41] It appears to have caused many Highlanders to sell off their cattle stock — an act which immediately rendered them more mobile, and more likely to seek refuge in the Lowlands, or in America. For some emigration was an act of desperation — it required them to sell their only asset, their cattle, and to reduce themselves to penury in the hope of rapid revival in North America. The famine marked the start of two decades of sustained emigration which compounded the anxieties of landlords fearful that the basis of their own existence was being drained away by the loss of their people. They continued to live in a psychology of depopulation, unaware of the demographic realities of their times.

From 1783 to 1803 it is likely that 20,000 people left Scotland, mostly from the Highlands. As Donaldson has noted:

Emigration from the Highlands tended, at least for many years, to be peculiarly communal or corporate, reflecting the close-knit character of highland society. Moreover, it was usually a movement under leadership, as one would expect of people accustomed to clan life.

Before 1775 sheepfarming was very little mentioned among the causes of emigration. But where commercial sheepfarming had infiltrated the southern Highlands it began to count among the complaints of the migrants — in 1775 departing emigrants from Appin in Argyllshire claimed that a third of the land in their district had been converted to sheep pasture.[42] Over the next five decades sheepfarming gradually added its weight to the general pressures already manifest in the Highlands. From the 1780s onwards, references to the new sheep economy were increasing by the year. Margaret Adam emphasised the importance of the growing familarity of ordinary people with American prospects, and the rapid extension of chain migration to particular locations, for example, the connection of Barra and South Uist with Cape Breton Island. Emigrants were recruited by itinerant agents whose work was strongly assisted by the profound impact of the 1782-3 famine. There was undoubtedly a continuing fear of its recurrence. Adam discounted the conventional explanation which attributed the departures to rackrenting, the consolidation of farms and the expulsive impact of sheepfarming. But she conceded that there exists substantial evidence of the displacement effect of sheep against which, however, she pits the fact that population growth continued even in the sheep counties. She believed that the intro-

duction of sheep often operated simply to occupy previously
vacant areas of the Highlands, and displaced no one at all. For her,
sheepfarming had been greatly over-rated as a force of social and
demographic change. The population upsurge itself rendered emigration inevitable — it was 'nothing but a dead weight upon the
scanty resources of the islands'.[43] J.M. Bumsted has taken the argument several stages further in his contention that the eighteenth-
century emigrations were 'undertaken at the initiative of the
common people ... rather than at the conscious instigation of the
landlords'. He suggests, cogently, that emigration was a highly
selective process which excluded those who could not pay the relatively high costs of passage. Those who left did so in response to
the positive call of America and, in some degree, as a pre-emptive
move 'to avoid modernisation'. He discounts entirely the notion
that emigrants from the Highlands, before 1815, were refugees
from landlordism; they 'were not so much innocent victims as
conscious actors, makers and masters of their own destiny in the
New World'.[44]

Bumsted and Adam are concerned to correct the opinion that
Highland landlords were uniquely responsible for the devastation
of the region, associated with clearance and emigration. Yet,
though the extreme view may be partially amended, it remains true
that landlords increased rents in line with market forces; it is also
true that the rationalisation of land use (again under market influences) rendered much of the population redundant and virtually
landless; similarly it is true that landlord policies uprooted the
people, shifted them about the great estates, and necessarily
caused them to contemplate the radical step of emigration; and it
is no less true that eventually many landlords simply evicted their
people without any provision for the future.[45] There were, indeed,
many indications that landlord policies, notably through their
rental policies and tenurial modernisation, were reinforcing the
effects of land hunger consequent upon population growth,
already accumulating by the 1770s. The upward pressure on rents
persuaded tenants, and especially tacksmen, to consider alternative
opportunities in North America. They would have considered emigration as a forced choice.

Until about 1815, however, the general incentive to rid the
Highlands of its people was relatively slight. A larger population,
especially where it was settled on the coasts to subsist on small
plots of land with opportunity to produce kelp, potatoes and fish,

could yield a good and rising rent. Notwithstanding the painful memories of famine, there was optimism that the region could develop employment to the benefit of both lord and peasant. Moreover it was not clear yet that the population had increased much, and the demands of military service, especially in the 1790s, made it reasonable to think in terms of actual shortages of labour. Thus, for several decades, despite recurrent famine and endemic poverty, confusion prevailed until the scale of the great structural change that had overtaken the region became inescapably apparent in the years after 1815. Until the end of the French Wars the evidence that clearance had caused massive emigration is not decisive — for, while landlords increasingly cleared people from potential sheep farms, many encouraged their small tenants to remain on their estates; even where eviction occurred the dispossessed were often welcomed by adjacent proprietors. Some of the evicted ended up in the proletarianised villages of the north, others fled to the Lowlands, others to North America. There can be little doubt that agrarian reorganisation rendered the population more geographically mobile.

The early paradoxical attitude of landowners to population growth was caught in the words of Sir John Macdonald of Sleat in 1763. He had been engaged in subdividing his lands in order to accommodate all, even the poorest, tenants on his estate. The scheme had not been an economic success, but he commented: 'Yet I cannot help rejoicing in the flourishing condition of the country when it overflows with people.'[46] For another forty years the virtue of numbers remained the conventional assumption of Highland thinking; it came to be challenged only at the turn of the century, the years in which Malthus emerged as a central figure in British economic thinking, and when a great debate developed about the wisdom or otherwise of mass emigration from the north of Scotland.

Notes

1. Quoted by P. M. Hobson, 'Congestion and Depopulation, a Study in Rural Contrasts between West Lewis and West Sutherland', unpublished PhD thesis, University of St Andrews, 1952.
2. Patrick O'Farrell, 'Emigrant Attitudes and Behaviour as a Source for Irish History', *Historical Studies*, vol. 10 (1976).
3. R. H. Campbell and J. B. A. Dow, *Source Book of Scottish Economic and Social History* (Oxford, 1968), p. 2.

4. M. W. Flinn, 'The Stabilisation of Mortality in Pre-industrial Western Europe', *Journal of European Economic History*, vol. 3 (1974), p. 309.

5. R. D. Lobban, 'The Migration of Highlanders into Lowland Scotland (c. 1750-1890) with Particular Reference to Greenock', unpublished PhD thesis, University of Edinburgh, 1969. Some variations on the 'proximity argument' is offered in the recent paper of T. M. Devine, 'Highland Migration to Lowland Scotland, 1760-1860', *Scottish Historical Review*, vol. 62 (1983).

6. This is the central theme of J. M. Bumsted's extended treatment of the pre-1815 emigration to Canada — see *The People's Clearance*. See also Marianne McLean, 'Peopling Glengarry County: the Scottish Origins of a Canadian Community' in Dona Johnson and C. Lecelle (eds.), *Historical Papers* (Ottawa, 1982).

7. On the definition of Alan Macfarlane, *The Origins of English Individualism* (Oxford, 1978), pp. 10-11. On the peasant question see Carter, 'Changing Image', pp. 9-15.

8. Devine, 'Temporary Migration', p. 359.

9. C. E. Carrington, *The British Overseas* (Cambridge, 1950), p. 498.

10. Hugh MacPhee, 'The Trail of the Emigrants', *TGSI*, vol. 46 (1969-70), p. 174.

11. Ibid., p. 176. There is a most useful survey of the evidence of early emigration to America in W. R. Brock, *Scotus Americanus* (Edinburgh, 1982), ch. 4.

12. *Johnson's Journey*, p. 90. On the early American emigration there are two detailed studies: Duane Meyer, *The Highland Scots of North Carolina, 1732-1776* (Chapel Hill, 1961) and I. C. C. Graham, *Colonists from Scotland: Emigration to North America 1707-1783* (Ithaca, 1954); see also Jacqueline A. Rinn, 'Scots in Bondage. Forgotten Contributors to Colonial Society', *History Today*, vol. 30 (1980), p. 18. The quotation about Sutherland gentry is from Brock, *Scotus Americanus*, p. 77.

13. There is a useful discussion of the numbers involved in S. D. MacD. Carpenter, 'Patterns of Recruitment of the Highland Regiments of the British Army, 1756 to 1815', unpublished M Litt thesis, University of St Andrews, 1977.

14. Pennant quoted by Graham, *Colonists from Scotland*, p. 54.

15. Gordon Donaldson, *The Scots Overseas* (London, 1966), p. 58.

16. *Johnson's Journey*, p. 85.

17. Donaldson, *Scots Overseas*, ch. 5.

18. R. J. Adam (ed.), *John Home's Survey of Assynt* (Scottish History Society, Edinburgh, 1960), pp. xix, xxiv, xxvi.

19. Michael Flinn (ed.), *Scottish Population History* (Cambridge, 1977), pp. 231-3.

20. In Eric Richards, *The Leviathan of Wealth* (London, 1973), p. 161.

21. *Edinburgh Evening Courant*, 25 September 1773, 10 November 1773.

22. *Scots Magazine*, 17 August 1772; see also J. P. Maclean, *An Historical Account of the Settlements of Scotch Highlanders in America Prior to the Peace of 1783* (Glasgow and Cleveland, 1900), Appendix C.

23. George Patterson, *A History of the County of Pictou, Nova Scotia* (Montreal, 1877), pp. 79-85. See also Graham, *Colonists from Scotland*, pp. 100-1; MacPhee, 'Trail of the Emigrants', p. 189; Donald Mackay, *Scotland Farewell: the People of the Hector* (Scarborough, Ontario, 1980), Bumsted, *The People's Clearance*, pp. 63-5.

24. J. Knox, *A View of the British Empire, More Especially Scotland* (London, 1978), p. 124.

25. Quoted in Iain R. Mackay, 'Glenalladale's Settlement, Prince Edward Island', *Scottish Gaelic Studies*, vol. 10 (1963), pp. 16 ff.

26. W. MacGill, *Old Ross-shire and Scotland as Seen in the Tain and*

Balnagowan Documents (Inverness, 1909), p. 50.
27. S. R. O. Seaforth Muniments, GD46/18/43, Seaforth, 8 May 1774.
28. Typed MSS of journal of Mathew Culley's 'Tour in Scotland of 1775', Culley Papers, ZCU43, pp. 71-3, Northumberland County Record Office. There is, in the literature, a recurrent notion that emigration was a form of social protest. See, for instance, Marianne McLean, 'Peopling Glengarry County', esp. p. 170, and Bumsted, *The People's Clearance, passim.* In a limited sense all emigration expresses a preference against the homeland; it is also true that some Highlanders left with a sense of repudiation of their landlords. But for most of the period reviewed in this volume emigration from the Highlands was similar in kind to, and probably part of, the general exodus from rural Britain. This vast nation-wide phenomenon was too comprehensive to allow much of it to be categorised as social protest.
29. Microfilm, Scottish Central Library, 'Emigrants from Scotland to America 1774-5', copied from PRO (T47/12) Lerwick: 'Report of the Examination of Emigrants from the Counties of Caithness and Sutherland on Board the Ship *Bachelor of Leith* bound for Wilmington in North Carolina'. This evidence is referred to in Richards, *Highland Clearances*, pp. 142-4. See also A. R. Newsome, 'Records of Emigrants from England and Scotland to North Carolina 1774-5', *North Carolina Historical Review*, vol II (1934), and *Oban Times*, 3 August 1895, 10 August 1895. The evidence is also discussed in Bumsted, *The People's Clearance*, pp. 17-18, 22, and there is further relevant material in MacPhee, 'Trail of the Emigrants', pp. 184-6, and in the letter of James Hogg, reprinted in W. K. Boyd, *Some Eighteenth Century Tracts Concerning North Carolina* (Raleigh, 1927), pp. 421-4; R. C. MacDonald, *Sketches of the Highlanders: with an Account of their Early Arrival in North America* (St John, New Brunswick, 1843). See also references to eighteenth-century Highland emigration in Bernard Bailyn, '1776. A Year of Challenge — a World Transformed', *Journal of Law and Economics*, vol. 15 (1976), and 'The Challenge of Modern Historiography', *American Historical Review*, vol. 87 (1982).
30. SRO Seafield MSS GD/248, Sir James Grant to Lord Advocate, 19 April 1775. On the agitation to restrict emigration see Graham, *Colonists from Scotland*, pp. 95-7.
31. Quoted in T. D. Mackintosh, 'Factors in Emigration from the Islands of Scotland to North America, 1772-1803', unpublished M Litt thesis, University of Aberdeen, 1979, p. 37. See also H. W. Meikle, *Scotland and the French Revolution* (Edinburgh, 1912), p. 84, and D. Macdonald, *Lewis, a History of the Island* (Edinburgh, 1978), p. 165.
32. J. H. St J. de Crevecoeur, *Letters from an American Farmer* (London, 1782; 1962 edition), pp. 73-5.
33. SRO, GD51/52/1-7, Report of Committee on Emigration, 12 January 1802. On the conditions of passage, including some more favourable reports, see Graham, *Colonists from Scotland*, pp. 100-2, and Meyer, *Highland Scots*, Ch. 4.
34. Bumsted, *The People's Clearance*, pp. 62, 216.
35. Janet Schaw, *Journal of a Lady of Quality*, ed. E. W. Andrews (New Haven, 1939), p. 281. The American end of the story has recently generated an interesting controversy. See, for instance, Forrest McDonald and Ellen Shapiro McDonald, 'The Ethnic Origins of the American People, 1790', *William and Mary Quarterly*, vol. 37 (April 1980), pp. 179-99, and subsequent correspondence.
36. See Meyer, *Highland Scots, passim.*
37. See above, Ch. 4.
38. Flinn, 'Malthus, Emigration and Potatoes', pp. 50-2. Although some Highland parishes recorded absolute falls in population, 'Emigration was clearly moderating only very slightly the impact of the natural rate of population growth';

Flinn, *Scottish Population History*, p. 444.
    39. See Meyer, *Highland Scots*, pp. 39-40. It is worth noting the report by Devine, 'Highland Migration', p. 141, that 'Detailed local studies have found difficulty in establishing any clear correlation between the spread of sheepfarming and population decline.' Parishes in Sutherland 1811 to 1831 must stand as a clear exception to this generalisation.
    40. See Meyer, *Highland Scots*, pp. 48-54, 63-4; Graham, *Colonists from Scotland*, pp. 188-9; Adam, '1770', pp. 281-2, '1783-1803', pp. 74, 79; Flinn, *Scottish Population History*, pp. 92-3, 249-50, 443; Bumsted, *The People's Clearance*, pp. xv, 9-10, Appendix A; Donald Mackay, *Scotland Farewell*, p. 63; Knox, *View*, pp. 8-11. At least some of the statistical confusion seems to result from printing or transcription errors. Knox, in the 1784 edition of his *View of the British Empire*, p. 11, says that between 1763 and 1775 'above 20,000 people' abandoned the Highlands; in the next edition of his book, 1785, p. 130, he says that 'between 1763 and 1775 above 30,000 people' emigrated. Thomas Garnett, who relied heavily on Knox in his *Observations on a Tour through the Highlands and Part of the Western Isles of Scotland* (1811 edition, p. 184), produces the larger figure, i.e. above 30,000, but for a shorter period, namely 1773 to 1775. Another confident guess is made by Bruce Lenman in *Canadian Journal of History*, vol. 18 (1983), p. 283.
    41. Flinn, *Scottish Population History*, p. 445. On Skye emigration see also Brock, *Scotus Americanus*, pp. 22-3. One of the greatest problems surrounding West Highland emigration concerns the remarkably high level of exodus achieved at various times in the eighteenth century — notably in the 15 years before the War of Independence, and again at the turn of the century. The continuing researches of the American scholar Bernard Bailyn and others suggest a very high rate of emigration in proportion to total population. Yet the rate of emigration in the nineteenth century is generally thought to have been relatively slow, and to have provided insufficient relief from congestion — which became the characteristic problem of the region. At present there exists no satisfactory explanation for this apparent change in the West Highlander's propensity to emigrate.
    42. Donaldson, *Scots Overseas*, p. 68. On numbers involved see Flinn, *Scottish Population History*, p. 443.
    43. Adam, '1783-1803', p. 87.
    44. Bumsted, *The People's Clearance*, pp. xvi, 46, 221.
    45. See, for example, the evidence of a group of emigrants to North Carolina in 1792, cited in Meikle, *Scotland and the French Revolution*, p. 84.
    46. Quoted in James M. Cameron, 'A Study of the Factors that Assisted and Directed Scottish Emigration to Upper Canada, 1815-1855' unpublished PhD thesis, University of Glasgow, 1970, from NLS MS 1309, Devine Papers, pp. 228-9.

8
THE EMIGRATION DEBATE

As the Evil [of emigration] at present seems to arise chiefly from the Conduct of Landowners, in changing the Economy of their Estates, it may be questioned whether Government can with Justice interfere, or whether any essential Benefits are likely to arise from this Interference.

Thomas Telford, 1802[1]

At the turn of the century the question of emigration from the Highlands (and elsewhere) had become highly contentious. Most landlords (anxious about losing tenants and rent), were against it, but some were beginning to argue that emigration was necessary and therapeutic and ought to proceed unhindered. The emigration question was in a transitional phase.

It was not yet clear that the population of the Highlands had grown to a level beyond its employability; nor that sheepfarming and general agrarian rationalisation were incompatible with the retention of the people: the new locations along the coasts or in villages had not yet failed. When Thomas Garnett toured the north in 1798 he was fully optimistic that the town and vicinity of Inverness, where hemp and flax manufacture employed more than 10,000 people and where cotton production and tanning were thriving, could easily absorb most of the people displaced in the interior county:

Since the introduction of sheep, the small tenantry are gradually wearing away, and the country becomes thinned of population; but fortunately, those who are thus driven from their farms find employment in the manufactures of the town, which has increased in population in a greater proportion than the country has diminished.[2]

201

Furthermore many west coast landlords were not sure that a greater population was not in the best interests of the kelp industry and the fishing (and therefore of their own rentals). These pervasive uncertainties inevitably led to public controversy at a time when emigration was a large and visible drain of people from particular districts throughout the region. Large emigrations were common at this time: for instance, in 1802, some 800 people from Barra crossed the Atlantic under the leadership of their Roman Catholic priests, and in the following year 1,000 people connected with the Glengarry Fencibles went with their priests to Upper Canada.[3] Yet in neither case is it possible to assess the degree of compulsion that attended the upheavals, because the circumstances of these migrations are simply not sufficiently well documented to allow a clear statement of their motivations. By contrast, we know that in the early clearances in Sutherland (in 1806) many of the people involved had rejected the alternative coastal accommodation offered by their landlord, and chose to migrate to America. In this case, as in many others no doubt, there was a combination of pressure and choice in the emigration. Clearance uprooted the people and precipitated their decision to leave altogether. The one choice which they were denied was that of the *status quo*.

I

Alexander Irvine, in 1802, published a paper on Highland emigration which argued powerfully that population was pressing dangerously near the limits of subsistence. The common people had 'great patience of hunger', he observed, but

> To equipoise population, they spread themselves begging. For instance, the higher parts of Inverness-shire in summer pour in upon the Counties of Perth and Angus so that I have seen, in seasons of scarcity, twenty or thirty served at a door, in one day, consisting mostly of women and children. The prevalence of beggary in the Highlands, requires attention, if it be caused by a defect of economy or arises from excessive population.[4]

Irvine's opinion was interesting because he insisted that, in many respects, the Highlanders were better off than ever before and that they emigrated because their aspirations were rising. Many remained poor, he said, because they were victims of their own indolence. He was also prepared to blame estate managers for oppressive policies which discouraged the people: emigration took away the best of them and positive measures, such as the introduction of manufacturing, were required to stem their departure.

The *Farmer's Magazine,* published in Edinburgh, provided perhaps the most important forum for debate on the emigration question. In 1807 it gave a classic description of a Highland emigration, written by an opponent of depopulation:

> The inhabitants of one district were required to pay an augmented rent for their possessions on which, at the time, they barely kept soul and body together. Perhaps a proud recollection of their kindred to the chief, of their bearing his name, of the battles they had fought abroad and at home under his banners, made the sudden demand for money go the worse down. They therefore took the unanimous resolution of seeking a new habitation in the wildest region of America. They, however, first sent a deputation to London, to try if Government would extend its parental Care to them, by the adoption of some general measures for the preservation of their race ... Finding their case hopeless, their deputies returned from London by Glasgow, where they hired vessels to transport 500 people to Canada; and the whole district took their departure — men with their pregnant wives, their children running at their feet and clinging to the breast — all, all took their departure, casting many a longing look at their well known and favourite mountains. Those who witnessed the embarkation describe in affecting terms, the manly tears starting from the eyes of the men, the howling and lamentations of the women and children, in terms that leave no doubt the peoples' attachment to their native spot, nor their deep regret at being compelled to leave it. I could not describe those unhappy people's sufferings on a long journey through a tempestuous ocean, nor the miseries and hardships they experienced on landing in a strange country, as wild as they had left, without leading the reader to discover the particular emigration I describe, and exposing an individual proprietor to more than his share of blame.[5]

In conditions of war, and of an increasing demand for military recruits, combined with the rising value of kelp production (which was, of course, highly labour-intensive), landlords became apprehensive again about the scale of emigration from their estates. Clearance was obviously not the only cause of emigration and most landlords had little interest in diminishing their tenantries, though their rental exactions probably contributed strongly to that end. In 1793 Colin Macdonald of Boisdale informed Sir James Grant that he could raise men for the regiments only with the greatest difficulty. His son had been engaged in recruiting a company for Breadalbane, but 'men being so scarce on this Estate, by Emigrations, for three years past that I am afraid he will have difficulty to make out his Company of men here'.[6] It was a widespread gripe. Eight years later the agents of the Clanranald estate rejected the suggestion that the Highlands were overpopulated and warned that emigration 'must be carefully guarded against'. While the people of the Uists had shown little propensity to flee, the local factor Robert Brown reported: 'I am confident however that there has of late been emissaries amongst them and who I suspect have been very busy ... I likewise suspect that one of our clergy there may join in the recruiting of Emigrants.' This hinted at the organising role of ministers which was a feature of several large communal emigrations at the turn of the century: the type of emigration described as 'concentrated and coagulated' by recent historians.[7] Brown himself was nervous about the South Uist people — he remarked that 'The poorness of the people and the highness of the freight to America are our greatest securities ... from the prevailing rage for emigration.' He advocated the provision of leases to the people in order 'to fix the tenants for effectively it would be ought [*sic*] of their power to move during the currency of the lease'. But Brown restricted this opinion to the insular parts only of the Clanranald properties: indeed he believed that on the mainland a partial outflow might prove beneficial so long as it did not become generalised. He observed that, in any case, 'to try to stop it injudiciously would only be to promote it'. During the following four decades the circumstances of the estates in South Uist altered drastically, as did Brown's opinions. The collapse of kelp sales and the transfer of the estates to trustees led to the eventual sale of the lands to Gordon of Cluny. In the end, Brown was converted to the promotion of emigration and Gordon of Cluny became one of the most notorious exponents of forced emigration in the 1840s.[8]

Sensitivity to the emigrant departures was apparent until 1815. When John Blackadder reported on the agriculture of Skye and North Uist in 1799-1800 (for the advice of Lord Macdonald's Commissioners), he was unable to avoid the opinion that any commercial reorganisation of the estates was likely to provoke emigration. He predicted that

> the Islander who is turned out of his possession will emigrate, unless another way of gaining his bread is pointed out to him. In improving an estate in such a situation as this, besides advancing the Rental, retaining a number of inhabitants is an object of the utmost importance; and all reasonable allowances should be made to prevent emigration.[9]

It was rare for the question to be stated with such clarity.

Emigration across the Atlantic occurred simultaneously with a similar flow to the Lowlands. Incoming Highlanders certainly helped to reduce labour shortages in the early phases of industrialisation and agricultural improvement in the south of Scotland. The famous enterprise of Lord Kames to drain Kincardine Moss near Stirling in 1768 gave work to 170 families, primarily from the Perthshire Highlands; and the great cotton mills of David Dale at New Lanark were receiving Highlanders in large numbers in 1791. Many Scotsmen believed that it was better for the national interest that Highlanders settled in the south than emigrated altogether, and clergymen were urged to promote the lesser of the two evils.[10]

Many of these fears were inflamed by a campaign against emigration that reached a crescendo in the period 1801-3. Much of the propaganda was blatantly alarmist, but there was no denying that a new peak of emigration had been reached.[11] Typical of established opinion was the advice offered by Sir W. Porter to Sir William Pulteney at the beginning of 1802. He reported that great preparations were under way for massive emigration from the Western Highlands. He believed that the government should intervene and offer the prospective migrants certain incentives — 'to encourage the Highlanders to collect themselves into towns in Britain, rather than see them add strength to other nations by leaving this kingdom'. Porter couched his report in terms of a humanitarian concern for the welfare of the people themselves.

They who emigrate know not where they are going; America is

not now what it was when best known to Highlanders, I mean before the Civil War of 1774 — they found it then a Paradise where they have nought to do but pluck and eat, now they shall find it as the land of Egypt in the days of the Plagues of the Pharoah.[12]

In fact there is good evidence to indicate that the motives of most landowners apprehensive about emigration were less tenderly philanthropic than those claimed by Porter. They were alarmed at the loss of rental that they believed would follow a diminution of population.

A year later there were sensational reports relating to the 'Buzz of Emigration' which threw a clarifying light on the connection with clearance. It was put about that a full two-thirds of the entire population of the Skye parishes of Strath and Sleat (and many from Trotternish) had already subscribed part of their passage money to America. These people, it is important to say, were in no sense victims of clearance. Lord Macdonald's factor bemoaned the problems of estate management which would be left in the wake of the predicted emigration — he did not know how to cope with 'those that remain as there are some Farms where two emigrate, some three, and others there is not above one left'. He thought that it might be best to remove the residue 'into such towns as are most adapted for small tenants, and the remainder left vacant for gentlemen or such strangers as the Commissioners think it proper to introduce'.[13] This was an especially significant exposition because it illustrates a reversal of the normal sequence of tenurial change in the Highlands: in this case the voluntary evacuation of small tenants prompted the landlord to rationalise his lands into the hands of more capitalistic in-comers.

Until 1803-4 many northern proprietors thought that official government policy was giving decided encouragement to emigration to North America. Highland landlords complained angrily when Lord Hobart recommended that a Canadian regiment be raised 'as an Expedient for relieving the supposed distresses' of the Highlanders. Hobart's advice combined the twin evils of military recruitment and emigration. As a consequence, according to Hope, the Lord Advocate of Scotland, 'The whole Highlands were thrown open [and] Agents' misrepresentations and falsehoods as to this country, held out the same delusive prospects as to America, which had been done by the agents of Lord Selkirk and others.' Hope claimed that the psychological effect had been great: that the government should encourage emigration

> shook the whole Highlands to the very foundations. The conse-
> quence was that Thousands, instead of hundreds, were eager to
> enlist into this Regiment ... Few of the officers are Highlanders
> or speak the language — consequently the recruiting has been
> carried on by low crimps who used arts and practised false-
> hoods, which I have no doubt, the officers did not know, much
> less countenance.

He described the manner in which the people's expectations had been played upon, claiming that the men were promised land in Canada immediately on arrival, and that they would be 'called out and drilled so many days a week, like the Volunteer Corps they had been accustomed to at home'. Land in exchange for military service was, of course, a traditional reciprocation in Highland society, and in this instance the bargain was incorporated into a scheme for emigration.[14] The northern proprietors were in a high state of alarm.

II

The government's attitude to emigration from the Highlands became the object of powerful and relatively sophisticated political agitation in the first years of the new century. A vigorous cam-paign of persuasion was orchestrated by a committee of the High-land Society of Scotland, a society instituted in 1787 to promote northern development (and preserve the population). The eventual outcome was the Passenger Vessel Act of 1803, an essentially Machiavellian piece of legislation in both conception and exe-cution, which assuaged the fears of the Highland proprietors that their estates would suffer unwanted depopulation by emigration. The campaign was a classic example of the operation of sectional pressure in the pre-democratic polity.

The committee of the Highland Society began its campaign pro-gramme by surveying opinion in the Highlands,[15] and by gathering information on the extent of plans for emigration. It was then in a position to offer a series of recommendations to the Society and to government. The voluminous reports submitted in 1802 and 1803 exposed the landlords' perceptions of the state of Highland society. The reports were highly critical of the departure of so many High-landers, and of the distress said to be the normal experience of many emigrants. They reported the presence of many emigrant vessels along the west coast; for example, 130 people had been taken from Ullapool to Nova Scotia, 565 from Fort William, and another 125 from Mull, all within a very short space of time. Whole populations were contemplating departure to North America. A questionnaire response had yielded various statistics — that more than 5,000 had departed in 1801-2, and that more than 10,000 were to go in 1803.[16] In one analysis of the geo-graphical source of the people in the first period, particular attention was drawn to Aird, Strathglass, Urquhart, Glengarry, Knoydart, Arisaig, Moydart, Lochaber, Rannoch, Appin, Glencoe, Sutherland, Glenelg, Kintail, Lochalsh, Macleod's Coun-try, Rum, Eigg, Barra and the Uists. The most popular destina-tions had been Pictou, Baltimore, Upper Canada, North Carolina and Cape Breton. It was believed that those who left were the most spirited and in the best circumstances — on average they took with them £30 in capital, a sizeable sum made possible by the relatively high price of cattle at the turn of the century.

For the immediate future it was reported that further substantial outflows of migrants could be expected from Strathglass, Aird, Sutherland, Lewis, South Uist, Barra, Knoydart, Breadalbane, Lochalsh and Glenmoriston. One correspondent observed

> that all the Islands from the butt of Lewis to Barra Head are in a ferment; every measure has been taken by the Tacksmen to avert the Spirit of Emigration, but it appears to have taken too deep a root.

It was significant that these investigations, while they emphasised the allegedly irrational behaviour of the migrants, as well as the trickery of the transport jobbers (who effected their business 'by forging letters from Emigrants, by beating up with a bagpipe and a flag, and by distributing vast quantities of spirits' to the disaffected people), did not leave the landowners unscathed. For instance, one writer from Lochbay blamed proprietors who 'substituted sheep for men, without regard to the moral or political tendency of the measure [and] who have no other object than an immediate aug-mentation of Rent'. He believed that 'the maxims of Dr Adam

Smith' did not properly apply to the emigration question, and that heavy duties should be imposed on all emigrant vessels.[17]

The evidence generated by these inquiries revealed a division of behaviour within the ranks of the Highland landlords — between those who made efforts to 'preserve' their tenantry and those who ousted them without compunction. A respondent to the Committee of the Highland Society was candid about the question.

Proprietors look too little into the affairs of their people — A Rent receivable from one great accountable Tenant suits their ease and Indolence and Cupidity and Extravagance ... I delight in this disheartening tale to be able to quote the respectable Names of the Duke of Argyle, the Duke of Gordon (as yet), Lord Seaforth (till now), the Laird of Grant (if he has lost a few it was from a Country within the sphere of Contagion), Argaivai, Locheil, Gairloch, Applecross, Cromarty and Harris — and a few others who cherish their people — and attend to whatever can promote their interest which in fact is Officially securing their own, to as valuable an extent and on a far surer basis, and I should think with far happier feelings — than a sheep rent could give, which desolated a Country and turned adrift its population to Chance, Despair and Emigration.

The body of evidence generated by the committee yielded a careful analysis of the range of forces which were promoting Highland emigration at the turn of the century — clearly the pressure of sheepfarming was now combined with the attractive forces of American prosperity, liberty and propaganada.[18]

There can be little doubt that the recruitment of emigrants from the Highlands had been developed into a fine art. The *Caledonian Mercury* had already criticised the enticing propaganda of emigration agents in 1791 in the strongest terms.[19] The ministers of the church co-operated in several places — the church doors were used to advertise emigration schemes and some clergy, especially of the Catholic districts, were instrumental in the actual business of organisation. It was claimed that 200 people left Barra within twelve months to be settled in Nova Scotia 'being inveigled thither by a Mr F. upon promises of the undisturbed profession of their religion, (being all Roman Catholics)'.[20]

But the causes of the emigration, as identified by the Highland Society, were manifold. Correspondents repeatedly alluded to the growth of population and the consequent shortage of opportunities for gainful employment; some landowners were removing their old tenants in order to introduce more efficient cultivators who would pay better rents, and were replacing black cattle with sheepstock. Rents had trebled and population had grown 'beyond the Industry and Employment of the Country'.[21] But beyond these reasons was the recurrent allusion to 'the change in the feudal manners of the Highlands' which had destroyed the old bonds of loyalty. There had been a 'moral' change which, according to one analysis, was much more radical than had been fully understood:

It is a spirit of discontent roused among them partly by Dissemination of the Principles of Jacobinism for which such pains were taken about ten years ago, now revived by the peculiarities of their own Situation; and partly by the recent acts of some ill-disposed persons who join the motive of gain to that of Sedition, and who work on the minds of the People by the Representatives of the Slavery they endure in their own Country, contrasted with the Freedom and Equality they may enjoy by emigrating to another.

These prospects, he continued, were strongly reinforced by alluring accounts of the transatlantic voyage, and of the reception in America — the emigration and transport agents operated like 'Crimp Sergeants beating up for Recruits, and meet with great success'. Indeed this report exposed the receptivity of the people to propaganda of a quasi-political character. The success of the emigration agents may provide a guide to popular mentalities in the Highlands at this time. It was reported that 'the People always conceive an Interest in Government opposed to theirs, and look to the power of leaving their Country as an escape from some hard restraint'.

One recruiting agent confessed to having circulated amongst potential migrants a letter from America which was avowedly political in content:

the aim of the writer was to rouze up the spirit of his Countrymen *to throw off the Yoke of Bondage and the Shackles of Slavery*, to quit the land of Egypt, and to come to this Land of Canaan ... How can I say otherwise ... when I never know what *actual freedom, or the Spirit of Equality* was till I came to Canada.

To anyone in authority these were alarming ideas, subversive of the entire structure and equilibrium of society — they were the means 'to disgust the people with their present situation, and to sow the seeds of Democracy and Sedition among them'.

The Committee of the Highland Society directed its main attack at the conditions experienced in the course of emigration. The only evidence of dissatisfaction among previous migrants that it produced was a letter from a Uist man who had left in 1792 and had written back to his cousin in the following terms:

Dear Angus, you may tell Boisdale about the people who left Uist that they are crying every day saying if Boisdale knew their condition that he would send for them again, but if you hear of them talking of coming to this place [in America], for Godsake, advise them to stay where they are else they would repent.

Though the Society had difficulty in producing adverse evidence about settled immigrants in America,[22] it was able to accumulate much better, and more damaging, information about the appalling conditions on board the transatlantic vessels. Hence the migrant ships became the target of the people who sought to staunch the Highland evacuation. There was much information about the gross crowding of the passengers, the dreadful condition of food and water, the disease and filth, as well as the lack of safety on the ships involved in the trade. The Society reported one case of a ship which had set off from Skye in 1791 with 400 people aboard — dismasted after twelve weeks at sea, it had returned to Greenock, a blessing to its passengers who, it was claimed, would have faced death from disease had they continued. The shipwrecked Highlanders declared that they were emigrating 'altogether owing to their wanting bread at home, and high rents, joined with several successive bad seasons'.[23] Two vessels from Fort William, aggregating 559 tons, had carried 700 people across the Atlantic — extraordinary crowding, even by the standards of eighteenth-century slave trading. One report claimed that 53 passengers had died *en route*.[24] These inhuman conditions gave the Highland Society a perfect ground for seeking government intervention in the great Highland migration.

III

The committee of the Highland Society eventually offered several key recommendations. It advocated that the government should generate greater levels of employment by the means of bounties on fishing and manufacturing in the north. In addition it advised Highland proprietors to cultivate greater patience when re-arranging agriculture on their estates: a more gradual approach would help them to retain the population they dislodged. But it is clear that its most effective recommendation was to do with legislative regulation of conditions aboard the migrant ships. It suggested that the Society should press for stringent rules to govern, for example, the ratio of tonnage to passengers, the provision of food and medical facilities, and the introduction of a measure which would withhold from a ship's contractor all passage money until evidence was produced to demonstrate that the passenger had been landed alive on the other side of the Atlantic. These recommendations contained a strong humanitarian appeal — but the sharper intention was apparent.

> It cannot be denied that even to prevent the horrors of the Passage must by every friend of humanity be a step of the highest and most beneficial consequence — but if the measures which the Committee are for that end to suggest promise also a tendency indirectly to check the evil of Emigration itself they will, with submission be entitled to a double share of approbation.

At each point the humanitarian benefits were perfectly matched by restrictive effects on the actual volume of migrant traffic.

The Society was patently exploiting humanitarian considerations to serve the perceived economic interests of the Highland proprietors. The report was entirely candid about the likely consequences of the legislation:

> But it is not dissembled that one Consequence of the Enactment would be to render the expense of Emigration ... so heavy that more deliberation would be used than at present in resolving to take this step. A Highlander at present thinks £8 or £10 a sacrifice worth making for the Chance of the Comfort and even riches he is made to expect he shall acquire. He never reflects,

indeed he has no room to suspect, that he is in addition to place the hazard of his life in the scale ... The expense of a decent passage will be such as will leave them to think deliberately before they give up the Substance in pursuit of the Shadow.

The report suggested that government regulations designed to protect the people would achieve the Society's objective indirectly, and in fact more effectively, than a prohibition on emigration. The report adverted, significantly, to 'the suspicious temper which leads the Highlanders to feel but a stronger bias in favour of Emigration from knowing it to be adverse to wishes and opinion of the higher classes'. There could hardly have been a more telling comment on the state of class relations in the Highlands. It is questionable, of course, whether they had ever been much different.

The Highland Society's agitation was substantially instrumental in creating the case for the first Passenger Act of 1803; and the regulations reflected the Society's recommendations. The government had responded to the Society in 1802 by sending Thomas Telford to survey the cost and the central Highlands, with a view to identifying possibilities for development and industry in the region which would discourage emigration. Telford estimated that almost 10,000 Highlanders would emigrate in 1803, which he attributed primarily to the introduction of sheepfarming.

It has been argued by modern historians that the Passenger Act was 'a normal reaction to the facts of suffering and mortality as disclosed', that the support of the Highland Society was neither disingenuous nor Machiavellian, and that the Act pioneered the mechanism of administrative reform which became typical in the early nineteenth century.[25] Nevertheless the internal evidence of the time is weighted against an interpretation so sympathetic to the Society and to its clients. The documents of the Society quoted above are entirely unequivocal and candid, and leave negligible room for doubt about the priority of motives. Dr James Hunter has effectively discredited the ostensible humanitarian impulses of the Society. Hunter examined the role of Charles Hope, the Lord Advocate in Scotland and MP for Edinburgh, who drew up the Passenger Vessels Act of June 1803. Hope admitted in the following year that the Act,

[although] professedly calculated merely to regulate the equipment and victualling of Ships carrying Passengers to America,

... certainly was intended, both by myself and other Gentlemen of the Committee ... indirectly to prevent the effects of that Pernicious Spirit of discontent against their own Country, and rage for emigrating to America, which had been raised among the people ... by the Agents of Lord Selkirk and others, aided no doubt, in some few cases, by the impolitic conduct of the landholders, in attempting changes and improvements too rapidly.[26]

Hope argued that the 'discontent and delusion of the people' was a strictly temporary phenomenon. Indeed, many contemporaries saw the real meaning of the legislation. Selkirk put it lightly when he remarked, 'Some people may be inclined to doubt whether humanity was the leading motive of the Society.'[27] In much more modern Highland history the landowners have been denounced without a proper balancing of the evidence. In the case of the Passenger Act the contemporary evidence clearly indicates a blatant cynicism about which there can now be little argument.

Humanitarian considerations were more prominent among Lowland interests who supported the case of legislative intervention. Dundas himself lent his assistance, and John Ramsay of Ochtertyre went much further and advocated full-bodied protection of the Highland people from the ravages of their landlords. He expressed the hope that 'the Legislative will interpose and discountenance depopulation and oppression in whatever form they may appear ... lest ... this brave and original people, depressed and scattered purely to enrich their superiors, will be forever lost to this nation'.[28] Ramsay's words were a far cry from the intentions of the Highland Society and were not acted upon for almost a century.

Despite many difficulties in its enforcement the Passenger Act proved an effective means of deterring emigration from the Highlands. It imposed severe regulations of conditions on board the emigrant vessels and, as Professor MacDonagh has observed, it introduced 'a revolutionary principle to English law ... the interference of the legislature with the freedom of contract'. The cost of a fare to Nova Scotia, which had been less than £4, thereafter was at least doubled, in some cases trebled.[29] Within days of the passage of the Act through Parliament, John Campbell of Kingsburgh wrote:

The Emigration is almost entirely knocked on the head and I do not suppose that one third of those who once talked of it will go ... one of Lord Selkirk's transports has arrived at Oronsay but has taken none on board yet.

Two weeks later he reported from Strath and Sleat on Skye that

The emigration is entirely stopped now from the Act of Parliament which puts it out of the poor people's power to pay the increase of freight — those who intended to emigrate are now a burden on the Country and from the total failure of the crops last year they will be reduced to indigent circumstances before Harvest — I am really at a loss how to manage the great population and little employment here is really depressing.[30]

More than a decade afterwards, by which time reigning assumptions about Highland population had shifted, the great sheep-farmer, Patrick Sellar, characteristically denounced government interference in the emigrant traffic: in his robust opinion the Passenger Act, particularly in requiring minimum food provision on migrant vessels, was an absurd obstruction to the natural exodus from the Highlands. Sellar believed that the voyaging Highlanders had no need for meat as specified by the Act, for they were normally able to survive on oatmeal.[31] He had no doubt that the Act was designed to impede rather than protect migrants. There was some irony in the fact that, within a decade or so of the Passenger Act legislation, the Highland proprietors found themselves hoist with their own petard.

There was a second prong to government policy in the Highlands. With encouragement from the Highland Society, the government poured further resources and subsidies into the development of facilities and industry in the north of Scotland, so extending policies of the previous two decades. The most spectacular example was the decision to construct the Caledonian Canal, which employed more than 300 men from Skye alone, but there were several other programmes for public works, especially roads and bridges. The express motivation was the creation of employment in order to retain population in the Highlands. Deterrence to emigration and the provision of employment both operated to maintain the population. However, it has often been argued that this interference with emigration rendered the region even more vulnerable to Malthusian crises, and exacerbated the long-run problems of the local economy.

Yet though government policy helped to reduce the 'fever of emigration', it did not succeed in terminating the flow. In October 1803, for instance, John Campbell reported from Skye that the poor harvest had created great strain and rising rent arrears among the tenantry. A group of people from Sleat had emigrated, and had 'drained the country of ready money'. He reported that

> Ninety to a hundred families have sailed for North Carolina and paid their passage at the rate of £12.12.0 a head. Their having done so shows that no expense or situation, if they are able to pay it, will deter them from their wandering schemes.[32]

In this case, and many more, the emigration took place in the teeth of the landlord's disapproval; it was in no sense a consequence of clearances or sheepfarming. Four years later the *Inverness Journal* bemoaned the continuing flight of Highlanders suffering what it called the 'most Criminal Infatuation' with North America. The newspaper commented:

> With so many incitements to industry and the means of employment afforded by the Caledonian Canal and other public works carrying on in the North of Scotland, it might naturally be expected that the rage for emigration among the Highlanders should be repressed if not altogether extinguished. Yet it is to be regretted that within those few days a ship was cleared out of the Custom-house of Thurso, for Pictou, in America, with a number of families of these deluded people, consisting of 130 persons in men, women and children, none of whom were under the necessity of leaving their native country.[33]

The contemporary belief that the Highlanders were seized by a 'frenzy' for emigration cannot be entirely discounted. Nor can the influence of propagandists, including Lord Selkirk and Francis Horner, be ignored. The dislocation of the old patterns of settlement by improving landlords created a readiness for change. But the most potent determinants were the general pressures on subsistence, exposed in the near famines of 1802-3 and 1806, and higher rents and meal prices. There are few statistics of annual emigration during these years, but it is certain that the transatlantic flow continued, probably at a lower level, after 1803. It did so despite government regulations designed to impede emigration, despite efforts to generate employment in the north, despite the continuing boom in kelp, despite the renewal of war, and despite the great poverty of the people and the costs of passage.[34] The basic Malthusian forces, it would seem, were strong enough to overcome the conditions acting to retain the people. It is likely that sheepfarming, while not insignificant, remained for some time a relatively weak element among the expulsive forces.

IV

Within a decade of the first Passenger Act these forces working in the Highlands were redoubled. But it was not until the 1830s that assisted emigration enabled the poorest members of this society to make a choice of destination. Many simply walked out of the Highlands along the road to Lowland agriculture and industry; seasonal migration, however, acted simply to delay the final departure. To finance emigration many Highlanders sold off their entire stock, so arriving in North America with nothing. Moreover it was several decades before landlord opinion shifted decisively towards the positive assistance of emigration. Meanwhile, for at least twenty years, there was a noisy debate between the proponents of emigration, led by the energetic Lord Selkirk, and those who believed that the Highlands should retain its people.

There quickly emerged an influenial body of opinion in the north which advocated emigration as the logical and progressive stage by which civilisation would be extended into the Highlands. Emigration, said a correspondent to the *Farmer's Magazine* in 1809, was not a proper cause for lamentation. He was convinced that 'the Highlands are more likely to be brought into a state of high and rapid improvement by southern industry, than by the pitiful exertions of the aboriginal inhabitants'. Another writer pointed out that all change is attended by 'circumstances of regret', but the benefits to the *émigrés* were unequivocal: 'By one great effort, by one leap across the Atlantic, they escape from a prison in which all their moral and physical qualities lye immured.' The same author was able to construct a grand theory from his beliefs:

The recent emigration from the Highlands, is a step in the

political progress of mankind; a link in the great chain that connects together the two extremes of civilization and barbarism. The revolution that had already taken place in the south of Scotland, travelled northward, and paved the way for a similar change in that extensive part of the island lying on the other side of the Forth. This change in the political system resembles the paroxysm of disease in the human body, when it is about to pass into a state of good health.[35]

Selkirk, of course, believed that the best solution for the recurrent destitution of the Highlands (and to the problems associated with agricultural improvement) was to facilitate emigration to British North America. He managed to obtain official sanction to develop settlements on Prince Edward Island and Upper Canada: In 1803 he arranged the migration of 800 west coast and island folk across the Atlantic. The saga of these enterprises, especially that of his Red River settlement, have been well documented elsewhere:[36] the entire story rang with melodrama and ended in débâcle, but it is evident that, with his agents, Selkirk effectively whipped up a spirit of emigration in the Highlands. The common people were receptive, and he had noteworthy success in Sutherland during the great clearances between 1811 and 1816. Indeed he had little difficulty in persuading many of the people cleared to depart for Canada instead of taking the lots on the coasts of the estate which had been reserved for their future accommodation.

Selkirk's correspondence during these years is of great value because it reflects the condition of the people who responded to his plans as he perambulated the Highlands over a period of almost two years. For instance, Selkirk found that many people of the Macdonald of Glenalladale estate 'have not even leases, but have a verbal promise of a Lease'. Many of the people of Skye and Wester Ross had been able to pay for land in Canada, but 'a few remained who from poverty could not'. There was a preference for large blocks of land in order to provide for brothers and cousins. Another party of people arrived in Canada in 1803, direct from the isles of Uist, and Selkirk described them as very poor and 'ill-selected for the object intended, having much too large a proportion of useless hands'. Selkirk generally found that the people would only migrate in large family groups which were not always ideal for Canadian conditions:

The difficulty is not always easy to obviate because from the social clannish disposition of the Highlanders it was impossible almost to take a small number — they would not go without their friends, and to refuse a part might have disgusted the whole, and driven them to abandon the plan and return to the idea of following their neighbours to Carolina.

Perhaps typical of the migrants who followed Selkirk to Canada in 1803-4 was a family evicted from their land in Rannoch, Perthshire; they sold off their four cows for £60, which proved sufficient to redeem their famine debts and pay for their fares across the Atlantic; they were penniless on arrival at Pictou in Nova Scotia. This family was therefore compelled to accept day labour for some time — which involved a loss of social esteem for the common Highlander — but eventually they were able to buy a plot of land which they planted with potatoes. Within three years they had plenty of food, a house and a good income.[37]

Selkirk's net was cast also into the northern Highlands where he ran into conflict with the Sutherland estate, which was in the middle of a massive programme of reorganisation associated with the introduction of commercial sheepfarming. The Sutherland estate management regarded him as a provocative nuisance, stimulating disaffection among the people, and disturbing their plans. Other landlords equally regarded Selkirk as a threat, a man who would seduce their people away. In Sutherland it was the clear policy of the proprietor, Lady Stafford, to discourage emigration: her elaborate programme was specifically designed to retain the entire population of the estate notwithstanding the introduction of sheep. In 1805, on the brink of the clearances, Lady Stafford was full of confidence in her plans; she told her wealthy husband that

> so much work is awaiting the people [who were to be resettled] in the way of canals, roads and bridges, that we foresee in spite of Lord Selkirk that in a few years this Country will be benefitted by preserving its people to a reasonable degree.[38]

The suggestion of Lord Webb Seymour in 1807 that the Staffords should actively facilitate and encourage emigration was rejected.[39] Only gradually did their opposition to emigration weaken. Emigration they regarded as the antithesis of their plans, a sign of failure. Indeed the factors of the estate believed that the common people threatened to emigrate as a bargaining counter to achieve better conditions within Sutherland. Forced emigration was not part of these clearances. When, in 1809, a group of 60 people left the estate it was, as Lady Stafford put it, because 'they would not come into the plans laid down for being Cottars at home'. In this case she had little regret, for the people would not pay for the land by military service, and 'if they will not adopt the other means of improvement for the country universally done elsewhere [i.e. by means of lotting] they must quit it to enable others to come to it'.[40] This became the standard attitude of the Sutherland administration for the next four decades. The success of Selkirk's overtures was a rejection of the Sutherland plan, and displayed clearly enough the attitude of the people to the clearances. The loss of status reinforced the loss of land as a cause of emigration.

When Selkirk toured Sutherland in 1812-13 he found a dislodged and mutinous people, especially in Kildonan, eager for emigration once they had been cleared by Lady Stafford's agents. Both then and in 1806 many had spurned the resettlement lots offered by the estate. 'They determined on emigrating all in a body,' said Selkirk, who received applications from 700 people. In early 1813 he had employed recruiting agents to travel about the north of Scotland, to engage people both for the Hudson's Bay Company and as settlers for his own colony. Selkirk met Lady Stafford in London in April 1813 to discuss the question of emigration — she had been surprised that the idea was strong with the people because she understood that they 'again appeared quiet and willing to settle in the manner proposed'. They had agreed that the decision to emigrate should be left entirely to the people. Lady Stafford pointed out that 'if our Agents were to make any proposal to them with a view to sending them to America they would suspect they had not fair play and that it would defeat its own purpose'.[41] It was a further reflection on the poor state of relations between landlord and people; it also indicated the proprietrix's desire to rid herself of disaffected and 'useless' elements among the common folk.

Selkirk achieved instant success in his recruitment drive, and the Sutherland managers made no effort to prevent the exodus because it would relieve pressure on the inadequately prepared resettlement zones.[42] At the end of June 1813 Selkirk had arranged for the despatch of more than 100 of the people. The terms he imposed were relatively stringent for a poor peasantry: each emigrant needed £10 for the passage, and 5s an acre for land, but they also needed funds for their immediate livelihood on arrival. The circumstances of the emigration were complicated by the popular resistance to the clearances, and by the concurrent plans to raise recruits for regiments in Canada;[43] there were also problems in organising transport. Only one-seventh of the original applicants departed under Selkirk's auspices. The voyage was not happy: typhus broke out among the seasick passengers and an unspecified number died *en route*. On arrival in Canada they faced horrifying conditions — fever raged through them, food was meagre, and shelter existed hardly at all. Temperatures fell 60°F below freezing point. The migrants had been told that it was unnecessary to take money, clothing and articles of furniture. At least one biographer of Selkirk portrays the enterprise as a series of botched episodes which, for many of the migrants, ended only in tragedy. Nevertheless further voyages followed and Selkirk continued to receive migrants from the Northern Highlands in the Red River Settlement.[44]

During his northern tour of June 1813, Selkirk recorded many of his responses to the condition of the people at the moment of their clearance. His eye-witness account drew a clear connection between eviction, alienation and the rush to emigrate:

The Sutherland Estate and indeed most of the country has remained hitherto in the occupation of small tenants under the old system, the proprietors having embarked largely in the rising of men for military service. Within these few years that system has been broken in again, and sheepfarming is now making rapid progress. It has been pushed on with considerable harshness, has excited very general discontent. In the parishes of Clyne and Kildonan, one great sheep farm has led this year to the dispossing of more than 100 families. These people (with their neighbours who are dreading the same fate) had so much of the Old Highland Spirit as to think their land their own, and attempted to resist the change *vi et armis* but this attempt was soon quelled, they determined on emigrating all in a body. They were however much at a loss how to proceed when I stepped in, and they have with joy accepted my proposals of settling them in Red River.

At that time Selkirk had been overwhelmed by the wholeheartedly enthusiastic response to his offers. He remarked:

The Sutherland men seem to be both in person and in moral character a fine race of men: there are great numbers among them who have property enough to pay their passage, and settle themselves with little or no assistance and many capable of paying in cash for their lands.

They were, he said, 'rigid Presbyterians', possessing 'a great deal of the old Highland pride and warmth of feeling, and I apprehend they will be much attached to any marks of personal attention and kindness'. In their anger and frustration at the Sutherland clearances, they had come to the point of violence. Selkirk's reflection on these events provides a precise indication of the assumptions of the people in relation to the land. He wrote in relation to the recent riots:

The circumstances of the case were such that I cannot consider their conduct on that occasion as any great imputation on their general character. According to the ideas handed down to them from their ancestors, and long prevalent among high and low throughout the Highlands, they were only defending their rights and resisting a ruinous unjust and tyrannical encroachment on their property.[45]

It seems more likely that emigration helped to siphon off some of the riotous elements during the Kildonan resistance. Emigration may have operated as an alternative to more sustained opposition to the clearances.

In the outcome, the migrants who joined Lord Selkirk's enterprise experienced fearful conditions which demanded further forbearance and stoicism. The voyage to Hudson's Bay was ravaged by the usual sequence of storm, seasickness and ship fever. Once disembarked, they were required to walk 900 miles overland to the Red River. The survivors then began to make a settlement with their bare hands, ice-bound and inadequately provisioned. Thereafter they found they were in the midst of a bloody conflict between feuding parties in the fur trade. They needed all the fortitude they could muster. Selkirk himself was the subject of an official inquiry and found wanting. He died in 1820, a broken man.[46] Yet, despite the unhappy experience of many Canadian emigrants, the exodus to North America was unstaunched and the streams continued to be fully supplied in the 1820s.

Within the Sutherland administration, which kept in step with most of the Highlands in this respect, proprietorial opinion moved towards the view that some degree of emigration was inevitable. Only Patrick Sellar took an extreme view — he believed that the people should be cleared out altogether, and preferably to America, in the cheapest possible way. For the others, Lady Stafford included, emigration signified the partial failure of their overall plan for the redesign of the estate. But, they thought, it was also a measure of the bloody-mindedness and suggestibility of many of the people. There exist some statistics for the later clearances in Sutherland, in 1819, which indicate that of 3,331 people removed, only 2 per cent left Scotland. This figure almost certainly understates the ultimate scale of the exodus. Clearance was often the first move that led, by stages, to expatriation. The landlords at this time gave no encouragement to emigration plans, but in Sutherland it was privately acknowledged that the departure of the less useful parts of the population would be desirable, and admitted that many would prefer emigration to settlement on the new coastal lots. The factors spoke of a predominance of 'inferior tacksmen who were compelled to be mere lotters' amongst the emigrants. The landlord, however, had no active role and, at all times before the famine of 1847, all initiative for emigration came from outside the Sutherland estate management.[47]

The Sutherland story was replicated in most of the north. After about 1815 landlords ceased to resist the operation of Malthusian forces. Indeed they frequently facilitated the process by further dislodging the population and readying them for the emigration agents. The expulsive forces were liberated, and the landlords now co-operated with the apparent necessities of depopulation.

Notes

1. Quoted in Campbell and Dow, *Source Books*, pp. 44-5.
2. Garnett, *Tour*, II, pp. 8-9, 12-13.
3. Donaldson, *Scots Overseas*, p. 68.
4. Alexander Irvine, *An Inquiry into the Causes and Effects of Emigration from the Highlands and Western Isles of Scotland* (Edinburgh, 1802), p. 7n.
5. *Farmer's Magazine* (1807), p. 322.
6. SRO, Seafield MSS, GD/248/683/2, Macdonald to Grant, 27 March 1793.
7. Ian Levitt and Christopher Smouth, *The State of the Scottish Working Class in 1843* (Edinburgh, 1979), p. 243.

8. This paragraph is based on Robert Brown to Hector Buchanan, 17 June 1801, from the Brown Correspondence (Lennoxlowe Muniments), quoted in Cameron, 'Scottish Emigration', p. 329. I am grateful to Dr Cameron for access to his important thesis.

9. SRO, RH/2/8/24, Report of John Blackadder.

10. *Caledonian Mercury*, 2 August 1792. Norman Murray, *The Scottish Handloom Weavers 1790-1850* (Edinburgh, 1978), p. 31; Bumsted, *The People's Clearance*, pp. 49, 76, 99; Garnett, *Tour*, pp. 235-6. Some of the western isles, notably Islay, had shown signs of overpopulation and emigration (some of it to Ireland) in the 1760s according to *The Rev. Dr Walker's Report on the Hebrides*, pp. 30. 97, 140, 153.

11. The fullest account of the politics of the emigration debate is found in Bumsted, *The People's Clearance*, Chs. 4-7.

12. SRO, British Fisheries Society Papers, 1773-1877, GD9/160/2, Porter to Pulteney, 10 January 1802; see also C. Fraser-Mackintosh, *Letters of Two Centuries* (Inverness, 1890), p. 343.

13. SRO, Lord Macdonald MSS, GD221/53, John Campbell to John Campbell (Edinburgh), 4 April 1803.

14. SRO, RH2/4/89, Home Office (Scotland) Correspondence, Hope to Grant, 3 September 1804.

15. There had been a previous inquiry into Highland emigration, in 1791, undertaken by the Society for the Propagation of Christian Knowledge. See J. Barron, *The Northern Highlands in the Nineteenth Century* (3 vols., Inverness, 1907-13), III, pp. 395 *et seq.*

16. Contemporary estimates are examined critically in Bumsted, *The People's Clearance*, p. 128.

17. SRO, RH2/4/89, Home Office (Scotland) Correspondence, Hope to Grant, 3 September 1804; SRO, GD9/166/23, letter from Lochbay, 27 December 1802.

18. Ibid.

19. D. Campbell and R. A. Maclean, *Beyond the Atlantic Roar: a Study of the Nova Scotia Scots* (Toronto, 1974), p. 9, n. 13.

20. On religious factors activating emigration in the western isles, see Mackintosh, 'Factors in Emigration' *passim.*

21. SRO, Melville Castle Muniments, GD51, H. Mackenzie to Lord Melville, 28 February 1803.

22. Such evidence would not have been impossible to discover. Reports of distress among Highland immigrants in North Carolina over the previous thirty years were in the correspondence of the Home Office. In December 1772, for example, Governor Josiah Martin had written: 'Between six and seven hundred people have lately arrived in Cape Fear River, from the Scottish Isles, one hundred and sixty of which I hear are absolutely pennyless, many of the People are said to have perished in this country of late years and few of them are thought likely to become profitable settlers, being for the most part unskilled in the Arts of Agriculture.' Quoted in Mackintosh, 'Factors in Emigration', p. 41. See also MacPhee, 'Trail of the Emigrants', pp. 182-4. On conditions aboard the migrant vessels see Edwin C. Guillet, *The Great Migration* (Toronto, 1933), pp. 10-11. See also the evidence of hardship experienced by the South Uist migrants to Cape Breton Island in 1791: NLS, Highland Society of Scotland Correspondence, Adv. MS 73.2.23, fo. 27.

23. For a full report see Knox, *A View of the British Empire, More Especially Scotland* (3rd edition, London, 1785), pp. 622-9.

24. SRO, Melville Castle Muniments, Papers of the Family of Dundas of Melville Castle, GD51/1/5/52/1-7, 'First and Second Reports of a Committee of

the Highland Society of Scotland on Emigration', 12 January 1802, 28 June 1802.
   25. See Oliver MacDonagh, *A Pattern of Government Growth 1800-1860* (London, 1961), pp. 55-8; Donaldson, *Scots Overseas*, p. 66.
   26. Hunter, *Crofting Community*, p. 25; Donaldson, *Scots Overseas*, p. 66; SRO, RH2/4/89, Hope to Grant, 3 September 1804. The motives of the Highland Society were long ago clarified by Stanley C. Johnston, *A History of Emigration from the United Kingdom to North America* (London, 1966 edition), p. 182.
   27. Selkirk, *Observations*, pp. 147-9, 152-3, and [Homer], *Observations on a Short Tour*, pp. 109-12.
   28. John Ramsay, *Scotland and Scotsmen of the Eighteenth Century* (2 vols., Edinburgh, 1888), II, p. 522.
   29. Hunter, *Crofting Community*, p. 25; but see also Guillet, *Great Migration*, p. 12, and MacDonagh, *Pattern*, pp. 59-60. One of the requirements of the Passenger Act was that foreign vessels taking passengers from the ports of the United Kingdom 'should be permitted to take only one person for every five tons'. John Quincy Adams had noted the unfavourable effect on American shipping and received an explanation from Castlereagh who 'insisted that the policy of the Act was not the discrimination of shipping, but to check emigration'. See *Writings of John Quincy Adams*, ed. W. C. Ford (New York, 1968), VI, p. 54.
   30. SRO, Macdonald MSS, GD221/53, Campbell of Kingsburgh to Campbell, Edinburgh, 20 June 1803, 4 July 1803.
   31. See Eric Richards, 'The Mind of Patrick Sellar (1780-1851)', *Scottish Studies*, vol. 15 (1971), p. 16. Some of the most devastating criticisms of the Passenger Act came from Francis Horner in 1805. He pointed out that the Bill had originated with the Highland Society, which had advocated ludicrously high standards for emigrant vessels:

so large an allowance of butcher's meat as 3¼lb for every passenger [weekly], even for infants at the breast, must appear strange to those who know that animal food is so rarely tasted in the Highlands by the lower order of tenantry, that, in the survey published by the Board of Agriculture, it is stated, that, among the farmers, there is not 5 lb of meat consumed in the family throughout the year.

The Highland Society had actually recommended 7 lb per week per head. Horner remarked, 'Nobody will entertain a doubt that their real purpose was to enhance the expense of the voyage, and so render it less within the means of the poor tenants.' He believed that its primary effect was to render the emigrants poorer, and that it produced the opposite effect to that expected by the humanitarian supporters of the Passenger Act. *Economic Writings of Francis Horner*, p. 127.
   32. SRO, Macdonald MSS, GD221/53, Campbell to Campbell, 26 June 1803.
   33. Barron, *Northern Highlands*, I, p. 6.
   34. Bumsted, *The People's Clearance*, pp. 191-2, indicates that the growth of the Canadian timber trade with Britain operated to depress the costs of the emigration passage and thereby diminish the impact of the new regulations.
   35. *Farmer's Magazine* (1809), pp. 43, 178.
   36. See J. P. Pritchett, *The Red River Valley 1811-1849. A Regional Study* (Toronto, 1942), p. 119, and J. M. Bumsted, 'Settlement by Chance: Lord Selkirk and Prince Edward Island', *Canadian Historical Review*, vol. 59 (1978), pp. 170-88.
   37. P. C. T. White, *Lord Selkirk's Diary 1803-4* (Toronto, 1958), pp. 33-5, 39, 51.
   38. R. J. Adam, *Papers on Sutherland Estate Management* (Scottish History

Society, 2 vols., Edinburgh, 1972), II, p. 39.
39. Ibid., p. 64.
40. Ibid., p. 90. John Campbell, factor to Lord Macdonald in 1801, had pointed out that status was a crucial consideration in the decision made by the poorer people of the Highlands. Given the choice of becoming cottars to tacksmen, or settlement on crofts or in villages, he said that 'they would rather try their choice in other countries'. Quoted in Mackintosh, 'Factors in Emigration', p. 94.
41. Adam, *Sutherland Estate Management*, I, pp. 143-4.
42. Ibid., II, pp. 192-3.
43. See Pritchett, *Red River Valley*, p. 119.
44. Gray, *Lord Selkirk of Red River* (London, 1963), pp. 86-7; Donald Gunn, *History of Manitoba* (Ottawa, 1880), Chs. 3 and 4.
45. Public Archives of Canada, Ottawa: Selkirk Papers, Selkirk to Miles Macdonell, 16 June 1813, MG19, EI I(2), pp. 650-61.
46. See Richards, *Leviathan*, pp. 216-19. NLS, Dep. 313, Sutherland Papers, Estate Management III, Box 10, Annotations of James Loch on printed letter of Francis Suther to the *Scotsman*, 13 August 1819. The Sutherland planners could not understand the desire of the people for emigration. In May 1813 William Young wrote, 'I really cannot account for the Emigration from Rogart — there is not a man who has been disturbed but with a view to make him better and that in place of having his land in runridge it may now be in one lot on a 19 year lease.' This was a measure of the social miscalculation at the centre of the Sutherland experiment. Ibid., Box 19, Young to Lord Gower, May 1813.
47. See MacPhee, 'Trail of the Emigrants', pp. 199-201.

9

THE HIGHLANDERS OVERSEAS AND OVERLAND

The Scottish Highlanders will ere long disappear from the face of the earth; *the mountains are daily depopulating*; the great estates have ruined the land of the Gael, as they did ancient Italy. The Highlander will ere long exist only in the romances of Walter Scott. The tartan and the claymore excite surprise in the streets of Edinburgh; they disappear — they emigrate — their national airs will ere long be lost, as the music of the Aeolian harp when the winds are hushed.

Jules Michelet[1]

Without discounting the 'pull' incentives of better conditions in America, the antipodes and the Lowlands, it appears likely that emigration from the Highlands during much of the nineteenth century was primarily a response to expulsive Malthusian forces. The incidence of famine conditions and the recurrent dependence of a large proportion of the population upon charity were undoubtedly dominant influences on the lives of people. Despite their tenacious attachment to their holdings, in the period 1815-55 many small tenants begged their landlords to help them emigrate. The main problem of historical interpretation concerns the degree to which the evicting and rental policies of the landlords, as a class, reinforced and accelerated the outward flow. There are enough unequivocal cases of clearances and emigration to demonstrate that compulsion was not uncommon, though such examples do not prove the typicality of the association. The fact that most agricultural regions of Britain, including many much better favoured than the Highlands, witnessed a drift from the land in these years operates as a check to the notion that the Highland proprietors were uniquely inhospitable to their tenantries.

The Highland case was more critical because the moment of its most rapid demographic increase, the 1810s, coincided with the precipitate decline of its most important income sources. The people's dependence on the potato was thereby redoubled, and their ability to pay a realistic return on landed capital diminished. Even the most tender Highland proprietors — David Steward of Garth, for instance — found themselves burdened with a growing and uneconomic tenantry, and sought to encourage their emigration. For many landlords and tenants alike the costs of passage rendered this solution implausible. Government policy moved only hesitantly towards the idea of assisting the emigration of the poor: in the 1820s there was much public opposition to the idea of 'shovelling out paupers'.[2] It was not until the 1830s that Wakefieldian ideas made experiments in subsidised emigration to the colonies acceptable. In the following decade there was a maturing of schemes to bring into accord the labour needs of colonies (notably those of Australia) and the depopulating policies of landlords (especially those of the Highlands and Ireland). By then chain migration had become a regular mechanism and the real cost of trans-oceanic emigration had been much reduced. But for several decades emigration from the Highlands continued to be unsystematic, improvised and subject to the 'fevers' of the common people, and the behaviour of individual landlords.

I

Reports from migrants were wildly inconsistent and it is almost certain that people left the Highlands with little accurate knowledge of the life they would face. Much evidence about the migrant experience was tainted by the propagandist needs of emigration agents, landlords and colonial governments — letters were edited, doctored, fabricated and presented on a highly selective basis.[3] Migrant letters are therefore an uncertain but potentially important source for penetrating the mental world of the *émigré* Highlanders.

Andrew Kennedy was almost certainly not representative. He had emigrated to America from the parish of Assynt, Sutherland, in 1809 with three other families. Between them they had £700. After an eight-week passage to New York, they proceeded a further 200 miles to the back settlements in search of land. There they met old acquaintances who had emigrated about thirty years before, but were now so miserably poor they could not offer even temporary quarters. The inhospitable and heavily wooded land cost £5 an acre. Greatly disappointed by their circumstances, the three families returned to their native country in July 1810 as they had so little encouragement to them remaining in America from the destitute state of the people who had been settled there for many years'. Kennedy testified that Highlanders lived in America in abject poverty and were not nearly so comfortable as the coastal cottars whose settlement had been catered for by the Sutherland estate. 'Thousands of them would willingly come home if they could procure a passage.' This evidence was quoted with great satisfaction at a time when the estate management was concerned to staunch the exodus from the estate, but it is to be noted that the Kennedy letter ran contrary to much other evidence which reported the success of the early emigrations from northern Scotland.[4]

The human face of emigration tends to be lost in a discussion of Malthusian pressures and the broad determinants of the great movements of people across the globe. The rarity of eye-witness accounts gives special value to a description written by Aiton of Strathavon in August 1805. He was in the middle of a survey of the Aviemore district and came across a party of emigrants *en route* for America. It was just after the Ruthven Fair and Aiton was accommodated in an already crowded inn.

> I was obliged to sleep in a room over a hall where common travellers are entertained, but before I got asleep, I heard the noise of a large company in the hall under my room, who I con-jectured were people returning from the fair; they made so much noise as kept me from sleep, and I could discover that some of them were in tears. Hearing a servant in the next room, I inquired who they were that occupied the hall, and what was the cause of their lamentations, when she told me they were a colony of Highlanders who had come from beyond Inverness, and were on their way to America, and that their tears had not dried up since they had begun their journey. This information removed all fears for my own safety, but my sympathy for these poor people was so much raised that I did not sleep one moment during that night, though I had travelled on foot from Blair Drummond to Aviemore on the three preceding days, nearly fifty miles each day. Every groan from below reached my heart. As a shilling was demanded for each bed, none of them could afford to pay that price, and they all remained in the hall.

They had worship performed with great solemnity and apparent devotion. I never saw so many people together so much dejected; *though the whole had been under sentence of death they could not have been more cast down*; their sighs and tears made an impression on my mind which will continue while I live.[5]

The condition on board the migrant ships, in defiance of the Passenger Act of 1803, varied alarmingly. Some vessels were undoubtedly ghastly. For instance there was the plight of a group of people who had been cleared from the Sutherland estate in 1819: they sailed from the port of Cromarty in conditions aboard ship which eventually provoked much public indignation. Even though the Customs officers had given approval for the voyage, the state of the ship was scandalous: the water was foul, the bread mouldy, and the half-cured pork was putrid. There were too many passengers aboard. When it reached Orkney it was wrecked and the rescued people were regarded as lucky in that they were spared the voyage across the Atlantic.[6]

II

The government remained decidedly lukewarm in its encouragement of emigration. The Report of the Select Committee on Emigration from the United Kingdon in 1827 was broadly sceptical of the proposition that overpopulation could be permanently remedied by emigration, even though it allowed for that possibility in some of the western isles. In the private sphere a few landlords financed their own schemes of emigration in the 1820s, in the hope of relieving the burden of numbers, but such arrangements did not develop in earnest until the 1840s. In 1823 Maclean of Coll had tried to obtain government assistance to transport his tenants from Rum to Canada, but without success. Taking the task into his own hands, in 1826 he despatched about 300 emigrants to Cape Breton Island at a cost of £5 14s per adult, generally described as 'crofters'. In this case the evidence suggests strongly that the people of Rum were given virtually no option but to emigrate: the episode was tantamount to clearance and forced expatriation. Maclean, however, did cancel all arrears, and provided passage money and a small fund to help settlement on arrival. 'Instead of a population of 350 people', the parliamentary inquiry was told, 'there is a population now of 50, and one person has taken the whole island as one farm, and of course he is able to pay a higher rent, as he has not to maintain so many people'. The man who organised the evacuation acknowledged that some of them had been reluctant: 'they did not like to leave the land of their ancestors'. In the same year Donald McNeill, the new owner of Canna, helped pay for the migration of 200 people and, even before, Grant of Glenmoriston had employed a similar device to reduce the burden of population on his estate.[7]

A great deal of the emigration from the Highlands passed unrecorded or was poorly documented, and it was rare for the precise circumstances of the departure to be defined. Even the dimensions of the exodus are unknown, still less the motives and the circumstances. Nevertheless there is some good evidence collected in the recipient countries, especially in Canada, which tracks some of the Highlanders to their destinations.[8] Thus, for the period 1815-38 we know that Nova Scotia alone received 39,000 immigrants, of whom 22,000 were Scots, and it is known that most of the latter were Highlanders. One agent, the vigorous Archibald Niven, circulated the information that he had 'shipped 12,000 Highlanders to the maritime colonies in the dozen years 1820-1832'. The historian of those great shifts of humanity wrote of 'the total disregard of many who dealt in this traffic for the welfare and fate of their passengers'. For instance, diseased, exhausted and penniless Highlanders arrived in Nova Scotia in 1827; their pitiful condition angered the local residents and placed strain on the capacity of the colonial hospitals. This was, indeed, a recurrent feature of mass peasant emigration in the nineteenth century, despite the regulations decreed by successive British governments.

The Canadian record of these years is packed with descriptions of the pathetic poverty of incoming Highlanders. In 1816 there arrived 'a very considerable number of Highlanders' at Pictou; in March 1817 400 more followed, including some of Selkirk's Sutherland recruits, from Orkney; in 1819 there were 435 from Tobermory and Lochaber and it was said that at least 750 more Highlanders arrived at Quebec. The flood continued: in 1821 at Sydney there disembarked a reported 350 from Barra followed in the next year by people from Muck. In 1826 Cape Breton Island received hundreds of people, including 500 said to have come 'at their own expense'. This deluge of people — probably over 2,000 in two years — caused the local authorities great anxiety. Many of these Highlanders were wracked with smallpox, dysentery and hunger: many deaths occurred *en route*, attributed by the surgeon to 'the confined, crowded and filthy state of the vessels'. But, in general, conditions on board were not detailed in the official record.

The brig *Stephen Wright* took on 170 passengers from Tobermory in September 1827. During the voyage one-third had been afflicted with smallpox, and many others with dysentery. Three of them died during the passage, another 10 while the vessel was in port, and a further 2 on landing at Sydney on Cape Breton Island. The *Harmony* carried 200 people from Stornoway, of whom 5 died on board and 22 on landing: they died 'on an uninhabited spot by measles, dysentery and starvation'. The local surgeon spoke of 'these poor creatures from the Highlands and Islands of Scotland [who arrived in Canada] to meet famine, disease and death on the shores of Cape Breton'. In 1828 two ships from Stornoway brought 673 people to the Canadian east coast, one ship reported to be so crowded that six families lived in the long boat for the duration of the voyage. Each year brought further batches of penniless migrants. In 1830 a shipload of 220 Highland emigrants were almost all stricken by severe fever during their transatlantic voyage. The death of 9 was ascribed to bad water which had been stored on board in palm oil casks. In the same year a group of 49 families from Skye were given a special grant of 4,000 acres on Cape Breton Island, but many immigrants began their colonial life begging for the relief of their immediate distress and the local communities were constantly pressed for charity.[9]

The flow of emigration was uneven but unceasing.[10] Sutherland in 1830 was said to have been possessed again by 'a fever of emigration'; more than 900 departed for Canada. Two years later 1,092 people from Stornoway and Tobermory arrived at Sydney in Nova Scotia.[11] In few of these cases were the details of the people's backgrounds recorded. Direct clearances onto the emigrant vessels were unusual but not impossible. Many came from the Macdonald estates, although it had been the proud boast of Lord Macdonald that 'not a man had been compelled to emigrate from his property ... and not one tenant had his goods sequestrated from the time his lordship came to the estates'. Such virtue was claimed, presumably, in contrast to the behaviour of his predecessors and his contemporaries. Yet within four years Macdonald's successor was assisting in arrangements for the expatriation of several hundred of his people to Cape Breton Island. It was reported that 'Two respectable agents, Islesman themselves, had chartered vessels for the purpose, partly as a trading speculation, partly as an act of philanthropy.' In some way the passage cost had been set in the extraordinarily low price of £2 per head,[12] for which the passengers received fresh water, but were obliged to find their own provisions for the voyage. As the *Inverness Courier* remarked:

> Highlanders, it is well known, can exist on very little when necessity requires them to do so. If each grown person, therefore, lays in one boll of oatmeal and another of potatoes, there is no fear of him starving, and thus for the sum of four pounds he will reach the promised land.[13]

Such arrangements enabled even some of the poorest to get out of Skye, but increased the risk of dependence and indigence in the receiving colony, of which there is much evidence.

While the direct impact of clearance is difficult to verify, there can be no doubt that these dislocations of humanity reflected the pressure of rising population, and the deterioration of living conditions in the Highlands. The falling price of cattle in the post-war years was especially critical for the people: they could not pay their rents, or sustain a tolerable existence on the land, which, in any case, was being competed for by sheepmasters. The peaks of emigration are not easily identified but appear to coincide with subsistence crises in the north, most notably in 1837-8 and 1847-53. There is enough evidence of distress and suffering among newly arrived emigrants in Canada and Australia to indicate that the agonies experienced in the homeland were compounded by both the conditions of the voyage and the rigours of settlement. In the few decades after Waterloo the Highland economy was, to borrow Gray's phrase, 'in travail'. The decline of economic activity occurred concurrently with the continued growth of population, which undoubtedly created conditions even riper for emigration than before. But the clearances helped further to set the population adrift. A dependent and poor population, however, lacked the means of emigration, and the more depressed the economy became (especially in the north-west) the more difficult it became for them to leave. It may be that, for the lowest strata, worsening conditions diminished the reluctance of the Highlanders to leave their native lands — but poverty made it impossible for them to raise the passage money. In this paradox was the root of much continued suffering in the Highlands.

For many of the very poorest, salvation came through a mechanism of chain migration by which earlier migrants paid for the subsequent passage of relatives. The evidence for this practice is substantial. A large proportion of migrants departed with the intention of joining kinsmen, especially in Nova Scotia and Cape Breton. Entire communities appear to have departed, such as the bulk of the Clan Chisholm, which went to America about 1834.[14] There is reference to the cohesiveness of the migrant groups in the supercilious comments made by John Howison in 1825 about the uncultivated newcomers in Glengarry, Upper Canada:

> Great numbers of emigrants from the Highlands of Scotland, have lately taken lands in the upper part of Talbot Settlement. These people, with the *clannishness* so peculiar to them, keep together as much as possible; and, at one time, they actually proposed among themselves, to petition the government to set apart a township, into which none but Scotch were to be admitted. Were this arrangement to take place, it would be difficult to say which party was the gainer, the habits of both [Highlanders and other] being equally uncouth and obnoxious.

He added that the Highlanders quickly adopted American democratic ways and lost all respect for rank.[15] Other reports, from Nova Scotia, suggested that Highlanders made relatively poor farmers:

> accustomed to a hard and penurious mode of life, they are too easily satisfied with the bare existence that even indolence can procure in this country, and care little for raising themselves and their families to a state of comfort and abundance.[16]

As for the morale of the departing migrants from the West coast ports, there were contradictory reports. Some appear to have left in an atmosphere of tragic despair; others were almost lighthearted, according to accounts. It almost certainly depended on the social stratum from which they were drawn, and the prevailing conditions in the Highlands. In 1835 more than 3,500 Highlanders left from the ports of Campbeltown, Oban and Tobermory. Lord Teignmouth witnessed the remarkable bustle of emigration from Tobermory where he found four ships full of people bound for Quebec and Nova Scotia.

One contained 200 persons, from the Long Island, emigrating in consequence of a difference with their landlord. They had received no assistance in the prosecution of their undertaking from any quarter; were in high spirits, and much encouraged by the accounts which they had received from their friends who had preceded them.

One of these people, Teignmouth recorded, had raised £40 from the sale of his property on Mull — including his house, two cows and a horse. A family of five could get to Cape Breton for £9 fare plus £4.10s for provisions.[17] He noted that most of the old obstacles to emigration had now been removed.

In the following year, 1836-7, famine again fell on the north, and increased the desire of the poorest to leave the Highlands, while again diminishing their capacity to pay the fares. The *Inverness Courier* lamented: 'We know not that the history of the British people ever presented such pictures of unmitigated want and misery as one exemplified at this moment in the case of the poor Highlanders.'[18]

III

In a general context of growing pressure on the land, the first step to emigration was often occasioned by the reorganisation of estate leases by the estate factor, or outright eviction. Small tenants might be dislodged and offered a little potato land, or inferior crofts on poor ground, or they would seek temporary asylum (at a high rent) on a neighbouring estate. The Kilcoy estate, the Gairloch estate in Urquhart and the Cromartie estate at Strathpeffer all offered refuge to small tenants removed by adjacent proprietors. Similarly the coastal villages also gave temporary or permanent sanctuary for the displaced, usually by the hospitality of a relative. Once mobilised, however, the people looked to wider horizons, even to emigration.[19]

Some, perhaps most, of the people who left the north simply journeyed out of the Highlands, into the Lowlands and into England, to the apparent promise of a more secure life in the industrial centres of the British economy. There is little evidence of the scale of this migration and of the reception of the Highlanders in the south. They captured little attention except where they became a social problem and entered public institutions. But Malcolm Gray has argued plausibly that the greatest drain of population from the Highlands, especially the south and east, 'was not in the departure of the emigrant ship ... but in the silent and steady and unplanned shifting, mainly of the border population ... towards the Lowlands'.[20] As early as the 1780s and 1790s people displaced from the southern Highlands were pouring into the Clydesdale area — into 'bleachfields, printfields, cotton mills, and many other branches of manufactures, in which previous intro-duction and preparation is not required'.[21] Some were directly recruited by southern employers; the Rothesay millowner, Dugald Bannatyne, took people from Mull, and declared the children better value than their parents as factory labour.[22] In 1810 the northern newspapers carried advertisements by Glasgow manu-facturers offering lodging and work for Highland families, while the Owen and Atkinson company of New Lanark sent a 'preacher' to the north in an effort to engage workers for their cotton factory. In Sutherland local managers hoped they could persuade Owen to transfer some of his operations to the north rather than lure away the people of the estate.[23] Direct recruitment of Highlanders to southern factories continued spasmodically until at least the 1850s, and there were repeated but unconfirmed allegations of gross exploitation of the innocent immigrants by powerful employers.[24]

The dependence of areas of the Scottish Lowland economy upon Highland labour — both seasonal and permanent — attests to the northerners' adaptability to modern southern discipline. The scale of the seasonal movement demonstrates both the mobility of the Highland labour force and the vital role of seasonal income in propping up peasant life in the Highlands. In 14 days in August 1824 more than 2,500 Highland shearers passed along the Crinan Canal in steamboats, and four years later the *Inverness Courier* offered another glimpse of this seasonal tide of humanity:

> Hundreds of Highland peasants, male and female, are now migrating to the South for employment during the harvest. On

Monday we met about 150 near Moy, journeying in parties according to their respective districts, and each accompanied by a piper. The greater part were from Sutherlandshire and the Black Isle, in Ross-shire. The sound of the bagpipes seemed to give a tone of gaiety to the scene, but there was often more of sorrow than of merriment in the strain.[25]

Seasonal migration, of course, had for many decades offered a preferred alternative to outright emigration, a means of sustaining peasant life in the north. There is fragmentary evidence that even this support was threatened in the 1830s when the Lothian harvest (a great and traditional employer of itinerant Highlanders) came into competition from seasonal Irish labour, generated by circumstances very similar to those in the north of Scotland.[26] In 1841 it cost less than a shilling to get from Northern Ireland to Glasgow but the fare from Skye was at least ten shillings.[27]

Recent research by Dr. Lobban on the internal exodus of Highlanders has identified a number of important themes which relate to the inter-regional adjustment of labour numbers. There appears to have been little friction on a general level, in the acceptance of northerners in the south. Though there were occasional criticisms of alleged indolence, work-shyness and dirty or verminous appearance, the record shows a relatively easy merging of Highlanders into Lowland society.[28] In 1836 a census taken by a Gaelic minister in Glasgow recorded 22,050 Highlanders in the city (almost certainly an underestimate), of whom 5,356 were less than ten years of age. It was thought that Edinburgh attracted only a tenth as many. In 1838 another estimate claimed that one-fifth of Glasgow's population came from the Highlands; in 1841 it was recorded that there were 30,000 in the city, a rise of 8,000 since 1822 (there were 50,000 Irish in Glasgow in 1841). The Census of 1851 indicated that about 10 per cent of all immigrant adults in Glasgow were Highlanders.[29] Norman Macleod remarked that

A very large proportion of that number [he estimated 30,000 in 1850] are incapable of receiving religious instruction except through the medium of their own language; while, from their own poverty, they are unable to pay for seat rents — a system unknown in the districts from which they come.

In 1851 a total of 85,400 people born in the primary Highland counties were living in the rest of Scotland.[30]

The actual experience of Highland emigrants in southern towns is little recorded, though there is some indication that they confronted initial difficulties similar to those of emigrants to Canada. It was often alleged, for instance, that aged and feeble Highlanders drifted into Edinburgh and Glasgow to become extra burdens on their relief facilities. It is known that, in 1836, 70 out of 110 patients treated at the Edinburgh Infirmary were Highlanders, mostly very recent immigrants from the remote islands. It was said that 'To the neglect of vaccination, and to the practice of it with impure lymph, deteriorated perhaps in the transmission, must be ascribed the prevalence of smallpox among the Highlanders.' Some further evidence of this was furnished in the statistics of out-pensioners at the Charity Workshops in Edinburgh in 1841 when there was a clear disproportion of Highlanders.[31] C. B. Baird, the honorary secretary of the Glasgow committee for the assistance of Highlanders made destitute by the famine of 1837, noted that they had suffered by the economic competition from the incoming Irish. He pointed out that it was more difficult for a Highlander to get to Glasgow than the Irish, who were also better labourers. He was robustly critical of his north countrymen:

> Above all, they are peculiarly subject to diseases from their mode of life and from their filthy habits, and especially from their want of inoculation. On looking over the reports regarding our infirmary, I find an amazing number of Highlanders among the inmates; and I found that in Albion Street Hospital, according to Dr Perry, in one year 40 per cent of the patients were from the Highlands and islands.[32]

In his evidence before a parliamentary inquiry, Baird said that the Highlanders were chiefly labourers and their families, and that their moral, social and economic condition was deplorable. A subsequent witness, the well-known champion of Highland causes, the Rev. Norman Macleod, denied these suggestions, and also rejected the allegation that most of Glasgow's prostitutes were girls from the Highlands. He did confirm, however, that the Highlanders were prone to measles and smallpox, thereby reinforcing the belief that they were careless of inoculation in the West Highlands.[33] Some of the internal migration of the Highlanders can be traced through the Census statistics — the drifts to Glasgow and beyond, to London as well. But not even the censuses detected the short-distance relocation of people within a parish, into coastal lots or villages, the most widespread consequence of agrarian change in the Highlands. As the Rev. John Macleod of Morvern testified in 1841:

> The people are compelled to congregate together in villages ... by looking to the population lists of my parish, it will appear that the population has not undergone any great change for the last two or three periods of the census; but a great part of the parish has been depopulated and other settlements have been formed, so that while one part was depopulated another was overpeopled.[34]

Intra-parochial movement of this order was, naturally, complemented by the voluntary movement of rural people to the villages and farms within and beyond the Highlands.

All these trails of Highlanders — abroad, to the Lowlands, to villages and farms — reduced the scale of demographic increase in the region but did not prevent an absolute rise of population until the mid-nineteenth century in most places. In this respect the Highland experience conformed with that of Ireland and other agricultural counties in Britain. Emigration was neither sufficiently large nor rapid enough to relieve fully the pressure on food resources in the ailing economy of the Highlands.

IV

During the 1830s the parlous condition of much of the Highland population, perhaps for the first time, began to impinge upon the national consciousness. As was so often the case, the Highlands followed in the wake of the Irish experience. More than anything else it was the famine conditions of 1836-7 that generated a new measure of concern — despite the competing demands for charity from the poor in the great new urban conglomerations of industrial Britain. The failure of two successive crops in 1836 and 1837 focused attention on the vulnerability and squalor of the northern peasantry. The crisis coincided with the organisation of free and subsidised emigration to Australia so that, for the first time, considerable numbers of Highlanders were directed to the southern hemisphere. For some years thereafter Australia and Canada became rival destinations for emigrants: both sought the young and the healthy, unencumbered by elderly and sick relatives. The emergence of Australia as a destination had been helped by a radical reduction in the costs of passage during the previous decade.[35]

A large proportion of the people recruited for the sponsored emigration to Australia in the 1830s were refugees from the crumbling economy of the Highlands. They were the forerunners of the concerted mass migration that developed more fully in the 1850s. Eventually the migrant needs of the Australian colonies seemed to coincide so closely with the needs of Highland landlords that it was widely believed that clearance and emigration were two sides of the same coin.

As early as 1815 there had been talk of Australia as a destination for people dislodged by clearances.[36] There had been a notable migration of Macleods to Van Diemen's Land in 1820. Donald Macleod of Talisker, Skye, who had been a major in the 56th Regiment, decided in 1819 to sell off his lands, which had been in the family for two centuries, and to emigrate to the Australian colony. His father-in-law, Alexander Maclean of Coll, appears to have financed the passage of Macleod's kinsmen.[37] Macleod travelled with a party of 36 Highlanders of his connection. Securing a grant of 2,000 acres in Van Diemen's Land, he became a considerable man in colonial society, and joined a network of West Highland immigrants of this class, mainly from the tacksman stratum, whose income and mobility had been much enhanced by military service in the French Wars. They chose Australia or Canada rather than the circumscribed environment of post-war Skye. Often they claimed to be leaving the Highlands because of the lack of military employment and the renunciation of their leases; many had experience in sheepfarming. There are many examples of these successful Highlanders — men of capital able to finance development in Australian land. They demonstrated the social mobility and acquisitive drive of the old middle-ranking Highlanders who had now cut themselves adrift. Australia presented an exotic opportunity for adventurous Highland families with more than the usual degree of capital and initiative. The relative success of this class of immigrant contrasted sharply with the pauperised masses who followed from the north-west coasts of Scotland in the following decades. Yet each, in different ways, was the product of the expulsive forces at work in the post-war Highland economy.

Great shortages of agricultural labour in Australia in 1836-7 coincided with the worst subsistence crisis in the Highlands since 1816-17, marked by bad harvests, a widespread potato famine and starving cattle. Demands for large-scale emigration became more insistent. Landlord opinion had moved closer towards the direct encouragement of emigration and many of the people were evidently keen to get out. The great impediment of course was the cost of the voyage — even the relatively short journey to Canada was beyond the purse of most common people; Australia might as well have been on the other side of the moon.

From Stoer on the extreme west coast of Sutherland, the parish minister petitioned the landlord on behalf of the people in March 1836:

> those, who are in indigent circumstances, solicit the favour of your ascertaining whether you could procure any aid for them from Government — or failing that, whether her Grace would be pleased to give any, as very few of them can pay their passage [to America], unless some aid be obtained for them ... If emigration could be encouraged it would effectively relieve and benefit those who remain and without some resource or other to provide for the redundant population, it is impossible to predict what shall become of them soon.[38]

Two years later the Glasgow Statistical Society received a report which predicted catastrophe. For instance, at Ullapool, they were told that

> The bulk of the people are idle and in very great misery. They are, at least many of them are, quite prepared to emigrate; but, alas! they have not the means; and the chance is, unless they receive assistance, that, after pining away a few years in their present state of wretchedness, their numbers may be thinned by famine or disease.[39]

The 'redundancy' of the population was acknowledged not only by landlords and ministers, but also by the beleaguered people themselves. It would clearly be inaccurate to ascribe the emigration of such people to direct force exerted by landlords: the people sought, indeed begged, for their own expatriation. The responsibility for the creation of the conditions in the Highlands which prompted this act of despair is a larger question.

Many, perhaps most, landlords remained reluctant to 'emigrate' their people by providing full subsidies. Partly the hesitation was connected with the fear of public criticism which would inevitably link subsidised emigration with the allegation that the common people were being levered out of the Highlands. Thus, the Duchess of Sutherland was prepared to offer a prospective emigrant a few pounds to help his departure, but explicitly refused to involve herself in the business of organising an exodus, or negotiate directly with shipping agents. One of her advisers believed that it would be in everybody's interest if half of the entire population emigrated, and 'more especially if one could get quit of the worthless, retaining the more respectable'.[40] Yet it was still some years before landlord subsidies became at all significant: emigration remained unsystematic and probably marginal, responding primarily to the demands of the people and limited by the availability of landlord funds.

In the severity of the famine in 1836-7, which brought reports of 'unexampled destitution and even starvation from the west',[41] the government at last made a positive move for emigration. Wakefieldian doctrines, in London and in Australia, had taken considerable hold, and the use of colonial land revenues for the payment of emigration costs had received general acceptance. In response to the urgent demand for labour in Australia, the British government sponsored a trial exercise in subsidised emigration: in October 1837 3 shiploads of Highlanders departed for New South Wales, followed by a further 17 vessels which, in total, carried about 4,000 emigrants. The recruitment was specific — the people were to possess 'good characters' and be under 35 years. In May 1838 the *Inverness Courier* reported the atmosphere created by the promise of free emigration:

After some months of expectation and anxiety, Dr. Boyter, the Government emigration agent for Australia, arrived at Fort William. The news of his arrival, like the fiery cross of old, soon spread through every glen in the district, and at an early hour on Monday, thousands of enterprising Gaels might be seen ranked around the Caledonian Hotel, anxious to quit the land of their forefathers and to go and possess the unbounded pastures of Australia. While we regret that so many active men should feel it necessary to leave their own Country, the Highlands will be considerably relieved of its overplus population.[42]

The operation was well planned and the demand from potential emigrants was great enough to persuade the government to extend the scheme for two extra years. There were no reports at this time of opportunistic landlords taking advantage of the situation to expel tenants from their estates. The exercise almost certainly revealed the latent demand for overseas emigration in the region: it was enough to overcome the common prejudice against New South Wales.

In more general terms the Australian experiment was a mixed experience for the people involved. Conditions aboard some of the ships were bad, and there were damaging allegations that the passengers had been treated no better than transported convicts. The officials tended to attribute the squalor, disease and death on some voyages to the poor condition of the people before their embarkation — as one of them said, they come from 'an extremely distressed district in a state of great want'. A full account of the reception of the Highlanders in Australia cannot be given here, but one aspect illuminates the mentality of the departing Highlanders. The Wakefieldian assumptions of the emigration programme required that the people present themselves as labourers on arrival in the colony. The subsidisation scheme was based on the premiss that they would not be able to set up as independent occupiers of land for some years after disembarkation. However, many of the Highlanders had migrated on the false understanding that they would receive land for themselves as soon as they got to the colony. As a consequence of this misunderstanding many Highlanders, on arrival, refused to accept hired employment and claimed they had expected to be given land and that they 'had been induced to emigrate, by the hope held out to them of being enabled to settle in one neighbourhood, so as to be within reach of religious ordinances administered in their native tongue'. The colonial authorities were reluctant to accord the Highlanders special treatment, but the persuasion of the redoubtable cleric J.D. Lang prevailed, and some of them were given special settlement grants in the Hunter Valley. Local employers were critical that the Highlanders had become 'occupiers of land on their own account, instead of being forced to work for wages as farm labourers', in proper conformity with colonial ideas. The episode illustrated the land hunger of the Highlanders and their basic aspirations: they had left Syke because they possessed insufficient land for their welfare; they crossed the world to become owners of land denied to them in Scotland. It was the old peasant mentality.

The recruitment of people for Australia continued through 1838 and the supply was almost overwhelming. It was a clear measure of the desperation of the population. The scheme was given active support by church ministers and although there was much criticism of the administrative conditions of the emigration, there was considerable popular gratitude expressed to Dr Boyter who had, by 1840 organised the transit of about 5,200 Scots to Australia, most of whom were probably Highlanders.

The Australian experiment of the 1830s helps to clarify the question of the relationship between Highland emigration and the clearances. The lack of ill-will among emigrants to the antipodes suggests that direct expulsion by landlords was entirely absent. The alacrity and enthusiasm for emigration was not the result of clearances — it was a response to the severity of the seasons 1836-8, to the general dilapidation of the Highland economy, to the pressure of rents (which had not fallen in line with other prices), and to the propaganda of the Australian emigration agencies. The thing that cannot be doubted is the spontaneous enthusiasm for emigration: Dr Boyter and his men were deluged with applications. Thus, for instance, in May 1838 more than 1,200 people of Lochaber alone had pledged themselves to emigrate to Australia under the Colonial Act — and this number, it was reported, was only a part of an even larger 'emigration of a voluntary and unaided character [that] had taken place from Lochaber and neighbouring districts during the past two years'.[43]

Emigration to North America continued in the late 1830s despite vigorous competition from Australia. In the summer of 1840 it was calculated that 403 people left the northern Highlands for Canada; in August 550 left Uig and Tobermory for Prince Edward Island. In most of these cases it is usually impossible to discover the precise circumstances which caused the emigrants to leave the Highlands; but when in April 1841 a ship left Scrabster with 190 emigrants, many from Reay parish, it is likely that more than a few were victims of a series of notorious evictions conducted at the behest of a tacksman, James Anderson.[44] Voluntary and involuntary emigration were intertwined.

In a number of other contemporary episodes the expulsive pressure of the landlord was also impossible to conceal. In 1837 Stewart Mackenzie of Seaforth expressed the view that emigration was the only permanent remedy for the population problem of

Lewis. He thought that clearances for sheep should be associated with schemes for subsidised emigration. Aware of these impending changes in estate policy, the people of Uig petitioned Mackenzie for free passages and land in Canada. In 1838 a group of 70 people emigrated from the Seaforth estate. It was recorded that 'They did not wish to go, but the farms were cleared for the purpose of being made sheep-walks, and the expense of the passage was paid by the proprietor.' Another group of people cleared from the Seaforth property arrived in Quebec in 1841 in a condition described as 'destitute and penniless'. It is also known that large numbers of people from the Skye and North Uist estate of Lord Macdonald continued to reach Cape Breton Island and Prince Edward Island in the years 1833 to 1842 — assisted by Destitution Committees in Edinburgh and Glasgow, as well as their proprietor. In this case there is no doubt that philanthropy rode in tandem with landlord pressure to secure a vigorous exodus of the people.[45] More publicity was attached to the induced emigration from Borve in Harris in these years — the first efforts in 1834 and 1838 were unavailing despite the offer of free passages and the cancellation of arrears. In 1839 troops were employed to evict the uncooperative people, yet even then they would not emigrate. Only in 1841-2 did they agree to go — a total of 631 people.[46]

These cases illustrate the total breakdown of social and economic relations on some Highland estates, and give some credence to the more sensational stories linking clearance and emigration in the mid-nineteenth century. Neutral reporting of the process was rare and consequently there is unusual interest in the relatively disinterested opinion of Highland emigration recorded privately by Lady Seymour in her journal of a tour of the north undertaken in 1839. She observed, 'A ship for Australia is collecting passengers at Tobermory in Mull, and the system of extending the Farms is still going on and obliging emigration as a resource to the Peasantry.' Local opinion approved 'on the ground of the Tendency of the Sons of Small Farmers to remain encumbrances on their families in preference to becoming Labourers'. Seymour had no doubt that the chiefs had caused 'the forced emigration of thousands of Highlanders', a process now further accelerated by the advent of 'Deer Stalking' which she described as 'the luxury of the age, or rather one of the means of excitement'.[47]

The context of emigration was created by general and particular pressures, not easily separated. As population pressure accumulated in mid-century, and as governmental and philanthropic assistance began to emerge, the most distressed stratum of Highland society came to dominate the emigrant lists. The most impoverished emigrants from the Highlands were those who departed in the famine decade, 1845-55, the subject of the next chapter.

Notes

1. Quoted in an anonymous pamphlet, *On the Neglect of Scotland and her Interests by the Imperial Parliament* (Edinburgh, 1878), p. 8.
2. See, for instance, H.J.M. Johnston, *British Emigration Policy 1815-30* (Oxford, 1972), *passim*.
3. On this question see Allan Conway, *The Welsh in America* (St Paul, 1961), Preface.
4. Quoted in Richards, *Leviathan*, p. 219. The most significant recurrent themes in the literary record were the frightful and hazardous conditions aboard the ships, followed by back-breaking experiences in the initial phases of settlement. Only subsequently did the great uprooting produce a better life.
5. *Treatise on Moss* (Ayr, 1811), p. 351, quoted in an article by W. G. Yorstoun in *Journal of Agriculture* (1842), p. 533. Emphasis in original.
6. Barron, *Northern Highlands*, I, p. 168; *Military Register*, 11 August 1819.
7. *PP* (1826-7), V, Select Committee on Emigration from the United Kingdom, pp. 287-92; Johnston, *British Emigration Policy*, p. 2; Cameron, 'Scottish Emigration', p. 295; cf. Flinn, *Scottish Population History*, p. 445. In 1827 Clanranald tried to gain government assistance for the emigration of 'the poorer class of Subtenants and Cottars' whom he wished to clear from his heavily encumbered estates in Benbecula, Canna and South Uist. In this case the connection between clearance and emigration was transparent. See J. L. Campbell, 'Eviction at First Hand. The Clearing of Clanranald's Islands, *Scots Magazine* (January 1945), pp. 297-302.
8. In particular see Campbell and Maclean, *Beyond the Atlantic Roar*.
9. Most of this information comes from J. S. Martell, *Immigration to and Emigration from Nova Scotia, 1815-1838* (Halifax, 1942), especially the Appendix. See also D. B. Blair, 'On the Early Settlement of the Lower Provinces by the Scottish Gael: Their Various Situations and Present Prospects', *Transactions of the Celtic Society of Montreal* (1884-7); Colin S. Macdonald, 'Early Highland Emigration to Nova Scotia and Prince Edward Island, 1770-1853', *Nova Scotia Historical Society Collections*, vol. 23 (1941).
10. See Flinn, *Scottish Population History*, p. 446.
11. Barron, *Northern Highlands*, II, pp. xxvii, 78.
12. It is not easy to chart the course of emigration costs. A passage from Skye to North Carolina was £12 12s per head in 1802; from Rum to Cape Breton in 1826 adults cost £5 14s and the expense from Tobermory to Quebec in 1847 was £4 per head. SRO,GD221/58, Campbell to Campbell, 7 October 1803; Cameron, 'Scottish Emigration', p. 337; *PP* (1826-7), p. 287.
13. Barron, *Northern Highlands*, II, pp. 61-2.
14. Ibid., p. 150.
15. John Howison, *Sketches of Upper Canada* (Edinburgh, 1825), p. 173.
16. Ibid. On Highlanders in Canada see also Macdonald, *Sketches of the High-*

landers; Barbara Kincaid, 'Scottish Immigration to Cape Breton, 1758-1838', unpublished MA thesis, University of Dalhousie, 1964; S. L. Morse, 'Immigration to Nova Scotia, 1839-1851', unpublished MA thesis, University of Dalhousie, 1946.

17. Lord Teignmouth, *Sketches of the Coasts and Islands of Scotland and of the Isle of Man* (2 vols., London, 1836), I, p. 80; *The Topographical, Statistical and Historical Gazeteer of Scotland* (Edinburgh, 1844), p. 788.

18. Quoted in MacPhee, 'Trail of the Emigrants', p. 194.

19. See I. R. M. Mowat, *Easter Ross 1750-1850* (Edinburgh, 1980), p. 46; Thomson, *The Little General*, pp. 48-9; Richards, *Highland Clearances*, pp. 232, 342-3.

20. Gray, *Highland Economy*, p. 64.

21. *Old Statistical Account*, III, Lochgilphead and Kilmorich, pp. 185-6.

22. Leigh, 'The Crofting Problem', pp. 1, 268.

23. NLS, Sutherland Papers, Dep. 313, III, Box 19, Young to Gower, 17 August 1810, 2 October 1810, 16 October 1810, 28 October 1810.

24. N. J. Mackinnon, 'Strath, Skye, in the Mid-Nineteenth Century', *TGSI*, vol. 51 (1978-80), pp. 179-80.

25. Barron, *Northern Highlands*, II, pp. 53-4; I, p. 245.

26. *PP* (1833), V, p. 128, Report from the Select Committee on Agriculture.

27. Mackinnon, 'Strath, Skye, in the Mid-Nineteenth Century', p. 177.

28. Lobban 'Migration of Highlanders'; allegations about Highlanders' work habits are quoted in James E. Handley, *The Navvy in Scotland* (Cork, 1970), pp. 35, 59-61; Murray, *The Scottish Handloom Weavers*, p. 31. As early as 1784 George Dempster had argued that rising expectations were the cause of Highland migration. He wrote, 'I do not believe the people live worse than they did but on the contrary by means of the potatoes rather better ... The people have got Ideas of living more comfortably, and believe it easier to effect elsewhere than at home and in the present state of the Highlands it certainly is so.' Quoted in Brock, *Scotus Americanus*, p. 161.

29. Teignmouth, *Sketches*, Appendix, p. 314; Arthur Redford, *Labour Migration in England, 1800-1850* (Manchester, 1964), p. 65.

30. NLS, Sutherland, Papers, Dep. 313, II, Box 45, Letter of Norman Macleod (printed), 10 January 1850, Macleod to Duke of Sutherland, 25 January 1850. Flinn, *Scottish Population History*, p. 462.

31. *Scotsman*, 16 January 1841.

32. Robert Cowan, *Vital Statistics of Glasgow* (Edinburgh, 1838), pp. 30-1.

33. Select Committee on Emigration (Scotland), *PP*, (1841), VI, pp. 51-2, 115-20. On distinctions between the Irish, West Highlanders and North Highlanders, see the evidence of William Dixon in 1836, quoted in Campbell and Dow, *Source Book*, p. 8.

34. SC on Emigration (Scotland) (1841), p. 101.

35. See Frank J. A. Broeze, 'Private Enterprise and the Peopling of Australasia, 1831-1850', *Economic History Review*, vol. 35 (1982), p. 237.

36. See Richards, *Leviathan*, p. 216.

37. D. S. Macmillan, *Scotland and Australia, 1788-1850: Emigration, Commerce and Investment* (Oxford, 1967), pp. 81-5.

38. SCRO, Sutherland Collection, D593/K, Gordon to Loch, 15 March 1836.

39. Allan Fullarton and Charles R. Baird, *Remarks on the Evils at Present Affecting the Highlands and Islands of Scotland* (Glasgow, 1838), p. 50.

40. SCRO Sutherland Collection, D593/K, Loch to Baigrie, 23 March 1836, 16 May 1836, Horsburgh to Loch, 15 April 1836. Macmillan, *Scotland and Australia*, p. 323.

41. Macmillan, *Scotland and Australia*, p. 278.

42. Ibid., quoted p. 261. On this situation in Lewis, see Macdonald, *Lewis*, pp. 166-7.

43. Barron, *Northern Highlands*, II, p. 225; George Dunderdale, *The Book of the Bush* (London 1898), p. 222. On the disposition of the population to emigrate see the decisive evidence of the survey of 52 parishes conducted by the Glasgow Destitution Committee in 1837-8, quoted by T. Cameron, 'The Changing Role of the Highland Landlords Relative to Scottish Emigration during the First Half of the Nineteenth Century' in *Proceedings of the Fourth and Fifth Colloquia on Scottish Studies* (Guelph, 1971), pp. 80-1.

44. See Richards, *Highland Clearances*, pp. 441 ff.

45. See Levitt and Smout, *Scottish Working Class*, pp. 239, 248.

46. SC on Emigration (Scotland), (1841), p. 174; Cameron, 'Scottish Emigration', pp. 358, 392-3.

47. Warwick County Record Office, CR114A 379, Journal of a Tour of Scotland by Lady Seymour and Sir Francis H. Seymour, 1839.

10
EMIGRATION AS A FINAL SOLUTION

All our readers know what a clearance is; and all will admit that it is a ready expedient. A shipful of human beings may be sent across the Atlantic at a trifling cost; and that cost is less to the proprietor, when it is paid from the proceeds of their own holdings. Heart-rending as such clearances are, tearing the poor from their hearths and their homes, and driving them aboard ship like a herd of cattle, is the mildest part of this awful ceremony. If the inconvenience of a long sea-voyage, and the mere *removal* of masses of people from their native soil were the worst, it might be suffered; but what becomes of them after crossing the Atlantic?

Elgin and Morayshire Courier, 26 October 1849

By 1840 the 'Highland Problem' had achieved sufficient prominence in the national consciousness to generate almost as much concern and alarm as the Irish case. Recurring famine (together with the evidence of the Census) strengthened the view that the Highlands were overpopulated and that the population should be reduced by systematic emigration. Even when the subsistence crisis receded in 1839-40 public pressure for government-assisted emigration was sustained. A petition from Inverness asked Parliament to apply the balance of the destitution relief monies to the promotion of emigration.[1] Relief committees established in Glasgow, Edinburgh and London continued in existence, and their services were again in demand in 1840 when yet another partial failure of the potato crop occurred in the north of Scotland.

In February 1841 the MP for the county of Inverness, Henry Baillie, brought the matter of Highland conditions before the attention of the House of Commons, and pressed for an inquiry into 'the expediency of a general and extensive system of emigration to relieve the destitute poor of the Highlands'. Significantly, Baillie presented the problem primarily in terms of the burden which overpopulation placed upon the northern land-owners who, he said, sought government assistance to emigrate their people. He tried to convince the House with the story of one unfortunate proprietor whose rental was inadequate to pay the settlements fixed for his younger brothers in time of booming kelp prices. This man had given up his entire estate to his brothers, and had himself gone out to Australia as a sheepfarmer. More gener-ally Baillie argued that the common Highlanders deserved govern-ment assistance: despite misery and distress, the people had committed no outrages. They had maintained an extraordinary and laudable stoicism in conditions of great hardship, far worse than anything endured by the negroes of the West Indies who, he noted, had been favoured by government help. At a cost of £3 a head, the people could get to Canada. In the event the government sanctioned a parliamentary inquiry even though the prospect of financial assistance was expressly discounted, and despite the fact that distress existed in many other parts of the British Isles. At that very time Britain was descending into perhaps the worst industrial depression of the century.

The Report of the Select Committee on Emigration of 1841, Scotland, came to the startling conclusion that there were between 45,000 and 60,000 people too many living on the West Highland zone of Argyll, Inverness and Ross. The essence of the Report was that wholesale emigration was the only feasible solution to the problem of poor relief in the West Highlands. The government, however, steadfastly refused to become directly involved except by applying colonial land revenues to subsidise migration to the anti-podes. Philanthropic bodies, such as the Glasgow Emigration Society, continued to offer assistance in a small way and some landlords provided direct support from their own coffers. In 1842, for instance, Sir Colin Mackenzie of Kilcoy provided for the emi-gration to Canada of a group of cottars from his Strathbraan estate in Ross.[2] But there could be no avoiding the odium that sur-rounded the idea of landlord-sponsored emigration: the line between encouragement and compulsion was indistinct if not actu-ally invisible. Frequently newspaper reports felt it necessary to distinguish particular emigrations as 'voluntary'[3] — itself testimony to the extent of the belief that many emigrations from the High-lands were other than voluntary. And there remained a body of opinion in the 1840s (and indeed to the present day) which denounced emigration, and demanded improved methods of cultivation and security of peasant tenure as the proper solution to the poverty problem. This view was fundamentally opposed to the quasi-Malthusian diagnosis that the 'Highland Problem' was a consequence of demographic causes rather than landlordism. A middle position was adopted by the editor of the *Inverness Courier*, who, in 1842, voiced ' unqualified censure to the manner in which whole districts had been hastily cleared and turned into sheep walks, but does not think that emigration can be avoided'.[4]

The parliamentary report of 1841 distinguished between various types of motivation which caused landlords to encourage the emigration of their own tenantry. It was rarely simply a question of expelling the people to make way for sheep and deer which would yield a better rent. In some cases no rental increase could be expected when the population was diminished by emigration. The benefit that accrued to the landlord in such circumstances (which were general) lay in the reduction of his obligation to relieve his tenantry during times of recurrent subsistence crisis. Duncan Shaw, a factor managing estates on Harris and North Uist, pointed out in evidence that Colonel Gordon, the new owner of South Uist (which had a population of 3,000) had concluded that his rental could not be increased even in the event of a large emigration. In bad seasons the proprietor was obliged by custom to import meal for the relief of his tenantry, although, as Shaw pointed out, he was under no legal compulsion and could 'claim for the price of that meal on the tenantry if he chooses to enforce it'. In reality, of course, bad seasons costs the landlords not only the price of the meal but also a loss of rents. Lord Dunmore in Harris expected to recover less than one-third of his recent expenditure on emergency supplies for his people. Eventually both Dunmore and Gordon became heavily implicated in forced emigrations.[5]

I

Through the 1840s the uncoordinated drain of the people from the Scottish Highlands continued. They responded to opportunities as they arose, to the state of the harvest, to letters from abroad and to the urging of their landlords. Often emigration worsened the sex imbalance in the population as well as the dependency ratio. The poverty of the people, together with the low rate of return on investment in the land, persuaded an increasing number of land-lords to subsidise the exodus of their tenants. The long and painful years of the Potato Famine, 1846 to 1851 (and longer in some places), caused further resort to that solution. The evidence from these years yields a striking variety of action among landlords — from direct physical compulsion to modest and restrained moral suasion and humanitarian care.

In July 1849 there was a report that

> On the 13th inst, the barque *Liscard* sailed from Loch Hourn for Quebec, with 214 passengers, emigrants of various ages from the east of Glenelg. They proposed to join their country-men in Canada, where there was a district named Glenelg, with a Gaelic-speaking population. The proprietor, Mr James Ewan Baillie, had cancelled arrears of rent, and provided the means for emigration.[6]

This was typical of newspaper accounts of many apparently uncon-troversial sailings from the west coast, and often the migrants expressed unqualified gratitude for the financial assistance received from their landlords. But the desperation of some of the people was attested in occasional reports — for example, only a month after the sailing of the *Liscard,* another vessel, the *Tusker,* set off from Gordon of Cluny's estate in South Uist, of which it was said: 'The people go away quietly, and are most anxious to leave, offering to sell their clothes, or to do anything to get away.'[7] Amid the propaganda of the emigration officials and the enthusiasm of the landlords and their agents, the trauma of these people only rarely reached the surface in official reports and letters.

It was inevitable that arrangements entered into between land-lords and penurious tenants frequently masked the primary purpose, that of clearance. Sceptics came to regard these sub-sidised emigrations as equivalent to eviction, especially where, at the last moment, the migrants suddenly changed their minds — and were then sometimes with physical force, compelled to keep to their contract, written or not. The waiving of rents and arrears, the compensation for crops and property, and the provision of fares, appeared to many contemporaries as no more than a sugaring of the pill of eviction.[8] The odium was made worse when landlords were seen to draw upon philanthropic relief funds and government grants to supplement the cost of such evictions. And there were, without doubt, many ugly and emotional scenes which coloured the public image of emigration schemes throughout the period of the famine.

A recent historian of Scottish emigration to Canada, Dr James Cameron, has surveyed landlord policies during these years and has provided basic data for judging the extent of compulsion in the general process. The great Argyll estates during the famine were beset by severe destitution, and the management certainly promoted emigration in a mood of desperation. Between 1846 and 1851 the estate spent £6,500 on the subsidised evacuation overseas of about 2,000 of its people from Mull, Iona and Tiree — an expenditure additional to the costs of relief undertaken during the famine itself. The attitude of the estate to the people was far from complimentary. An agent wrote in 1849 of the folk of Tiree:

> They are too indolent and idle to move, but move someday they must, and the less given them here the sooner they will better themselves, not but many will be on the eve of starvation ere they move, indeed many actually starve before they move, but this must come some day and the sooner they are prepared for exerting themselves the better.[9]

Of a list of 761 emigrants drawn up in March 1841 many more than half were totally destitute, and only 35 of them could pay their own passage even when the arrears of rent were forgiven. The mentality of the management was transparent in an agent's letter penned in June 1847: it would be beneficial for Tiree if the 'really destitute and worthless characters' were despatched, otherwise they would remain a dead burden on the estate. Those who remained, though poor, were at least industrious and also 'less likely to break out into open violence' — which he predicted would follow the termination of relief supplies. Emigration, in effect, became the central concern of estate policy.

In December 1849 the Duke of Argyll was told that many of his 'poorest' and 'most worthless' tenants had departed, and that 'the benefit resulting from the emigration of last season is very sensibly felt there are not now the number of poor applying for aid as in former years'. The goals of the landlord and his agents are clear enough, but the exact degree of inducement applied in the promotion of emigration is more obscure. In a public statement made in 1851, the Duke's chamberlain claimed that no person 'was forced to emigrate from their property, or asked to go'. In reality, as Dr Cameron shows, the estate undoubtedly issued summonses for removal of people in arrears of rent, and these people inevitably became far less resistant to the idea of free emigration. Yet in 1851 the Duke decided no longer to volunteer assistance for emigration; the people themselves had to take the initiative and seek his aid. He had taken umbrage at the generalised imputation that the only beneficiaries of emigration were the landlords. There appear to have been few cases of direct forced emigration on the Argyll estates, and the main expulsive pressure was derived from the severe economic conditions of the time.

Much more notorious, and more widely publicised, was the case of Gordon of Cluny, who had bought his way into Hebridean property in 1840.[10] His enthusiasm for the improvement of the crofters swiftly evaporated, and his estates became the prime examples of destitution and crofter misery. Emigration on a large scale had begun in 1848, and several shiploads from South Uist departed for Canada in the following three years, assisted by Gordon. In 1851 petitions from Gordon's estates presented to Parliament indicated that nearly 3,000 people wanted to emigrate. This expression of the popular will was particularly important in the light of the obloquy subsequently attaching to Gordon's emigration schemes. At considerable expense, he assisted several thousand people to Canada and Australia, including a total of 1,700 in 1851 alone. The condition of many on their arrival abroad became a matter of national scandal. Dr Cameron's account of the events dwells on the question of the force which, allegedly, was applied to Gordon's recalcitrant people at the time of the emigration. He suggests that in only 20 cases were people actually manhandled into the waiting ships. Moreover, although these emigrations have been the subject of continuing recrimination in Highland folklore, Gordon is due some credit for his large expenditure on the welfare of the migrants, and many of the difficulties which overtook the people were, apparently, the fault of the authorities in Canada. Cameron takes the view that 'while it can be argued that more liberal aid should have been provided, the magnitude of the problem and the social attitude of the landowner ruled out such a possibility'.[11] At the root of the problem was the fact that population growth and remoteness had created a crisis of such proportions that Gordon felt compelled to cut the Gordian knot, even at great cost to himself and to his reputation.

James Matheson, the phenomenally successful merchant in the Orient, bought the island of Lewis in 1844. He enjoyed a reputation in total contrast to Gordon's. Matheson, a philanthropic and benevolent landlord, lavished his fortune on the improvement of the people of Lewis. Nevertheless there emerged a close parallel between the estates of these two men. Congestion on Lewis, according to later studies, had little or nothing to do with sheep-farming, but much to do with the fecundity of the population and the failure of the kelp industry.[12] In 1844, however, Matheson believed that no emigration from his estates was necessary: six years later he was convinced that at least 20 per cent of the population should leave the island, and that the 'redundancy of population' was an inescapable fact of life. From that time he was much involved in the promotion of emigration to Canada. He offered liberal terms he cancelled rent arrears, provided clothing, arranged the sale of the people's stock, paid their fares, and 'engaged to have them conveyed to any spot in upper or lower Canada which they might select'. He made arrangements to pay the salaries of emigrant ministers, and it is clear that most of the people who left Stornoway followed in the path of relatives. Despite the obvious liberality of these terms, it is evident from internal estate correspondence that even Matheson exerted pressure upon the people to leave his property. He told his agents that if anyone — other than the sick and the aged — refused to emigrate, he should be summonsed to remove, and be 'deprived of his lands'. In fact many summonses were served in 1851: there can be no doubt that the Matheson policies required compulsion if not actual physical force. Between 1851 and 1853 Matheson subsidised 3,200 people to emigrate to Canada, and a smaller number were despatched to Australia.[13]

The story was much the same on the great debt-ridden estates of Macdonald: here again the management clearly compelled the people to shift and they became reluctant emigrants. The Sollas and Suishnish cases are well known.[14] The Macdonald policies were closely associated with the philanthropic activities of the Highland and Island Emigration Society. When the Society launched its programme in the West Highlands it sought the co-operation of landlords. The attitude of the Macdonald estate was expressed lucidly in a letter written in June 1852:

It would be absolute insanity not to take advantage of the present opportunity of getting rid of our surplus population and I can hardly believe that my Trustee will allow such a one to slip ... I have no doubt he will at once see how beneficial to the Estate on outlay of two or three thousand pounds will be.[15]

The Society provided landlords with a cheap way of despatching large numbers of people to the Australian colonies. Both Lord Macdonald and the Duke of Sutherland were deeply involved in the promotion of emigration in the famine years. Sutherland expended about £6,000 on a basis as liberal as that of any landlord in the north — but even here philanthropy was guarded with the most stringent regulations. Thus, when an emigrating tenant received financial assistance from the Sutherland estate, he was required to sign a pledge. For instance, on 5 April 1848 William Mackay, of the Tongue district, signed the following statement with his mark:

As you have agreed to provide a passage for me and my wife and family — numbering together eight — to Canada, I hereby bind myself to be forward at any port you may fix, and on such day as you may name, to join the Vessel, under a penalty of fifty pounds for failure over and above any expense which I may thereby create to his Grace. Farther I now renounce and give up the Lot and premises presently held by me in Tongue, and bind myself to leave the same in their present condition without receiving meliorations therefore. I also bind myself to procure my mother's resignation of her hold on the Lot and premises.[16]

There was a measure of inducement in the act of benevolence.

The people themselves often wavered in their choice of destination; sometimes whole districts set their faces against Canada for several years and then it ran into favour against the competition of the Australian colonies. In May 1848 the senior factor on the Sutherland estate reported these shifts, while also exposing the dissimulation and pressures which he and the church ministers employed to influence the prospective migrants:

Now, the tide runs in full force in favour of Autralia. I believe some hundreds of them are preparing and have entered their names to emigrate to that place, and it will be good riddance and a good way to get clear of them, as the utmost we shall have to pay is for their passage by sea to Leith, a mere trifle in comparison with the charge for taking them to Canada, but as I continue the policy ... to seem indifferent whether they go or remain, I know little of what the ultimate result of this move will be, except what I hear from Rutherford, the Agent, and even he is very much in the dark, and will be until he sees them embarked for the voyage ... the Free Church Ministers are availing themselves of their influence in the Pulpit and in their daily intercourse to dissuade the poor deluded people from leaving this country, but fortunately not with any great effect hitherto. Your Grace will no doubt observe that their sinister object is to secure the continuance of a large population around them, that they may more readily drain their pittance of wages, towards the upholding of the Free Church, and more especially the Sustenation Fund.

Despite the factor's optimism many of the intending migrants did indeed withdraw from the plan at the last minute.[17]

In some cases — notably at Knoydart — the connection between emigration and clearance was unambiguous, and confirmed the impression that the people were forced to leave by the combined pressure of poverty and landlord coercion. The people had no option even where the landlord could afford patience. More pervasive was the compulsion of destitution. In October 1853 there was yet another exodus of people from Lochaber. The *Inverness Courier* remarked:

There can be no better proof that migration from parts of the Highlands is necessary than the fact that these people have voluntarily left possessions under one of the most indulgent landlords in the county. They found that even without paying rents, they could not exist but in misery and wretchedness, and they determined to take advantage of the only alternative left them. Even this they could not have accomplished had they not been aided by the Highland and Island Emigration Society — a society deserving the support of all interested in the improvement and prosperity of the Country.[18]

It was a graphic indication of the destitute and miserable condition of the emigrant peasant, endless thousands of whom fled the outer periphery of Western Europe after the great famine.

II

In reality, the motives of landlords who involved themselves in migration were mixed. It was advantageous to a landlord to emigrate his people even at a substantial cost. In the long run future maintenance expenses at times of poor harvest were avoided and the value of the land was enhanced by the diminution of its population. It was also a humane act to provide the people with a better set of opportunities abroad than was conceivable in the Highlands. The people themselves were often in such fearful poverty that emigration came as a blessed release. But emotional attachment to the homeland and the memory (possibly softened by the passage of time) of better years in the past undoubtedly rendered most departures painful and affecting. Sometimes the people were confronted with a choice only of evils: emigration or eviction. In the end the entire business of emigration reflected the narrowed circumstances of an economy gripped by famine and low income levels and caught in a classic Malthusian trap. It may be utopian to expect the landlords as a class to have behaved any better than they did; it appears improbable that they could have found better solutions. It is not surprising that some landlords held out inducements to their small tenants to leave their estates; nor is it surprising that the moral criteria by which those episodes have been judged have become confused. In effect the story of emigration merged into the history of the clearances precisely because they were both expressions of the melancholy poverty of a region the control of which lay in the hands of a landlord class, incapable financially or intellectually of finding a solution.

The famine of 1846-8, of course, required massive relief schemes as well as subsidised emigration. Much aid was received from external sources of charity, but some landowners (notably the Duke of Sutherland) were able to relieve their people from their own resources. Two landowners, apparently bound by the obligations of ancestral pride, broke their estates in efforts to relieve their famished tenantries. Macleod of Dunvegan ruined himself in the process, paying over £255 a week from his own pocket in relief until his reserves were utterly emptied. Lord Macdonald did so much that, eventually, he came under the comprehensive control of his trustees.[19] Even the unloved Gordon of Cluny poured huge amounts of money into relief, before his patience ran out. But none of these cases has been fully investigated, and they remain a little-known aspect of landlord economies.

During the famine years assistance from outside bodies focused in the first instance on the business of immediate relief, although the general view held by even the most philanthropic was that any permanent amelioration depended on emigration. Yet policies of individual landlords to promote emigration continued to arouse suspicion and even resistance. This attitude was ventilated by a newspaper correspondent in November 1850:

> Where the proprietors have sought to diminish the pressure of the population upon the means of subsistence by issuing notices of removal, accompanied by offers of liberal assistance to emigrate, many have generally been met by a sullen refusal or turbulent resistance, and by clamorous complaints of injustice.[20]

The problems of the landlords, and the plight of the people, intensified in 1850 when relief monies began to dry up after several years of famine. For three or four years the Highland economy had been propped up by external charity. In January 1851 the Glasgow section of the Highland Destitution Board terminated its relief operations on a sombre note: in the previous year the Board had spent more than £21,000 on relief and the construction of roads and piers but, it confessed publicly, the expenditure had had no impact on the prevailing condition of the people. The plain fact was that they were worse off than they had been in 1846. The Board pointed out that efforts to introduce fishing in Mull, Barra and Harris had failed miserably. On the question of crofter rents, the Board cited the position in Barra, which typified the west coast: rents were unquestionably too high for the crofters, partly because the owner, Colonel Gordon, had landed himself in financial difficulties after the failure of his attempt to revive kelp production in the island. Gordon, whose reputation had been blackened by his recent emigration policies, had expended £5,609 beyond the income of his estates, but again with little permanent improvement to show for the expenditure.

Relief and improvement schemes appeared to have failed. The Royal Patriotic Society in Inverness estimated that there were 50,000 destitute in the Western Highlands and Islands,[21] and another contemporary estimate calculated that, of a total population in the Highlands of 148,492, some 46,300 should be removed altogether.[22] It was amid this atmosphere that the most systematic public effort to co-ordinate Highland emigration was initiated in 1852 under the leadership of Sir Charles Trevelyan, Assistant Secretary to the Treasury, 1840-59.

Trevelyan sought to exploit the apparent complementarity of interest that existed between the needs of the Australian colonies and those of the Highlands. The gold rushes in Victoria had generated a vast expansion of activity in Australia and created a serious shortage of labour in all sectors. Many parts of Australia had suffered severely from the outrush of labour to the gold-fields in 1851, and had gained little (or so it was believed) from the expensive subsidisation of immigration, as migrants commonly rushed off to Victoria once they landed in, for example, Sydney or Adelaide. Colonies such as South Australia had a clear preference for migrants who were likely to take root. It was argued, credibly enough, that family migration was likely to be more stable, especially where the families belonged to a larger cohesive grouping with whom they migrated. Similarly, in the Highlands of Scotland it was obvious that the migration of entire families (to include young and old dependants) was socially desirable, though difficult to accomplish.

The satisfaction of these two interests was the stated purpose of the Highland and Island Emigration Society, formed early in 1852. In Trevelyan's words, the intention of the Society was to transfer 'the surplus of the Highland population to Australia' — and he appears to have envisaged an exodus of 40,000 people. For finance the Society attracted donations from the philanthropic public, from the British government, and from the recipient colonial governments (in connection with land sales). In addition the Society required Highland proprietors to pay one-third of the cost of the emigration of their tenants which, it was emphasised, must be of families rather than individuals. The passage in 1851 of the Emigration Advances Act enabled landlords to borrow from public funds to pay the costs of emigration for their tenants. It was evident that landlords who did not pay would not be relieved of their paupers. This, naturally, was the most contentious aspect of the entire scheme: Trevelyan was obviously appealing to the landlords' self-interest. It was possible to view the entire enterprise as a substitute for conventional clearances which had become extremely odious to the British public. Indeed there were cases in which estate factors were employed directly in the recruitment of emigrants, a connection which generated allegations of compulsion and cruelty of a sort commonly associated with the process of clearance. Once more it was the detail of specific episodes which created most of the adverse discussion at the time: those instances where the line between the encouragement of emigration and the physical compulsion of the people was blurred. Hence the operations of the Highland and Island Emigration Society were clouded by its alliance with landlords wanting to divest themselves of small tenantry who were no longer economic. The Society gave the appearance, in a number of dramatic cases, of actually promoting clearances. Yet, at the same time, the realities of destitution in the north persuaded most literate opinion that emigration had become inevitable.

The Society became entangled in several extreme cases.[23] In the Knoydart clearances landlords applied pressure to migrants, and physical force was used against uncooperative tenants. The people of Suishnish and Boreraig in Skye, who eventually left for Australia in 1855, were certainly refugees from clearances. Some of the people of Sollas in North Uist, whose repeated eviction and resistance were widely publicised, were among emigrants aboard the ill-fated *Hercules* which voyaged to Australia in 1852. The Sollas people were profoundly embittered by their treatment, and the memory of their hatred is hardly yet forgotten.[24] The regulations imposed by the Society upon the Australian emigration had the effect of accelerating (or indeed initiating) the marriages of many young women in the Highlands. The emigration of single men was discouraged and, as the *Inverness Courier* remarked in 1852,

> The consequence has been that numerous marriages have taken place all over the country, the newly-wedded pairs proceeding immediately southward, under the charge of the agents of the Commissioners to embark for their future home in the land of promise.[25]

It was ironic that the Sutherland estate, which had imposed notorious anti-marriage regulations on its small tenants for many years, now found itself party to hurried unions. A particular case from Elphin may be cited, where in September 1853 Donald Gunn asked the local factor, Evander MacIver, to arrange a passage for him to Australia. He wrote:

Perhaps it may not be out of place for me to mention that young
men got a passage from Skye to Australia along with a sister or
any female who chooses to go along with them. If I get a
passage in that way so much the better. But if not it can't be
helped, as if I didn't get in that way I'll marry before I lose a
passage.

Gunn had several acquaintances already in Van Diemen's Land.
Maciver remarked:

He will get a wife if he can't go without one — but he would
prefer to go out single, and take a sister with him. I think there
is much force in Sir John MacNeill's remark that many of the
marriages made for the purpose of making the parties eligible
emigrants do not turn out well.[26]

In more general terms the efforts of the Society achieved limited
success. Although its original impetus was considerable (in 1852 it
organised 17 ships to Australia, with 2,605 emigrants), its operations
did not run smoothly and by 1855 the flow of people had diminished
to a trickle. The decline reflected, in part, the improved condition of
the Highland economy and, to a lesser extent, the consequences of
unfavourable reports sent home by early migrants. It was perhaps
significant that, in 1855, a group of Skye people retracted their
understanding to emigrate when a shipload of potatoes and oatmeal,
paid for by charity, arrived at the island. Sheer hunger and the
depression of opportunities were the most potent forces for emigration. The Society wound up its operations in 1858, by which time it
had despatched about 5,000 Highlanders to the Australian
colonies.[27]

Throughout the period of famine less systematic forms of emigration continued to reduce population pressure in the region. In
some places landlords persuaded crofters to migrate in order that
their vacated crofts could be made available to new crofters
cleared from interior glens. Where a landlord accepted responsibility for maintaining a bare minimum standard of welfare among
his people, it was sometimes cheaper to pay emigration expenses
than to undertake permanent improvements for the crofts. On the
Sutherland estate, in April 1852, an area at Lothbeg was leased out
to a large tenant, Innes, whose entry to the land was dependent on

the shifting of the small tenants who were described as 'wretchedly poor'. For the estate managers it was a question of 'how are they to be disposed of?' The Duke of Sutherland hardly ever moved people without offering them alternative accommodation on the estate, but in this case emigration was recommended because it gave 'the advantage to get rid of the whole beggarly set for a far less outlay than will be required to help in building their houses as was provided'.[28] The benefits and costs of emigration were counted on all sides.

III

The story of the Highland migrants abroad, as retailed in the Scottish newspapers, tended to understate the initial difficulties facing these people who were, in almost all aspects, refugees. For, while the expatriation of the Highlanders solved the most basic problem of the landlord, allowing him to reorganise his estate and rationalise his rents, for the migrants, in contrast, the departure was often the prelude to a further chapter of trauma and deprivation. Like other refugees of other times, many of these people usually possessed nothing to tide them over the transition until they found employment and habitation. They were lucky if they landed abroad to find instant employment and security. It was likely that they would be required to journey again, overland and up country, to an isolated place and little welcome — especially if they were thrown on local charity as soon as they arrived. Their language was a problem, as was their sickliness. Many groups of emigrants disembarked amid a deluge of immigration to find all the jobs already taken — and so they suffered alarming and humiliating times. Emigration was no guarantee of security or hope. In the long run the great majority of these people found better circumstances which enabled them to sustain themselves with less physical and mental stress. Only then was emigration a solution to the Highland problem. The success of Highland migrants may be measured in the remittances they sent back home — payments which, like the proceeds of seasonal migration to the Lowlands, enabled the Highland economy to sustain its remaining people better than would otherwise have been the case.[29]

Departure from the Highlands was the emotional climax of the emigrant experience, and the contemporary records contain many classic accounts of the scene, heavy with literary pathos. The last farewell and embarkation of the people of Locheil and Ardgour in September 1849 was one such moment and the report contained vivid detail (and some poetic licence):

> A correspondent, who chanced to be on board the steamer when the embarkation took place, describes the scene in the most moving terms. He states that it was heart piercing to hear them wailing — the Highland wailing — and when the bagpipes struck up 'Lochaber no more', the passionate outburst of their grief broke through all restraints. It was at midnight this scene took place, and by the aid of the steamer's lights alone they were able to take their last look at the hills of Lochaber, from the great bosom of which they were thus wrenched — Australia, not Canada, is their destination. Our correspondent spoke to one poor widow, whose distress was extreme, and by suggesting Gospel consolations succeeded in somewhat soothing her. She was accompanied by three boys and a girl, and her total means of meeting the expense of a few months' voyage amounted to just £17 for the five souls, derived thus — value of croft £11, allowance from Locheil, from whose estate she was removed £3, and from the poor's fund £3. The distress of many of the emigrants was greatly aggravated, owing to their being compelled to leave members of their families behind, from inability to pay the passage money.[30]

These people, able to raise some part of their passage money, must have come from a stratum of crofter society slightly above the most destitute. The latter were able to leave only when emigration was fully subsidised.

The voyage to the colonies was sometimes a purgatory for these refugees. Of many affecting accounts, a letter from Melbourne by John Mackinnon of Skye may be cited. Of his voyage to Australia he wrote:

> Oh, Sandy, throwing out my two into the deep sea, it will never go out of my heart. The youngest died with the measles crossing the line, and the other six days later with a bowell complaint. Disease raged greatly in our ship among children. Fifty three children, died, and two woman in childbed, and one sailor. We had too many on board.

Surprisingly Mackinnon was happy to recommend to Sandy, and others in Skye, that they also emigrate to Victoria.[31]

The voyage of the *Hercules* was perhaps the worst example of the migrants' passage. A large frigate, sailing under the aegis of the Highland and Island Emigration Society, it was 'a naval ship, nicely fitted up, sufficiently manned, and excellently managed'. The *Hercules* left Campbeltown in Argyll on Boxing Day 1852, bound for southern Australia. It carried 619 emigrants, many of whom had suffered considerable privations during the long drawn out saga of the Sollas clearances. Soon after departure, while still in Scottish waters, the *Hercules* ran into a storm which raged for four days during which there were two deaths. The ship put into Rothesay on the Clyde where it stayed until 14 January 1853. On its second departure smallpox and typhus broke out among passengers and crew and it was forced to put into Queenstown, Cork, where the people were further detained until 14 April (and some left altogether at this stage). There were allegations made that the ship had been contaminated before the voyage, but the sickness must also have reflected the careless attitude of the Highlanders towards inoculation. There were 237 cases of fever and smallpox and 38 deaths in Ireland and at sea. Several children from North Uist were orphaned. There were reports that some of the survivors were compelled to sell their blankets and part of their clothing before they reached Australia. There were further testimonies about repeated suicide attempts by two of the passengers, and several burials at sea. The surviving immigrants arrived at Adelaide 104 days after their original embarkation.[32]

The official records of the emigrant vessels provide some of the fullest documentation available for the individual circumstances of the Highlanders during these years. It is evidence relatively untainted by its source, and the simple factual descriptions of each emigrant provide vivid indication of the plight of the people, and the narrowed employment opportunities of the post-famine economy of the Highlands. Many of the records establish a clear connection between clearances and emigration. On board the *British Queen* and the *Panama, en route* for Australia in January 1853, were many who were casualties of the famine, and also of the eviction policy of their landlord, Clarke of Ulva. Among them was Dugald MacFarlane, aged 40, of Tobermory, who was accompanied by his wife aged 35, an infant of eight months, and six other children under 15 years. The descriptive note of the Emigration Society official was plain:

> Has been a crofter, was dispossessed of his land about 10 months ago, by Mr Clarke of Ulva. Has supported his family by catching lobsters and other shell fish. Price of lobsters 2/- per dozen. Has not earned 20/- for the last month. Inhabits one room for which he pays 7d per week. Very destitute family. The Revd W. Ross states that he found Mr MacFarlane and two of his children last winter lying in a state of exhaustion for want of food.

There were other such cases from the Ulva estate, including a family destined for Van Diemen's Land having been evicted from Clarke's crofts several years previously; of the father it was written that he had supported 'the family by gathering shellfish. Was long on the Destitution fund.'[33] The descriptions attached to the names of passengers aboard the *Hercules* extend the picture of misery:

> 'Lately dispossessed of croft. Very destitute family.'
> 'Very destitute — children nearly naked.'
> 'Has neither land, cattle nor employment — very poor and destitute family.'
> 'Dispossessed of croft in May. Employed in the fishing for a few months. Poor family.'
> 'Maintains herself by spinning, can earn about 3/- per week.'
> 'Rents a small croft. Has maintained his two brothers for the last four years. Had employment in the South six months ago but left to emigrate.'
> 'Went annually to the Herring fishing.'
> 'Supports herself by spinning.'
> 'Shoemaker, work very precarious, can earn 8/- per week when fully employed. Children small and helpless.'

The *Hercules* was relatively well adapted for emigrants: it was unlucky to be racked by storm and disease. But its passengers were fortunate to arrive at their destination — Port Adelaide and Melbourne — at a time when the local labour market was buoyant. They were accommodated in a temporary fashion by the local immigration officials, and provided with an interpreter to help them seek employment. By 1855 many had saved enough from their earnings to pay off their debts to the Society. But tragedy continued to dog others. Individual catastrophes were recorded — such as Christina McCaskill, aged 30, from Harris, who died soon after her arrival, in the Adelaide Destitute Asylum, as did two other people; at least ten of the *Hercules* folk entered the Adelaide Hospital. They experienced the problems common to newly arrived immigrants — as one official observed, before they established themselves they were thrown into great poverty because of sickness. Moreover, despite the principles of the family emigration scheme, many of the Highland groups were broken up and dispersed once they arrived in the colonies.[34]

There were too many individual tragedies among the emigrants to allow recent historians' optimistic view of emigration to remain unmodified. Emigration, in reality, was frequently a second or third catastrophe which followed those of clearance and famine. When, for instance, the *Priscilla* left Liverpool for Port Phillip in the second week of October 1852, it carried 298 souls, mainly from the Macdonald and Skeabost estates, but also a number of people from St. Kilda, the most distant and isolated of the Outer Hebrides. A newspaper account of their departure remarked that

> Mr McLeod, the humane proprietor of the island came to Glasgow to see them of, and it was very affecting to observe them crowd about him, and, in their own expressive language, wishing God to bless him as each of them shook him by the hand.

On their arrival at Melbourne the Immigration officials found that the children of these indigent people were in dire need of clothing. Thereupon emerged the appalling story of the MacQueens, a St Kilda family of whom there were originally nine. The medical officer recorded their experience without comment.

> The father, mother and one child are dead — leaving 6 orphans, viz Donald aged 18, recovering from Scarlatina; Meron, aged 16 now suffering from phthisis, consequent upon Scarlatina; Catherine aged 12, Nanny aged 8 ill of anasarca, Neil aged 6, Findlay aged 4 dying of marasmus, and they have had the misfortune to lose all their clothes by the burning of the bark hut in which the four younger ones were living, so that nothing but the few fitting rags which scarce [cover] them, left. They are at present

aboard the *Lysander*, and as I see no probability of any of them being able to leave the station for months, if ever, I have the honor to request that a requisite supply of wearing apparel may be forwarded them.[35]

Nevertheless some of the survivors eventually fared well enough in Victoria to send remittances home to Hirta.

During the years of mass emigration there were similar stories of suffering Highlanders in Canada. The deplorable condition of many of the migrants at the Canadian ports created heated controversy about the legal and moral limits of the responsibilities of the respective landlords and the relief committees. There was a view that the emigrants should be provided with fares and subsistence until they settled in a place; some landlords felt they had discharged their duties when the migrant reached the point of disembarkation. Between 1848 and 1852 to that part of Quebec alone, more than 7,000 people were 'assisted' by their Highland landlords.[36] It was well known that many Highlanders left Scotland in a desperate condition. In August 1849, for instance, two shiploads of people from the Argyll estates arrived at Quebec almost totally destitute, 'many of whom had not the shirts on the backs' and were also infected with cholera. Typically, it was necessary to assist such people to Upper Canada with government help and private charity. The Argyll estate sometimes provided some a little — some 'miserably poor' people from Tiree were given clothing because 'they were so naked', as well as money for travel up country when they arrived in Canada.

In 1848 Gordon of Cluny, who combined a policy of eviction with assisted emigration, sent a body of 150 South Uist emigrants as far as Cape Breton Island, and a larger number went to Quebec and New York in 1849, from whence they were forwarded inland by government agency. It was in 1851, however, that the Gordon estates attracted unprecedented adverse publicity: five shiploads of his people were despatched to Quebec between August and October. The people were penniless on arrival and Buchanan, the emigration agent in Quebec, remarked that they were 'without the means of leaving the ship or of procuring a day's subsistence for their helpless families on landing'. The local authorities had no alternative but to subsidise their continuing travel: their transport inland to Hamilton cost £674 10s. Though the people were relatively healthy, the Medical Superintendent at Grosse Isle observed that: '[I] never during my long experience at the station saw a body of emigrants so destitute of clothing and bedding, many children nine and ten years old had not a rag to cover them.' The people understood, wrongly, that Gordon had paid their passage as far as Hamilton. The newspaper, the *Dundas Warden*, in October 1851 exclaimed that the emigration of these people was worse than banishment:

> Their last shilling is spent probably before they reach the upper province — they are reduced to the necessity of begging. But again, the case of these emigrants of which we speak is rendered more deplorable from their ignorance of the English tongue. Of the hundreds of Highlanders in and around Dundas at present, perhaps not half a dozen understand anything but Gaelic.[37]

In his study of Canadian immigration Dr Cameron found that even after the people arrived in Hamilton they were disadvantaged by their lack of employable skills and their equal lack of English. They continued to exist in considerable distress.[38]

Other landlords appeared to be more liberal in their assistance. More than once in the 1840s Malcolm of Poltalloch provided generous if not lavish assistance to tenants from Argyll to reach the London district of Upper Canada. Baillie of Dochfour gave some assistance for the post-disembarkation phase to his Glenelg people. Matheson ensured that emigrants from Lewis received food, clothing and a passage, followed by one week's rations on arrival and a fare to the eventual destination. He continued to sponsor emigrants from the Long Island into the 1860s, as did other landowners such as John Ramsay of Kildalton, who subsidised 600 people to leave the western isles.

There were, naturally, many success stories among the *émigré* Highlanders in all parts of the globe, and they left their mark in too many spheres of life to be enumerated here. The local histories of former colonies are full of stories of the rise to wealth and eminence of the descendants of Highlanders who had been part of the great diaspora. Sometimes these *émigrés* adopted the standards and values of colonial expansionism and financial ambition with extraordinary vigour and enthusiasm. Sometimes too they bought their success at a high price. The story of successful Highland settlement among the squatterdom of Gippsland in Victoria, Australia, is stained by the blood of massacred Aborigines, perpetrated by men who, ironically, sought profit from large-scale sheepfarming. It was an ugly story, not restricted to Australia, which casts long shadows across the reputation of Celtic civilisation.[39]

Much of the evidence about mid-century Highland emigration, both to Canada and Australia, accords with results derived from systematic research conducted by the historian Michael Katz into an immigrant city, Hamilton in Ontario. On the whole, first-generation immigrants achieved a generally low rate of economic success which was probably connected, in part, with the trauma of the emigrant passage. But in rural settlements the story may sometimes have differed, and a study of Tiree immigrants (also in Ontario) suggests the effectiveness of community solidarity and self-help despite initial setbacks.[40]

IV

For many of the peasant emigrants from the Highlands the great attraction of Canada and Australia lay in the apparently unlimited access to land, and the security associated with it. Emigration also offered a final release from the tyranny of arbitrary landlordism, a liberation from centuries of compulsory deference. Since there is little in the extant record of the actual consequences of emigration for most of these people, it is not possible to gauge the fulfilment of their collective or individual aspirations. Yet there are some fragments which convey a sense of the transplanted Highlanders' emotional responses to new environments.

In Adelaide, South Australia, in 1855, some of the islanders who had travelled from Skye aboard the *Switzerland* found themselves not only in a weakened, sickly condition, but also difficult to employ. They were in an increasingly desperate plight, and the tenacity of their kinship[41] made them reluctant to split into smaller groups and disperse. In these circumstances ten of the menfolk petitioned the colonial Governor for a grant of land. The petition read:

> We humbly beg your Lordship, this government would grant each family of us, more or less land, in the manner that we would be able to live by it, or we would pay the whole amount to government by instalment. In the next place, we the under-

signed as all head of familys, should we scatter hear and there in search of work, we don't know what to do with our familys, and we have no money to uphold them during our absence. We do humbly expect to have better prospects through your Lordship's influence.

The petition gave rare voice to the profound abhorrence of separation; it also represented the land hunger of a dispossessed peasantry, seeking to re-establish a status that they had lost in the Highlands. But colonial Wakefieldianism was almost as immovable as Highland landlordism, and no land grants were possible.

Land and independence were the great themes of many letters from the colonies. In 1834 a migrant from St Clair River in Upper Canada wrote in no uncertain terms about the benefits:

Urge my brothers to come out if they ever wish to free themselves from bondage; this is the land of independence to the industrious — the soil that will repay the labourer for the sweat of his brow — and where grinding lairds that harrass and oppress the poor of Scotland are unknown.[42]

Similarly triumphant in tone were the words of Duncan Ferguson from Yarmouth in Upper Canada, written in September 1837 to his brother back in Argyll:

It is not for other people that we are working as you are, but for ourselves and family, and suppose we work hard, we know we will have the benefit in the end. Men in that country [Scotland] are only working for their living and a property beside. Every one that came here has got land in some shape or other ... It is my advice to you, come! If you had come when I came you would be an independent man now. I am glad that I came ... This is a good country, fertile land, mild climate, very healthy, very palatable food, and genteel way of taking it.

These sentiments were given more radical and more vigorous expression in a piece published in a short-lived Gaelic newspaper which began publication in Australia in February 1853. *An Teachdaire Gaidhealach* celebrated the successes of Highlanders at the gold diggings and elsewhere, and remarked on the presence of a Highland camp at virtually every rush. The newspaper described the enduring camaraderie of the Highlanders, and the ubiquitous tones of the accompanying bagpipes. It then drew a wider lesson learned by the Highlanders:

> What a contrast, as we look with indignation on days gone by, when suffering under the tyranny of Lairds and Factors, in the Highlands, where sheep meet with more consideration than men — where all means are used to increase the former and diminish the latter — where marriage is prohibited under the penalty of ejectment — Tyranny is the rule, and justice the exception. The poor man who rents the croft which has descended to him from his father and his father's father, must, when required for the accommodation of sheep, turn out family and all to seek another home where he may. If he ventures to use opposition or resistance the most diabolical means are taken to carry into effect their infamous laws. I need not mention one instance which occurred two years ago in Kincardine of Ross-shire. On this occasion the sheriff accompanied with an armed force, ejected about twenty men and women from their homes; and without the slightest provocation, made a furious and brutal attack upon them, wounding many of them severely; — and afterwards carried several to prison. When we look back on such a country, we cannot but feel that all we have to regret is our dear relations, and our Gospel Ministers left behind, because we know that Pharaoh is still alive, and that his heart is as hard as ever.

Away from this tyranny, said the correspondent, the migrant found himself in a new world of fraternity and equality: 'Here a man is respected as a man, and Jack is as good as his Master.'[43]

V

The place of emigration in the history of the Highlands and the clearances in the period 1770 to 1860 remains problematic. It is, of course, common to hold responsible for the distress and exodus a landlord class whose cupidity knew no bounds. An alternative view gives greater emphasis to the larger forces of economic decline and population pressure, a Malthusian interpretation recently reactivated by M. W. Flinn. James Hunter represents the former emphasis in that he regards emigration as the clear consequence of the landlord's 'determination to extract profits from the land'. It was the logical culmination of the clearances, and the last act in the great struggle for the possession of land, a lopsided contest between landlord and crofter. Emigration was induced by the landlords, either directly or by way of generalised impoverishment for which they were ultimately accountable. Class interest was at all times dominant and Hunter is not prepared to concede that any humanity entered the landlord's sponsorship of emigration.[44] Professor Donaldson, by contrast, takes a markedly benign view: he derides the opinion that emigration was compulsory and that clearance was commonly associated with dispossession or forced expatriation. He remarks that

> The notion that scheming landlords, for their own financial profit, shipped to America tenants who were living in plenty, or even comfort, at home is preposterous. The truth is that people who had experienced the miseries of life in the Highlands in the 1840s clamoured for assistance to enable them to leave the country.

He believes that the natural exodus was also much stimulated by letters from relatives abroad and by general propaganda.[45]

There can be no doubt that in the 1830s and 1840s many landlords as well as their tenants had concluded that emigration was the only feasible solution to their respective economic difficulties. It is also true that some landlords simply could not afford to subsidise emigration, and that many people were extremely reluctant to depart despite the material squalor of their lives. There were varying degrees of cupidity and humanitarianism, of patience and opportunism; but beyond all this was the inescapable poverty of the region and the fact that the prevailing economic structure could not cope with the swollen population of the Highlands. The most productive way to consider the question of emigration is in the terms in which the society tried to accommodate this population imperative.

Flinn's approach, derived from Malthusian premises and informed by a wider, European, context, offers the most useful framework for an analysis of the responses of both crofters and landlords. The Highland economy, he suggests, was in constant battle with demographic forces, of population outstripping its means of support. The role of emigration was to stave off the gathering crises at various times after 1750. The exodus of 1772 to 1775 represented a recognition by the people of the dangers facing them; it also 'played a part in keeping Malthus at bay'. The pressure of continuing population growth, up to 1815 perhaps, was also contained by other developments — by military service, by subdivision and the miraculously productive potato, and by the labour-intensive employment in kelp. Thus, though migration continued sporadically, most of the natural increase was retained: 'between 1770 and 1815, the society of the northwest had continued to prevent the axe of the positive check from falling'. Landlords also interfered in the natural play of Malthusian forces — by discouraging emigration and by resettling people on coastal crofts. The growth of regional wealth, by way of kelp, cattle, sheep and military service, was increasingly siphoned off by the landlords in the form of inflated rents. The policy of retaining population in these circumstances helped to compound the vulnerability of the people to an eventual Malthusian crisis.

The crisis developed after 1815: population growth continued while sources of income, for the crofters, diminished. Dependence on the potato necessarily intensified, and the power of the region to purchase imports was reduced. Flinn estimates that out-migration reduced the natural increase but, nevertheless, by 1840 there were an extra 10,000 people in the West Highlands, becoming dangerously dependent on potatoes. He quotes W. P. Alison's observation, made in 1847: 'When we find a population ... living chiefly on potatoes, and reduced to absolute destitution, unable to purchase other food when the potato crop fails, we have at once disclosed to us the undeniable fact, that that population is redundant.' Highly vulnerable, this population had no choices when the potato failed — as in 1836-7 and then, overwhelmingly, in 1846-8. The famine was undoubtedly a watershed in Highland history. It was a demographic turning point after which the population was reduced to more sustainable levels. There was virtually no starvation (in contrast to Ireland), a result attributed to the combined efforts of government, landlords and charities which averted the full consequences of the blight. The true adjustment was achieved by emigration which, calculated Flinn, reduced the population by a third between 1841 and 1861. Other responses helped: the sex and age structure shifted to such an extent that negative rates of population growth came into operation.[46]

The gravamen of this formulation is that the Highlands were, through these years, gripped by demographic imperatives. The only real relief, as Alison and his contemporaries reluctantly conceded, was extensive emigration. It had been delayed until 1845 by temporary and unstable improvisations, such as crofting, sub-division and seasonal migration. After 1845 sustained emigration, together with changing marriage and reproduction patterns, altered the framework of the Highland problem. In Flinn's acount emigration was a safety valve, relieving some of the Malthusian pressures, spasmodically until 1815, considerably but insufficiently until 1847, and thereafter decisively altering the balance of resources and population. It is a view which invests the population factor with an overwhelming and ostensibly autonomous role in the creation of the Highland problem. This interpretation does not rest comfortably in the same bed as the idea that all the problems of the Highlands were attributable to landlordism.

VI

It is difficult to know the precise scale of Highland emigration during the age of the clearances: the movements of people internally and externally were not registered at the time. In August 1849 the *Scotsman* reckoned that in the previous ten years something like 20,000 Highlanders had emigrated to Canada alone.[47] Some further rough estimates may be made from the Census returns[48] by the very simple procedure adopted below. Assume a 10 per cent net natural increase per decade, and then subtract the actual population at the end of the decade from the projected population which would have been reached with 10 per cent growth had there been no emigration.[49] This yields the estimates shown in Table 10.1 of the population outflow for the eight Highland counties (Argyll, Inverness, Perth, Ross and Cromarty, Sutherland, Caithness, Orkney and Zetland).[50]

This exercise is based upon a key speculation about the size of the population had emigration not occurred. It is a heroic assumption which begs the most fundamental question which remains unanswered both in this exercise and in the evidence currently available: it is not possible to say to what degree emigration reduced demographic pressure in the Highlands during the classic period of the Industrial Revolution. It is clear, however, that the population of the Highlands grew much less than in other parts of Britain.[51] For instance, the population of England and Wales doubled between 1781 and 1831, but that of the Highlands grew by less than 40 per cent. It seems almost certain, therefore, that emigration over that long period channelled away a large part of

Table 10.1: Highland Migration Estimates, 1801-61

	Actual Population	Actual Decadal Increase	Required Decadal Increase for 10% growth	Estimated Decadel Migration Outflow
1801	428,400			
		23,986 (5.6%)	42,840	18,854
1811	452,386			
		47,955 (10.6%)	45,239	−2,716
1821	500,341			
		30,701 (6.1%)	50,034	19,333
1831	531,042			
		2,460 (0.5%)	53,104	50,644
1841	533,502			
		698 (0.1%)	53,350	52,652
1851	534,200			
		−20,260 (−3.8%)	53,420	73,680
1861	513,940			

the demographic increment, and rather more than many contemporaries appeared to understand. The comparatively brisk emigration reduced the vulnerability of the region to the extreme consequences of famine, and cushioned the economic and social consequences of the introduction of sheepfarming. Within the estimates of emigration it appears that the outflow was relatively slight in the first quarter of the new century, and consequently demographic difficulties continued to accumulate. The acceleration of Highland emigration in the 1830s indicates a similarity with the Irish experience, and both regions appear to have undergone substantial demographic adjustment some time before the onset of the great famine of the 1840s.[52] It was not until mid-century that the net emigration and reproduction rates combined to cause an absolute reduction of population. As in much of Ireland, continuing seasonal migration served as 'a means of consolidating peasant property, at least temporarily' and as a way of 'avoiding full proletarianisation'.[53]

More broadly, the exodus from the Highlands may be seen as part of a general British phenomenon which produced 'a continuous redistribution of population from the periphery to the

core'. Throughout rural Britain in the middle decades of the nineteenth century 'the increment of population was slackening and
migration from the countryside accelerating'; everywhere from
west Wales to East Angia and the south-est, rural reservoirs were
drained of their younger people, and natural increases declined.[54]
It is, indeed, possible to argue that the rate of decline was slower
and later in the Highlands than in much of the rest of agricultural
Britain. Recent studies have suggested that, after about 1855, emigration was not sufficiently vigorous or sustained to relieve poverty
and congestion, especially along the north-western seaboard.[55]
Part of the explanation lies in the general revival of the Highland
economy, and also in the fact that thenceforth landlords eschewed
the policy of outright eviction. In the 1880s there was a legislative
consolidation of crofting and this strengthened the tenacious hold
on land for which the crofters were renowned.

The estimates in Table 10.1 obscure the intra regional variations which were of immense significance for the north-west in
particular. As early as 1812 John Walker had identified the crucial
pattern in his analysis of population figures since 1755: he pointed
out that population increases had been least in those parts of the
Highlands which adjoined the Lowlands and Clydeside. The
greatest increases had been in the north-west: Walker correctly
attributed the difference to differential migration.[56] The most
plausible interpretation is that the north and west were caught in a
Malthusian low-level income trap.

The demographic experience of the Highland counties may be
compared with other predominantly pastoral districts of Scotland
and the rest of Great Britain. It is striking, for instance, that while
the population of the Highlands showed a small net increase in the
decade 1841-51, an actual fall was registered in the counties of
Wiltshire, Merioneth, Montgomery and Radnor. More generally
demographic decline in the Highlands was of the same order of
scale and timing (though usually a decade earlier) as the southern
Scottish pastoral counties of Wigton, Berwick, Roxburgh and
Dumfries. As Malcolm Gray has said, 'From 1801 to 1851, most
areas and most agricultural parishes showed increases of population well below any credible rate of natural increase.'[57] It must be
obvious that large-scale forces were at work in the shifting patterns
of population in nineteenth-century Britain. Alexander Russel
pointed out in 1857 that the decline of population since 1801 in
the three Lowland countries of Haddington, Berwick and

Dumfries had been 28 per cent compared with 30 per cent in the Highlands — yet these counties contained large acreages of wheat production, high rents, large mining populations, thriving towns, fertile straths and 'a fishing station more productive than all the Highland fisheries put together'. Selkirkshire was less densely populated than Inverness-shire, Peebles than Ross-shire. In the light of acreage per person, Russel asked:

> By what possible process of reasoning, or even of some senti-
> mentality, are people to lament that the quaking bogs of the
> Hebrides sustain a population only three times greater than the
> green hills and smiling haughs of Ettrick and Yarrow?[58]

A large proportion of the social and economic problem of the Highlands was derived from the landless character of much of the population. In 1855 there were 800 cottars without land in Lewis alone; in 1883 West Sutherland was populated by 360 crofters, 200 cottars and 100 paupers.[59]

The idea of a mechanical operation of Malthusian pressures in the Highlands has been subject to recurrent criticism since the time of the clearances. The influential commentator on emigration and colonisation ideas in the 1830s, Herman Merivale, had been critical of Robert Torren's proposals to mitigate the Irish problem by emigrating one million people to America. As evidence Merivale cited the example of the island of Skye from whence 8,000 of a total population of 11,000 apparently had emigrated in the mid-eighteenth century. Yet, within a generation the population had regenerated to a point beyond the previous maximum. In this case, the Highland example appeared to disprove the long-term benefits of mass migration. It was significant for both Ireland and the Highlands that, by 1861, Merivale was prepared to recant; he then accepted that emigration could effect a permanent diminution of population.[60]

The response of the Highland community to the demographic forces remains the central historical question. Indeed it is possible to argue that the landlords (by encouraging kelping and crofting) exacerbated the Malthusian pressures on the common people, and that the people themselves were tied to patterns of inaction which seriously inhibited a positive response to the deepening demographic crises of the period. M W. Flinn, indeed, has emphasised the role of the landlords who, by their almost medieval control of the society, encouraged population growth on the fringes of the region, while they siphoned off the increments of income derived from the lucrative sheepwalks and kelp grounds. After 1815 the same landlords reversed their policies and prohibited subdivision, and subletting and early marriages, and pressed the people outwards from the region. 'Having contributed by clearance to the overcrowding of the coastal areas, landlords then aimed to use their power to complete the process by creating the conditions in which the surplus of population had no choice but to emigrate.'[61] In these ways the landlords increased the pressures on their people, and then offered them relief by means of expatriation. Neither action earned them much credit with the general public or posterity.

Emigration therefore forms a surprisingly complex relationship with the question of the Highland clearances and the persisting problem of the Highland economy. At the centre of the web of causes was the growth of population in the late eighteenth century. In his studies of geographical mobility in both Lowland and Highland Scotland, Malcolm Gray has argued that migration was the critical mechanism of adaptation. He says that 'From some time in the second half of the eighteenth century rural arrangements were threatened by a rising rate of natural increase.' By 1800 rural communities in Scotland were confronted with a population growth of more than 18 per cent per decade. Without extensive reserves of good or unused land the swollen population could only be accommodated at the cost of subdivision, underemployment, declining productivity per capita, and intensified susceptibility to subsistence crises. Even with the help of the potato and some forms of rural industralisation there were no districts capable of sustaining 'the productivity per head of a congested rural population'. In reality most rural communities divested themselves of their growing population, thereby helping the remaining people to raise output while supplying the industrial zones with the demographic surplus. This was the form of adaptation in the Lowlands and in the most southerly parts of the Highlands. But the north and west resisted the mechanism and the problem of congestion was compounded. It was the slowness rather than the rapidity of emigration that characterised the demographic experience of most of the Highlands in the age of the clearances, and it was this fact that dammed up the problem for the second half of the nineteenth century. Dr Hildebrandt points out that the crofting population grew by 30 per cent between 1851 and 1891 and that 'congestion and not emigration was a primary problem at a sub-regional level'. The propensity to emigrate among the north-western crofters in the late nineteenth century was low and falling, and Hildebrandt argues.

> that the incentives to mobility introduced during the nineteenth century in the wake of economic and social change were not strong enough to outweigh the constraints imposed by a peasant society still accustomed to a subsistence living in the remoter areas.[62]

In the twentieth century emigration from the Highlands has been explained in terms of the failure of crofting to yield 'an income which is acceptable in terms of the rising opportunity cost of croft labour'. But the older peasant tenacity continues to inhibit the fully rational adjustment of factors. The same economist says: 'Most crofters are willing to accept a much lower money income from crofting than that which they would earn for the same effort in alternative employment'.[63]

The demographic dimension in Highland history was also part of the wider set of economic constraints which bound the region and which set the framework of the clearances, and of the human tragedy which caused so large a proportion of the population to suffer and migrate. The final verdict on the landlords must comprehend the extent to which they were, individually and as a class, able to manipulate the general conditions which gripped the Highlands in these years. This question is addressed in the last part of this volume. Before that, however, it is logical to contemplate the degree to which the people of the Highlands co-operated with their betters, and the manner in which landlord plans provoked active resistance among the tenantry.

Notes

1. Barron, *Northern Highlands*, II, p. 274.
2. Ibid., III, p. 10.
3. Ibid., p. 11. The drift to the east coast was also significant. As late as the 1880s the Pennells found many families from the western isles living in the town of Nairn and able to speak only in Gaelic. Pennell, *Tour*, p. 139.
4. Barron, *Northern Highlands* III, p. 12.
5. SC on Emigration (Scotland) (1841), pp. 200-1.
6. Barron, *Northern Highlands*, III, p. 184.

7. *Scotsman*, 11 August 1849.
8. Cynicism was not new. T. C. Smout quotes a section of Sir John Clark's memoirs of the famine of 1740, where he explains that thousands of bolls of relief meal had been imported by local gentlemen at a cost of £2,000. Resignedly, Clark reported that the common people 'asserted that all was done for our private advantages, not believing it possible that we had bought meal for them at a 3rd or 4th dearer than we sold it to them'. A century later the Highland lairds found it impossible to dispel the very same type of feeling. T. C. Smout in L. M. Cullen and T. C. Smout (eds.), *Comparative Aspects of Scottish and Irish Economic and Social History 1600-1900* (Edinburgh, 1977), p. 25.
9. Quoted by Cameron, 'Scottish Emigration', p. 337. Much of the next section owes a debt to Dr Cameron's important thesis.
10. See Richards, *Highland Clearances*, Ch. 14.
11. Cameron, 'Scottish Emigration', pp. 345-56; Barron, *Northern Highlands*, III, p. 235.
12. Hobson, 'Congestion and Depopulation'.
13. Cameron, 'Scottish Emigration'.
14. See Richards, *Highland Clearances*, Ch. 14.
15. Quoted in Cameron, 'Scottish Emigration', p. 368.
16. William Mackay to Horsburgh, 5 April 1848, quoted in Eric Richards, 'Problems on the Cromartie Estate, 1851-3', *Scottish Historical Review*, vol. 52 (1973), p. 154, n 2.
17. NLS Sutherland Papers, Dep. 313, II, Box 41, Gunn to Duke of Sutherland, 7 May 1848. The Free Church consistently resisted the idea of emigration and spoke loudly against it in the 1880s, at the time of the Crofter Commission. See Rowland Hill Macdonald, *The Emigration of Highland Crofters* (Edinburgh, 1885), p. 33. On the instability of emigrants' attitudes to Australia and Canada, see Levitt and Smout, *Scottish Working Class*, p. 245.
18. Quoted in the *Scotsman*, 20 October 1853.
19. See W. H. Murray, *Islands of Western Scotland* (London, 1973), p. 224. Cf. Flinn, *Scottish Population History*, pp. 431-3.
20. Barron, *Northern Highlands*, III, p. 215.
21. Ibid., III, pp. 220-1.
22. SRO, GD221/15, 'Population List of Certain Districts in the Highlands and Islands of Scotland — Exhibiting Total Population and Number which should be Removed out of Each District'.
23. They have been documented in Richards, *Highland Clearances*, Chs. 13 and 14. On Trevelyan's philosophy of improvement and emigration see Jennifer Hart, 'Sir Charles Trevelyan at the Treasury', *English Historical Review*, vol. 75, no. 29 (1960), pp. 96-101.
24. Richards, *Highland Clearances*, pp. 426-8.
25. Quoted in the *Scotsman*, 12 June 1852.
26. Quoted in Richards, 'Problems on the Cromartie Estate', p. 154, n 3.
27. See Macmillan, *Scotland and Australia*; Eric Richards, 'The Highland Scots of South Australia', *Journal of the Historical Society of South Australia*, no. 4 (1978). As early as June 1852 there had been publicly expressed fears of actual labour shortages in the Highlands. *Ross-shire Journal*, 19 June 1852.
28. SCRO, Sutherland Collection, D593/K, Gunn to Loch, 12 April 1852. Alexander Smith in *A Summer in Skye* (Edinburgh, 1912 edition), describes similar landlordly urgings in Skeabost in 1864, pp. 470-4.
29. See Napier Commission, Appendix A, Rev. Archibald Clark, p. 32; and Devine, 'Temporary Migration', *passim*.
30. *Inverness Advertiser*, quoted in *Stirling Journal and Advertiser*, 14 September 1849.

31. 'Historical Pamphlets of Inverness-shire', I, 'Emigrants from Skye to Australia', Inverness Public Library.
32. See Richards, 'Highland Scots', *passim.*
33. Mitchell Library (Sydney), A3071, records of *British Queen* and *Panama.*
34. See Richards, 'Highland Scots', *passim*
35. La Trobe Library (Melbourne), 53/B2246, Hunt to Grimes, 20 February 1853; Grimes to Col. Secretary, 2 March 1853; *Scotsman* 6 October 1952; *Inverness Courier*, 9 May 1850. Similar tribulations were experienced by the typhus-ridden Highlanders aboard the *Persian* which arrived at Hobart, Tasmania, at the end of October 1857. Argument over quarantine prevented disembarkation until the ship was towed to Impression Bay where it remained until January 1858. Local authorities described them as 'very inert, and not disposed to exert themselves' and 'the most unsatisfactory people who have been introduced at the public expense'. I thank Ms Jane Beer of Balwyn, Victoria, for this information. See also Tom Steel, *The Life and Death of St Kilda* (Edinburgh, 1965), pp. 41-4, and Charles Maclean, *Island on the Edge of the World* (London, 1972), pp. 124-7.
36. Landlords, in their turn, criticised the cruelty of some of the Canadian authorities, particularly with regard to the imposition of an Emigrant Tax. See NLS, Sutherland Papers, II, Box 45, Correspondence on complaints by emigrants of treatment in Prince Edward Island, 1849. The statistic quoted is from Cameron, 'Changing Role', p. 84.
37. Quoted in John Murray Gibbon, *Scots in Canada* (London, 1911), p. 132. See also MacPhee, 'Trail of the Emigrants', pp. 195-7.
38. Cameron, 'Scottish Emigration', pp. 345-56. See also W. S. Shepperson, *British Emigration to North America* (Minneapolis, 1957), pp. 46-7.
39. See Richards, 'Highland Scots', pp. 33-64; Dunderdale, *The Book of the Bush*, pp. 222 ff; and Don Watson, *Caledonia Australis* (Sydney, 1984).
40. Michael Katz, *The People of Hamilton, Canada West* (Cambridge, Mass., 1975); Margaret Mackay, 'Nineteenth Century Tiree Emigrant Communities in Ontario', *Oral History Journal*, vol. 9 (1981), pp. 49-60.
41. See Richards, 'Highland Scots', pp. 51ff.
42. Quoted by Cameron, 'Scottish Emigration', p. 584, from emigrant letters published in *Sequel to the Counsel for Emigrants* (Aberdeen, 1834), pp. 38-9.
43. *An Teachdaire Gaidhealach*, 1 August 1857. Propagandists of Highland emigration provided considerable, if partial, evidence of successful expatriation. See, for example, Macdonald, *Emigration of Highland Crofters*, *passim.*
44. Hunter, *Crofting Community*, pp. 73-87.
45. Donaldson, *Scots Overseas*, pp. 78-9.
46. Flinn, *Scottish Population History*, pp. 33, 441-54.
47. *Scotsman*, 25 August 1849.
48. On the vicissitudes of census taking in mid-century see the sobering account 'Recollections of a Highland Census', *Chambers's Journal*, 29 June 1881, p. 75.
49. The assumed 10 per cent growth rate is derived from Flinn, *Scottish Population History*, pp. 307-8. A similar exercise is undertaken by Gaskell, *Morvern Transformed*, p. 123. See also Gustav Sundborg in Charlotte Erickson (ed.), *Emigration from Europe, 1815-1914* (London, 1976), pp. 25-9. On the general problems of estimating emigration, see E. A. Wrigley and R. S. Schofield, *The Population History of England, 1541-1871* (London, 1981), pp. 219-28.
50. A similar exercise in Flinn, *Scottish Population History*, pp. 436-7, concludes that 'the potato famine led to an outflow of population from the western Highlands and Islands of almost one-third of the pre-famine numbers, or possibly 60,000 people'.
51. See, for instance, Richards, *Highland Clearances*, p. 99.
52. Cf. Cormac O'Grada, 'Demographic Adjustment and Seasonal Migration in

Nineteenth Century Ireland' in L. M. Cullen and F. Furet (eds.), *Irlande et France* (Paris, 1980).

53. Ibid., p. 189.

54. See Richard Lawton, 'Regional Population Trends in England and Wales, 1750-1971' in John Hobcraft and Phillip Rees (eds.), *Regional Demographic Development* (London, 1979), esp. Figure 2.4.

55. See R. N. Hildebrandt, 'Migration and Economic Change in the Northern Highlands during the nineteenth century with particular reference to the period 1851-91', unpublished PhD thesis, University of Glasgow, 1980.

56. J. Walker, *An Economical History of the Hebrides and Highlands of Scotland* (2 vols., Edinburgh, 1812), II, pp. 399ff. Similar calculations were done by Sir John McNeill in 1851 which likewise showed the differential population growth and vulnerability to famine as between the north-west Highlands and the south-east Highlands, as reported by W. R. Greg, 'Highland Destitution and Irish Emigration', *Quarterly Review*, vol. 90 (1851), p. 178.

57. Malcolm Gray, 'Migration in the Rural Lowlands of Scotland, 1750-1850' in T. M. Devine and David Dickson (eds.), *Ireland and Scotland 1600-1850* (Edinburgh, 1983), p. 105.

58. *Edinburgh Review*, vol. 106 (1857), pp. 489-91. For a modern comparison of the experience of the Highlands and the border country, see Robert A. Dodgshon, 'Agricultural Change and its Social Consequences in the Southern Uplands, 1600-1780' in T. M. Devine and David Dickson (eds.), *Ireland and Scotland 1600-1850* (Edinburgh, 1983), pp. 46-59.

59. Hobson, 'Congestion and Depopulation', pp. 31, 50.

60. Herman Merivale, *Lectures on Colonization and Colonies* (London, 1861 edition). Cf. Flinn, *Scottish Population ...*, p. 445.

61. Flinn, 'Malthus, Emigration and Potatoes'.

62. See Gray, 'Migration in the Rural Lowlands', esp. pp. 107-9, and Malcolm Gray, 'Scottish Emigration: the Social Impact of Agrarian Change in the Rural Lowlands, 1775-1875' *Perspectives in American History*, vol. 7 (1973). On the crucial importance of rural migration during the age of demographic revolution see W. A. Armstrong, 'The Influence of Demographic Factors on the Position of the Agricultural Labourer in England and Wales, c. 1750-1914', *Agricultural History Review*, vol. 29 (1981), esp pp. 71-5. Hildebrandt, 'Migration', pp. 29,73.

63. D. R. F. Simpson, 'An Economic Analysis of Crofting Agriculture', unpublished PhD thesis, Harvard University, 1962, pp. 4, 15.

PART THREE

THE REACTION FROM BELOW

The Song of Foxes
(Oran nam Balgairean)

My blessing be upon the foxes, because that they hunt the sheep —
The sheep with the brockit faces that have made confusion in all
the world,
Turning our country to desert and putting up the rents of our
lands.
Now is no place left for the farmer — his livelihood is gone;
Hard necessity drives him to forsake the home of his fathers.
The townships and the shielings, where once hospitality dwelt,
They are now nought but ruins, and there is no cultivation in the
fields.

There is no filly, nor mare with foal by her side.
Gone too are the heifers that suckled their calves.
No need is there of dairymaids, for every fold is broken and
scattered.
No lad can earn a wage save only the shepherd of the sheep.
The good useful goats, they too are gone ...

Deeply do I hate the man who abuses the foxes,
Setting a dog to hunt them, shooting at them with small shot.
The cubs, if they had what I wish them, short lives were not their
care.
Good luck to them, say I, and may they never die but of old age.*

Duncan Ban Macintyre, c. 1790-1804

---

* A translation by J. L. Campbell from the Gaelic, quoted in J. A. S. Watson,
'The Rise and Development of the Sheep Industry in the Highlands', *THAS*, 5th
Series, Vol. 44 (1932), p. 10.

11
AN ELUSIVE PEOPLE

The peasant past, its concern for daily detail, its perpetual hand-to-hand combat with a sly and brutal world of nature, is nearly impossible to recover in the western world, especially within close reach of the city dweller.[1]

Mass emigration from the Highlands was predominantly an expression of the failure of the economy to develop in a manner which could adequately sustain the much augmented population of the region. But, as the previous chapters have argued, it was not simply an automatic reflex response to economic failure. Emigration was also a manifestation of social change: within it was often contained a sense of collective rejection by the people of the new order in the north, reinforced by the attraction of life in the south and overseas. The evidence of surviving emigrant letters is striking — for the writers refer repeatedly not only to their new-found ease and affluence, but to their exultation in colonial freedom and to their contempt for the landlord class back in the Highlands.

There is, however, a record of more direct and explicit opposition to the clearances in various forms of social protest, to which much of the next four chapters is addressed. It is a chronicle of discontent perhaps not untypical of such a peasant society, half-stunned by the enormity of the changes taking place about it. It is true that social protest in the Highlands failed in the sense that the evictions proceeded without much interruption; but the record of protest is significant in that it voiced popular attitudes, and placed a range of checks (however minimal) upon landlord action. Moreover popular resistance in the Highlands drew upon most of the techniques of protest normally employed in other peasant societies under threat. The attitudes and forms of communal behaviour by which the Highland peasantry responded to the clearances bear comparison with the models of pre-industrial protest which have been explored by several modern historians of other European societies, most notably in the work of Charles Tilly and George Rudé.[2] In most such societies, peasant resistance to social and economic change was usually constrained by problems of geography, social solidarity, rudimentary organisation and leadership, and by the burden of deference and limited political awareness.

While most of the story of the Highlanders' response to the evictions is consistent with historical expectation, the case of Patrick Sellar does not conform, and requires separate attention. The popular assault on the great sheepfarmer in 1815-16 was marked by a degree of co-ordination and sophistication relatively unusual in the annals of British agrarian protest. Sellar is singled out for special treatment in Part Four partly because he epitomised the alien influence of sheepfarmers and factors in the new Highlands, and partly because his reputation outlasted all other elements in the collective memory of the Highland clearances. His story became part of the new folklore of the region, and crystallised the communal revulsion of the people from their masters.

I

The reconstruction of the Highland economy and society in the late eighteenth century was imposed from above by landlords who were acting entirely within their legal rights. The people whose lives were thus transformed and literally dislocated had initially no connection with the great changes except as the often hapless objects of the policy. Co-operation and consultation were concepts totally unknown at that time. It is exceedingly difficult to obtain any direct evidence of the people's response to the clearances and to the new world created over their heads by the landlords.

Most of the people of the Highlands spoke only Gaelic — a language in sharp decline in many parts of the region by the time of the clearances, and often despised by the improvement ideologues of the new age. The Gaels, so far as written records are concerned, were careless of posterity. Moreover a large proportion of them lived in remote communities with little access to newspapers or to spokesmen who would take their experience to a wider court. The Highlanders, for virtually all of the eighteenth and nineteenth centuries, were beyond the political nation. In 1890 two American visitors to the north wrote angrily that 'If the Highlands were represented by 85 members, all wanting Home Rule, more would have been heard about destitution in the Hebrides.'[3] The crofters had virtually no parliamentary representation until the last quarter of the nineteenth century; as soon as they were enfranchised they achieved rapid legislative gains.[4] Their case gained expression only through sympathetic outsiders. The scantiness of historical material from the Highlanders has necessarily reinforced the idea that their reaction to the clearances was undemonstrative and unresisting. The belief was widespread that the common people had been pacified, and that this represented an authentic quietism: in effect, the Highlanders were not angered by their fate.

Ian Grimble asserts firmly that 'when the history of the Celtic clearances in Scotland is written at last, the voices of Gaels themselves must provide the most important evidence, as they do in the history of all peoples'.[5] Yet such a declaration presents serious technical problems for a historian because the surviving evidence is slight and not easily interpreted. In the written record it is true that the volumes of the Napier Commission in 1883-4 provide eloquent testimony of the legacy of emotion stored in two generations after the great clearances: it is an oasis of information in what is otherwise a desert of evidence about the common people. There exist also the memoirs of men who claimed to speak for the crofters — of Donald Sage, Donald Macleod, Hugh Miller, Donald Ross, Alexander Mackenzie and others.[6] Inevitably the evidence tends to be indirect and retrospective: little of the response of the people themselves issues directly from their own mouths; there is little immediately contemporaneous evidence. Herein lies the classic problem of producing 'history from below' from a pre-literate, poor, isolated, peasant world.

There is another source. Some relief from the tyranny of the written evidence may be derived from the popular poetic memory which has continued to flow since the time of the clearances. The oral tradition, captured in the surviving fragments of Gaelic poetry, expresses something of the collective psyche, and may be claimed to be the richest source relating to the mental world of the peasantry. Despite much apparent loss there survives a substantial corpus of poetic testimony.[7] It is a difficult source for a historian untutored in Gaelic and the oral tradition, and the problem of what weight to attach to this form of evidence is compounded by the difficulty of judging its veracity and representativeness. However, if the poetry of the time was the authentic expression of the popular mind — and this has yet to be demonstrated — then it opens wide windows on to the inner mentality of the Gaelic peasant, the object of the clearances. For this we must rely on the translations, and on literary interpretation.

Dr Donald Meek has argued that, in the Gaelic Highlands, 'verse (or more strictly song) rather than prose was until recently the principal medium or popular journalism', and that, despite the loss of the majority of this oral tradition, 'much has survived [which] is of immense value in providing an insight into popular views of the movement for local law reform'. Gaelic poetry therefore provides an access into 'the emotional reactions of the Highland people generally, and helps to give some idea of the most important factors in producing these reactions'. In the latter sense it may be possible to achieve a view of the social and moral priorities within the peasant society which may be juxtaposed with the record of physical resistance. But it is a tenuous exercise requiring assumptions about the typicality of poetic sensibility, a point which Dr. Meek is prepared to concede.[8] The poets possibly spoke only for themselves, though their popularity and survival suggest otherwise. Clearly it is evidence to be considered in parallel with other sources: no one would write a history of enclosure in England exclusively on the basis of a poem by Goldsmith.

Sorley Maclean, the distinguished Gaelic poet, half a century ago analysed with great insight the entire poetic tradition of the age of the clearances.[9] It is worth summarising his arguments. He restricted his study to the poetry directly concerned with evictions, pointing out that the intimately connected theme of emigration loomed even larger in the tradition. Maclean's general theme is that the Gaelic poetry of the nineteenth century in its 'weakness, thinness and perplexity' reflected the relative weakness of physical resistance to the clearances. A secondary theme he detects is the 'absurd tendency to blame the factor more than the landlord' which, together with the influence of both Established and Free churches, operated to undermine any active resistance by the people to limit their landlords' behaviour. Maclean is adamant: 'the Highlanders' resistance, physical and moral, was bound to be very weak, and the poetry of the period reflects this impotence'.[10] The poetry was pathetic, depressing and hopeless in tone until the crofters were galvanised into action in the 1880s (notably inspired by the example of the Irish). Until then the Highlanders made little headway, poetically or intellectually, in fathoming the basic causes of their fate. Their poetry expressed this confusion directly.[11]

The poetry of the earliest clearances — in the third quarter of the eighteenth century — was more robust in spirit and tone. The elimination of the tacksmen in the 1770s appears to have produced some glee, and provied expression to 'the old view of the clan's right to the territory'. Moreover Maclean tells us that the poetry of Ailean Dall, in its description of the desolation of the cleared Highlands, also expresses.

> with great power an even physical contempt for the Lowland shepherds or shepherd farmers, their manners, their talk, their whole being, but not a disparaging word of the noble landlords whose pockets were being filled by the high rents paid by the shepherd farmers.

In this poetry the shepherds are offered as 'a personalification of all that was extinguishing the old Gaeldom of song, wine, bardic patronage and Gaels'.[12]

There were few direct poetic assaults on the specific landlords, though factors, for example Young, Sellar and the Ardnamurchan tacksmen, felt the full blast of contempt.[13] By 1820, however, there was 'a great decline in full-bloodedness of matter' in Gaelic poetry, in conjunction with 'a more persistent feeling for humanity', probably influenced by religious elements. It produced in some cases 'a union of anger and piercing sorrow', expressed primarily in 'a vague generalised regret without a definiteness even of indictment, a common failure to face the real cause'. It was allied with a number of repeated themes — 'an uncritical idealisation of the pre-clearance period', and 'a common execration of the Lowland shepherd and shepherd farmer'. Maclean agrees with Watson that it added up to the 'wail of a harrassed and dejected people', the poetry of a period of hopelessness.[14]

Maclean, in accord with his general thesis, shows that the clearances were a relatively minor focus of Gaelic poetry:

> Nostalgia is the most common sentiment in nineteenth century Gaelic poetry, and there is a huge body of verse that says nothing especially about the Clearances, but ... an emigrant's sadness pervades. Indeed some poets specialise in a generalised nostalgia that neither explains nor attacks.

Maclean is heavily critical of the poetry of vacuous melancholia and he makes the important point that most of the poetry about the clearances was retrospective rather than contemporaneous with events.[15]

Eventually in the 1880s, the poetry of nostalgia was overtaken by a stronger strain, the poetry of resurgence,[16] for which Maclean has greater respect, even though the poet followed rather than led the movement for crofter agitation. Maclean's study of the Gaelic poetry of the entire period of the clearances is a penetrating, critical survey which identifies various elements in the popular response which support impressions drawn from other sources. It emphasises the lingering faith in landlords; the revulsion from the new forces and changes in society; the intellectual and emotional confusion and the general pathos. Maclean points out the tendency towards caricature and inaccuracy. In all, it is a tradition highly suggestive of the popular mentality. It leaves unanswered the question of typicality: after all there is little known about the provenance of this evidence. To say that the poetry of the clearances speaks for the evicted Highlander requires a leap of faith. Nevertheless the poetic evidence may be set beside other elements — the pattern of protest itself meshes with the poetic tradition plausibly enough, and frequently vindicates the poetic source.

Dr Meek has taken the analysis of the surviving Gaelic tradition into the late nineteenth century, and, while he confirms much of Maclean's interpretation, he also suggests certain key values central to the convictions of the poets and, by extension, the Gaelic community. Though the political content of the poetry is slight, there is some indication that 'At the centre of such arguments lay the view that the land was the property of the people, and not of any feudal superior', and that, therefore, 'evictions were an unjust violation of a natural, albeit unwritten law. Landlords were often viewed as imposters, usurping the role of the benevolent chieftains of an earlier day, and misusing the land.'[17]

In summary, the Gaelic poetry of the age of the clearances seems to illuminate the communal psychology. But the poetic tradition may be unrepresentative, and may give a melodramatic version of popular opinions; it was usually created long after the event. Its provenance, even its authorship and dating, are usually unclear. Its survival depended upon the highly selective process of the oral tradition, and the poetry may well reflect what people wanted to believe about the past, rather than the way the past seemed at the time.[18] However, in the last two decades, scholars have been able to collect and systematise the surviving oral record just as more of the literary documentation has become available. It is now possible to connect two sides of the popular response: the poetry of the people and the actual record of physical resistance.

II

The Highlanders' reaction to the clearances was directly visible in the statistics of emigration and in the record of actual resistance to the policy of clearance. The exodus from the Highlands speaks clearly enough for their perception of the relative benefits of the new bases of life in the region compared with the attraction of abroad and of the south. Evidence of physical resistance to the clearances provides the most obvious and tangible measure of the popular response to the policies adopted by the landords. Yet there is an important and telling paradox in the testimony of resistance. There is a widely held notion that the Highlanders were stoically passive and pathetically supine in their reaction to the landlord policy of clearance; in the face of extraordinary incitement their resistance was feeble; yet a large proportion of *all* the evidence about the clearances is derived from those episodes of clearance which were sufficiently resisted to generate legal and journalistic attention. Much of our knowledge of the clearances is derived from reports generated by the physical expression of popular resistance to the evictions. Indeed the surviving evidence of disturbance and riot is hard to square with the received wisdom on the subject.

The general historical record of social response to eviction and enclosure, even within the British Isles, is very mixed. In parts of Wales, for instance, there was extensive and vigorous popular resistance to rising rents and enclosure, most of which conforms to the modern category of 'reactionary collective violence'.[19] In Ireland there were times when the peasantry struck back at the landlords in prolonged bouts of agrarian terrorism and assassination; they were held together by secret societies noteworthy for their rational choice of target, and for a sophistication of organisation. Eviction was resisted by sporadic violence which frightened the established order.[20] In England the record is much quieter — the enclosure movement of the late eighteenth century seems to have created little rural disorder. E. P. Thompson has written that 'enclosure riots [in England] were rare, not because enclosure was not unpopular, but because people learned early that to riot was hopeless'.[21] Perhaps the English were less slow to learn that the Irish and the Highlanders; their compliance may also reflect the greater degree of systematic organisation that accompanied the English enclosure movement, and the fact that wholesale eviction was unusual. Total dispossession and ejection mainly affected the class of squatters. For the rest the dislocation was generally less complete and less cataclysmic than the events in the Celtic regions. Much the same is true of Scotland south of the Highland line: there the process of enclosure and agricultural transformation was usually gradual and caused less social upheaval than in Ireland.

The Highland experience was more similar to that of parts of Ireland. Large-scale clearances, with or without resettlement provision, created a far greater degree of social havoc than agrarian transformation in the south. John Ramsay had predicted that the selfish behaviour of the landlords would eventually provoke the common people into open violence. He believed that Parliament would eventually have to intervene on behalf of the people.[22] Yet contemporary observers, marvelled at the stoicism of the people, and normally explained the Highlanders' apparent submission in terms of their good nature, or their native fatalism, or their broken psyches — their collective will had been destroyed by the treachery of their landlords and by the pacifying doctrines and influence of their ministers. Specific comparisons with their Irish counterparts were common: not untypical was W. R. Greg, in 1851, who observed that the Highlanders 'resembled the Irish in much of their character and in most of their habits; they were a somewhat indolent and unenterprising race — far less turbulent than Irish, but fully as impracticable and less energetic'.[23]

In much of the literature the good nature and docility of the Highlander has become a cultural if not racial stereotype, a part of some broad 'ideology'[24] of existence which is invoked to explain their social behaviour. Lord Teignmouth testified in 1835 to the extreme lawfulness of the Highlands in the face not only of landlordly provocation but even of famine itself. He wrote:

> The natives of Skye suffered much distress during the last year; and yet, to their credit be it recorded, on the assurance of a principal tacksman and proprietor, that not a single sheep was

stolen from him. This gentleman mentioned to me that he had
known a whole family slink away from this island, unable to
bear the disgrace which had been brought on them by the delin-
quency of an individual member of it.[25]

In 1838 two members of the Statistical Society of Glasgow, men
of science, ruminated on the same question. They were amazed
that such an illiterate and ill-educated peasantry should be so
orderly:

> Our astonishment is, that so much ignorance, combined with
> the want of employment so complete as that existing in the
> Highlands, should not ere now have produced the riot and dis-
> order usually attendant upon such a state of things — and we
> cannot but consider it as a circumstance highly honourable, to
> the national character of the people, that nothing of the kind
> has been even threatened.[26]

Sheepfarmers, factors and landlords were not unconscious of the
economic benefits of such relative peaceability. Thus, in 1830 one
agricultural adviser calculated that the real rent of one great Highland estate was worth 20 per cent more than its nominal level
because it had 'no *Tythes,* poor *rates* or *Incendiaries* to contend
with'.[27] And a recurrent theme in much of the anti-landlord criticism in the mid-nineteenth century was that the proprietors were
courting disaster — that continued clearances would eventually
goad the people into violence.

Hugh Miller, like so many defenders of the Highlanders against
their landlords, was consumed with frustration at their inertia and
submissiveness. Although he appears never to have publicly
incited direct physical resistance, he knew well the political utility
of violence. In 1846 he contrasted the peaceable Highlanders with
the violent Irish, and suggested that direct physical action was the
only way to attract the attention of Parliament.[28] Henry George
thought that the Highlanders were 'as tame as sheep', and asked an
audience in Glasgow in 1884, 'Those poor cowed people in the
Highlands, trembling under the eyes of their factors, what can they
do for themselves?' But by then the crofters had begun to stir
themselves.[29]

Historians during the past century, until recently,[30] have echoed
the contemporary opinion. The general interpretation of the popular response[31] to the clearances was stated succinctly in 1969 by

H. J. Hanham. After 1745 the more martial Highlanders, he remarks, became pacified, tamed and domesticated to such an extent that, in the clearances, 'scarcely a hand was raised against the destruction of much loved homes'. By the mid-nineteenth century the Highlanders had become 'notoriously god-fearing and law-abiding, and unwilling to cause trouble'. There is an important corollary to the received interpretation on the question of popular response to the clearances. It is that the crofters' war of the 1880s sprang into life without precedent: without warning, the peaceful world of the Highlands exploded. It has come to be regarded as a genuine historical discontinuity. The 'Battle of the Braes' is thus regarded as a unique moment in Highland history: on this view, it was not until 1882 that the Highlanders at last shook themselves into action; only then was the value of resistance by the common people realised, and a measure of success achieved. Even then, it is said, the crucial factor in the victory was the recruitment of outside support which made the crofters' case audible to the nation. Thus the story is one of pathetic peasant stoicism which showed no cracks until 1882. Like so much Highland history, it emphasises the special, perhaps uniquely Highland, response to the pressures of the new economic age.[32]

Many years before, J. P. Day put the case similarly — 'The people of the Highlands and Islands, dependent by tradition, training and sentiment upon the land magnates, were extraordinarily patient upon their sufferings, sinking gradually towards a state of hopeless apathy.' He connected the discontent that erupted in the 1880s with the general currents running in Western Europe against the system of unrestrained property in land (associated with the views of Laveleye, Walras and Henry George).[33] Another late-nineteenth-century observer of the events of the 1880s asserted that 'the teachings and the incitement of professional agitators ... has resulted in the people throwing off the restraints of customary submissiveness'.[34] At much the same time, a pair of American tourists, Joseph and Elizabeth Pennell, declared that the Highlanders had awoken from their passivity and had become 'far more determined and daring' than their Irish counterparts. In the past, they said, 'the Highlands have been laid to waste, their people brought to silence. But now the people themselves have broken their long silence, and a cry has gone up from them against their oppressors'.[35] Similarly a correspondent of the *Athenaeum* in 1883 felt it necessary to stress the wonderful forbearance shown by the people who were driven out. Their poetry shows how bitterly they felt their expulsion from their homes; but the whole history contains no record of a single agrarian murder by the oppressed. Yet in many instances they suffered from a long series of tyrannical acts.[36]

The tradition of docility has provided the foundation for one of the more perplexing puzzles of modern Highland history. There can be no doubt about the antipathy of the common people of the Highlands to the great changes subsumed in the phrase 'the clearances'. Nor did the Highlanders lack eloquent spokesmen; yet the passionate literature of protest seemed to be unmatched by an equivalent physical resistance on the part of the people. Apart from occasional eruptions, the Highlands became a pacific fringe contrasting with the social turmoil of the new industrial order to the south, or the troubles of peasant Ireland. *Prima facie* the distance from centres of military force, the difficulty of the Highland terrain, and the derisory local sources of law and order, all favoured communal resistance to the hated landlord policies. It is not unreasonable for D. G. Macrae to ask: 'Why didn't the Scots peasant shoot his landlord?'[37]

Among the proprietorial class in the Highlands there persisted, for many decades, an entirely different understanding of the relative quiescence of the common people. Many landlords honestly believed that, notwithstanding the years of eviction, a genuine feeling of mutual respect and clan loyalty had survived into the mid-nineteenth century. Traditional ties of affection held Highland society together while industrial Britain and agrarian Ireland lost all semblance of social cohesion. In this fashion the entire question of Highland pacifism was turned on its head — the common people did not riot because they continued to receive and accept the social leadership of their landlords. This philosophy was voiced most strikingly in the journal of Elizabeth Grant (1797-1885), who was brought up in a well-to-do family in Rothiemurchus in the Highlands, and then married a small landlord in Ireland, Colonel Smith of Baltiboys. She was perhaps uniquely placed to make comparisons, and in January 1840 she observed the apparent breakdown of order in the manufacturing districts of England, and in her adopted country, Ireland:

It is impossible not to dread future events, and the links which used to connect the different ranks of society together have been so rudely cut asunder by the haughty bearing of the *aristocracy* of birth that very unkind feelings have been created between classes which have been mutually agreeable and together most useful to the community at large. A little of the *Highland* manners would have done more for the good of the empire than people are perhaps aware ... When did anyone hear of Radicals in the Highlands? Are there any Chartists there? And where can be found such a society of *gentlemen* as her chiefs and nobles. There was nothing struck us so remarkably when I first came here [Ireland] as the tenants marrying their children — setting them up in different trades etc, without ever saying one word about it to their landlord. It went through their whole conduct — we were to them only the receivers of a much grudged rent. It has been my endeavour faithfully pursued through many discouragements to establish a more affectionate intercourse between us. I have certainly succeeded in a great degree.[38]

There is considerable evidence of residual deference in the Highland community in the mid-century and part of Elizabeth Grant's testimony rings true. Nevertheless her recollection was undoubtedly an idealisation of old Highland society from a patrician viewpoint; it took no cognisance of the palpable disintegration of social connections, and was entirely innocent of the record of resistance which, despite common perceptions, was already substantial.

III

In its main thrust the conventional view of the efficacy of Highland protest is correct. The Highland clearances were not halted by popular resistance; there was no general and co-ordinated obstruction of landlord action; there were no assassinations and the record of rural terrorism and disorder was slight in comparison with that of the Irish. For more than a century Highland proprietors executed clearances without a full confrontation with the united forces of popular opposition. Nevertheless it may be argued that the orthodoxy does scant justice to the actual behaviour of the people and to the difficulties which impeded concerted resistance. It also distracts attention from the long continuum of popular Highland protest which erupted in every decade after 1780, and underrates the modest efficacy of the various forms of opposition which were practised in the Highlands during the clearances. The next two chapters attempt to delineate that pattern of protest and its connection with the mental world of the Highland peasantry as it faced the radical transformation of its economic and social foundations.

Notes

1. E. L. Jones and R. S. Parker, *The European Peasant and his Market* (Princeton, 1975). Afterward by Eric Jones, p. 329.

2. See, for instance, Charles Tilly, 'Collective Violence in European Perspective' in H. D. Graham and T. R. Gurr (eds.), *Violence in America: Historical and Comparative Perspectives* (New York, 1969); and 'The Pre-Industrial Crowd' in George Rudé, *Paris and London in the Eighteenth Century* (London, 1970).

3. Joseph Pennell and Elizabeth Robins Pennell, *Our Journey to the Hebrides* (London, 1890), p. 210. Their work was first published in *Harper's Bazaar*.

4. Richards, *Highland Clearances*, Ch. 15.

5. Ian Grimble, *Scottish Gaelic Studies*, vol. 10 (1963), pp. 113-14.

6. See above, Ch. 2 and 3.

7. The Outer Hebrides possess the richest storehouse of oral tradition in Western Europe, according to Donald MacCormick, *Hebridean Folksongs* (Oxford, 1969), Preface.

8. D. E. Meek, 'Gaelic Poets of the Land Agitation', *TGSI*, vol. 49 (1974-6), pp. 310, 318. More generally see Derick Thomson, *An Introduction to Gaelic Poetry* (London, 1974), Ch. 6. General criticism of oral tradition may be found in Bumsted, *The People's Clearance*, esp. p. 62

9. Samuel Maclean, 'The Poetry of the Highland Clearances', *TCSI*, vol. 38 (1937-41).

10. Ibid., pp. 296-7.

11. This is confirmed, on the whole, by Dr Meek: 'Gaelic poetry tends to be concerned with direct statements and it is mainly narrative in style, scarcely offering an analysis of the situation described.' Even during the land agitation in the 1880s it remained 'largely parochial and non-political'; 'Gaelic Poets', p. 315.

12. Maclean, 'Poetry of the Highland clearances', p. 300. On the eighteenth-century tradition see Grimble, *The World of Rob Donn*. esp. Ch. 11; and Thomson, *Gaelic Poetry*, pp. 194-217. The earlier tradition is considered in MacCormick, *Hebridean Folksongs*, esp. pp. 17-18, and Campbell, *A Collection of Highland Rites and Customes*.

13. Maclean, 'Poetry of the Highland Clearances', pp. 302-3.

14. Ibid., pp. 306-9. For specific anti-factor feeling see John Smith quoted in Macdonald, *Lewis*, pp. 43-4, and the Gaelic material presented and translated in Ian Grimble, 'Patrick Sellar' in Gordon Menzies (ed.), *History is my Witness* (London, 1977), pp. 36-66.

15. Maclean, 'Poetry of the Highland Clearances', pp. 312-14.

16. Ibid., p. 316.

17. Meek, 'Gaelic Poets', p. 323.

18.　Fear of the political uses of the romantic poetic evocation of the crofter past was expressed in Lawson, 'The Poetry and the Prose of the Crofter Question', pp. 592-606. The poetic tradition appears to have neglected the Disruption of 1843 and gave virtually no attention to the famine of the 1840s; see Thomson, *Gaelic Poetry*, p. 233, and Eric Cregeen, 'Oral Sources for the Social History of the Scottish Highlands and Islands', and 'Oral Tradition and Agrarian History in the West Highlands'.

19.　See David J. V. Jones, *Before Rebecca. Popular Protest in Wales 1793-1835* (London, 1973), esp. pp. 34-6, 43-9, 57, 199. Interestingly the poetry of protest was substantially more vigorous in Wales than in Gaelic Scotland. See Thomson, *Gaelic Poetry*, p. 229.

20.　See, for instance, the study by Michael Beames, 'Rural Conflict in Pre-Famine Ireland: Peasant Assassinations in Tipperary 1837-1847', *Past and Present*, no. 81 (1978), pp. 75-91, and the papers by Maureen Wall and Joseph Lee in T. Desmond Williams (ed.), *Secret Societies in Ireland* (Dublin, 1973).

21.　E. P. Thompson, 'English Trade Unionism and Other Labour Movements before 1790', *Society for the Study of Labour History*, Bulletin no. 17 (1968), p. 20. But see E. P. Thompson, 'History from Below', *Times Literary Supplement*, 7 April 1968. Anti-enclosure resistance is considered in W. E. Tate, 'Parliamentary Counter-Petitions during the Enclosures of the Eighteenth and Nineteenth Centuries', *English Historical Review*, vol. 59 (1944), pp. 392-403, and 'Opposition to Parliamentary Enclosure in Eighteenth Century England', *Agricultural History*, vol. 19 (1945), pp. 137-42. See also John W. Leopold, 'The Levellers Revolt in Galloway in 1724', *Scottish Labour History Journal*, vol. 14 (1980); Jeanette M. Neeson, 'Opposition to Enclosure' in A. Charlesworth (ed.), *An Atlas of Rural Protest in Britain 1518-1900* (London, 1983), pp. 80-2.

22.　Ramsay, *Scotland and Scotsmen*, p. 536.

23.　Greg, 'Highland Destitution and Irish Emigration'.

24.　See T. C. Smout, 'An Ideological Struggle: the Highland Clearances', *Scottish International*, vol. 5, no. 2 (February 1972), pp. 13-16.

25.　Teignmouth, *Sketches*, II, p. 151.

26.　Fullarton and Baird, *Remarks on the Evils at Present Affecting the Highlands and Islands of Scotland*, p. 73.

27.　SCRO, Sutherland Collection, D593/K, Young to Loch, 5 December 1830.

28.　See Mackenzie, *Hugh Miller*, pp. 190-1, and Ch. 2 above. Most of the claims about the orderliness of the Highlanders emanate from periods of relative quiescence in the north.

29.　George, *Scotland and Scotsmen*, pp. 13, 18.

30.　Some modifications have been suggested in Eric Richards, 'Patterns of Highland Discontent, 1790-1860' in J. Stevenson and R. Quinault (eds.), *Popular Protest and Public Order* (London, 1976) and 'How Tame were the Highlanders?' in Hunter, *Crofting Community*, Ch.6; and K. J. Logue, *Popular Disturbances in Scotland, 1780-1815* (Edinburgh, 1977), Ch. 2.

31.　For examples see Richards, 'How Tame were the Highlanders?', pp. 35-6.

32.　H. J. Hanham, 'The Problem of Highland Discontent, 1880-1885', *Transactions of the Royal Historical Society*, vol. 19 (1969), pp. 22-67.

33.　Day, *Public Administration*, p. 182.

34.　Macdonald, *Emigration of Highland Crofters*, p.7.

35.　Pennell and Pennell, *Our Journey to the Hebrides*, pp. 151, 210, 225.

36.　*Athenaeum*, 3 March 1883, pp. 2-6.

37.　Review of Gray's *Highland Economy* in *Economica*, new series, vol. 25 (1958).

38.　*The Irish Journals of Elizabeth Smith 1840-1850*, ed. David Thomson and Moyra McGusty (Oxford, 1980), p. 6.

12
POPULAR RESISTANCE TO THE CLEARANCES: THE PATTERN ESTABLISHED

Are we alone, of all the proprietors of land in the Kingdom, to be prevented from acting according to our judgement, and from turning our estates to the best account; and forced to make them nests of misery?

Sir George Mackenzie, 1806[1]

In the record of popular disturbance in the great period of the clearances, 1780 to 1855, the most striking impression is one of sporadic but repeated eruption of spontaneous resistance to established authority. Among the eruptions, varied in scale, there were at least three episodes of unusually ambitious resistance, marked by sustained and co-ordinated pressure: the events in Ross-shire in 1792, the campaign against Patrick Sellar in 1814-16, and the riots in the Culrain district in 1820-1, appeared to pose a generalised threat to the progress of the clearances. For the most part, however, resistance was usually highly localised and unconnected. In all, there were at least 50 occasions during the clearances when the forces of law and order were challenged by the will of the common people. Not only was there a continuity in this period; there was also a marked recurring pattern in the mode and techniques of popular protest. The main purpose of this chapter is, rather than to retail every episode, to sketch this pattern of social action.

I

Highland disorder was favoured by the fragile system existing for the maintenance of civil peace in the north. Geographical isolation, the awkwardness of the terrain, and the minimal establish-

301

ment of police and militia inevitably stretched the capacity of the authorities to maintain a sense of security in the region. This helps to explain the condition of near-hysteria that often infected law officers and landlord agents during times of disturbances. The line of communication from Whitehall to Edinburgh, then to Inverness or Fort William, and then to the location of resistance, was long and easily broken. There were times — especially during the French Wars — when the availability of troops to put down recalcitrant Highlanders was extremely uncertain.

Within the Highlands it was often difficult to raise constables who could be trusted wholeheartedly to put down local skirmishes. In 1813 Sidmouth, Home Secretary, was informed that, in the Highlands,

> most of the local Militiamen are either themselves of the number who are to be dispossessed, or entertain the same sentiments. A Military Force of a different description has become necessary. There are however few troops in the North of Scotland.[2]

In 1821 it was difficult to get constables to do the unsavoury work of clearing the common people from the straths of Easter Ross. There is good evidence that at Coigach in 1853 the authorities were exceedingly pessimistic about the pertinacity of not only local but even Glasgow policemen in the task of evicting obstinate and riotous crofters. The constables were lukewarm towards the work, and generally sympathetic to the people. Thus, when the authorities did act — calling in troops, despatching naval vessels, and mobilising police from Glasgow — they gave the impression of using a steam hammer to crack a nut. Nevertheless the over-response of authority in several instances may be one powerful factor explaining the general lack of sustained opposition by the people.

The events in Easter Ross in the summer of 1792 (described in detail elsewhere[3]) were the first and virtually the last time that an effort was made to arouse the entire Highlands against the invasion of sheep and the disruption of the old way of life. In this sense it was an exception to the 'classic' form of Highland protest behaviour; moreover its widely publicised failure, impressed on the mind of the Highlanders, may have acted to inhibit subsequent thoughts of insurrection on a grand scale. Nevertheless even the events of 1792 encompassed several recurrent features of the general model of 'pre-industrial' Highland protest. Before the drama of 1792, there existed already a record of disorder and breakdown of co-operation. There was, for instance, widespread disaffection in the mid-eighteenth century on the Argyll estates where the landlord's ambitious plans were frequently frustrated or at least restrained by a spirit of resistance. There was sporadic trouble elsewhere in the north. Dr. Logue has recently documented an episode at Letterfinlay, Lochaber, in 1782, when a visiting sheepfarmer from the south was set upon by a body of women and given rough treatment. A second attempt at intimidation was accompanied by abuse, threats and several gunshots, but no further action. Presumably the opposition in Lochaber fizzled out. So also did a reported 'combination' designed to steal and destroy the sheep stock of Geddes, a southern sheepfarmer who rented land from Sir John Ross of Balnagowan.[4] At the end of the century John Ramsay was predicting a physical collision from the rising tension of the times: 'The indifference and selfishness of many landlords have converted the love and veneration of the common people into hatred and alienation which will undoubtedly break out into violence in some fresh provocation.'[5]

There can be no doubt that the incoming sheepfarmers felt the hostility of the native people. In 1795, for instance, two border farmers, pioneering sheepfarming in Inverness-shire and searching for new pastures, were 'somewhat alarmed and apprehensive of not being relished by the present possessors or others'. Such hostility was widespread and sustained, though it was not necessarily expressed in a physical form. A visitor to Sutherland in 1808 noted how Lady Stafford was 'very much abused for turning off last year a great number of small tenants who had held land under the family for upwards of two hundred years, and making sheep farms'. Often this feeling became manifest in a chronicle of low-level intimidation of the sheepfarmers, normally by way of sheep thefts, the constant complaint of the new men after 1780.[6]

The 1792 episode was, of course, a direct clash between cattle-grazing peasantry and incoming sheepfarmers. Widespread opposition to sheep farms was aroused and activated without much difficulty; it is unlikely that the plan could have developed at all without the considerable tacit support of the community at large. The strategy employed was naïve: the incoming sheepfarmer was given rough treatment, bruised and humiliated; but the main thrust of the uprising was a direct attack on the sheep themselves — to chase them out of the northern Highlands altogether. The local gentry were rapidly brought to the point of panic, and although there were rumours of gunpowder-running from Inverness, and of radical conspiracies, the entire business lacked not only violence but any suggestion of serious political consciousness.[7] The whole affair evaporated with extraordinary rapidity as soon as troops appeared in the district. The 'uprising' was poorly organised, childishly optimistic, and it lacked any sustained plan or foresight. It was, in a technical sense, an unsophisticated (though grandiloquently ambitious) piece of resistance. Given the weaknesses in its organisation, the most remarkable feature of the episode was its duration (several weeks) and the tenacity of the resistance while it lasted.

II

As far as is currently known, most clearances passed with little or no overt opposition; for large tracts of the Highlands and for long stretches of time the record is silent. All that remain are the grumblings of posterity about the fate of the Highlanders, without precise evidence of the actual events in most districts. In Sutherland, however, the record is far from silent and the events in Kildonan during the second phase of the great Sutherland plan vividly illustrate the recurrent form of Highland protest behaviour. The reaction against renewed clearances in Kildonan began in December 1812[8] in response to plans for removing at least 60 families; they were scheduled for resettlement along the coast, while their land was marked out for a new sheep farm. It is perfectly clear from the evidence in the factors' correspondence that the people of Kildonan were smouldering with discontent at the landlord's programme of change. In January 1813 they presented a petition asking the proprietor to cancel the removal. They declared that they had been promised the occupation of the land when they 'furnished men for the 93rd Regiment'. Patrick Sellar, acting at this time on behalf of the estate, reckoned that the undertaking had expired in 1808, but the people were adamant that they would certainly keep hold of the land until the men returned from service at the Cape of Good Hope.[9] Valuers who travelled to

Kildonan to mark out the sheep farm and negotiate compensation were given short shrift by the mutinous people of the strath: they were ejected and threatened with violence should they return. Sellar reported that 150 men were involved in the opposition to the clearance, and that they were led by 'their Orators' declaring that they were entitled to the land. The people refused to sign a bond of peaceful behaviour and the main estate administrator, William Young, was extremely apprehensive that any stranger, but especially any sheepfarmer, would be subject to reprisals and harassment in Kildonan. Sellar believed the mutineers capable of assassination. There was no chance that they would comply with the law: 'How could they sign a Bond of Law ... with respect to men who would ruin them and their families, and against whom they therefore entertain enmity in their hearts'.[10] William Young described the popular opposition as 'a premeditated design to remain among the mountains in spite of every reasonable proposal to the contrary'.[11] There was also a strong suggestion that the people of Kildonan were in league with rebellious tenants in the Reay Country in a plan (reminiscent of 1792) to eject all sheep from the country.[12]

The people had spurned the resettlement plans made for them by the Countess of Sutherland. The factor was at his wits' end, fearing that if the uprising was not quashed his plans for improvement would be totally subverted. He believed that the Kildonan affair was encouraging a spirit of insubordination across the Highlands: the people were driven by the notion that not only could they halt the clearances, but also previous clearances would be reversed. Whitehall was apprehensive of rumours of a 'Highland Rebellion'. Alarmed estate administrators detailed the events to Sidmouth at the Home Office. The Sheriff Depute of the county, George Cranstoun, was warned that the rebellious insubordination might easily spread across the entire country, and that 'the whole people are anxiously watching the issue of the contest, for so it must now be called, some to resume farms they have formerly possessed, others to follow the same plan of resistance to other projected arrangements'. It was a reasonable interpretation of the events and there can be no doubt that the people were acting in total opposition to the plans of the landlord. The people declared that their sons were defending the nation from Napoleon, and that they would unite to protect their lands from strangers.[13] It has a straightforward contest for the control of the land.

On 20 February 1813, when the news of possible military inter-vention had been made known to the people, Young met the ringleaders of the resistance and managed to extract from them 'partly from fear … a petition to Lord and Lady Stafford begging forgiveness'. In fact the disturbances continued into March and troops, called into Kildonan from Fort George, travelled north by fishing boats to put down what Cranstoun termed 'a very extensive and well organised combination among the tenantry'. On the arrival of these troops (who had recently served in Ireland) the people became 'perfectly submissive', according to the estate factors. The ringleaders were rounded up but later released. Both William Young and Lord Gower, the heir, met representatives of the people, explained the resettlement and removal programme again, and attempted to pacify their feelings and remove their fears. This was the closest the House of Sutherland came to con-sultation with the subjects of their clearances. Patrick Sellar regarded these conciliatory moves as a public demonstration of the weakness and spinelessness of the Sutherland management, cal-culated to encourage the people of Strathnaver to launch their sub-sequent assault upon Sellar himself.[14] In his anger he claimed that the management, in effect, had capitulated to the rioting conspira-tors. They had been allowed to get off scot-free: 'I saw six of the ringleaders feasted in Rhives parlous, Mr Young drawing ale for them,' he recalled bitterly.[15]

Another aspect of the Kildonan affair throws light on the men-tality of the people during the clearances. The protesting people of Kildonan drew attention to their plight by a number of actions embarrassing to the landlord. The physical resistance had been enough to draw the attention of newspapers in Inverness and Edinburgh: in addition reports were sent — very probably by the people's representatives — to the London newspapers, notably the *Star*. This was unwelcome publicity for the Stafford family, but its effect was compounded by a petition sent to the Prince Regent and to Lord Sidmouth, requesting intervention against the landlord or, failing that, assistance for emigration to Canada. A spokesman, a half-pay soldier and former recruiting sergeant in the 93rd Regi-ment, went to London to press the case. In the upshot these public demonstrations forced the Stafford family to negotiate with the people, even to the point of making promises concerning future action. Thus, although the concessions were small, and the threat of military intervention was crucial (Young remarked: 'We shall never again have ... occasion to bring Military into the Country and our plans called into question'), some of the people's objectives were met, merely by the attraction of public attention. The rebellion collapsed, but the estate administrators were left regretting that 'the disturbances had ... become in some degree of a public nature'. Action against the leaders could not be contemplated: the landlord's camp was expressly afraid that the subject would come before the House of Commons. As one agent wrote, regretfully,

> we have a publick here to regard whose opinion on the subject is very material; to stand right in their eyes is of much consequence — even if it should most unfortunately delay your final statement [i.e. the clearance programme] for a few weeks.[16]

Thus, while the appeal of the people to a higher and distant arbiter of their case demonstrated a naïve faith in the benevolence of ultimate authorities, it nevertheless acted as an effective measure to embarrass and curb the landlord. The expectation of external intervention was a recurrent theme in peasant rebellion in the Highlands, as elsewhere in the history of popular protest.

There is little doubt that the Kildonan Rebellion (as it became known) was a direct challenge to landlords. As James Loch noted, 'The measure must be persevered in or the improvement of this Country must forever be abandoned and the Proprietors must resign their property to their Tenants and Dependents.'[17] He was confident that the common people had been brought to their senses. In the event he was proved too sanguine: the great campaign against Patrick Sellar erupted within one year of the Kildonan Rebellion. The currently available evidence is consistent with the view that the assault on Sellar was a continuation of the partly clandestine struggle against the policy of clearance. In many ways it was the most sophisticated technique of opposition employed through the history of the clearances.[18] In the last analysis it created a permanent stain on the reputation of the greatest landlord in the Highlands.

Sellar himself perceived a direct continuity from the Kildonan Rebellion in 1812 to the great campaign which culminated in his trial in 1816. The Sellar story was paralleled by other expressions of popular opposition. In July 1813 there had been a violent incident on the west coast of the Sutherland estate, in Assynt, about the installation of a new minister whose place was in the Countess's gift. Although it was far from being the first time that the induction of a minister had been resisted in the Highlands, the violence of the riot was singular.

Only two years previously, at Creich, a new minister had required protection for his introduction, and even this failed to prevent a riot.[19] The Assynt trouble of 1813 assumed serious proportions, following closely on the heels of the Kildonan skirmishes. William Young accompanied the minister to Assynt where the common people, who had their own preferred candidate, resisted fiercely. Young and the new minister had narrowly escaped from an angry crowd which had come close to putting the men out to sea, handcuffed together in an open boat. According to Sellar, the new minister was subject to substantial intimidation — his house was attacked at sunset, gutted of everything before morning 'and they transported man, wife and child, blankets, beds, chairs, and all et ceteras, to a heath near Glen Cool in Edrachylis about ten miles distance and left them there'. Sheriff substitute Mackid began a precognition, and Young remarked that the recent disturbances were even more dangerous to authority than the Kildonan riots. Sheriff Cranstoun called in a King's Cutter with 160 men of the Norfolk Militia from Leith Roads. In fact he had over-reacted (to the irritation of the Stafford family) since the disturbances had subsided completely before the troops arrived — and Cranstoun hurriedly ordered them not to land. Mackid arranged for five ringleaders to appear at the Inverness Assizes; the settlement of the minister proceeded.[20] Donald Sage later commented of the new minister that 'his appointment to Assynt was a personal arrangement between himself and Lady Stafford. *The people of Assynt were not consulted in the matter.* They however, took the liberty of thinking for themselves in the case.'[21] The new man never gained the co-operation of the people, and was transferred in 1817. One rioter taken to Inverness received nine months' imprisonment.

The Assynt Riot of 1813 was as much an expression of anti-landlord feeling as of religious conviction. Sellar himself argued that the people were set against the new minister because he had acted 'treasonably' in the Kildonan riot. He was alleged to have 'leagued with the factors' and told the landlord of the plans for rebellion.[22] The intimidation of the incoming minister was paralleled by threats alleged to have been made against sheep-farmers in the clearing zones. Sellar reported that 'shepherds had been ... hunted over the mountains from Kildonan to Bighouse, and a day was appointed for driving every south countryman out of the country'. In particular Mrs Reid, the pregnant wife of a sheepfarmer who had the lease of the disputed area of Kildonan, was threatened in 'a message, sent by the rioters to her family, that if she bore a boy it should be killed. If a girl they would save it because its mother was a Highlander.'[23] If the threat was made it was unfulfilled; assassination was not employed in any Highland protest.

Yet the assault on Sellar resembled an attempted assassination: the legal processes were exploited in a campaign to destroy the man and the policy for which he stood. Regardless of the veracity of the charges, the campaign necessitated elaborate organisation, the commitment of many of the people to petitioning and raising subscriptions and orchestrating the legal forms against Sellar. As Sellar said, 'they conspired by *Law* ... to take the life of the Agent'. It also attracted external publicity by its developing connection with the press in London, notably through articles in the *Star* and the *Military Register.* The leaders in the assault were almost certainly half-pay captains and tacksmen, middlemen in the old hierarchy, their economic status set at nothing by the clearances. The publicity generated by the affair was intensely embarrassing to the Stafford family; wisely, they did not underestimate the threat. Their anxiety was that the affair would eventually provoke the interest of parliamentary questions and inquiry. This was probably the greatest fear of the landlord class as a whole: that the noise emanating from the north would attract so much attention that Westminster would be compelled to intervene, even to the extent of clipping the wings of the landlords. It was not an entirely absurd fear, as events of the following fifty years eventually demonstrated. As for Sellar, he knew well the ferocity of the opposition and indeed the threat to his own life. As the Trial Report put the issue:

this was not merely the trial of Mr Sellar, but in truth a conflict between the law of the land and a resistance to that law: ... the question at issue involved the future fate and progress of agricultural and even moral improvements, in the country of Sutherland ... [It is] in fact, a trial of strength between the abettors of anarchy and misrule, and the magistracy as well as the laws of the Country.[24]

In other words, it was about the control of the land and the limits of landlord power.

III

The Sellar affair caused only a temporary halt in the Sutherland clearances. The third great phase of removals was spread over two seasons in 1819 and 1820. Once more the scale was so vast that disruption and conflict were virtually inevitable. Surprisingly there was no direct physical confrontation with the clearance parties. The common people appear to have put their faith in public appeal as their best hope of salvation: some superior authority, some higher moral agency, might intervene against the demonstrable unfairness of their landlord. It happened in the following way.

In the early summer of 1819 the principal Sutherland agent, in the midst of the clearances, reported that the people were 'inoffensive and timidly pliant'. True, he had found it necessary to burn the roofs of some houses to prevent reoccupation; but the ministers had accompanied the removal party 'to several towns and used their influence and arguments with the people to submit with cheerfulness to the will of the proprietors'. Nevertheless, despite the passivity, 'clamour' was rising on the fringe of the estate. It took an unusual form. Among the displaced persons of the clearances Thomas Dudgeon, a farmer and former factor, had formed the Sutherlandshire Transatlantic Emigration Society, ostensibly a friendly society, based at Meikle Ferry. With the help of a Tain teacher, and a half-pay captain and a publican, Dudgeon opened a subscription to assist the emigration of dispossessed Sutherland tenants. Their activity coincided with an outburst of public criticism in the *Scotsman*, where the Sutherland removals were described as 'more barbarous than anything [...] ever heard of in Ireland or anywhere else'.[25] The Association was clearly designed to create publicity adverse to the House of Sutherland, and its allegations included statements that during the 1819 clearances 271 houses had been demolished by fire, 43 smashed down by hatchets and mattocks, and a school house, a kiln and three corn mills destroyed. There was a further allegation that a woman's death had been caused by the removals. All of this was heatedly rebutted by the estate administration.[26]

Dudgeon held several meetings at Meikle Ferry, including one gathering with an attendance estimated at over 1,000 which produced a petition to the Regent and both Houses of Parliament pleading for a grant of land or aid for emigration. Opponents claimed that he had promised the people money, but instead had extracted subscriptions from them — sixpence or a shilling from 672 persons with 2,367 children. Dudgeon's campaign effectively concentrated attention on the Sutherland situation, gave a focus for concerted action, and excited the authorities into an advanced state of anxiety.[27] Mounting abuse and renewed allegations of atrocity filled the Scottish newspapers. Moreover, Dudgeon's association was sending emissaries over the entire Highlands. The less sanguine of the estate officials were beginning to panic in the face of collective action. One prospective sheepfarmer reported the mood of the people in October 1819:

> It is impossible for me to tell you here what he [Sergeant Mackay of the Association] revealed of the intentions of the people — not only against myself as an expectant of succeeding to their land [in the forthcoming 1820 clearances] — but against all law and authority. They declared they intended to resist being moved ... that they were determined to have blood for blood in the struggle for keeping possession.[28]

The northern authorities' greatest fear was the suspected danger that Dudgeon's Association had links with burgeoning southern radical movements. Informers' reports[29] were mixed. One described Dudgeon as 'a thorough *Radical* ... he is perhaps endeavouring to create a diversion by an appearance of a rising in the North', that is, as part of a radical conspiracy. Others denied any political connection. But landlords had to consider 'how far the police of the Country should permit a set of individuals, unconnected with it, to travel up and down and make the people dissatisfied with their condition so as to interfere even with the management of private property'. The common people of the northern Highlands were in the grip of demagogues.[30]

The Emigration Association countered the charges of radicalism in a manner potentially even more dangerous. At the end of 1819 Henry Brougham was told reassuringly by a landlord representative from the Highlands that '*our Rebellion* wants one most important feature of such a proceeding, namely it wants actors'. At that moment Dudgeon was organising another public meeting with the avowed object of refuting the aspersions that the Association was composed of thieves and rebels. To prove their point the Association offered its 'services in a military capacity' to the government. This doubled the anxiety of the authorities, some of whom believed that this was a pretext for drilling and arming the dissidents. Dudgeon's men were reported touring the north, 'using the most inflammatory language and infamous falsehoods' to raise support. The magistrates acted promptly: they declared Dudgeon's forthcoming meeting illegal under the Seditious Meetings Act. The meeting failed: Dudgeon did not appear and the leadership disintegrated. He was declared an imposter. But the authorities maintained a vigil — especially on Dudgeon's influence by way of 'his intercourse with the people through the pensioners' — that is, the half-pay captains who were seen as a constant source of discontent in the post-war Highlands,[31] and indeed represented the defeated elements in the new Highland society of the nineteenth century.

The Dudgeonite agitation in 1819-1820 did not develop into violence on the Sutherland estate, but was effective in maintaining a degree of raised consciousness that was probably significant in the explosion of physical resistance on the adjacent estate of Munro of Novar at Culrain in March 1820. Here the pattern of resistance was demonstrated in one of its fullest forms, in the manner to be repeated many times before the Battle of the Braes in 1882. A populous Highland area in Easter Ross had been marked out for clearance: 600 people were to be evicted without any alternative provision for their accommodation (in contrast to the removals on the Sutherland estate). In the first episode at Culrain, officers who were charged with the responsibility of delivering the notices of removal were set upon, humiliated and sent back; they had been threatened with 'the severest corporal punishment'. On the second attempt a party of constables 'were seized by men in women's clothes — beat — and the summons burnt in their presence'. The Sheriff then mustered a party of about 40 constables as well as armed militia —

> He went in person ... suppposing such a force more than sufficient for his purposes — but he had no sooner entered upon the grounds than he was attacked by columns of women and

young men — and pelted with stones as if forces from Hell had come forth. The men — I mean the Country people ... organised in the rear of the women — with firearms to give battle in case the latter were not successful — it is calculated about five hundred of them — upon the blowing of horns they advanced to their station from all quarters — and it is confidently believed there were a great number from Sutherland.

Two women and a boy were hurt when a mêlée occurred and shots were fired without orders; but the official force was driven back with its own lesser casualties. The common people apparently used only stones, the armed men (one report said there were 200) keeping their distance. The people had commanded a narrow pass into the estate. The officials were 'obliged to retire and leave the field to these amazons, some of whom were supposed to be *gentlemen* in female attire.'[32]

Another account of the same incident reported it thus:

They were opposed by an overwhelming number of men and women organised and armed to give Battle ... hundreds of young lads and women met them on the Boundaries of the Grounds to be removed from, who had there a Collection of Stones and of which they made in their fury such use that hardly a Gentleman present or soldier came back without being hurt and several severely — even Geanies [the Sheriff] was hit several times. These women paid no regard to the fire arms — but rushed through knocking about them — one woman was shot and it is supposed mortally, another was badly wounded in the mouth and eye by a bayonet and a young lad was shot in the legs which immediately took him down ... their principal force of reserve it was said were armed and reported to be about 200 ... but observing the number of women suffice in making the Military and Civil forces retreat they do not come nearer ... [the women] did not regard the Soldiers daring to shoot as they would sooner suffer in that manner than remove.[33]

In alarmist quarters it was believed that the Highland disturbances in 1820-1 were part of a national radical conspiracy and so the authorities maintained the closest vigilance. In the north the fear was that 'the evil may spread', and the influence of Dudgeon was widely suspected. A regiment and three pieces of cannon were sent for from Aberdeen. Meanwhile a heated public discussion ensued.

The *Scotsman* insisted that it was essential 'to separate this unfortunate [Culrain] business from the political discussions of the day and . . . to speak for a body of illiterate people' who had never heard of 'radicalism'. No provision had been made by the landlord for the 600 cleared people; they felt there had been a breach of promise by the landlord who, they maintained, had nothing to gain by the clearances in any case. Their desperate resistance lasted a fortnight and then was pacified largely by the intervention of the local minister, who publicly condemned the landlord's action, denied that the rebellious people had any connection with radicalism or with the Sutherland estate, and rejected the claim that the rebels had arms. He had calmed them to an acceptance of their fate.[34]

In the wake of Peterloo and the Six Acts, the newspapers were emphatic that Culrain had nothing whatever to do with radicalism. The minister, MacBean, reported that

> The disgraceful scene of 2nd March was wholly the deed of the women and a few of the male youth, who, goaded to distraction at the dismal prospect before them (nearly 600 souls to be removed, without a place of residence provided for one of them — not knowing under the canopy of heaven where to go) in their folly and ignorance resorted to this way of averting the threatened danger. Of the 600 souls there are almost 100 bed-ridden and aged persons, whose locks are grown hoary on the soil, under the fostering kindness of the late excellent Sir Hector Munro, whom no earthly power can remove, till death came to their relief.

They had no guns, they were not in arrears, and they had been paying a rent higher than the tacksman who was to succeed them. The minister pleaded that 'There is no occasion for a body of 500 men and three field pieces to come among us.'

Sidmouth's informant in the north, Henry Monteith, put the whole episode in a fuller perspective. The Culrain business, he said, had nothing to do with politics. The proprietor had been unwise and probably harsh and cruel to his tenants. The riot had been much employed by southern radicals as an inspiration for greater vigour among their own people: 'The Radicals hold up the women in that part of Ross-shire, as an example of fortitude, not fearing to advance on the very bayonets of the soliders.' The minister, said Monteith, had behaved admirably: 'He restored peace there, when the Sheriff and Militia could not.'

The Culrain rebellion remained in the public memory of the district for at least three decades and the inspiration was invoked in the food riots of Easter Ross in 1847.[35] It was not an isolated episode of physical resistance, even in 1820. The Sutherland estate — close to the last of its great clearances — was especially nervous. 'In these times', wrote the chief agent to his man in the north, 'depend upon it every motion is watched and if you do anything at all which will occasion public observation it will be brought before the house of commons.' The use of fire in the ejection was forbidden. Local officials were instructed to use better informants in their surveillance of the Dudgeonites. It was reported that the Culrain rebels had told the Assynt people (at Unapool) that 'if they had the spirit to resist they would come in a body to their assistance'. The estate official tried to scotch Dudgeonism at Unapool by ejecting one of the adherents — but the Sheriff's men were 'opposed by a party of women who rushed on us like furies, and told us they were determined to resist the man's being turned out'. The officers persisted and the restance petered out. Meanwhile the clearances passed without violence, although often the people had to be physically dislodged from their homes in the interior.[36]

Soon after, in 1821, however, violence occurred on the same estate at Gruids. Once more a Sheriff's party serving notices of removal was deforced. It was reported that 'a great number of Women (or I should rather imagine men in female attire) attacked the party and stripped the clothes off them and sent them home *stark naked* and tore all their papers'. The authorities quickly gathered a force of 60 constables, but the Gruids people were also 'mustering and preparing all sorts of weapons', and 'prepared to oppose whatever species of force may be brought against them'. Rather than force the issue, the local law officers decided to delay their assault.[37]

While the Gruids' resistance simmered, another spasm of violence occurred — at Achness on the Sutherland estate. This was taken seriously, for it seemed that the contagion of revolt was spreading. A precognition was taken and 100 fusiliers with artillery were put at the ready for service in Sutherland. Any delay, it was said, would keep 'Sutherland in a flame'. Additionally, it was believed that the Achness people were expecting 'their friends in Caithness, the heights, and Ross-shire ... to join them there', while others disturbances were developing in Caithness estates. At Gruids, in March 1821, another Sheriff's officer was deforced — again stripped naked. The situation led one landlord's agent to complain that 'the Civil Power of this country is inadequate to eject them', and that the constables were 'lukewarm' in their task of ejecting the people since they partook of 'the general feeling of the natives in their cause'. James Loch opined that there was 'a regular organised system of resistance to civil power' throughout the north, and that it had been allowed to go too far. 'We shall be put into a state that will require all the energy of Government and its disposable force to put down'.[38]

In April 1821 troops arrived — 70 men of the 21st Regiment under Major Tallon. They toured the trouble spots. 'Their presence seems to have operated like magic', reported one observer, 'and proves the importance of a distinct demonstration that the civil authority is to be supported by the government.' At Achness the men 'took off up the hillside like mountain deer'. Letters of removal were affixed to the deserted houses and the roofs of the huts were pulled down. Eventually three prisoners were taken. The number of troops was then increased to 200 at Bonar Bridge whence they travelled to Gruids. But no opposition was offered. More prisoners were taken. The Achness people, it was reported 'skulk from one place to another', trying to get help to emigrate. The local factor remarked that:

All the people are now convinced that they will not be supported by government — the appearance of the soldiers put an end to all their hopes. I never saw people who boasted as they did so crestfallen, they are completely cowed and I am certain we shall have no more trouble.[39]

'You must not ... in your future transactions', the Sutherland agent was told,

cast them [the Achness people] on the wide world, ill as they have behaved — let the less guilty have lots on their signing that they are sorry for their conduct and that they acknowledge the kindness of Lord and Lady Stafford. It would produce a great sensation here [in London] that any set of people were wandering about without habitations.

The weight of public opinion rested heavily on the Stafford family. They specifically requested Major Tallon to stay in the country for the few remaining clearances. In the event there was virtually no resistance. 'We are extremely busy just now with our removings', said a factor, 'which God be praised will be completed effectively and without a whisper on Wednesday.' Thenceforward only minor clearances were undertaken in Sutherland. The management expressly acknowledged that the pressure of publicity had checked the full exercise of the policy of clearance. Nonetheless they had executed the greatest of all the Highland clearances with only minor resistance.[40]

The turbulent events at Culrain and Gruids were part of a pattern of resistance which continued to unfold in the subsequent clearances, indeed until the Crofters' War. The essentially apolitical character of the resistance was already fixed; the sporadic but petty violence was established; the fragility of leadership, the prominence of women and the general lack of co-ordination were continuing elements. The role of the military and the clergy was a further recurrent feature, together with the common belief that the people held a moral right to occupy the land regardless of the economic interest of the proprietor. Also significant was the location of protest and resistance, particularly the place of the borderlands of Easter Ross and Sutherland which repeatedly staged the strongest resistance. The concentration of a swelling village population, comprising refugees from the sheep farms and a vigorous subculture of fishermen, was fertile ground for discontent and united action.[41] It was from such sources that the most active resistance continued to come.

Notes

1. *Farmer's Magazine* (August 1806), p. 289.
2. Quoted in Richards, 'Patterns of Highland Discontent', p. 88.
3. Richards, *Highland Clearances*, Ch. 9. For the tactics of the authorities see letter of Donald Macleod to Munro Ross of Pitcalny, 16 August 1792, in SRO, Ross of Pitcalnie Muniments, GD199/225. See also Logue, *Popular Disturbances*, pp. 58-64.
4. Logue, *Popular Disturbances*, pp. 54-5.

5. Ramsay, *Scotland and Scotsmen*, p. 536.
6. Fraser-Mackintosh, *Letters*, p. 330; *Correspondence of Charlotte Grenville, Lady Williams Wynn*, ed. Rachel Leighton (no place, 1920), p. 127.
7. Henry, Lord Spence, in November 1792, reported that a Gaelic version of Tom Paine's work was circulating in the north. During the food riots of April 1793, in Inverness, the magistrates blamed Paine's book and 'its damnable Doctrines' which they said had been eagerly embraced by the lower classes. Quoted in Logue, *Popular Disturbances*, p. 47.
8. See Adam, *Sutherland Estate Management*, II, p. 266.
9. *Star*, 16 March 1813.
10. Adam, *Sutherland Estate Management*, II, pp. 176-7.
11. Ibid., p. 266.
12. See Logue, *Popular Disturbances*, p. 69.
13. Quoted in Adam, *Sutherland Estate Management*, II, pp. 180-1.
14. See below, Ch. 15.
15. See Richards, *Leviathan*, p. 180.
16. *Military Register*, 28 June 1815; SCRO, Sutherland Collection, D593/K, Loch to Young, 3 April 1813.
17. SCRO, Sutherland Collection, D593/K, Loch to Inglis, 6 March 1813.
18. See below, Ch. 15.
19. Huw Scott, *Fasti Ecclesiae Scoticanae* (3 vols., Edinburgh, 1915-28), I, pp. xii, 33.
20. SCRO, Sutherland Collection, D593/K, Young to Loch, 11 July 1813, Loch to Cranstoun, 7 August 1813, Cranstoun to Loch, 8 August 1813, Gower to Mackid, 7 August 1813, Adam, *Sutherland Estate Management*, II, p. 283.
21. Donald Sage, *Memorabilia, Domestica, or Domestic Life in the North of Scotland* (2nd edition, Wick, 1899), p. 182.
22. Adam, *Sutherland Estate Management*, II, pp. 282-3.
23. Ibid.
24. Alexander Mackenzie (ed.), *The Trial of Patrick Sellar* (Inverness, 1883), p. 47.
25. *Scotsman*, 10 July 1819, 25 December 1820; *Military Register*, 25 August 1819.
26. *Scotsman*, 2 October 1819, 22 January 1820.
27. *Military Register*, 4 August 1819.
28. SCRO, Sutherland Collection, D593/K, Mackay to Suther, 28 October 1819.
29. Captain John Grant, a half-pay captain, had been employed in this capacity and reported that he had been 'afforded the means of discovering the acts practised by the disaffected to inflame their minds and instigate them to resist the civil authorities'. He had passed on such information to the Sheriff of Ross. In September, 1819 he sought a naval officer's post in Van Diemen's Land. See Macmillan, *Scotland and Australia*, p. 120.
30. SCRO, Sutherland Collection, D593/K, Loch to Gunn, 17 November 1818, Loch to Lady Stafford, 9 November 1819, Loch to Mackay, 14 December 1818, Mackenzie to Loch, 10 November 1818. *Military Register*, 29 December 1819.
31. *Military Register*, 17 July 1816, 19 January 1820; SCRO, Sutherland Collection, D593/K, Loch to Brougham, 27 December 1819.
32. SCRO, Sutherland Collection, D593/K, D593/K, Mackenzie to Loch, 30 March 1820, Mackay to Loch, 4 March 1820; *Military Register*, 22 March 1820; *Inverness Courier*, 9 March 1820; *Scotsman*, 11 March 1820.
33. SCRO, Sutherland Collection, D593/K, Sutherland to Loch, 5 March 1820.

34. SRO, Home Office (Scotland) Correspondence, RH2/4, fos. 181ff, 255-6, 284; *Scotsman*, 11 March 1820; *Inverness Courier*, 9 March 1820.
35. See Eric Richards, *The Last Scottish Food Riots* (London, 1982).
36. SCRO, Sutherland Collection, D593/K, Loch to Sutherland, 26 March 1820.
37. Ibid., Mackenzie to Loch, 14 August 1820.
38. Ibid., Loch to Mackenzie, 23 March 1821.
39. Ibid., Grant to Loch, 17 April 1821.
40. Ibid., Loch to Sutherland, 30 March 1821.
41. See Richards, *The Last Scottish Food Riots, passim.*

13
THE PATTERN CONFIRMED

The year 1821 was the end rather than the beginning of an active phase in the record of popular disturbance against clearances in the Highlands. In the following two decades, despite continuing clearances in many parts of the region and despite the recurrence of major famine (in 1836-7) and the general rundown of the Highland economy, the tempo of protest was slow. For years on end the Highlands got scant mention in the Scottish and even less in the London newspapers. Public comment within the Highlands was restrained and few voices were raised beyond the region.

There were surprisingly few radical critics of landlord authority in these decades. The common people threw up few spokesmen of their own. On rare occasions Scots newspapers took up the Highlanders' cause in political terms.[1] William Cobbett was perhaps the only national figure to question publicly the legal framework that permitted the clearances. At Paisley in 1832 he addressed a public audience:

> What, have we not the right to be upon the land of our birth? Are we to be told, that we are bound in duty to come out and venture our lives in defence of that land against a foreign enemy, and yet that we can be swept off from it when the landowner pleases?[2]

Both the Swiss economist Sismondi and Karl Marx found the Highland clearances a spectacular example of the abuse of landlord power,[3] and their work was greeted warmly by some Scots critics. But, for the most part, local writers held back from any direct challenge to 'the land monopoly' until the 1840s when, with the writings of Donald Macleod, Hugh Miller and Donald Ross, a radical current began to flow in the Highlands.

I

At the end of the 1830s a sudden outburst of protest was occasioned by several large clearances. In July 1839 there were disturbances on the estate of Lord Dunmore in Harris where 50 families were to be removed. In essence it involved a plan for the introduction of a large sheepfarmer and the forced emigration of the people of the estate. In this case the resistance, physical and relatively prolonged, was reputedly encouraged by recent events in Skye where Macleod of Macleod had been the target of threatening letters. Moreover, 'Inflammatory proclamations of the same description were posted on the church doors, and some sheep belonging to a sheep grazier were houghed [i.e. mutilated] and killed.' These actions had gone unpunished and the Dunmore people resolved to ignore their summonses of removal: it was also said that they believed that 'no military would be sent to so remote a corner'. Local law officers despatched to the scene were 'defied and severely maltreated', and the Sheriff was unable to impose his authority; there was talk about 'a conspiracy for resisting the law [which] existed in all this quarter of the West Highlands, which, if not at once checked, would lead to consequences no lover of order would care to think of'. When a party of 30 troops from Glasgow was brought in, the resistance collapsed instantly. Five ringleaders were taken but subsequently released, and Lord Dunmore expressed his forgiveness of the tenantry. He also gave them another year's grace before their removal. 'Thus terminated an outbreak which, but for the prompt measures of government in sending the military would have thrown the West Highlands into confusion for many years'. Other opinion at the time claimed that the leniency shown to the people in Harris encouraged resistance to the law elsewhere in the northern counties.[4]

In the following years, 1840, trouble flared up at Culrain — twice before the scene of anti-landlord violence. This time, according to one incensed spokesman of the landlords, 'A strong body of civil officers employed to execute warrants of Removing by a principal Tacksman against his sub-tenants was deforced. The farmstead of the Tacksman was set on fire and twenty cattle consumed. Yet no Criminal Trial followed.' He reported too that the people 'called out that they *expected aid from the people of the Reay Country* (including Durness)', suggesting an anticipation of wide support which here, as elsewhere, failed to materialise.[5] But the Culrain episode of 1841 was further evidence, not only of strong popular abhorrence of the clearance policy, but also of the crumbling cohesion of Highland society. The tacksman, so far from being the leader of popular feeling, had become the enemy of the people.

The fear that landlord policy and famine would inflame the population into violence of Irish proportions was never far from the thoughts of concerned observers of the Highlands. The Rev. Norman McLeod raised this spectre in his evidence to a Select Committee in 1841. If emigration were not given urgent priority, he warned, the landowners and the government would face

> not only ... the piteous wailing of want and famine, not only the sad spectacle of a once moral people becoming, through the hardening and animalizing influence of grinding poverty, the reckless slaves of low passion, but ... the still more alarming though not more woeful, spectacle of a loyal and peaceable people giving themselves up to robbery and rapine. The flocks of large sheepfarmers are annually thinned by those who feel the pinching of famine; and to such an extent is this system carried that it has led to the proposal of establishing a rural police throughout the island, which is expected to come into immediate operation, a measure completely unprecedented in the history of the Highlands.

Norman McLeod believed that the Highlands was on the edge of economic and social explosion:

> I would say that the country is just now threatened with an apoplectic attack; it must be bled; the homeopathic system will not melt the pressure of the malady upon the system; that something immediately must be done, or consequences will take place, to which the country cannot close its eyes.

In the same report Murdo Mackenzie, a resident proprietor in Lochbroom, testified to a disturbing level of petty violence in the crofting community. He contended that the common people's isolation from decent society accounted for their wildness and lack of civilisation: 'outrages and barbarities are committed which are nowhere else heard of in Scotland'. Cattle had been driven into the sea, horses had been flayed alive and their throats cut, wood had been destroyed, sheep stabbed and houghed, and a woodkeeper had been shot at. Such Irish behaviour was, by all other accounts, rare in the Highlands.[6]

Norman McLeod, as it turned out, had exaggerated the dangers. The Highlands weathered not only two severe famines in the years 1836-7, and 1847-50, but also several sensational clearances, none of which produced any generalised uprising of the people. Nor should it be thought that landlord tyranny was the sole cause of communal violence in these years. Inevitably there were internecine disputes, some involving the deliberate maiming of livestock. In 1835 there was a report from the west coast of Sutherland:

> A very barbarous act was perpetrated ... in Assynt. Some young men of Clachtoll most barbarously cut off the ears of some horses belonging to the people of Store, which were found trespassing upon their grass. The apology they offered was that they had pounded their horses several times and that they had always been released by force.[7]

The old communal land grazing system in which individual rights and obligations were not clearly delimited generated such disputes, as well as indiscriminate grazing which was the bane of the life of many sheepfarmers. As the Minister of Portree parish said in 1837:

> This mode of tenure is productive of many disadvantages and evils; it occasions disputes and quarrels among the immediate neighbours in possession; it excites in their minds envy, anger and even malice to one another. It is highly injurious to the interest of the tenants, and equally prejudicial to that of the tenants, and equally prejudicial to that of the landlord; it encourages and protects sheep-stealing.[8]

The subletting middlemen in the Highlands were often authors of the most insensitive clearances. In 1841, at Durness (near Cape Wrath), James Anderson — fish-curer and tenant originally of Lord Reay and later of the second Duke of Sutherland — decided to cease fishing and convert his lands to sheep pasture. Anderson, a ruthless entrepreneur, had encouraged subtenants to settle on the smallest patches of land; subdivision went unchecked and the fishermen sank into his debt.[9] By 1840 Anderson decided that their fishing no longer gave a sufficient return on his capital. He thus embarked on a programme of eviction quite independently and beyond the control of the landlord. He provided no alternative accommodation and no compensation for amelioration. He simply evicted on the shortest notice. He had already cleared Shegra in 1840. In August 1841 the officer delivering summons of removal to the Durness people was opposed by 'a large body of men and women' who took his papers and burnt them. The people addressed a petition to the Duke of Sutherland for 'shelter against the threatened and expected storm of tyranny'. Thirty-one families, 163 people, had been summoned to remove at 48 hours' notice. While the Duke dallied, awaiting the appointment of a new district factor, Anderson arranged for a party of special constables to force through the eviction on Saturday, 18 September. The people said they would depart on the Monday. The officials declined the offer and, in the course of the attempted eviction, were successfully resisted, and eventually put to flight — the people saying that they would rather break the law on a Saturday than on the Sabbath. The Minister explained that 'the serving officers were resisted by almost all the females of the district ... when no prospective opening was provided for so many destitute people, public sympathy could not possibly be suppressed'. The Sheriff's party retreated to Durnine Inn but was there attacked, manhandled and ejected. The next inn was 20 miles away and some of the officers hid among the corn and rocks till daylight. It was reported that the people threatened to throw Sheriff Lumsden into Smoo Cave and the Sheriff himself recorded that his party had 'been deforced, assaulted, threatened with instant death, and expelled at midnight ... by a ferocious mob'. He believed that the minister had fomented the insurrection, and then sat quietly by his fireside while the mob did its worst. Lumsden alleged also that the Durness mutineers were in correspondence with the Culrain folk who had resisted authority only a few months before, and that the Harris episode had also created a precedent: 'the Durness rioters often called out that they had as good a right to resist as the *Culrain Tenants* had'. Moreover, reported Lumsden, 'no consideration will induce any of these officers to go back on such a mission to Durness without the aid of military force'.[10]

The Durness incident was a sensation in the Highlands and was widely reported in the newspapers. The landlord's agent observed that 'it will leave an unpleasant feeling throughout the country' and there was rumour of 'a Tongue uprising'. Sheriff Lumsden, in a state of continuing panic, sent alarmist letters to Sir William Rae, the Lord Advocate in Edinburgh, insisting that he could not return to the scene and that infantry should be sent by sea to catch the ringleaders. There was considerable criticism of Lumsden's personal timidity and alarmism — and Rae described him as 'the fool of a sheriff'. Calm was required, the people should be talked to, and Rae was keen to know 'the real causes which led to this outbreak and all the alleviating circumstances which have attended it'. The rumour of military intervention had an effect in Durness — the women were reported to have dispersed to neighbouring Edderachilles. Eventually, with the help of arbitration by both the local minister and the landlord, the dispute was settled in mid-October. Findlater, the minister, met the assembled people and was able to say that they repented and that the military would not be required. The people apparently apologised to Anderson and petitioned for a delay of clearance. This was granted — until May 1842 — and no criminal prosecutions followed. Findlater blamed Anderson for his lack of prudence, while Rae complacently observed that the Sutherland rebellion was over. Anderson was castigated by the Duke of Sutherland. For the latter the lesson was clear — even small clearnces could provoke outrages which were probably not worth enduring — indeed, the memory of Durness was used as counsel against further clearances as late as the mid-1850s.[11]

II

While most of the currents of national life — including Chartism — left the Highlands unmoved, repeated outbursts of anti-clearance discontent broke the surface calm. In June 1842 at Lochshiel an eviction party was resisted and driven off by 'a party of women' obstructing a plan to form a sheep farm then occupied by 300 people. In April of the same year the Glencalvie people successfully held out against Sheriff's officers, seizing and burning papers on two occasions. Another attempt was made in 1843 — when 'the women met the constables beyond the boundaries, over the river, and seized the hand of the one who held the notices, whilst some held it out by the wrist others held a live coal to the papers and set fire to them'. The Glencalvie people were again given notice in May 1844 to remove in 1845 — by which time the correspondent of *The Times* was on the spot to give national publicity to prevailing conditions and to the treatment of ordinary people in the Highlands. Further resistance occurred and the clearance was not implemented until 1846 when, on the advice of the Free Church minister, the people removed peacefully. In August 1843 Sheriff Lumsden's authority was once more resisted on the west coast when he attempted to eject a single tenant at Balchladdich. He was told that '*The whole people of Assynt*' would rise, and they might gain the support of the returning herring fishermen. The incident, however, petered out and four prisoners were taken.[12]

The Sollas evictions in North Uist in the late summer of 1849 were described by Alexander Mackenzie as almost the only case in the history of the clearances 'where the people made anything like real resistance'. It was one episode among several during the post-famine clearances in which emigration was offered as Hobson's choice to a population about to be evicted. By mid-century landlord policy and most public opinion converged in the belief that the only solution to the general subsistence problem was mass emigration. Details of the Sollas riots have been provided elsewhere.[13] The pattern of the action had now become familiar: there was clearly a high level of participation from the population at large; there was the usual preliminary petty humiliation of the serving officer; there was a system of signalling to alert the people of the approach of the constables; the womenfolk behaved most vociferously; there was stoning, but no other arms were employed; and the angry confrontation was resolved by the intercession of the local minister who negotiated a small compromise on behalf of the people. The reporter of the episode in the *Scotsman*, unaware of the long-established pattern of Highland resistance, remarked, 'Their conduct altogether was very unlike what Highlanders might be expected to exhibit.'[14] The Sollas affair provoked large-scale publicity in Scotland and the fate of the people was still a matter of public concern twelve months after the riot. Their action was effective in the sense that they achieved a delay of clearance, and some of them avoided the emigration that was being forced upon them. But they lost their lands on North Uist. The trial of the four Sollas men was more a triumph for the people. They were convicted by the jury, but then dealt with extraordinarily leniently 'in consideration of the cruel, though it may be legal, proceedings adopted in ejecting the whole people of Solas'. As Cockburn, who presided at the Session, remarked: 'This statement will ring all over the country. We shall not soon cease to hear of this calm and judicial censure of incredible but proved facts.' Cockburn was disgusted by the landlord's action and wrote of hereditary roofs being pulled down while 'the mother and her children had only the shore to sleep on — fireless, foodless, hopeless. Resistance was surely not unnatural, and it was very slight.'[15]

The 'public fury' which greeted the detailed story of the Sollas proceedings did not deter several landlords from pursuing identical policies of clearance. Indeed, though the pace of clearance accelerated in the early 1850s, most cases went unrecorded in the press, and probably unresisted. The island of Skye was more turbulent. On the Strathaird estate in 1850 the threatened eviction (of 620 persons) was opposed, despite the offer of assisted emigration.[16]

In April 1851 the Sutherland estate administration was successfully resisted by the people of Elphin and Knockan in an episode which caused the local factor, Evander MacIver, to fume in barely controlled anger. He reported:

> I found these people in a very insolent spirit — quite proud of their illegal conduct and not one of them would admit they did wrong. On the contrary they think they were quite justified in resisting the officer of the law — and seem quite resolved to do so again.

The people had resisted an effort to serve them with notices of removal: the law agents

> were surrounded by a mob of men and women who would have mastered them if they had resisted — the officer was surrounded by a drove a women who rifled his pockets and took from them the papers ... there was no personal injury but if he had resisted they would have resorted to any violence so excited were they.

MacIver blamed newspapers for whipping up poisonous antipathies, 'calculated to destroy the feelings of attachment which exist among the smaller tenantry towards their superiors'. Great support was given by the Free Church ministers 'who take peculiar delight in fulminating their anathemas against the landlords, while every thing done in this Country is either misrepresented or grossly exaggerated'. Here was the authentic voice of the embattled West Highland factor.[17]

On the north-east mainland, particularly at Wick, the elections of 1852 provided an opportunity for political comment on land-lordism in the Highlands. James Loch, the sitting member, and closely identified with the Sutherland policies for forty years, was subjected to a barrage of public abuse which drew on the accumulated hatred of the clearances. Loch's political agents described Wick as 'a den of radicalism' under the 'misrule of demagogues'.[18] The rival candidate, supported by the local newspaper, was able to capitalise on the anti-clearance issue, and thereby demonstrated the possiblities of political opposition to Highland landlordism. Loch was defeated. Some landlords clearly jibbed at the prospect of such public enmity. The Sutherland family faced the dilemma again in 1852-3 at Coigach on the isolated west coast of Ross, where stout resistance to a tentative effort to resettle the people was sufficient to reverse landlord policy, despite mounting arrears. The Sheriff's officers were deforced by the women: 'The men formed the second line of defence in case the women should receive any ill treatment.' The Coigach people held out for more than two years and eventually the estate managers and the land-lord gave up the effort to resettle them. In February 1853 the land-lord had ordered a final determined attempt to impose her authority on the resistant community. The officer sent to the dis-trict to serve the summonses had no success.

> the summonses were forcibly taken from him and destroyed and himself grossly maltreated though fortunately without any serious injury to his person ... The officer was entirely stripped of his clothes by these rebels, and was put into the boat in which he went to Coigach in a state of almost total nudity.

Four weeks later the entire episode was re-enacted when a party of six constables took on the assembled womenfolk of Coigach, but with no greater success. For the landlord there was extreme frus-tration. The entire affair had been conducted in a blaze of publicity which raised larger questions concerned with the maintenance of property rights and the authority of the law. As an agent said, 'the people in that district have lost all respect for Constituted Authority'. Another declared that 'the people must submit for there is a prevalent feeling over all the West Coast north and south that the Government are not serious in their desire to enforce the law'. It was transparently obvious that the clearance could not be achieved without military intervention, and the landlord was not prepared to stomach the odium of such an action. The Coigach people stayed. The whole episode vividly exemplified the weakness of local resources of law and order. Underlying the landlord's attitude was a fear of Highland radicalism and a widening (though far from universal) sensitivity to public opinion. But there was also a developing confidence among the crofters. Indeed the success of the Coigach people may have reinforced the resolution of other crofters to resist clearances in the following two years. Equally, it may have strengthened the determination of other landlords to crack down upon any opposition before its infection spread. In the event it was no more than a prelude to some of the most violent confrontation and resistance that had been witnessed in the Highlands.[19]

Non-violent resistance occurred also on the Macdonald estates in Skye in 1853. At Suishnish and Boreraig 32 families were being cleared for a sheep farm. No resettlement provision had been made. The estates' trustees were ineffectually opposed and three men were taken into custody by the accompanying police. At the subsequent trial, with the assistance of a good solicitor paid by charitable donations in Inverness, the Skyemen were acquitted 'to the cheers of an Inverness crowd'. The *Inverness Courier* commented that 'the sympathies of the public were strongly with the Skyemen, and there was a general impression that the proprietor himself sympathised with them'.[20] It did not prevent the subsequent eviction of these people. Adverse publicity also attended clearances on the Macdonell of Glengarry estate at Knoydart in the same year. Four hundred souls were evicted, many of them directly onto the emigration ships. Although indignation ran high, no resistance was made. The newspapers, although attentive, had only publicity to offer. Many clearances passed without even this — for example, the Strathconan clearances, which over a decade dispersed several hundred peasants.

The most infamous case of all was at Greenyards, near Bonar Bridge, in the spring of 1854, on the estate that had witnessed the Glencalvie incidents in 1845. The resistance, similar to that of the Coigach people, was almost certainly influenced by the publicity attracted by that episode. On their first attempt to serve notices of removal the Sheriff's officers were assaulted by a crowd, stripped naked, and their papers burnt. The *Northern Ensign* noted that the officers were deposited 'at the braes of Dounie where the great Culrain riot took place thirty years before' — a symbolic act of defiance. The subsequent spasm of violence was caused primarily by the failure of the usual mechanism of compromise which had resolved previous confrontations. The posse, now augmented to 30 constables, returned at the end of March 1854, and was received, it was reported, by a crowd of 300, two-thirds of them women. The women were lined in front, the men behind, and the only arms mentioned were sticks and stones. The constables apparently wielded their batons freely and, while sustaining no injuries themselves inflicted between 10 and 15 serious wounds on the women. In this case the landlord was sufficiently determined and thick-skinned to force the action to its logical conclusion. The police, primed to their task by their colleagues' humiliations at Coigach, were in no mood for shilly-shallying. Donald Ross wrote of the pools of blood and the butchery at the hands of the police. 'The Ross-shire Haynaus have shown themselves more cruel and more blood-thirsty than the Austrian women-floggers.'[21] The *Inverness Courier* considered that the police had over-reacted and criticised their failure to induce a compromise. At the Inverness trial one man received 18 months' hard labour and a woman was imprisoned for a year.[22]

In the 1850s, partly in response to the publicity generated by the harrowingly dramatic stories of the Greenyards clearances, the current of radicalism ran strongly. Pubic debate was more vigorous within and beyond the Highlands. Newspaper comment in the north of Scotland became increasingly audacious; the *Elgin Courier* in particular helped to bring the land question into political focus for the first time. Radical newspapers were now widely read and the tone of criticism seemed to pose a growing threat. A literature of protest was emerging which gave moral support to the crofters, and gave landlords cause to hesitate before stimulating further resistance. In 1855, the Duke of Sutherland was told that there had 'arisen a feeling among the people that they would soon resume possession of what they conceived to be the possessions of their fathers'. It was said that a new political influence was at work: 'A radical feeling is abroad propagated from Wick — that most radical of the radical towns of Scotland.'[23] A writer in the relatively conservative *Inverness Advertiser* in

November 1850 had warned that 'Proprietors of land in the Highlands must understand that in this age of improvement and reform, abuses of every description and class must be corrected' and that 'No human being should have a right to evict, nor to be tempted with such power. Even good men cannot be safely trusted with it.' He warned that all clearing landlords were being watched very carefully: 'The most searching inquiries will be made into the whole system of Highland clearances, and means will be taken to obtain from the Government of the country some redress, should any attempt be made to resort to further depopulation.' In a sense these words were prophetic of the events of the 1880s, but they had singularly little immediate influence in the 1850s.[24]

The record after 1855 suggests that landlords trod more carefully in their efforts to change the use of land. There were few if any large-scale clearances, though smaller and more gradual adjustments continued to be made. Landlords perhaps learned to be patient with their uneconomic crofters; most of the work of large-scale clearance may have been done already, and the balance of land occupation may have reached a new equilibrium. The fear of further popular protest, public opprobrium and violent resistance almost certainly operated as a deterrent to the prospective evictor. There was a long hiatus in the struggle for land; in the next phase, in the 1880s, the initiative for change came from the crofters rather than the landlords. They were, at last, roused to regain their long-lost land rights, and to regularise their occupation of the land to which they so precariously clung. It was then that they concerted into an assault upon landlord authority.

The social discontent evident in the literature as well as the acts of protest during the 1850s therefore did not yield positive political results until the 1880s. The Battle of the Braes in Skye in 1882[25] was the start of a remarkable phase of sustained agitation which exhibited an unprecedented cohesion in Highland discontent. It generated incongruous spectacles such as the march of 1,400 men up Strathnaver in 1884 — ostensibly supported by their landlord — chanting: 'Give us back our Bonnie Strathnaver,' and 'Highlands for the Highlanders'.[26] Certainly the style of Highland agitation changed in these years towards a strategy of direct action which yielded greater results than ever before. An anonymous handbill of November 1884 attempted to rouse the crofters and the cottars to 'stand up like men before your oppressors. Demand restoration of the rights of which you have been robbed. Do not rest satisfied until you have obtained them. If they are refused, act for yourselves.' This exhortation called for the destruction of property, cutting telegraph wires, sabotaging railways, the firing of heaths and the poisoning of game dogs. It identified as enemies of the people 'the landlord, the agent, the capitalist, and the Parliament which makes and maintains inhuman and iniquitous laws'.[27] Crofter action fell somewhat short of these standards of violence, but during the 1880s, popular action was sufficiently physical and well directed to persuade the government to intervene in the form of the Crofter Commission Inquiry of 1884. The landlords' long-standing fear became a reality.

The crofter agitation of the 1880s was separated by several decades from previous examples of Highland resistance; it was also considerably more successful in achieving its objectives, and consequently the Crofters' War is often represented as a genuine historical discontinuity in the history of popular protest. Nevertheless, as this chapter argues, the events of the 1880s may sensibly be seen in a larger perspective. In several respects the action of the people of Skye was in a century-long tradition of sporadic popular resistance in the Highlands.

III

Taken in isolation each Highland riot seemed an ephemeral convulsive reaction of a stupefied peasantry. However, historians of riots have come to treat social responses of this sort with more understanding in recent times, discerning greater rationality in the record of communal protest, especially in pre-industrial societies as they reached the transition into modern conditions. If individual instances of riot are juxtaposed and analysed, some recurrent patterns emerge which illuminate not only the events as they happened, but also the mentalities and social divisions from which the events sprang. In the case of the Highland clearances much of our historical knowledge derives from the episodes of protest and resistance. A major hazard of this evidence is that it tends to exaggerate the sporadic nature of the clearances which, as had been argued, were in fact a much more continuous process than is suggested by the history of resistance.

A regular pattern may be discerned amid the many cases of popular resistance to landlord policy. The common people through many decades and across a wide territory seen to have conformed to an almost stylised mode of action. From these cases one can create a composite picture of a Highland disturbance as a graduated, four-stage challenge to landlord authority:

(1) The local law officer or the landlord's agent would attempt to serve the summons of removal on a village. The first time he might simply be turned away. The second time he would be subjected to some kind of petty humiliation, usually at the hands of the womenfolk of the village. They might seize his papers and burn them under his nose. Sometimes the officer was stripped naked and chased off the land — or even pushed out to sea in a boat without oars.

(2) A posse of constables led by a Sheriff and his assistants would arrive, often very early in the morning. Real resistance would follow: they would be assaulted with volleys of stones and sticks from a massed group of the common people. In the front line of the latter were, invariably, the women and boys, making most noise and taking the worst injuries. Sometimes men were reported at the front — often dressed as women. But most of the menfolk were to the rear, apparently as a second line of defence. The resistance was usually sufficiently vociferous and violent to push back the posse. Meanwhile the common people might have made an appeal to some distant authority: the Prince Regent, the press, local worthies or even the landlord.

(3) Higher legal authorities would be alerted: the Solicitor General, or the Lord Advocate, or perhaps the Home Office. Repeatedly the local landowners, in an advanced state of panic, would attribute the disturbances to agitators with suspected connections with 'Radicalism'. Sometimes there was inflated talk of a 'Northern Rebellion' which helped persuade the authorities that military intervention was required — from Inverness, Fort William, Aberdeen or Glasgow.

(4) The news of impending intervention was usually enough of itself to lead to a collapse of resistance. Troops intervened on at least ten occasions but were never actually engaged in physical hostilities. The termination of resistance was frequently facilitated by the mediation of the local minister who produced a face-saving formula for the people. It generally took the

form of a delay of removal, but rarely did anything to prevent the eventual clearance.

Most of the incidents show the marks of spontaneous desperation — unpreparedness, absence of arms, lack of co-ordination, no clear leadership, and collapse in the face of military intervention. In the majority of Highland disturbances women took a prominent, often a dominant, role. Frequently the menfolk seem to have held back, in wait of further developments. Highland riots were women's riots. At Culrain in 1820 and at Gruids in 1821 the women were at the forefront of the confrontations. At Durness in 1841 the women assaulted and humiliated the Sheriff's officers. At Sollas in 1849 the women confronted the officers; at Lochshiel in 1842 the eviction party was driven off by the womenfolk; at Glencalvie in 1843 it was the women who took the lead. At Greenyards in 1854 the local women bore the brunt of the armed attack by the constables, and the women sustained the worst injuries. It was a similar story at Knockan and Elphin in 1852, at Coigach and at Ullapool in 1852-3. Women were, later, a prominent element in the 'Battle of the Braes' in 1882. Still later, in December 1887, in crofter action against the landlord in Assynt (Sutherland), women, accompanied by men in women's clothes, were at the front of the resistance to the law — using strong language and throwing stones. They had blackened their faces and drew their shawls across their faces.

The conspicuous place of women, and the transvestite element — of men dressing as women — were both recurrent features of Highland disturbances. Parallels with the French Revolution, and the Rebecca Riots, come to mind. Of the former Olwen Hufton has argued forcefully that 'to appreciate the nearness of women to the Revolution one must understand their role in the family economy'.[28] Like the womenfolk of Rebecca's Wales, Highland women shared fully in the most laborious tasks of the peasant economy. Nevertheless it is not altogether evident how family roles are to be related to the propensity to violence and protest. A Sutherland agent remarked in 1821 that 'the opinion of the people here is that a woman can do anything with impunity'; it was thought (on both sides) that the constables and the troops were less likely to injure women than men. As well as this, it seems probable that direct female activism was a characteristic of pre-industrial societies in conflict. It is well known that food rioting generally engaged high levels of female participation, probably because their conventional sex-roles exposed them most immediately to the threat of high food prices. Similarly, in a semicommunal peasant life the women directly involved in the domestic economy may have placed themselves in the front line when the fabric of social existence was under attack by way of eviction.[29]

Some of the weaknesses of Highland popular protest are reasonably obvious. Outbreaks of resistance were sporadic and spontaneous — they never cohered into a continuous threat to the landlords. Inchoate, dispersed, unarmed, apolitical and rural-based, Highland discontent was unsophisticated in comparison with the methods of the new urban and industrial working class of central Scotland and England. The Highland discontents lacked leaders: they appear to have been too few in number and inadequate in organisational abilities. Although the terrain was ostensibly ideal for Hobsbawmian rebels and myths, no outstanding figures emerged.

The poverty of leadership may be related to the polarisation of Highland society and the demise of the tacksman — many had emigrated,[30] others had thrown in their lot with the landlords. Fragmentary evidence suggests that returned army captains often led the discontented, but never openly.[31] Thomas Dudgeon and Robert Mackid were the only men who stood out as co-ordinators, but both lacked the charisma of leadership. Where one can identify the leaders during the disturbances they seem to be men of 'middling rank' — a schoolmaster, a publican, a small landowner, a failed land agent, several half-pay captains. On the whole they lacked the ability to co-ordinate the rebellions. Eventually the ministers of the Free Church effectively assumed the leadership of popular protest, but for the most part they choose to divert the stream away from direct action towards forms of spiritual introversion. The absence of arms diminished the threat of revolt significantly — and there is little evidence of agrarian terrorism which was employed with some success in contemporary Ireland. Deaths and serious injuries in the Highlands occurred almost entirely among the protestors.

As for the ministers of the established church, they have gained an unenviable reputation: they are regarded as the quislings of modern Highland history. Alexander Mackenzie wrote angrily: 'The professed ministers of religion sanctioned the inquity [of the

clearances] and prostituted their sacred office and high calling.'[32]
W. C. Mackenzie concurred:

> The attitude of the clergy during the expatriation of the High-
> landers was almost uniform in the absence of outspoken denun-
> ciation of an iniquitous injustice; ... they were passive
> spectators of it; with hardly an exception, they showed them-
> selves unworthy of their calling.[33]

Certainly the influence of the clergy was considerable — as Eric
Cregeen has said, 'In the nineteenth century the tacksman's role as
a social leader and educator was largely taken over by the
minister.'[34] But the connection between religion and social action
is a notoriously subtle and complex question. The relationships
between landlord policy, religious dissidence and popular protest
in the nineteenth-century Highlands have yet to be properly
established. There were, for instance, many occasions when the
ministers of the established church spoke, and wrote down, the
case for the common people against the landlords. A reading of
some of the Highland sections of the *New Statistical Account* (as
well as government reports) demonstrates how critical and unsyco-
phantic some ministers could be. (This applies to Sutherland in
particular — the county often represented as the most abused in
this respect.[35]) But the ministers, even those of the Free Church,
did not lead the people in physical resistance. T. C. Smout has
offered a general psychological proposition: that the church provided a refuge into which passions were channelled away from violent opposition to landlords. In a vivid phrase he says that 'the
people fled towards the compensations of an intense spiritual
enthusiasm like leaves before the storm'.[36] In preaching a fatalistic
acceptance of landlordism the ministers probably saved lives and
avoided futile resistance: they dissuaded their people from violence in the face of the overwhelming power of the authorities. For
the most part the role of the Highland ministers was not unlike that
of Catholic priests in Irish rural disturbances of the early nineteenth century.[37] They gave solace and mediation. They were
leaders *of* the people, from *within* the crowd, but they cast their
influence against the spontaneous resistance of the people. Nevertheless it is not the case that the ministers invariably deserted the
common folk. It is quite likely that the conventional view of the
Highland clergy is close to a caricature.

Religion was of course one area of life in which the Highlanders were prepared to stand firm against the will of the landlord, and in which they were able to concert with unprecedented (though not total) unanimity. The rioting against the induction of unacceptable ministers in the early nineteenth century was only a degree less violent than the anti-clearance agitation. The Disruption of the church in the Highlands, in the years after 1843, was a saga of social protest which produced a measure of solidarity remarkable for its contrast with the weakness of organisation in the anti-clearance protests. Apart from the Disruption, rioting on religious issues (notably about the induction of new ministers) took much the same form as the anti-clearance disturbances.

The widespread desertion of people and ministers to the Free Church in the 1840s — in the face of considerable persecution — for once showed Highlanders effectively pitted against secular authority. The intensity of the conflict between landlords and people was severe, and the steadfast resistance of individuals and congregations often involved deprivation, self-sacrifice and eviction. There is a moving passage in the *Journal of Henry Cockburn* which bears witness to the extraordinary fortitude of the people. He wrote:

The favourite malice is for the deluded lords of the soil to refuse sites for churches or schools ... The Ministers of the county of Sutherland, having suffered most, were each asked lately to say whether there was anything, and what, in his circumstances, which gave him a claim for consideration in the distribution of the Sustenation Fund. There is nothing more honourable to Scotland, and little more honourable to human nature, than the magnanimous answers by every one of these brave men. Not one of them made any claim. Each abjured it. One of them stated that though he had been turned out of a hovel he had got into last winter, and had been obliged to walk about thirty miles over snow, besides the cart which conveyed his wife and children to another district and had nothing, he was perfectly happy, and had no doubt that many of his brethern were better entitled to favour than he was. These are the men to make churches! These are the men to whom some wretched lairds think themselves superior![38]

It was, of course, a most powerful psychological victory over the landlords, a unifying experience which helped build the communal confidence necessary for the assault which emerged in the 1870s and 1880s.

Another salient weakness of Highland protest was the fundamental lack of any rallying ideology for the common peole. Certainly the people believed that they had traditional right to their lands, and that the clearing landlords were usurping those rights and acting against real justice. This basic assumption was not given effective political expression until the 1880s. So far as one can tell, the collective thinking of the ordinary Highlanders was essentially backward-looking. There was much discussion of lost rights — but little radical thought was devoted to any consideration of the future of the Highland society and economy — or even to any notion of an alternative to landlordism. The voluminous evidence of the Napier Commission in the 1880s demonstrated the tenacity of this way of thinking. As T. C. Smout has written, there was 'no reasoned economic argument against clearance' and 'the intellectual trumpets of the Scottish left gave forth no certain sound whatever'.[39] It was, of course, difficult for anyone to demonstrate conclusively, in short-run economic terms, that the Highlands could be rendered viable — even if the institutional structure were altered in the most radical fashion. Through the nineteenth century there was an intermittent rumbling of anti-landlord journalism in the north: it was able to frighten Highland proprietors who knew the potential power of a literary protest to act as catalyst on the people. And there were those like Hugh Miller who were ready to assert that, in net practical terms, the clearances cost the landlords far more than any financial benefits that they derived. On the whole, however, the intellectual case against the proprietors was not well sustained.

But this was not only a Highland failure: British radical thinking as a whole failed to generate much effective questioning of the political and legal bases of landlordism. It was not until the emergence of Irish pressure after the famine that the Highlanders found any kind of political model or focus. Before that virtually all the intellectual penetration had come from outside. From within Scotland only Hugh Miller and John Stuart Blackie were able to budge the prevailing complacency of public opinion.

Direct and physical social protest was generally less effective than the passive resistance which, although much more difficult to define, was virtually universal during the clearances. Inevitably passive resistance is less easily identified and gauged in its impact than physical protest. Nevertheless this was the other side of the coin of 'Highland fatalism'. A land agent in 1841 put the matter plainly enough: 'I was always afraid of this passive sort of resistance, and, if resorted to it will no doubt create a vast deal of difficulty and trouble to all concerned.'[40]

Passive resistance entailed a sullen refusal to partake in landlord plans, a withholding of co-operation — and an implicit rejection of all the assumptions of the landlord-directed transformation of the Highland economy and its society. It proved more decisive a weapon than violent resistance in some areas. Of course landlords varied — some evicted their people without compunction and for them the relative passivity of the people was totally irrelevant. But for those landlords who wished not only to clear but to reconstruct the local economy, for those who sought to promote secondary industry, the social response was crucial.

A strong case could be made that in both Argyll and Sutherland radical landlord policies, involving heavy investment, and containing a reasonable chance of generating a new basis for Highland economic life, foundered on the rocks of social resistance by the common people. Grim apathy, mixed with malevolent pleasure when failure occurred, was an impenetrable barrier to development. This attitude — all pervasive even into the twentieth century — may have been half the tragedy of the Highland problem. Economic plans which ignored the social response that they engendered carried within them the seeds of their own destruction. It would have been a miracle of planning for even the best-intentioned landlord to have rendered the clearance of the people palatable. As it was, the social response was ignored and the investment plans, for the most part, came to naught.

The work of Eric Cregeen on Argyll points this way. There was, he notes, 'a legacy of mistrust and hostility' which 'proved an almost insurmountable obstacle to the Argylls when in the eighteenth century they launched programmes of economic reform that required trust and co-operation from their tenants.' Of the project in Tiree of the fifth Duke of Argyll, Cregeen has written: though

> impeccable in theory, the scheme was a total failure in practice. It embodied many of the defects of doctrinaire planning and was highly unpopular. With the spirit of resistance

spreading through the island and giving rise to plans of emigration, the Duke seized the first pretext to withdraw his plan.

Emigration from the Highlands had many causes but it was, as much as anything, a final expression of the polarisation of Highland society.[41]

The popular campaign against Patrick Sellar in Sutherland in 1815-16 was neither violent nor passive. It employed relatively unusual tactics to draw attention to the circumstances in Sutherland, with the object of destroying Sellar and reversing the clearances to the point where the land would be returned to the people. T. C. Smout has drawn attention to the 'ritual national hatred of Sellar', and has suggested that there has never been a proper intellectual rebuttal of Sellar's way of thinking: 'he was unkind and a bit rough', but unanswered.[42] There is a suggestion in this that only on the most radical assumption — in effect, only when the criterion of profit maximisation is relegated to secondary importance in the Highland economy — were Sellar's views at all assailable. This, however, may be too generous to the Sutherland sheepfarmer and his kind. Sellar can be impeached without recourse to such an extreme assumption. The critical point is that Sellar's attitude to social relations *of itself* gravely impeded the economic development of the Highlands. It was an attitude which, when translated into estate policy, necessarily entailed a disruptive social response. The restructuring of the economy and the collapse of social cohesion were central factors in the Highland tragedy. The fatal weakness of the Sellar mentality — and though he was an extremist in his views the direction of his thinking was followed by most clearing landlords — lay precisely in its failure to take into account the response of the common people. Their co-operation was never properly sought and they were thoroughly alienated by the arrogance of the planners, and by the communal agony which was the practical consequence of even the most constructive landlord's plans.

The significance of Patrick Sellar and his ideology was that he helped to build that mountain of hatred which destroyed for a century any chance of a co-operative and radical attack on the Highland problem by the landlord and the people. Social breakdown dislocated positive investment programmes during the clearances and left a legacy of burning distrust. It was expressed in the fatalistic apathy of the people which even today is not fully dispersed.

The long history of economic experiments in the Highlands — from the Duke of Argyll to Lord Leverhulme — demonstrates the unwisdom of neglecting the social context of economic planning.

IV

The discontent of the Highlanders was eventually mobilised and channelled into the so-called 'Crofters' War' in the 1880s. H.J. Hanham's incisive analysis specifically raises the questions, 'Why ... did such disturbances occur? And why, in particular, did they start early in 1882?'[43] Hanham, one of many writers who have stressed the apparent discontinuity in the outbreak of the Braes disturbances, maintains that in the year 1882 the Highlanders stopped being passive and at last fought for their rights. Hence the 'Crofters' War' requires a special historical explanation. Hanham answers his questions in terms of the current political and social context, the over-reaction of the local authorities, and the widespread press coverage. 'Once the attention of the outside world has been attracted, the character of the land problem in the Western Highlands changed dramatically.'

Hanham states categorically that 'There was no tradition of resistance to government and no desire to use the land agitation for general political purposes.'[44] Yet virtually all the features of the crofters' agitation had their forerunners in the pattern of protest that had been repeated so often in the previous eight decades. The main contrast was the ultimate success of the agitation as a movement — though even there, remembering Coigach, success was not totally unprecedented. Otherwise, the 1882 agitation was within a long-established continuity of sporadic protest in the Highlands.

The Skye events of 1882 seem to have begun with the attempt to serve notice of ejectment on a group of people following a dispute over lost grazing rights. Hanham's analysis shows that the people were acting in defence of what they regarded as traditional rights to their land. The first summons had been burned by 'some crofters and their wives'. During the main confrontation with the police force the womenfolk played a prime role. A newspaper reporter gave a description reminiscent of many such scenes earlier in the century of clearances:

The women with infuriated looks and bedraggled dress ... were shouting at the pitch of their voices, uttering the most fearful imprecations, hurling forth the most terrible voices of vengeance against the enemy ... The women, with the most violent gestures and imprecations, declared that the police should be attacked.

The people possessed no firearms and no apparent leader was picked out. The action had had ' a religious counterpart in the riot of Strome Ferry in 1883'. Hanham does not mention any intervention by the minister but reports that the dispute was eventually settled quite amicably in December 1882.[45]

The authorities blamed the events on 'agitators'. It was found that 'the forces of law and order in Skye (a pitiful fiction) were far too weak to serve writs or notices on tenants determined not to receive them'. Thus police from Glasgow were requisitioned. Hanham notes a reluctance on the part not only of the police, but also the army and the navy, to become involved. He writes, 'There is no suggestion [in the reports] that an attack at dawn on the houses of god-fearing Free Churchmen by a large body of police from Glasgow is an odd way of arresting five crofters in Skye.'[46] It was in fact a well-tried way of dealing with recalcitrant crofters. As it was, the force proved to be insufficient for the task and the resistance continued. The 'Battle of the Braes' and the early stages of the Crofters' War possessed many of the characteristics of earlier Highland riots in terms of participation, organisation and community support. Had the conflict halted at this point the episode would have fitted exactly the long-established model of the Highland riot.

In the outcome, the Skye episode became part of a much wider Highland conflagration unprecedented in its level of sustained agitation, its geographical solidarity, and the positive legislative response which it eventually elicited. As Hanham points out, the connections with the Irish land leaguers, the sympathy of expatriate Highland societies and the excellent press coverage were each important factors. It may be argued that external support was not entirely unprecedented: several land agitators had given vent in previous Highland disturbances — the writing of Donald MacLeod, David Ross, Hugh Miller, Karl Marx and Sismondi in the early 1850s had provided some inspiration or incitement for a crofters' revolt. In 1855 landlords in the north were fully aware of 'a strong feeling among the people that they would all resume possession of what they conceived to be the possessions of their fathers'.[47] The Duke of Sutherland was warned that if landlords 'persevere in pursuing a mistaken policy they do more to hasten their downfall than the wildest Leveller could hope to accomplish'.[48] Press coverage of Highland protest was not new — most riots were reported, and newspapers such as the *Military Register*, the *Scotsman* and *The Times* at various times took up a stridently sympathetic attitude to the crofters — in the 1810s, 1840s and 1850s. It was not therefore a new development: nor was expatriate assistance unprecedented. In 1822, for instance, 'The Expatriated Highlanders of Sutherland' in India, in addition to voicing criticisms of landlordism, had raised subscriptions for victims of the clearances. These were important elements of continuity in the story of Highland protest.

Another argument in explanation of the crofter agitation of the 1880s concerns the general economic condition of the Highlands. It is undoubtedly true that a succession of poor grain harvests, combined with the failure of the potato crop and the fishing, and a catastrophic fall of stock prices, created great difficulties for many crofters. Gains in living standards over the previous 25 years were at risk, rising expectations were suddenly frustrated. The conjuncture of such circumstances may indeed have created some of the necessary conditions of revolt. Simultaneously the profits of sheepfarming were in sharp decline which, for landlords, reduced the opportunity cost of eventually relinquishing lands to the crofters. Nevertheless the Highlands had seen all the elements of economic decline many times before, but never before had popular protest developed in such a co-ordinated form.

There are so many elements in the Crofters' War which were common to previous riots that the pressing historical question would seem to be not 'Why did they start early in 1882?' but 'Why, in the 1880s, did the disturbances yield such rapid returns?' Since the character of the disturbances appears to have changed little, the tenacity and ultimate success of the agitation may be best associated with the changing receptivity of both public opinion and the authorities to the demonstrations of Highland crofters. While increased press coverage undoubtedly helped, as did the Irish parallels, the most important element was probably the least definable — public opinion in the south. During the last quarter of the nineteenth century a national social conscience had emerged in Victorian Britain; it was particularly sensitive to highly publicised injustice in remote regions. The government, itself precariously placed, was required to respond to this sensitivity in a manner inconceivable fifty years before. But the pattern of Highland discontent itself had changed hardly at all. It is inconsistent with the historical record to consider the crofters' agitation of 1882 as a unique case of Highlanders rebelling against established order. The Highlanders in 1882 had not suddenly become untamed. The Skye people revolted in the manner that employed much the same methods as had been used throughout the clearances. The crofters' success was, in part, a victory for the new sensibility of Victorian public opinion and its faintly condescending concern for lesser elements on the fringe of society.

In 1847 the legal writer J. Hill Burton made an incisive but (in the event) premature remark to the effect that

> against any repetition of those multitudinous and simultaneous clearings, which more resembled the removal of a flock of sheep from their grazings, than the termination of so many contracts between landlord and tenant, there is now the protection of public opinion, which has generally condemned the system.[49]

In 1847 public opinion was a half-formed instrument of political restraint. Twenty-five years later the social conscience of the British upper middle classes had changed decisively, and constituted a highly receptive sounding-board for the crofters' agitation. The Highlanders themselves had changed hardly at all.

V

John Stuart Blackie, writing in 1885, contemplated the question of direct resistance in the Highlands: examining the record of resistance, he argued that the 'recent experience has amply proved that they might have been better treated, if they had at an earlier period, and with greater observance, applied to the Government accustomed to act only on compulsion from below, the highly stimulant recalcitration of a Kenmore or Killarney squatter'. Blackie stated clearly his opinion that 'the lawbreakers in the Highlands were less to blame for recent disturbances than the lawmakers'.[50] When it was put to Professor Blackie that his views effectively incited violence in the Highlands, he vehemently denied the aspersion. His opponents had distorted his words and the newspapers had misunderstood him too. In the same breath he added:

My own conscience is perfectly free. I never told anyone not to pay rent. I never told anybody to shoot landlords from behind a hedge; what I have stated is that it was a strange thing that the Irish, who were guilty of such things, should get lollypops, while the quiet Highlanders got stripes and nothing else.[51]

In a similar vein were the remarks of W. C. Mackenzie that 'so long as the Highlands remained quiet, neither of the great political parties paid heed to the miseries of the voteless and voiceless proletariat; but when the agents of the law were defied, public opinion fired the government into action'.[52]

There is of course a danger in concentrating attention on this single aspect of the Highland question since it inflates the importance of disturbances in the history of the clearances. Nevertheless there is an equal danger in understating the significance and extent of popular Highland resistance before 1882. It would be a mistake to write off the record of Highland protest as futile. In functional terms the resistance performed three important tasks: it attracted public attention which eventually had a cumulative effect; it checked the full exercise of landlord power; and it sabotaged plans of economic reconstruction. Resistance, or the threat of it, helped to define, increasingly restrictively, the tolerable limits of landlord behaviour and thereby reduced some of 'the legalised brutality' of the clearances. It acutely embarrassed the more sensitive of the lairds. In Sutherland it certainly produced a degree of caution in, and later a suspension of, the clearance policy. At Coigach (as well as at Elphin and Knockan) it prevented a clearance. But in the long run, it was passive resistance that was more permanent and decisive in its consequences. The most common response of the Highlanders was a sullen refusal to co-operate.[53] Symptomatic was the comment of James Loch that, once uprooted, the people would rather emigrate several thousand miles than accept accommodation 26 miles away from their old homes. It was a rejection of all the alternatives offered by the landlords. In real terms it was this attitude — itself the product of 'the clearances' — that dealt the fatal blow to several ambitious plans for economic reconstruction. Implicitly the great plans in, for instance, Argyll, Sutherland and

Lewis, which required considerable landlord investment, assumed a degree of co-operation which the very act of clearance made impossible. As T. C. Smout has remarked:

> It was madness to assume that any lasting agrarian prosperity could be built except on a basis of carrying the local population with the landowners. The positive response of the tenantry was the whole key to the success in the lowlands.[54]

It may also be the key to failure in the north. If the Napier Commission Report was an acceptance of the crofters' ancient claims to the land, then the deadening immovability of the Highlanders had proved its power. It was also a victory for what Smout has described as 'the Highland ideology', by which 'the crofter put home before wealth, the possession of land before the dubious opportunity to gain enrichment by a better move as an industrial worker, or even as a landholder overseas'.[55]

In comparing the Highlanders' response to the clearances with known reactions of other agrarian societies, one is struck by several similarities. Indeed the forms of protest employed by the Highlanders correspond extraordinarily well with the types of social action that are now well known in other pre-industrial societies. The apolitical character of the riots, the spontaneity, the sporadic incidence, the composition, the absence of arms, the role of women, the motives, the fragility of effective leadership — all this accords well with the established patterns of the typical pre-industrial forms of protest. From studying the experience of other pre-industrial societies Charles Tilly has defined an analytical category which he terms 'reactionary collective violence'. Such disturbances, he says, are usually

> small in scale, but they pit either communal groups or loosely organised members of the general population against representatives of those who hold power, and tend to include a critique of the way power is being wielded ... The somewhat risky term 'reactionary' applies to their forms of collective violence because their participants were commonly reacting to some change that they regarded as depriving them of rights they had once enjoyed; they were backward-looking.[56]

It might be fair to say that the occurrence of food riots in the Highlands into the 1840s (they had virtually disappeared in the rest of Britain by 1830) is a further symptom of survival of the essential 'pre-industrial' mode of life there.[57] More generally, on these comparative criteria, the Highlanders' action during the clearances, far from being especially tame, was a good average for such a society. The Highlander was not so much naturally submissive as technically limited in his possibilities of effective protest; his ability to organise the population was less developed; deference continued to retain its grip on social attitudes; a consciousness of collective social resistance had not emerged. In the main the Highlanders behaved and reacted in a manner that historians have come to expect of a pre-industrial society in such circumstances.

The implication of much historical discussion about the Highlands is that there has been something uniquely Celtic in its character and institutions. This applies to such questions as the common Highland attitude to the profit motive, to social protest, to religion and to economic development. It may be more helpful if social historians considered the Highland experience in relation to similar societies. It is not necessary to deny the special qualities of life in the nineteenth-century Highlands to see it as an essentially pre-industrial society in an increasingly industrial age.

Opposition to the clearances was a record of discontent perhaps typical of a peasant society half-stunned by a cataclysmic economic change. In the last resort social protest in the Highlands failed in the sense that the clearances proceeded without much interruption. The evidence of resistance, together with the poetic recollection of collective anger, leave no doubt about the reaction of the people to the clearances. And, while the Highlanders' protest fits comfortably within the models of pre-industrial crowd action, it remains incontrovertible that they fell far behind their Irish cousins in terms of violence and sustained resistance. Parts of contemporary Ireland responded to rackrenting and eviction with a much larger range of rural violence, including elaborate clandestine associations and assassination.[58] In the perspective of recent studies of rural protest, the Highlanders' relative peaceability was more typical of pre-industrial society than was the Irish turbulence.

Notes

1. There was an unconfirmed claim that Robert Carruthers, editor of the *Inverness Courier*, had, in 1844, 'managed to stop an extensive series of evictions in Ross-shire by drawing the facts to the attention of the government'; E. M. Barron (ed.), *A Highland Editor. Selected Writings of James Barron of the Inverness Courier* (Inverness, 1927), p. 50.

2. Cobbett, *Rural Rides*, III, p. 89.

3. See above, Ch. 3.

4. First Report of the Select Committee on Emigration (Scotland), *PP* (1841), VI, p. 199; Barron, *Northern Highlands*, II, p. 251; SCRO, Sutherland Collection, D593/P/22/1/7, Lumsden to Rae, 6 October 1841.

5. Barron, *Northern Highlands*, II, p. 251. SCRO, Sutherland Collection, D593/P/22/1/7, Lumsden to Rae, 6 October 1841.

6. SC on Emigration (Scotland), 1841, First Report, p. 80, Second Report, p. 26. James Wilson in *A Voyage Round the Coasts of Scotland and the Isles* (Edinburgh, 1842) used very similar language to describe the broken spirit of the Skye people:

The most distressful feature of the poverty of these people is its demoralising influence. The flocks of sheep farmers are yearly thinned by the reckless hand of want, goaded on by the approaching famine, and uncontrolled by the now dissevered chains of feudal affection. (quoted in Derek Cooper, *Road to the Islands* (London, 1979), p. 94)

7. SCRO, Sutherland Collection, D593/K, Loch's Report, 1835.

8. *New Statistical Account*, Inverness-shire, Skye, Portree, pp. 227-8.

9. Teignmouth, *Sketches*, II, pp. 17-24; see also Richards, *Highland Clearances*, pp. 442-4.

10. SCRO, Sutherland Collection, D593/4, Anderson to Loch, 2 August 1841 and accompanying correspondence.

11. Ibid., Horsburgh to Loch, 20 October 1841, 13 October 1841, Loch to Anderson, 6 November 1841, D593/P/22/1/7. Barron, *Northern Highlands*, II, pp. 314-16.

12. Barron, *Northern Highlands*, III, pp. 185, 190. SCRO, Sutherland Collection, D593/K/22/1/7, Sinclair to Lumsden, 5 August 1843, Lumsden to Duke of Sutherland, 7 September 1843.

13. See Richards, *Highland Clearances*, Ch. 13.

14. *Scotsman*, 28 July 1849.

15. Henry Cockburn, *Journal of Henry Cockburn, 1831-1854* (2 vols., Edinburgh, 1874), II, p. 247. *Nairnshire Mirror*, 22 September 1849.

16. Barron, *Northern Highlands*, III, p. 207.

17. SCRO, Sutherland Collection, D593/K/1/3/39, MacIver to Loch, 4 April 1851.

18. Wick had a reputation for radicalism in 1832 when it was described as having 'suddenly risen from a trifling village to a great population composed of emigrants from all quarters of the Kingdom, with radical principles and no leading family to control or guide them since the MacLeays became extinct'. SRO, Loch Muniments, Robert Bruce to James Loch, 20 August 1832.

19. A more thorough treatment is offered in Richards, 'Problems on the Cromartie Estate'.

20. Barron, *Northern Highlands*, III, pp. 293, 297.

21. Ibid., pp. 302-9; Richards, *Highland Clearances*, pp. 460-8; Ross was quoted in Mackenzie, *History of the Highland Clearances*, p. 136. The Austrian general Haynaus had outraged world opinion by his psychopathic conduct during

his reign of terror in occupied Brescia.

22. The imprisoned man, Peter Ross, protested total innocence of the offence. The Rev. Gustavus Aird interceded on his behalf and his term in Perth prison was reduced to twelve months. His relatives emigrated to Melbourne, Australia; other tenants went to Langwell. This information is derived from a letter from Aird to the Rev. A. Patterson, 4 September 1855, displayed in Tain Museum and kindly brought to my attention by Mrs Mackenzie.

23. SCRO, Sutherland Collection, D593/K, Loch to the Duke of Sutherland, 19 February 1855.

24. *Inverness Advertiser*, 20 November 1850.

25. See Hanham, 'Highland Discontent', *passim.*

26. *Northern Ensign*, 7 October 1884, 16 October 1884.

27. Quoted in *Inverness Courier*, November 1884.

28. On the general proposition about women in riots and their role in the domestic economy see Olwen Hufton, 'Women in Revolution, 1789-1796', *Past and Present*, no. 83 (1971), pp. 92-5; and Richard A. Cloward and Frances Fox Piven, 'Hidden Protest: the Channelling of Female Innovation and Resistance', *Signs* (Summer 1979), pp. 657-8; Jones, *Before Rebecca*, pp. 43-9.

29. On the role of women in Highland life see Alexander Nicolson, *History of Skye* (Glasgow, 1930), pp. 315-16. See also Logue, *Popular Disturbances*, pp. 199-203.

30. See Schaw, *Journal of a Lady of Quality*, p. 28.

31. Cf. Logue, *Popular Disturbances*, pp.209-10.

32. Mackenzie, *History of the Highland Clearances*, p. 22.

33. W. C. Mackenzie, *A Short History of the Scottish Highlands and Islands* (London, 1908), p. 289.

34. Eric Cregeen, 'The House of Argyll and the Highlands' in I. M. Lewis (ed.), *History and Social Anthropology* (London, 1968), p. 189n. See also James Hunter. 'The Emergence of the Crofting Community: the Religious Contribution, 1798-1843', *Scottish Studies*, vol. 18 (1974).

35. Cf. evidence of critical comment by ministers in Gordon E. MacDermid, 'The Religious and Ecclesiastical Life of the North West Highlands, 1750-1843', unpublished PhD thesis, University of Aberdeen, 1967, esp. pp. 142-8.

36. See Smout, *History of the Scottish People*, p. 464.

37. Galen Broeker, *Rural Disorder and Police Reform in Ireland 1812-1836* (London, 1970).

38. *Journal of Henry Cockburn*, II, p. 79.

39. Smout, 'Ideological Struggle', pp. 13-16.

40. Richards, 'Patterns of Highland Discontent', p. 108.

41. Cregeen, 'The House of Argyll and the Highlands', pp. 154ff.

42. Smout, 'Ideological Struggle', p. 16.

43. Hanham, 'Highland Discontent', p. 30. Much the same problem exists for the timing of successful agrarian agitation in Ireland, 1879-82. See Samuel Clark, *Social Origins of the Irish Land War* (Princeton, 1979), *passim.*

44. Hanham, 'Highland Discontent', pp. 22, 65.

45. Ibid., pp. 24, 30, 53. On the question of internal and external leadership see Hunter, *Crofting Community*, pp. 129ff and 'The Politics of Land Reform 1873-1895', *Scottish Historical Review*, vol. 53, (1974).

46. Hanham, 'Highland Discontent', pp. 30, 54.

47. SCRO, Sutherland Collection, D593/K, Loch to Duke of Sutherland, 19 February 1855.

48. Ibid., Davidson to Duke of Sutherland, 3 August 1855.

49. [J. Hill Burton,] 'Celtic Clearings', *Edinburgh Review*, vol. 86 (1847), p. 503.

50. Blackie, *Scottish Highlanders*, pp. 192-202. Napier Commission, Evidence, Q. 45888.
51. Blackie, *Scottish Highlanders*, loc. cit.
52. Mackenzie, *A Short History of the Scottish Highlands and Islands*, pp. 321-2.
53. See Hugh Miller, *Leading Articles on Various Subjects* (Edinburgh, 1870), p. 420.
54. Smout, *History of the Scottish People*, p. 360, and 'Ideological Struggle', p. 16.
55. Smout, 'Ideological Struggle', p. 14.
56. Tilly, 'Collective Violence in European Perspective', p. 16.
57. See Richards, *The Last Scottish Food Riots*.
58. See Beames, 'Rural Conflict in Pre-Famine Ireland'. On the effectiveness of threatened violence as a restraint on eviction see Joseph Lee, 'The Ribbonmen' in T. Desmond Williams (ed.), *Secret Societies in Ireland* (Dublin, 1973), pp. 32-5.

14
SOCIAL CHANGE AND CONTROL IN THE HIGHLANDS

If any harshness was used during the evictions, Lord Stafford cannot be fairly blamed, but the agent employed. However, it was never proved that such had been the case. The lies and calumnies did their dirty work, and for years, a kind of stigma attached itself to those, and even the descendants of those, who had carried out these vast improvements in the condition of their people and estates.

Lord Ronald Gower[1]

The character and significance of social change during the age of the clearances is the least-known part of the Highland story. There has been virtually no systematic research on the subject, and the theoretical problems have not even yet been broached. Dr Hunter has argued cogently that while the economic development of the Highlands has been explored in recent research, much of this work has been conducted

> at the expense of neglecting the social changes and adaptations necessitated by them ... [and] the way in which the crofting community, considered as a social and cultural entity, was created out of the commons of the clans remains something of a mystery.[2]

Untouched also is a range of questions concerning the cohesion of Highland society. They begin with the nature of the pre-clearance social structures — the integrity of 'the clan system' and the question of its vitality. Authority invested in the chiefs within the old society seems to have been delegated effectively to the tacksmen who, often by ties of kinship and patronage, connected the top with all other levels of the society. The social influence of the landlords and their tacksmen allegedly provided the society with a solidarity and sense of community which sustained it through subsistence as well as military crises. We know too little about the distribution of wealth and authority in the society, and about the levels of social and psychic welfare. Instead, our understanding of pre-clearance Highland society depends primarily on presumption reinforced by the collective nostalgia identified in the Napier Commission Report of 1884.

Dr Hunter has suggested that even as early as the latter part of the eighteenth century the Highlanders were 'a confused, disturbed people' in the throes of a 'cultural disintegration' marked 'by the steep decline in Gaelic culture as the language was abandoned by the upper classes and as the old certainties gave way to growing doubt and perplexity'. The common people had been left to 'fend for themselves in a strange new environment in which the land of the kindred could be bought and sold for cash and the people who lived upon the land treated as an element in a calculation of profit and loss'.[3] Where communities were evicted their place was taken by solitary shepherds, and the original population dispersed far and wide. More significant, however, was the transplantation of Highland communities into crofting settlements along the coasts as in Sutherland and the western islands. These settlements provide one aspect of social readjustment in the early nineteenth century. Another was represented by the residual uncleared populations in their original places in many parts of the Highlands, even as late as 1850.

Within these communities there were obvious shifts. Rapid changes in land ownership brought several waves of proprietorial types to the Highlands, from the nabobs of the 1780s to the industrialists of the 1850s (the Baird brothers paid over a million pounds for Highland estates at this time), and soapmakers and Americans at the end of the century. The social consequences of these repeated changes were uneven. Highland society bifurcated. The sheepfarmers and estate factors indeed became a separate caste, isolated from the population at large with virtually no social and economic connection. As Robert Somers put it in 1848:

> there are only two ranks of people — a higher rank and a lower rank — the former consisting of a few large tenants ... and the latter consisting of a dense body of small cottars and fishermen ... The proverbial enmity of rich and poor in all societies has

received peculiar development in this simple social structure of the Highlands.[4]

A correspondent for the *New Statistical Account* in the 1830s pointed out that the middle classes, which he defined as those paying between £10 and £50 rent, had been virtually suppressed. He bemoaned the fact that the lower classes had no body of people to emulate, and that it had become difficult to find 'men suitable for being ordained elders'. It had been divested of its natural magistrates, JPs and officers in the army. The society had become 'plebeian', as another writer put it. The sheepfarmers employed private teachers and the local schools lost the children of the respectable classes.[5] The polarisation of Highland society was almost complete. The landowners, even where the old families survived, seemed to become increasingly absentee for most of the year. The new breed of Highland proprietors, including some who aped the old lairds, did not generate much of the social warmth which they thought characterised the old world. The influx of sportsmen after 1840 was strictly seasonal and did little for social cohesion: they emphasised the exoticism of the Highlands and had little stake in the Highland community.

I

The sheepfarmers were generally wealthy, resourceful, extraordinarily capitalistic, and usually strangers to the local community. Of their origins only a little is known. The first wave of sheepfarmers into the southern Highlands, after 1755, included men from New Cumnock, Clydesdale, Tweeddale and Nithsdale. James Loch, who was well placed to know, described the stockmen of Sutherland in 1817 as 'the Northumberland sheepfarmers'. They included the partnership of Atkinson and Marshall which had invested £20,000 in the county by 1820. James Hall, however, was an ex-shepherd from Roxburghshire; Walter Grieve hailed from Selkirkshire; Thomas Geddes was from Perthshire; the Cameron brothers, who settled at Kildermorie, were from Lochaber; Culley and Morton came from Northumberland; Patrick Sellar was a native of Moray. Gilchrist came from Ospidale and Captain Mackay was a Highlander.[6] When estate owners advertised for new tenants they appeared glad to be able to say that they had already attracted 'enterprising Farmers from Northumberland'.[7] 1849 Charles St John noted that the new sheepfarmers brought with them their own border shepherds. They were 'a fine stalwart race of men, Armstrongs, Elliots, Scotts and others', and he added, revealing a trace of bias, that 'the genuine Highlander has not, I think, yet sobered down into a good shepherd; the border men still form the most persevering and careful guardians of the large flocks which now fill the northern mountains'.[8] According to Lord Teignmouth, the sheepfarmers were 'chiefly from Northumberland and the lowlands', and it is known that in the parish of Farr in the north-west extremity of the region all the sheepfarmers were absentees who left their stock in the hands of managers. As late as 1861 the Sutherland estate was still recruiting its sheepfarmers from the pastoral districts of the south of Scotland. Nevertheless all this may overstate the case. When, in 1820, James Loch enumerated the large leaseholders on the Sutherland estate, he found that 17 came from the county itself (probably remnants of the old tacksmen class), 4 were from Northumberland, 2 each from Moray, Roxburgh and Caithness, and 1 each from the Merse and Midlothian.[9]

The sheepfarmers were denounced from all quarters, both within and beyond the Highlands. When a correspondent of *The Times* in 1850 contemplated the allegedly dilapidated state of Highland society, he deplored the neglect of social duty by the

> sheepfarmers: graziers from the south, who, taking large sheep walks, sweep away the profits to the lowland districts, where they reside, and leave the peasantry without sympathy, encouragement or support. It is not difficult to see what the condition of a population must be in a purely pastoral district, with absentee tenants; yet such is, to a great extent, the conditions of the West Highlands.[10]

As T. C. Smout remarks, they 'were almost as much a colonising alien class as European settlers in Kenya's White Highlands'.[11]

The response of the indigenous population to the sheepfarmers is not well recorded, but there are many traces of a general hostility which was often combined with anti-English attitudes. During the riotous resistance to sheepfarming in Sutherland in 1813 there were clear reports that the invasion of the sheep was regarded specifically as an English abomination. At one point the Kildonan

people alleged that the sheepfarmers had caused the current inflation of meal prices and rents, and the shepherds were denounced
as 'those English Devils'.[12] Almost everywhere the sheepfarmers
kept their distance from the local people. Furthermore, even
between themselves the sheepfarmers had great difficulty in
developing a sense of solidarity, or even of ordinary social connection. It is true that they met at sheep and wool markets, and
that they conducted collective campaigns against foxes and
'depredations' on their sheep. But they were not a cohesive
element in the Highlands: they lived far apart; many were absentees, and unlike southern arable farmers formed few agricultural
societies and clubs.[13] They were an excellent example of 'economic
man' in classical political economy, perfectly competitive,
unobstructed by any interference with market forces. They
naturally attracted much of the opprobrium generated by the
transformation of the Highlands.[14] And even within the management of the great estates there were qualms about the scale and
aloofness of the sheepfarmers. An English adviser to the
Sutherland estate in 1831 felt that the organisation of land holding,
alien to his southern expectations, was deficient in several respects.
He advocated that middle-sized farms be inserted between the
'higher and lower classes — evidently a link is wanted to unite a
society that would entertain proper feelings towards each other,
the reverse being the case at present'.[15] This point was re-echoed
through the following decades but was rarely acted upon because
the economics of sheepfarming was heavily loaded in favour of
large-scale operations. But the economic efficiency of the great
sheepfarmers was unmatched by any contribution to the working
of Highland society.

At the end of the nineteenth century some of the new breed of
sporting landlords attempted to reconstruct social relations on
Highland estates. Some even created the semblance of social harmony. But it is difficult to avoid the view that the crofters offered
deference from a position of dependency and even demoralisation,
and that the good feeling evident on a number of estates arose
from an artificial structure of social relations which left little room
for genuine dignity.[16]

Throughout the trauma of revolutionary social and economic
change in the Highlands there emerged the crofting community
itself, the elements of which have been analysed with penetration
and subtlety by Dr Hunter. It is easy to categorise crofting as an

anachronism which impeded emigration, and exacerbated the problems of congestion and rural squalor. Yet crofting provided a haven in an alien world, and created the means of communal solidarity and cultural survival for a population on the brink of subsistence crises and even extinction. There were times in the nineteenth century when crofting gave food and employment for a surplus population which the rest of the economy could not support. Crofting absorbed 'the residual surplus of population' because it was labour-intensive; it coped with its aged and its sick, and it gave solace to the evicted. Though the level of welfare was often appallingly low, it was the crofting system which sustained the disinherited Highlanders for much of the nineteenth century.[17] At the same time it could be argued that crofting prolonged the agony of adjustment to the processes of modernisation.

Crofting occupied a half-way house between the status of an independent peasantry and that of a totally dispossessed proletariat. In many parts of the Highlands and Islands the pressure of population, much reinforced by landlord policies of reorganisation and clearance, operated to disperse the old population. Many entered villages and became farm servants or casual day-labourers in the model widespread in the rest of Britain during agrarian transformation. Some Highland landlords deliberately set out to obliterate all independent holdings, including crofts and cottar lands. The consequences for economic welfare depended on the timing of the change and on the opportunities for alternative employment in the locality. The change was not necessarily inconsistent with an improvement of living standards, and the process of proletarianisation was clearly sanctioned in the tablets of classical political economy. Nevertheless, the response of the people was virtually uniform — day-labour was repugnant, the time discipline was alien, and the loss of status was psychologically damaging. This blank resistance to social change represented the gulf between the improvement mind and the mentality of the peasantry. It goes much of the way to explaining the extraordinary tenacity with which crofters adhered to their small holdings.

II

A recurrent theme in much nineteenth-century discussion about the Highlands was the great rift that had developed in the com-

munity — between the crofters and the proprietors. Some landlords continued to entertain notions of social leadership
throughout the years of the clearances. In 1820, on the collapse of
resistance in Sutherland, James Loch remarked that 'the good that
has sprung out of the late proceedings is that it has brought the
people more back than they have been for some time to their
natural leaders, the ancient Nobility of the lands'.[18] It was a
despairing thought, and many landowners, having reorganised
their estates had good cause to regret the apparent diminution in
warm feeling between them and their small tenantry. They could
no longer depend on an automatic deference and loyalty from
their people. It is significant too that the cause of this social decline
was attributed to the erosion of the middling ranks of Highland
society — the elimination of the social gradations between the two
extremes of the social spectrum. The problem of social leadership
was necessarily related to this question. Clearly the sheepfarmers
provided none and the elimination of the tacksmen created a
'social vacuum'.[19] To some degree the Highland crofting communities appear to have survived without much visible leadership
from above. They seemed to turn inwards upon themselves, partly
perhaps to exclude the alien world, partly to nurse the injuries of
social change. It may go some of the way towards explaining their
low political consciousness through much of the early nineteenth
century. It may help explain, too, the relatively slight degree of
resistance to the clearances.

Eventually leadership appears to have fallen into the hands of
the dissident clergy. In the early nineteenth century various eccentric or unorthodox religious movements gained a surprisingly tenacious grip on the minds of the common people, who appear to
have easily fallen under the sway of articulate outsiders — notably
schoolmasters and journalists. After the Disruption there is little
doubt that the Free Church ministers seized hold of social leadership and eventually helped the crofting community to organise
itself against the landlords and sheepfarmers.

The common Highland people were easy prey to itinerant
preachers and to the religious revival movements that crossed
through the region in the early nineteenth century.[20] A
demoralised people, they were enticed by 'millennial visions of
social justice' that were associated with revivalism. Hunter has
argued plausibly that 'the origins of this "deep and stirring
religious awakening" are to be found in the social and psycho-

logical consequences of the collapse of the old order' — in the disorientation of a people robbed of their traditional leadership. In effect, revivalism provided the bond which eventually created sufficient cohesion to permit the crofters to challenge the landlords. In this argument there is a connecting rod between the early religious movements, the Disruption of 1843, and the land leagues of the 1880s. Hunter says that

> in the north-west Highlands the Free Church came into existence as a profoundly popular institution, the hero to a long tradition of religious dissent ... In 1843 ... a majority of the crofting population stood up to their landlords for the first time. And they won.[21]

The victory was comprehensive. In Sutherland, for instance, out of a population of 25,000 only 219 people remained with the established church.[22]

The ultimate role of the Free Church ministers in creating the political consciousness of the crofters, and then leading them into a prolonged and successful confrontation with the landlords, was critical. Their efforts drove some landlords into paroxysms of frustration and rage. When an agent of the Duke of Sutherland, Thomas Purves, drew up a memorandum on the crofting question for the Napier Commission in 1883, he gave vent to some of this accumulated frustration. The Gaelic language, he claimed, was at the root of most of the crofters' difficulties:

> [It] paralyses the energies of the Highland people. It keeps up the remembrance of the old clan system, for ever done away with; makes them look on every stranger as an enemy forgetting in the past their greatest oppressors were their kinsmen and clansmen and their real foes were those of their own name. It makes them the willing tools of a priesthood in many cases as ignorant and superstitious as themselves and destroys that power of action and liberty of thought which is the birthright of every Briton. What but the Gaelic and the ignorance thereby engendered makes them the cats-paws, and believers of such shady philanthropists and agitators as the Blackies, Mackays and Mackenzies, who came to them trusting in their ignorance and simplicity to gain a spurious and unhealthy population ... What do they offer them, or what practical solution have they

ever proposed for the real grievances of the Highland crofters? Thank God if the Education Act does nothing for the Highlands but abolish Gaelic as a spoken language, it would not be passed in vain and there will be some recompense for the grievous burden laid on the backs of Highland lairds and Highland Tenants.[23]

The religious passion of the Highlanders was not easily understood by many of the landlords or their agents. On a tour of the north-west in October 1835 James Loch was astonished to come across a great crowd of 3,000 people on the side of a mountain, drenched in teeming rain: they were there 'to hear preaching; the rain pouring incessantly. The English service *in the Church* was attended by about 12 individuals. The celebration of the Sacrament at this time of the year ought certainly to be avoided.'[24] Fifty years later Colin Macdonald displayed similar incredulity about the survival in the Highlands of 'terror-preaching of a most fanatical type, in which threats of a literal eternal fire largely preponderated[. It] was quite common and, indeed, strange to say, pretty generally relished in the Highlands.' It was the type of belief which later came to be labelled 'the chiliasm of despair'.[25]

The religious history of the Highlands in the nineteenth century almost certainly reflected the extent to which the general population had become alienated from its secular masters. It represented the assertion of the popular will against the wishes of the landlords in one area of life which had been jealously guarded against intrusion. This tradition connected the anti-patronage riots of the early nineteenth century[26] with the Disruption and later the Crofter Revolt. For, although traditional deference in landlord/crofter relations continued, the record of religious resistance suggests a deeper sense of discord. Indeed the history of religion provides a parallel to the chronicle of protest during the clearances.

III

Highland estate factors have an unenviable reputation not only as the instruments of landlord policy, but also as men who egged on their masters in the eviction of the common people. Often they became the scapegoats for the social dislocation of the Highlands.

They were represented as cunning, shifty and mercenary, men without heart. The people blamed them for the clearances partly because they would believe only the best of the proprietors; and the landlords, especially when they fell bankrupt, would lay blame on their agents. Not untypical was the insolvent laird in 1836 who ranted against 'cursed Edinburgh lawyers. I thought I was living very quietly on a third of my income, and when I came to examine into matters, I found myself obliged to sell half my property.'[27]

The image of the Highland factor in the nineteenth century was not unlike that accorded to the tacksman of the previous century.[28] Indeed there was a considerable transfer of functions, with some vital differences, between the two categories of men who controlled the detailed operations of Highland society. Each, of course, derived his authority from above, and each possessed a wide scope for individual discretion; both exercised their authority through a hierarchy of management. Each stood at the centre of the social framework. During the era of the clearances landlords strove to eliminate the tacksmen altogether as an act mutually beneficial to themselves and the common people. The Sutherland management, for instance, genuinely believed that the small tenants regarded the tacksmen as cruel and detestable: Lady Stafford wrote of them in 1805, 'The hopes of having their Farms under us, instead of being subset ... in future, gives them universal joy.' She sent spies to find out what rents the tacksmen extorted; these would 'in future be transferred from their pockets to ours, and produce an amazing increase, also to the joy of these people from the change of masters'.[29] In place of the tacksmen came the professional managers, the factors, whose role it was to oversee the allegedly beneficial change, which inevitably antagonised the most influential stratum in Highland society, and worked painfully against the reconstitution of social harmony.

Few people loved a factor. All credit for landlord benevolence, whenever it was visible, was directed to the fountainhead; all abuse for his rigour, for his evictions, was sheeted home to his factor. Undoubtedly a factor wielded considerable powers, particularly if the owner was absentee and the lines of management were long and little supervised. Corruption, negligence and oppression sometimes followed.[30] But the factor was never more than an employee, and could be dismissed at any moment and rendered practically unemployable in the network of the great estates. A sacked factor was as virulent a critic as the redundant tacksman, and both were prominent in the public denunciation of the landlord class.

Alexander Irvine, writing in 1802, was unambiguous about the power of the factors in the north:

> It would be tedious and irksome to enumerate the various methods by which a factor may get rid of a person whom he hates, or let in (as it is termed) one whom he loves ... He that could bear the tyranny of small masters, might have been born a Mohemetan![31]

Throughout the century the Highland factor lost none of this public character; the implementation of the policy of clearances made him the object of abuse.[32] The Earl of Selkirk, himself a southern landowner, said that the factors of Highland estates were invested with so much power that the temptations were 'almost too great for human nature'; but he argued that public odium was more properly directed at their masters 'who suffer such abuses to be committed in their name'.[33] Thomas Garnett went further and suggested that the pressure was merely transmitted from the land-lords:

> The steward or factor, hard pressed by letters from the gaming house, or Newmarket, demands the rent in a tone which makes no great allowance for unpropitious seasons, the death of cattle, and other accidental circumstances; the laird's wants must be supplied.[34]

Certainly a Highland factorship was no sinecure. The poverty of the ordinary people and the intractability of the environment made the job far more onerous than its southern counterpart. Often a Highland factor was called upon to perform managerial miracles. During the clearances they had to prepare the minds of the people for changes which in their nature were entirely unpalatable; they were expected to maintain the landlord's standing while the lives of the people were revolutionised. In 1822 the Countess of Sutherland prescribed 'gentle management' for the refugees she had recently uprooted from Strathnaver. She told the ground officers to be 'very humane and interested in their welfare ... Having got them removed and settled, we must treat them as gently as they deserve.' The factor was called upon 'to nurse them and encourage them'.[35]

The factor on a Highland estate had few supports within a community bereft of any middle stratum. Isolated, and lacking adequate powers of law and order, he was often a lonely man who conducted much of his estate business by correspondence with hypercritical superiors in legal offices in Inverness, Edinburgh or London. The sheer distances involved in Highland property made it a career on horseback and added great strain to the daily round of duties. Good men were not easily recruited; cases of corruption were matched by dedication and the breakdown of health. Charged with the collection of rents, the removal of tenants and the forced implementation of improvements, a factor could scarcely avoid unpopularity. It was a gruelling job which ruined good men as well as bad.

The advantages of the position were not inconsiderable. In addition to a salary, most factors leased their own farms on the estate, usually on favourable terms. The factor for the western district of Sutherland in the mid-century became a wealthy man and actually implemented clearances on his own account.[36] Anonymous letters to landlords, an interesting but slippery source of popular attitudes, frequently contained allegations of fraud or negligence or peculation by the factor. The manager of the Rosehall estate in 1814 got into debt, took money and then committed suicide.[37] Patrick Sellar in Sutherland was reckoned guilty of holding back rents to solve their own short-term liquidity problems.[38]

The recruitment of factors was also a matter of controversy. As the key instruments of improvement agriculture, estate agents were selected to avoid prior contamination by old Highland ways and attitudes. Sir John Sinclair advocated the employment of non-Highlanders as part of a general philosophy for the encouragement of southern influence in the Highlands.[39] Hence many Lowlanders were recruited to Highland management and, failing that, a southern-educated man was preferred. MacIver in Sutherland was a Highlander, educated at Edinburgh University, and by 1845 he was earning an annual salary of £400. But the lower echelons of estate managements were usually populated by local men — ground officers who had the benefit of detailed local knowledge and bilingualism, but were not always good bookmen. These men were charged with the details of local management such as the extraction of rent, the eviction of tenants in arrears, supervision of improvements, and even a strict watch on the morals of the people. Inevitably many came into conflict with local opinion; they were frequently the special enemies of the ministers of the Free Church. Before the Napier Commission in 1883 the minister of Melness declared that the landlord — the Duke of Sutherland — was often moved by benevolent motives, but 'the agents of his Grace are his hands, his eyes, his ears, and his feet and in their dealings with the people they are constantly like a wall of ice between his Grace and his Grace's people'.[40]

The essential unpleasantness of the factor's work was captured in the conduct of Evander MacIver in 1850. MacIver was a Lewisman of great experience and dominating personality who, for fifty years, ruled over the western quarter of Sutherland known as Scourie, full of small tenants and profound poverty. He was certainly unpopular, and he undoubtedly pursued hard policies, often ahead of his master, the Duke of Sutherland. With MacIver it was an article of faith that the people required rigid discipline — without it, both they and their landlord would be overtaken by the effects of indolence and disorder. In 1850 he had attempted to rearrange some of the small tenantry of Kinlochbervie into lots of lands in which, he claimed, they would become more economically secure. He remarked:

> The poverty of a large portion of the Tenantry in this District naturally poor and ungenial is very striking; and it is difficult to decide how one is to deal with the case of an able-bodied man with eight children in arrear two Rents — and without stock to meet these arrears — his children partially naked — and no food except what he earns by his labour.

Faced with this dilemma, MacIver said:

> Humanity prompts one to leave such a man in possession of his lot. Duty to my Constituent compels me to give the lot to some neighbour who will pay the rent of it — moreover examples must be made as a warning to others. I have a dozen cases in Kinlochbervie District alone.

MacIver was thus fully aware of the moral tension in his work: and, because of his belief in the necessity of rigid social control, he tended to a greater rigour than his employer. The entire question became more lively when MacIver tried to relocate the people: they physically resisted the process and the episode brought public odium on the head of an angry Duke of Sutherland.[41] Such was the furore that the factor was overruled and the Duke prohibited any further attempted clearance. MacIver protested vigorously, saying that his authority was undermined and that the capitulation was 'damaging ... to the future management of these townships'. He threatened resignation but, in the event, stayed in the management for a further forty years.[42]

During this episode the Sutherland management came to regard the Free Church ministers as direct rivals for the control of the common people of the west coast. The local press had poisoned the minds of the people, and had promulgated 'doctrines of a nature calculated to destroy those feelings of attachment which exist among the smaller Tenantry towards their superiors, and to injure an entire social system'. Worse still, 'the Free Church party reiterate the same sentiments and take peculiar delight in fulminating their anthems against the Landlords'. According to the agent it rendered management almost impossible.[43] Evander MacIver, his hands firmly tied by the Duke of Sutherland, seethed with frustration. He could neither clear the tenants, nor punish the riotous. And the people themselves showed no contrition. According to the factor:

> so long as they are left unpunished they will remain in the same spirit — it makes the management of them so difficult ... for when there is no fear of punishment there is no check or restraint to their violence and disorder ... If I had my own way I would have gone every length the law permitted to get them punished, and the longer this is left undone, the more turbulent and unruly they will become.[44]

MacIver predicted that unless a sterner attitude were adopted it would become impossible to execute any removal in either Assynt or Sutherland as a whole. While he was hot for a vindication of factorial authority, his master the Duke had no stomach for the business and MacIver's advice was discarded.

Highland management was already by 1850 in process of qualitative change. James Loch tried to lecture MacIver on the theme that public opinion now had to be taken into account just as much as the old principles of managerial control. The role of the factor had altered — his actions, said Loch, would be viewed differently by a large part of the public of this country and by a majority of the press from what you do ... it is ... the tribunal by which we shall be judged. We must not therefore run against it.

Loch continued his unwelcome advice to MacIver:

Formerly Highland management differed materially in several respects from that of lowland property: [it] has altered much; the Highlanders are more acquainted with their rights than they were and in which they are maintained by others, whose designs are in many instances questionable, and unless they are treated as their lowland neighbours are, they never will be contented.

Loch's advice implied that the arbitrary authority of the old Highland factor no longer could be exercised without reference to public opinion, and to newly prevailing liberal standards of behaviour.

James Loch offered MacIver some measures of sympathy since he knew the appalling isolation of the factor's work: 'The more so, in your District, where you have no equals to advise with, and above all have to perform the mixed and not always the concurrent duties of Factor and of Magistrate' — a position which Loch decried as totally anomalous. It was indeed widespread practice in the Highlands for the factor to perform virtually all public offices connected with the Poor Law, the magistracy and road works. As Loch put it:

This combined duty of being the administrator of the public law and at the same time manager of the landlord's affairs, has always appeared to me to be one of the great sources of the Factor's difficulties and of the unpopularity of the management.[45]

Factorial pluralism was one of the most virulent sources of contention in all Highland administration, and the root of several scandals during the middle decades of the century. Henry George, after detailing a number of cases of factorial authoritarianism, declared that, in Skye, 'the factor there is everything except the parish minister'.[46] Even at the end of the century the anomalies remained prominent in public criticism. The highly critical

American tourists, the Pennells, complained bitterly of the plight of the crofter: 'He is wholly at the mercy of the factor, who usually holds all the highest offices on the estate, and has the power, as at Barra, to disenfranchise the entire island.' The people were kept in subjection by this system; it was a 'state of terrorism under which the small tenantry live through the insolent threats of subordinate officials, whose impudence increases in proportion to the smallness of their authority'.[47]

On instructions from their masters, estate factors commonly refused the small tenantry any direct access to their landlords; all business must pass through the factor's office. This arrangement, standing in the way of any expression of popular feeling, caused great frustration. Sometimes the people gathered together a petition which would reach the eye of the landlord without the intervention (and censorship) of his managers. Only a few of these untutored but eloquent documents, which give rare voice to the people, have survived. The fear of eviction and the comprehensive power of the factor were expressed boldly in a petition to the landlord written by five crofters from Airdeon in Benbecula, South Uist, in January 1852.

at Benbecula 3rd January 1852

My dearest Lord
    I have to tell you the oppression they are to do on us we are here five poor men without a boat or horse to support ourselves but we are hardly making of crop what would support us for half a year and the rest maintaining ourselves with fish and with what we would get for it now our possession is given to another man by Master William burne's order we are saying that we will never remove from our possession till this Complaint be sent before your honourable first because we got leases During 7 years It is [alm?] we got the lots first by Doctor MacLeod's order for we were unable to pay a better place he saw it proper to us to come to it and laid 5 shilling sterling rent on us the first year of our lease Mr William Young laid on us one pound sterling yearly of rent during the severe years the first of them we paid the rent honourably by kelp just carrying the seaweed on ourback without horse very scarce of food besides all every one of them will be on the parochial board except few because they are old without Assistant but if they are left where they are they

will help themselves as well as they can and they will be dilligent to pay their dues after making improvements and dykes they wanted us to go to worse place where we cannot get any seaweed neared than a m[ile].

this letter is not well written but I hope your honour will excuse me for I had no learn and we would not get any person at Uist that should write for us supposing they would kill us for fear of the factor and ground officer We have 4 acres of moss apiece and the manure is ... at the end of each croft for it is so favourable for us as it is We hope your honour will have pity on us for it is said by the factor that we will be sent away from your estate at Whitsunday because we refused to go to the bad place they want [us] to go We have no more to add this is the name of our place Airde on Benbecula South Uist[48]

Petitions were total anathema to Highland estate managers not only because they encouraged the crofters in an unusual unity of purpose, but also because they threatened to undermine the factor's arbitrary local authority.

It was undoubtedly easy for crofters and landlords to regard the factors — who were placed between the needs of both — as the root cause of their respective difficulties. Their position certainly gave them great local authority and some behaved with odious arrogance. But their employers could not be absolved from responsibility and it is too facile to generalise the sins of a small sample of these men into a general condemnation of their profession.

Patrick Sellar, though he was an estate agent for only a short period, has come to typify the entire body of Highland estate factors. Sellar provided a remarkable torrent of commentary on all Highland issues in the age of the clearances. His career, the subject of the following section, is instructive not only as a mirror of the social dislocation of the Highlands and the responses to which it gave rise, but also as the source of the most persistent preoccupation in the collective memory of the Highland clearances.

Notes

1. *My Reminiscences* (4th edition, London, 1885), p. 62.
2. Hunter, 'Emergence of the Crofting Community', p. 95.
3. Ibid., p. 96.
4. Quoted in ibid., p. 110.
5. *New Statistical Account*, XV, pp. 104, 816.
6. SCRO, Sutherland Collection, D593/K, Loch to Lord Bathurst, 3 December 1817; J. Henderson, *General View of the Agriculture of the County of Sutherland* (London, 1812), p. 27; Watson, 'The Rise and Development of the Sheep Industry in the Highlands', pp. 9-14.
7. *Inverness Journal*, 31 July 1812, advertisement for the farm of Armadale.
8. Charles St John, *A Tour in Sutherlandshire* (2 vols., London, 1849), I, pp. 241-3.
9. *New Statistical Account*, Farr, p. 79; Lord Teignmouth, *Sketches*, I, p. 39; SCRO, Sutherland Collection, D593/P/24/2/1, George Loch to Duke of Sutherland, 7 June 1861; Loch, *Account of the Improvements*, p. 63.
10. *The Times*, 2 January 1850.
11. T. C. Smout, 'Scotland and England: is Dependency a Symptom or a Cause of Underdevelopment?' *Review*, vol. 3 (1980), p. 616.
12. See Logue, *Popular Disturbances*, pp. 58, 65, 67.
13. See L. Kennedy and T. B. Grainger, *The Present State of the Tenancy of Land in the Highland and Grazing Districts in Great Britain* (London, 1829), p. 95.
14. See press clipping from *The Times*, SCRO, Sutherland Collection, D593/K/1/8/27, 'Great Show of Cheviot Sheep'.
15. NLS, Dep. 313, Sutherland Papers, Box 12, Lewis to Loch, 15 September 1831.
16. See the interesting discussion in R. H. Campbell, Introduction to 1980 edition of Gaskell, *Morvern Transformed*, pp. xiv-xvi.
17. Cf. Colin Heywood, 'The Role of the Peasantry in French Industrialisation, 1815-80', *Economic History Review*, (1981). On the prevalence of mutual support among crofters see SC on Emigration (Scotland) (1841), pp. 24, 100.
18. NLS, Sutherland Papers, III, Box 23, James Loch to Lord Stafford, 7 December 1820.
19. See E. R. Cregeen, 'The Tacksmen and their Successors', *Scottish Studies*, vol. 13 (1969), p. 134.
20. See, for example, John Macinnes, *The Evangelical Movements in the Highlands of Scotland 1699-1800* (Aberdeen, 1951); Mowat, *Easter Ross*, Ch. 5; Kennedy, *Days of the Fathers, passim*; and MacDermid, 'The Religious and Ecclesiastical Life of the North West Highlands 1740-1843', *passim*. The theme has been treated sociologically by Steve Bruce, 'Social Change and Collective Behaviour: the Revival in Eighteenth Century Ross-shire', *British Journal of Sociology*, vol. 34 (1983), pp. 554-72.
21. Hunter, 'Emergence of the Crofting Community', p. 112.
22. Figures cited in *Scottish Notes and Queries*, 3rd series, vol. 5 (1927), p. 163.
23. SCRO, Sutherland Collection, D593/K/1/8/20.
24. SCRO, Sutherland Collection, D593/N/4/1/1C. On the relationship between Presbyterianism and social change in the Highlands, see Smout, *History of the Scottish People*, pp. 358 *et seq.*
25. [Colin Macdonald,] 'Transition in the Highlands of Scotland', *Scottish Review* (July 1888), p. 125; E. P. Thompson, *The Making of the English Working*

Class (New York, 1963), p. 375.

26. Sometimes anti-clearance and anti-patronage feeling was expressed simultaneously in a broadly based attack on a landlord. See Logue, *Popular Disturbances*, pp. 173-4.

27. C. Lesingham-Smith, *Excursions through the Highlands and Islands of Scotland in 1835 and 1836* (London, 1837), p. 68.

28. See the fine study by Cregeen, 'The Tacksmen and their Successors'.

29. NLS, Sutherland Papers, II, Box 25, Countess of Sutherland to Lord Stafford, 1 August 1805.

30. See, for example, the allegations against a factor in June 1819 in Warwick County Record Office, CR229, Malcolm of Poltalloch Papers, NRA DR2, and Richards, *Leviathan*, p. 286.

31. Irvine, *Inquiry*.

32. See Catherine Sinclair, *Scotland and the Scotch* (Edinburgh, 1850), p. 174.

33. Selkirk, *Observations*, pp. lv-lvi.

34. Garnett, *Tour*, I, p. 180.

35. SRO, Loch Muniments, GD268/360, Lady Stafford to Loch, 18 July 1822, 20 July 1822.

36. MacIver evacuated the island of Handa in 1848 and converted it into his own sheep farm. See Hobson, 'Congestion and Depopulation', p. 30; Roderick R. Houston, 'The Impact of Economic Change in Sutherland 1755-1851', unpublished PhD thesis, University of Edinburgh, 1980, p. 120.

37. Reading University Library, Rosehall Memorandum Book 1806-1821, entry for 1814.

38. See below, Ch. 16.

39. Sir John Sinclair, *General View of the Agriculture of the Northern Counties of Scotland* (London, 1795), p. 166. See also Joseph Mitchell, *Reminiscences of my Life in the Highlands* (London, 1883), p. 93.

40. Napier Commission, Q. 25259; see also Q. 168.

41. SCRO, Sutherland Collection, D593/K/1/3/38, MacIver to Loch, 22 March 1850.

42. Ibid., MacIver to Loch, 8 March 1850.

43. Ibid., D593/K/1/3/3a, Fraser to Loch, 24 March 1851.

44. Ibid., MacIver to Loch, 22 April 1851.

45. Ibid., Loch to MacIver, 30 May 1851.

46. George, *Scotland and Scotsmen*, p. 12.

47. *Our Journey to the Hebrides*, p. 128. On pluralism see Hunter, *Crofting Community*, pp. 121-2.

48. This petition is understood to have been saved from a bonfire of South Uist, Gordon Cathcart estate papers and was kindly shown to me by Dr J. L. Campbell of Canna, to whom I am much indebted.

PART FOUR

PATRICK SELLAR

I was long a passionate declaimer against the only reasonable improvement of which the Highlands are susceptible. I mean the removal of the people to fishing ground — to allotments where a man in ten minutes in many seasons may catch as many fish as his family can eat in four and twenty hours — and stocking the interior with sheep. The effects of such arrangements in advancing the estate, the country to which it belongs — the very people who oppose it — in wealth, civilisation, comfort, industry, virtue and happiness, are palpable — ask Sir William Grant what his Grandfather was — a removed tenant! But for the *just* views of the proprietor this great man would have been now in a place like Scottany and at a rent of £5 — following two or three Highland poneys with a cocked bonnet on his head and a Red top to it, and a ragged philiby reaching half way down his leg, afflicted I doubt not by a hereditary itch which all the brimstone in Scotland would be tardy to cure.

Patrick Sellar, June 1815

15
THE MAKING OF A MYTH

Myths and symbols are said to perform complicated and important functions in most societies. Patrick Sellar has been a particularly fruitful symbol in several ways. He has embodied the powerful oral tradition of the popular response to the Highland clearances, and has served as a convenient target upon which much collective anger has been expended. The almost ritualistic invocation of Sellar has even helped to simplify and sharpen the moral issues of the clearances. He has become, even in modern accounts, a demonic figure who personified the forces of cruelty and alien domination against which there appeared to be no defence, either of arms or reason. Pitted against such manifest evil, the Highlanders were simply victims: their consolidation lay in religion and in an undying hatred of the forces which Sellar came to represent. Yet, it may be argued, the repetitive denunciation of Sellar, while it gave vent to the emotional turmoil of the community, also helped to obscure the larger task of confronting the intellectual and political challenge entailed in the economic transformation of the Highlands. The enduring collective hatred which blames Sellar for the destruction of the old Highland society has been an evasion of realities: it has enabled the community at large to escape the responsibility for a workable understanding of the problems of their economy and society. It encouraged them to ignore the task of generating plausible alternatives to sheepfarming and crofting; it encouraged their fatalism rather than an active response to their circumstances. In its extreme form, it was an attitude that paralysed most forms of positive collective action.

Sellar was a useful personification in another way. He was a loquacious, and indeed eloquent, spokesman of the improvement mentality of his day, and offered, furthermore, a consistent and logical contemporary diagnosis of the Highland problem of the nineteenth century. The mind of Patrick Sellar provides a key to

373

the dominant intellectual response to the circumstances in which the clearances were implemented. Sellar's vigorous opinions captured perfectly the liberal philosophy which sanctioned all measures promoting economic efficiency, regardless of the temporary social cost. Sellar's ideology ignored most of the complications inherent in a society run exclusively along market lines. Sellar's mentality was a one-eyed vision of improvement which declined all responsibility for any act of compensation or amelioration. Ultimately it was a philsophy which converted the Highlands into a sheepfarming monoculture, and discouraged the possibility of any more broadly based development for the economy. There was a fatal aridity in Sellar's thinking and outlook which helps to explain how the rulers of the Highlands failed to recruit the co-operation of the people of the north for the reconstruction of the Highlands. Sellar himself was instrumental in the polarisation of Highland society and the alienation of the people. It was inconceivable in such circumstances that there could be a collective assault on the economic and demographic problems which burdened the Highlands for more than a century.

Sellar's career brings together much of the emotional and intellectual response to the clearances. His trial by jury for murder in Inverness in April 1816 was a climacteric moment in the history of the Highlands. It brought into confrontation the conflicting elements in Highland society — the philosophies of the peasantry and the improvers, the power of the law and the rising fear of collective resistance. The episode demonstrated the extent, and the limits, of power of the landlords. It illuminated most of the essentials that constituted the tragedy of the clearances, as well as the origins of a potent myth.

I

Sellar was perhaps the most successful of the great entrepreneurial sheepfarmers who transformed the economic use of the Highlands in the age of the clearances. He was the opportunistic capitalist *par excellence,* fortunate to start his career in pastoral farming in the first decade of the new century, when wool prices were high and rents relatively low. But his success was not based on luck: his technical expertise and business acumen were recognised by everyone in his field; he was also extraordinarily energetic and ambitious. He was enterprising, innovative and always drove a hard bargain; he became the most reliable of tenants and reinvested heavily in the development of the northern sheep economy. The achievement of high productivity in Highland wool production, and the expansion of regional income, owed a great deal to the energy, skill and dedication of the new sheepfarmers, and none could better Sellar's record of economy and output. Nor was his success entirely selfish: he expended much of his time in advising fellow sheepfarming of the best methods he had devised, and in supporting sheepfarmers' associations and markets.[1]

Sellar was the son of a Wesleyan family in lowland Moray. His father, a well-known Elgin solicitor who acted on behalf of a clientele of wealthy landowners, was evidently well versed in the latest improvement thinking. He is known to have developed a remarkable swift method of settling estate populations, on previously unused land, of rationalising the land system, and of raising rents without incurring large capital outlays. His business as factor/solicitor was sufficiently lucrative for him to buy the substantial Westfield estate in 1808; with the help of his son Patrick he converted it into a model of efficiency. It eventually yielded capital for investment in sheepfarming in Sutherland though the younger Sellar was already a considerable capitalist before he inherited this wealth.

Patrick Sellar was educated at Edinburgh University during the ascendancy of Dugald Stewart. He trained for a legal career, joined his father's practice in Elgin and quickly rose to the position of Procurator-Fiscal. In 1809 he joined a consortium of businessmen who developed commercial plans for expanding trade in the northeast of Scotland. They were led by another energetic agricultural improver, William Young, also from Moray. Sellar and Young joined forces and came to the opinion that Sutherland presented almost unlimited scope for improvement. To them it was like a colony ripe for exploitation, an entirely new field for enterprise. The story of the Sutherland connection is now familiar. The two Moraymen began to exert a dominant sway over the Sutherland family, already committed to radical change on its vast estate. They became tenants of an arable farm at Culmaily in 1809, and soon after Young was installed as commissioner of the Sutherland estate, with Sellar acting as his right-hand man. Between them they gained a considerable degree of control over the design and implementation of the economic plan for the estate. Most important of

all, the Moray speculators helped to persuade the noble proprietors that an expanding coastal economy could be established
on a foundation of fishing and diversified industrial activity. Thus
evolved the Sutherland experiment in social and economic
engineering: the clearance of the inhabitants of the straths to the
coasts where they were intended to engage in new and improved
modes of subsistence. The interior tracts would be turned over to
sheep; rents would rise with productivity, the people would no
longer be susceptible to periodic famine, nor would the landlord be
liable for expensive relief measures. These were the assumptions in
the planners' minds.

Sellar's personal role in these great changes was twofold.
Although he began as adviser, he soon was taken into employment
as a factor to the Sutherland family, responsible to Young; but he
also emerged as a sheepfarmer. In December 1813, apparently
without much premeditation, he decided to bid for the lease of a
great deal of Strathnaver which was marked out for the clearance
of its relatively dense population. Within ten days of this successful
negotiation Sellar issued notices to quit to various groups of
tenants in Strathnaver. Meanwhile his factorial duties continued.
They were defined thus:

> to collect rents, keep accounts of the expenditure, pay attention
> to the various rights of the tenants, to their fulfilment of the
> conditions in their Tacks, to enforcing the laws for preserving
> the plantations and the Game, transactions with Ministers,
> Schoolmasters, farming Tacks and other writings.[2]

For almost a decade Patrick Sellar, as sheepfarmer and factor, was
the most visible instrument of the policy of clearance. His estate
duties, as well as his interests as a sheepfarmer, brought him into
direct confrontation with the common people of the country. For
not only did Sellar collect their rents, he was responsible for the
small detail of estate management including game-keeping; most
important, he was responsible for their removal and, if necessary,
their eviction. He personally gained most from the prompt and
rigorous execution of estate policy.

In 1814-16, in the middle of these momentous events, the confrontation between Sellar and the people of Sutherland broke into
open and indeed sensational conflict. Sellar was eventually accused
of murder and tried before a jury at Inverness in April 1816. The

trial, as will be argued below, represented not only an elaborate assault on the sheepfarmer but also a dangerous threat to the entire policy of clearance.

Sellar, however, was acquitted and, once he became disengaged from the Sutherland management in 1818, spent the rest of his life in sheepfarming. By the early 1840s he farmed land in three counties. He paid a rent of £2,200 to the Duke of Sutherland alone, and he invested almost £30,000 in the purchase of the Ardtonish estate in Argyll, one of the ancient seats of the Lords of the Isles. He thus became a laird in his own rights, and adopted the expensive proprietorial habits which he considered appropriate to his newly elevated position. Sellar was also ambitious for his family and his descendants achieved considerable respectability in Victorian society. His nine children became a veritable dynasty of talented and aspiring Sellars who made their mark in the late nineteenth century: of his seven sons, four were prominent merchants in Liverpool, London and Melbourne, one succeeded him as a great sheepfarmer in the Highlands, one represented Partick in the House of Commons, and another became a Professor of Humanity and wrote books on Roman poets. An Australian scion celebrated their collective achievement in a volume published in Melbourne in 1910.[3] 'I have studied to act the part of an industrious honest man and a good subject,' Sellar once wrote; he regarded himself as a self-made man in whose life virtue and industry had been properly rewarded. On his own terms Patrick Sellar was a resounding success.

The entire career was, of course, always clouded by the sensation of his trial in 1816, and neither he nor his descendants were able to disperse the infamy that has attached so decisively to his name. The resilience of this tradition of Sellar in the history of the Highland clearances is partly to be accounted for by the scale and intensity of the conflict over his trial, partly by the manner of the man himself, and partly also by the utility of the myth in subsequent Highland thought. Each of these elements may be treated in turn.

II

The trial of Sellar in April 1816 was the climax of a series of events which stretched back to 1813 and which may be interpreted as the most elaborate and co-ordinated response mounted by any body of the common people during the clearances. There was a paranoid side to Sellar's personality which may have led him to exaggerate the extent of the conspiracy, but there can be no doubt that the process by which he was brought before the law required an unprecedented degree of planning, solidarity and concerted action. The campaign against Patrick Sellar was a form of social protest which fits uncomfortably in the received models of pre-industrial crowd behaviour.

The events may be stated briefly. In September 1813 Sellar had finished his collection of the rents from ten parishes on the Sutherland estate. It was the culmination of a major effort to regularise the estate accounts and press for the payment of all arrears, large and small. He pursued backsliders with rigour and generally sought to impose social control on the estate population which, in both Kildonan and Assynt, was already turbulent. He agreed with William Young that they should bring 'rogues of every description to punishment ... if sheep-stealers are convicted we shall be able to rid the country of some very bad characters'.[4] In December 1813 he made his successful bid (against the competition of the resident tenantry) for Strathnaver, which he planned as a sheep farm. The minister for the parish explained the legal documents to the people in Gaelic: they would be cleared at Whitsun 1814.

In the intervening months Sellar added to his reputation as the hard man of Sutherland, collecting rents and issuing notices of removal, and accepting no excuses. There can be no doubt that he regarded the entire business of estate administration as a contest between the factors and the people.[5] In May 1814 the great clearance of Strathnaver was in frenetic process: within 14 days more than 430 families were removed from Strathnaver, many to be resettled at Brora on the coast, where they were expected to become fisherfolk. 'They require to be thoroughly brought to the coast where industry will pay,' said Sellar, 'and to be *convinced* that they *must* worship industry or starve.'[6] Sellar was in the very thick of the removals, directing a team of assistants and ensuring the clearance of land which he himself would occupy as sheep-farmer.

Six weeks elapsed before some of the cleared tenants of Strathnaver raised a petition to the Stafford family complaining that Sellar had illegally demolished their houses[7] and set fire to their heaths, and complained also that he had given insufficient notice of removal. There was no allegation of murder. The petition was transmitted by the Sheriff Substitute, Robert Mackid, and received by the Stafford family, who were not surprised because they had already received many complaints about Sellar's harshness towards the people. The Stafford family urged the Sheriff Deputy, George Cranstoun, to investigate the complaints and 'award what pecuniary damages he might see due, after a full investigation', a process in which Sellar concurred. Cranstoun, absent in Edinburgh, directed Mackid to undertake the precognition (i.e. a preliminary examination of witnesses) in the latter months of 1814. The upshot of this inquiry is obscure, but it is known that it did not address any question of murder.[8]

Only in February 1815 (ten months after the events) did a second, and vastly more serious, set of allegations emerge. A new petition was generated in which it was claimed that Sellar had caused the death of unspecified persons during the 1814 removals — that he had fired buildings in which there were aged and bedridden people who, though they managed to escape the flames, died a few days later in an outhouse, caused by 'the affright, precipitancy and circumstances of such a removal'. These allegations were again communicated to the Stafford family by Robert Mackid who, from 23 to 25 March 1815, conducted a second precognition into the allegations of murder.[9]

Mackid's precognition required the examination of a large number of witnesses from among the number who had been cleared from Strathnaver. The investigations encouraged the common people to organise a subscription to assist in the effective prosecution of the sheepfarmer. There can be no doubt that a considerable communal effort was exerted; equally the Stafford family raised no hand to impede the progress of the case. Moreover the entire events were efficiently communicated, in lurid detail, to a radical newspaper in London, the *Military Register*, which brought the episode to attention of the government and the nation.

Many of the witnesses before Mackid's precognition spoke no English and the report of their testimony was subject to Mackid's own interpretation. According to the *Military Register*, the people of Strathnaver proved their case beyond any doubt; a list of atrocities was produced and the names of seven victims of Sellar's evictions were detailed. Sellar was alleged to have set fire to the houses, property and food stores of the people and to have caused the deaths of three of the inhabitants. The scorched blanket of one of the people, Margaret Mackay, was brought before Mackid's proceedings. '*The Sherriff was so affected by the detail that he fainted in court, overpowered by his feelings.*' Mackid moved swiftly after the precognition — he immediately arrested Sellar and incarcerated him in the felon's side of the county gaol at Dornoch. A very large bail was tendered but Mackid refused it; it was reported that there was great rejoicing among the people of Dornoch.[10] Mackid wrote to Lord Stafford that 'a more numerous catalogue of crimes, perpetrated by an individual has seldom disgraced any country, or sullied the pages of a precognition in Scotland!!!'[11]

The date of Sellar's release from the Dornoch gaol is unrecorded but he remained there for long enough to suffer intense distress and a feeling of profound humiliation. His emotional state was further exacerbated when a second precognition, this time in the hands of George Cranstoun in September 1815, found enough corroboration of Mackid's previous unsatisfactory and irregular inquiry to confirm that there was a case against Sellar. Moreover, the Rev. David Mackenzie (who has sometimes been regarded as a 'quisling' minister in the pocket of the Stafford family) pointedly refused to deny 'the circumstances regarding Mr Sellar since they have a foundation, however highly exaggerated'.[12] Sellar was not actually brought to trial at Inverness until April 1816, eleven months after Mackid's second precognition.

From the moment of his arrest until his acquittal Sellar sustained a level of intense indignation; he poured out his shock and exasperation to the Stafford family and the principal agent, James Loch. Hotly and repeatedly he contended that there was a widely based campaign against him, worked up by Mackid and fellow intriguers who had plotted to ruin Sellar and to break the entire clearance policy. Mackid, he asserted, was his sworn enemy because Sellar had caught him poaching in 1813, while Mackid had made counter-allegations that Sellar had misappropriated estate rents and wished to take Mackid's legal position as Sheriff Substitute. Mackid, Sellar alleged, had manipulated the people to attend his precognition, and had fabricated or distorted their testimonies. In private correspondence Sellar acknowledged that he had experienced difficulty in budging the people from his farm in Strathnaver and that fire had been used to destroy the house of a recalcitrant tinker — the man Chisholm, whom he described as a bigamist, a squatter and a sheep thief. Sellar had given strict orders that any infirm people cleared be left undisturbed in their houses. He claimed that a sick woman, named in the homicide charge against him, had actually died later, in the summer, of old age and had been 'buryed after the manner of the country'.[13]

The charges against him, said Sellar, were implausible on two counts. First, the delay between the alleged commission of the crime and the publication of the charges rendered the process farcical: it was ludicrous to think that twelve months would elapse before a prosecution was initiated. Second, there could be no motive. As Sellar said to Loch in October 1815:

Can you believe my good sir, that I, a person not ... escaped from a madhouse, should deliberately, in open day, by means of an officer who has a wife and family, with three witnesses *called to attest his process*, burn a house with a woman in it! or that the officer should do so, *instead* of ejecting the tenant — the said tenant and woman being persons of whom we have no felonious intent — no malice or ill-will![14]

III

Nothing could have been better designed to draw public attention to protests against the clearance than a trial for murder of one of the leading sheepfarmers of the day. The lairds were undoubtedly fearful that recurrent commotion in the north would provoke demands in Parliament for an inquiry. Reports of the precognition filtered to London in a garbled form: some declared that Sellar had been found guilty of homicide and other atrocities even before the trial had occurred. The trial of Patrick Sellar was unquestionably a vital moment in the progress of the clearances.

The internal correspondence of the Sutherland estate at the time before the trial illuminates not only the character and reputation of Sellar but also the degree of support that he received from his masters. James Loch, for instance, spoke of Sellar's 'hurried and improvident ejection of the people'. William Young testified to Sellar's great unpopularity among the people; he had many enemies and should have 'steered a middle course' during the clearances in Strathnaver. Loch, who had on many occasions restrained the sheepfarmer's sarcasm and arrogance towards the people, agreed that he had made 'many enemies ... who will make the most of any act of hasty imprudence which he may have committed'. Although Loch could not believe Sellar guilty of murder,[15] the Sutherland estate management was noticeably cool towards Sellar during the period before the trial. If Sellar was to be found guilty they had no wish to be implicated; nor did they wish to be involved in any influence upon the course of justice. Sellar seems to have received little aid. James Loch was generally uncooperative and not particularly encouraging; he took great pains to make it clear that Sellar had acted in his capacity as tenant, not as under-agent, during the Strathnaver removals. The *Military Register* went so far as to commend Lady Stafford for refusing to support Sellar[16] and despite subsequent allegations to the contrary,[17] Sellar appears to have been left to his fate. It was at one stage suggested to Sellar that popular feeling was so inflamed against him that he would be well-advised to press for a trial in Edinburgh rather than in Inverness.[18]

The result of the Inverness trial was in no sense a foregone conclusion. Representatives of the Stafford family were conspicuously absent from the court, though close contacts were kept with the proceedings. A legal adviser to the family remarked that 'I look with anxiety to the issue of the trial,' for, though he considered the charge against Sellar was exaggerated, he nevertheless feared that his conduct may have been culpably harsh.[19]

IV

The trial lasted for 15 hours. The only detailed account of the proceedings was reconstructed from the notes of Robertson, Sellar's junior counsel; it was issued as a pamphlet and was expressly designed to counter the 'clamouring of the disaffected', particularly in the *Military Register*.[20] The jury was composed of eight landed proprietors, three or four large tacksmen or farmers, two merchants and a lawyer. There were many allegations of corruption and undue influence. It was claimed, also, that Sellar had possessed the best legal assistance, and was 'backed by all the influence of the family of Sutherland', and that the evidence of some of the principal witnesses had been refused. It was alleged also that 'all the exculpatory witnesses brought from Strathnava [sic] were sumptuously entertained at Sellar's House of Culmaily on their way to the trial'. Victimisation and bribery were claimed to have been employed with the assistance of 'copious libations of whisky'. It was pointed out that Lord Pitmilly, who presided over the trial, was the brother of Lady Stafford's law agent in Edinburgh.[21] Sellar himself had similar but opposite doubts about Pitmilly because he was connected by his brother with the influences in Sutherland which 'did at the first foster and bring forward this and similar oppressions against me'.[22]

The crucial element in the trial was the fate of the old woman who had been in William Chisholm's house when it was set on fire by the eviction party, and which caused her death. Sellar's defence was that Chisholm was properly evicted by the Sheriff's officers, who had the correct legal warrants. The house had actually been unroofed before Sellar himself arrived at the spot. Sellar had been told about the old woman remaining on the premises and Chisholm's resolve to reoccupy the house. Sellar had ordered that Chisholm be given 6s for the roof timber, and gave instructions that the rest was to be burned, which was done by the local people. The old woman, he claimed, was already relocated in a nearby byre, some 30 yards from the burning house. The entire case hinged on the relative credibility of the opposing sets of witnesses,[23] on the legality of Mackid's proceedings, and on the character of the accused. In his summing up, Pitmilly stressed that Sellar appeared to have acted with humanity in regard to the sick; that various testimonials presented established his 'humanity of disposition'; and that the legality of the actual removals was not in any doubt. The jury had to decide eventually between the contradictory records of the prosecution and defence witnesses.

The verdict was unambiguous: Sellar was acquitted on all charges. Pitmilly addressed Sellar. It was about 1.00 a.m. and the court room was packed. The judge spoke:

> Mr. Sellar, it is now my duty to dismiss you from the bar; and you have the satisfaction of thinking, that you are discharged by the unanimous opinion of the Jury and the Court. I am sure that, although your feelings must have been agitated, you cannot regret that this trial took place, and I am hopeful it will have due effect on the minds of the country, which have been so much and so improperly agitated.[24]

After the trial, Sellar's senior counsel, in triumph, reported that the happy result 'was calculated to display the arrangements on the

Sutherland Estate and Sellar's own conduct for moderation and humanity in the removal of the people in the most favourable light'. Lady Stafford's legal adviser reported that

> in short, nothing can be more complete than Sellar's exculpation and Mackid is made as black as possible. The trial has had an amazing effect in changing the Current of prejudice which ran against Sellar and has turned out a fortunate Circumstance for him contrary to the most sanguine expectations of his best friends. It lasted 14 hours. Sellar bore up very well but when the Verdict of Acquittal was pronounced, he burst into tears which had a great effect on the Audience.[25]

James Loch and the Stafford family were jubilant. Loch wrote to Sellar that 'such a termination was equally essential for the future progress and prosperity of Sutherland as it was for your comfort and happiness ... I went to Cleveland House where I found everyone most happy'.

V

Sellar's acquittal at Inverness has been questioned on many occasions and the folklore of the Highlands, including modern fiction, has uniformly assumed that the sheepfarmer was guilty. Many writers have doubted that a jury and judge of Sellar's own class could have considered the case impartially. The controversy flared up on many occasions after the trial; Sellar was persecuted throughout his life and his sons were unable to remove the taint. Sellar continues to be found guilty by many historians, though Dr Phillip Gaskell has warned of 'the absurdity of the Sellar folk-lore which persists in Scotland', and suggests that the trial report offers evidence that a fair trial was conducted by Pitmilly.[26]

Amid so much controversy only a few propositions stand with much certainty. It is impossible to say whether Sellar or his adversaries lied. Sellar himself was certainly an objectionable and provocative man; he dislocated the life of the people of Strathnaver in a way which was crude and inhumane. The accommodation for the people he removed from the interior to the coast was not ready until a matter of days before their forced ejection. There is no doubt either that Sellar had set fire to at least one house in the strath. Equally certain is the fact of Robert Mackid's long-standing feud with Sellar; Mackid's legal proceedings against Sellar had been highly irregular. It is no less certain that the Strathnaver people had been incited to opposition by skilful propaganda, and there was indeed a popular conspiracy to overturn Sellar and the policy he represented. In the trial itself many witnesses examined in the precognitions were not called; the language problem created great difficulties; moreover, given its provenance, complete reliance cannot be placed upon the only surviving report of the trial.

The physical circumstances of the 1814 clearances may also be considered. The forced resettlement of 430 families was bound to create cases of appalling hardship. Evicting octogenarians and nonagenarians, even in spring, was likely to accelerate their death, even if they were not manhandled. Sellar's closest associates believed that he was capable of culpable harshness in the use of his authority. There was a striking contrast between the high praise of Sellar's character presented to the jury at the trial of 1816 and the candid reports on the man in private estate correspondence.

Nevertheless, balancing the probabilities, it is difficult to imagine this pedantic, calculating man committing acts of pointless, sadistic cruelty against the Kildonan peasantry. For their part, the people abominated the clearance system. They were on the edge of hysteria and violence. In the belief that they could stop the clearances it is possible that they were persuaded to inflate their complaints into charges of homicide against the hated Sellar. They had been provoked by the man's arrogance. But their action was also the consequence of an economic policy that entailed the instant transformation of an ancient way of life.

VI

The aftermath of the trial produced further light on the contest that had been fought, and gave more evidence of Sellar's standing in Highland society. Of the popular reaction to Sellar's acquittal in Sutherland, little is known. During the trial there were a few episodes of apparent protest: the throats of twenty of Sellar's sheep were slit open, as was that of Lady Stafford's prize Tibetan goat. Changes in the management of the estate, the abatement of rent by 25 per cent, and the descent of near-famine conditions may have dampened any further expression of fury among the people.

Resistance after the Sellar affair tended to be less co-ordinated and therefore less threatening to the managers of the Sutherland clearances.[27]

Sellar's post-trial euphoria rapidly gave way to thoughts of retribution against his defeated assailants. Alluding to the crisis of authority in the Highlands, and to the long-standing conspiracy against himself, he told the Stafford family that they should not forget that the day had been appointed, by the conspirators, 'for driving every South countryman out of the country'. 'It occurs to me to be very essential', he wrote, 'to find out and punish the leaders of the people.' Sellar's determination was strengthened by renewed libels against him appearing in the *Military Register.* The people 'have *insinuated* and *sneaked* and *whispered* calumnies through every indirect channel', he complained, and it was time that the lies were finally broken. The troublemakers must be rooted out: 'now is the happy hour to give them battle'.

The triumphant sheepfarmer directed his main attack against Robert Mackid, whom he intended to ruin financially and publicly, and hound out of the county of Sutherland. He began legal proceedings, but in September 1817, on the advice of James Loch, decided to settle with Mackid without extracting his pound of flesh.

> I found the miserable man involved in such difficulties on all hands, and his family of I believe 9 or 10 young children so certainly about to be beggars by my bringing him to Trial, that I was well pleased to wash my hands of them.

Instead Sellar obtained a letter of confession from Mackid to the effect that the precognition of 1815 had been full of misstatements and that he was 'fully ashamed' of what he had done. Mackid said, 'From the aspersions thrown on your character I trust you need not doubt that you are already full acquitted in the Eyes of the World.' He pleaded with Sellar, now that he had resigned his office of Sheriff Substitute of Sutherland, not to destroy his 'innocent family' by pressing a legal case for damages against him. It was a document of almost total abasement. Sellar replied that since Mackid 'is no longer possessed of the power illegally to deprive a British subject of his liberty and otherwise to oppress him under the form of law', he would take pity on Mackid's family and drop his suit. Mackid paid Sellar £200 and met Sellar's costs.[28]

Mackid was effectively destroyed. In answer to all later critics, Sellar was always able to present Mackid's confession as complete proof of his own innocence. The fact that Mackid had written the letter under threat of financial ruin tended to weaken its impact.[29]

As for the appointment of a new Sheriff in Sutherland, Sellar again left no room for doubt about his own feelings: it was of 'great consequences that our new Sheriff ... be no "Gael" nor "Mac" — But a plain, honest, industrious *South* country man'. It was a principle which, he was convinced, ought also to apply to all 'Parsons and Schoolmasters'.[30] Sellar's aversion to native Highlanders was an extreme example of a common attitude among improvement landlords and factors.

There was a second sequel to the trial of Patrick Sellar. While the apparatus of the law was being reconstructed in the county, the Sutherland estate administration itself underwent radical transformation. The regime of William Young and Patrick Sellar was swept away: both men resigned under pressure from their employer. The Sutherland family distanced itself from Sellar in particular. Even before the Inverness trial Sellar had been in bad odour with its commissioner, James Loch. He remarked that the sheepfarmer had a 'quick, sneering, biting way of saying good things in the execution of his duty which I do not think has made him popular with anybody whether in the management of affairs or otherwise'.[31] Only a few months later Loch described Sellar as 'a faithful and zealous person'.[32] Nevertheless Loch advised him to take care to

> avoid a certain ironical mode of expression, which does you more mischief than you are aware of ... believe me the number of enemies a man makes by doing his duty steadily and honestly are few, the mode of doing it however makes the case very differently.[33]

In May 1816, soon after the trial, Loch again recommended Sellar to avoid taunting the people, and to use moderate language in order to establish a new relationship with the inhabitants of the estate. Loch was clearly dissatisfied with Sellar's attitudes and methods in the management of the Sutherland estate and he attributed much of the unpopularity to Sellar's 'satirical turn which does him so much harm'.[34]

Loch's opinion of Sellar was shared by Lady Stafford. From the beginning she had regarded him as a clever writer and accountant, but he was over-zealous and exceeded his instructions; he was excessively ambitious and lacked judgement; he was too sharp, 'full of law Quirks' and pedantry; his general strictness kept the common people in a state of tension. Another estate adviser remarked decisively that

> whereas taste, temper, or feeling is required, or even ordinary discretion, he is deficient beyond what I ever met in any man, so that I don't know one in the whole circle of my acquaintance so ill-calculated as him to fill the office of a Factor and in such a County as Sutherland.

In a final scathing confidential indictment Loch said that Sellar possessed 'less discrimination that it is easy to believe [and] was really guilty of many very oppressive and cruel acts'.[35]

Sellar's career as a factor and confidant to the Stafford family was ended. The old management was dislodged and a new agency was established which was more directly answerable to Loch. Sellar was thereafter consigned to sheepfarming, and though he continued to be consulted on technical and agricultural matters of policy, there was never again any cordiality in the relationship. Occasionally outright hostility broke forth, but the mutually lucrative commercial arrangement was maintained for the rest of his life.

Perhaps most significant was the role which the Stafford family now attributed to Sellar. He was held responsible for the collapse of good relations between landlord and people during the transformation of the estate economy. In Loch's view Sellar's factorship had been an unmitigated disaster, and he was blamed for much of the antagonism and social dislocation that attended the early clearances in Sutherland. Sellar, he said, had caused 'much injury ... in disposing the minds of the people against all reasonable change'. The former sheepfarmer had become the scapegoat for the social consequences of the clearances. Indeed, by promoting this diagnosis of the course of events, the Sutherland managers were implicitly concurring in much of the simplifying folklore that flowed out of the Highland clearances. They were prepared to attribute at least part of the failure of landlord policies to the adverse personality of a single factor. It became a substitute for a more thorough and realistic construction of events during the clearances.[36] Moreover, the repeated and exhaustive analysis of Sellar's character by his colleagues and his employers yielded a conclusion that Sellar was indeed capable of cruelty and even inhumanity towards the people. The mythology of Patrick Sellar had at least some basis in contemporary opinion, even from the side of the landlord.

Most extraordinary of all, Sellar seems to have understood at least part of his own psychological weakness. Sometimes, amid a great flow of words and introspection, he penetrated to the very centre of his own personality. He was prepared to concede that his approach to the business of estate management in the Highlands was not necessarily appropriate. He once wrote:

> I fear I have been bred to too much precision and possess too much keenness of temper to be so useful in my office [as factor] as I ought and as I sincerely wish to be. A man less anxious might better suit the situation and the nature of the people.[37]

It was a self-judgement with which few of his colleagues would disagree.

Outcast though he was, Sellar nevertheless personified the ruling perception of the needs of Highland society. Extreme though his views patently were, he nevertheless expressed the basic assumptions and principles which dominated the economic and social framework which was imposed upon the Highlands in the age of the clearances. The next chapter explores the nature of that understanding.

Notes

1. This section draws upon Richards, 'The Mind of Patrick Sellar'. In her important paper 'The Highland Clearances', Rosalind Mitchison discusses at length 'the special heat that attaches to the clearances, to the neglect of other wrongs of the propertyless'. She identifies 'the deep and continuing feeling of the people involved and of their descendants' as a central historical question in its own right.

2. NLS, Sutherland Papers, EM Box 7, Document of Agreement between the most Noble the Marquess and Marchioness of Stafford ... and ... Young ... and Sellar, *c.* 1810.

3. P. L. Selkirk, *The Langs of Selkirk* (Melbourne, 1910).

4. SCRO, Sutherland Collection, D593/K, Young to Sellar, 1 September 1813.

5. Ibid., Sellar to Young, 25 March 1813, Young to Loch, 27 March 1813, Patrick Sellar, 'Statement by Patrick Sellar, Sometime Factor to the Earldom of

Sutherland, in Answer to Certain Misrepresentations, Concerning his Conduct, while he Held the Above mentioned Situation', unpublished pamphlet, 1825; copy in SCRO, p. 3.

6. Quoted in Richards, *Leviathan*, p. 184.

7. It was not unusual for houses to be destroyed during evictions or changes of lease. It prevented reoccupation and the buildings had no value to the sheepfarmers. As the *Farmer's Magazine*, reported in May 1806, p. 229, 'the huts of the aborigines [*sic*] farmers can be of little or no use to the new tenant'.

8. Adam, *Sutherland Estate Management*, II, pp. 208, 236.

9. *Military Register*, 5 April, 1815.

10. *Military Register*, 28 June 1815; cf. Donald Macleod, *History of the Destitution in Sutherlandshire* (Edinburgh, 1841), p. 12.

11. SCRO, Sutherland Collection, D593/K, Cranstoun to Loch, 7 August 1815, Gower to Loch, 29 September 1815, Mackenzie to Loch, 25 August 1815, Sellar to Loch, 11 September 1815, 13 September 1815.

12. Quoted in Richards, *Leviathan*, p. 189.

13. SCRO, Sutherland Collection, D593/K, Sellar to Loch, 15 June 1815, 28 June 1815; Adam, *Sutherland Estate Management*, II, p. 240.

14. SCRO, Sutherland Collection, D593/K, Sellar to Lady Stafford, 17 July 1815, Sellar to Loch, 14 September 1815, 16 October 1815.

15. Ibid., Young to Loch, 15 June 1815.

16. *Military Register*, 4 October 1815, but see 15 May 1816. SCRO, Sutherland Collection, D593/K, Sellar to Lady Stafford, 1 July 1815.

17. For example, in June 1817 David Stewart of Garth told Colonel David MacPherson of Cluny, with reference to Lady Stafford:

> You will be astonished to learn that when her old and faithful adherents, who had given her such repeated proofs of their attachment, were cruelly oppressed by a factor, that she refused to listen to their complaints, and when that factor was tried for his life on charges of cruelty, oppression and murder, it is most unaccountable that her ladyship should exert all her influence to screen him from the punishment which he so richly deserved. (quoted in 'More about Sellar and the Sutherland Clearances', *Celtic Magazine*, vol. 9 (1884), p. 489)

18. Adam, *Sutherland Estate Management*, II, p. 279.

19. SCRO, Sutherland Collection, D593/K, Mackenzie to Loch, 21 April 1816.

20. Mackenzie, *The Trial of Patrick Sellar.*

21. *Military Register*, 15 May 1816, 15 July 1816, 20 July 1816; cf. 28 July 1819.

22. Adam, *Sutherland Estate Management*, I, p. 211, n. 1.

23. Thomas Sellar, *The Sutherland Evictions of 1814* (London, 1883), p. 81.

24. Mackenzie, *The Trial of Patrick Sellar*, p. 49.

25. Adam, *Sutherland Estate Management*, II, p. 279.

26. J. S. Blackie, *Altavona* (Edinburgh, 1882), Dialogue V; Sellar, *Sutherland Evictions*, Appendix, p. xcix; NLS, MS 2644, fo. iii; Gaskell, *Morvern Transformed*, pp. 38-40.

27. SCRO, Sutherland Collection, D593/K, Sellar to Loch, 7 May 1816, 25 May 1816, Sellar to Lady Stafford, 2 June 1816; *Military Register*, 5 June 1816.

28. SCRO, Sutherland Collection, D593/K, Sellar to Grant, 23 September 1817, Sellar to Loch, 24 September 1817, Lady Stafford to Loch, 9 October 1817.

29. The letter is printed in Sellar, *Sutherland Evictions*, Appendix. Also SRO, GD136/2661.

30. SCRO, Sutherland Collection, D593/K, Sellar to Loch 31 May 1816.

31. Ibid., Loch to Adam, 10 June 1815, Loch to Young, 9 June 1815.

32. Ibid., Loch to Lord Stafford, 14 August 1815.

33. Ibid., Loch to Sellar, 26 October 1815.

34. Ibid., Loch to Sellar, 15 May 1816, Loch to Grant, 8 June 1816.

35. Adam, *Sutherland Estate Management*, II, pp. 152-3, 203, 229.

36. SCRO, Sutherland Collection, D593/K, Mackenzie to Loch, 19 October 1816, Loch to Lady Stafford, 3 October 1816.

37. Ibid., Sellar to Loch, 13 October 1815.

16
THE TYRANNY OF DOGMA

I

Too arrogant, even brutal, for estate management, Patrick Sellar was effectively dismissed from the service of the Sutherland family,[1] but he was too valuable a sheepfarmer to lose as a tenant, and in any case the Sutherland estate was already contracted to him for the lease of further sheeplands to be cleared in 1817. Having recently inherited substantial property, he was keener than ever to expand his operations in Sutherland. However, the Sutherland family were now wary of his methods. Lady Stafford remarked that 'as Sellar is so strict a lawyer ... he will adhere to the letter of any promise from us [therefore] we must not give him any promise of entry ... unless sure of being able to keep to it' — her implication being that he would insist upon entry to the lands even if it entailed cruelty to the people involved in the removals. Lady Stafford also noted that Sellar 'exaggerates in everything relating to them [i.e. the common people], and by beginning in that line he has probably drawn upon himself more attacks from them than he would otherwise have had'. She also commented (in November 1818) that 'Sellar is too sly and refining upon his plans by concealing half'.[2]

Although his commercial and technical advice was sought, and although he became one of the richest men in the north, Sellar was isolated from good society in the county. His phenomenal success in sheepfarming gave him little social prestige in Sutherland and probably explains why he established himself in a certain proprietorial style at Morvern in Argyll. His relations with the Sutherland family were cool and professional, sometimes even hostile. He nursed the idea that his role in the financial success of the estate economy had not been recognised. He undoubtedly saw himself as the instrument of progress and efficiency, and an important figure in the extension of modern business practice to the Highlands. He considered that the sheepfarmers, who had vastly increased the value of the Highlands by their energy, example, intelligence and capital, were not accorded sufficient credit for their efforts.

Sellar's career as a sheepfarmer stretched across four decades marked by considerable commercial difficulty until the recovery of the early 1840s. He conducted a continuous and argumentative correspondence to extract the best terms from his landlord. In 1822, for instance, Sellar complained bitterly of the fallen wool prices and suggested that he deserved a temporary rent reduction — after all, he pointed out, he was the tenant 'who is most extensively embarked on his own capital and on that for which I pay his Lordship $6\frac{1}{2}$ per cent interest per annum' (Sellar had borrowed £1,500 from Lord Stafford). He asked plaintively that the estate 'do not insist on the ruin of my wife and children' — and he received some accommodation. Other problems were less easily settled. In 1836, for instance, Sellar's hostility to the estate agents surfaced over questions of policy on muir-burning and deer forests. He suggested that many of the estate officers were not trustworthy, and were prejudiced against him; in some cases, he maintained, they were 'men who have been, themselves, dispossessed to make room for sheep, or the descendents and relatives of men so situated'.

Recurrent irritations continued. The estate administrators, especially James Loch, were never happy with the size of Sellar's leases. In the late 1840s thought was given to the idea of breaking up the larger sheep farms on the estate — partly to create a 'middle class' of occupiers, partly to mollify public opinion. Sellar had a ready answer in his own case — he paid £2,200 a year to the Duke of Sutherland, and he paid it regularly — if his lands were split this would prove much more difficult. He wrote:

> If your Grace succeeded in taking it out of our frugal management to put it under 'hand-loom' conduct [i.e. of smaller occupiers], at the very point of time when the profession is discovering the impossibility of competing successfully against the untaxed growers of foreign provisions unless on the factory system, you would greatly lose by doing so.

The Duke conceded the point, but replied that there were 'other considerations ... involved in this concern' beyond the 'pecuniary point of view'. Sellar had not only neglected 'the improvement of the condition of the people' but was an absentee, one of the 'monopoly of ... a few rich capitalists' in Sutherland who had contributed little to its social leadership. The Duke lectured Sellar:

> you must consider how essential it is for the good of the country to have resident Gentlemen to act as Magistrates, to give assistance in supporting the poor, in attending to the concerns of those who require their assistance in a thousand ways, and not merely to attend to private affairs for their own immediate gain.

As a sheepfarmer he was regarded as an unqualified commercial success; but the social consequences of Patrick Sellar were no less evident to the second Duke and his aides whose minds were exercised in ways of erasing the shadow of past misadventures in estate planning.[3]

It is important to emphasise the persistent ambivalence which marked the relationship between Sellar and the Sutherland estate during these decades. It defines the limits of the influence of his ideas and attitudes. Sellar's commercial success and his excellent record of rent payment had to be set against his continuing unpopularity, his crude ambition and his negative attitude to community-building on the estate. Although his opinion on agricultural matters was genuinely valued, even here he was a prickly and acrimonious correspondent, and small disagreements with James Loch over matters of estate policy left him disproportionately hurt and indignant.

II

What Sellar may have been denied in ordinary social intercourse in Sutherland was offset by a large, eloquent and continuous correspondence with his landlord, his agents, political economists, politicians, the newspapers and agriculturalists. He had a hard analytic mind, and a trenchant literary style, which he employed unceasingly to advocate the absolute necessity of rational progress. His inspirations were the Bible, and, most of all, the political economists; he quoted Adam Smith, Ricardo and Malthus as though they possessed divine authority. While many of his contemporaries drew back from the full rigour of his logic, he expressed with great clarity the fundamental assumptions on which the Highland economy had been transformed in the age of improvement. His was the *laissez-faire* mind *par excellence* and it was this philosophy which determined the direction of the Highland economy throughout the nineteenth century until the Crofters Act of 1886.

Sellar's own intellectual development seems to have paralleled the evolution of northern landlords' thinking on the Highland question. In the first decade of the century he was an apostle of 'developmental' improvement, heavy investment in construction and agricultural reclamation, and the dense settlement of small tenants on moorlands. At that stage, in his own recollection, he was entirely opposed to the clearance system, but his exposure to the realities of 'feudalism' and congestion on introduction to Sutherland converted him to the opposite view in about 1810. Thereafter he believed that political economy and common sense demanded the rapid transformation of land use — the hills and the interior straths were for sheep; the people must be cleared to the coasts, and they must depend exclusively on fishing for their future livelihood. Any compromise on this issue, he believed, would render the resettlement programme self-defeating. If the people were unable to make a living at fishing then there was little hope for them. He insisted that sheepfarming in the Highlands was logical, inevitable and, on individual and national criteria, truly beneficial. He wrote in 1820 that 'if the country goes on at the rate it has done during the last century, every part of the Highlands will assuredly be put under stock, although General Stewart ... may not live to see it'; the population and wealth of Britain had grown at such a rate that the demand for wool could not fail to increase.[4]

Sellar could see no sense in subsidising (by periodic relief and by low rentals) the common people in the hills when better rents could be obtained from sheepfarmers: the people would be better off along the coasts. In March 1817, in the midst of famine, Sellar told Lady Stafford that he was

> convinced that the time will come when Sutherland, instead of robbing the industrious mechanic of his meal to support a useless population among ye hills, shall send food as well as clothing to other countries, and if the people on the coast take to fishing as they seem inclined to do, they will already diminish the scarcity among themselves very considerably.[5]

When the schemes came under public criticism in 1816, Sellar consoled Lady Stafford with the thought that

Every reformer of mankind has been abused by the established *errors, frauds and quackery* — from Martin Luther to Mr. Coke, and from that prince of improvers to such a miserable cobler [?] as myself, but where the reformers have been right at bottom, they have by patience ... and their unabating zeal and enthusiams got forward in spite of every opposition, and so I trust shall your Ladyship in your generous exertions to better the people in this country.[16]

There was an almost Messianic element in Sellar's faith in 'improvement'.

Patrick Sellar's evaluation of the positive character of the great changes in the Highlands was outlined in an article which he published in 1831. He catalogued the output of the newly reconstructed Sutherland economy. It exported '180,000 fleeces annually and 40,000 sheep to feed the English manufacturer', 50,000 barrels of herring, together with corn, whisky and cattle. The tillage lands of the county, he maintained, were

chiefly available for the esculent food and the refuge during winter months which it affords to the weaker portion of the flocks which occupy the great extent of pastoral country, with which it is by the wise provision of nature connected.

He personally accounted for one-twentieth of the entire output of the county. In his own operations he regularly employed 26 people at Golspie and Morvich and a further 90 on a seasonal basis, in addition to his 11 married shepherds and 8 young men on the sheep-walks. His employees were in far better circumstances than previously:

with a more dense population than ever existed there at any former period of time, there are no tithes, no poor-rates, and no drunkards or beggars ... Nay, one meets with few peasants' sons, of this district, who have not, from slender wages ... been taught to read, write, and perhaps, to cast an account ... If tolerable proficient, away he goes to 'seek his fortune'.[7]

This was the meaning of improvement to Sellar. It was the difference between importing grain for the maintenance 'of idle smugglers' and 'the export of food and raiment towards the support of the British Empire'.[8]

The Elgin sheepfarmer was never patient with the recalcitrant attitudes of the common people of Sutherland. In August 1814 he bitterly condemned their backward and obstructive ways: they were

> a parcel of beggars with no stock, but cunning and laziness. Sutherland is a fine farm badly stocked. The people have often succeeded against industry — they have wearied out the agents in subversion by their craft and their intrigue and combination; and although they are driven at present pretty much from their original habits, the mass requires a great deal more yeast yet before it shall become leaven.

He continued:

> The interior of this country is clearly intended by providence to grow wool and mutton for the employment and maintenance and enrichment of industrious people *living in countries suited to manufacture.* It is part of the territories of the 'beasts of the field' where it was not meant that '*man* should dwell in cities' — and the present population of this interior, are, of all others best calculated, when driven to it, for making real, and moving form this latent state, our other branch of wealth. I mean the myriads of valuable fish with which every creek is periodically filled, and which are not sent there to die a natural death or for the feeding of whales and sharks.[9]

Sellar seems to have believed that political economy combined with 'Providence' to provide the complete justification for the clearances.

Much of Sellar's thinking on the subject of land use and crofting is crystallised in a report for the Sutherland estate on the newly acquired Reay area of the county in 1832. In general he believed that the people were little more than beasts of burden sunk in great indigence and discomfort, 'the dry husks of misgoverned poverty'. The crofting population lacked capital, and was irregularly employed, and its labour was applied to the most absurd purposes. Of one crofting community he remarked that 'besides trouble, deterioration of ground and expense of different sorts, 50 p.cent of the annual value of the ground ... [continues] to be sacrificed, on purpose to keep a mass of population from generation to gener-

ation in a state of beggary'. Reorganised, this land could yield
more with one man and a pair of horses than with 20 families of
cottars. Sellar evidently believed that crofting was totally uneconomic, a misuse of good land, and that it would be better if the
people were completely abstracted from the land, into villages or
into fishing or else persuaded to emigrate. 'You have your choice
between sheep, fishing and pauperism ... where you can have fishing foster them. Where you can't, place sheep. To plant cottars
without a view to fishing is to sow paupers.' Education was the
long-term answer — the only cure for all

> the prejudice and ignorance which checks emigration, and for
> that implicit obedience to the passions, which inducing among
> the Highlanders, the Irish, the illiterate manufacturers, and all
> barbarians professing Christianity, premature and reckless
> marriages, reduce the mass of the people to abject poverty, by
> the increase of their numbers, beyond the means of subsistence.

In effect Sellar was saying that Sutherland would be better off
without crofters, that the policy of resettlement of people cleared
from the interior was ill-advised. Sutherland, he maintained, was a
magnificent province which would be best occupied by 20 to 30
men of capital (perhaps worth £10,000 each) who would pay their
rents without even the interposition of factors. They would be men
of business (like Sellar himself), without pretensions 'to Grey-
hounds, Galloping horses, livery servants' or, he added with
boundless scorn, 'the company of idle and bankrupt Lairds'.[10]

For the culture of the Highlanders, Sellar had only contempt.
Like many other factors and sheepfarmers he spoke no Gaelic and
regarded the language as a gross impediment to all progress. In
1811 he argued that working people could not possibly study two
languages since it would divert their energies from writing, arith-
metic and trade, and that without English the great mass of
Highlanders would be 'shutt out from every useful Service'. Consequently, he said, 'I would therefore Suppress the reading of Gaelic
and induce the Study of English.'[11] He returned to the same theme
at the time of his trial in 1816. Highland civilisation was moribund
and corrupt. There was a population of several hundred thousand
souls who possessed no 'principle of truth and candour'. These
people, he believed, constituted

the sad remnant of a people who once covered a great part of Europe, and who so long and so bravely withstood the invading strength of the Roman Empire. Their obstinate adherence to the barbarous jargon of the times when Europe was *possessed by Savages*, their *rejection* of any of the several languages now used in Europe, and which being sprung or at least improved from those of the greatest nations of antiquity, carry with them the collected wisdom of all ages, and have roused their possessors to the most astonishing pitch of *eminence* and *power* — Their seclusion, I say from this grand fund of knowledge, places them, with relation to the enlightened nations of Europe in a position not very different from that betwixt the American Colonists and Aborigines of that Country.

The Highlanders were low in the scale of civilisation; their 'brutishness' could only be contrasted with the 'knowledge and cultivation' of their neighbours; like the Amerindians the Highlanders were 'fast sinking under the baneful effects of ardent spirits'.[12] According to Sellar, the Highlanders lived 'in the same degree of civilization as their fathers had done 500 years ago'. Contempt for the peasant mode of existence was widespread in early-nineteenth-century thought,[13] but Sellar took the attitude to its logical extreme.

In similar vein was Sellar's denunciation of 'the aborigines' when plans for further removals were being prepared in 1817.[14] He declared that the sheepfarmers would not be able to get forward until the people and their cattle were completely cleared from the interior districts. 'The aborigines drain from *us* a full rent, and they *beg or steal too from the proprietor's pocket* what *we pay him,*' and in return, said Sellar, the sheepfarmers had 'the pleasure of feeding these animals, the enjoyment of seeing them destroy and damage everything in their reach, and the satisfaction of being abused and misrepresented in return for our forbearance'. The people were 'in a state of worse than entire inutility. I thank God the thing is so near a termination.'[15] In the following year Sellar rejoiced that 'the aborigines — the common people, are effectively cowed' by the properly unbending vigour of the management in its plans for the forthcoming removals. 'We shall march steadily forward at Whitsunday [1819], and shall make our clearance of the Hills ... once and for all,' he told James Loch.[16]

It came to be Sellar's view that there were too many people

altogether in Sutherland.[17] He quoted the Reverend Malthus several times with approbation. In 1815, for instance, he directed Loch's attention 'to a very fine passage' in Malthus' work which

> shews irresistably how the increase of population is independent of every other circumstances except the increase of food ... and in the experience of all countries and ages nothing is more certain than that the country commanding most food, will contain most people, command most labour and contract most strength.

In 1816-17 the supply of food fell short in Sutherland; acute suffering was created. Sellar's analysis of the problem pointed out that until recently the local population had been sustained partly by 'the circulation of Lord Stafford's money' (meaning capital expenditures mainly on the new coastal economy), partly by the expenditures on Highland road construction, partly by 'annual drainage to the armies', and partly by the unusually high prices of black cattle. These special circumstances, he reasoned, had eased the pressure of numbers on the local means of subsistence; but the position had since been reversed.

> Population in spite of everything, increases by returns from the army and from the south, and many families and individuals to whom I have denied any footing on the estate ... set up a turf cabin under the shelter of a brother or father, or go into family with friends.

Moreover employment opportunities had been reduced and the land of the interior people produced insufficient corn; thus the people were able to '*create nothing to export to other countries* in exchange for the supply of these wants'. The price of their cattle had fallen so catastrophically that they could not afford to buy food for themselves, let alone pay their rents. They would either have to emigrate or be freed from the obligation of paying rent.[18]

Sellar considered emigration the logical and only practical remedy to the population problem of the Highlands, and in this opinion he was, at least in the early days, far more radical than his landlord. He saw no other solution to the famine problem of 1816-17. There were, he figured, between 12,000 and 15,000 people on the Sutherland estate who would be 'destitute of three or four months food'. Most of them possessed 'little or no property to exchange for food — nothing but labour such as it is'. He continued that

> the people have 'no skill or capital', they do not convert the produce of the ground into any quantity of value proportional even to the low rents. They conserve of what little they produce, an excessive proportion, in maintaining a multitude of idle families. They are of consequence without property to exchange for meal — money they have none.[19]

Lord Stafford organised some relief measures in the form of meal and potatoes. Sellar commented that

> This supply of meal and potatoes, with economy, should keep us until the mildew comes again, perhaps about 1821. It is a most charitable donation from a Great Family to a distressed tenantry, but the true benevolence to them is to render them independent of such supplies by setting as many as the country and its fisheries can keep on low ground, and enabling the rest to emigrate to a country more suitable for them.[20]

When it came to Sellar's attention, in 1816, that a number of small tenants in Strathnaver were contemplating emigration, he remarked:

> I confess I think it would be a most happy thing if they did, both for themselves and for this estate. They are just in that state of society for a savage country, very different from the London and Manchester tradesmen, when landed in the woods of America.

The landlord should consider seriously the possibility of subsidising their departures: 'Here you feed them to continue in beggary. By the other [i.e. paying their passages to America] you feed them to remove from beggary to independence.' Even better, they might be inclined 'to carry a swarm of their dependents with them'. Sellar assured Lady Stafford that 'you really will not find this estate pleasant or profitable until by emigration or by draining to your coastside you have got your mildewed districts cleared'.[21]

Governmental efforts to humanise and regulate the emigrant traffic were, to Sellar, meddling and misguided. He regarded the introduction of minimum food requirements on migrant vessels as an absurd obstruction to the exodus from the Highlands — Highlanders did not need so much meat as regulated, they could live on oatmeal. A similarly characteristic response of Sellar came in 1819 when he heard that, instead of settling on the coastal reception zones on the Sutherland estate, many of the recently cleared people of the interior were departing for Skibo and Caithness. 'Upon the whole', he commented, 'Skibo and Caithness are two receptacles and they have unloaded you a great deal of trash, of which you are well rid.'[22]

A quarter of a century later the tone of Sellar's thoughts on emigration had not noticeably changed. The Potato Famine created great difficulties in the west and north of Sutherland, and the second Duke and his agents mobilised relief on an unprecedented scale. As always, Sellar was ready with gratuitous advice. It was more sensible, he wrote in March 1847, to use ships for exporting destitute people rather than for importing food. Available ships should be employed

> in summer, to carry the redundant population to locations of various sorts in Canada, and kindly and paternally, settling them there, *where provisions are comparatively cheap* ... The Sons and grandsons of the men you send and *settle there*, in a *spirit of kindness*, would 'stand a wall of fire' betwixt you and the Yankees.

A few weeks later Sellar returned to his theme:

> If facilities were given for emigration, there would be a general wish to get abroad. The *difference in cost* of eating Indian corn in America, besides eating it at home would pay the expense of their transport. Ten millions spent in applying the remedy would be a profitable remedy, but ten millions applied, merely to pass through the bowels of the misgoverned people is worse than thrown away. It destroys their self-reliance — makes them a mistletoe on the British oak.[23]

Once more the clarity of his opinion was matched by his forceful prose.

III

Sellar's responses to his critics were also resolute and illuminating. Repeatedly provoked by allegations concerning his conduct in the clearances of 1814, the resentful Sellar took every opportunity to abuse his assailants, and to clear his own name with the public. Armed with Mackid's signed apology and with the successive Census returns (showing a continuous though marginal increase in the Sutherland population to 1831), he retorted to a long line of authors and newspapers. In 1825, for instance, he pursued Major-General David Stewart of Garth regarding a section of his first edition of *Sketches ... of the Highlanders of Scotland* which implied that, notwithstanding the Inverness trial verdict, Sellar had been guilty of heinous crimes. Sellar considered Stewart an ignorant, interfering, impertinent man — 'a selfish, petty Highland laird who sees no further than the limits of the little sovereignty where Donald approaches him with fear and trembling — hunger in his face — a tattered philibeg of Stewart on his other end'. Not only did he regard Stewart as an incompetent and impecunious estate-manager, typical of his class; he was also hypocritical — he was prepared to drink the health of Lady Stafford at the Celtic Society — a Society which, Sellar sarcastically noted, was established 'on purpose to oppose the demoralisting effects of *civilisation* upon Highlanders'. And, though Stewart was basically unrepentant, he substantially toned down the offending sections of his influential book in its subsequent edition.

The resurgence of criticism — led by Donald McLeod — in several Edinburgh papers in 1841 was the occasion for further indignation from Sellar. 'Radical newspapers', he exclaimed, were devoting their energies to exciting 'the mob against the powers that be'. The libels against the Sutherland family 'are decidedly part of a system adopted by this paper [the *Chronicle*] to stir up the unwashed part of mankind against those who wash and wear a clean shirt'. When a body of Sutherlanders rioted at Durness in the same year he turned his rhetoric in their direction — they were 'the most lying, psalm-singing, unprincipled peasantry in the Queen's dominions'. Yet it should be said that, in this instance, the Sutherland estate administration regarded the Durness people as at least partly justified in their grievances against a particularly rapacious middleman.[24]

Two years later Sellar consoled the Duke of Sutherland when

further newspaper attacks were launched against the estate. He told the Duke that no peasantry in Scotland were treated half as kindly by their landlord. He pointed out that he himself would happily pay twice the rent that the people were paying for their lands 'saving to your Grace the expense of two extra Agents and a host of Bailiffs attached necessarily to the existing circumstances'. Criticisms directed against the Sutherland estate, he urged, were the machinations of seditious, wrongheaded, desperate vagabonds, egged on by Free Church ministers and by what he termed 'the worst of all tyrannies, that of an unprincipled and democratical press!'[25]

Sellar's critics were not silenced. In 1847 *Tait's Magazine* had published the accusation that, in the 1810s, he had 'made cold four or five thousand hearths'. In his angry rebuttal Sellar appealed to the evidence of the official Census:

> to shew that we did *not* depopulate Sutherland, that we did *not* diminish the number of people, but that we *did increase them*. The official census will convince you that in 1810, when the improvement began, the people of Sutherland numbered 23,629, and in 1821 they were 23,840. I leave it to you, Sir, to judge how this *undesirable fact* can be reconciled with the alleged extinction of 5,000 hearths.

IV

Patrick Sellar's blinkered personality profoundly affected both his role in the clearances and his reasoned response to the economic problems of the Highlands. Everyone, including his closest colleagues, acknowledged that he was the poorest manager of men, and quite incapable of foreseeing the response that his actions were likely to provoke. His indignation against the common people derived partly from his legal entanglements, and partly from his inability to view a situation from any standpoint other than his own. Social protest against the clearances in Sutherland existed before Sellar entered the county, and it continued after his death, but it was he, more than anyone else, who inflamed the feelings of the people against the landlord. His methods were provocative and, on his own admission, he confronted the people in a deliber- ately combative frame of mind. The Sutherland family was misguided in delegating to him so much of the implementation of the elaborate plans for the radical reorganisation of their estate. They chose a man who antagonised even his own associates. His ambition and his insensitivity to the temper of the people cannot be discounted in the accumulation of hatred against the landlord and his representatives. The internal evidence of estate correspondence tends to confirm at least part of the legend of Patrick Sellar.

During the proceedings of the Royal Commission into the condition of the crofters and cottars in 1883, Sellar's son, Thomas (then 63 years of age) conducted a lengthy defence of his father's career against the renewal of the old allegations of inhumanity. He made one interesting concession in his argument:

> I take it, and I say it frankly for myself, that the compulsory clearances are things of ruder times long gone by when the views as to the rights of landlords over land were very different from what they are today — moral rights.[27]

Sellar and the ideology of which he was an extreme proponent, helped to destroy, for a century any chance of a co-operative and radical attack on the Highland problem by the landlord and the people. It helped to reinforce among the common people a fatalistic apathy which even today is not fully dispersed. It dislocated positive investment programmes during the clearances and left a legacy of burning distrust. The weakness, even the collapse, of social cohesion was a central factor in the Highland tragedy, and the Sellar mentality was one of the pervasive causes.

Sellar's constricted attitudes to social interaction were paralleled by his extreme but influential version of the 'ideology of improvement' in the newly cleared Highlands. He pushed prevailing ideas beyond their contemporary currency among lairds and sheepfarmers, and pressed the basic propositions to their logical (and sometimes unacceptable) conclusions. James Loch, an Edinburgh intellectual himself and a man of relatively severe economic principles, repeatedly warned Sellar that 'the strict rules of Political Economy' could not be applied to the management of Highland estates. Sellar, of course, expounded the underlying principles of political economy governing the development of the Highlands in the nineteenth century with clarity and astonishing bluntness. His guiding light was 'improvement', in the shape of the calculated rationalisation of economic activity. Whatever the roots of his thinking, he became an extreme example of the *laissez-faire* philosophy of the early nineteenth century: he believed that what he did was right because it was founded upon the precepts of political economy. Patrick Sellar reflected many of the preoccupations and anxieties of the 'colonists' from the south in the Highland economy. But it would be a misjudgement to say that he was typical of the improving mentality. His intellectual fanaticism took him beyond the sympathy of his fellows — so that he became a rather lonely caricature of the new entrepreneur in the Highlands.

The questions which Sellar brought into focus were often fundamental and philosophical issues, moral, political and economic, which underlay the great dilemma of the Highland problem. Why not make over the Highlands to men of business and capital? Why not lease it to sheepfarmers who could maximise the productive output of the land and serve the needs of the British economy in the most efficient commercial sense? Why should Highland proprietors accept low rents from inefficient small tenants when they could increase their rentals (and diminish their costs of management) by leasing the land to great sheepfarmers? Why give people crofts when more rent could be obtained from capitalists? Why indeed should landlords subsidise a poverty-stricken population who, in the long run, would be far better off as migrants to the south or abroad? What was the point of subsidising a population which could not support itself at tolerable levels of welfare, and which bred beyond its means? Why encourage Free Church ministers when they used their influence to alienate the people from their landlords, and why permit a 'democratical press' when it defamed the innocent with impunity? Why impede the decline of feudalism and the antique Gaelic language when they kept the people in poverty and ignorance? Why, he implied, should the Highlands and the landlords be subject to different standards and economic principles from the rest of the world?

Though much of Sellar's rhetoric was unacceptable to his peers, the general direction of his thinking was entirely consistent with the prevailing practical response of the landlords and their advisers, and the government, to the problems of the Highland economy in the nineteenth century. Classical political economy was immensely influential in defining the role of capital, labour and land, and diagnosing the solutions to the Highland problem. It carried an almost irresistible intellectual authority, a clear formula for evaluating estate policy on every question. It persuaded most people in authority that the free operation of the market solved all problems optimally.

The *laissez-faire* prescription — which Sellar proselytised with uncommon vigour — solved the problems of the Highlands by way of regional specialisation and out-migration. It produced a monoculture and, eventually, depopulation. Its solution dismissed the possibilities of balanced economic development and ignored the unequal consequences which derived from the dominant industrial economy of the south. It was, therefore, at odds with the economic philosophy of the developers of the late eighteenth century and the planners of the twentieth.

The common people created a mythology which enabled them to ascribe their fate to forces of evil. The followers of Sellar's philosophy believed the economic machine worked mechanically according to prescribed formulae. Both sides of the community were thereby equally freed from the need to find further explanation of the plight of the Highlands in the nineteenth century.

Notes

1. Cf. Sellar, *Sutherland Evictions*, p. 41, in denial of the opinions of A. R. Wallace in *Land Nationalisation* (London, 1882; 3rd edition, 1883), which Wallace was later persuaded to retract. See the triumphant and basically accurate report of Sellar's dismissal in *Military Register*, 30 December 1816.
2. SCRO, Sutherland Collection, D593/K, Lady Stafford to Loch, 31 October 1817, 11 November 1818.
3. Ibid., Sellar to Duke of Sutherland, 28 September 1847 and associated correspondence.
4. Ibid., Sellar to Loch, 30 March 1820.
5. Ibid., Sellar to Lady Stafford, 22 March 1817.
6. Ibid., Sellar to Lady Stafford, 26 January 1816.
7. *Library of Useful Knowledge: Farm Reports, and Accounts of the Management of Select Farms*, No. 3, communicated by Patrick Sellar, 6 January 1831.
8. Sellar, writing in 1813, quoted in Adam, *Sutherland Estate Management*, II, p. 181.
9. SCRO, Sutherland Collection, D593/K, Sellar to Loch, 1 August 1814.
10. Ibid., report by P. Sellar concerning Durness, 10 May 1832, and associated correspondence.
11. NLS, Sutherland Papers, Sellar to Lord Stafford, 3 April 1811.
12. Quoted in Adam, *Sutherland Estate Management*, I, pp. 175-6.
13. See C. J. Dewey, 'The Rehabilitation of the Peasant Proprietor in Nineteenth Century Economic Thought', *History of Political Economy*, vol. 6 (1974), p. 17.
14. This was not of course exclusive to Sellar. Donald Sage used the term in his

memoirs; see *Memorabilia Domestica* (1889 edition), p. 77.

15. SCRO, Sutherland Collection, D593/K, Sellar to Loch, 16 October 1817.
16. Ibid., Sellar to Loch, 13 April 1818.
17. Sellar had expressly denied this view in 1811 when he and William Young advised Lady Stafford on the boundless possibilities of her estate. See Eric Richards, 'The Prospect of Economic Growth in Sutherland at the Time of the Clearances, 1809 to 1813', *Scottish Historical Review*, vol. 49 (1970), and Adam, *Sutherland Estate Management*, II, p. 146.
18. SCRO, Sutherland Collection, D593/K, Sellar to Lady Stafford, 17 April 1817.
19. Ibid., Sellar to Loch, 2 December 1816, 11 December 1816, 29 December 1816.
20. Ibid., Sellar to Loch, 22 March 1817.
21. Ibid., Sellar to Loch, 16 October 1816, 20 October 1816, 27 October 1816, 11 December 1816, Sellar to Lady Stafford, 10 April 1817.
22. Ibid., Sellar to Loch, 22 June 1819.
23. *Ibid*, Sellar to Loch, 6 March 1847, 17 March 1847.
24. See Richards, *Highland Clearances*, pp. 439-44.
25. SCRO, Sutherland Collection, D593/K, Sellar to Duke of Sutherland, 28 November 1843, 2 September 1847.
26. Ibid., Sellar to the Editor, *Tait's Magazine*, 20 September 1847.
27. Napier Commission, Evidence, p. 3187.

PART FIVE

THE ECONOMICS OF THE HIGHLAND CLEARANCES

It would be a hard man, and a philistine, to wish much economic progress onto the mountains and waters of Scotland's empty quarter.

The Economist, 18 February 1978

17

THE HIGHLAND ECONOMY, THE INDUSTRIAL REVOLUTION AND THE CLEARANCES

When we understand that local distress is incidental to general progress, we shall not indeed try to stay general progress in order to escape the local distress, but we shall try to mitigate the local distress by diverting to its relief some portion of the general access of wealth to which it is incidental. To mitigate the penalties of failure, without weakening the incitements to success, and to effect an insurance against the disasters incident to advance, without weakening the forces of advance themselves, is the problem which civilisation has not yet solved. No wonder, for it is only just beginning to understand what the problem is, and to recognise the 'deeply inherent limits' within which it must be solved.

Phillip Wicksteed, 1910[1]

'The penalties of failure' were high and seldom mitigated in the Highland economy of the nineteenth century. Failure was expressed in the clearances, in depopulation and emigration, in rural squalor and communal bitterness, and in the low levels of social welfare which marked the region even at the end of the century. It became a classic 'regional problem' of the twentieth century, its poverty and underdevelopment a challenge to the planners who regarded it as an anachronistic survival, inadequately integrated into the national economy.

This chapter will argue that the experience of the Highland economy — and therefore the clearances — can best be understood as an aspect of the much broader process of industrialisation in Britain and Western Europe. The fate of the Highlands (in common with other peripheral parts) presents a reverse side of the coin of industrial advance, and the region experienced those 'penalties of failure' identified by the political economist

411

Wicksteed. Herbert Heaton, the economic historian, also conscious of the unsuccessful elements in the classic age of industrialisation, suggested that the Industrial Revolution could be usefully reconsidered, and perhaps better understood, if it were written from the point of view of those who, in the general process, failed.[2] Similarly, when A. H. Dodd wrote his *Industrial Revolution in North Wales* in 1933 he remarked, somewhat reproachfully, that if his book 'induces some student to turn his gaze away from Lancashire, Yorkshire and the Midlands, it will have served its purpose'.[3] These observations have a special pertinence for regions such as the Highlands and the west of Ireland. The failure of some parts of the national economy finds its origins in the evolution of complicated inter-regional relationships during the process of industrialisation. The failure of the Highland economy is a component of the generic problem of the retarded region in an industrialising economy. In this is contained most, though not all, of the explanation of the economic and social tragedy of the clearances.

Economic historians and others argue cogently that economic development in Britain was contingent on a nation-wide process of regional specialisation within the developing economy of Britain. The benefits of specialisation were crucial for the growth of the economy — it was vital for Britain *as a whole* that such regions as the Highlands should produce efficiently commodities such as kelp, fish, wool, meat and sporting facilities. Where regions were slow to integrate into this national network of exchange, the growth of the whole was impeded. François Crouzet explained the point succinctly in his consideration of the survival of 'quasi-autarkic subsistence ... in extensive areas ... acting as a brake on the growth of the economy as a whole'.[4] In the late eighteenth century, as this chapter contends, the Highlands followed the path of specialisation and structural change, but eventually developed an economy which was unable to support its population on a tolerable basis. The social costs were enormous and the history of the clearances is the epitaph to that tragedy. Indeed it was the role of the clearances to facilitate the reorientation of the economy along the path governed by the forces of regional specialisation. The continuing growth of population exacerbated the social and economic consequences. As E. H. Hunt has written, 'Like Ireland, the Highlands exhibited the remarkable propensity of peasant communities occasionally to allow population to grow beyond the level resources could comfortably sustain.'[5]

Regional retrogression was in no sense unique to the Highlands. As the economist Myrdal wrote, 'the play of forces in the market normally tends to increase rather than decrease the inequalities between regions'. There were several areas in Britain whose experience diverged from that of the rest of the national economy. The persistence of backwardness and poverty, the loss of population and the failure of industry may be seen in the west of Ireland, in rural areas in England and in Wales, and, in more recent times, in the old industrial areas left behind in the continuous readjustment of the world economy in the twentieth century. In the early nineteenth century the collapse of native industry could be seen in many parts of rural Britain.[6] Cormac O'Grada argues that deindustrialisation in Ireland was a consequence of a shift in the terms of trade towards agriculture and that 'Britain's Industrial Revolution ensured that Ireland's comparative advantage — outside the north west — would lie in agriculture for the forseeable future'. A. H. Dodd, in his discussion of North Wales, described a universal mechanism:

At first developments in transport promised to be a further stimulus to local industry, and each successive trade boom brought with it a fresh crop of investors and prospectors; but as each tide receded it washed away some of the shakier outworks of industry, narrowing the area of successful production to a few more fortunate centres ... As the locomotive penetrated further and further into the heart of the country, the products of these better equipped regions ousted one local manufacturer after another from the home market, and brought North Wales into ever closer dependence on the great industrial centres.[7]

It was a pattern repeated many times over on the periphery of industrialisation: it was integral to the general flux and adjustment of the Industrial Revolution.

There is in the literature of British and European economic growth and regional development a particular and continuing argument about the role of agriculture and of labour specialisation. Economists frequently postulate that a key problem for any developing economy is to induce the traditional agrarian sector to contribute to the modern industrialising sector, particularly by means of increased output, greater efficiency from all the factors of production, and the release of labour. Sidney Pollard suggests that there is an 'economic logic' of industrialisation which requires regional shifts and works in an inexorable manner. Similarly, Arthur Redford thought that the geographical redistribution of population was 'part of an evolutionary process by which the rural population of each district was specialising in the kind of agriculture to which the district was physically and climatically suited'. Brinley Thomas, in relation to the Welsh experience, considers the concomitant 'rural exodus' as 'a necessary consequence of economic growth', one of the 'growing pains' associated with development. The implication seems to be that, if the process of regional change had not been allowed to occur, the very mechanism of national growth itself would have been jeopardised. However, the achievement of an increased supply of a primary product in an agrarian sector (as in the Highlands) could permanently impair the capacity of a region to develop in the cumulative manner that is the defining characteristic of industrialisation.[8]

In terms of social welfare the experience of regions such as the Highlands diverged from that of the mainstream of the national economy. The regional interest and that of the nation were at odds; there emerged an imbalance in the economic system. The persistence and intensity of the Highland problem provides powerful evidence against the extreme doctrine that economic growth possesses self-equilibrating qualities by which regions tend to adjust continuously towards the achievement of similar levels of *per capita* income and welfare. As Stuart Holland says, capitalist development, in practice, has been grossly unbalanced and has created enormous regional problems for which theory makes no allowance. The modern discussion of regional imbalance has served primarily to emphasise the extraordinary difficulty of the task of establishing the conditions of economic advance in regions left behind in the wake of industrialisation.[9] In the nineteenth century, in the age of the clearances, there was a failure, both in theory and in practice, by both private and public sectors, to tackle the great human problem of accommodating the surplus population, and giving security to the cultivator of the soil. Yet they were probably contradictory objectives: it is arguable that the retention of an inefficient agrarian peasantry was inimical to the growth of the economy at large.

A region of retardation, the Highland economy in the nineteenth century failed to provide tolerable levels of welfare and security for its growing population. The purpose of this chapter is to locate the policy of clearance among the sources of poverty and distress. It contends that landlord policy contributed positively to the general dilapidation of the regional economy, and that the landlords as a class must bear a substantial proportion of the responsibility for the outcome. At the same time it is argued that the landlords were constrained within a framework itself much influenced by external forces, which were beyond their control. Moreover it is by no means certain that the behaviour of Highland landlords was markedly different from that of landlords elsewhere.

In earlier chapters it was maintained that the demographic forces operating in the Highlands (as elsewhere) created unprecedented pressure on resources in the decades after 1760. To this must be added the preponderantly adverse consequences for the Highlands of the dynamic expansion of the industrial economy in the south. As these forces grew in the early nineteenth century, the conclusion became inescapable that the Highland economy could not generate a structure of employment capable of absorbing its swollen population. The role of the clearances was contributory in that the introduction of sheepfarming exacerbated the problem of excess labour. Yet, as is contended below, sheepfarming was itself only one influence among many which radiated from the centre of the new industrial economy. Essentially the Highlands was a peasant economy on the periphery of national industrialisation; it was affected by a series of forces generated at the centre which were, virtually, irresistible.

The parallel with the Irish experience in the century before the famine, despite certain geographical differences, is obvious and appropriate. In a recent reinterpretation of Irish economic history L. M. Cullen has analysed the strength of the external forces which wrought economic retardation in nineteenth-century Ireland. Cullen, speaking of the potency of the 'environmental' pressures upon the Irish economy, has remarked that 'It is far from clear whether there was any alternative to the course events took, or to what extent, well-directed human resources or economic policies might have overcome the environment.'[10] Such an exposition comes perilously close to a doctrine of economic inevitability, yet the question of the realistic limits of action is irrepressible. It applies with equal force to the Scottish Highlands and is, in the last analysis, a matter of hypothetical alternatives.

I

The essence of the argument has already been foreshadowed.[11] It has been contended that the old Highland economy of the eighteenth century was, at all times, a precarious structure, liable to famine, and productive of only low material standards of living for the great majority of its peasant population. It was suggested, primarily on the evidence of literary sources, that the region was subject to more severe crises of subsistence, and had a smaller capacity to absorb rapid population growth, than most of the rest of the British Isles. This long-standing susceptibility to recurrent famine and Malthusian setbacks was revealed at many times in the eighteenth century, and with especial force in the 1770s and 1780s. In this peasant economy the considerable authority of the landed proprietors had probably been constrained, until the late eighteenth century, by habits of self-interested paternalism and social convention. All the distinguishing features of under-development (even by the standards of that century) were displayed: scattered cultivation, low *per capita* incomes, high birth and death rates, poor communications, low levels of capital formation, high dependence on agriculture, seasonal migration and sporadic emigration, and a strong attachment to 'traditional' attitudes (in the Rostovian sense[12]). There was an equilibrium of low-level subsistence, a 'primitive stability' as Samuel Johnson put it.

The unusual element in this essentially peasant economy was its substantial commitment to an export sector. The development of the cattle trade from the late seventeenth century introduced an important, indeed vital, commercial trading element within the basically subsistence framework of life. Hence this northerly outlier of both the Scottish and the British economy had already achieved a positive response to favourable market opportunities in the south a hundred years before the primary industrialisation of the British economy. Income derived from cattle exports permitted a degree of specialisation within the peasant economy, and allowed the region (itself deficient in cereals) to organise its food supply on a basis of regular imports of meal from the east and the south. It facilitated a greater division of labour, a higher level of subsistence and, presumably, an augmented population. The crucial characteristic of the cattle sector of the peasant economy was, to adopt D. C. North's phrase, 'the technological nature of its production function'.[13] In common with kelp, but in total contrast to sheep production, the cattle economy was heavily labour-intensive. Moreover the economies of scale and the capital requirements were never so overwhelming as to exclude the small-scale and semi-communal producers. Though some pressures in the direction of 'ranching' developed in the 1770s[14] the effects were not comparable in scale with those of sheepfarming in the following half century. If the purpose of economic activity in the Highlands was to retain as many people as possible, cattle and kelp (abetted by the potato) were perfectly adapted to its needs.

The landlord and tacksman classes were well placed to tap the income derived from exports (first cattle, then kelp, then wool) by squeezing rents upwards wherever possible. The total dominance of the landed proprietors and the glaringly unequal distribution of income gave the region as a whole a genuine opportunity to generate the basic conditions of continuous development by permitting the accumulation of capital. This became a responsibility — Adam Smith himself had defined the role clearly — which rested squarely upon the shoulders of the landlords.[15] The growth of export earnings provided an unprecedented and realistic chance to develop the resources of the region, as proprietors channelled into their own purses the wealth of the cattle trade.

In the outcome the landlords failed — partly because general economic circumstances eventually made the difficulties of development much greater than could have been anticipated, but also because landlords as a class misused the financial resources of the region.[16] In this judgement it is important to acknowledge the significant exceptions to the rule — to recognise the efforts of a handful of proprietors who used their capital creatively and with the intention of generating self-perpetuating investment; but the rest of the account is less than edifying. Indeed one of the most mystifying aspects of the Highland story is the manner in which so many of the landlord class consumed their way into bankruptcy. The demise of Highland families in the period 1770-1850 suggests that, in financial terms, the class committed suicide.[17] Although there have been no systematic studies of the economic behaviour of Highland proprietors, there is evidence that much of the funds generated internally (especially from the export staples) was squandered on conspicuous non-reproductive consumption in the Highlands, or, even worse, on competitive personal extravagance in Edinburgh and London. At the end of the eighteenth century the social pretensions of the Highland lairds in London and in

Edinburgh outran their incomes, and they consumed their capital. This leakage of resources from the region was undoubtedly debilitating for the economy.

John Ramsay commented on the radically altered patterns of economic behaviour among the lairds of the eighteenth century. In an age of inflated rents, he said, the laird was generally well placed to afford the increased price of 'all the necessaries and luxuries of life'. However, many landowners had radically raised their levels of consumption and, consequently, the

> unavoidable enlargement of his scale of expense is more than sufficient to swallow up the additional rental. This will be most severely felt by such as have, in a greater measure, deserted their country seats. Whether the education of children, or their love of more polished life, makes them take this step, it will seldom contribute either to the standing or aggrandisement of their families.[18]

These were prophetic words, not merely for the maintenance of hereditary dignity but also for the development of the Highland economy. The classic example of wasteful expenditure of the windfall gains which fell like ripe fruit into the laps of the *rentiers* was the case of the sixth Duke of Argyll. A notorious rake and outrageous spendthrift, he was described by a descendant as a complete reprobate whose 'sheer carelessness, idleness and want of purpose in life, did nothing but dilapidate his great inheritance'. He is said to have single-handedly reduced the family fortune by a cool £2 million.[19] This, in the first instance, had been extracted from the pockets of peasants, kelp farmers and sheepfarmers. But the inflowing profits of colonial trade and military service were similarly neutralised by Highland landlords. For instance, Sir Hector Munro, who made a notable fortune in India, spent £70,000 on his house at Novar — a seventh of it on his garden alone, and a great deal more on exotic furnishings and art work.[20] Much external income both from the colonies and from English industrial and agricultural fortunes was expended in this way.[21] Sometimes local income-generation was enhanced; but more often than not income flooded out of the region in pursuit of aristocratic pleasure. Robert Somers, writing in 1848, made the same point:

> the profits of kelp brought the Highland chiefs within the reach

of the same temptations to which the English and lowland barons had yielded a century earlier. They introduced them into the splendid warehouses and saloons of London, filled with the richest handwork and the rarest and costliest luxuries which the ingenuity of man could devise, or the unwearied energies of commerce could collect. There, too, were the English aristocracy, with their princely equipages and their glittering wealth, to excite emulation and to ruffle pride. The effect was the same as when a hawker of the backwoods spreads out his toys, and trinkets, and firemakers, before a tribe of Indians. The vanity of the Highland chiefs was intoxicated, and the solid advantages which the new tide in their affairs had opened up to them were bartered for the merest baubles. There is a staircase-window in Lord MacDonald's mansion in Skye which is said to have cost £500. In residences, dress, furniture, equipages, pleasures, and style of living, the Highlands chiefs copied the English model; and while they necessarily lost their power by this new way of life, the only resources by which their rugged country and its untutored inhabitants could have been brought into a cultivated and civilised condition, were wasted in the vain attempt to rival the magnificence of an aristocracy who possessed much richer domains and larger revenues.[22]

It is undoubtedly true that consumption levels among the Highland lairds rose sharply in the late eighteenth century. It was not entirely a break with the past — the chiefs, for centuries, had been known for a relatively sophisticated manner of living which had always depended upon imported luxuries. Nor were they unique in Britain — many landowners in the south found themselves in financial straits after the turn of the century. Of the Highland proprietors who became bankrupt some were candid enough to curse their ill luck at gambling, but others blamed their lawyers in Edinburgh, or else their agents.[23] But the most decisive factor was the decline of agricultural prices after 1813 which reduced rent receipts in advance of consumption. By then many proprietors had incurred debts and accepted familial obligations (probably the biggest drain of all) which, sooner or later, crippled them. Whatever the cause, the effect on Highland investment and on the security of the people was negative. Investment in the Highlands (excluding the relatively safe zone of sheepfarming) was at all times fraught with high risk. The Highlands had perhaps more than its share of economic behaviour which, in terms of the conventional criteria of investment, was 'irrational'. The economic behavior of the land-lord class diminished the possibilities of economic progress in the Highlands.

Yet, notwithstanding the problems of landlordly dissipation, there were times when the Highland economy faced opportunities for expansion. It has been suggested that the period from about 1780 to 1815 presented the region with a respite, or remission.[24] For, although population growth built up pressures and caused sporadic and substantial emigration (which itself was accompanied by a leakage of capital[25]) this was counterbalanced by the action of several expansionary forces in the northern economy. There is no precise way of measuring the productivity trends of this economy during this (or the later) phase, but all the indications point to a radical expansion of output and real income up to 1815. The phenomenal productivity of the potato almost certainly multiplied severalfold the *per capita* output of food within a few decades. By 1808, it was said, half of the people of the Highlands lived mainly on potatoes for nine or ten months of the year, and by 1846 two-thirds of the food of the labouring classes was in the form of the potato.[26] Statistics for the island of Skye in the period 1801-41 demonstrated conclusively the vital dependence on this crop of the continuing population growth. Population in Skye rose by 42 per cent while the output of cereals remained static; meanwhile, how-ever, the output of potatoes increased sixfold. As William Skene said, the potato 'furnished the sole additional production to meet the requirements of the additional population'.[27] The miraculous growth of productivity from the potato was the *sine qua non* of the reduction of the size of holdings and the relocation of the Highland population associated with sheepfarming and the clearances. It was fundamental to the emergence of crofting, permitting population increase without any other adjustment in the economy, though it left the people at a bedrock level of subsistence and with little hope for any betterment.

There were two other sources of remission for the labour-intensive sector of the economy. The buoyancy of cattle prices until the last years of the French Wars allowed the ordinary small-time pastoralist to vie for land despite rising rents resulting from the mounting competition from the sheepfarmers. Kelp production was an even greater boon: perfectly adapted to the superabundant labour resources of the West Highlands, it required little fixed

capital and relatively simple entrepreneurial skills.[28] Linked ultimately to the soap and glass industries of the south, kelp may be
regarded as an early supply response to industrialisation; it yielded
substantial export income for the region, and reinforced further the
conviction of many landlords that the small tenantry could subsist
on minute allotments. Landlords subdivided land and encouraged
a concentrated population of small tenants.[29] Recruitment to the
regiments may also be regarded as a growth industry in these years
(mainly after 1780), and as equivalent to an export sector.
Government and landlord expenditure in the region — on roads,
bridges, harbours, fishing villages, the promotion of linen and
cotton manufacture, houses, hotels, agricultural improvements
(especially in drainage) and the Caledonian Canal — all generated
income to sustain higher levels of employment in the region. Fishing and linen expanded with modest success at the end of the century. The old domestic manufacturing industries — a wide
spectrum of activity from weaving to the production of shoes and
basic household utensils — persisted in the ancient ways, while
experiments to introduce more sophisticated methods of production continued into the second decade of the new century.

Although there were many signs of underemployment, and continuing expressions of anxiety about famine and the recurrent
recourse to emigration, the development of new sectors in the
Highland economy in the late eighteenth century permitted the
region to accommodate the swelling population seemingly without
any radical deterioration in average living standards, which were in
any case low to begin with. Landlords, of course, did extremely
well from what were virtually windfall gains: the rise of kelp,
potato production, army recruitment, cattle and wool output all
owed precious little to any initiative taken by the landlords and
were not consequential upon prior investment. Landlords reaped
returns simply by virtue of their ownership of the land. Some did
develop their estates along progressive lines, but only a small part
of the expansion of rent may be attributed to these efforts. The
classic form by which income was augmented was the introduction
of sheepfarming. In this the initial costs to the landowner were
slight — his main function was to find a sheepfarmer with capital
and expertise sufficient to exploit the land (and usually the sheepfarmers were eager enough to negotiate a lease); his second
function was to vacate the land of its resident population in order
to give the incoming farmer free range for his animals. If the

landowner incurred any expenditure at all it was connected with the purely optional business of relocating the people removed to new facilities on the coastal fringes of the estate. The financial benefits from sheepfarming flowed completely from the market opportunities created by the textile industrialists of Yorkshire, and the expansion of demand associated with the early stages of industrialisation.

Most of the developments before 1815 possessed strong backward and forward linkages within the regional economic structure. They were relatively labour-intensive, with only slight leakages out of the region; capital works expenditure (e.g. on roads and canals) generated considerable multiplier effects through the economy. Sheepfarming, in contrast, was greedy of land and used little local labour or skills; the income derived was quickly leaked out of the Highlands: the sheepfarmers spent little time within the Highlands (they even educated their children in the south) and the landlords, to whom much of the income accrued, seem to have spent a large proportion of the wealth unproductively. James Walker, writing in 1812, described the changed pastoral economy:

> A stock of black cattle requires many hands, both for tillage and for the dairy. A sheep farmer on the hills of the South of Scotland or of the North, requires neither of these, but can live and make rich in a desert, with his sheep, and a very few servants.[30]

The form of the structural changes induced by these various pressures was peculiar: the expansion of economic activity in the region accommodated the growth of population, but pressed the mass of the people on to smaller shares of the land. The combined effect of the growth of kelp and fishing industries and of manufacturing villages, accompanied by increased cultivation of potatoes, was to allow the common people to subsist on a substantially smaller proportion of the land than before. In essence, the lucrative profits in sheepfarming caused a great shift in the relative returns on land use to the point at which the sheep came to monopolise great tracts of the Highlands. The sheepfarmers took over land which had been used very little in the past, in addition to much of the old cattle-grazing land, as well as parts which had been arable. Landlords therefore benefited at every turn — both from the more intensive use of the coastal zones, from their monopsonistic control of kelp sales, and from the greater utilisation of the grazing lands. In these circumstances it appeared to be in their interests to discourage the emigration of the common people — a policy which, in retrospect, has been regarded by many historians as both foolish and cynical.[31]

All too soon the new structure that evolved in the Highlands proved to be a false and tragic framework. It failed to lift the standards of life for the common people; on the contrary, it left them vulnerable to the old-fashioned crises of subsistence which had become anachronisms in the south of Britain. After about 1815 most of the props of the old economy collapsed and the entire structure became ramshackle. Many of the old traditional as well as the new infant industries lost their earning power: kelp, linen, cattle and fishing industries became a disappointment, leaving the people more than ever dependent on the dangerous monoculture of the potato. Meanwhile population growth continued — especially from 1811 to 1831 — and the demographic adjustment to economic decline was agonisingly slow. Sheepfarming remained as virtually the only paying sector in the northern economy. Landowners found themselves in increasing financial difficulty; land changed hands rapidly; the burden of poor-relief rose swiftly. In the new era there were simply too many Highlanders to find tolerable subsistence; even if the land had been in communal occupation, it is unlikely that the demographic pressure could have been contained. Clearances continued and the population piled up until, aided by recurrent famine and perpetual poverty, the forces for emigration gained strength, especially in the 1830s and 1840s.

The Highlanders had procreated as rapidly as most of the rest of Western Europe in this age, but, like the Irish, they had not begotten industry or indeed any vigorous and enduring new labour-intensive economic activity. The region failed to industrialise. The reverse occurred — the indigenous manufacturing of the Highlands fell into decay. This was the context of the post-war clearances, and the reason why the tragedy of eviction was compounded by the lack of alternative employment for the human resources of the region. The people on the margin became redundant.

II

The turning point in the story of structural change was marked by the collapse of prices in about 1813 and the beginning of the secular downward trend of prices until about 1847.[32] The Highland economy was disabled by a series of long-term influences, concomitant with further clearances, which reduced the level of new investment and income in the region. The cumulative impact of these adversities was to reduce the population to the barest subsistence level and to a still greater dependence on their crofts — and hence on potatoes, oatmeal and seasonal employment in fishing. The Highland economy was, of course, not self-sufficient in foodstuffs and was repeatedly forced to import large quantities of meal, particularly during recurrent famines. As the population increased and became more congested, its vulnerability to these shortfalls (despite improved yields from potatoes, and of wheat in the east) was compounded. As its capacity to pay for these imports had, traditionally, rested upon cattle and kelp revenues, the collapse of these sectors devastated the peasant economy. Moreover the entry of sheep and the takeover of the land by sheepfarmers, diverted regional income into the hands of people who did not need to employ the crofters. The scale of this problem cannot be doubted. Early in the transition, in 1802 for instance, the island of Skye alone imported £25,000 worth of meal, at a time when 'the fall of markets ... prevented them [the smallest tenants] turning their cattle into money'.[33] When the cattle economy languished after 1813 this problem was central to the subsistence and rent-paying capacity of small tenants and crofters.

Despite continuing emigration, the number of people continued to rise in most parts of the Highlands until the famine of 1847-9. The common people, mainly crofters now, were thrown back on a primitive self-sufficiency in a peasant economy. In some parts, during the 1830s, there was a reversion to barter transactions among the small tenants.[34] Apart from the sheepfarming sector, this was an economy in retreat. The condition of the people was further aggravated by the continuing pressure exerted by landlords seeking, in an environment of falling or static rents, to extend sheepfarming on their estates in order to buttress their rentals. As sources of non-agricultural income diminished (a subject explored below) so the pressure on land use increased. Land hunger — the contest between crofters, cottars, squatters, sheepfarmers, sporting tenants and landlords — became the dominant characteristic of this economy. Clearances therefore became even more necessary for the sick finances of many landlords. Although opposition and opprobrium became more vociferous, emigration accelerated: the consequences of Malthusian pressures were scored across the entire economy.

The economic history of the Highlands in this phase was largely the outcome of its relationship with the growth of industrialisation in other parts of the national economy. Most of the retarding influences were derived from outside the region, and the region could not withstand these forces. These influences require individual analysis.

The fate of the kelp industry encapsulates the problem of most parts of the Highland economy. The industry exploited seaweed resources, mainly on the west coast and in the Outer Hebrides, to meet the needs of glass and soap makers in Liverpool.[35] The commitment of large numbers of small tenants and their landlords to kelp was a backward linkage of the newly industrialised chemical industry — the demands of which pressed so much against supplies (especially in wartime) that the price of the raw material increased tenfold between 1750 and 1810. After 1810 the use of imported foreign substitutes killed the industry in the West Highlands — the price of kelp halved by 1820 and then collapsed at the end of that decade. The reduction of the duty on foreign alkali in 1822-3 was a further heavy assault on the industry; the blow was strongly reinforced by the discovery of a process by which a cheaper alkali could be extracted from common salt. The result was decisive and kelp became practically unsaleable. There could have been no better illustration of the strength of external influences upon this peripheral region. Malcolm Gray summarised the consequences:

> The expansion of the industry, proceeding within communities balanced on the traditional combination of fishing and agriculture, stimulated a growth of population which fishing and agriculture alone could never support; contraction left a large semi-industrial population precariously dependent on shrunken stocks of cattle (made even less profitable by the fall in livestock prices), small arable holdings, and intermittent inshore fishing.[36]

The collapse of kelp revenues was a prime cause of the sale of property by lairds after 1815, and of the introduction of a new class of proprietor to the Highlands. It reduced crofters' income and their power to accumulate savings which might tide them over the recurrent shortfall in the grain and potato crop. The collapse of kelp also destroyed the logic of the early clearance policies, which had provided for the resettlement of the peasantry on the coasts: without kelp the crofter economy was incapable of maintaining even the most minimal levels of social welfare. Equally it reduced the landlord's ability to perform his traditional relief function during emergencies. The effect was simultaneously to reduce the income of the region, to create unemployment, to reduce its effective claim on external supplies, and to exacerbate the demographic dangers.

These dire consequences had been accurately predicted in 1813 when the tariff protecting kelp was under consideration. A group of West Highland proprietors had met in August of that year to consider the problem: they claimed that the profits on kelp were very small and that, often, the only reason that landlords continued production was to give 'employment to the lower class of the people on their respective properties'. They pointed out that 20,000 people were employed in kelp-making and that it complemented fishing as a seasonal employment. If protection were abolished, they claimed, the kelp industry would collapse; it 'might create serious disturbances, and certainly would render emigration inevitable'.[37] Ten years later Seaforth wrote that the Highland proprietors had depended on buoyant kelp prices 'to meet the debts and obligations incurred in past times of expense and high prices'. He was critical of his fellow proprietors who, he contended, ought now to provide their people with alternative means of employment, or else help them to emigrate. Seaforth believed that some lairds had been actuated by 'sordid motives' in their promotion of kelp shores in the time of good prices; he said that the population was in danger of becoming 'a starving mass' unless humanitarian measures were introduced to protect their future subsistence.[38] In the event the government remained intransigent on the issue. There would be no protection.

The collapse of the Highland kelp industry in the 1820s brought consequences not unlike those that faced the handloom weavers of Lancashire, the nailmakers of the Black Country, the straw plaiters of East Anglia and many domestic trades in other parts of Britain during industrialisation. They were casualties of economic progress, vainly attempting to compete with new, cheaper, substitutes, the products of efficient industrial enterprise. The longer they lingered in the doomed trades the worse their conditions of life became. This bitter story has been replayed endlessly over two hundred years of modern industry to the present day.

III

The story of the kelp industry exemplified the general dilemma facing the Scottish Highlands in the nineteenth century. It was a problem inherent in the relationship of this region to the national economy in an age of demographic revolution. That is to say, the acceleration of economic growth in the south of Britain in the late eighteenth century effectively eroded the autarky of the Highland economy, and dissolved its insulation along with that of other quasi-regional economies within the British Isles. The widespread improvement of transport, commercial and banking facilities in the British economy at large was part of the general integrating mechanism of the Industrial Revolution; but the prime moving force in the late eighteenth century was the basic shift in demand schedules achieved by the combined effect of population growth and industrialisation. Effectively these forces levered open regional economies to the influences of economic specialisation and rising productivity by orienting their production towards the developing exchange markets of the national economy. As Pollard and Crossley have remarked, regional specialisation was one of the most potent forces making for an increase in national output in the period of industrialisation.[39] Southern industrialisation created new commercial opportunities, and thus there were better export markets, rising prices, rising profits and rents for particular products, new types and levels of consumption, and a changing use of resources. By a process of regional specialisation in response to these opportunities the Highlands (as other regions) could gain large rewards. However, the transformation entailed serious problems of adjustment which bore particularly heavily on this region. The social consequences were fundamentally dislocating, and the new opportunities for specialisation in the Highlands quickly became irresistible imperatives which virtually dictated the direction and form of economic activity in the Highlands in the nineteenth century. Moreover regional specialisation, by definition, rendered the Highlands vulnerable to sudden changes in national and international markets. In essence, a structural change was imposed upon the Highlands and the transformation was complex and disturbing in both its benefits and its costs. It was in this context that the clearances were pursued.

Until about 1815 the economic consequences for the Highlands were evenly balanced between advantage and disadvantage. Mainly negative in its social consequences was the spread of sheepfarming which was, of course, a direct and scarcely stoppable response to the demand for raw wool in the south. It required the relocation or outright eviction of the resident population; it saw the import of capital and expertise in the shape of the sheepfarmers. It undoubtedly raised the aggregate income of the region, and the benefit to the landlords was expressed in their increased rent rolls.[40] The economic problem with sheepfarming was obvious to all, and was the subject of great debate in the literature of agricultural improvement: it employed little labour in an economy in which labour was already oversupplied. Sheepfarming possessed poor backward and forward linkage effects, and had little internal multiplier and accelerator effects. The point was well expressed by David Lawrie in 1810:

the truth is, there is scarcely one link of connexion by which the wealth of the sheep farmer can be transfused into the society with which he is necessarily intermingled ... [often] their rents and the whole substance of their labours pass directly southwards, leaving the country swept and desolate.[41]

Hence the introduction of sheepfarming into the Highlands reduced still further the value of labour in the economy and, simultaneously, sharpened the pressure on landed resources. In terms of the existing disposition of resources and population in the Scottish Highlands, sheepfarming was a disaster. The beneficiaries were the farmers (many but not all of whom were outsiders), the landlords and 'the national interest', in the sense of an efficient supply of wool for both production and consumption.[42]

Responding to essentially similar stimuli, kelp was a growth point in exactly the right place, the densely populated west coast. It too required structural adjustment, but its consequences ran in the opposite direction because of the nature of its factor requirements. Its intensive labour demands matched perfectly the existing factor endowments of the region, and it required virtually no land. Cattle prices, entirely contingent on the demands created in the south, were also relatively buoyant until about 1810. This buttressed the old economy and permitted the small tenantry to maintain a long drawn out competition for land with the sheepfarmers. Taken together, kelp, cattle and the potato were expansive elements in the old Highland economy and made possible the partial accommodation of the population within the region in the eighteenth century. It is true that the demands of the landlords creamed off the lion's share of the gains; nevertheless, by its exports the region was able to generate claims against other regions, and to expand activity internally. These developments reduced visibly the economic autonomy of the region, so that the determinants of the level of activity became almost entirely external.

In the expansive phase, up to about 1815, the Highlands also witnessed important deliberate efforts to promote both general and specific development. Government assistance reinforced private initiative in the creation of a more efficient infrastructure — in the form of roads, canals, harbours, villages, mails and lighthouses. There were also moves to advance domestic industry in the region — there was, for instance, some initial success in linen and cotton textiles which ran parallel with similar growth in rural Ireland before both regions experienced the full competitive force of imports from the industrialised centres in England, central Scotland and Ulster. A.J. Youngson has examined the efforts to advance flax and linen manufacture in the Highlands before 1800,[43] which were followed by similar efforts to promote cotton and woollen manufactures, coal production, potteries, brickmaking, saltpans, lime works and much more. The Highlands had long been self-sufficient in many basic commodities; most household goods were manufactured in the home and by a few craftsmen such as weavers, tailors, blacksmiths and shoemakers.[44] The new initiatives introduced a degree of specialisation to the non-agricultural part of the Highland economy (though usually on the basis of pre-industrial technology). Fishing was similarly promoted by public and private investment.

The objectives of the enterprise and capital lavished on the Highlands in these years were threefold: to employ labour, to stem emigration and to reap benefits of the sort generated by the new industry in the south. Moreover, the buoyancy of prices in the economy encouraged landlords and entrepreneurs to venture capital in all directions in the Highlands. There is evidence of some clear progress before 1815. In 1807 in Perthshire, for instance, it was said that 'By the industry of the people here in raising flax and in spinning yarn for sale, all the rents as well as the tradesmen's accounts due by the tenants are paid from the produce of the linen yarn.' From many parts of the north at this time there was news of similar expansion of a sort which might be categorised as 'proto-industrialisation'. In many places it took the shape of village development — new settlements designed to concentrate employment opportunities for the expanding population which, as the result of agrarian transformation, was becoming increasingly detached from the land. Fishing, of course, was the great hope of many landlords and the British Fisheries Society, and was another response to a growth of external demand (of which kelp had been the outstanding example). The influence of exogenous stimuli was paramount, and the impact was powerfully reinforced in several cases by concurrent landlord initiatives (such as those on the Argyll and Sutherland estates). Urged on by the propagandists David Loch, George Dempster, Sir John Sinclair and others,[45] a number of landlords began efforts to reproduce in the Highlands the conditions of economic progress achieved in the south. They were encouraged even more by the trend of prices for Highland commodities.[46]

After 1812, or thereabouts, these exogenous forces turned against the Highland economy in an almost uniformly disastrous fashion. Old industries, especially in textiles, collapsed. But also obliterated were the mushroom growths of wartime. The deflationary price trends at the end of the French Wars, associated partly also with the sharpened competitive impact of imports into the region, had a crippling effect on a great deal of Highland enterprise. The demise of kelp was obvious and sensational. The linen industry everywhere ceased to exist as a commercial activity: it could not compete with the low-cost production of factories in the Lowlands and England, nor in the Baltic. In the long run, no local manufacturing could resist the competition of the southern factories — the bedrock wage levels of the Highlanders were eventually undercut by the economies of scale ceaselessly generated by mass production. After Waterloo the deindustrialisation of the Highlands became virtually inevitable. Locational advantages, economies of scale and externalities achieved in Lanarkshire and

Lancashire (and elsewhere in industrial Britain) had made almost impossible any similar expansion in peripheral regions. Virtually without exception the development of secondary industry in the Highlands in the war years was erased: the region lost practically all its industry and, just as seriously, lost all possibility of any future growth of industrialisation. The unquenchable optimism of the Countess of Sutherland, Sir John Sinclair and George Dempster was proved false, while the unpopular scepticism about Highland industry associated with the doctrines of the Earl of Selkirk[47] was vindicated.

The economic experience of the Scottish Highlands was not unique, but part of a wider process by which the effects of industrialisation were radiated across the British and European world. The impact was confined neither to the Highlands nor to peripheral British regions. Francois Crouzet has referred to the process as 'pastoralisation' and remarks that 'countries like Spain, Portugal, and Sweden which fell into the economic orbit of England during the wars suffered a crisis or a collapse of their traditional industries without any compensating rise of new ones'.[48] Sidney Pollard has located the question within a general thesis about the European economy and the evolution of a geographical division of labour: 'Regional specialisation associated with modernisation, for example, in pottery, in cutlery, and toolmaking, or in woollen textiles was tantamount to de-industrialisation elsewhere.'[49] That is to say, the consequence of development at the centre of the British economy was denuding industry in outlier regions which, if they were lucky, found other compensating forms of specialisation. This phenomenon constituted a developmental process which was forced along by the sheer competitive urgency of industrialisation. The regional impact was highly varied and requires close examination at that level, for, as Francois Crouzet has pointed out, 'After all, the Industrial Revolution was not made in England but in a few small districts of England — South Lancashire, some sectors of the East Midlands and Yorkshire, Birmingham, and the Black Country.'[50] The regional experience of the Highlands was in strong contrast and, indeed, corresponds more closely with the story of western regions of Ireland where the decline of linen and woollen manufacture seriously weakened the general economic structure. There was an almost exact parallel with the Highlands: 'The growth of population, accompanied by a decline in domestic industry, signified that Ireland was becoming more rural, more agricultural, than it had been.'[51]

The consequences, social and economic, for the Highlands were no less severe. The local manufacture of yarn and cloth had almost disappeared by the 1840s. Not only did the region cease to export such manufactures; it now clothed itself by imports, including footwear. Imports of cheap manufactured goods — even in the abysmally poor north-west — proved overwhelming, and destroyed local crafts. Coal came to be imported in increasing quantities, and began to displace peat production (which had always been intensely laborious). Imported iron ploughs began to replace local wooden varieties; timber, hemp and sailcloth, slates and bricks all made rapid progress against local products. But the invasion of Lowland dress and habits, and the fashion for cottons and 'exotic' woollens had the most visible consequences.[52] The position was much the same as in Ireland where, by 1838, local production of textiles had been reduced to a mere 14 per cent of the Irish market. The decay of linen spinning and weaving in Aberdeenshire was complete by 1843, and even the knitted stocking industry, which had been a crucial source of cash income in the eighteenth century, was dead by 1850. The substantial town of Inverness had difficulty in maintaining even a vestige of its textile manufacturing.[53] The once thriving linen and woollen manufactories of Orkney were in decline, 'being supersed by the perfect machinery now in use'; there also straw plaiting (which had employed 3,000 women) had been devastated by the caprice of fashion.[54] It was the same story in Moy and Dalrossie.[55] In Reay, in the north-west of the mainland, home-made blue duffle cloaks had given way to silk and muslin gowns, shawls and bonnets, all imported — so that farmers' wives had given up their old industry.[56] In the parish of Inverness linen yarn and worsted thread which had once been produced for local consumption were, by 1840, 'almost wholly superseded by the produce of the great manufacturing establishments of the south'.[57] From Kiltearn, in Ross and Cromarty, it was reported that all manufacture had ceased, 'even the home-made stuffs, which the peasantry used to wear, are now nearly discontinued, as they find it cheaper to purchase than manufacture them'.[58] The process at work was obvious to all: in Durness in 1840, it was said that

> Instead of the tartan or kelt coat and trousers, spun and dyed at home, when each family had their own wool, hardly anything is

to be seen on the young but the fustian jacket and trousers, or the lighter tartan of the shops, and, here and there, the blue and fancy cloths of Leeds.[59]

Most traditional industry in Sutherland was in retreat by the 1820s.[60]

There were some minor exceptions to the rule, most notably the woollen manufactures in Harris which, in 1846, were reported as a survival (based on local consumption but providing the basis for later export development). A contemporary account of Harris remarked that

The natives wear clothes entirely of their own manufacture. They dye their stuffs with an infusion extracted from some native plants; and as a number of the females are taught to ply the shuttle, they get up their coarse webs at a comparatively small expense.[61]

But almost everywhere else the shadow of southern industrialisation spread over Highland enterprise and smothered both old and new growths in the economy. As Malcolm Gray put it, 'the enticements of industry had proved false' — they had been proved false by the movement of prices and the competition of the factories. It was, again in Gray's words, 'the deep running tendency of the time — the tendency of mechanised industry in the metropolitan country to break into the cruder self-sufficiency of the remote areas and to enforce a growing specialisation between industrial and agricultural areas'.[62] Exogenous forces had created implacable imperatives for the peripheral economy.

Mrs Grant of Laggan, in an oft-quoted passage, remarked that 'a Highlander never sits at ease at a loom; 'tis like putting a deer in the plough'.[63] There has been, indeed, a long-standing notion that the Highlander was in some constitutional (or perhaps biological) sense unsuited to and unemployable in industry or fishing. There is little evidence to support the idea, and the welcome the Highlanders received both in the Glasgow mills and the Caithness fisheries makes it untenable.[64] It is difficult to argue that the supply of labour as such was ever a serious problem for Highland industry. Nevertheless there has been a long and perplexing history of failure among incoming entrepreneurs who have been unable either to recruit the co-operation of local people or raise a suitable labour force.[65]

IV

The other props of the Highland economy also weakened and crumbled in the years after Waterloo. Cattle prices halved between 1810 and 1830 and this staple of the small tenants' economy, the means of payment for rent and imports and the insurance against harvest shortfall, failed the people. Demand had diminished at the end of the war. In part it was also the consequence of competition in the cattle trade — the two Celtic supply regions, Ireland and the Highlands, drove down prices to their mutual disadvantage. And since the price of cattle (in relation to rents) was almost certainly the main determinant of living standards among the crofters, the effect was to worsen the rising pressure of population on the slender resources of the region.

Fishing, which had expanded with some vigour since 1780, proved to be an unreliable and unprofitable activity except in a few favoured centres, notably Wick and Thurso. The habits of the herring were capricious and their migration caused the west coast fishery increasing difficulties, and the winter fishing seemed to be beyond the capabilities of northern fishermen. The withdrawal of bounties on herring fishing in the 1820s was a disincentive, particularly to the smaller communities, and the rapid decline in the market for cured herrings in Ireland and the West Indies put further pressure on the marginal producers in the industry. Eventually most activity was centralised in the great seasonal bustle of the Caithness ports. The demand for fishing nets helped to keep womanfolk employed — in Farr, for instance, they switched from the lapsed tartan manufacture to the preparation of hemp for herring nets.[66] But, in general, fishing failed to provide an adequate basis for life in the congested districts of the west.

Even wool prices sagged in the period after 1812,[67] but in this sector the response was an expansion of supply which brought with it greater pressure on land resources. The switch towards sheep production was accelerated by the differential increase of wool over cattle prices in the years after 1840. A witness before the Select Committee on Emigration in 1841 pointed out that

The rearing of black cattle had a direct tendency to support a greater proportion of population; but, since turnips have been so successfully introduced, and applied to the feeding of sheep, and since prices of cattle have fallen so low and prices of wool have for some years risen so high, the farmers find it in their interest to change black cattle for sheep; and it is alleged that this has been done to an extent not compatible with the welfare of the people, and in some instances without much regard to their feelings and interests as human beings.[68]

Until 1840, rental income either stabilised or fell, and landlords, for example the Duke of Sutherland, reduced their estate expenditures and ceased to develop their properties; similarly the expenditure of government funds on roads, lands and harbours also came to an end. There was, of course, a consequent negative multiplier effect from both sectors. The sudden contraction of government and landlord investment expenditure necessarily reduced regional income and employment, and added substantially to the other downward pressures already at work. Government policy was doubly unsympathetic — it impeded the efflux of population by its Emigration Acts, and it exposed kelp and fishing industries to foreign competition. The final cause of structural changes was the shift of demand and supply curves in both manufacturing and raw material sectors, most notably in textiles, chemicals and fishing. In the long run the heavy commitment of the Scottish Highlands to wool production brought the region into global competition with other places — Australia, South Africa, Argentina — which had also specialised in this way.

These pressures acting upon the Highland economy exacerbated the fundamental difficulties facing the region. While its population continued to rise, the region was thrown back on to its pre-industrial foundations, and on to a virtual monoculture of potatoes. The ability of the crofters to pay a competitive, economic rent diminished. Because sheepfarming and deer forests remained the only effective sources of cash income for the landlords, the pressure on land was sharpened. The people were pressed out to the fringes of the Highlands; their crofts yielded little beyond subsistence, and many people were simply thrust out of the region. Because the supplements to rural subsistence dried up after 1815, the population became increasingly mendicant and famine-prone, to a degree which was almost certainly comparable with the vulnerability of the pre-industrial population of the Highlands. For, though there were some improvements within the crofting economy — in the use of wheeled vehicles, housing, ploughs and better cattle breeding, for example[69] — the possibilities of improved cash income were tightly constricted. Emigration and intermittent landlord philanthropy were the only respites in the tragedy of the Highland economy. Hence the accelerated emigration from the region, and the greater resort to seasonal emigration to the south of Scotland. Ironically it was here that the peasant economy of the Scottish Highlands made contact with that of Ireland — Highlanders came into direct competition with the migrant Irish for the worst-paid jobs in Glasgow.[70]

The consequence of the Highlands' failure to diversify its employment structure was that in the new world of economic specialisation it was forced further into pastoralism, and its expanded population faced the alternatives of emigration from the region or privation within. These imperatives were determined beyond the Highlands.

After 1815 the Highland economy, apart from its primary growth sector, sheepfarming, had degenerated. Sheep and deer clearances continued; congestion and the shortage of arable land sharpened; dependence on potatoes increased, and the continuing growth of population threw the entire structure closer to the Malthusian margins — a point demonstrated vividly in the famines of 1817-18, 1836-7 and 1847-50. Bankruptcy among the landlord class became prevalent, and the crofting population became increasingly dependent on the output of a few acres supplemented by the proceeds of seasonal employment elsewhere. It became abundantly clear that, in terms of actual agricultural efficiency in the prevailing market context, much of the small tenantry was redundant — it was uneconomic in terms of the rewards to factors of production, and also in terms of the marginal productivity of labour and capital. It is not unlikely that the marginal productivity of labour in the Highlands was negative. Moreover the society was now marked by deep social divisions, and by an atmosphere of profound suspicion, not diminished by the partial replacement of the old hereditary rulers by new landlords with only a meagre acquaintance with the people.[71] The Highland economy was not merely deindustrialised; apart from the enclave of sheepfarming, it sank back into its classic peasant mould, now burdened with a much larger population critically dependent, in the west especially, on the potato.

The Industrial Revolution, which at first had created promising opportunities for this economy, had finally closed off all chances of a diversified economic structure. The Highlands became a classic case of regional retrogression (in terms of employment opportunities and social welfare for its resident population) on the periphery of the national economy. The Highlands paid the penalty for its inability to participate in the labour-intensive industrial sector of the new national economy — it was a penalty exacted in the form of debt and poverty, accompanied by a long-term draining of its population to more hospitable zones. Pressed into a specialisation in pastoralism, the region was unable to support its people. This has remained the status of the region until the final quarter of the twentieth century. The problem for present-day planners is as intractable as it was for their less well-endowed predecessors.

V

George Kitson Clark advanced the view that 'The Industrial Revolution was to a large extent a blind force, almost as blind, as unconscious of its results for humanity, as the increase in population.' He developed his point in an even more vivid simile:

> It probably should be considered as nearly as void of moral significance as a change in the weather which happens to produce in some year a good harvest ... It was in fact morally neutral. It was not directed with any certainty to any particular end. It might bring good and it might bring evil. Indeed, as men realised from the beginning, it did bring good and did bring evil to different people at different times, and if it were to be made safe for humanity its propensities for evil must be brought under control or compensated.[72]

It has been argued in this chapter that, for the Highlands, the negative elements were large and, in the context of time and place, could neither be controlled nor be much mitigated.

The Highland economy was caught in a web of regional specialisation which established narrow limits on the possibilities of economic development. These circumstances constrained all sections of the people of the region. The landlords were the effective controllers and leaders of this society. The next chapter considers the range of their responses to the problems of the Highland economy, and the limits of landlord policy in such a constricted environment.

Notes

1. Phillip Wicksteed, *The Common Sense of Political Economy*, I (2 vols., London, 1910), quoted by Brinley Thomas, *The Welsh Economy* (Cardiff, 1962), p. 197.
2. Quoted by Jacques Barzun in *The Modern Researcher* (New York, 1977), p. 179n.
3. A. H. Dodd, *The Industrial Revolution in North Wales* (Cardiff, 1933; 1951 edition), p. xi.
4. F. Crouzet, 'England and France in the Eighteenth Century: A Comparative Analysis of Two Economic Growths', in R. M. Hartwell, *The Causes of the Industrial Revolution in England* (London, 1967).
5. E. H. Hunt, *Regional Wage Variations in Britain 1850-1914* (Oxford, 1973), p. 180n.
6. See, for instance, Dennis R. Mills, *English Rural Communities. The Impact of a Specialised Economy* (London, 1973), *passim*; Sidney Pollard, 'Industrialisation and the European Economy, *Economic History Review*, vol. 26 (1973); L. M. Cullen, *An Economic History of Ireland since 1660* (London, 1972), p. 106; T. W. Freeman, *Pre-Famine Ireland* (Manchester, 1957), pp. 6, 75-6; John Saville, *Rural Depopulation in England and Wales 1851-1951* (London, 1957); Holland, *Capital versus the Regions*, p. 47; O'Grada, 'Seasonal Migration', p. 184. For a recent review of relevant economic theory see Albert O. Hirschman, *Essays in Trespassing* (Cambridge, 1981), *passim*, and, more specifically, Staffon Burenstom Lindner, *Trade and Trade Policy for Development* (New York, 1967), pp. 141-8, 171-2.
7. Dodd, *Industrial Revolution in North Wales* (1951 edition), pp. ix-x.
8. Jan de Vries, *The Dutch Rural Economy in the Golden Age, 1500-1700* (London, 1974), p. 214; Pollard, 'Industrialisation', p. 638; Thomas, *The Welsh Economy*. On the French and European experiences in early industrialisation, during which time some 'rural areas became more exclusively agricultural than they had been for centuries', see Charles Tilly, 'Did the Cake of Custom Break?' in John M. Merriman (ed.), *Consciousness and Class Experience in Nineteenth Century Europe* (New York, 1979). Redford, *Labour Migration in England*, p. 79.
9. See, for instance, Holland, *Capital versus the Regions, passim.*
10. L. M. Cullen (ed.), *The Formation of the Irish Economy* (Cork, 1976), p. 123. A sophisticated quantitative analysis of the causes of Irish poverty has since been produced by Joel Mokyr in *Why Ireland Starved.*
11. Richards, *Highland Clearances*, Part I.
12. W. W. Rostow, *Stages of Economic Growth: A Non-Communist Manifesto* (London, 1960), pp. 4-6.
13. D. C. North, *The Economic Growth of the United States 1790-1860* (Englewood Cliffs, 1960), p. 4.
14. See above, Ch. 7.
15. See above, Ch. 1.
16. This view concurs with that of T. C. Smout, who attributes the 'wastage' of export income 'to the weak bargaining position of Highland tenants vis a vis their landowners'. He says that the landowners were 'not the best recipients for extra income from the point of view of the development of the Scottish economy' because

of their tendency towards conspicuous consumption; 'Scotland and England: is Dependency a Symptom?' p. 615.

17. On the turnover of estates see Sir Kenneth S. Mackenzie, 'Changes in the Ownership of Land in Ross-shire, 1756-1853', *TGSI* (1897). This is not to suggest that indebtedness was a new element in the Highlands, but that the velocity of breakdown accelerated.

18. Ramsay, *Scotland and Scotsmen*, II, pp. 526-7.

19. Gaskell, *Morvern Transformed*, p. 23. Duke of Argyll, *Autobiography and Memoirs*, I, pp. 28, 67-8, 129.

20. Robert Carruthers, *The Highland Notebook* (Inverness, 1887), p. 333. Cf. Campbell, 'Eviction at First Hand', pp. 297-8, on Clanranald's expenditures.

21. In the balance sheet of capital movements some recognition must be accorded to the considerable outflows associated with the emigration of tacksmen; see, for example, the evidence in Macmillan, *Scotland and Australia*, pp. 80-1.

22. Robert Somers, *Letters from the Highlands* (London, 1848), pp. 102-3.

23. Lesingham-Smith, *Excursions through the Highlands and Islands*, p. 68; see also Mowat, *Easter Ross*, pp. 88ff. The Highland community in general tended to blame the landlords for the collapse of their estates. When Campbell of Islay lost his patrimony, a kinsman in Australia wrote: 'He certainly must have been a very weak-minded thoughtless person, in not having the presence of mind sufficient to have pulled up in time to save his much to be respected family and princely property from ruin.' He also commented on the fate of the Highlands in broad terms: 'That primitive and unsophisticated race are gradually and effectively giving way to the inroads of the stranger, and what the force of arms for centuries could not accomplish, is performed through, the means of unbridled extravagance and folly of their unfeeling landlords.' SRO, GD64, Campbell of Jura Papers, McDougall to Campbell, 1 June 1849.

24. See Richards, *Highland Clearances*, Ch. 4.

25. See, for instance, Bumsted, *The People's Clearance*, pp. 134-5.

26. Day, *Public Administration*, p. 80.

27. William Skene, *Celtic Scotland* (Edinbrugh, 1880), pp. 374-5. Mention should also be made of the substantial improvements made to productivity in wheat production on the eastern margins of the Highlands.

28. See Malcolm Gray, 'The Kelp Industry in the Highlands and Islands of Scotland', *Economic History Review*, vol. 4 (1951), pp. 198ff.

29. Unlike the Irish case, there is no doubt on this score, Cf. W. A. Maguire, *The Downshire Estates in Ireland 1801-1845* (Oxford, 1972), p. 247.

30. James Walker, *An Economical History of the Hebrides and Highlands of Scotland* (2 vols., Edinburgh, 1812), I, p. 407.

31. See for instance, Hunter, *Crofting Community*, Ch. 2.

32. On prices see A. Gayer, W. W. Rostow and A. J. Schwartz, *The Growth and Fluctuation of the British Economy 1790-1850* (2 vols., Oxford, 1953).

33. SRO, GD222/53, John Campbell of Kingsburgh to John Campbell, Edinburgh, 7 October 1803.

34. SC on Emigration (Scotland), *PP* (1841), VI, p. 214.

35. On the industrial use of kelp see L. F. Haber, *The Chemical Industry during the Nineteenth Century* (Oxford, 1958), pp. 6, 11.

36. Gray, *Highland Economy*, pp. 136-7; and see also Greg, 'Highland Destitution and Irish Emigration', p. 177n.

37. SRO, GD22/33, Minute of a Meeting of the Proprietors of Kelp in Scotland and their Agents, Edinburgh, 1 April 1813.

38. SRO, GD46/17, vol. 44, Seaforth to Gladstone, 11 June 1823.

39. Sidney Pollard and D. W. Crossley, *The Wealth of Britain* (London, 1968), p. 159.

40. See Richards, *Highland Clearances*, pp. 121-2.
41. David Lawrie in *Farmer's Magazine* (June 1810), p. 159.
42. An instructive comparison with the effects of sheepfarming in the southern uplands has been drawn by R. A. Dodgshon. He points out that the full force of social disruption was diminished because the people displaced were absorbed in the textile trades which offered a 'local solution'. The whole process was less violent and less terminal. See 'Agricultural Change and its Social Consequences in the Southern Uplands.
43. Youngson, *After the Forty Five*, *passim*, and Richards, *Highland Clearances*, Ch. 2.
44. See, for example, Gray, 'Economic Welfare', pp. 48-9; *The Topographical, Statistical and Historical Gazeteer of Scotland*, pp. 46, 184; Barron, *Northern Highlands*, I, p. xxx; Leigh, 'The Crofting Problem', pp. 206-8; Teignmouth, *Sketches*, I, pp. 318-22.
45. Many contemporary writers, particularly Irvine, believed that industrialisation could be achieved in the Highlands and some advocated tariff protection for the process.
46. See Appendix.
47. Selkirk, *Observations*, pp. 106-7.
48. Crouzet, 'Wars, Blockade and Economic Change', pp. 577-80.
49. Pollard, 'Industrialisation', p. 638.
50. Crouzet, 'England and France', p. 159.
51. Cullen, *Economic History of Ireland*, p. 119. On Irish deindustrialisation see also Brenda Collins, 'Proto-industrialization and Pre-Famine Emigration', *Social History*, vol. 7 (1982), esp. pp. 138, 146.
52. See Gray, 'Economic Welfare', pp. 48-9; this phenomenon is identified in Hirschman, *Essays in Trespassing*, p. 66.
53. *New Statistical Account*, II, pp. 30-1.
54. Ibid., XV, p. 32. On the decline in Orkney see Thomson, *The Little General*, p. 39.
55. *New Statistical Account*, XV, p. 18.
56. Ibid., XV, p. 22.
57. Ibid., XV, p. 106.
58. Ibid., Ross and Cromarty, p. 326. On Easter Ross see also Mowat, *Easter Ross*, pp. 53-8.
59. *New Statistical Account*, XV, p. 97.
60. See Beriah Botfield, *Journal of a Tour through the Highlands* (Norton Hall, 1830), p. 153.
61. Quoted in Barron, *Northern Highlands*, III, p. 92.
62. Gray, *Highland Economy*, p. 59.
63. Ann Grant, *Letters from the Mountains* (3 vols., London 1807), II, p. 103; see also Youngson, *After the Forty Five*, Postscript; see also *Chambers's Journal*, 15 January 1848, quoted in Handley, *The Navvy in Scotland*, p. 35.
64. There is a useful discussion of the question of Highland adaptability in Murray, *The Scottish Handloom Weavers*, pp. 59-61.
65. See, for example, Nigel Nicolson, *Lord of the Isles* (London, 1960).
66. *New Statistical Account*, XV, p. 74; Teignmouth, *Sketches*, I, p. 129; James Thomson, *The Value and Importance of the Scottish Fisheries* (London, 1849), *passim*. The definitive work on fishing is Malcolm Gray, *The Fishing Industries of Scotland 1790-1914* (Aberdeen, 1978).
67. On wool prices see Teignmouth, *Sketches*, I, p. 129, and Appendix below.
68. SC on Emigration (Scotland) (1841), p. 215, evidence of Mr Thomas Knox.
69. See James Loch, *Facts as to the Past and Present State of the Estate of Sutherland* (published anonymously, 1845). One measure of the change was the

increase in the number of blacksmiths in the region: in 1796 there were 2 black-smiths between the Ord of Caithness and Bonar Bridge; in 1830 there were 38. J. H. Dawson, *The Abridged Statistical History of the Scottish Counties* (Edinburgh, 1862), p. 1039.

70. See above, Ch. 9.

71. See, for example, *Inverness Courier*, 17 May 1823, quoted in Barron, *Sketches, Northern Highlands*, II, pp. 3-4; Archibald Geikie, *Scottish Reminiscences* (Glasgow, 1904), p. 185; Teignmouth, I, p. 52.

72. G. Kitson Clark, *The Making of Victorian England* (London, 1962), p. 108.

18
THE RESPONSE OF THE LANDLORDS

> We have heard again and again that the position of a landlord does not pay; if it did not, the landlords would sell their estates tomorrow.
>
> Joseph and Elizabeth Pennell, *Our Journey*, 1888

Down through the years of the clearances Highland proprietors complained endlessly that they were misunderstood, and that the problems they faced were underestimated. The agricultural reporter, James Macdonald, who was particularly eloquent in the cause of Highland landlords, remarked in 1811:

> People in London, and in our large cities and places of great resort, know nothing of the hardships of a humane Hebridean landlord's situation. They have no idea of the difficulties attending the removal of tenants from lands, or persons of every description from the homes to which they have succeeded as by right of heritage from a long line of ancestors, connected perhaps by blood with the landlords to whom they are now a burden, and whose estates they serve merely to encumber and to deteriorate; and they have no idea of the expense and trouble of removing poor people's families from one island, or one estate to another.[1]

Macdonald thought that the southern public had little comprehension of the practical problems involved in clearing small tenants. Within a few decades the same public totally rejected the notion of clearances, and generally regarded the Highland lairds as a selfish and mercenary, unworthy descendants of the clan leaders immortalised in the novels of Sir Walter Scott.

The property rights of nineteenth-century landowners, generally, were well protected by the prevailing political philosophy;

442

their common interests were well served by existing law enforcement procedures; they had power, used it, and generally did not undermine each other. Yet in a political and social sense the Highland landlords were not well organised, and they were not well placed to defend themselves against sophisticated opposition. They possessed few organisations to bring them into alliance. Only under unprecedented threat, during the crofter agitation, did they develop any unanimity — most notably in their support for 'The Liberty and Property Defence League' in 1882. By then, however, their cause was almost lost.[2]

I

There can be no doubt that the Highland proprietors confronted greater moral and economic problems than those elsewhere in the British Isles, with the obvious exception of their Irish counterparts. By the nineteenth century few English landlords were bothered by a large population of allegedly redundant small occupiers: the peasantry had long disappeared in most places and any superfluous population was relatively easily absorbed by neighbouring towns; and, in any case, many of the social problems of the agrarian south were confronted and cushioned by a middle stratum of large tenant-farmers. Yet even the relatively favourable conditions of English agriculture were no guarantee against rural conflict, such as that associated with 'Captain Swing', during periods of rural underemployment and displacement. In the Highlands (as in Ireland) the peasantry remained and grew, and there was little alternative employment for them. The incoming capitalist entrepreneurs — the sheepfarmers — accepted no responsibility for the anachronistic small tenants. Nineteenth-century Highland landlords confronted the problem of a peasantry locked into a modernising agriculture. They faced the transition two centuries later than many of their British counterparts, and their moral dilemma was compounded, for not only was its scale greater than before, but the public conscience itself was more vigilant for any departure from the codes of social behaviour that emerged after 1800. Since the Highland predicament was different in kind from the condition of English agriculture, so there existed a gulf of incomprehension between the Highland landlords and the southern spectators.

The response of the landlords as a class to the structural changes discussed in the previous chapter was varied. In the long term, the outcome of their policies was much the same — the sheep and the deer triumphed, little or no secondary industry survived, and the entire region, in terms of balanced development, fell behind the rest of the kingdom. But, in the short run, landlords pursued their sometimes idiosyncratic, individual paths. In the age of the clearances they were faced with the allurement of rapid rental increases, but also with the recurrent problems of famine. They frequently recognised a continuing moral obligation for the welfare of their people, often in response to the traditional invocation of the special Highland feeling between chief and clansmen; but they also acknowledged the obligation to conduct rational improvement as demanded in the manuals of the new political economy. They faced the temptations of ostentatious consumption and the enticements of southern comfort which frequently attended the early stages of the drift into landlord bankruptcy.

From the record of landlord behaviour in the Highlands, it is evident that some landlords followed their direct economic interest with little or no restraint: they simply pushed up their rents and cleared. Others tempered the full force of the adjustment and attempted to effect a compromise with the forces making for radical economic and social change. Others again delayed all change for as long as possible — until, in some cases, the demographic crisis engulfed both them and their people. The proportional distribution of landlord responses among these categories is unknown; the record has yet to be fully explored.

There was a marked discontinuity in the story of the Highland landlords. Before 1815 landlord behaviour was relatively positive in character — plans for development were pursued with considerable spirit: sheepfarming would be allied to industry, and the growing population would be retained within the region. The promise of development was dashed after 1815, although even then some landlords came to the Highlands with visions of progress. The best examples are Matheson in Lewis, Gordon of Cluny in South Uist, and the most famous visionary of all, Leverhulme, who enlivened the history of Harris and Lewis in the early twentieth century. There was another class of proprietor, his fortune made in trade or the army, or by inheritance, who bought a quasi-feudal dignity at a relatively low price. The Highlands seemed to them an attractive region in which to nourish their rising egos.[3] However, more typical of landlord behaviour after 1815 was a retreat from the idea of development — for example, the second Duke of Sutherland, who imposed a regime of retrenchment, and contented himself with the hope that his Highland empire would yield better returns to his descendants. Some landlords shed tears for the tragic condition of their people and their own impotence. Many sold out, or teetered on the edge of bankruptcy while their estates were placed in the hands of trustees whose room for manoeuvre was constricted by Scottish law and problems relating to entail.[4] Others made sure that they married well, usually into commerce and/or English capital, and maintained their estates by indirect subsidisation. Many families used wealth from other sources — from the colonies, from the iron and steel industry, from English estates — to prop up the finances of their Highland estates. Many landlords left the problem in the hands of their factors. Perhaps the most pervasive response was acceptance of the assumption that a fully economic return on crofting agriculture was extremely unlikely, and that, in general, a Highland estate would yield a lower rate of profit than most alternative investments.

II

The economics of landlordism in the Highlands is exposed in the estate records of the period. The realities of the times can be glimpsed in the way landlords (or, more likely, their factors) wrestled with their finances and their consciences. Representing the position at the turn of the century when conditions favoured economic expansion, was the report by the land-surveyor, John Blackadder, to Lord Macdonald in 1799, relating to Skye and North Uist. His instructions typified the economic assumptions of the age. Blackadder had been asked to consider

all kinds of productions on the estates which may be used in manufactures, and Report how the people may be employed to their advantage and comfort, in case any of those should be put out of their Farms, and give up an account of any other arrangements.

The question at issue was the future of the common people when new arrangements, perhaps clearances, were instituted. It implied also that the fate of the people was a responsibility proper to the landlord. Blackadder described in detail the existing terms of land occupation and the disposition of the people.

> At present every Family in the Country is a kind of independent Colony of itself. They turn up what part of the soil is necessary to suppport them with meal and potatoes, take their own Fish, Manufacture, and make most of their own cloathes and Husbandry utensils. Their Cows supply them in Summer with Butter and Milk, after which a few of them are sold to pay [rent] for the small spot on which they live. While at work they labour hard, but it is with a view to have soon the same proportion of ease. They are ill fed, and unable to make a continued exertion. By their methods of management a great deal of time is lost, and much industry ill-applied. Twelve people having Families possess one Farm, and each one turning up his proportion of arable ground with the crooked spade, will not do more work among the whole than one man with a pair of good horses, when the plough can be used.

Blackadder believed that the runrig system was exceedingly inefficient for both arable and pasture. He advocated wholesale reorganisation whereby the people would live in villages with small lots of land and employment in kelping; the rest of the land should be used for sheep-walks and for modernised cultivation on large farms.

Blackadder estimated that his recommendation would reap an increase of rent to the landlord of more than 50 per cent — but he warned that the common people were extremely resistant to all change. Moreover he emphasised that the alteration should be implemented gradually for otherwise the population would simply emigrate. He encapsulated the priorities of his time in a sentence: 'In improving an estate in such a situation as this, besides advancing the Rental, retaining a number of inhabitants is an object of the utmost importance, and all reasonable advances should be made to prevent emigration.'[5] He claimed that the products of the sea could sustain virtually unlimited numbers of small tenants at living standards better than those presently prevailing. Kelp was the staple of the country and the means of 'encouraging a number of inhabitants to settle or remain on it'. Blackadder effectively represented the *fin de siècle* model of the Highland economy

— change was inescapable; the people were poor and ill-directed in the existing runrig system; new methods and tenures were indispensable; the small tenants would be better off on the coast in a more diversified structure of existence; both arable and pastoral production should be modernised and rents should be raised. Most important of all, in his view, none of these propositions was incompatible with the retention and augmentation of the population — indeed this was a desired objective in any policy for economic reform. Comprehensive economic change would benefit the entire community so long as it was engineered with care and patience.[6]

The latter virtues were put to test by the pressures of the time. Another landlord, Macdonell of Glengarry, voiced the dilemma facing him in 1802 in a letter to the Secretary of State. He had surveyed his estate in order to determine its real value — that is, its value if let to the highest bidder, presumably a sheepfarmer. Macdonnell's purpose was calculating — he wished to know what sacrifice he would make in setting a rent 'to my numerous Tenants and Dependents'. In the circumstances he thought that a new rent at about 10 per cent below the real value of the land would constitute a magnanimous gesture to his people even though it involved a substantial increase upon the prevailing level of rent. However, to his chagrin, the tenantry responded poorly to his altruism:

> Upon my return about a month ago, I was very much surprised to learn that the Tenants, for whose comfort and encouragement I had proposed to make the above sacrifice, in general wished to surrender their leases, and that they all (with very few exceptions) signed engagements to go to America (Canada I believe).

This was an accurate reflection of the effect on the potential returns to land-use caused by the sensational profitability of sheep-farming — the existing population, in most cases, simply could not compete. Macdonell feared that, despite his generous restraint, he would be accused of oppression. He warned the Secretary of State that 'if the Government or the Legislature do not speedily and decisively interpose, the Highlands will be *depopulated*', and added what he regarded as the clinching point: the Highlands contributed ten Fencible Regiments (in addition to Regulars) to the nation's military strength.[7] Glengarry's lucubrations nicely caught the prevailing landlord mentality: there was a desire to reap rental increases without any diminution of population or public esteem. The price of 10 per cent, it seems, was Glengarry's valuation of the bonds of kinship and popularity.

In the last years of the eighteenth century many Highland estates were caught in a net of financial and familial problems which constricted agricultural policy and transmitted economic pressure directly on to the backs of the peasantry. The relatively small estate of Shirvan in Argyll[8] may represent the plight of many such embarrassed properties at the end of the century. Estate management, spurred on by the bankruptcies which had already crippled old families such as Dumstaffnage, Glenfeochan, Gallanoch, Inverliver, Ederline and Comby, eventually hatched plans which required a severe dislocation of prevailing tenurial arrangements. Shirvan was inherited in 1788 by Archibald Graham-Campbell, aged two, and was placed in the control of three guardians[9] who wrestled with the financial problems of the infant proprietor. The difficulties in the first instance were the product of the lavish expenditure of his predecessors. When the guardians came to arrange the education of young Archibald they sent him to Europe with a tutor (at the cost of £750 per annum) to avoid the 'disippation and expensive habits' which would prove to be the 'foundation for the ruin both of his fortune and his morals — both his uncle and his Father splitt upon that Rock. They spent their Estate before they succeeded to it.'[10] The second source of financial disarray was a series of family obligations: the estate was responsible for annuities to two illegitimate great-uncles, to two unmarried great-aunts and to the heir's mother and his younger brother; estate revenues were also committed to pay off the debts of a grandfather whose investments in the West Indies had come unstuck in the American War.

The third administrative problem was the physical condition of the estate itself: it was crowded with small tenants and cottars and, though the rent had increased substantially, the property was clearly underrented by local standards. To increase the income of the estate required the removal of the population and the consolidation of small holdings into a large farm with a much increased rent, on the approved models of agricultural modernisation. It created the classic dilemma of the Highland landlord, and the guardians debated the question over the entire period of the heir's minority. The debate hinged primarily on how fast the transformation might be undertaken. The managers resolved to resettle the displaced people in crofts and at a new village to be created on the Crinan Canal (then under construction). One guardian was sensitive of the moral obligations which had been incurred in oral informal agreements made with the cottars. He favoured giving 'the dispossessed' long leases for their crofts to encourage them to build and to enclose, and also recognised what he termed 'the natural claims of the poor people in possession'. He insisted that they be given a decent period of notice to quit, with exemption for 'old wives and others who had no holdings but were real objects of compassion'; he pleaded that there should be no 'attempt to higgle with or undermine these poor people'. Nevertheless he recognised equally the 'irritancy' of the small tenants; their presence was associated not only with low rents but also with 'the destruction of wood, game, and black fish, illegal distilling and attending vagrant preachers'.[11]

The plans of the guardian managers were substantially frustrated by the unwillingness of the small tenantry to accept the accommodation offered for them in crofts on the banks of the Crinan Canal, 'although such possessions alone are fit for such trumpery tenants and cottars as swarm especially on the farm of Dunamuck'. This response caused one guardian to fulminate against these 'triffling tenants', 'idle useless people', who stood in the way of 'tenants who will do some justice to the land'. He pointed out the model of the larger estates:

> Great men possessed of enormous estates do not seem to consider it a sound policy to sacrifice good spacious tenements to be destroyed and mismanaged by a rabble hardly deserving the name of tenants, and who would be infinitely better situated in small crofts, and possessions suitable to their circumstances and awkward mode of cultivation.[12]

Consequently the small tenantry on the Shirvan estate were levered off the land in a manner which, though tempered by the staying hand of one of the guardians, reduced them to the status of crofter or day labourer. It was a result forced by the rise of population, cattle prices and rents, and by the vicissitudes of landlord finances. Most striking in the Shirvan case was the heavy weight of the landlord's relatives hanging on the net rental. The young Graham-Campbell himself died in early adulthood, and by the

terms of the settlement, the load of dependency on the estate was
again increased. Proprietorial demands on estate income always
rose in proportion to any growth of rent. The burden never seemed
to ease, even in good times.

III

The years from 1803 to 1815, from the Emigration Act to
Waterloo, represented an intermission in the emergence of the
Highland economic problem. High wartime prices for Highland
commodities and the continuing rise of rents masked the weakness
of much recent development, as well as the accumulating pressure
in the west of the region.[13] In this phase emigration remained a
matter of much controversy. The consequences of the recent anti-
emigration legislation were accurately predicted as early as 1803
by John Campbell of Kingsburgh. Here was another view from the
estate factor's office. The exodus from the Highlands had stopped,
he argued, because the people were too poor to pay the extra cost
now imposed. Furthermore, he claimed:

> Those who intended to emigrate are now a burden on the coun-
> try and from the total failure of the crops last year they will be
> reduced to indigent circumstances before Harvest — I am really
> at a loss how to manage the great population and little employ-
> ment here is really distressing.

Campbell faced the recurrent elements of recent Highland history:
harvest failure, underemployment, indigence and the rising contest
for land between large and small tenants. As he himself put it:

> There are a great many Tennants in want of lands and it rests
> with Lord Macdonald and his commissioners to determine
> whether they will prefer high rent from a respectable Tenant or
> give it to the poor Tennants who have been disappointed in
> their want of Emigration.[14]

The moral tangle was inescapable and was forced on landlords by
the structural shift in the economy at large. But, until the collapse
of prices, many landlords remained blithely confident, sustained by
their zest for improvement. The Earl of Breadalbane, in January

1812, exclaimed, 'All is peace and tranquillity. The improvement of the Land, and the better management of rural concerns seems now the great object with all classes.'[15]

After the war the economic climate deteriorated radically and most landlords eventually appear to have reduced their rents and tightened their belts. Many (but again we do not know the proportions) were enmeshed in family obligations accumulated in the years of high profits and rent. Excessive generosity to younger children, complicated entails and unwise wills all contributed to a dead weight on estate finances, the real burden of which rose sharply during the post-war deflation. Some simply went bankrupt or sold off their estates. The experience of agricultural depression was not exclusive to the Highlands, nor were the lairds the only landlords in Britain to fall into debt — indeed, the extent of aristocratic indebtedness in England remains a lively debate among economic historians.[16] Nevertheless, although statistics are meagre, all the signs suggest a far greater rate of elimination among the Highlanders than elsewhere.

The pattern of landlord response in the post-war years may be further charted in estate records, for instance, those of Shaw, Clanranald's factor for the Uist properties. In 1823 Shaw summarised the economic problems now besetting his master, in company with most other West Highland proprietors. The tumbling price of kelp and the completion of the Caledonian Canal and other public works had greatly diminished employment opportunities. The consequences of several decades of population growth were now manifest:

> The population is excessive much beyond what the lairds can maintain... [and] the allotments of land owing to the number of inhabitants are so small that in bad years the Tenants, even with the additional spur which the division of the Estate into Lots has given to their Industry, cannot raise provisions sufficient for themselves.

Shaw catalogued the recent shortfalls in harvest — 1811-12, 1816-17, 1817-18, 1822; on each occasion meal imports had been required of the landlord, and many cattle and horses had died from a scarcity of fodder. In previous times Clanranald had normally been able to recover his outlays on meal imported for relief when the small tenants sold their cattle. The fall of cattle prices — itself a

calamity for the crofting economy — overturned all normal expectations. Hence, 'the factor is totally unable to say, with certainty,
what part of the arrears due by the Tenants now in possession of
Lands from Clanranald may be desperate or what recoverable'.

The Clanranald estate, in common with many other Highland
properties, turned away from further subdivision of small tenants'
lands (into lots) and towards the outright encouragement of emigration. The current population of the estate was about 5,500 but
the factor believed that it could properly support only 3,000,
which, he suggested, was 'a number quite sufficient for the kelp
manufacture and fully as many as the property can maintain, in the
way in which they ought to live'. In that his calculation was
premised upon a continuance of kelp manufacture, his statement
was wildly over-optimistic.

Shaw penned a perfect statement of the Highland economic
problem as seen from the landlord's viewpoint:

> In order to accommodate the Population now living in his
> Estates, Clanranald has been obliged to divide these lands into
> Allotments so small that the Tenants can barely, in favourable
> seasons, raise a sufficiency of provisions for themselves, and in
> unfavourable seasons they must depend on the Proprietor for
> support. To the Proprietor, in name of rent, they give nothing
> and can give nothing but labour. The Estate is more fitted for
> pasture than tillage, and the attention of the Tenantry ought to
> be directed, principally, to the rearing of cattle; but so small is
> the allotment of Land which can be given to each family, that
> they cannot rear cattle by the sale of which they might pay a
> rent to the landlord, or furnish necessaries for themselves.

Added to the small tenantry was the unofficial population of the
estate — relatives of the small tenants and squatters whose numbers compounded the burden. Population control was not feasible,
for while 'every measure has been taken to prevent this subdivision
of allotments ... it is unnecessary to say that marriages cannot be
prevented; and of course parents will not see their children starve'.
It was a proposition in fair concurrence with the known population
history of the region, for the birth-rate did not decline significantly
until much later in the century.[17]

In Shaw's view, representative of a growing part of landlord
opinion, the surplus people were 'worse than useless' because they

could not even repay the costs of their own periodic relief. Turning to the condition of the island of Canna, he advised that it was worse still because

> the Population is so closely packed that it resembles a village. Here the inhabitants depended entirely on the wages earned at the Public Works for their support. Since the works have ceased the Tenants have never paid a sixpence of rent nor even been able to maintain themselves.

Inevitably, caught in such crippling circumstances, these people could not pay for their own emigration. Shaw contended that:

> It is impossible to expect that Clanranald is to pay the expense of sending such a multitude of people across the Atlantic, and it is equally unreasonable to suppose that he is to continue to make such sacrifices for their maintenance here ... he now finds it absolutely necessary to arrange his Estates so as to draw a rent from the Lands, and the arrangement is incompatible with the residence of the Tenantry even holding Land directly from himself. As to that part of the Population which depended on the Public works they must in any event be removed or Starve.[18]

Clanranald, in common with other proprietors during the 1820s, asked the government (which was exceedingly reluctant to become involved) for assistance to help the people emigrate. From Shaw's exposition comes a vivid sense of the economic pressures bearing upon tenantry and landlord alike. It is often said that the landlords in these years reaped the whirlwind which they themselves had sown — they had promoted population growth, they had subdivided their lands to maximise rents, and they had waxed fat on the profits of kelp. They had also discouraged emigration during the good years. While it may be difficult to feel sympathy for such people, it does not diminish the magnitude of the human tragedy with which they were all now confronted.

IV

The Highland economy lurched through a series of crises and remissions. The famine of 1836-7 was a severe and unambiguous warning: it is probable that, in intensity, it compared with the rigours of 1782-3, but it failed to generate the old peaks of mortality because relief was now much more efficiently mobilised. It was followed, as earlier chapters have shown, by a stiffening of landlord resolve to attack the root causes of destitution (and of their own poor rents). The language of estate administrations matched the firmer resolution. Thus, on the estate of Lord Macdonald in North Uist, in 1839, the factor reported:

> The population in the Estate is greater than the Land, the kelp being abandoned, can maintain. Tenants are so small that they cannot maintain their families and pay the Proprietor the rent for which the Lands are worth if let in larger Tenements. It becomes necessary therefore that a number of the small tenants be removed; that that part of the Estate calculated for grazings be let as grazings; and that the allotments, on that part better calculated for small tenants, be so enlarged as to enable the Tenants to raise a surplus of produce for the payment of the rents.[19]

Such removal policies brought landlords into direct conflict with the small tenants and, increasingly, with public opinion in the south.

Many Highland estates were in a financial stranglehold by the 1840s, gripped by the accumulation of debt and annuities, and unable to squeeze better rents from their tenants (though sheep farms began to improve in value at this time). Some of these estates are well documented because financial desperation generated thorough investigations of all possible sources of income. The case of the Riddell family, owners of the Ardnamurchan and Sunart estates, may be used to illustrate the landlord mentality. In 1829 the nominal rent of these properties had been just above £7,000. There were long-winded discussions within the estate administration about the possibility of clearing off the small tenants and redirecting them into the Strontian lead mines, forestry, fishing or seasonal employment in Glasgow. But little was achieved in this direction, and during the following twenty years debts accumulated on the estates until it became necessary for trustees to take over the management. In 1848 Riddell came to the view that he must sell part of his estate in order to liquidate the debt, which had now swollen to £50,000. He attributed his plight to his 'outlay on improvements, and to the continually recurring expenses of such an Estate, in the Highlands of Scotland'. The improvements he listed as 'Buildings, Roads, Enclosures, Drainage ... repairs' which were additional to 'the constantly recurring outlays incidental to landed property'. In forty years more than £52,000 had been sunk into the estate; some clearances for sheep had been executed, but arrears remained high. The arrears position was intractable because 'any attempt to force payment would ruin the Tenants and prove very injurious to the Proprietor'. Caught in this situation, the estate chose not to proceed with further clearances — instead all future improvement was suspended and the salary of the factor reduced. Hence the problem of an excess human population remained, and the estate continued to be rented below its potential economic value.[20]

The general impact of economic adversity upon the people of the Highlands depended to a large but unknown degree upon the behaviour and resources of individual landlords. Individual action, for such matters as famine relief, clearance procedures and emigration policy, was generally guided by an unwritten code of acceptable behaviour among the lairds as a class. But there were important variations within the class. Many landlords — for instance, the Lords Reay in Sutherland — were incapable of living within their income, or improving their estates, or supporting their people. They effectively abrogated any responsible role as landlords, and eventually sold off their estates.[21] Other landlords — for example Major General David Stewart of Garth — walked a tightrope in their estate finances: they pressed their tenants for as much rent as they thought decent; they reorganised their estates to permit larger tenancies to emerge without causing wholesale dislocation of the population; they used income from external sources (perhaps the East or West Indies) to bolster their Highland properties; they gave gentle or forceful encouragement to emigration, and they tightened their own belts. Mostly they lived a life of excruciating financial anxiety. Some landlords, of whom there were several cases during the famine of the 1840s, crippled themselves in attempting to relieve poverty and destitution — and even where they survived they were ripe for takeover in the following years.

Some contemporaries believed that landlord poverty was the root of the economic problem of the Highlands, and that the only solution was the free inflow of commercial capital. It was well expressed by the editor of the *Elgin and Morayshire Courier* in 1849:

> The crowning evil of the Highlands is — a proprietary without capital — an aristocracy living in splendid poverty. Their estates are beyond their means; and those lands which a free dissemination of capital would turn into fruitful fields, are a barren waste. The result is, that the people as well as their superiors, are poverty-stricken. Where enterprise and capital would produce comfort and plenty, misery and wretchedness prevail. In order to get rid of the poverty-stricken people, the landlords resort to a method repugnant to humanity and contrary to the first principles of justice.[22]

The cases of the Duke of Sutherland and the tycoon-merchant James Matheson form a separate category because they had access to vast wealth from outside sources and were able to channel large sums into their northern estates. The consequence was that they were able to maintain levels of economic activity above the norm — but such policies were possible only because the proprietors were prepared to sink vast amounts of imported capital into the Highlands with the almost certain prospect of very low rates of return on that capital. By any conventional criteria of investment, these policies were extremely inefficient and could be justified only by reference to non-economic (for example psychic or humanitarian) benefits, and to distant returns spread across future generations of the family.

The example of Matheson's estate in Lewis[23] is salient because it provides a test of the effects of a policy which did not include wholesale clearances. Lewis had the benefit of relatively stable ownership and control through the nineteenth century, and the island was in the hands of proprietors who developed close sympathies with the people (which were not always, notably in the 1870s, fully reciprocated). Lord Seaforth, who eventually sold out to pay off his debts, is said to have been offered double rent by Lowland sheepfarmers, but replied 'that he would not turn his people out under any consideration or any rent that could be offered'.[24] Despite such protestations there was undoubtedly a series of unsensational removals in the 1820s and 1830s; but population almost trebled between 1750 and 1844, when Matheson took full possession. The population of Lewis was then estimated to be double the level calculated as optimal in relation to the island's resources. Both Seaforth and Matheson were widely regarded as uncommonly liberal landlords. James Matheson, a native of Sutherland, had returned from China at the age of 46 with an immense fortune made in the Hong Kong trade in the firm of Jardine, Matheson and Co. He began buying Highland property in 1840. It was said that 'He was proud of the land and the people, and did his best for the improvement of both, not always with pecuniary profit to himself.'[25] The new proprietor spent more than half a million pounds to make the island more cultivable and to establish new modes of employment. J. P. Day, writing with the benefit of hindsight, said that 'The main result of this expenditure was that the population continued steadily to increase at a time when in the rest of the crofting areas, it was decreasing.'[26] Admitting failure, Matheson reluctantly came to the conclusion that the most humane policy was to provide elaborate and, by the standards of the time, generous assistance to the islanders to emigrate. After his death in 1878 the estate was forced to retrench its expenditure which, together with a series of poor seasons, helped to generate conditions on Lewis ripe for the flowering of land agitation. Yet Matheson had apparently drawn no net revenue from his island estate for the entire period 1844 to 1878. For, despite such propitious landlordly attitudes and policies, Lewis remained one of the worst and most dilapidated parts of the Highlands — and, in later years, was a standing challenge to the zeal of Lord Leverhulme, and to the scientific planning of the Highlands and Islands Development Board. Looking back over the nineteenth-century story it is difficult to blame the landlords for the poverty of Lewis, except perhaps in the special sense that Matheson, in the long run, may have exacerbated the problem by his kindness.[27] As for Sir James Matheson and his family, they received a bitter reward in the crofters' agitation in the 1880s. Alexander Shand commented on the irony of events in noting that 'the late Sir James Matheson ... probably expended for the benefit of Lewis nearly as much as the original purchase money, and ... [his] heirs in return for his generous sowing, have been reaping a rich harvest of ingratitude'.[28] They confronted as much civil disobedience and abuse as any Highland landowner of the day.

A tolerance of low rates of return was, for most, a condition and a penalty for the ownership of Highland property. The dimensions of this phenomenon have yet to be determined by systematic quantitative measurement,[29] but the literary record is compelling in its own way. The real costs of Highland proprietorship (that is, the potential revenues forgone) were offset by the indubitable psychic benefits of possession which included a sense of territoriality and social exclusivity, and the access to some of the most sought-after scenery and sport in the British Isles. For many of the mid-nineteenth-century owners, Highland proprietorship was a form of conspicuous consumption and, in that sense, its costs were calculated in a fully rational manner. Yet, whatever the motivation, each style of ownership involved an implicit or explicit cross-subsidisation of the small tenantry. A tolerance of low rental return on capital was a concession to the enormous difficulties of inducing economic growth in the region after 1815, and to the unacceptable social costs connected with the extraction of the full return upon capital.

The landlord response to the difficulties after Waterloo was generally expressed in the curtailment of any plan for expansion, a retrenchment of expenditure and the maintenance of rents as high as the times would allow. Horizons contracted and the idea of rapid growth in returns on investment simply evaporated. Some simply left: the most famous case was the chief of Glengarry who, in 1840, took his family and dependants to Australia, together with timber houses and agricultural implements.[30]

John Ramsay had made some penetrating remarks on the psychology of this form of landlord capitulation half a century before. He contended that, before the great transformation in the Highlands, the old proprietorship, whenever faced with financial embarrassment, always seemed to survive their tribulations. By whatever stratagem, they would weather the storm 'till some man of more conduct or better fortune than his predecessors arose and retrieved matters'. In the new age the old resolution and tenacity had gone, and, owing 'principally to the new-fashioned expensive way in which people now live' estates were sold up swiftly, and fell into the hands of speculating southerners.[31] To their number were now added the sporting breed, the Nimrods who were roundly condemned for their uncouth lordliness by the pen of John Stuart Blackie.

V

There was an ineluctable paradox at the heart of the Highland problem. For, despite the widely-known poverty of the region and the low return on capital, land prices continued to rise more rapidly than these circumstances would be expected to permit. In part this reflected the general contemporary philosophy that land, though it gave a poor current yield, was the safest form of long-term investment. It was consonant also with a high valuation placed upon the non-economic returns to the ownership of Highland property. The influx into the Highlands of Lowland capital — both Scottish and English (and subsequently American if we include Andrew Carnegie) — was another chapter in the story of the channelling of industrial and commercial wealth into broad acres and rural serendipity. Moreover, as land prices were pushed upwards by these pressures, so the cost of retaining the crofters increased and the internal contradictions of the situation intensified.[32] The government took virtually no interest until the 1880s; before then the only form of restraint imposed upon landowners was public opinion and the distant threat of peasant resistance.

There was a further element which complicated the picture of landlord motivation. Incoming landowners were sometimes zealots full of an almost missionary passion for improvement. They regarded the Highlands as a challenge as well as a retreat, and believed that they could conquer the poverty of the region: better management, more calculated policies, and a measure of persuasion applied to the crofter population would raise the whole mode of existence out of feudal, primitive backwardness. The history of the nineteenth-century Highlands is replete with such improvement psychology — from the Duke of Argyll to the Marquis of Stafford, through Matheson to Leverhulme. Matheson had been much encouraged by the enthusiastic advice of the vastly-experienced agricultural innovator, Smith of Deanston, who, in 1844, told an audience in Glasgow that improved modes of life and husbandry, if properly introduced, could enable the island of Lewis to 'maintain twice the number of inhabitants'. This turn of mind combined a philanthropic urgency with commercial confidence verging on arrogance. As one ironic observer wrote in 1846:

No spot is now safe, by its remoteness, from the access of

remedial alteration. The Isle of Islay is fast increasing its agricultural productiveness; light is about to descend on the smaller Island of Tiree; Mull is beginning to move; the distant Lewis is threatened with the much-dreaded agricultural revolution.[33]

Almost invariably the zealots underestimated the intractability of the Highland problem. Occasionally they thought they were winning in the battle for modernisation. In 1835, for instance, James Loch of the Sutherland estate reviewed the consequences of the resettlement programme over which he had presided for twenty years. He firmly believed that the people whom he had cleared from the glens to the coasts were better off, and substantially less prone to famine, than before. Comparing the new settlers on the coast with the uncleared population, he remarked:

> They are a remarkably tall and fine race and especially the females, contrasting singularly with the wretchedness of their houses and cultivation ... Kirkaig is composed of persons who were removed there. Their houses are far better; their industries, considerable; their cultivation ... extended — altogether they were in better condition — confirming an observation that has always been very striking that it is only necessary to move the people from the lands, as originally occupied by them, and to disturb them in their original mode of holding in order to excite industry and improvement.[34]

Nevertheless even James Loch, the improver *par excellence*, was compelled, at the end of the day, to admit at least partial failure in his lifelong effort to hoist the Highlanders out of their poverty. Relatively impartial observers of the Highland scene believed that 'the agricultural revolution' in Sutherland had been forced through too violently for 'the sum of human happiness', and that the Highland people required 'long patience and much kindly forbearance'. But such humanitarianism always ran into the teeth of Malthusian imperatives.[35]

In reality it is not feasible to separate the motivations of landlords into different categories: motives were almost always mixed. But some of the landlords of the newer style came to the Highlands with the belief that their best approach would be a straightforward pursuit of 'rational' policies. It is evident, for instance, that some of the clearances in mid-century were executed, not in desperation by bankrupt proprietors, but by men who followed the logic of optimal land use as governed by prevailing market conditions. When Gordon of Cluny contemplated the western isles and their economic prospect, he made no allowance for any intrinsic difference from his properties in Aberdeenshire, where the application of capital and expertise had reaped large rewards. Gordon clearly believed that the introduction of improvement agriculture to the Hebrides would raise both rents and the condition of the people out of their notorious and primitive backwardness.

In 1836 Gordon's representatives examined the Clanranald estates, on Benbecula and North Uist, and initiated a series of negotiations with the owner. These interchanges provide some indication of the level of expectation in the mind of the prospective buyer. One letter remarked:

> The price is not yet fixed nor indeed has Mr Brown instructed us as to advertising. But I mentioned to them that the price would likely range from £110,000 to £120,000, and that with £30,000 laid out judiciously in improvements, the rental would be doubled. You are aware that Gordon is the richest commoner in Scotland, or perhaps in England, but his adviser Duguid is reckoned very sharp and cunning.[36]

The Clanranald trustees emphasised the sheer size of the property and its potential profitability. Clanranald himself was energetically opposed to the sale, but he was powerless to prevent the trustees pressing forward with their plan to sell. They regarded the estate merely as a burden to be rid of; Clanranald did not have the authority to stop them — 'No doubt you can do both [establish the Missives of sale and the Disposition] without him, but it is certainly better to carry him along with you.'[37] When Gordon came to the point of making a serious offer he was anxious about such questions as the length of existing leases, the actual rents paid, and the policy concerning the payment of ameliorations to tenants. As the agreements were drawn up it was insisted that

> If any further sums are found justly due to the Tenants at the Removal of all, or any of them, from their different possessions when the Leases expire, the Purchaser is to be relieved, by the Exoner paying the amount whatever may be the amount due to them.

This precautionary clause symbolised the manner of thinking, and the expectations, of Gordon and his advisers.

The Gordon-Clanranald negotiations brought face to face two extreme exemplars of the old and new styles of landlordism. Clanranald, reduced to financial impotence by a combination of inefficiency, bad luck and sentimentality, appealed to the better nature of Gordon, a man whose fortune was based on a single-minded devotion to maximising his return on literally every penny. In the middle of the protracted negotiations which he himself opposed, Clanranald told Gordon that his debts — which amounted to £45,000 — were entirely the result of 'bad and expensive management and neglect' by his factors. He opposed the 'alienation of ... my last remaining possession', and tried to retain part of his estate by striking a bargain with Gordon by which 'I should be allowed the happy prospect of spending the remainder of my days among the affectionately disposed tenantry, whose forefathers and mine have ever been united by ties of no ordinary degree of mutual attachment'. Gordon was not a man to countenance this type of soft-headedness. Clanranald tried a further stratagem in May 1839 when, in defiance of his trustees, he was reported as perambulating his lands 'calling on the Inhabitants and promising them Leases of their Possessions at Reduced Rents, stating that he is to keep possession of the Estates'. His tenacity was to no avail. Gordon of Cluny eventually acquired not only the Clanranald lands but, in 1841, the bankrupt estates of MacNeill of Barra. He attempted to apply Aberdeenshire methods of 'improvement' to the islands, and proclaimed his intention of retaining the native population at a higher standard of life. But it all turned sour and Gordon, like many others, eventually came to the view that evacuation was the only solution to his problem. His course of action was a set piece in the transition of attitudes. He became one of the greatest and the most loathed of the clearing landlords.[38]

VI

After the famine, for a quarter of a century, conditions in the north were somewhat better than for several decades. Nevertheless, though living standards must have improved, the region in its continuing rural squalor lagged far behind the majority of the nation.

Prices of agricultural commodities here, as elsewhere, were buoyant, and the sheepfarmers did remarkably well. But the problem of the dual economy remained undiminished: the crofting population eked out its restricted livelihood with small benefit to the landlords, and the large tenant-farmers continued to provide much the larger part of the growing rental income of the great estates. A measure of the cost of an excessive population was provided on the Argyll estate. Following the famine there was a great exodus from the island of Tiree which presented the Duke with the possibility of rearranging the tenancies. In consequence, the rent rose from £700 in 1847 to £2,260 in 1853.[39] It was a story common to much of the West Highlands for, while emigration had eased some of the population problem, congestion and immobility continued to mark the crofting economy. The Malthusian adjustment of the Highland economy was decisive, but always gradual.

The landlord perception of the changed environment was demonstrated in the remarks made by Balligall, factor of the Macdonald estates in Skye and North Uist in 1851-2 when, at last, the effects of famine had begun to recede. With reviving confidence, he reported that

> The stability of the Rental may not only be depended on, but it is expected to improve. Considerable rises in rent have been obtained recently in two large farms ... and measures are in progress which will very materially improve the condition of the small tenantry.[40]

In the event, this opinion turned out to be over-sanguine. The improvement of rents in mid-century came almost exclusively from the large tenants — sheepfarmers and sportsmen — while the crofting population, in many parts of the Highlands, paid little more in 1880 than they had in 1840, despite the rise in prices, including cattle prices. Throughout the period the small tenantry was generally regarded as uneconomic. In Kilmuir parish, for instance, Balligall noted that the small tenants continually squabbled about their common pasture, and that they failed to make full use of their land. The system, he thought, should be remodelled, but he warned that both the social and economic consequences might be serious. Any change would require

to be cautiously gone about owing to many of the poor cotters possessing a few sheep on the common hills [who] would undoubtedly become paupers were the Test removed whereby an Inspector can debar their admission from the Relief Roll.

The operation of the Poor Law, despite its notorious inadequacies, provided some restraining influence on landlord action.

Balligall's investigations provide useful windows into the nature of landlord/crofter relations in mid-century. He described the predicament of a large farmer of Snizort parish in Skye, who was encumbered by a number of crofters who would not get off his land. The factor recommended that 'in the event of re-let in 1858 they should be cleared away, if this is done the Rental might be maintained'. At the same time, in 1851, Balligall was able to look back over half a century of economic change in the parish of Portree on the same island. There was a specific farm which, he discovered, had been

> valued in 1810 by Mr Blackadder at £447 Stg. The advance since that period to the present rent of £847 Stg. shows the immense advantage to the Proprietor encouraging the system of clearing croft farms adjoining the larger possessions and the cultivation of the cheviot breed of sheep to which causes this rise is mainly attributable.

But much of the island property remained uncleared and, he argued, great tracts would be much more productive under the Cheviot regime. He gave the example of two farms at the banks of Loch Sligachan where there were 34 lots each with souming (that is, communal grazing) for two cows. Balligall remarked:

> These two farms are very troublesome, the crofters being on the confines of the deerforest their crofts will continue to be liable to damage from game. It would be very desirable could they ... be removed entirely and established elsewhere, they are miserably poor and always in arrear. Although the advantages of their situation for white fishing is unlimited they do not prosecute it.

Balligall was an unexceptional adviser whose views were echoed in the correspondence of many Highland factors during these years. It was practically a truism among these men that the land

would be better placed under sheep and deer; but they acknowledged, with almost equal unanimity, that the people could not
simply be heaved out of the country. In Balligall's perception the
people were dependent and childlike:

> Nor are the people altogether to be blamed for the distress
> nurtured by overpopulation during the paling [sic] days of the
> kelp trade; for then there was every encouragement held out for .
> an increase of population in addition to the natural one of a
> community in a healthy thriving condition. In the present
> reduced state of the lower class it is not for them but their
> superiors to devise such means as many permanently directly or
> indirectly improve their social condition.[41]

About their social and economic condition there was abundant
evidence. When Sir John MacNeill toured the famished region on
behalf of the Home Office in 1851, his conclusions were unambiguous. He reported that crofters existed on holdings which were
inadequate to the purpose of providing enough food for an
average family, and not enough to keep them for more than half a
year. Hence they had to provide half their subsistence — their rent,
clothing and everything else — out of wages won in a market which
had little demand for hired labour.[42] It was inevitable that they
would depend heavily on seasonal labour in the south. The fact
that they preferred this arrangement to final emigration was a
measure of their attachment to the Highlands.[43] It was also a fact
of life in the operation of the Highland economy.

The final burst of great clearances in the Highlands occurred in
the years 1852 and 1855. The famine had persuaded landowners
that clearance and mass emigration were the only solutions to the
economic problems of their estates and, by extension, those of the
region itself. After 1855, for two decades the Highland economy
settled into an increasingly ossified duality, reinforced by the
renewed development of deer forests in the region. Landlords were
relieved to see their sheep farm and sporting rents rise strongly
throughout the 1850s and 1860s. But they were inhibited from any
further pursuit of clearance by the noise that such events now
invariably generated. Some minor adjustments of crofter tenancies
were achieved, but mostly the small tenants were left alone, toler-
ated grudgingly by their landlords. Moreover, despite quite severe
recurrence of potato blight — in 1862-3 and 1872 — the crofters,

in their reduced numbers, were able to survive perhaps more comfortably than at any time in the previous four decades. Emigration continued to carry away substantial numbers, expecially the young and the fit, but the general level of exit was lower than in the period 1845-55. In effect there was a lull in the contest for land in the Highlands, probably a reflection of the relatively buoyant state of the northern economy. Aggregate rents rose rapidly for the landlords, but the increase came primarily from the non-crofter sector. In these circumstances most landlords were prepared to leave their small tenants alone. It is likely that the real income of crofters rose substantially in these years as a consequence of improved cattle prices. Rents for crofts, in contrast, remained stable on most estates and the improvement in real income was not passed on to the landlords who derived rent increases almost exclusively from the large farmers and sporting tenants.[44]

The good years ended in the late 1870s when, once again, the prices of Highland products declined precipitously and crops failed over a number of seasons. Once more rancour erupted between crofters and landlords: the edge of conflict sharpened dangerously and a new political consciousness was aroused, inspired in part by the concurrent agitation over the Irish question. The deepening depression in the northern economy in the quinquennium 1878 to 1883 accelerated the growth of crofter agitation.[45] The parliamentary inquiry into crofting in 1882-3, prompted by the agitation, exposed the vast social divisions in Highland society; it also revealed much detail about the economic status of the crofting population. For the estate of Sutherland, for instance, there were statistics from three north-west mainland parishes of the rental income derived from the crofters, with the landlord's annual expenditure on poor rates and school rates.

Table 18.1: Rental and Rates on Sutherland Estate (£)

	Rental	Poor and school rates
Tongue	904	780
Farr	679	1,226
Reay	544	270
	2,127	2,276

The factor of this part of the Sutherland estate commented:

> This shows that the proprietor would be a gainer of many thousands a year in saved rates and extra rental, if he had no crofters whatever. This is not meant as an argument for their extinction or eviction but as showing the difficulty of dealing successfully with a great evil and the great danger of extending the system.[46]

He believed that even if the Duke of Sutherland gave the crofters their land entirely free of rent they would not be appreciably better off: their annuals rents were equivalent to only four weeks' wages, and the crofts were too small for their maintenance.

Adversity in the crofting economy was matched by a rapid decline in many prices from the late 1870s until the mid-1890s. It represented not a mere cyclical downturn but another external shock which imposed further structural change on the Highland economy. Improved co-ordination of raw material markets on a global scale brought Highland sheepfarmers into competition with those of the new world, notably in South Africa, Argentina and Australia. It was an unequal competition and the economies of scale achieved by colonial producers drove down the prices of wool and meat. The writing was on the wall by 1879. A Sutherland factor told the estate commissioner, Sir Arnold Kemball, that 'the adverse elements of competition which affected the agricultural and grazing interests of the country ... have ... been intensified'. He believed that the competition would worsen yet further, especially from the American prairie producers aided by the science of refrigeration for meat. Added to this was 'the stagnation and disastrous condition of things at home [which] are driving the best and most energetic of our farming population abroad to become, in their turn, keen competitors in the home market'.[47] Australian and New Zealand wool production was too competitive for Scotch producers who were handicapped also by poor seasons which decimated the sheep population.

From the crofter's point of view the debilitation of the sheep economy had little significance except in the sense that it made their own demands for extra land seem less resistible. Indeed the depression of prices in the sheep economy necessarily diminished the likely costs of land reform in the Highlands. However, the reduced profitability of sheep also increased the trend towards the substitution of deer for sheep in many parts. The development of deer forests in the north of Scotland represented a curious repercussion of British industrialisation. In the last chapter it was argued that the main effect of industrialisation had been to create intense demands for raw materials from the Highlands, and to reduce its levels of employment. In this phase, however, the profits of southern industry were directed into the Highlands as a form of consumption. The extension of the railway system made the Highlands accessible to southern sportsmen whose 'rage' for the sport, according to the Earl of Malmesbury, had begun in 1833. They undoubtedly helped to sustain aggregate rent levels in the Highlands. Deer forests probably exerted a greater employment effect than sheepfarming and it was part of the nature of the sport that the participants were seen to spend as ostentatiously as possible.[48] In 1857 Alexander Russel reported that 'an enormous amount of London money [was] being spent in the Highlands', and he commented that 'we cannot see the harm, at least to anybody in the Highlands, from the Dublin banker, the London "brewer", or the English "lordling" choosing to pay it'. It was certainly better than the preceding outflow of landlord capital into high living in London.[49]

Deer farming was a seasonal and capricious industry, a service sector which required isolation from the native population of the region. It helped to bolster estate finances and to support land prices in the north. It may have helped to keep crofter rents down in some places, by cross-subsidisation, but deer forests did nothing to generate broadly-based development in the north. I. F. Grant expressed this attitude in a paper written in 1928:

It is humiliating that so large a part of our country should be dependent upon the luxury tastes of the rich people who rent Highland moors and forests, but were it not for these sporting tenants it is impossible to see how the proprietors could provide the steadings and permanent improvements that are essential to modern standards of agriculture, or how the local revenue for providing the customary social services could be raised.[50]

The tourist trade, like other forms of seasonal employment, helped to make life tolerable for the residue of the crofting population. But crofting itself remained a marginal existence, and the ideal of a self-sustaining prosperous peasantry in the Scottish Highlands was mainly illusion, even in the twentieth century.

The coexistence of deer stalking and crofters' poverty was too provocative for some Victorian opinion. The moral response was best expressed in the damaging and influential words of John Stuart Mill in 1865:

> The pretension of two Dukes to shut up a part of the Highlands, and exclude the rest of mankind from many square miles of mountain scenery to prevent disturbances to wild animals, is an abuse; it exceeds the legitimate bounds of the rights of landed property. When land is not intended to be cultivated, no good reason can in general be given for its being private property at all; and if anyone is permitted to call it his, he ought to know that he holds it by sufferance of the community.[51]

VII

The record of the response by the several elements in the Highland community to the economic circumstances of the nineteenth century did not always adhere to the expectations of classical political economy. Had the landlords pursued the maximisation of returns on capital and land without restraint, it is likely that the population of the region would have been considerably smaller than it actually was in 1850 to 1880; had the crofter population responded more positively to wage differentials between the Highlands and the rest of the world, they would have abandoned their crofts much earlier, they would have engaged more in fishing, and they would have emigrated earlier and in larger numbers. In fact the poorest lingered in the north and the west the longest. The market determinants, though enormously and pervasively powerful, were not the only forces of influence in the region. The sheepfarmers conformed most closely to the model of rational economic behaviour: they invested their capital with great efficiency and at all stages looked for the best return. The crofters were to an important degree insulated from the dictates of the market, not only by their particular way of life and their lower material expectations, but also by their smaller involvement in the cash economy. The landlords themselves, as this chapter has argued, did not behave uniformly: they were influenced in different degrees by changing perceptions of their social, economic and moral obligations in the community. In many instances their actions were based upon either poor or eccentric calculations of the rate of return on their capital.

On the evidence of individual estates, investment in Highland property appears to have yielded very low monetary returns compared with alternative opportunities offered in the rest of the British economy. The record, which has never been analysed systematically, seems to confirm impressions that, at least for the middle nineteenth century, landlords reaped very small, or even negative, returns from their Highland estates. There are statistics, gathered by W. R. Greg, which claim to demonstrate the actual return on capital in the years of the destitution to about 1851. For example, between 1846 and 1850 Rainy, proprietor of the island of Raasay, was reported to have spent £1,672 beyond the rental income of his estate, mainly on draining, trenching and road-making in an effort to sustain local employment. Yet the condition of the people did not improve, nor did the rental respond to the investment. The Duke of Argyll experienced an almost identical result with respect to his operations on Mull, 'yet without being able to check the increasing poverty of the people'. The same source reported that Forsyth of Sorne, in 1849, spent £1,296 on wages and material for his estate, yet received only £113 of the nominal rent of £305 per annum. Clarke of Ulva spent more than his rent; so did Lord Dunmore on Harris, and Maclean of Coll's expenditure was only £7 less than his rent of £1,171. Gordon of Cluny, whose policies were among the most controversial of all landlords, spent £4,834 more than his rental during the famine years; for the entire period 1843 to 1851 his estates in South Uist and Barra produced a revenue of £25,606 while his total expenditure amounted to £19,752. In 1847 alone, the Duke of Sutherland, with a rental of about £39,000, spent £78,000 on the Sutherland estate, exclusive of his outlays on the reconstruction of Dunrobin Castle. For the period 1811 to 1883 the Dukes of Sutherland almost continually overspent their income in the Highlands. Not all these expenditures can be categorised as productive investment or even relief expenditure. Some of it was obviously a form of conspicuous consumption. Nor are the figures precise enough to allow a firm calculation of rates of return. But the fact remains that, regardless of motive, capital was pumped into the estates in contrast to the extractive policies of the pre-clearance era.[52]

The best example of all landlord expenditure relates to Sir James Matheson, who channelled much of his commercial wealth into the Long Island — in a mere five years, 1845-50, he undertook works costing £101,875, and outlays on education and charity totalling £73,870 — a figure far beyond the revenues of the island. A few years later Alexander Russel, editor of the *Scotsman*, cast a jaundiced eye over Matheson's incredible outlays and judged that 'the condition of the people is in no whit improved socially or morally, and it is no secret that, as for pecuniary return, the proprietor might as well have sunk his treasure in the sea as in the bogs'. Russel provided other evidence of well-meaning landlord investment in small farm development which had come to nothing. Lord Macdonald had spent £100,000 on improvement on Skye, yet his heir 'was lately obtaining literally not one shilling from the whole of his far stretching territory'. Macleod of Macleod, who had resisted the idea of clearances, ended up with a starving tenantry and himself bankrupt. Sir F. Mackenzie of Gairloch spent large amounts on the improvement of small holdings to no positive result — the people could not feed themselves, let alone pay their rent.[53]

Landlord expenditures during the famine years may have been exceptional, but evidence from individual estates for other periods of the century confirms the general impression of low rates of return. In many cases these expenditures were only possible because proprietors were able to draw upon non-Highland resources. For many of the new owners of Highland property in the mid-nineteenth century, land in the north of Scotland was a way of enjoying their financial success earned in other parts of the British economy (associated in some cases with the challenge of improvement in such a backward zone). The 'psychic returns' were certainly a considerable compensation — people bought land for 'the glamour of the West Highlands' and they knew that losses would occur. As Phillip Gaskell points out, 'it seems most unlikely that anyone could have made a return on the purchase price'.[54] Some of the new landowners undoubtedly regarded the ownership of land in the Highlands as a form of consumption rather than a productive investment.[55] But as long as the land prices remained buoyant, low annual returns could be at least partly compensated for by capital gains on eventual sales. Highland landowners sometimes appear to have been easy prey to fast-talking southern advisers who conjured with visions of great rent-rolls. Land was regarded as the best very long-run security for the placement of capital, and they may have sensed a dearth of other suitable investment opportunities in this category. Landlords repeatedly miscalculated the likely return on their outlays. Poor and amateurish economic management cannot be discounted.

These changing patterns of land ownership and tenancy in the late-nineteenth-century Highlands produced a remarkable juxtaposition of some of the most successful entrepreneurs of the Victorian age with the least modernised agrarian margin. The qualitative consequences are difficult to assess. It is not uncommon for the decline of Highland culture to be attributed to the alleged breakdown of the old social solidarity and the poverty of social leadership in the new regime. On this subject there are many imponderables and few reliable criteria or measures for comparison. Certainly the composition of land ownership had changed rapidly, even in the eighteenth century. In 1825 it was reported that wide areas of Strathconan, Ardoss, Muirtown and Milncraig had been bought up by 'gentlemen of the law in Edinburgh'.[56] English and Scottish bankers were prominent, as were Glasgow merchants. Lord Teignmouth in 1835 identified another stratum:

> East Indians and half-pay officers have also obtained in smaller portions, a large share of Highland and Insular property, often selecting it in the neighbourhood of their birth and early youth — a gratifying proof of their strength of local attachment and hereditary predilections.[57]

Sir Alexander Geikie, somewhat later, testified to the widespread extinction of old families renowned for their pride of pedigree who, by poverty, were compelled to make way for rich merchants, bankers, brewers, ironmasters and manufacturers.[58]

Undoubtedly the upper echelons of Highland society witnessed a rapid change of composition in the age of the clearances — the elimination of the tacksman class and the entry of many non-Highland shepherds, factors and landowners altered the complexion of the society. An alien land ownership may have persuaded the small tenantry to turn inwards into their own community, and into the hands of the Free Church ministers. The social distance between the common people and the higher strata almost certainly widened. Society was polarised. Absenteeism, though there is no basis for comparison with the rest of Britain, probably widened the gulf. In 1841, in the distressed areas of the west, it was estimated that 46 out of 195 proprietors were absentee.[59] Many contemporary observers believed that the consequence was neglect and oppression. Thus Catherine Sinclair, the novelist and philanthropist, wrote in 1850:

> The Highland tenantry, like those in Ireland, are suffering beneath the iron rule of absentees, who employ what the Scotch appropriately call 'grieves', Anglice bailiffs, to be resident managers, and who look upon an estate as a mere machine for making money, while thousands of our countrymen are hurrying to Australia or Canada.[60]

Yet there was nothing new in absenteeism; a hundred years before complaints had been equally long and loud.[61] Thomas Brassey, the great railway contractor, in 1857 had similarly caustic remarks for the influence of agents and landlords:

> Land and island owners, glorying in their £60,000 per annum, hardly wrung from a poverty stricken tenantry, so far from endeavouring to improve the condition of their tenants, are wont to expend their whole substance in the gaieties of the London season; while the entire care of the property appears to be entrusted to a set of factors who, to the sole advantage of their privy purse, habitually exact double rental. No areas of redress exists for the unhappy tenants, whose complaints, addressed to the proprietor are, by him, of course, referred to the astute and pitiless factor.[62]

In such remarks there was always the danger of facile caricature. Just as southern owners came to the Highlands with unrealistic visions of profit and improvement; it was likely that external observers underestimated the sheer difficulty of Highland estate administration and the intractable problems of poverty in the crofting community. Nevertheless internal evidence, derived from estate records, provides enough examples of landlord neglect and factorial arrogance to indicate that at least part of the indictment was valid.

Notes

1. James Macdonald, *General View of the Agriculture of the Hebrides* (London, 1811), pp. 730-1.

2. See Bristow, 'The Liberty and Property Defence League and Individualism'. On the weakness of the landlords' response see Reginald MacLeod, 'The Crofters: How to Benefit them', *Blackwood's Magazine*, vol. 1139 (1886), p. 563.

3. See, for instance, the story of Traill and Burroughs, well told in Thomson, *The Little General.*

4. See, for instance Dr Mackenzie to Sir George Grey, 12 September 1846, on the problems of Scottish wardship; *PP* (1847), LIII, Correspondence from July 1846 to February 1847 Relating to the Measures Adopted for the Relief of the Distress in Scotland, pp. 25-7. On entail see R. C. Michie, *Money, Mania and Markets* (Edinburgh, 1981), p. 79.

5. SRO, RH2/8/24 Report of John Blackadder, land surveyor, on the agriculture of Skye and North Uist, 1799-1800.

6. Ibid.

7. SRO, RH2/4/87, fo.151 (Home Office Papers), A. Macdonell of Glengarry to Pelham, 21 March 1802.

8. This section is based upon an unpublished paper by Mr David Graham-Campbell entitled 'An Argyllshire Estate during a Minority 1800'. I am most grateful to the author for allowing me to quote from this paper.

9. MacNeil of Gigha, John Campbell W. S. of Edinburgh, and George Howe of Paxton, Roxburghshire (ibid.).

10. Ibid., George Howe to John Campbell, 17 August 1801.

11. Ibid., John Campbell to MacNeil, 27 January 1801, 23 December 1803, 25 March 1804.

12. Ibid., MacNeil to Campbell, 2 February 1804; the northern part of the Shirvan estate was sold to Malcolm of Poltalloch in the 1810s and some of the dispossessed tenants probably settled in the new village of Lochgilphead belonging to the neighbouring laird, Campbell of Auchendarroch.

13. See Eric Richards, 'Structural Change in a Regional Economy: Sutherland and the Industrial Revolution, 1780-1830', *Economic History Review*, vol. 26 (1973).

14. SRO, GD221/58, Campbell to Campbell, 4 April 1803.

15. SRO, Breadalbane Muniments, GD112/74/18, letter of 5 January 1812.

16. See David Cannadine, 'Aristocratic Indebtedness in the 19th Century: the Case Re-opened', *Economic History Review*, vol. 30 (1977); and the exchange with D. Spring in ibid., vol. 33 (1980).

17. See Flinn, *Scottish Population History*, pp. 335-48.

18. SRO, Clanranald Papers, GD201/1/352; GD201/5/1217/46.

19. SRO, Lord Macdonald MSS, GD221/38, Report of North Uist factor as to arrears, 14 December 1839.

20. SRO, Riddell Papers, AF49/3, Report of Thomas Anderson, 1829; AF49/6 Report of Thomas Goldie Dickson; AF49/5, Trustee accounts, August 1851; GD1/395/26, Correspondence and Memorial Relative to a Disentail of Ardnamurchan by Sir James M. Riddell, Bart, November 1848.

21 Reay sold his ancestral estates and bought a villa in Ealing. SRO, Loch Muniments, GD268/224, Lady Stafford to Loch, 1 December 1832.

22. *Elgin and Morayshire Courier*, 26 October 1849.

23. On Lewis see Macdonald, *Lewis*, on the infusion of imported wealth in Easter Ross, see Mowat, *Easter Ross*, pp. 18, 21-2, 32.

24. His rents, nevertheless, grew very rapidly. In 1810 he exulted in a 'gloriously successful' expedition to the north when he let Lewis for £11,000, Brahan for £4,200 and Kintail for £2,000, all exclusive of kelp and timber revenues. SRO, NRA (Scot) 1454, Adam of Blair Adam Papers, General Correspondence 1810, Seaforth to Adam, 27 November 1810.

25. Barron, *Northern Highlands*, III, p. xlx. See also the discussion in Hobson, 'Congestion and Depopulation', pp. 30-9. On Matheson, see *Proceedings of the Royal Society of London* (1879), pp. xxi-ii; letter of Hugh M. Matheson to *The Times*, 27 January 1888.

26. Day, *Public Administration*, pp. 183-4.

27. Ibid., pp. 183-5; Smout, *History of the Scottish People*, p. 353; Macdonald, *Lewis*; Caird, *Park*, p. 3. On Leverhulme, see Nicolson, *Lord of the Isles.*

28. Quoted in Cooper, *Road to the Isles*, p. 142.

29. See Eric Richards, 'An Anatomy of the Sutherland Fortune: Income, Consumption, Investments and Returns, 1780-1880', *Business History*, vol. 21 (1979), pp. 58-63.

30. *Inverness Courier*, 22 January 1840. The emigration was a disaster. Glengarry lost most of his money and returned to Scotland to die.

31. Ramsay, *Scotland and Scotsmen*, p. 529.

32. See, for example, Richards, 'Problems on the Cromartie Estate', pp. 158-61.

33. Smith is quoted in Barron, *Northern Highlands*, III, p. 59; the 1846 comment is from [J. F. W. Johnston,] 'On the State and Prospects of British Agriculture', *Edinburgh Review*, vol. 84 (1846), p. 428.

34. SCRO, Sutherland Collection, D593/N/4/1/1c, Loch's tour of Sutherland and Reay, 1835.

35. See Richards, *Leviathan*, pp. 277-8; Johnston, 'State and Prospects of British Agriculture', pp. 418-19.

36. SRO, Clanranald Papers, GD201/5/1223, Hunter Campbell to Duncan Shaw, 24 May 1836.

37. Ibid., Campbell to Brown, 22 June 1836.

38. Ibid., Macdonald to Gordon, 2 December 1839; Duguid to Hunter, 16 February 1837; Brown to Hunter, 22 June 1836. See Richards, *Highland Clearances*, pp. 402ff.

39. Cregeen, 'Oral Sources', *passim.*

40. Quoted in Leigh, 'Crofting Problem, p. 139.

41. SRO, GD221/77, Report by Mr Balligall, factor on the Macdonald estate, 1851.

42. Day, *Public Administration*, p. 102.

43. See Devine, 'Temporary Migration', *passim.*

44. See, for instance, Richards, 'An Anatomy', pp. 70-8, and below, Ch. 19. On the impact of public burdens on estate finances in Orkney, see Thomson, *The Little General*, p. 121.

45. See Richards, *Highland Clearances*, Ch. 15.

46. SCRO, Sutherland Collection, D593/4/1/8/20, Thomas Purves, 23 June 1883. Napier Commission, Evidence, pp. 2776ff.

47. SCRO, Sutherland Collection, D593/N/2/4, Crawford to Kemball, 22 June 1881.

48. The employment effects of deer stalking have been the subject of debate. In 1873 a Royal Commission was told that sheep farms kept six to ten times as many inhabitants as deer forests or grouse moors. Recent studies have been more critical. The employment effects have been considered (in relation to concurrent changes in sheepfarming) by Orr, *Deer Forests*, pp. 107-18, App. IX, and also Hunter, *Crofting Community*, pp. 108-9. *PP* (1873), XIII, Report from the SC on Game

Laws, Q. 3490. On rents see Earl of Malmesbury, *Memoirs of an Ex-Minister* (London, 1885), p. 41.

49. Russel, 'Men, Sheep and Deer', pp. 505-6. By 1885 one-third of the Highlands was let to sportsmen; see Robert Hall, *The Highland Sportsman and Tourist* (London, 1885), pp. 27-9.

50. I. F. Grant, 'Some Accounts of Individual Highland Sporting Estates', *Economic History*, no. 3, Supplement to *Economic Journal* (January 1928), p. 411.

51. Quoted in W. L. Guttsman (ed.), *The English Ruling Class* (London, 1969), pp. 93-4, Cf. Orr, *Deer Forests*, p. 148.

52. Figures derived from Greg, 'Highland Destitution and Irish Emigration', pp. 167-8; R. Elliot, *Special Report on Sutherland and the West Highlands* (pamphlet, 1848), p. 9. See also evidence presented in Orr, *Deer Forests*, especially pp. 93-4. Some complication of the question of low rates of return on Highland land ownership is created by the inflation of land prices during the nineteenth century. There were times when prices appeared to move ahead much more rapidly than, and almost independently of, current rental income. Capital gains were substantial and relatively predictable, and may have reflected a deferred return on capital — which was not otherwise apparent in the annual rates of return.

53. [Russel,] 'Men, Sheep and Deer', pp. 482-3. Napier Commission, Appendix A, p. 154; Evidence, pp. 1144 *et seq.*

54. Gaskell, *Morvern Transformed*, p. 60.

55. Lord Tweedmouth bought large tracts of the central Highlands in 1855 for the 'great natural beauties and ... good grouse shooting. For these reasons, I purchased the property at what was then, before railway days, considered a fancy price. I certainly did not purchase it on account of its rental.' Sir John William Rawson also bought into the Highlands. He said, 'My first inducement was to obtain a deer forest, but I wished, in addition to that, to become possessed of a large extent of wild land which would give me the opportunity of planting and draining and improving it according to my wishes.' Napier Commission, pp. 2930, 2949.

56. Barron, *Northern Highlands*, II, pp. 3-4. See Mowat, *Easter Ross, passim.*

57. Teignmouth, *Sketches*, I, p. 52.

58. Geikie, *Reminiscences*, p. 185. The mobility of ownership was not new; see Mowat, *Easter Ross*, pp. 17-18.

59. Leigh, 'Crofting Problem', p. 430. See also Mowat, *Easter Ross*, pp. 43, 89.

60. Sinclair, *Scotland and the Scotch*, p. 174.

61. Bumsted, *The People's Clearance*, p. 31.

62. Quoted in Cooper, *Road to the Isles*, p. 108.

19

ECONOMICS, MORALS AND ALTERNATIVES

As the evil at present seems to arise chiefly from the Conduct of the Landowners, in changing the Economy of their Estates, it may be questioned whether Government can with Justice interfere, or whether any essential Benefits are likely to arise from this Interference.

Thomas Telford, 1802

A country is poor because it is poor.

Ragnar Nurkse, 1953

I

Why did the Highlands remain a zone of poverty and rural backwardness throughout the nineteenth century while Britain became the most successful economy in the world? Why were its people hauled through the tragic dislocation of the clearances? How could such a sequence of events occur in the richest and best organised country in Europe? The past two chapters have outlined some of the pressures and imperatives that propelled the region into a series of painful choices. The circumstances of the Highland economy set the limits on these choices, and defined the boundaries of landlord action and the crofter response.

Nevertheless, despite the strength of these arguments, it would be an over-simplification to suggest that the events in the Highlands were entirely governed by economic determinants, or were otherwise inevitable. A large part of the Highland experience in the nineteenth century hinged upon the structure of authority which allowed the proprietors to make decisions on behalf of the entire society, without consulting the interests of the majority of its people. In many respects these men, and a few women, were the true descendants of the pre-1745 autocrats who had ruled the Highlands with an ancient arbitrary authority. Their actions, in their turn, were influenced by their perceived social roles and moral obligations, and by old and new patterns of consumption and investment. The collective psychology of the landlord class in the age of the clearances was crucial in determining the direction of adjustment of the Highland economy. The common people's attitude to land, their reproductive behaviour, their response to economic incentives, their will to resist and their rhythm of labour all influenced the general response of this society to the structural changes in the employment of Highland resources. The character of social leadership was also crucial in determining how this society came to terms with the pressures of population growth and economic change. The obliteration of the tacksman class, the continuous drain of youth by migration, the social abdication of many of the landowners and the invisibility of the sheepfarmers all undoubtedly diminished the ability of this society to shape its own future. It left the Highlands bereft of its old social leadership and created a vacuum which was filled by the new ministers of religious extremism — the revivalists, and the hard men of the Free Presbyterian Church who triumphed in the Disruption.

Analysis of trends in income distribution during the age of the clearances is much handicapped by the deficiency of data. Statistics of regional income are almost entirely lacking and there are few figures for the main indicators of production and consumption. Little is known about the quantities of cattle, whisky, wool, kelp, oatmeal and potatoes produced, and there is only fragmentary evidence for trends in rent. At bottom, much of the controversy about the Highland experience has been about the allocation of benefits and losses consequent upon the great economic changes.

The peasant sector of the economy presents the historian with the largest problem because it is notoriously difficult to gauge production in a regime of near-subsistence agriculture. Like many peasant societies, the crofters' input and output in economic life were, to a large extent, not measurable. The great cash-export commodity of this economy, cattle, appears to have expanded rapidly throughout the eighteenth century, and the Highlands in general benefited from a favourable movement in the terms of trade between the region and the rest of the country. After 1815 the trend was reversed and income from cattle exports declined.

The same arc was followed by kelp and whisky production, both of which generated widespread employment effects, together with fishing and linen production. The introduction of potatoes increased the productivity of arable land in a sustained fashion, and was a vital addition to the expansion of the economy because it used the ample factor of production, labour, and required little land and virtually no capital. The peasant economy was buttressed by income derived for seasonal labour and service in the Highland regiments. The introduction of sheepfarming into the region greatly augmented its income. Before 1815 it helped to induce an atmosphere of expansion and confidence which persuaded landlords to invest in many types of development — most notably in agricultural improvements, villages and road construction, as well as the construction of opulent homes. Though sheepfarming had feeble employment and linkage effects, it swelled regional income and generated some minor local expansion.

The economic effects of these developments were complex. Much of the growth drew strongly on the abundant factor of production, labour, and helped to sustain *per capita* incomes despite the growth of population. Processing employment in kelp and linen expanded vigorously and nascent factory production in cotton began in, for instance, east Sutherland in the 1790s. But the advance was narrowly based and soon checked: no indigenous chemical industry developed to employ the products of kelp; industrialised woollen manufacture did not develop in the Highlands; there was no linen or cotton weaving; tanning of sheep hides was very slight; and the only authentic forward linkage that developed was in fish processing which created useful urban growth in Caithness and eastern Sutherland. Most landlord enterprise, directed to labour-intensive manufacturing, was easily snuffed out in the adverse conditions after Waterloo.

The benefits of increased regional income were not evenly distributed. Much of the income derived by the region as a consequence of its trade with other regions was effectively cornered by the landlords, whose consumption habits caused a large part of the gain to leak away from the Highlands. The potential benefits by local consumption and by productive investment were negated by a landlord class which seems to have spent itself towards bankruptcy with suicidal enthusiasm. As Malcolm Gray has written, the landlords 'swept away the greater part of the new peasant surplus'.[1] Any of the surplus retained was dissipated by the overwhelming growth of the peasant population. And when the pillars of the economy crumbled the peasantry, harried by clearing land-lords, reacted slowly to the changed circumstances. Population growth continued into the period of economic contraction, and emigration was relatively slow to drain away the surplus. Rent fell slowly and fragmentary evidence, where available, suggests that the marginal productivity of labour was close to zero. Almost certainly the standard of living of small tenants fell between 1810 and 1850.

Sheepfarmers, on the whole, weathered the difficulties until wool prices rose again in the mid-1830s: greater efficiencies in breeding, winter feeding and marketing appear to have assisted their survival. Landowners, from 1815 to 1840, had to cope with reduced rental incomes and greater demands on their resources during intermittent famines. Many went under. They sold out to men who sometimes brought investment capital to the north; but whoever gained possession of the land was confronted with the problem of the persistently low rate of return on capital. Maxi-misation of income required switching land use between crofters, sheepfarmers and sportsmen. In most of the rest of Britain land-lords were able to deploy their lands to the best personal advantages, primarily because further agricultural adjustment to market forces, being relatively gradual, caused little social dis-location after the 1830s.

In the Highlands, the relocation of the people demanded whole-sale emigration because the region was unable to offer alternative employment appointments. Crofting itself was a ramshackle device for the retention of the old peasantry and solved none of the eco-nomic and few of the social problems of the Highlands.

The demographic impact of agrarian transformation throughout Europe at this time depended to a large extent on the labour intensity of the new agriculture and the growth of industry.[2] The demographic historian E. A. Wrigley has remarked that it was a great good fortune for England in these years 'that the Industrial Revolution rescued her from what must otherwise have been a period of great stress due to the pace of population increase'.[3] It is plain that the Highlands of Scotland were not rescued from this fate, and the story of the clearances is an aspect of that 'period of great stress'. The Industrial Revolution mitigated some pressure of numbers by providing, in England and central Scotland, some absorption of the outflow of the Highland population. But it also exacerbated the problems of the local economy by destroying most of its native industrial structure and stifling the development of new industry.[4] After 1815, in the long slump of prices, Highland industry capitulated to southern competition.

It is clear therefore that Highland proprietors confronted a moral dilemma greater than most of their southern counterparts. They were expected, both then and in retrospect, to forgo rent increases and to preserve an expanded population in an obsolescent agriculture. Had the Highland lairds followed the dictates of market forces they would have evicted most of the small tenantry without compunction, and without alternative accommodation. In reality most landlords retreated from the full violence of *laissez-faire*; many came to an unsatisfactory compromise which combined clearance with the retention of the small tenantry on crofts, a solution that perpetuated the problem of overpopulation and compounded the fundamental problem of land shortage. Some landlords were held back by a sense of social duty, by the increasing effectiveness of public opinion, and by the fear of political consequences. In the end they were hamstrung by the remarkable legislation (deriving from the Napier Commission Report of 1884) which gave the crofter almost absolute security of tenure and the right to an independently fixed rent so that, as D. R. F. Simpson has observed, 'the landlord has actually no economic relations with his crofter-tenant'.[5]

Undoubtedly there had been cases of ruthless eviction (which have been documented elsewhere), but the full fury of economic adjustment was tempered by the restraint of some (perhaps most) of the landlord class towards the tenantry. This, of course, is tantamount to saying that though the social catastrophe of the clearances was severe enough, it could have been even worse.[6]

An anonymous writer in 1838 addressed himself directly to the double-standard which seemed to condemn the Highland laird yet absolved his Lowland equivalent. He argued that when the landlords converted their lands 'to valuable sheep instead of a dwarfish and profitless race of black cattle', and shifted the people to the seaside 'to manufacture formerly useless sea ware', there was good common sense in their actions. They could not have been expected to predict the collapse of the kelp industry; nor was the turn in fortune any different from events in the rest of the country. He pointed out that:

Landlords in the South have vastly increased their rentals by suffering manufactories to be established on their properties. The proprietors of these works have amassed enormous wealth, but are they held responsible for the redundant and indigent population, of which a glut in the markets, or stoppage of trade, is the secondary, but they themselves, the original cause? Certainly, until it is considered wise policy to check by the imposition of some such responsibility the extravagance of commerce and reckless speculation throughout the kingdom at large, it cannot be just or expedient in respect to landlords in the Highlands, where the ability to bear such an infliction is totally wanting in most of them.[7]

In terms of the distribution of income, it seems likely that, from 1815 to about 1850, the crofter class suffered not only an absolute decline in welfare (from the fall of cattle prices) but also a deprivation disproportionate to the rest of the Highland community. Rents seem to have fallen more slowly than the prices of most of the staples of crofter production. But from the famine of 1847 until the 1870s the reverse tendencies almost certainly applied: small tenants' rents rose, if at all, less than prices, and the living standards improved roughly parallel with the experience of small tenants in Ireland.

II

In the last resort, the economics of the clearances is about the returns to the factors of production, during and after the transformation of the Highland economy. The outcome was influenced by the manner in which incomes were generated in the region, and the proportions in which these incomes were distributed between the three main categories: crofters, sheepfarmers and landlords. The exercise is complicated because the composition of the economy, the balance of production and the relative sizes of the main sectors changed radically over time. The transfer of land first to graziers and later to sportsmen necessarily reduced the crofters' relative contribution to regional income and rent. The movement of prices and productivity of the key staples of the region determined the aggregate output of the several sectors, and the population growth rates inevitably influenced the trends of social welfare.

The economics of the sheepfarming sector of the Highlands is relatively straightforward. Incoming sheepfarmers, sustained by high prices for wool and sheep, gaining great economies of scale and importing their own capital, were able to pay the escalating rents of the years 1780 to 1815. The landowners, who contributed relatively little to the cost of innovations or reorganisation, reaped extraordinary gains, as the trend of rents followed that of wool prices.[8] The clearances enabled the landlords to take advantage of these prices virtually without investment outlay of their own. To those landlords, for example the Sutherland family, who connected a policy of clearance with positive investment schemes in non-pastoral activity, the return on capital outlay was derisory. Indeed, throughout the nineteenth century, the return on land was almost entirely determined not by internal investment policies of landlords but by externally determined price trends. After Waterloo wool prices fell rapidly. There was a modest recovery in the 1830s and then prices increased strongly between 1850 and 1880. Landlords, usually after some time lag, adjusted rents in line with these trends, while improved productivity helped maintain the sheepfarmers and their landlords during the years of depression.[9]

The crofting economy is altogether more difficult to analyse. In part, the crofter was a subsistence farmer, usually engaged in both arable and pasture activities; but he also sold on the market, cattle being his great cash crop, and bought and sold meal, potatoes and other products of the family economy. He might exchange output on a barter basis — for instance leather goods, yarn, cloth and cheese. Some crofters travelled annually to the fishing centres on the east coast, some to the southern harvests, while others would work locally as part-time day labourers. Some income was derived from the 'black economy', from whisky sales. The crofter's purchases varied over time — during shortfalls in potato production, increased expenditure on meal could have a devastating effect on the wealth-holdings of the peasantry. As the taste for southern consumer products (especially textiles) expanded, the demand for local handicrafts inevitably declined.

In these circumstances, it is exceedingly difficult to provide an index of crofter income during the age of the clearances. Although price trends may be sketched, it is not possible to determine aggregate or *per capita output* over time. Crofter welfare was heavily dependent on the price of cattle which contemporaries regarded as the most important single source of cash income for the small tenantry in the Highlands. Cattle numbers and values were decisive because they provided the fund from which rents were paid and meal purchase financed.[10] It is important to note Malcolm Gray's educated guess that, despite the sheep clearances, the number of cattle in the Highlands was maintained remarkably well, although it did not keep pace with population growth in the years to 1845. 'On the whole it seems that a broadly unchanged total stock divided among an increased number of families allowed each family somewhat smaller possessions.' Living standards therefore depended on cattle prices, the availability of supplementary incomes and the share of peasant income appropriated by the landlord through his rent. Much of the information on relative incomes is not available and, until the 1850s, most rents are not disaggregated to show the differential contribution of small and large tenants. Moreover, in the early phases of the clearances, the rent received by the landlord from the people was first paid to the tacksman, who took his cut. Many rents were still paid in kind or in labour services. The clearance dislodged the small tenants from their old holdings and some, notably the kelp-makers, were left with hardly any land at all. Evaluating the trends in rents is greatly complicated by changes in arable boundaries, the availability of pasture, changes in labour services, and initial payments, improvements made by either tenant or landlord or both, the exaction of rates, the treatment of arrears and the quality of the land. To compare the rental burden of the small tenants before and after the clearances has to take account of these factors.

These difficulties do not obstruct all understanding of the broad trends. Cattle in the eighteenth century rose in value (and size) and prices accelerated upwards at the end of the century. It is likely that cattle prices more than quadrupled between 1750 and 1815, and in the period 1800-13 alone they increased by 70 per cent. This rising income in the peasant sector, augmented by income from kelp, fishing and regimental service, was to a large extent channelled into landlords' purses through the mechanism of rent increases. These flows, however, are not easily documented, though Malcolm Gray concluded that 'a larger share of total money income was diverted to the pockets of landlords: almost the whole of the peasant's money income as derived from the land, was handed over in rent'.[11]

During periods of depressed prices, most landlords resisted any reduction in rent. During the second price phase in the Highlands, this was a marked tendency. After Waterloo most prices fell rapidly and remained low for twenty years. Wool prices on the Inverness market fell from 42s in 1818 to 10s 6d in 1823, and still further by 1830. Improved efficiency among the sheepfarmers, and some reduction in rent demands, helped to cushion the impact for the sheepfarmers until the gradual improvement in prices in the 1830s. Cattle prices declined by perhaps 40 per cent — rather less than wool prices but nevertheless a devastating blow to the small tenants — and remained low until mid-century. On some estates arrears were allowed to accumulate and then written off at a later time. Landlords were reluctant to commit themselves to an acknowledged reduction of rent. The pinch was felt keenly and undoubtedly helped to increase the propensity for emigration among the growing population. It is most likely that rents did not fall as much as prices in this period[12] — on the Cromartie estate, for instance, rents were kept up into the mid-1820s and were then reduced less than prices; Sutherland followed a similar policy. The middle period, from about 1815 to about 1850, therefore saw a tightening of belts, but the peasants felt the greatest pressure.

The third period — 1850-82 — is in many ways the most interesting and the most enigmatic for the economic and social history of the Highlands. Price trends favoured producers and living standards, admittedly from a very low base, improved for almost the entire community. The two key indicators are wool prices (which rose by a third between 1850 and 1880) and cattle prices (which doubled in the same period).[13] The wages of labour were also much improved and, though the price of oatmeal advanced, the terms of trade for cattle farmers improved out of sight. The response of the landlords to these trends in the income of their lands was curiously varied. There was the predictable lag between the price rise and the augmentation of rents — but the rent increases demanded from the sheepfarmers were discernibly steeper than those required of the crofters. It was as though the landlords had relinquished the idea of a full payment of rent from the crofters.

A large quantity of data relating to prices, incomes and rents emerged before the Napier Commission in 1883. This information, though much of it was self-serving, tends to reinforce the impression derived from estate records and contemporary observation. Unfortunately the material is not uniform: conditions varied markedly from district to district, and estate to estate.

Reasonably representative of perhaps the majority of the crofters' evidence was the testimony of a man of Broadford in Skye. Looking back over forty years, he said that his rent had been increased from £11 to £15 per annum; meanwhile the price of a cow had risen from £5 or £6 to £7 or £8 and the price of a stirk from £1 to £4; sheep prices, he thought, had almost doubled, and wages had increased by 50 per cent.[14] On the Macdonald estates, crofter rents had increased 12.7 per cent since 1830, while those of sheepfarmers rose by 74.4 per cent.[15] At Bernisdale, over a similar period, there had been a reduction of crofter rents, while on the Clanranald estate rents had been virtually stationary. On Barra, crofter rents declined by 72 per cent (in association with a reduction of land area) while large rents rose 44 per cent between 1836 and 1883. On Benbecula crofter rents fell 26 per cent, while large farm rents rose 90 per cent. Most of the evidence confirms the proposition that sheepfarmers' rents rose rapidly, sporting rents still more so, while crofters' changed very little. On the Lewis estates, for instance, the new sporting rents accounted for practically all the increase in total rents. On many estates the small tenants faced no rent increases until the 1870s. Following the upsurge of prices in the 1870s several landowners seized the advantage, and it appears that most rent increases occurred in the late seventies. The perception of many estate managers was typified in William Gunn's testimony:

> Although the croft rents may be said to have been stationary for 50 years, the farm rents in the same district have in several instances risen 100 per cent, and in some cases even more ... the small tenants get fully a half more wages now than 30 years ago, while they get nearly double the price for their cattle that they could have got even twenty years ago.[16]

On the Gairloch estate, crofter rents had fallen 13 per cent since 1853, while sheepfarmers paid 28 per cent more, and sporting rents had risen from nought to 35 per cent of the total.[17] On the Inverishie estate of Sir George MacPherson Grant the non-sporting rents increased by 12 per cent while the sportsmen increased their contribution fourfold.[18] There may have been marked variations in some of the accuracy of the reporting, crofters may have lost some grazing rights, some may have been over-rented at the beginning of the period, but the weight of the evidence gives an overwhelming impression that crofters' rents rose less than those of other tenants, and much less rapidly than their real incomes. Part of the improved living standards was expressed in more adventurous consumption habits, and some observers commented on the allegedly baneful effects of tea and tobacco in the crofter's life.[19]

The elaborately kept records of the Sutherland estate bureaucracy tell the same story: total rental income rose about 75 per cent in the period 1856-76, but the increase was spread disproportionately. The large sheepfarmers (who paid the lion's share) found themselves paying 54 per cent more; the sportsmen paid an increase of 275 per cent (about one-sixth of total rents at the end of the period). Meanwhile the small tenants experienced a rise of 16 per cent. It is plain that the rental policy was discriminatory and that the crofters had become a relatively insignificant source of revenue (in 1876 only one-eighth), although they continued as a source of managerial disturbance.[20]

The boom in sporting rents in the third quarter of the century together with the buoyancy of wool prices fuelled the inflation of land prices in the Highlands. Sometimes the capital gains were spectacular. The Duke of Leeds bought Applecross in 1854 for £135,000 and made two forests of it, which six years later sold for £213,000. One part was bought by Lord Hill for £76,000; after spending £14,000 on it, he sold it for £191,000. The Monar Forest was sold in 1838 for £16,000, converted to a deer forest and two-thirds sold off in 1850 for £40,000. Harris was sold for £60,000 in 1831; half of it was converted to deer and in 1871 that half fetched £155,000.[21] Only in the last decades of the century did the boom diminish.[22]

The implication of these figures is that, in relative terms, the crofters' rents had become insignificant to the landlords in many places. It is also evident that many landowners, during the good years, did not press rent increases proportional to price rises, and on the whole refrained from evicting tenants. Thus increases were substantially below the potential rental capacity of the land. Often the crofters were of such low economic utility to an estate that it would have been more valuable without them. This of course was the logic of the clearances on many estates. The residual crofting population had been reduced to economic insignificance by the advance of sheep and deer.

The case of the Rousay estate in Orkney (a relatively favoured part of the region) may have been somewhat extreme, but indicated the timing and direction of change in rental policy of many landowners. The proprietor Burroughs attempted to push up rents in line with rising prices in the 1870s, and to maintain them when prices fell in the 1880s. The crofters had gained the edge in the good years, but felt profoundly threatened in the depressed years. As Thomson says, 'Rent threatened to erode advances they had made between 1850 and 1870 and these new increases coincided with their final loss of grazing rights.' It generated an angry clash of interests between landlord and people.[23]

It was ironic that, when conditions turned towards depression, the crofters were able to exert political influence in the Highlands which gave them control of the land far beyond their economic significance. The real test of authority came when agricultural prices declined in the 1880s: there was a *de facto* increase in real rents after forty years of stable or falling rents. As in Ireland, these were propitious times for social revolution.

The experience of the small tenants in the Highlands indeed appears (once more) to correspond with that of their peasant counterparts in Ireland. The recent reinterpretation of Victorian Irish history (by Solow, Donnelly, Macguire and Vaughan) has described the land war of 1870s primarily in terms of 'a revolution of rising expectations', in which the tenantry attempted (successfully, in the event) to protect their previous gains at a time when agricultural prices began to deteriorate rapidly. It was a reaction to depression rather than 'the product of an intolerable rapacious land system which finally cracked'. In a survey of 50 Irish estates in the years 1851 to 1881 Vaughan calculates an average rent increase of 20 per cent at a time when livestock prices rose by more than 40 per cent, implying a considerable redistribution of agricultural income away from the landlords towards the tenantry. In essence, the landlords failed to exploit fully the rental capacity of their estates and, presumably, thereby lost the whip hand for the coming times of agricultural depression when the tenantry successful objected to the decline in real income represented by stationary rents.[24]

It is not difficult to transpose this interpretation to the Highland case. Indeed, it was argued in remarkably similar terms as long ago as 1888 by Colin Macdonald. Commenting on the continuing crofter agitation at that time, he claimed that the true causes were depression and education. He remarked that

While prosperous times ruled, and the prices of cattle and farm produce were high, as every one can remember them to have been for many years up to about the year 1880, very little was heard about crofters 'grievances', and there was certainly no perceptible agitation.

He maintained that the high cattle and potato prices had 'enabled the average crofter to make a pretty comfortable living'. Moreover the demand for labour had been strong, partly sustained by landowners' expenditures on land reclamation which gave much employment to crofters. Ploughmen and shepherds had practically doubled their wages in the thirty years since 1850, while domestic servants' wages had trebled in the Highlands. Earnings in Scottish fishing had doubled in the good years. But from 1882 to 1888 the severe depression halved the prices of cattle and potatoes. Macdonald claimed that the combined effect of these unfavourable changes was a loss to the crofters of perhaps £20 per year, and that, since the crofters usually paid less than £5 per year in rent, 'it would manifestly be but a slight compensation for the loss sustained to remit to the crofters, in these circumstances, their full rent'.[25]

Macdonald's hypothesis corresponds with most of the evidence for the period 1820-88. When the Crofter Commission eventually came to adjudicate rents, the reductions imposed were relatively small; it actually raised some rents despite the depression of prices. Rents, however, were only one part of the crofters' agitation — much of their case was avowedly historical. It concerned not so much current rents as the loss, perhaps eighty years before, of lands and rights (especially of grazing). The fact that real rents may have been stationary or falling for thirty years was omitted from their case. Undoubtedly their expectations were rising; they were prepared to resist the decline of incomes during the years of depressed prices. But their grievances were directed to historical injustices, the main expression of which were rent strikes, and, more directly, land raids. It was, in James Hunter's words, a sense of expropriation which rankled permanently in the folk memory.[26] The peasants were activated to reverse the distribution of landed wealth that had occurred, they believed, during the clearances of the early nineteenth century. Macdonald argued a case frankly based on economic determinism:

It is important to bear in mind that the irritating struggle to keep up the expensive tastes of prosperous time on the diminished income of the days of agricultural depression explains a good deal of the murmuring discontent heard among crofters and others during the recent, and to some extent still enduring, 'agitation'.[27]

There can be no doubt that conditions deteriorated rapidly. The winter of 1882-3 was thought to be the worst ever experienced in the western isles; the fishing was a total failure; the potato crop was diseased and a great storm destroyed the stooked corn. Many were left destitute. The Bernera riot in Lewis, and the land raids, occurred in a society much ravaged by the elements.[28]

One objection to Macdonald's interpretation was that the crofter agitation began to stir before the onset of depression in 1882: substantially heightened consciousness was evident by 1878-9. In Macdonald's defence, it can still be said that the agitation reached radically higher levels in the depression, and that some of the initial turbulence may be associated with the belated efforts of some landlords to raise rents towards the end of the period of high prices.

During the last two decades of the century, crofters' living standards — which were never generous — were again depressed by the effects of adverse price trends. Volumes of evidence published by the Crofter Commission demonstrated the unsatisfactory levels of welfare of the congested districts. The crofters indeed were near the bottom of the *per capita* income levels of the British workforce: close perhaps to those persisting among the farmworkers of late Victorian England who, though they worked in more efficient and richer agricultural conditions, continued to subsist in primary poverty, and typically failed to reach B.S. Rowntree's minimum of 'physical efficiency'.[29]

The question of physical living standards undoubtedly exercised the crofters at least as much as their landlords, the Poor Law inspectors and the many travellers who poured through the region in the late nineteenth century. Nevertheless, it would be an over-simplification to reduce the entire matter of social welfare to a statistical relationship between indices of prices and rents. Landlords and sportsmen paid high prices for the non-economic benefits of a Highland estate; the ineffable rewards to the crofting life were not less valued. The social history of the Highlands in the nineteenth century demonstrates clearly that spiritual and cultural matters counted for more in the crofting life than the value of material comfort. The tenacity of the crofter community, and its inner strength in the face of economic adversity, must be part of any explanation for the generally slow rate of emigration from the region. There was indeed no simple equation between material comfort and spiritual ease.[30]

III

In 1825 John Anderson, in his *Prize Essay* on the state of the Highlands of Scotland, challenged the critics of the landlords. He wrote:

> I believe I am not mistaken when I say, that none of those who have been so ready to espouse the popular side of the question, have ventured to show in what condition the people would have been, had they not been disturbed from their stationary indolence. This was a speculation into which they were unwilling or unable to enter; or else it escaped them to consider what the consequences would have been had no change been effected. To those possessed of the talent of observation who are acquainted with the habits of the Highlanders, it is obvious that misery and wretchedness would have resulted to the population, and beggary to the proprietors, while the country would have continued in idleness.[31]

There is, indeed, a counterfactual argument implicit in most writing about the Highland clearances, though it is not always stated in the tendentious terms used by Anderson.[32] One hypothetical alternative attempts to identify the possible and realistic options to the policies actually pursued by the landlords in the nineteenth century — in effect, were the clearances really necessary? In part, it expresses a resistance to the dominant tradition in British economic history which has almost always discounted the possibilities of modernisation through the agency of the peasantry.[33] The critical question is whether a different allocation of resources in the Highlands could have produced a better basis for supporting a population of the size reached in, say, 1841. There is an argument common in the literature which, explicitly or implicitly, contends that if the resources (notably the land itself) of the Highlands had been organised differently, and had been more equally distributed, the population of the region could have been sustained at a more acceptable level and, presumably, with less involuntary emigration.

Ultimately this contention rests on an assumption, that if the crofters had had clear possession of the land they could have created tolerable living conditions for themselves. It is further assumed that the retrogression of the region could have been halted, and a balanced development achieved by some form of co-operative utilisation of resources. Often this line of argument draws on the experience of other allegedly comparable places — the Faeros, the Åland Islands, the Danish mainland, and even Scandinavia as a whole. Examples are offered in which small land-holders appear to have created an agriculture which sustained an undiminished population, and in which the popular culture was not destroyed by the type of economic convulsions which undermined the Highlands. Unfortunately these parallels have never been systematically investigated, and constitute, at present, only comfortable speculations by latter-day critics of Highland landlordism. The argument requires verification and evidence well beyond the scope of this study.[34]

At the opposite pole is the view that all small producers, such as crofters, were doomed to extinction in the manner of the workforce employed in domestic industries throughout Britain, most notably the handloom weavers.[35] Sydney Checkland, who describes the clearances as 'the liquidation of Tribal Pastoralism', tends to this view when he suggests that 'the transition to new modes of production could not be stopped' — except by extraordinary measures of state intervention.[36] There was a similar theme in the views of Margaret Leigh, who asserted that

> In the agricultural history of every nation the time comes sooner or later, when small-scale family farming gives way to large capitalist enterprises in which a smaller proportionate expenditure of money and labour will secure a higher return from the land. The process of adaptation is not an easy one, and unless overseas settlement or other alternative assumptions are open to the displaced cultivator, there is bound to be much difficulty and hardship.[37]

Leigh also asked the critical question — would the crofters have

made a better living if, as they sought, the land had been redistributed into their hands for them to obtain the gains of sheepfarming? To this question, she remarks that sheepfarming was a
highly skilled and capital-intensive activity, buffeted by severe
fluctuations, and with high fixed costs. She points out that where
crofters had tried to operate collectively in sheepfarming, they had
signally failed — 'Club farm sheep stocks, even with a good
shepherd, are as a rule less efficiently managed, and the small co-
operators have less reserve to tide them over a period of
depression and enable them to back wool or stock.'[38] This is slender
evidence on which to reject the possible alternative of communal
enterprise, but it seems that sheepfarming was technically less
amenable than, say, dairying in parts of Scandinavia.

The recent revival of the long-running historical discussion
about 'the transition from feudalism to capitalism', primarily in
Western Europe, has many points of interest for the debate about
the relatively late agrarian transformation of the Scottish Highlands. At the centre of both debates is 'the peasant question' — the
small independent or communal producer represented by Adam
Smith, Karl Marx and a legion of others as the dead hand of
feudalism, and the obstacle to all progressive change, to commercialism, to the achievement of economies of scale, and, most of all,
to the emergence of capitalism. From the time of the 'improvers'
until the present day, the Highland peasant (in his various forms)
has been cast in the role of an enemy of progress. It may not be
extravagant to say that the Highlands saw the last flicker of resistance to the passing of feudalism in Britain. The persistence of
feudal anachronisms was the prime target of the eighteenth-
century critics of Highland society; Marx said plainly enough that
the demise of the peasantry was inevitable; and twentieth-century
planners tend to the opinion that crofting is too small in scale to
exist without subsidy from the rest of the country. The clearances
were simply part of the inevitable eradication of the feudal, the
small-scale and the inefficient. In the recent debate about the
transition from feudalism several arguments have been erected to
oppose this interpretation. In particular it is contended that the
peasant economy is generally more resilient, flexible and progressive than is conventionally allowed, and that the historical
record in Western Europe is replete with examples of commercialised, efficient and adaptive peasantries who led the way to
agrarian capitalism.[39]

The Highland case presents the basis for some comparison. It is clear that the concentration of property in the Highlands was highly propitious for the evolution of capitalist modes of production. The landlords were able to transfer their lands to large capitalist tenants when the need arose, when market opportunities offered rapid returns, and without restraint. Their legal and military strength was matched by the complementary weakness of the small tenantry. Feudalism, the *bête noire* of improvement writers, was swept away in the agrarian transformation of which the clearances formed so large a part. The peasantry, according to this view, was eradicated in the name of economic progress.

There are, therefore, many echoes in the modern debate. In the Highlands the waters are muddied somewhat because the small tenantry had been involved for more than a century, in a perfectly successful competitive exchange economy, before they came to be regarded as an obstacle to progress. The eighteenth-century cattle economy, on any criterion, was an export-oriented commercial system which operated effectively within the peasant system. It has to be said, also, that the Highland peasantry was already psychologically adapted to commercialism long before the coming of sheep. There was never any problem of inducing peasant co-operation in the cattle economy. Indeed it was the landlord class which used its anachronistic powers to modify the operation of the market economy — in the late eighteenth century there were many efforts to reimpose or redouble labour services, and to increase arbitrary taxes and rent: all reminiscent of behaviour identified in thirteenth-century England by M. M. Postan.

It is difficult to sustain the claim that the crofters, in the new age of sheepfarming, could have maintained themselves at decent levels of welfare had they been given reasonable access to land, and to the profits of the pastoral economy. It seems likely that the landlords chose the large sheepfarmers, not from any doctrinaire aversion to small farmers (though that existed without doubt), but because the larger operations were palpably more efficient and yielded much better rents. It was, in essence, a matter of agricultural capital and technique — whereas the old cattle economy was assimilable within the peasant economy, the sheep economy was simply not adaptable to the peasant mode.

The population loss in the Highlands in the second half of the nineteenth century was fully consistent with the demographic experience of the rest of rural Britain. Even where there was a buoyant demand for agricultural labour, population drifted from the land through good times and bad. The largest agricultural county in England, Salop, was repeatedly embarrassed by rural labour shortages in the years 1880 to 1914. From the Highlands the drift was relatively slow and, to an extent, obstructed by the resilience of crofting, and the tenacious peasant attitude to land. The question of demographic adjustment of the Highlands may be sensibly associated with another counterfactual proposition which resides in much of the modern literature on the subject. Assumed rather than demonstrated, there is a widespread notion that, without the clearances, the population of the north of Scotland would have fallen victim to the Malthusian catastrophe, perhaps on a scale comparable with the Irish disaster of mid-century. The argument is grounded upon the premiss that overpopulation and monoculture combined to place the region at critical risk. The fact that the famine of the 1840s in the Highlands was not associated with a rise in mortality rates was, in this argument, a tribute to relief measures and to the availability of employment in the south. It did not demonstrate either economic resilience or demographic equilibrium. The Malthusian counterfactual has been reinforced in the last decade by the research of Scottish historical demographers.[40]

If the question of economic feasibility is fraught with counterfactual difficulty, the political possibilities of the age are still more problematic. To have given the crofters possession and control of the land in the Highlands would have required a revolution.

Was it possible for an expropriation of the landlords to occur in the nineteenth century? John Ramsay at the end of the eighteenth century gave a discouraging, but probably accurate, diagnosis when he observed that

If Parliament were to interfere on general grounds, their [i.e. the landlords'] clamours would drown the cries and complaints of the poor. To prohibit the extension of sheep farms would be like fighting nature, and resented by a very powerful body as a violation of the rights of property.[41]

However, when Parliament eventually acted in the 1880s, the legislation was too late to turn back the clock of agrarian change, and by then the resistance of the landowners was surprisingly shallow.[42]

It remains difficult to believe that the conversion of the Highlands into a vast sheep run mainly to supply English industry was the best way of maximising the economic, social and cultural welfare of the people of the Highlands. It produced an exceedingly unbalanced economy which had little use for its abundant factor of production, its human population. Perhaps the most realistic observation on the economic problem of the Highlands came from the minister of Portree in 1841. He wrote that the best course for the island of Skye was to consolidate the land into sizeable pastoral farms 'of sufficient extent to support a family'. Such farms, he said, should be given, on twenty-year leases, to people with the capital, stock and skill to make the best use of the land. However, he was forced to concede that 'with the present immense population, in a place without commerce, without manufactures, without agriculture, and without any kind of permanent employment for the people, no system that can be adopted will render them comfortable'. His own solution, prompted by humanitarian sentiment of the highest order, would cater only for a relatively small proportion of the existing population of the island. By implication his humanitarianism entailed the removal of a substantial part of the people of Skye. The minister of Portree pointed out that every type of experiment had been tried with a view to accommodating the people — 'it is perfectly evident that no liberality on the part of proprietors can render the present immense surplus population in any measure comfortable'.[43] It was the despair of experience.

IV

The realities of the clearances and Highland poverty were, of course, set within the prevailing framework of *laissez-faire* and a growing freedom of trade. There was no shelter from the devastating competition of Lowland and English industry, of foreign alkali manufacturers and fishermen, of antipodean sheepfarmers or the competitive rents offered by leisured sportsmen from England, North America and Australia. The impact of improved transport over the century after 1746 was precisely the same as that of the abolition of tariffs — it permitted a much freer play of factors of production and offered both opportunities and dangers to a semi-autarkic economy such as that of the Scottish Highlands. It was unlucky that the prevailing disposition of its resources propelled the Highlands in the direction of unbalanced economic growth.

The regional benefits and costs of *laissez-faire* raise a further counterfactual question about the Highland experience in the age of the clearances.[44] Had the region possessed some degree of autonomy by which to protect itself (which would have required at least the reversal of the Act of Union), the region conceivably may have been in a position to mitigate the extreme social costs of structural change. As a previous chapter argued, the fate of the Highlands in the nineteenth century was one of the unhappiest consequences of industrialisation in Britain, and the Highlanders bore too much of the cost of national economic advance. The contemporary debate about the Highlands was contained entirely within the free trade context and its assumptions, and, as in Ireland, the possibility of achieving regional development by 'protection, manipulation of exchange rates or major fiscal variations [was] ... excluded from debate'.[45]

Some Irish historians have identified the imposition of free trade by Westminister as the source of Irish economic retrogression. Thus Oliver MacDonagh has charged 'what perhaps virtually determined the ruin of the Irish economy [was] the establishment of a free trade area within the British Isles, followed by the rapid abandonment of protection for this area from external competition'.[46] But the thesis has not passed unchallenged, even in the Irish case. Louis Cullen has recently offered an utterly opposed view:

> Irish conditions were in many ways akin to those of other agricultural countries, or in agricultural regions of industrialising Britain ... Likewise industrial decline in the nineteenth century in Ireland was paralleled in rural areas elsewhere ... To a large extent the decline was inevitable; after mid-century decline was true less dramatically of rural England as elsewhere. There is no easy explanation of decline ... It is far from clear whether there was any alternative to the course events took, or to what extent well-directed human resources or economic policies might have overcome the environment.[47]

Such speculations apply as much to the Highlands as to Ireland. The poverty and lack of a progressive economic structure were connected to the tyranny of an environment of which the clearances were the most dramatic expression. The experience of the Highlands was part of a dynamic process of great shifts in land use, of the strong pushing out the weak, of land hunger and land pressure, and of technological change. The introduction of new breeds of sheep to the Highlands in the 1760s was as much a technological change as the application of steam power to textile production. The restructuring of land use in Britain was generally drawn out over several centuries. In the case of the Highlands, the episode was concentrated into a few decades, sometimes with a force bordering on violence. It was not fundamentally different in kind from the adjustments forced upon other regions in Britain in the course of economic change.

These economic circumstances imposed a constricting framework on the range of choice facing the people of the region. It is not readily clear how alternative policies, apart from subsidisation by, or protection from, the other regions of Britain, could have made appreciable difference to the actual outcome in terms of the loss of population and the development of large pastoral farms. It may be argued that in Sutherland, in Argyll and in Lewis at different times, landlords actually pursued policies which were as elaborate and as ambitious as any a government could have executed. In no case did they make any permanent impression on the essential problem of the Highland economy: the efforts made to retain population and diversify employment did not work. These failures speak eloquently of the fundamental intractability of the problem.

The clearances were, therefore, part of a much larger problem which had several dimensions. The great clearances such as those of Sutherland and North Uist drew great publicity and notoriety, but, in quantitative terms, the effect of 'natural' drift from the region was probably greater. Many landowners held back from clearances for several decades. Some of the clearances were managed, as far as was possible in such circumstances, with considerable humanity; and many were not. It was not until the 1880s, when the crofters collected themselves into co-ordinated political pressure, that the power of the landlords was emasculated. After the Crofters Act had been implemented, it became clear that rent control and compensation were not the solution to the problem of poverty in the Highlands. It provided an historical example of Angus Maddison's precept that 'Any system which freezes rents or fixes maximum sizes of individual holdings is likely to effect resource allocation adversely in the long run. For this reason, land reform should never be regarded as a final utopian panacea.'[48] The Highlands remained a backward periphery of the British economy, a rural slum, until the mid-twentieth century.

The Scottish Highlands has, throughout its modern history, been a poor country in both resources and income. Few people made much of a fortune out of its natural resources, though the landlords did well out of kelp, and the sheepfarmers were prosperous for half a century. But the poverty of the people was not specifically a consequence of the expropriation of their 'surplus' by the landlords; it was the product of their low productivity. Nor was this an economy in the classically colonial mould in the sense that income was continuously extracted out of the region to satisfy external investors. Many of the greatest landlords were net importers of capital and so were most of the sporting tenants. The destinations of the profits of sheepfarming are not well researched, but the greatest of them all, Patrick Sellar, invested most of his money in the purchase of a Highland estate. In general terms, it would be misleading to brand the nineteenth-century Highlands as 'an extractive economy'.

The experience of the Highlands is not reducible to explanations such as 'economic retardation', or the influence of economic geology, important though they no doubt were. Nor was it simply a matter of what landlords did to the peasantry, or the inexorable forces of agrarian transformation. Any explanation of the history of the clearances must take account of the response of the people and their leaders to the agrarian crisis precipitated by the Industrial Revolution. The region was itself partly responsible for its own fate.

Defining the underlying determinants of Highland economic retardation does not, of course, absolve the landlords of all responsibility for the poverty of the region, but provides an understanding of the objective limits of that responsibility. The relationship between the persistence of poverty in the Highlands and the impact of the clearances was complicated. Poverty certainly predated the clearances; poverty was worst and most intractable in the uncleared parts of the Outer Hebrides. Emigration was greatest from the most favoured parts of the Highlands. The continuing accumulation of population in the most isolated and least hospitable zones, partly encouraged by landlords in the age of kelp, built up conditions of demographic crisis by the 1830s. Landlord policies had perplexing consequences — clearances dislodged many people and cast them adrift in a region which offered little alternative employment; but where landlords sought to retain their people, often for the most philanthropic reasons, they generally aggravated the long-term problem of redundancy and poverty. The voluntary exodus of people was probably greater than that forced along by the landlords. Sheepfarming, a classic enclave economy,[49] increased regional income but distributed the gains so unequally that the fructifying effect on the economy at large was slight. The economics of large-scale sheepfarming virtually precluded the possibility of participation by the old peasantry.

In the last analysis, the morality of the landlord is to be judged against the pressure of the circumstances, and in comparison with economic behaviour in the rest of contemporary Britain. It was, finally, a national question — why did the most advanced country in the word allow this poor, overpopulated, peripheral region to shoulder a disproportionate share of the costs of industrialisation? And why did this country permit a succession of aristocrats, nabobs, plutocrats and Edinburgh lawyers to determine the fate of tens of thousands of poor clansmen? No government of the nineteenth century possessed the knowledge, the will, or even the machinery to counter the adverse effects of rapid economic growth.

Notes

1. Gray, *Highland Economy*, p. 65.
2. See, for instance, the Swedish case in Christer Winberg, 'Population Growth and Proletarianization' in S. Akerman, H. C. Johansen and D. Graunt (eds.), *Chance and Change*, (Odense, 1978).
3. E. A. Wrigley, 'The Process of Modernisation and the Industrial Revolution in England', *Journal of Interdisciplinary History*, vol. 3 (1972), p. 257. In a recent analysis of rural poverty in England, W. A. Armstrong has argued powerfully for the paramountcy of the demographic factor. The universal growth of population imposed a pressure and strain on all rural economies, and its continued growth in the countryside was 'indicative of behavioural inertia'. Emigration from rural England was extraordinarily slow: 'few, if any, occupational groups stood to gain more than farm labourers from emigration to foreign parts. Yet modern research suggests that they were distinctly underrepresented among emigrants from the United Kingdom'. It is an argument which applies to the Scottish Highlands. See Armstrong, 'Influence of Demographic Factors'.
4. See, for instance, Irvine, *Inquiry, passim*; and the pages of the *Farmer's Magazine* in the years 1800 to 1820. Mackenzie, *Letter*, p. 17.
5. Simpson, 'An Economic Analysis of Crofting', p. 4.
6. Cf. Raymond D. Crotty, *Irish Agricultural Production* (Cork, 1966), pp. 42-5.

7. Anon., *Observations on the Causes and Remedies of Destitution in the Highlands of Scotland* (Glasgow, 1838), p. 13.

8. See Appendix.

9. See below, Appendix; Teignmouth, *Sketches*, I, p. 129; Gray, *Highland Economy*, pp. 142, 241; Walker, *Report on the Hebrides*, pp. 157-8, 209; Ramsay, *Scotland and Scotsmen*, II, pp. 222ff; M. M. Edwards, *The Growth of the British Cotton Trade, 1780-1815* (Manchester, 1967), p. 33; Richards *Highland Clearances*, pp. 121-2; James Hunter, 'Sheep and Deer: Highland Sheep Farming, 1850-1900', *Northern Scotland*, vol. 1 (1973), pp. 200-3; Youngson, *After the Forty Five*, pp. 175, 182.

10. See for instance, SC on Emigration (Scotland) (1841), Q. 2101, and Gray, 'Economic Welfare', p. 3.

11. Malcolm Gray, 'The Consolidation of the Crofting System', *Agricultural History Review*, vol. 5 (1957), pp. 37-8.

12. Ibid., p. 38. Gray states that landlords held rentals near top levels despite the price falls. This was not exclusive to the Highlands — see SC on Agriculture (1833), which indicates that many rents in England did not fall as rapidly as prices.

13. Cattle prices rose in the 1850s and by 1857 were about 57 per cent above the mid-century figure. They fell about 12 per cent during a short depression which lasted until the mid-1860s, and then they rose until 1871. There followed a slight decline until 1879; another peak achieved in 1882-3 was succeeded by a steep decline. See Appendix below, and also Hunter, *Crofting Community*, pp. 107-8, and Orr, *Deer Forests*, pp. 11, 154-64, 166.

14. Napier Commission, p. 235.

15. Ibid., pp. 476-7.

16. Ibid., p. 1822. On prices see ibid., pp. 68, 124, 2209.

17. Ibid., p. 1868.

18. Ibid., p. 2968.

19. Ibid., Appendix V, p. 11. Cf. Macdonald, *Lewis*, pp. 18-20.

20. Richards, 'An Anatomy', pp. 58-63, 70-5.

21. Report of RC on Game Laws, *PP* (1873), XII, Q. 5075; see Richards, *Highland Clearances*, pp. 484-5.

22. See Gaskell on Lochaline, *Morvern Transformed*, pp. 30-1, 102. On deer forests see Orr, *Deer Forests*, Ch. 2, Appendix VIII; Tables XIII, XIV. On sports rents and prices of land see Hunter, 'Sheep and Deer', p. 218.

23. See Thomson, *The Little General*, p. 109.

24. See especially W. E. Vaughan, 'Landlord and Tenant Relations in Ireland between the Famine and the Land War, 1850-1878' in L. M. Cullen and T. C. Smout (eds.), *Comparative Aspects of Scottish and Irish Economic and Social History 1600-1900* (Edinburgh, 1977), and W. E. Vaughan, 'An Assessment of the Economic Performance of Irish Landlords, 1851-1881' in F. S. L. Lyons and A. A. J. Hawkins (eds.), *Ireland under the Union* (Oxford, 1980). See also B. L. Solow, *The Land Question and the Irish Economy, 1870-1903* (Cambridge, Mass., 1971).

25. Macdonald, 'Transition in the Highlands of Scotland', pp. 114-15.

26. Hunter, *Crofting Community*, p. 128.

27. Macdonald, *Lewis*, p. 114.

28. Ibid., p. 129.

29. Quoted in Armstrong, 'Influence of Demographic Factors', p. 79. Cf. Hunter, *Crofting Community*, p. 111.

30. See the remarkably apt statement of the paradox in Otter, *Life and Remains of the Rev. Edward Daniel Clarke*, p. 230.

31. John Anderson, *Prize Essay on the State of Society and Knowledge in the Highlands of Scotland* (Edinburgh, 1825), pp. xviii-xix.

32. There is a useful and caustic exposition of the centrality of counterfactual propositions in the literature in R. H. Campbell's Introduction to the second edition of Philip Gaskell, *Morvern Transformed* (Cambridge, 1980), pp. ix-xvi.

33. On this see, for example, the reply of E. Le Roy Ladurie in the debate on 'Agrarian Transformation' in *Past and Present*, no. 79 (May 1978), esp. p. 59, and the article by Heywood, 'The Role of the Peasantry in French Industrialisation'.

34. Ian Grimble, on the evidence of arctic fishing communities in Scandinavia, provides some basis for optimism, and A. J. Youngson has explored the temporary success of timber production in late-nineteenth century Norrland. But generally the question always seems to return to Youngson's doleful formula: 'The problem is to discover a policy that would provide reasonable prosperity in the Highlands at an acceptable cost in terms of subsidy from the rest of the community.' Most modern commentators on the Highlands would agree that small farming in the north is an anachronistic labour-intensive system and that growth in the region must depend on planned growth in non-agricultural sectors. See Ian Grimble, 'Unsceptred Isle' in D. S. Thomson and Ian Grimble (eds.), *The Future of the Highlands* (London, 1968); Youngson, *After the Forty Five*, p. 200; Anon., 'Landed Tenures in the Highlands', *Westminster Review*, vol. 34 (1868), p. 288; Simpson, 'An Economic Analysis of Crofting Agriculture', Ch. 1. For a discussion of the historical possibilities of the 'endogenous transformation of traditional peasantries', see E. J. Hobsbawm, 'Scottish Reformers of the Eighteenth Century and Capitalist Agriculture' in E. J. Hobsbawm (ed.), *Peasants in History* (Calcutta, 1980), esp. pp. 19-24.

35. This was the prediction of Sir Charles Wood, quoted in David Spring, *English Landed Estates in the Nineteenth Century: their Administration* (Baltimore, 1963), p. 111.

36. S. G. Checkland, 'Scottish Economic History', *Economica*, vol. 21 (1964), pp. 307-8.

37. Leigh, 'The Crofting Problem', p. 137.

38. Ibid., p. 138. Cf. Orr, *Deer Forests*, p. 83.

39. See D. Goodman and M. Redclift, *From Peasant to Proletarian* (Oxford, 1981); and the debate in *Past and Present* inaugurated in no. 70 (1976) by Robert Brenner, 'The Agrarian Roots of European Capitalism', but especially the contribution of J. P. Cooper, ibid., no. 80 (1978), Croot and Parker, no. 78 (1978) and Ladurie, no. 79 (1978).

40. See Richard Perren, 'The Effects of Agricultural Depression on the English Estates of the Dukes of Sutherland, 1870-1900', unpublished PhD thesis, University of Nottingham, 1968, and Flinn, *Scottish Population History*, passim.

41. Ramsay, *Scotland and Scotsmen*, pp. 536-7.

42. On the contemporary debate on peasant ownership and land and the rights of property see R. N. Lebow, *J. S. Mill and the Irish Land Question* (Philadelphia, 1979).

43. *New Statistical Account*, Inverness-shire, p. 235.

44. A contrary opinion on the general question of economic dependency has been voiced by T. C. Smout in a stimulating paper which contemplates the impact of economic union between Scotland and England. In opposition to much theoretical discussion, and to some recent Irish historiogrpahy, Smout believes that Scotland, the weaker party to the Union of 1707, fared extraordinarily well on the evidence of most economic indicators. Significantly Smout makes a clear exception of the Highlands from his generalisation about Scotland, in terms which are entirely consistent with the argument of this chapter. Smout, 'Scotland and England: is Dependency a Symptom?' esp. pp. 614-20.

45. R. D. C. Black, 'The Irish Experience in Relation to the Theory and Practice of Economic Development' in A. J. Youngson (ed.), *Economic Development in the*

Long Run (London, 1972), p. 194. The problem has been identified in similar terms by E. J. T. Collins in a fine essay which draws illuminating comparisons between the Highlands and the rest of upland Britain during industrialisation: 'The Economy of Upland Britain, 1750-1850' in R. B. Tranter (ed.), *The Future of Upland Britain* (2 vols. Reading, 1978). There is a particularly incisive statement of the conflict between development and welfare in Stephen Hymer and Stephen Resnick, 'A Model of an Agrarian Economy with Non-Agricultural Activities', *American Economic Review*, vol. 59 (1969), pp. 505-6.

46. MacDonagh, *Ireland,* p. 6. See also F. S. L. Lyons, *Ireland since the Famine* (London, 1971), p. 55. The influence of this view is extensive. See G. Hallett, P. Randall and E. G. West, *Regional Policy for Ever?* (London, 1973), pp. 3-4.

47. Cullen, *Formation of the Irish Economy*, pp. 113-23. The efficacy of protection for West European industry is argued by Crouzet, 'Wars, Blockade and Economic Change', *passim*. For a recent discussion of regional retardation in a common market see E. Victor Morgan, 'Regional Problems and Common Currencies', *Lloyds Bank Review*, no. 110 (October 1973), pp. 19-30.

48. Angus Maddison, *Economic Progress and Policy in Developing Countries* (London, 1970), pp. 150-2. Cf. Simpson, 'An Economic Analysis of Crofting Agriculture', p. 18, concerning the 'misplaced generosity' towards the crofter, 'inspired by a feeling of guilt', which did little to solve the fundamental problems of Highland poverty.

49. See Albert O. Hirschman, *The Strategy of Economic Development* (New Haven, 1965), pp. 110-11.

APPENDIX: HIGHLAND RENTS, PRICES AND WAGES

Highland Rents

The following remarks and series relating to changes in rents over the period of the clearances are intended to sketch a broad impression, and not a precise and detailed picture. Ideally, one would like to know how money rent changed for a given piece of land with associated costs and rights held constant, how the composition and level of landlords' incomes changed, and what contribution the investment policies of landlords made to income increases. Clearly, information of the first kind cannot be had in aggregate; and even at the level of the individual crofter holding, for which evidence is available, there are problems: the pattern of effective change in the cost of renting land can be clouded by changes in the rights and services attaching to occupation of the croft. For consistent comparisons, it would be necessary to allow for changes in the burden of rates, labour dues and other payments in kind, in pasture rights (as to both the number of beasts to be grazed, and the quantity and quality of land available to the tenant), and in the acreage and location of arable; additionally, regard would need to be paid to policy on rent arrears, and to maintenance expenditures and capital improvements, such as drainage, fencing, fertilising and reclamation (distinguishing that part of improvement due to the tenant's efforts).

Unfortunately, there is not as yet a sufficient body of detailed studies of individual Highland estates to support a confident synoptic view. The evidence here referred to has been subjectively sifted and weighed. The reduction of the selected series of rents to index form in the accompanying tables is intended to render comparison easier between estates, between landlords' rental income and crofters' rent outlay, and between changes in rent and other

504

Figure A1: Wool — Prices, Production and Retained Imports, UK, 1775-1877

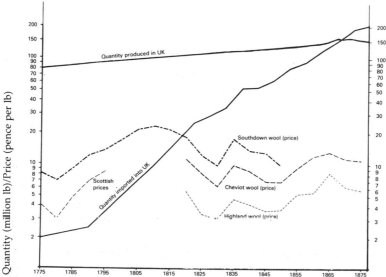

Note: Data are plotted on a semi-logarithmic ratio scale in which equal vertical distances represent equal percentage changes.

Source: The import and production series are based upon Committee on Industry and Trade, *Survey of Textile Industries* (HMSO, London, 1928), p. 275, and upon B. R. Mitchell and P. Deane, *Abstract of British Historical Statistics* (Cambridge, 1962), pp. 495-6. For the sources of the price series, see Tables A10-A12 below.

prices. But it must be emphasised that these indices are not to be relied on as anything more than broad indicators of rent trends.

The impressionistic evidence is overwhelmingly of considerable rent increases in the late eighteenth-century Highlands, as well as the Lowlands. Commenting on increases in Black Isle rents 1795-1814, Mowat attributes the rise mainly to the increased acreage of arable. Doubling of rent was not unusual. Gray catalogues increases for the following estates: Breadalbane, Perthshire section (1774-84, 53 per cent; 1784-95, 86 per cent; 1799-1811, 75 per cent); Dunvegan (1724-54, 63 per cent; 1754-69, 66 per cent; 1784-92, 51 per cent; 1792-1811, 238 per cent); Torridon (1772-98, 275 per cent); Lochalsh (1758-98, 266 per cent); Badenoch (1762-85, 237 per cent); Glengarry (1786-1825, over 800 per cent). On Skye, the McLeod estate rentals rose over 200 per cent in the first decade of the nineteenth century; Lord Macdonald's Skye rentals rose by 155 per cent in the same period.

Figure A2: Comparative Price Movements, 1740-1885
(av. 1818-22 = 100)

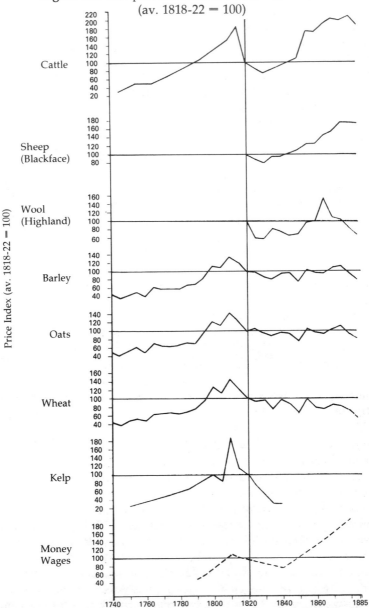

Note: This graph is based on the price series used in compiling the Appendix. It is intended only to suggest broad comparisons of changes in price movements.

The sharp rises in rents associated with the Napoleonic Wars appear to have held up longer in the Highlands than further south, as landlords sought to preserve the value of incomes severely depleted by sharp post-war reductions in the demand for Highland exports. The policy of maintaining nominal rents while allowing increase of arrears and discretionary abatement of rents effectively held small tenants in thrall and enabled landlords to siphon off more easily the benefits of occasional price improvements. Unfortunately, it vitiates assessment of just how closely Highland rent movements paralleled the southern decline of the twenties, stability of the thirties, and commencement of upward movement in the forties.

There were abundant claims by crofters appearing before the Napier Commission in 1884 of rent increases over the rates prevailing in the 1840s and 1850s. Some claims were disputed by the estates, but they were in general unchallenged. Whether this evidence is entirely representative of the general pattern of change is unclear. It appears that rents not uncommonly remained unchanged for as long as thirty years: even then, percentage increases were not necessarily large. The range of alleged increases in crofters' rent was wide — Uig, 1852-80, between 55 per cent and 130 per cent; Lephin, 1830-80, 67 per cent; Husabost, 1838-84, 56 per cent; Balta Sound, 1839-83, 52 per cent; Shetland, 1850-83, between 17 and 90 per cent; Orkney, 1851-83, between 38 and 100 per cent; Lewis, 1843-83, 100 per cent; Achiltibuie, unchanged 1850-80, but then a 25 per cent increase; Tyree, 1850-80, 180 per cent; Dervaig, 1857-83, 29 per cent; Port Ramsay, 1853-83, 8 per cent; Roster, 1856-83, 116 per cent; Lord Lovat's estate, 1850-80, 38 per cent (crofters' rent), 30 per cent (large farms); Kilcoy, 1854-83, 85 per cent; Macdonald estate, 1830-83, 13 per cent (selected crofters), 75 per cent (large tenants). Other evidence relating to large estates shows higher percentage increases applying to large tenants than small tenants. For example, on the Sutherland estate, percentage increases in rental were as follows, over the period 1853-7 to 1876-82:

Location	Large Tenants	Small Tenants
Scourie	66	18
Tongue	113	32
Dunrobin	85	−20 (decrease)

508   *Appendix*

It would be a mistake to assume that higher rent proceeds in land-lords' hands meant proportionately greater payment by crofters: larger agricultural and pastoral tenants and sporting tenants contributed not only greater absolute increases, but also greater proportionate and more rapid increments to landlords' rent rolls than did the crofters. (This was consistent with the usual distribution of improvement expenditures). Thus one must be cautious in drawing inferences from rental series: they do not necessarily represent the pattern of cost changes experienced by the crofter; nor do they represent the net benefits received by landlords, as they ignore investment expenditures, and may not be net of operating expenses. As Table A5 shows, landlords' investment in improvements may have little effect on net operating income. A rising rent roll may accordingly be associated with a declining rate of return on landlords' capital.

Sources: See evidence of David Low, SC on Agriculture (1883), Q.11353; R.J. Thompson, 'An Enquiry into the Rent of Agricultural Land in England and Wales during the Nineteenth Century' in W.E. Minchinton (ed.), *Essays in Agrarian History* (Newton Abbot, 1968); Gray, *Highland Economy*, pp. 146-8; Hunter, *Crofting Community*, p. 37; Mowat, *Easter Ross*, pp. 40-1, 61, 88, 99; Napier Commission, *passim*, but especially pp. 82, 93, 395,415,424, 554, 574,693, 711, 764, 1054, 1295, 1336, 1423, 1427, 1471, 1481, 1560, 1569, 1632, 1665, 1692, 1704, 1768, 1791, 1821-2, 1850, 1948, 2011-12, 2138, 2277, 2351, 2412, 2423, 2600, 2867, 2885, 3207 and Appendix A, pp. 11, 308.

Table A1: Rents — Lochalsh, Lochcarron and Strathconan, 1852-82

[Index of sporting rents (1862 = 100)]

	1852	1862	1872	1882
Lochalsh				
Sporting rents	105	100	87	469
Other rents	93	100	107	82
Lochcarron				
Sporting rents	n.a.	100	250	881
Other rents	87	100	132	107
Strathconan				
Sporting rents	70	100	110	145
Other rents	96	100	91	110
Average of 3 estates				
Sporting rents	69	100	121	282
Other rents	91	100	115	98

Source: W. Orr, *Deer Forests, Landlords and Crofters* (Edinburgh, 1982) p. 93.

Table A2: Rents — Rousay, 1855-85

[Index of rents received (1855 = 100)]

1855	100
1860	116
1865	137
1870	136
1875	161
1880	236
1885	224

Note: These rents appear to have been for crofts. While there was no change in the estate size over this period, grazing rights were reduced in the seventies.

Source: W. P. L. Thompson, *The Little General and the Rousay Crofters* (Edinburgh, 1981), p. 105.

Table A3: Rents — Sutherland Estate, 1856-76

[Index of total, sporting and small tenants' rents (1857-8 = 100)]

	Total Estate	Small Tenants	Sporting Rents	Sporting Rents (Tongue)
1856-7	97	109	85	71
1858-62	109	94	112	114
1863-7	119	101	125	116
1868-72	131	101	148	147
1873-6	160	106	n.a.	240

Source: Derived from estate records relating to Tongue, Scourie and Dunrobin managements referred to in Eric Richards, 'An Anatomy of the Sutherland Fortune', *Business History*, vol. 21 (1979), pp. 70-5.

Table A4: Rents — Sutherland Estate, 1771-1876

[Index of rental income (1851-5 = 100)]

1771	8	1848	95
1785	11	1849	87
1802	15	1851	101
1803	16	1853	101
1804	16	1856	98
1805	16	1857	104
1806	16	1858	105
1807	19	1859	113
1808	29	1860	115
1809	31	1861	117
1810	31	1862	120
1811	33	1863	120
1812	41	1864	124
1813	47	1865	125

Table A4 continued

1814	52	1866	127
1815	55	1867	128
1820	55	1868	130
1824-5	48	1869	132
1826	51	1870	135
1827	56	1871	140
1828	54	1872	148
1829	48	1873	160
1833	75	1874	168
1839	79	1875	170
1842	69	1876	173

Note: There are serious discontinuities in this series, and it is offered only tentatively as in indicator of landlord receipts.
Source: As for Table A3.

Cattle

Gray and Haldane remark on the difficulty of compiling an index of cattle prices: the evidence relates to disconnected markets, and price and quality differences between them weaken conclusions as to details of trends over time. Nevertheless, the general picture of price movements seems well agreed. Highland cattle prices doubled in the second half of the eighteenth century, with sharp rises in the eighties and nineties, after a brief decline about 1770-2. There was a rapid jump in the first decade of the nineteenth century, with prices reaching a peak in 1815 (or perhaps a little earlier) at £5-£6 per stirk — possibly 60 to 70 per cent above the turn-of-the-century level. After 1815, prices fell steeply to pre-war levels, and remained till mid-century at about £3-£4 per stirk.

Whetham's series of cattle prices for the second half of the nineteenth century, while not relating to Scottish sales, displays a pattern of change which is broadly consistent with the course of prices of Scotch beef on the London market reported by Orr, and also with the little specific material the Napier Commission has about cattle price changes over time. When it was hearing evidence, cattle prices were at their all-time high; there are numerous general observations about the unprecedented price of cattle, double the level of twenty or thirty years before.

Table A5: Rents, Acreage and Outlays on the Sutherland Estate, 1872-88

| | Acreage Let | | Rental (£) | | | | Operating Outgoings (£) | Net Income (£) | Permanent Improvements (£) | |
| | | | Arable | | Pasture | | | | New Buildings | Drainage, etc. |
	Arable	Mountain or Hill Pasture	Rent Agreed	Rent Rec'd	Rent Agreed	Rent Rec'd				
1872	7,136	817,697	8,473	8,450	28,251	26,987	11,345	24,092	4,136	6,863
1873	7,176	817,697	8,361	8,338	28,935	27,471	11,759	24,050	4,688	5,639
1874	7,356	820,297	9,237	9,237	29,581	28,117	12,827	24,527	7,984	18,390
1875	7,406	820,297	9,197	9,197	29,296	28,170	12,939	24,428	9,333	42,620
1876	7,874	822,697	8,518	8,518	29,859	28,708	12,344	24,882	5,115	36,287
1877	8,611	822,697	8,948	8,925	30,524	29,143	11,900	26,168	3,322	25,837
1878	9,535	779,697	10,515	10,515	30,956	29,854	11,787	28,582	1,743	21,195
1879	9,570	779,697	9,655	9,655	31,009	31,291	10,582	30,364	2,149	12,640
1880	9,579	763,277	10,179	10,156	31,490	29,415	8,448	31,123	1,475	17,115
1881	9,634	763,277	11,002	10,979	30,350	22,925	9,141	24,763	586	14,516
1882	9,654	719,657	10,983	10,960	29,223	22,601	9,099	24,462	1,907	3,472
1883	9,036	686,707	10,446	10,398	27,264	26,344	9,518	27,224	329	1,897
1884	9,119	674,972	11,005	10,932	26,875	22,711	10,522	23,121	343	1,915
1885	9,553	708,322	11,163	10,251	27,091	24,599	11,123	23,727	701	8,461
1886	9,786	658,822	10,141	9,963	25,003	23,900	10,237	23,626	950	1,940
1887	10,048	677,056	9,907	8,375	21,600	19,112	9,181	18,306	785	1,059
1888	10,014	660,704	9,595	7,515	19,195	17,269	8,221	16,563	54	793

Note: Operating outgoings include rates, repairs and management expenses. Net income is income from property after payment of operating expenses.

Source: *PP* (1896). XIV, Royal Commission on Agriculture, Appendix to Second Report, pp. 51-2.

512   *Appendix*

Table A6: Indices of Cattle and Beef Prices, Quinquennial
Averages, 1851-92
[1851-2 = 100]

	Store Cattle	Beef, Prime & Middling (av.)
1851-2	100.0	100.0
1853-7	147.5	133.4
1858-62	143.6	131.9
1863-7	160.7	141.9
1868-72	171.4	154.8
1873-7	168.1	171.4
1878-82	178.3	158.0
1883-7	157.5	143.4
1888-92	145.8	127.3

Source: Based on E. H. Whetham, 'Livestock Prices in Britain, 1851-93', *Agricultural History Review*, vol. 11 (1963), p. 29.

Obviously the extent to which the crofters enjoyed the benefits of these increased prices depends on whether their cattle numbers were maintained. Gray finds that cattle holdings of small farmers and cottars had declined by 1850. There is much evidence before the Napier Commission of reduced grazing rights or privileges, and of reduced cattle holdings. Landlords disputed their tenants' 'right' to traditional grazing, which was seldom covered by any written agreement: it was, according to one landlord, a 'privilege', not taken into account in determining earlier rents. Crofters' claims are overwhelmingly of reduced cattle-grazing entitlement and of lower stock holdings, in some cases down to half their numbers of fifty years before, in others to zero. The development of specific payment for grazing complicates judgment of the net effect on crofter incomes: this practice gave some support to the level of crofters' cattle holdings albeit at increased cost (in the absence of offsetting rent reductions following reduction of pasture 'privileges'). Despite some contrary instances of increased cattle holdings the evidence points to the conclusion that cattle numbers were not kept up, and so crofters did not experience the rise in incomes that a simple comparison of cattle prices from mid-century to the time of the Napier Commission might seem to suggest.

Sources: Day, *Public Administration,* esp. pp. 83, 180; Gray, 'Economic Welfare and Money Income in the Highlands, 1750-1850', *Scottish Journal of Political Economy,* Vol. 2 (1955), pp. 56, 68; Gray, *Highland Economy,* pp. 142-3, 241, 244; A. R. B. Haldane, *The Drove Roads of Scotland* (Edinburgh, 1968), pp. 58-9,

205-6; Orr, *Deer Forests*, pp. 71-6, 217-19; Whetham, 'Livestock Prices in Britain'; Youngson, *After the Forty Five*, pp. 38, 45, 175, 182; Napier Commission, pp. 362, 415, 424, 427, 479, 574, 919, 959, 1312-13, 1340, 1378, 1394, 1570, 1957, 1961, 2071, 2184, 2200, 2209, 2275, 2277, 2284, 2385-8, 2423, 2905, 2926, 3170, 3207, App. I, p. 68.

Grain

Table A7: Prices at Haddington, Quinquennial Averages, 1738-1829

[Average price (in shillings) per imperial quarter]

	Barley	Oats	Wheat
1738-42	15.4	12.2	26.3
1743-7	12.8	11.0	22.7
1748-52	14.4	13.1	27.6
1753-7	16.6	15.1	30.2
1758-62	13.7	12.2	28.0
1763-7	21.2	17.7	37.3
1768-72	19.7	16.4	37.3
1773-7	20.5	16.1	38.5
1778-82	20.0	16.4	37.3
1783-87	22.7	18.1	39.3
1788-92	23.9	17.7	44.4
1793-7	28.9	21.2	56.2
1798-1802	39.2	30.5	76.4
1803-7	37.9	28.9	67.3
1808-12	46.9	35.9	88.7
1813-17	41.7	31.2	71.4
1818-22	34.7	25.2	60.8
1823-7	37.5	28.6	58.4
1828-9	36.3	24.7	62.8

Note: Rosalind Mitchison remarks that 'no reliable series survives for the seventeenth or eighteenth centuries for anywhere north of the Great Glen', and that even south of it regional fiars prices, which generally moved consistently with each other from the mid-eighteenth century, nevertheless occasionally diverged. See R. Mitchison, 'The Movements of Scottish Corn Prices in the Seventeenth and Eighteenth Centuries', *Economic History Review*, vol. 18 (1965), esp. pp. 279, 288; Alexander Stewart observes that the Haddington prices are 'considerably higher than the average fiars prices of Scotland'; 'On the Prices of Grain' (see Source), pp. 226, 231. See also Flinn, *Scottish Population History*, pp. 489-98, Appendix B, Fiars prices 1629-1826.

Source: Based on Alexander Stewart, 'On the Prices of Grain from 1647 to 1829', *Transactions of the Highland and Agricultural Society of Scotland*, vol. 8 (1831), pp. 226-31.

Table A8: United Kingdom Grain Prices, Quinquennial Averages, 1818-87

[Average price (in shillings) per imperial quarter]

	Barley	Oats	Wheat
1818-22	36.0	24.5	65.9
1823-7	35.9	25.7	60.6
1828-32	33.7	23.1	63.2
1833-7	29.9	21.5	48.5
1838-42	33.5	23.1	64.7
1843-7	34.4	22.8	55.3
1848-52	27.2	18.4	42.9
1853-7	37.4	25.3	65.2
1858-62	35.2	23.7	50.4
1863-7	34.2	22.7	48.2
1868-72	38.1	25.0	54.5
1873-7	39.7	27.0	52.5
1878-82	34.1	22.5	45.0
1883-7	29.0	19.5	34.8

Note: UK prices are not identical in amount with the Haddington prices reported in Table A7 for the period of overlap. However there is a high degree of conformity in the pattern of change for oats and wheat; there is a lesser conformity with respect to barley in the timing of price changes.

Source: Based on Mitchell and Deane, *Abstract of British Historical Statistics*, pp. 488-0.

Kelp

Table A9: Price per Ton of Kelp

	£ s d		
1740-60	2. 5.0		
1771-80	5. 0.0		
1781-90	6. 0.0		
1791-1800	9. 0.0	to	10.0.0
1804	7. 0.0	to	9.0.0
1806-10	16. 0.0	to	18/20.0.0
1815	10. 0.0	to	11.0.0
1816	8. 0.0	to	10.0.0
1820	8. 0.0	to	11.0.0
1825	7. 0.0		
1830	4.16.8		
1835	3. 0.0		
1840	2.10.0	to	4.0.0

Note: Malcolm Gray warns that quality differences affect the comparability of kelp prices over time, but concludes that the general pattern of rise, peak and fall is clear. See his article 'The Kelp Industry in the Highlands and Islands', *Economic History Review*, vol. 4 (1951), esp. p. 198n.

Source: *PP* (1914), XXXII, Cmnd 7564, Report on Home Industries in the Highlands and Islands, pp. 173-4. Prices for 1815-35 in this series are derived from the SC on Emigration (Scotland) (1841), p. 214, which also indicates quantities produced annually 1811-36 on the estate to which the quoted prices relate.

Sheep and Wool

Table A10: Scottish Wool Prices, Quinquennial Averages, 1750-96

	Laid Cheviot (pence per lb)
1750-2	3.2
1753-7	3.0
1758-62	3.5
1763-7	3.4
1768-72	3.6
1773-7	4.1
1778-82	3.1
1783-7	4.9
1788-92	7.0
1793-6	8.7

Source: Based on J. Hogg, *The Shepherd's Guide* (Edinburgh, 1807) quoted in C. Gulvin (ed.), 'Journal of Henry Brown' in *Scottish Industrial History: a Miscellany* (Scottish History Society, Edinburgh, 1978), p. 83.

Table A11: Scottish Sheep and Wool Prices: Quinquennial Averages, 1818-87

	Sheep		Wool	
	Cheviot Wethers (shillings)	Blackface Wethers (shillings)	Laid Cheviot (pence per lb)	Laid Blackface (pence per lb)
1818-22	22.1	19.0	11.6	5.6
1823-7	20.3	16.4	6.6	3.4
1828-32	20.5	15.2	6.3	3.3
1833-7	25.8	17.7	9.8	4.6
1838-42	26.7	17.9	8.7	4.2
1843-7	26.7	19.4	7.0	3.7
1848-52	26.3	20.8	6.9	3.7
1853-7	30.8	23.6	9.3	5.3
1858-62	31.0	23.5	12.2	5.6
1863-7	38.0	27.5	13.6	8.3
1868-72	38.8	28.9	11.9	6.1
1873-7	39.9	38.5	11.4	5.6
1878-82	40.4	33.3	9.5	4.5
1883-7	38.8	32.8	7.9	3.8

Source: Based on *THAS*, vol. 49 (1937), pp. 307-11.

Table A12: British Wool Prices, Quinquennial Averages, 1759-1845

	Southdown Wool (Raw) (pence per lb)		Southdown Wool (Raw) (pence per lb)
1759-62	7.5	1803-7	21.3
1763-7	8.1	1808-12	23.1
1768-72	7.3	1813-17	21.2
1773-7	8.1	1818-22	18.3
1778-82	7.1	1823-7	12.5
1783-7	9.1	1828-32	9.8
1788-92	12.6	1833-7	17.8
1793-7	14.1	1838-42	14.1
1798-1802	17.4	1843-5	13.8

Source: Based on Mitchell and Deane, *Abstract of British Historical Statistics*, p. 495.

Wages

Morgan's analysis of comparative wage rates in late eighteenth-century Scotland shows that Highland wages were anything from 30 to 80 per cent below the national average revealed in the *Old Statistical Account*. Moreover, the Highland region experienced the slowest rate of conversion to cash payments both before 1790 and into the nineties. She notes ministers' comments to the effect that the area had 'an incompletely developed money economy': food and shelter were the most important element in the labour contract.

Bowley's series reproduced here gives some guide to relative changes in the nineteenth century, but here too maintenance is a complicating factor. Its value cannot have remained constant over time; yet it cannot be assumed to have paralleled changes in money wages. The daily wage is calculated as the average of summer and winter daily wages. The annual wage is that of unmarried farm servants, who also received maintenance in kitchen or bothy. Bowley warns that these figures are 'not of great precision'. It is to be noted that they are not entirely consistent with Gaskell's wage figures for the Ardtornish estate (after recalculation to a nominal series).

Table A13: Day Labourers — Average Daily Wages, 1790-1881 (pence)

	1790	1794	1810	1834-45	1860	1867-70	1880-1
Scotland	11	13	20	18	27	28	33
N. Scotland	9	11	17	17	26	26	33
Selected counties							
Argyll	10	10	15	17	28	18	27
Caithness	8	10	(13)	17	23	(26)	33
Inverness	9	9	15	16	26	(26)	(30)
Perth	12	15	19	18	24	27	32
Ross &							
Cromarty	6	9	13	14	23	(26)	35
Sutherland	7	(9)	13	17	24	(24)	32

See Table A14 for notes and source.

Table A14: Farm Servants — Annual Wages, 1790-1881 (£)

	1790	1794	1804-14	1814	1834-45	1867-70	1881
Scotland	6	8	16	14	11	21	n.a.
N. Scotland	5.5	7	15	13	10	19	25
Selected counties							
Argyll	7	8	14	11	10	(17)	22
Caithness	3	6.5	(8)	8	7.5	13.5	18.5
Inverness	(7)	8	14	(11)	9	(19)	26
Perth	8	9	18	16	12.5	20	27.5
Ross &							
Cromarty	(4)	4	12	(10)	7	15	23
Sutherland	2.5	(6)	(11)	(9)	8	22	(22)

Notes: a. Figures in brackets (thus) are interpolated.
b. Bowley has defined Northern Scotland to include Perth, Forfar, Kincardine, Aberdeen, Banff, Elgin, Nairn, Argyll, Inverness, Ross and Cromarty, Sutherland and Caithness.
c. See also V. Morgan, 'Agricultural Wage Rates in Late Eighteenth-Century Scotland', *Economic History Review*, vol. 24 (1971), and Gaskell, *Morvern Transformed*, p. 177.
Source: A. L. Bowley, 'The Statistics of Wages in the United Kingdom during the Last Hundred Years (Part I) Agricultural Wages — Scotland', *Journal of the Royal Statistical Society*, vol. 62 (1899).

BIBLIOGRAPHY

Manuscript Sources

In the National Library of Scotland, Edinburgh:
Buchanan Autograph Letters   MS 740
Constable Letter Book   MS 792
Highland Society of Scotland Correspondence   Adv. MS 73
Lauriston Castle Collection, Devine Papers   MS 1309
Sutherland Papers   Dep. 313

In the Scottish Record Office, Edinburgh:
Adam of Blair Adam Papers   NRA1454
Balnagowan Castle MSS   GD129
John Blackadder, Report on Agriculture   RH2/8/24
Breadalbane Muniments   GD112
British Fisheries Society Papers   GD9
Campbell of Jura Papers   GD64
Clanranald Papers   GD201
Cromartie Collection
Fraser-Mackintosh Collection   GD128
Highland Destitution Papers
Home Office Papers (copies)   RH2/4
Lennoxlowe Muniments
Loch Muniments   GD268
Lord Advocate's Papers   RH
Lord Macdonald MSS   GD221
John Macgregor Collection   GD50
Mackay of Bighouse Papers   GD87
Maclaine of Lochbuie Papers   GD174
Melville Castle Muniments   GD51
Reay Papers   GD84
Riddell Papers   GD1 and AF49
Ross of Pitcalnie Muniments   GD199
Seafield MSS   GD248
Seaforth Muniments   GD46
Sinclair of Freswick Papers   GD136
Letters of James Skene   RH4
Skene of Rubislaw MSS
Sutherland of Rearquhar Papers   GD347
Tods, Murray & Jamieson Collection   GD237
Letters of James Traill of Ratter

In the Argyll & Bute District Archives:
 Malcolm of Poltalloch Papers
In the Hampshire Record Office:
 Mildmay Family Papers   15M50/1326
In the Northumberland County Record Office:
 Culley Papers   ZCU43
In the Stafford County Record Office:
 Sutherland Collection   D593
In the Warwick County Record Office:
 Gordon Letters   CR764
 Poltalloch Estate Papers   CR229
 Seymour-Conway Papers   CR114
Public Archives of Canada, Ottawa:
 Selkirk Papers
In private hands:
 Irvine Robertson Collection, Stirling
 MacPherson Grant Papers, Ballindolloch Castle
 Papers of the Graham-Campbell family of Shirvan

Parliamentary Papers

Select Committee on Emigration from the
 United Kingdom   1826-7 V
Select Committee on Agriculture   1833 V
Select Committee on Agricultural Distress   1836 VIII
Select Committee to Inquire into Education
 in Scotland   1837-8 VII
Select Committee on Emigration (Scotland)   1841 VI
Report on Relief of Distress in the
 Highlands (1837)   1841 XXVII
Correspondence from July 1846 to February 1847 Relating
 to the Measures Adopted for the Relief of the
 Distress in Scotland   1847 LIII
Report of the Board of Supervision for the Relief
 of the Poor in Scotland   1847-[annual]
Royal Commission on the Employment of Children,
 Young Persons and Women in Agriculture   1867-8 XVII
Select Committee on Game Laws   1873
Report of Commissioners of Inquiry into the Condition
 of the Crofters and Cottars of the Highlands and
 Islands of Scotland   1884 XXXII-XXXVI
Report of the Royal Commission on the Highlands and
 Islands (Deer Forest Commission)   1895 XXXVIII-XXXIX
Royal Commission on Agriculture   1896 XVI

Newspapers and Periodicals

Annual Register   *Military Register*
An Teachdaire Gaidhealach   *Nairnshire Mirror*

520   Bibliography

Blackwood's Edinburgh
 Magazine
Caithness Chronicle
Caledonian Mercury
Celtic Magazine
Dundas Warden
Edinburgh Evening Courant
Edinburgh Review
Elgin Courant
Elgin and Morayshire Courier
Farmer's Magazine
Glasgow Herald
Inverness Advertiser
Inverness Courier
Inverness Herald
Inverness Journal
John O'Groat Journal

North Star
Northern Chronicle
Northern Ensign
Notes & Queries
Quebec Times
Ross-shire Advertiser
Ross-shire Journal
Ross-shire Observer
Scots Magazine
Scotsman
Scottish Highlander
Scottish Notes & Queries
Star
Stirling Journal & Advertiser
Tait's Magazine
The Times
True Scotsman

Books, Pamphlets, Articles, etc.

Adam, M. I, 'The Causes of the Highland Emigrations of 1783-1803', *Scottish Historical Review*, vol. 17 (1920)
_____ 'The Eighteenth Century Highland Landlords and the Poverty Problem', *Scottish Historical Review*, vol. 19 (1922)
_____ 'The Highland Emigration of 1770', *Scottish Historical Review*, vol. 16 (1919)
Adam, R. J. (ed.) *John Home's Survey of Assynt* (Scottish History Society, Edinburgh, 1960)
_____ (ed.) *Papers on Sutherland Estate Management* (Scottish History Society, 2 vols., Edinburgh, 1972)
Adams, John Quincy. *Writings of John Quincy Adams*, ed. W. C. Ford (New York, 1968)
'Agricola'. 'On the improvement of the Highlands', *The Weekly Magazine of Edingburgh Amusement*, vol. 25 (1774)
Alison, W. P. *Letter to Sir John McNeill on Highland Destitution* (Edinburgh, 1851)
Alister, R. *The Extermination of the Scottish Peasantry* (Edinburgh, 1853)
'Amicus'. *Eight Letters on the Subject of the Earl of Selkirk's Pamphlet on Highland Emigration as they Lately Appeared under the Signature of Amicus in One of the Edinburgh Newspapers* (Edinburgh, 1803)
Anderson, James. *An Account of the Present State of the Hebrides* (Edinburgh, 1825)
Anderson, John. *Prize Essay on the State of Society and Knowledge in the Highlands of Scotland* (Edinburgh, 1825)
Anon., *Emigration from the Highlands and Islands of Scotland to Australia* (London, 1852)
_____ *Hints for the Use of Highland Tenants and Cottagers, by a Proprietor* (Inverness, 1838)
_____ 'Landed Tenures in the Highlands', *Westminster Review*, vol. 34 (1868)
_____ *Notes and Sketches Illustrative of Northern Rural Life in the Eighteenth Century* (Edinburgh, 1877)
_____ *Observations on the Causes and Remedies of Destitution in the Highlands of Scotland* Glasgow, 1838)
_____ *On the Neglect of Scotland and her Interests by the Imperial Parliament* (Edinburgh, 1878)

Argyle, Duke of (George Douglas Campbell). *Autobiography and Memoirs*, edited by the Dowager Duchess of Argyll (2 vols., London, 1906)
_____ 'A Corrected Picture of the Highlands', *Nineteenth Century*, vol. 16 (November 1884)
_____ 'On the Economic Condition of the Highlands of Scotland', *Journal of the Statistical Society of London*, vol. 26 (1883)
_____ *Scotland as it was and as it is* (2 vols., Edinburgh, 1887)
Armstrong, W. A. 'The Influence of Demographic Factors on the Position of the Agricultural Labourer in England and Wales, c. 1750-1914', *Agricultural History Review*, vol. 29 (1981)
Ashton, T. S. *The Industrial Revolution* (London, 1968 edition)
Bailyn, Bernard. '1776. A Year of Challenge – a World Transformed', *Journal of Law and Economics*, vol. 15 (1976)
_____ 'The Challenge of Modern Historiography', *American Historical Review*, vol. 87 (1982)
Balfour, R. A. C. S. 'Emigration from the Highlands and Western Isles of Scotland to Australia during the Nineteenth Century', unpublished M Litt thesis, University of Edinburgh, 1973
Barron, E. M. (ed.) *A Highland Editor. Selected Writings of James Barron of the Inverness Courier* (Inverness, 1927)
Barron, J. *The Northern Highlands in the Nineteenth Century* (3 vols., Inverness, 1907-13)
Bayne, Peter. *The Life and Letters of Hugh Miller* (2 vols., London, 1871)
Beames, Michael. 'Rural conflict in Pre-Famine Ireland', *Past and Present*, no. 81 (1978)
Bear, W. E. 'Obstruction to Land Tenure Reform', *Contemporary Review*, vol. 48 (1885)
Black, R. D. C. 'The Classical View of Ireland's Economy' in A. W. Coats (ed.), *The Classical Economists and Economic Policy* (London, 1971)
_____ 'The Irish Experience in Relation to the Theory and Practice of Economic Development' in A. J. Youngson (ed.), *Economic Development in the Long Run* (London, 1972)
Blackie, J. S. *Altavona* (Edinburgh, 1882)
_____ 'The Highland Crofters', *Nineteenth Century*, vol. 13 (1883)
_____ *The Scottish Highlanders and the Land Laws* (London, 1885)
_____ *Scottish Song* (Edinburgh, 1889)
Blair, D. B. 'On the Early Settlement of the Lower Provinces by the Scottish Gael: their Various Situations and Present Prospects', *Transactions of the Celtic Society of Montreal* (1884-7)
Botfield, B. *Journal of a Tour through the Highlands* (Norton Hall, 1830)
Boyd, W. K. *Some Eighteenth Century Tracts Concerning North Carolina* (Raleigh, 1927)
Brenner, Robert. 'The Agrarian Roots of European Capitalism', *Past and Present*, no. 70 (1976)
Bristow, Edward. 'The Liberty and Property Defence League and Individualism', *Historical Journal*, vol. 18 (1975)
Broady, M. *Marginal Regions* (Oxford, 1973)
Brock, W. R. *Scotus Americanus* (Edinburgh, 1982)
Broeker, Galen. *Rural Disorder and Police Reform in Ireland 1812-1836* (London, 1970)
Broeze, F. J. A. 'Private Enterprise and the Peopling of Australasia, 1831-1850', *Economic History Review*, vol. 35 (1982)
Bruce, Steve. 'Social Change and Collective Behaviour: the Revival in Eighteenth Century Ross-shire', *British Journal of Sociology*, vol. 34 (1983)

Bryden, John. 'Core-Periphery Problems – the Scottish Case' in Dudley Seers, Bernard Schatter and Marja-Lilsa Kiljunen (eds.), *Underdeveloped Europe* (London, 1979)

Bulloch, J. M. *The Gordons of Cluny* (Buckie, 1911)

Bumsted, J. M. *The Peoples Clearance: Highland Emigration to British North America 1770-1815* (Edinburgh, 1982)

_____ 'Settlement by Chance: Lord Selkirk and Prince Edward Island', *Canadian Historical Review*, vol. 59 (1978)

Burton, J. H. 'Celtic Clearings', *Edinburgh Review*, vol. 86 (1847)

Caird, J. B. 'The North West Highlands and the Hebrides' in Jean Mitchell (ed.), *Great Britain. Geographical Essays* (Cambridge, 1967)

_____ (ed.) *Park: a Geographical Study of a Lewis district* (Nottingham, 1958)

Cameron, James M. 'A Study of the Factors that Assisted and directed Scottish Emigration to Upper Canada, 1815-1855', unpublished PhD thesis, University of Glasgow, 1970

Cameron, T. 'The Changing Role of the Highland Landlords Relative to Scottish Emigration during the First Half of the Nineteenth century' in *Proceedings of the Fourth and Fifth Colloquia on Scottish Studies* (Guelph, 1971)

Campbell, D. & R. A. Maclean. *Beyond the Atlantic Roar: a Study of the Nova Scotia Scots* (Toronto, 1974)

Campbell, J. L. *The Book of Barra* (London, 1936)

_____ (ed.) *A Collection of Highland Rites and Customes, Copied by Edward Lluyd from the Manuscript of the Rev. James Kirkwood (1650-1709), and Annotated by him with the Aid of the Rev. John Beaton* (The Folklore Society, Cambridge, 1975)

_____ 'Eviction at First Hand. The Clearing of Clanranald's Islands', *Scots Magazine* (January 1945)

Campbell, R. H. *Scotland since 1707* (Oxford, 1965)

_____ & J. B. A. Dow. *Source Book of Scottish Economic and Social History* (Oxford, 1968)

Cannadine, David. 'Aristocratic Indebtedness in the 19th Century: the Case Reopened', *Economic History Review*, vol. 30 (1977)

Carpenter, S. D. MacD. 'Patterns of Recruitment of the Highland Regiments of the British Army, 1756 to 1815', unpublished M Litt thesis, University of St Andrews, 1977

Carrington, C. E. *The British Overseas* (Cambridge, 1950)

Carruthers, Roberts. *The Highland Notebook* (Inverness, 1887)

Carter, Ian. 'The Changing Image of the Scottish Peasantry 1745-1980' in R. Samuel (ed.), *People's History and Socialist Theory* (London, 1981)

_____ 'The Highlands of Scotland as an Under-developd region' in E. de Kadt and G. Williams (eds.), *Sociology and Development* (London, 1974)

Checkland, S. G. 'Scottish Economic History', *Economica*, vol. 21 (1964)

Chisholm, C. 'The Clearance of the Highland Glens', *TGSI*, vol. 5 (1876-7)

Clark, G. K. *The Making of Victorian England* (London, 1962)

Clark, Samuel. *Social Origins of the Irish Land War* (Princeton, 1979)

Cloward, R. A. & F. F. Piven. 'Hidden Protest: the Channelling of Female Innovation and Resistance', *Signs* (Summer 1979)

Cobbett, William. *Rural Rides*, ed. G. D. H. and Margaret Cole (3 vols., London, 1930 edition)

Cockburn, Henry. *Journal of Henry Cockburn, 1831-1854* (2 vols., Edinburgh, 1874)

Collier, Adam. *The Crofting Problem* (Cambridge, 1953)

Collins, Brenda. 'Proto-industrialization and Pre-Famine Emigration', *Social History*, vol. 7 (1982)

Collins, E. J. T. 'The Economy of Upland Britain, 1750-1850' in R. B. Tranter (ed.), *The Future of Upland Britain* (2 vols., Reading, 1978)

Conway, Allan. *The Welsh in America* (St Paul, 1961)
Cooper, Derek. *Hebridean Connection* (London, 1977)
_____ *Road to the Isles* (London, 1979)
_____ *Skye* (London, 1970)
Cooper, P. *The So-Called Evictions from the Macdonald Estates in the Island of North Uist, Outer Hebrides, 1849* (Aberdeen, 1881)
Cowan, Robert. *Vital Statistics of Glasgow* (Edinburgh, 1838)
Cowie, R. *Shetland, Descriptive and Historical* (Aberdeen, 1879)
Cregeen, E. R. 'The Changing Role of the House of Argyll in the Scottish Highlands' in N. T. Phillipson and Rosalind Mitchison (eds.), *Scotland in the Age of Improvement* (Edinburgh, 1970)
_____ 'The House of Argyll and the Highlands' in I. M. Lewis (ed.), *History and Social Anthropology* (London, 1968)
_____ 'Oral Sources for the Social History of the Scottish Highlands and Islands', *Oral History,* vol. 2 (1974)
_____ 'Oral Tradition and Agrarian History in the West Highlands', *Oral History,* vol. 2 (1974)
_____ 'The Tacksmen and their Successors', *Scottish Studies,* vol. 13 (1969)
Crotty, R. D. *Irish Agricultural Production* (Cork, 1966)
Crouzet, F. 'Wars, Blockade and Economic Change in Europe 1792-1815', *Journal of Economic History,* vol. 24 (1964)
Cullen, L. M. *An Economic History of Ireland since 1660* (London, 1972)
_____ (ed.) *The Formation of the Irish Economy* (Cork, 1976)
Darby, H. I. (ed.) *A New Historical Geography of England* (Cambridge, 1973)
Darling, F. F. *Island Years* (London, 1940)
_____ *The Story of Scotland* (London, 1945)
_____ *West Highland Survey* (Oxford, 1955)
Dawson, J. H. *The Abridged Statistical History of the Scottish Counties* (Edinburgh, 1862)
Day, J. P. *Public Administration in the Highlands and Islands of Scotland* (London, 1918)
de Crevecoeur, J. H. St J. *Letters from an American Farmer* (London, 1782; 1962 edition)
Dempster, G. *A Discourse on the Proceedings of the British Fisheries Society* (London, 1788)
_____ *In Memoriam* (privately printed, 1889)
Devine, T. M. 'Highland Migration to Lowland Scotland, 1760-1860', *Scottish Historical Review,* vol. 62 (1983)
_____ 'The Rise and Fall of Illicit Whisky-making in Northern Scotland c. 1780-1840', *Scottish Historical Review,* vol. 54 (1975)
_____ 'Temporary Migration and the Scottish Highlands in the Nineteenth Century', *Economic History Review,* vol. 32 (1979)
de Vries, J. *The Dutch Rural Economy in the Golden Age, 1500-1700* (London, 1974)
Dewey, Clive. 'Celtic Agrarian Legislation and the Celtic Revival: Historicist Implications of Gladstone's Irish and Scottish Lands Acts 1870-1886', *Past and Present,* no. 64 (1974)
_____ 'The Rehabilitation of the Peasant Proprietor in Nineteenth Century Economic Thought', *History of Political Economy,* vol. 6 (1974)
Dodd, A. H. *The Industrial Revolution in North Wales* (Cardiff, 1933; 1951 edition)
Dodgshon, R. A. 'Agricultural Change and its Social Consequences in the Southern Uplands, 1600-1780' in T. M. Devine and David Dickson (eds.), *Ireland and Scotland 1600-1850* (Edinburgh, 1983)
Donaldson, Gordon. *The Scots Overseas* (London, 1966)
Donnelly, J. S. *The Land and People of Nineteenth Century Cork* (London, 1975)

Dunbabin, J. P. D. *Rural Discontent in Nineteenth Century Britain* (London, 1974)
Dunderdale, George. *The Book of the Bush* (London, 1898)
Dunlop, Jean. *The British Fisheries Society 1786-1893* (Edinburgh, 1978)
_____ 'The British Fisheries Society: 1787 Questionnaire', *Northern Scotland*, vol. 2, no. 1 (1974-5)
Edmondston, A. *A View of the Ancient and Present State of the Zetland Islands* (2 vols., Edinburgh, 1809)
Edwards, M. M. *The Growth of the British Cotton Trade, 1780-1815* (Manchester, 1967)
Elliot, R. *Special Report on Sutherland and the West Highlands* (pamphlet, 1848)
Engels, F. *The Condition of the Working Class in England in 1844* (London, 1952 edition)
Erickson, Charlotte. *Emigration from Europe, 1815-1914* (London, 1976)
_____ *Invisible Immigrants* (London, 1972)
Extracts from Letters of the Rev. Dr McLeod, Glasgow, Regarding the Famine and Destitution in the Highlands (Glasgow, 1847)
Fairhurst, H. 'The Surveys for the Sutherland Clearances 1813-1820', *Scottish Studies*, vol. 8 (1964)
_____ & G. I. Petrie. 'Scottish Clachans II: Lix and Rossal', *Scottish Geographical Magazine*, vol. 80 (1964)
Fea, J. *The Present State of the Orkney Islands* (Edinburgh, 1775)
Ferguson, Wm. *Scotland 1689 to the Present* (Edinburgh, 1968)
Fergusson, Jas. (ed.) *Letters of George Dempster to Sir Adam Fergusson, 1756-1813* (London, 1934)
Findlater, E. J. *Highland Clearances: the Real Cause of Highland Famines* (Edinburgh, 1855)
Fischer, W. 'Rural Industrialization and Population Change', *Comparative Studies in Society and History*, vol. 15 (1973)
Flinn, M. W. 'Malthus, Emigration and Potatoes in the Scottish north-west, 1770-1870' in L. M. Cullen and T. C. Smout (eds.), *Comparative Aspects of Scottish and Irish Economic and Social History 1600-1900* (Edinburgh, 1977)
_____ 'The Stabilisation of Mortality in Pre-industrial Western Europe', *Journal of European Economic History*, vol. 3 (1974)
_____ *Scottish Population History* (Cambridge, 1977)
Forsyth, R. *The Beauties of Scotland* (5 vols., Edinburgh, 1808)
Fraser-Mackintosh, C. *Letters of Two Centuries* (Inverness, 1890)
Freeman, T. W. *Pre-Famine Ireland* (Manchester, 1957)
Fullarton, Allan & C. R. Baird. *Remarks on the Evils at Present Affecting the Highlands and Islands of Scotland* (Glasgow, 1838)
Garnett, Thomas. *Observations on a Tour through the Highlands and Part of the Western Isles of Scotland* (2 vols., London, 1811)
Gaskell, Phillip. *Morvern Transformed* (Cambridge, 1968; 1980 edition)
Gayer, A. *et al. The Growth and Fluctuation of the British Economy 1790-1850* (2 vols., Oxford, 1953)
Geikie, Archibald. *Scottish Reminiscences* (Glasgow, 1904)
George, Henry. *Scotland and Scotsmen* (Glasgow, 1884)
Gibbon, J. M. *Scots in Canada* (London, 1911)
Gillespie, J. 'The Cattle Industry in Scotland', *Transactions of the Royal Highland and Agricultural Society of Scotland*, 5th ser., vol. 10 (1898)
Goodman, D. & M. Redclift. *From Peasant to Proletarian* (Oxford, 1981)
Gower, Ronald (Lord). *My Reminiscences* (4th edition, London, 1885)
Graham, I. C. C. *Colonists from Scotland: Emigration to North America 1707-1783* (Ithaca, 1954)
Grant, Ann. *Letters from the Mountains* (3 vols., London, 1807)

Grant, I. F. *The Economic History of Scotland* (London, 1934)
_____ *Everyday Life on an Old Highland Farm, 1769-1782* (London, 1924)
_____ *Highland Folk Ways* (London, 1961)
_____ 'Some Accounts of Individual Highland Sporting Estates', *Economic History*, no. 3 (January 1928)
Gray, Alexander. *The Development of Economic Doctrine* (London, 1931)
Gray, J. M. *Lord Selkirk of Red River* (London, 1963)
Gray, Malcolm. 'The Consolidation of the Crofting System', *Agricultural History Review*, vol. 5 (1957)
_____ 'Economic Welfare and Money Income in the Highlands, 1750-1850', *Scottish Journal of Political Economy*, vol. 2 (1955)
_____ *The Fishing Industries of Scotland 1790-1914* (Aberdeen, 1978)
_____ *The Highland Economy 1750-1850* (Edinburgh, 1957)
_____ 'The Highland Potato Famine of the 1840s', *Economic History Review*, vol. 7 (1954-5)
_____ 'The Kelp Industry in the Highlands and Islands of Scotland', *Economic History Review*, vol. 4 (1951)
_____ 'Migration in the Rural Lowlands of Scotland, 1750-1850' in T. M. Devine and David Dickson (eds.), *Ireland and Scotland 1600-1850* (Edinbugh, 1983)
_____ 'Scottish Emigration: the Social Impact of Agrarian Change in the Rural Lowlands, 1775-1875', *Perspectives in American History*, vol. 7 (1973)
Greg, W. R. 'Highland Destitution and Irish Emigration', *Quarterly Review*, vol. 90 (1851)
Grierson, T. *Autumnal Rambles among the Scottish Mountains* (Edinburgh, 1850)
Grimble, Ian. *Chief of Mackay* (London, 1965)
_____ 'Emigration in the Time of Rob Donn, 1714-1778', *Scottish Studies*, vol. 7 (1963)
_____ 'Gael and Saxon in Scotland', *Yale Review*, vol. 52 (1962)
_____ 'John Mackay of Strathan Melness, Patron of Rob Donn', *Scottish Gaelic Studies*, vol. 10 (1964)
_____ 'Patrick Sellar' in Gordon Menzies (ed.), *History is my Witness* (London, 1977)
_____ 'The Rev. Alexander Pope's Letter to James Hogg, 1774' *Scottish Gaelic Studies*, vol. 11 (1966)
_____ *The Trial of Patrick Sellar* (London, 1962)
_____ 'Unsceptred Isle' in D. S. Thomson and Ian Grimble (eds.), *The Future of the Highlands* (London, 1968)
_____ *The World of Rob Donn* (Edinburgh, 1979)
Guillet, E. C. *Early Life in Upper Canada* (Toronto, 1933)
_____ *The Great Migration* (Toronto, 1933)
Gunn, Donald. *History of Manitoba* (Ottawa, 1880)
Guttsman, W. L. *The English Ruling Class* (London, 1969)
Haber, L. F. *The Chemical Industry during the Nineteenth Century* (Oxford, 1958)
Hall, J. *Travels in Scotland by an Unusual Route* (2 vols., London, 1807)
Hall, Robert. *The Highland Sportsman and Tourist* (London, 1885)
Hallett, G., P. Randall & E. G. West. *Regional Policy for Ever?* (London, 1973)
Hamilton, Henry. *The Industrial Revolution in Scotland* (Oxford, 1932)
Handley, J. E. *The Navvy in Scotland* (Cork, 1970)
Hanham, H. J. 'Mid-Century Scottish Nationalism' in R. Robson (ed.), *Ideas and Institutions in Victorian Britain* (London, 1967)
_____ 'The Problem of Highland Discontent, 1880-1885', *Transactions of the Royal Historical Society*, vol. 19 (1969)
Hansen, M. L. *The Atlantic Migration* (New York, 1961)
Hart, Jennifer. 'Sir Charles Trevelyan at the Treasury', *English Historical Review*, vol. 75, no. 294 (1960)

Hechter, Michael. *Internal Colonialism: the Celtic Fringe in British National Develop-*
ment, 1536-1966 (London, 1975)
Henderson, John. *General View of the Agriculture of the County of Sutherland*
(London, 1812)
Heywood, Colin. 'The Role of the Peasantry in French Industrialisation, 1815-80',
Economic History Review, vol. 34 (1981)
[Highland Emigration Society.] *Report of the Highland Emigration Society from its*
Formation in April 1852 until April 1853 (London, 1853)
Hildebrandt, R. N. 'Migration and Economic Change in the Northern Highlands dur-
ing the Nineteenth Century, with Particular Reference to the Period 1851-91',
unpublished PhD thesis, University of Glasgow, 1980
Himmelfarb, Gertrude. *Victorian Minds* (London, 1968)
Hirschman, A. O. *Essays in Trespassing* (Cambridge, 1981)
_____ *The Strategy of Economic Development* (New Haven, 1965)
'Historical Pamphlets of Inverness-shire', vol. I, 'Emigrants from Skye to Australia',
Inverness Public Library
Hobsbawm, E. J. 'Capitalism and Agriculture: the Scottish Reformers in the
Eighteenth Century', *Annales*, vol. 33 (1978)
_____ 'Scottish Reformers of the Eighteenth Century and Capitalist Agriculture' in
E. J. Hobsbawm (ed.), *Peasants in History* (Calcutta, 1980)
Hobson, P. M. 'Congestion and Depopulation, a Study in Rural Contrasts between
West Lewis and West Sutherland', unpublished PhD thesis, University of St
Andrews, 1952
Holland, Stuart. *Capital versus the Regions* (London, 1976)
_____ *The Regional Problem* (London, 1976)
Hollander, Samuel. *The Economics of Adam Smith* (London, 1973)
Homer, P. B. *Observations on a Short Tour Made in the Summer of 1803 to the Western*
Highlands of Scotland (London, 1804)
Horner, Francis. *The Economic Writings of Francis Horner in the Edinburgh Review*
1802-6, ed. F. W. Fetter (London, 1957)
Houston, George. 'Farm Wages in Central Scotland from 1814 to 1870', *Journal of the*
Royal Statistical Society, Series A, vol. 118 (1955)
Houston, R. R. 'The Impact of Economic Change in Sutherland 1755-1851',
unpublished PhD thesis, University of Edinburgh, 1980)
Howison, John. *Sketches of Upper Canada* (Edinburgh, 1825)
Hufton, Olwen. 'Women in Revolution, 1789-1796', *Past and Present*, no. 83 (1971)
Hughes, E. 'The Eighteenth Century Estate Agent' in H. A. Cronne, T. W. Moody and
D. B. Quinn (eds.), *Essays in British and Irish History* (London, 1949)
Hunt, E. H. *Regional Wage Variations in Britain 1850-1914* (Oxford, 1973)
Hunter, James. 'The Emergence of the Crofting Community: the Religious Contri-
bution, 1798-1843', *Scottish Studies*, vol. 18 (1974)
_____ *The Making of the Crofting Community* (Edinburgh, 1976)
_____ 'The Politics of Land Reform 1873-1895', *Scottish Historical Review*, vol. 53
(1974)
_____ 'Sheep and Deer: Highland Sheep Farming, 1850-1900', *Northern Scotland*,
vol. 1 (1973)
Hyde, E. D. 'The British Fisheries Society: its Settlement and the Scottish Fisheries,
1750-1850', unpublished PhD thesis, University of Strathclyde, 1973
Hymer, Stephen & Stephen Resnick. 'A Model of an Agrarian Economy with Non-
Agricultural Activities', *American Economic Review*, vol. 59 (1969)
Innes, Cosmo. *Sketches of Early Scotch History and Social Progress* (Edinburgh,
1861)
Irvine, Alexander. *An Inquiry into the Causes and Effects of Emigration from the*
Highlands and Western Isles of Scotland (Edinburgh, 1802)

Johnson, Samuel. *Johnson's Journey to the Western Islands of Scotland and Boswell's Journal of a Tour to the Hebrides with Samuel Johnson LL.D.*, edited by R. W. Chapman (Oxford, 1924)

Johnston, H.J.M. *British Emigration Policy 1815-30* (Oxford, 1972)

Johnston, J.F.W. 'On the State and Prospects of British Agriculture', *Edinburgh Review*, vol. 84 (1846)

Johnston, J.G. *The Truth, Consisting of Letters Just Received from Emigrants to the Australian Colonies* (Edinburgh, 1839)

Johnston, S.C. *A History of Emigration from the United Kingdom to North America 1763-1912* (London, 1966 edition)

Johnston, Thomas. *Our Scots Noble Families* (Glasgow, 1926)

Jones, David. *Before Rebecca. Popular Protest in Wales 1793-1835* (London, 1973)

Katz, Michael. *The People of Hamilton, Canada West* (Cambridge, Mass., 1975)

Kennedy, J. *The Days of the Fathers in Ross-shire* (3rd Edition Edinburgh, 1861)

Kennedy, L. & T.B. Grainger. *The Present State of the Tenancy of Land in the Highland and Grazing Districts in Great Britain* (London, 1829)

Kincaid, Barbara. 'Scottish Immigration to Cape Breton, 1758-1838', unpublished MA thesis, University of Dalhousie, 1964

Knox, J.A. *A View of the British Empire, More Especially Scotland* (3rd edition, London, 1785; London, 1978)

Ladurie, E.L. 'A Reply to Professor Brenner', *Past and Present*, no. 79 (1978)

Lawson, W.R. 'The Poetry and the Prose of the Crofter Question', *National Review*, vol. 4 (1884-5)

Lawton, Richard. 'Regional Population Trends in England and Wales, 1750-1971' in John Hobcraft and Phillip Rees (eds.), *Regional Demographic Development* (London, 1979)

Lebow, R.N. *J. S. Mill and the Irish Land Question* (Philadelphia, 1979)

Lee, Joseph. 'The Ribbonmen' in T.D. Williams (ed.), *Secret Societies in Ireland* (Dublin, 1973)

Leigh, M.M. 'The Crofting Problem 1790-1883', *Scottish Journal of Agriculture*, vol. 11-12 (1928-9)

Leopold, John. 'The Levellers Revolt in Galloway in 1724', *Scottish Labour History Journal*, vol. 14 (1980)

Lesingham-Smith, C. *Excursions through the Highlands and Islands of Scotland in 1835 and 1836* (London, 1837)

Letters to the Rev. Dr Norman Macleod Regarding the Famine in the Highlands (Glasgow, 1847)

Lettice, J. *Letters on a Tour through Various Parts of Scotland in the Year 1792* (London, 1794)

Levitt, Ian & Christopher Smout. *The State of the Scottish Working Class in 1843* (Edinburgh, 1979)

Leyden, J. *Journal of a Tour in the Highlands and Western Islands of Scotland in 1800* (Edinburgh, 1903)

Lindner, S.B. *Trade and Trade Policy for Development* (New York, 1967)

Lobban, R.D. 'The Migration of Highlanders into Lowland Scotland (c.1750-1890) with Particular Reference to Greenock', unpublished PhD thesis, University of Edinburgh, 1969

Loch, James. *An Account of the Improvements on the Estates of the Marquess of Stafford* (London, 1815; enlarged edition, London, 1820)

_____ *Facts as to the Past and Present State of the Estate of Sutherland* (published anonymously, 1845)

Logue, K.J. *Popular Disturbances in Scotland, 1780-1815* (Edinburgh, 1977)

Low, D. *On Landed Property and the Economy of Estates* (London, 1844)

Lyons, F.S.L. *Ireland since the Famine* (London, 1971)

McArthur, M. M. *Survey of Lochtayside 1769* (Scottish History Society Publications, 3rd series, XXVII, Edinburgh, 1936)
MacCormick, Donald. *Hebridean Folksongs* (Oxford, 1969)
MacCulloch, John. *A Description of the Western Islands of Scotland* (3 vols., London, 1819)
_____ *The Highlands and Western Isles of Scotland* (4 vols., London, 1824)
McCulloch, J. R. *A Descriptive and Statistical Account of the British Empire* (2 vols., London, 1854)
_____ *A Dictionary of Commerce* (London, 1834)
MacDermid, G. E. 'The Religious and Ecclesiastical Life of the North West Highlands 1750-1843', unpublished PhD thesis, University of Aberdeen, 1967
MacDonagh, Oliver. *Ireland* (Englewood Cliffs, 1968)
_____ *A Pattern of Government Growth 1800-1860* (London, 1961)
[Macdonald, Colin.] 'Transition in the Highlands of Scotland', *Scottish Review* (July 1888)
Macdonald, C. S. 'Early Highland Emigration to Nova Scotia and Prince Edward Island, 1770-1853', *Nova Scotia Historical Society Collections*, vol. 23 (1941)
Macdonald, D. *Lewis, a History of the Island* (Edinburgh, 1978)
McDonald, Forrest, & E. S. McDonald. 'The Ethnic Origins of the American People, 1790', *William and Mary Quarterly*, vol. 37 (April 1980)
Macdonald, James. *General View of the Agriculture of the Hebrides* (London, 1811)
MacDonald, R. C. *Sketches of the Highlanders: with an Account of their Early Arrival in North America* (St John, New Brunswick, 1843)
Macdonald, R. H. *The Emigration of Highland Crofters* (Edinburgh, 1885)
Macfarlane, Alan. *The Origins of English Individualism* (Oxford, 1978)
MacGill, W. *Old Ross-shire and Scotland as Seen in the Tain and Balnagowan Documents* (Inverness, 1909)
McGrath, John. *The Cheviot, the Stag and the Black Black Oil* (Kyleakin, 1974)
Macinnes, John. *The Evangelical Movements in the Highlands of Scotland 1699-1800* (Aberdeen, 1951)
Macintyre, L. M. 'Sir Walter Scott and the Highlands', unpublished PhD thesis, University of Glasgow, 1976)
Mackay, D. I. & N. K. Buxton. 'The North of Scotland — a Case for Redevelopment?' *Scottish Journal of Political Economy*, vol. 12 (1965)
Mackay, Donald. *Scotland Farewell: the People of the Hector* (Scarborough, Ontario, 1980)
Mackay, G. G. *On the Management of Highland Property* (Edinburgh, 1858)
Mackay, I. R. 'Glenalladale's Settlement, Prince Edward Island', *Scottish Gaelic Studies*, vol. 10 (1963)
McKay, Margaret. 'Nineteenth Century Tiree Emigrant Communities in Ontario', *Oral History Journal*, vol. 9 (1981)
McKay, Margaret M. (ed.) *The Rev. Dr John Walker's Report on the Hebrides in 1764 and 1771* (Edinburgh, 1980)
Mackenzie, Alexander. *The Highland Clearances — a Strange Return by the Highland Chiefs for the Fidelity of the Clans* (Inverness, 1881)
_____ *The History of the Highland Clearances* (Inverness, 1883)
_____ *History of the Macdonalds* (Inverness, 1883)
_____ *The Isle of Skye in 1882-1883* (Inverness, 1883)
_____ (ed.) *The Trial of Patrick Sellar* (Inverness, 1883)
Mackenzie, G. S. *Letter to the Proprietors of Land in Ross-shire* (Edinburgh, 1803)
Mackenzie, K. S. 'Changes in the Ownership of Land in Ross-shire, 1756-1853', *TGSI* (1897)
Mackenzie, W. C. *A Short History of the Scottish Highlands and Islands* (London, 1908)

Mackenzie, W. M. *Hugh Miller. A Critical Study* (London, 1905)
Mackinnon, N. J. 'Strath, Skye, in the Mid-Nineteenth Century', *TGSI*, vol. 51 (1978-80)
Mackintosh, T. D. 'Factors in Emigration from the Islands of Scotland to North America, 1772-1803', unpublished M Litt thesis, University of Aberdeen, 1979
McLauchlan, T. *The Depopulation System in the Highlands* (Edinburgh, 1849)
Maclean, Charles, *Island on the Edge of the World: Utopian St Kilda and its Passing* (London, 1972)
Maclean, J. P. *An Historical Account of the Settlements of Scotch Highlanders in America Prior to the Peace of 1783* (Glasgow and Cleveland, 1900)
McLean, Marianne. 'Peopling Glengarry County: the Scottish origins of a Canadian Community' in Dona Johnson and C. Lecelle (eds.), *Historical Papers* (Ottawa, 1982)
Maclean, Samuel. 'The Poetry of the Highland Clearances', *TGSI*, vol. 38 (1937-41)
Macleay, D. *Scotland Farewell. The People of the Hector* (Scarborough, Ontario, 1980)
Macleod, Donald. *History of the Destitution in Sutherlandshire* (Edinburgh, 1841)
MacLeod, J. N. *Memorials of the Rev. Norman Macleod* (Edinburgh, 1898)
MacLeod, Reginald. 'The Crofters: How to Benefit them', *Blackwood's Magazine*, vol. 139 (1886)
Macmillan, D. S. *Scotland and Australia, 1788-1850: Emigration, Commerce and Investment* (Oxford, 1967)
MacPhail, I. M. M. 'Prelude to the Crofters' War, 1870-1880', *TGSI*, vol. 49 (1974-6)
_____ 'The Skye Military Expedition of 1884-85', *TGSI*, vol. 48 (1972-4)
MacPhee, Hugh. 'The Trail of the Emigrants', *TGSI*, vol. 46 (1969-70)
MacSween, M. D. 'Settlement in Trotternish, Isle of Skye, 1700-1858', unpublished B Litt thesis, University of Glasgow, 1962
Maddison, Angus. *Economic Progress and Policy in Developing Countries* (London, 1970)
Maguire, W. A. *The Downshire Estates in Ireland 1801-1845* (Oxford, 1972)
Malmesbury, Earl of (J. H. Harris). *Memoirs of an Ex-Minister* (London, 1885)
Malthus, T. R. *An Essay on the Principle of Population* (London, 1972 edition)
Martell, J. S. *Immigration to and Emigration from Nova Scotia, 1815-1838* (Halifax, 1942)
Marx, Charles [Karl]. 'Sutherland and Slavery, or The Duchess at Home', *The People's Paper*, 12 March 1853
Marx, Karl. *The American Journalism of Marx and Engels* (New York, n.d.)
_____ *Capital* (3 vols., Moscow, n.d.)
_____ *Collected Works* (Moscow, 1976)
_____ *Ireland and the Irish Question. A Collection of Writings by Karl Marx and Frederick Engels* (New York, 1972)
_____ *The Poverty of Philosophy* (New York, 1963 edition)
Mason, J. W. 'The Duke of Argyll and the Land Question in Late Nineteenth Century Britain', *Victorian Studies*, vol. 21 (1978)
Meek, D. E. 'Gaelic Poets of the Land Agitation', *TGSI*, vol. 48 (1972-4)
Meikle, H. W. *Scotland and the French Revolution* (Edinburgh, 1912)
Mercer, John. *Hebridean Islands, Colonsay, Gigha, Jura* (London, 1974)
Merivale, Herman. *Lectures on Colonization and Colonies* (London, 1861 edition)
Meyer, Duane. *The Highland Scots of North Carolina, 1732-1776* (Chapel Hill, 1961)
Michie, R. C. *Money, Mania and Markets* (Edinburgh, 1981)
Miller, Hugh. *Essays* (Edinburgh, 1875)
_____ *Leading Articles on Various Subjects* (Edinburgh, 1870)
_____ *My Schools and Schoolmasters* (Edinburgh, 1874 edition)

_____ *Sutherland as it was, and is; or, How a Country may be Ruined* (Edinburgh, 1843)

Mills, D.R. *English Rural Communities. The Impact of a Specialised Economy* (London, 1973)

Mitchell, Joseph. *Reminiscences of my Life in the Highlands* (London, 1883)

Mitchison, Rosalind. *Agricultural Sir John. The Life of Sir John Sinclair of Ulbster 1754-1835* (London, 1962)

_____ 'The Highland Clearances', *Scottish Economic and Social History*, vol. 1 (1981)

_____ *A History of Scotland* (London, 1970)

_____ 'The Movement of Scottish Corn Prices in the Seventeenth and Eighteenth Centuries', *Economic History Review*, vol. 18 (1965)

Mokyr, Joel. *Why Ireland Starved. A Quantitative and Analytical History of the Irish Economy, 1800-1850* (London, 1983)

Morgan, E.V. 'Regional Problems and Common Currencies', *Lloyds Bank Review*, no. 110 (October 1973)

Morgan, Valerie. 'Agricultural Wage Rates in Late Eighteenth-Century Scotland', *Economic History Review*, vol. 24 (1971)

Morse, S.L. 'Immigration to Nova Scotia, 1839-1851', unpublished MA thesis, University of Dalhousie, 1946

Mowat, I.R.M. *Easter Ross 1750-1850* (Edinburgh, 1980)

Murray, Norman. *The Scottish Handloom Weavers 1790-1850* (Edinburgh, 1978)

Murray, W.H. *Companion Guide to the West Highlands of Scotland* (London, 1968)

Murray, W.H. *Islands of Western Scotland* (London, 1973)

Neeson, J.N. 'Opposition to Enclosure' in A. Charlesworth (ed.), *An Atlas of Rural Protest in Britain 1518-1900* (London, 1983)

Newsome, A.R. 'Records of Emigrants from England and Scotland to North Carolina 1774-5', *North Carolina Historical Review* vol. 11 (1934)

New Statistical Account of Scotland (15 vols., Edinburgh, 1835-45)

Nicolson, Alexander. *History of Skye* (Glasgow, 1930)

Nicolson, Nigel. *Lord of the Isles* (London, 1960)

Noble, John. *Miscellanea Invernessiana* (Stirling, 1902)

North, D.C. *The Economic Growth of the United States 1790-1860* (Englewood Cliffs, 1960)

O'Farrell, Patrick. 'Emigrant Attitudes and Behaviour as a Source for Irish History', *Historical Studies*, vol. 10 (1976)

O'Grada, Cormac. 'Demographic Adjustment and Seasonal Migration in Nineteenth Century Ireland' in L.M. Cullen and F. Furet (eds.), *Irlande et France* (Paris, 1980)

_____ 'Seasonal Migration and Post-Famine Adjustment in the West of Ireland', *Studia Hibernica*, vol. 13 (1973)

Okun, B. & R.W. Richardson. 'Regional Income Inequality and Internal Population Migration', *Economic Development and Cultural Change*, vol. 9 (1961)

Omand, D. *The Caithness Book* (Inverness, 1972)

Orr, Willie. *Deer Forests, Landlords and Crofters* (Edinburgh, 1982)

Otter, William (ed.). *The Life and Remains of the Rev. Edward Daniel Clarke LL D* (London, 1824)

Parker, W.N. & E.L. Jones (eds.). *European Peasants and their Markets* (Princeton, 1976)

Patterson, George. *A History of the County of Pictou, Nova Scotia* (Montreal, 1877)

Pennell, J.P. & E.R. *Our Journey to the Hebrides* (London, 1890)

Perren, Richard. 'The Effects of Agricultural Depression on the English Estates of the Dukes of Sutherland, 1870-1900', unpublished PhD thesis, University of Nottingham, 1968

_____ 'The Landlord and Agricultural Transformation, 1870-1900', *Agricultural*

History Review, vol. 18 (1970)

Picton, J. A. 'The Crofters' Cry for More Land', *Contemporary Review*, vol. 48 (1885)

Ployen, C. *Reminiscences of a Voyage to Shetland, Orkney, and Scotland in the Summer of 1839* (Lerwick, 1894)

Pollard, Sidney. 'Industrialisation and the European Economy', *Economic History Review*, vol. 26 (1973)

———— *The Genesis of Modern Management* (London, 1965)

———— & D. W. Crossley. *The Wealth of Britain* (London, 1968)

Prattis, J. I. *Economic Structures in the Highlands of Scotland* (The Fraser of Allander Institute Speculative Papers, no. 7, Glasgow, 1977)

Prebble, John. *Culloden* (London, 1961)

———— *Glencoe* (London, 1966)

———— *The Highland Clearances* (London, 1963)

———— *Mutiny* (London, 1975)

Pritchett, J. P. *The Red River Valley 1811-1849. A Regional Study* (Toronto, 1942)

Pryde, G. S. *Scotland from 1603 to the Present Day* (London, 1962)

Rae, J. 'The Crofter Problem', *Contemporary Review*, vol. 47 (1885)

Ramsay, John. *Scotland and Scotsmen of the Eighteenth Century* (2 vols., Edinburgh, 1888)

Redford, Arthur. *Labour Migration in England, 1800-1850* (Manchester, 1964)

Richards, Eric. 'Agricultural Change, Modernization and the Clearances' in D. Omand (ed.), *The Ross and Cromarty Book* (Inverness, 1984)

———— 'An Anatomy of the Sutherland Fortune: Income, Consumption, Investments and Returns, 1780-1880', *Business History*, vol. 21 (1979)

———— 'Australia and the Scottish Connection, 1788-1914' in R. A. Cage (ed.), *The Scots Abroad* (London, 1984)

———— 'The Highland Scots of South Australia', *Journal of the Historical Society of South Australia*, no. 4 (1978)

———— *A History of the Highland Clearances: Agrarian Transformation and the Evictions 1746-1886* (London, 1982)

———— 'How Tame were the Highlanders during the Clearances?' *Scottish Studies*, vol. 17 (1973)

———— 'The Land Agent' in G. E. Mingay (ed.) *The Victorian Countryside* (2 vols., London, 1981)

———— *The Last Scottish Food Riots* (London, 1982)

———— *The Leviathan of Wealth* (London, 1973)

———— 'The Mind of Patrick Sellar (1780-1851)', *Scottish Studies*, vol. 15 (1971)

———— 'Patterns of Highland Discontent, 1790-1860' in John Stevenson and Roland Quinault (eds.), *Popular Protest and Public Order* (London, 1976)

———— 'Problems on the Cromartie Estate, 1851-3', *Scottish Historical Review*, vol. 52 (1973)

———— 'The Prospect of Economic Growth in Sutherland at the Time of the Clearances, 1809 to 1813', *Scottish Historical Review* vol. 49 (1970)

———— 'Structural Change in a Regional Economy: Sutherland and the Industrial Revolution, 1780-1830', *Economic History Review*, vol. 26 (1973)

———— 'Varieties of Scottish Emigration in the Nineteenth Century', Bamforth Lecture, University of Otago, 1984

Rinn, J. A. 'Scots in Bondage. Forgotten Contributors to Colonial Society', *History Today*, vol. 30 (1980)

Ross, Donald. *The Glengarry Evictions* (Glasgow, 1853)

———— *The Russians of Ross-shire* (Glasgow, 1854)

Rostow, W. W. *Stages of Economic Growth. A Non-Communist Manifesto* (London, 1960)

Rudé, George. 'The Pre-Industrial Crowd' in George Rudé, *Paris and London in the*

Eighteenth Century (London, 1970)
[Russel, Alexander.] 'The Highlands — Men, Sheep and Deer', *Edinburgh Review,* vol. 106 (1857)
Sage, Donald. *Memorabilia Domestica, or Domestic Life in the North of Scotland* (Wick, 1889; 2nd edition, 1899)
St John, Charles. *A Tour in Sutherlandshire* (2 vols., London, 1849)
Saville, John. *Rural Depopulation in England and Wales 1851-1951* (London, 1957)
Schaw, Janet. *Journal of a Lady of Quality,* ed. E. W. Andrews (New Haven, 1939)
Scott, Huw. *Fasti Ecclesiae Scoticanae* (3 vols., Edinburgh, 1915-28)
Scrope, G. P. *Some Notes on a Tour in England, Scotland and Ireland* (London, 1849)
Selkirk, Earl of (Thomas Douglas). *Observations on the Present State of the Highlands of Scotland* (Edinburgh, 1805)
Selkirk, P. L. *The Langs of Selkirk* (Melbourne, 1910)
Sellar, E. M. *Recollections and Impressions* (Edinburgh, 1908)
Sellar, Thomas. *The Sutherland Evictions of 1814* (London, 1883)
Senior, N. S. *Journals, Conversations and Essays Relating to Ireland* (2 vols., London, 1868)
Seton, George. *St Kilda, Past and Present* (Edinburgh, 1878)
Shairp, J. C. *Glen Desseray and other Poems* (London, 1888)
Shepperson, W. S. *British Emigration to North America* (Minneapolis, 1957)
Simpson, David. 'Investment, Employment and Government Expenditure in the Highlands, 1951-60', *Scottish Journal of Political Economy,* vol. 10 (1963)
Simpson, D. R. F. 'An Economic Analysis of Crofting Agriculture', unpublished PhD thesis, Harvard University, 1962
Sinclair, Catherine. *Scotland and the Scotch* (Edinburgh, 1850)
Sinclair, D. M. 'Highland Emigration to Nova Scotia', *Dalhousie Review,* vol. 23 (1943-4)
Sinclair, John. *Address to the Society for the Improvement of British Wool* (Edinburgh, 1791)
_____ *Analysis of the Statistical Account of Scotland* (2 vols., London, 1825)
_____ *General Report on the Agricultural State and Political Circumstances of Scotland* (Edinburgh, 1814)
_____ *General View of the Agriculture of the Northern Counties of Scotland* (London, 1795)
_____ *Memoirs of the Life and Works of the late Right Honourable Sir John Sinclair, Bart* (2 vols., Edinburgh, 1837)
Skene, William. *Celtic Scotland* (Edinburgh, 1880)
Skinner, Andrew. *A System of Social Science* (Oxford, 1979)
Smith, Adam. *The Wealth of Nations* (Glasgow edition, 1976)
Smith, Alexander. *A Summer in Skye* (Edinburgh, 1912 edition)
Smith, A. M. *Jacobite Estates of the Forty Five* (Edinburgh, 1982)
Smith, Elizabeth. *The Irish Journals of Elizabeth Smith 1840-1850,* ed. David Thomson and Moyra McGusty (Oxford, 1980)
Smith, J. *General View of the Agriculture of Argyll* (Edinburgh, 1798)
Smout, T. C. 'Famine and Famine Relief in Scotland' in L. M. Cullen and T. C. Smout (eds.), *Comparative Aspects of Scottish and Irish Economic and Social History 1600-1900* (Edinburgh, 1977)
_____ *A History of the Scottish People, 1560-1830* (London, 1969)
_____ 'An Ideological Struggle: the Highland Clearances', *Scottish International,* vol. 5, no. 2 (February 1972)
_____ 'Scotland and England: is Dependency a Symptom or a Cause of Underdevelopment?' *Review,* vol. 3 (1980)
Society for the Support of Gaelic Schools. *Annual Reports* (Edinburgh, 1810-22)
Solow, B. L. *The Land Question and the Irish Economy, 1870-1903* (Cambridge,

Mass., 1971)

Somers, Robert. *Letters from the Highlands* (London, 1848)

Spring, David. *English Landed Estates in the Nineteenth Century: their Adminis-tration* (Baltimore, 1963)

Stark, W. (ed.) *Jeremy Bentham's Economic Writings* (London, 1952)

Statistical Account of Scotland, ed. J. Sinclair (21 vols., Edinburgh, 1791-9; reprinted 1975-)

Steel, Tom. *The Life and Death of St Kilda* (Edinburgh, 1965)

Stevenson, David. *Alasdair Maccolla and the Highland Problem in the Seventeenth Century* (Edinburgh, 1980)

Stewart, David. *Sketches of the Character, Manners, and Present State of the High-landers of Scotland: with Details of the Military Service of the Highland Regiments* (2 vols., Edinburgh, 1822; 2nd edition, 1825)

Sutherland, Alexander. *A Summer Ramble in the Northern Highlands* (London, 1825)

Sutherland, S.R. 'Ethics and Economics in the Sutherland Clearances', *Northern Scotland,* vol. 2, no. 1 (1974-5)

Tate, W.E. 'Opposition to Parliamentary Enclosure in Eighteenth Century England', *Agricultural History,* vol. 19 (1945)

_____ 'Parliamentary Counter-Petitions during the Enclosures of the Eighteenth and Nineteenth Centuries', *English Historical Review,* vol. 59 (1944)

Teignmouth, Lord (C.J. Shore). *Sketches of the Coasts and Islands of Scotland and of the Isle of Man* (2 vols., London, 1836)

Thomas, Brinley. *The Welsh Economy* (Cardiff, 1962)

Thomas, P.D.G. *The House of Commons in the Eighteenth Century* (Oxford, 1971)

Thompson, E.P. 'English Trade Unionism and Other Labour Movements before 1790', *Society for the Study of Labour History,* Bulletin no. 17 (1968)

_____ 'History from Below', *Times Literary Supplement,* 7 April 1968

_____ *The Making of the English Working Class* (New York, 1963)

Thompson, Francis. *The Highlands and Islands* (London, 1974)

Thomson, Derick. *An Introduction to Gaelic Poetry* (London, 1974)

Thomson, James. *The Value and Importance of the Scottish Fisheries* (London, 1849)

Thomson, W.P.L. *The Little General and the Rousay Crofters* (Edinburgh, 1981)

Tilly, Charles. 'Collective Violence in European Perspective' in H.D. Graham and T.P. Gurr (eds.), *Violence in America: Historical and Comparative Perspectives* (New York, 1969)

_____ 'Did the Cake of Custom Break?' in John M. Merriman (ed.), *Consciousness and Class Experience in Nineteenth Century Europe* (New York, 1979)

_____ 'Proletarianization and Rural Collective Action in East Anglia and Elsewhere, 1500-1900', *Peasant Studies,* vol. 10 (1982)

The Topographical, Statistical and Historical Gazeteer of Scotland (Edinburgh, 1844)

Tranter, R.B. (ed.) *The Future of Upland Britain* (2 vols., Reading, 1978)

Trevor-Roper, Hugh. 'The Invention of Tradition: the Highland Tradition of Scotland' in Eric Hobsbawm and Terence Ranger (eds.), *The Invention of Tradition* (Cambridge, 1983)

Vaughan, W.E. 'An Assessment of the Economic Performance of Irish landlords, 1851-1881' in F.S.L. Lyons and A.A.J. Hawkins (eds.), *Ireland under the Union* (Oxford, 1980)

_____ 'Landlord and Tenant Relations in Ireland between the Famine and the Land War, 1850-1878' in L.M. Cullen and T.C. Smout (eds.), *Comparative Aspects of Scottish and Irish Economic and Social History 1600-1900* (Edinburgh, 1977)

Viner, Jacob. 'Guide to John Rae's *Life of Adam Smith*' in John Rae, *Life of Adam Smith* (reprinted, 1965)

Walker, James. *An Economical History of the Hebrides and Highlands of Scotland* (2 vols., Edinburgh, 1812)

_____ *Report on the Hebrides in 1764 and 1771*, ed. M. M. McKay (Edinburgh, 1980)

Watson, J. A. S. 'The Rise and Development of the Sheep Industry in the Highlands', *THAS*, 5th series, vol. 44 (1982)

White, P. *Observations upon the Present State of the Scotch Fisheries* (Edinburgh, 1791)

White, P. C. T. *Lord Selkirk's Diary 1803-4* (Toronto, 1958)

Wicksteed, Philip. *The Common Sense of Political Economy* (2 vols., London, 1910)

Williams, T. Desmond (ed.). *Secret Societies in Ireland* (Dublin, 1973)

Wills, Virginia (ed.). *Reports on the Annexed Estates, 1755-1769* (Edinburgh, 1973)

_____ *Statistics of the Annexed Estates, 1755-1756* (Edinburgh, 1974)

Wilson, James. *A Voyage Round the Coasts of Scotland and the Isles* (Edinburgh, 1842)

Winberg, Christer. 'Population Growth and Proletarianization' in S. Akerman, H. C. Johansen and D. Graunt (eds.), *Chance and Change* (Odense, 1978)

Wood, G. H. 'Real Wages and the Standard of Comfort since 1858', *Journal of the Royal Statistical Society*, vol. 62 (1909)

Wrigley, E. A. 'The Process of Modernisation and the Industrial Revolution in England', *Journal of Interdisciplinary History*, vol. 3 (1972)

_____ & R. S. Schofield. *The Population History of England, 1541-1871* (London, 1981)

Wynn, C. W. *Correspondence of Charlotte Grenville, Lady Williams Wynn*, ed. R. Leighton (no place, 1920)

Yanaihara, Tadao. *A Full and Detailed Catalogue of Books which Belonged to Adam Smith's Library* (Tokyo, 1951)

Young, G. M. 'Scott and the Historians', *Sir Walter Scott Lectures, 1940-1948* (University of Edinburgh, 1946)

Youngson, A. J. *After the Forty Five* (Edinburgh, 1973)

INDEX

Oban 84, 235
O'Farrell, Patrick 179
O'Grada, Cormac 413
Orkney 118, 175, 230, 231, 432,
    475n, 487
Oronsay 215
Orwell, George 116
Owen and Atkinson, sheepfarmers
    236

Paine, Tom 318n
Paisley 320
Peebles 278
Pennell, Joseph and Elizabeth 296,
    366, 442
Pennant, Thomas 32n, 186
Perth Burghs 20
Perthshire 50, 202, 205, 219, 430
Peru 192
Peterloo 314
Pictou 187, 208, 216, 219, 231
Pitmilly, Lord 383-4
Plaid Cymru 157
poetry 290-3
Poland 60
police 302, 342
Pollard, Sidney 414, 427, 431
Poor Relief, system 62, 365, 464,
    475n, 490
population growth 6, 21, 93-4,
    109-10, 121, 129, 136, 159,
    480-1
Porter, Sir W. 205-6
Port Phillip 267
Portree 323, 464, 496
Portugal 431
Postan, M.M. 494
potato 15, 35, 52, 69, 94, 114, 121,
    123, 159, 166, 181, 196-7, 235,
    247n, 274, 436-7, 466, 479, 490
Prattis, J.I. 164-5, 166
Prebble, John 142, 143-5, 146, 167,
    170
prices 5, 17, 424-30, Chap. 19, 501n
Prince Edward Island 188, 218, 244
Pryde, George 134
Pulteney, Sir William 205
Purves, Thomas 358

Quebec 231, 235, 245, 246n, 252,
    268-70
Queenstown 265

Raasay 8, 13, 470
Radnorshire 277
Rae, Sir William 325
Ramsay, John, of Ochtertyre 214,
    294, 303, 418, 458, 495
Ramsay, John, of Kildalton 269
Rannoch 208, 219
Rawson, Sir John William 476n
Reay Country 190, 244, 321, 397,
    432, 466
Reay, Lord 109, 323, 455, 474n
Rebecca Riots 334
Redford, Arthur 414
Red River 37, 42, 218
Rees, J.F. 111
rents 10, 13, 16, 26, 38, 47, 51, 65,
    85, 90, 188, 480-2, 484-5
Rhives 306
Ricardo, David 69, 394
riots 36, 37, 41, 76, 151, 245, 293
    passim, 315
Robertson, Patrick 382
Robertson, William 141
Rosehall 362
Ross, Donald 289, 320, 330
Ross, Peter 349n
Ross, Sir John, of Balnagowan 303-5
Ross-shire 28, 36, 37, 41, 50, 278,
    301, 316
Rostow, W.W. 416
Rothesay 236, 265
Rothiemurchus 297
Rousay 175, 487
Rowntree, B.S. 490
Royal Patriotic Society 259
Roxburgh 277, 353-4
Rudé, George 288
Rufus, William 34
Rum 208, 230, 246n
Russia 60
Russel, Alexander 71, 277, 468, 471
Ruthven Fair 229

Sage, Donald 75, 81, 289, 407n
St. Clair River 271
St. Kilda 267
St. Charles, John 354
San Francisco 177
Scandinavia 120, 142, 146, 492-3
Scotsman the 71, 167-71, 275, 310,
    314, 326, 343
Scott, Sir Walter 44-5, 56, 72n, 97,
    141, 150n, 227, 442
Scottany, 371